THE WORLD ALMANAC®

Dictionary of Dates

THE WORLD ALMANAC®

Dictionary of Dates

Longman

New York & London

Published in Cooperation with World Almanac Publications

Longman, Inc., 19 West 44th Street, New York, N.Y. 10036
Associated companies, branches, and representatives throughout the world.

Library of Congress Catalog Card Number 81-71772
Longman, Inc. ISBN 0-582-28372-8
Newspaper Enterprise Association, Inc. ISBN 0-911818-25-1

Manufactured in the United States of America
9 8 7 6 5 4 3 2 1

CREDITS

Editor in Chief   Laurence Urdang

Editors   George C. Kohn

                             Kenneth D. Whitehead

                             Lois E. Anderson

Editorial Assistants   Nancy T. Peterson

                             Charles H. Ruhe

                             Diane A. Puklin

                             Diane H. O'Herlihy

                             Janet Turk Cohen

A NOTE TO THE READER

The World Almanac Dictionary of Dates is a unique, alpha-betically-organized chronology of major events and phenomena throughout history. The entries are written to be as concise as possible while still giving the basic information you need to iden-tify and date the precise event or phenomenon.

The book has been designed for easy use. Entry headings, in almost all cases, refer to the specific event or phenomenon, not the general category for which you are seeking a date. For instance, you will find the Hundred Years' War under precisely that listing, not under the general category of wars. If appropri-ate, cross-references to other entries are given.

Finally, *The World Almanac Dictionary of Dates* is not intended to serve as a biographical reference work. However, the names of peoples and quasi-historical figures who can be dated but would not appear in a biographical dictionary are included.

Hana Umlauf Lane
Editor, *The World Almanac*

Aachen (Aix-la-Chapelle), battle of, U.S. First Army, aided by allied aerial bombardment, defeated German forces and captured Aachen, first major German city to fall to Allies in WW II, **Oct. 13-20, 1944.**

Abbadids, Arab dynasty in Spain, ruled emirate of Seville, **1023-91**; became chief Moorish power in Spain, **c. 1050**; deposed by Almoravids, **1091.**

Abbasids, Arab dynasty of caliphs, ruled at Baghdad, **749-1258**; climax of dynasty during reign of fifth caliph, Harun al-Rashid [c. 764-Mar. 809,] **786-809**; caliphate at Baghdad destroyed by Hulagu Khan [1217-1265], grandson of Genghis Khan [1162-1227], **1258**; last Abbasid captured by Selim I [1467-Sept. 22, 1520], **1517.**

Abbey Theatre, national repertory theater, Dublin, Ireland, **1904**, featuring works of Irish cultural revival; fire destroyed original building, **1951**; new Abbey theatre built, **1963.**

Abe Lincoln in Illinois, play, **1938**, with selections from Lincoln's own words, by U.S. social dramatist and biographer Robert E. Sherwood [Apr. 4, 1896-Nov. 14, 1955].

Abenaki Wars, series of conflicts between white colonists and the Abenaki Indians in Maine, **1702, 1722, 1724.**

Abensberg, battle of, French and Bavarian forces under Napoleon I defeated Austrians at Abensberg, Bavaria, **Apr. 20, 1809.**

Abolitionism, antislavery principles and movement begun in the U.S., **early 19th century**; New England and New York preachers crusaded for emancipation of the slaves, **1820s-30s**; William Lloyd Garrison [Dec. 10, 1805-May 24, 1879] published *The Liberator,* **1831**; American Anti-Slavery Society organized in Philadelphia, **Dec. 1833**; American and Foreign Anti-Slavery Society formed, **1840**; Liberty Party formed, **1840**; Fugitive Slave Act, **1850**; *Uncle Tom's Cabin* published, **1852**; John Brown's raid on Harpers Ferry, Va. (now W. Va.), **Oct. 16, 1859**; Pres. Lincoln's Emancipation Proclamation, **Jan. 1, 1863.**

Abominations, Tariff of, U.S. Congress passed high protective tariff, increasing rivalry between northern mercantile interests and southern farmers, **May 13, 1828.**

Abraham Lincoln: The War Years, biography, **1939**, by U.S. poet Carl Sandburg [Jan. 6, 1878-July 22, 1967]; author's *Abraham Lincoln: The Prairie Years,* **1936.**

Abraham, Plains of, site of British victory, under Gen. James Wolfe [Jan. 2, 1727-Sept. 13, 1759], over French forces, under Gen. Louis Montcalm [Feb. 28, 1712-Sept. 14, 1759], **Sept. 13-18, 1759.**

Abscam, national scandal, **1980**, involved FBI investigation of some U.S. congressmen who met with agents posing as aides to bogus Arab sheiks willing to pay for favors; alleged bribery and conspiracy of congressmen.

abstract art, painting style, originated **c.1910**, eliminating recognizable subject matter and concentrating on color, form, line, and texture; pioneered in such paintings as *Dreamy Improvisation,* **1919**, by Russian painter Vassily Kandinsky [Dec. 4, 1866-Dec. 13, 1944].

abstract expressionism, New York art movement pioneered by Arshile Gorky [1905-July 21, 1948]; drip technique, **1947**, by Jackson Pollock [Jan. 28, 1912-Aug. 11, 1956]; Mark Rothko [Sept. 25, 1903-Feb. 25, 1970]; turned to AE school, **1948.**

Abukir, battles of, French-Egyptian forces under Napoleon I destroyed large Turkish army at Abukir, east of Alexandria, Egypt, **July 25, 1799**; British drove French from their position at Abukir during British invasion of Egypt, **Mar. 8, 1801.**

Abu Klea, battle of, British forces defeated the Mahdists during British military campaigns in the Sudan, **Jan. 17, 1885.**

Abyssinian Wars, conflict between Britain and Abyssinia (Ethiopia), **Jan.-Apr. 1868**; Britain defeated king of Abyssinia at Magdala, **Apr. 10, 1868**; conflict between Italy and Ethiopia, **Oct. 1935-June 1936**; Italians captured Addis Ababa, **May, 1936**; King Victor Emmanuel III [Nov. 11, 1869-Dec. 28, 1947] of Italy was made emperor of Ethiopia, **June 1, 1936**.

Academy Awards, annual awards, called "Oscars," first presented **1929**, for excellence in films; awarded by the American Academy of Motion Picture Arts and Sciences, founded **May, 1927**.

Academy of Design (*Accademia del Disegno*), first "academy"; artistic society, founded Florence, **1562**, to free artists from medieval guilds, by art patron Cosimo de' Medici [June 12, 1519-Apr. 21, 1574]; 19 academies active in Europe, **1720**; 100 active, **1790**.

Academy of Inscriptions and Belles-Lettres (*Academie des Inscriptions et Belles-Lettres*), society devoted to scholarly and artistic studies, founded Paris, **1663**; Berlin Academy, **1711**; Royal Portuguese Academy, **1720**; Spanish Royal Academy, **1738**.

Academy of Painting and Sculpture (*Academie de Peinture et de Sculpture*), royal society, founded Paris, **1648**, to promote the arts; headed, from **1663**, by classicist painter Charles Le Brun [Feb. 24, 1619-Feb. 22, 1690]; renamed Academie des Beaux Arts, **1816**, arbiter of official "academic" art.

Academy, The (of Athens), school of philosophy founded, **387 B.C.**, by Greek philosopher Plato [428?-347? B.C.]; closed **529** in an action directed against paganism by the Roman Emperor Justinian [A.D. 483-Nov. 14, 565].

Acapulco, battle of, Mexican liberals, led by Benito Juarez, [Mar. 21, 1806-July 18, 1872] defeated Mexican government troops led by Antonio Lopez de Santa Anna [Feb. 21, 1794-June 21, 1876] during Mexican liberal uprising, **Aug. 9, 1855**.

accident insurance, first, issued, **1863**, by Travelers Insurance Company of Hartford, Conn.

accordion, wind instrument in bellows form, first made in Germany, **1822**; key-

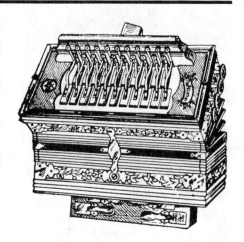

board added, **c. 1852**.

A.C. electric reciprocating engine, patented, **1889**, by Belgian-American inventor Charles J. Van Depoele [1846-1892].

Acemists, movement of Russian poets, founded **1910**, aiming at "classical" exactitude and discipline in style but with "romantic" subject matter.

acetic acid, discovered, **c. 800**, by Arabian alchemist Geber (Jabir) [722-815], through the distillation of vinegar. German chemist Adolph Kolbe [1818-1884] discovered a process for the synthetic manufacture of acetic acid, **1845**.

acetone, synthesized, **1911**, by Russian-English chemist Chaim Weizmann [1874-1952].

acetylcholine, secretion first isolated from autonomic nervous system c. **1915**, by English biologist Sir Henry H. Dale [1875-1968]; synthesized, **1921**, by German-American physiologist Otto Loewi [1873-1961].

acetyl coenzyme A, demonstrated to be essential substance in metabolism, **1951**, by German-American biochemist Fritz A. Lipmann [1899-].

Achaean League, confederation of Greek city-states on Gulf of Corinth, dissolved by Alexander the Great but reformed, **280 B.C.**; dissolved after war with Rome, **146 B.C.**

Achaean War, conflict between Achaean League and Rome, **147-146 B.C.**; Achaeans defeated at Scarphea and

Leucopetra, **146 B.C.**; Corinth destroyed, **146 B.C.**; Greece became Roman province, **Sept., 146 B.C.**

Achaemenids, ancient Persian dynasty, made strong by Cyrus the Great [600?-529 B.C.], **c. 550 B.C.**; developed advanced civilization, **550-330 B.C.**; dynasty ended after the battle of Issus, **333 B.C.**, and defeat of Darius III, **330 B.C.**, by Alexander the Great.

A.C. induction motor, invented, **c. 1888**, by Yugoslavian-American inventor Nikola Tesla [1856-1943]; multiphase system used, **1886**, in world's first hydroelectric plant at Niagara Falls and to illuminate Chicago World's Fair, **1893**.

Ackia, battle of, Chickasaw Indians, allied with the English, defeated French force led by Jean Baptiste le Moyne, Sieur de Bienville [Feb. 23, 1680-1768] at Indian village of Ackia, La., **May 26, 1736**.

Aconcagua, Mt., highest mountain in Western Hemisphere (22,835 ft.), on border of Argentina with Chile, first climbed by member of British expedition, Alpine guide Mattias Zurbriggen, **Jan. 14, 1897**.

acoustics, first scientific aspects developed, **1856**, by American physicist Joseph Henry [1797-1878].

Acropolis, elevated, fortified section in ancient Athens, Greece, having some of world's greatest architectural works; laid waste by Persians, **480 B.C.**.

ACTH (adrenocorticotrophic hormone), first used as a pharmacologic agent, **1949**, by U.S. physician Philip S. Hench [1896-1965] and associates; isolated in pure form, **1953**, by U.S. scientists at Armour Laboratories, Chicago, Ill.

actinium, element no. 89, discovered, **1899**, by French chemist Andre Louis Debierne [1874-1949].

Actium, battle of, site of the defeat of the land and sea forces of Mark Anthony [82-Aug. 30 B.C.] and Cleopatra [69-30 B.C.] by the force of Octavian (Augustus) [Sept. 23, 63-Aug. 19, 14 B.C.] under Agrippa, **31 B.C.**.

Act of Confederation, Germanic confederation for mutual defense formed by 39 German states, replacing old Holy Roman Empire, **June 8, 1815**.

Act of Indemnity and Oblivion, procured by Lord Oliver Cromwell [Apr. 25, 1599-Sept. 3, 1658], forgiving all state offenses committed before battle of Worcester, **Feb. 1652**.

Act of Grace, English parliament gave indemnity to all followers of James II except those in treasonable correspondence with him, **May 20, 1690**.

Act of Settlement, succession to the English throne passed to Sophia, princess of Hanover, granddaughter of James I [June 19, 1566-Mar. 27, 1625], and to her heirs, if they were Protestants, **June 12, 1701**.

Act of Supremacy, King of England and his successors were appointed Protector and only Supreme Head of the Church and Clergy of England, **1534**.

Acts of the Apostles, fifth book of the *New Testament*, **c. 90**, believed to have been written by the author of the *Gospel of Luke*.

Act of Uniformity, Cavalier parliament required England's clergymen, college fellows, and schoolmasters to accept everything in the *Book of Common Prayer*, **Aug. 24, 1662**.

Act of Union, England and Scotland were united to form Great Britain, **May 1, 1707**; Great Britain and Ireland were united to form the United Kingdom, **Jan. 1, 1801**.

Actors' Equity Association, U.S. association for actors founded at New York's Pabst Grand Circle Hotel, **May 26, 1913**; gained recognition as trade union of acting profession following 30-day strike, **Aug. 1919**.

Actors' Studio, professional workshop, founded New York City, **1947**.

Actor's Workshop, dramatic school, founded, Los Angeles, **1953**; New York City, **1973**.

Adairsville, battle of, Union forces of Gen. Sherman forced Confederates under Gen. Johnston to retreat at Adairsville, Ga. **May 17, 1864**.

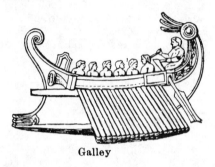

Galley

Adams-Onis Treaty, Spain gave up all claims to West Florida and ceded East Florida to U.S., which agreed to pay $5 million claims by U.S. citizens against Spain, **Feb. 22, 1819**.

adding and recording machine (key-set), patented, **1888**, by American inventor William S. Burroughs [1857-1898].

Addis Ababa, originally called Finfinnie, renamed, **1886**; made capital of Ethiopia, **1889**; captured by Italians and made capital of Italian East Africa, **1936**; recaptured by Allies in WW II and returned to Ethiopian rule, **1941**.

Addled Parliament, second parliament of King James I of England, which constantly quarreled with the king and produced no legislation, **Apr. 5,-June 7, 1614**.

addressing machine, patented, **1896**, by American inventor Joseph S. Duncan.

Aden, port on Gulf of Aden in southwest Arabia, held by Muslim Arabs, **7th-16th centuries**; British Crown Colony, **1935**; made capital of South Yemen, **1970**.

adrenalin (epinephrine), first isolated as pure hormone, **1901**, by Japanese-American chemist Jokichi Takamine [1854-1922].

Adrianople, battles of, Roman army and cavalry under Emperor Valens [c. 328-78] defeated by Visigoth cavalry, **Aug. 9, 378**; Byzantine Turks defeated Bulgarians, **1254**; Ottoman Turks captured city of Adrianople, **1365**; Turks made it their capital, **1366**; Bulgarians captured city, ending first Bal-

kan War, **Mar. 26, 1913**.

Adrianople, Treaty of, Russian and Ottoman Empire made peace, **Sept. 24, 1829**.

Aduwa (Adowa or Adwa), battle of, 80,000 Ethiopians under Menelik II [Aug. 17, 1844-Dec. 22, 1913] destroyed 20,000-man Italian army, assuring independence for Ethiopia, **Mar. 1, 1896**.

Aegospotamos, battle of, Spartan fleet under Lysander [?-395 B.C.] defeated Athenian fleet under Conon [?-392 B.C.], **405 B.C.**

Aegusa, battle of, Roman fleet defeated Carthaginian fleet, sinking 50 Carthaginian ships and ending first Punic War, **Mar. 10, 241 B.C.**

Aeneid, unfinished epic poem, **19 B.C.** by Latin poet Vergil [70-19 B.C.] recounts escape of Aeneas from Troy and his voyage to conquer Latium in Italy.

aerosol can valve mechanism, developed, **1953**, by American inventor Robert H. Abplanalp [1923-].

Aesop's Fables, stories of talking beasts, **500s B.C.**; illustrating moral lessons, by the semi-legendary Greek writer Aesop [c. 620-c. 560 B.C.]; definitive collection, **200s B.C.**

Aetolian League, military confederation of western Greek city-states that defeated, with Roman help, Macedonians at Cynoscephalae, **197 B.C.**; made subject ally of Rome, **189 B.C.**

Afghanistan, conquered by Genghis Khan, **c. 1220**; conquered by Persians, **1730s**; invaded by Soviet troops, **Dec., 1979**.

Afghan Wars, conflicts between British and Afghans, resulting from rivalry between Britain and Russia for Afghan buffer-state; first war, **1838-42**; second, **1878-80**; Treaty of Gandamak, **May 16, 1879**; third, **1919**; British recognized independence of Afghanistan by Treaty of Rawalpindi **Aug. 8, 1919**.

Agency for International Development (AID), U.S. federal agency authorized **Sept. 4, 1961**, by Pres. John F. Kennedy, to replace International Cooperation Administration (ICA) and Development Loan Fund (DLF).

Age of Reason, philosophical treatise in two volumes, **1794, 1796**, by English-U.S. thinker and publicist Thomas Paine [Jan. 29, 1737-June 8, 1809].

Agincourt, battle of, Henry V [1421-71] of England defeated the French in the Hundred Years' War, **Oct. 25, 1415.**

Agnadello, battle of, French army of King Louis XII [June 27, 1462-Jan. 1, 1515] defeated Venetian army in Cremona province, northern Italy, **May 14, 1509.**

Agricultural Adjustment Administration (AAA), former U.S. government agency established under the Agricultural Adjustment Act, **1933;** empowered to make loans to farmers on staple crops, **1938;** renamed Agricultural Adjustment Agency, **1942;** taken over by Production and Marketing Administration, **1945.**

Agricultural Wheel, farmers' political organization, founded in Arkansas, **1882.**

Agriculture, U.S. Department of, division of U.S. government established by Congress, **1862;** Secretary of Agriculture made U.S. Cabinet member, **1889.**

Aigun, Treaty of, China ceded north bank of Amur River to Russia, **June 29, 1858.**

Ain Jalut, battle of, Mamelukes of Egypt defeated Mongol army of Hulagu, the grandson of Genghis Khan, near the Sea of Galilee, checking Mongol invasion in the West, **Sept. 1260.**

air brakes, invented, **1867,** by American engineer George Westinghouse [1846-1914], as a railroad safety device.

air conditioning, invented, **1902,** by American engineer Willis H. Carrier [1876-1950].

aircraft carrier, first experimental vessel, **1910,** by U.S. Navy; improvised platform on U.S. Navy cruiser, *Birmingham.*

air force, air arm of a nation's defense forces, began with the French use of balloons, **1859;** first great air battle, Battle of Britain, **1940;** U.S. Air Force established, **1947;** U.S. Air Force Academy opened, **1955.**

Air Force, U. S. Department of the, U.S. Army Air Corps established by Congress, **July 2, 1926;** united with War and Navy departments to form a single department (Department of Defense), **July 25, 1947.**

air mail, carrying of mail by airplanes, demonstrated in the U.S. and England, **1911;** first regular U.S. civilian service began, **May 15, 1918;** first scheduled coast-to-coast (U.S.) service by air, **July 1, 1924;** first transpacific air mail introduced, **1935;** first transatlantic air mail introduced, **1939;.**

airplane, experimental, invented, **1896,** by American inventor Samuel P. Langley [1834-1906].

airplane, first manned, power driven, heavier-than-air flying machine produced by Orville and Wilbur Wright near Kitty Hawk, N.C., **Dec. 17, 1903;** 'ight lasted 12 seconds.

airplane, gasoline engine, first built, **1901,** by American mechanical engineer Charles M. Manly [1876-1927]; five-cylinder radial design, 52 hp, weight 125 pounds.

airplane, jet, first passenger service, **1952.** British DeHaviland Comet covered distance from London to Johannesburg, South Africa, in less than 24 hours.

airplane, jet first transatlantic passenger service, 1958, by British Overseas Airways Corp. and Pan American World Airways.

airplane, military, first used by the Italian army, **1911,** during Italo-Turkish War to observe movements of Turkish forces in Libya.

airplane, multiengine, first produced, **1913,** by Russian-American aeronautical engineer Igor I. Sikorsky [1889-1972].

airplane, multiengine flying clipper, first produced for transoceanic flight, **1931,** by Russian-American aeronautical engineer Igor I. Sikorsky [1889-1972].

airplane, solar-powered, first sunlight-powered airplane without storage batteries, crossed English Channel, **July 7, 1981;** called Solar Challenger; designed by American aeronautical engineer Paul MacCready [1926-]; drew electricity directly from 16,128 solar cells covering wings and stabilizer.

airplane, supersonic (TU-144), first demonstrated, **1968**, by Russian aircraft designer Andrei N. Tupolev [1888-1972].

airplane, turbojet, German, first flight, **1939**; He 178, designed by German aircraft engineer Ernst Heinkel [1888-1958].

airplane, turbojet engine, first experimental design flown, **1941**, with Whittle 1 turbojet engine; called Gloster E28/39; engine designed by English engineer Sir Frank Whittle [1907-].

airplane, turboprop, first went into service, **1948**; Vickers Viscount; combination jet and propeller driven engine.

airplane, U.S., jet, first domestic passenger service, **1958**, by National Airlines with Boeing 707 between New York and Miami.

airplane, V.T.O.L., tested, **1954**; Convair XFY-1; first to take off and land vertically.

airplane crashes, great, U.S. Army bomber crashed into Empire State Building, killing 13 persons, **July 28, 1945**; TWA Super Constellation and United DC-7 collided over Grand Canyon, Ariz., killing 128 persons, **June 30, 1956**; Air France Boeing 707 jet crashed on takeoff from Paris, killing 130 persons, **June 3, 1962**; Japanese Boeing 727 and F-86 fighter collided in mid-air, killing 162 persons, **July 30, 1971**; East German Aeroflot-Ilyushin-62 airliner crashed near Moscow, killing 156 persons, **Aug. 14, 1972**; Eastern Airlines Tristar jumbo jet crashed into Everglades, killing 101 persons, **Dec. 29, 1972**; Turkish DC-10 jumbo jet crashed on takeoff from Paris, killing all 346 passengers, **Mar. 3, 1974**; Pan Am 747 and KLM 747 jumbo jets collided on runway at Tenerife, Canary Islands, killing 579 persons in worst disaster in aviation history, **Mar. 27, 1977**; Air India 747 exploded after takeoff from Bombay, killing 213 persons, **Jan. 1, 1978**; Icelandic DC-8 jetliner crashed in storm at Colombo, Sri Lanka, killing 183 persons, **Nov. 25, 1978**; American Airlines DC-10 crashed on takeoff from Chicago, killing 275 persons in worst disaster in U.S. aviation history, **May 25, 1979**; Saudi Arabian Airlines Lockheed Tristar crashed on landing at Riyadh, killing all 301 persons aboard, **Aug. 19, 1980**.

airplane engine, Merlin, designed by English engineer Sir Henry Royce [1863-1933]; powered Hurricane, Mustang, and Spitfire fighter planes from **1934** to end of World War II.

airplane flight, first transatlantic flight, June **1919**, by British aviators Sir John William Alcock [1892-1919] and Arthur Whitten Brown [1886-1948], nonstop from Saint John's, Newfoundland, to Clifden, Ireland, in 16 hours and 12 minutes.

airplane stabilizer, first used, **1912**, on Curtiss seaplane; invented by American engineer Elmer A. Sperry [1860-1930].

air travel, commercial, introduced, **1910**, in zeppelin airship *Deutschland*, built by German inventor Count Ferdinand von Zeppelin [1838-1917].

Aisne, battles of, Germans stopped fierce Allied attack, marking start of stabilized trench warfare in WWI, **Sept. 15-18, 1914**; Germans checked French offensive, **Apr. 16-20, 1917**; German offensive pushed French armies back, **May 27-June 6, 1918**.

Aisne-Marne offensive, counterattack by French and 270,000 U.S. troops, **July 18, 1918**, between Aisne and Marne rivers, drove Germans back, **Aug. 6, 1918**; turning point in WW I.

Aix-la-Chapelle, Treaty of, ended War of Devolution, **May 2, 1668**; ended War of the Austrian Succession, **Oct. 18, 1748**.

Akron, U.S. dirigible *Akron* crashed off New Jersey coast, **Apr. 4, 1933**; 73 persons perished.

Alabama, formerly Georgia territory, admitted to the Union (U.S.) as 22nd state, **Dec. 14, 1819**; seceded from the Union, **Jan. 11, 1861**; readmitted, **June 25, 1868**.

Alabama letters, Henry Clay [Apr. 22, 1777-June 29, 1852] supported U.S. annexation of Texas if it could be done with Union consent and without war, **July 1-27, 1844**.

Alamein, battle of, British forces under Gen. Bernard L. Montgomery [Nov. 17,

1887-Mar. 24, 1976] defeated German forces under Field Marshal Erwin Rommel [Nov. 15, 1891-Oct. 14, 1944] in northern Egypt, **Oct. 23-Nov. 2, 1942**.

Alamo, the, mission-chapel-fort in San Antonio, Tex., that was defended unsuccessfully by 182 Texans against 3,000 Mexicans under Gen. Antonio Lopez de Santa Anna [Feb. 21, 1794-June 21, 1876], **Feb. 24-Mar. 6, 1836**.

Aland (Ahvenanmaa), battle of, Russian fleet overpowered and forced large Swedish fleet to retreat near Aland Islands during Great Northern War in Baltic region; first major Russian naval triumph in history, **July 14, 1714**.

Alaska, admitted to the Union (U.S.) as 49th state, **Jan. 3, 1959**.

Alaska pipeline, U.S. congressional bill to construct 799-mile Alaska pipeline signed by Pres. Nixon, **Nov. 16, 1973**; first oil flows from Alaska's Prudhoe Bay (North Shore) to port of Valdez, **July 28, 1977**.

Alaska, purchase of, U.S. Sec. of State agreed to purchase Alaska from Russia ("Seward's Folly"), **Mar. 30, 1867**; Senate ratified purchase treaty, **Apr. 9, 1867**; House of Representatives appropriated $7,200,000, about 2 cents an acre, for purchase, **July 14, 1868**.

Alaska Highway (Alcan Highway), all-weather road from Dawson Creek, B.C., Canada, to Fairbanks, Alaska, built by U.S. troops, **Mar.-Sept. 1942**; U.S. transferred control of Canadian part of road to Canada, **1946**; opened to unrestricted travel, **1947**.

Albania, republic on Adriatic, conquered by Turks, **1501**; proclaimed its independence from Turkey, **Nov. 28, 1912**; Communist dictatorship established, **1946**; broke with Moscow, **1961**; ended alliance with China, **1978**.

Albany Plan of Union, colonial union plan proposed by Benjamin Franklin [Jan. 17, 1706-Apr. 17, 1790] at start of Albany Congress, **June 19, 1754**.

Albany Congress, meeting at Albany, N.Y., in which a treaty was settled between representatives of seven British colonies and the Iroquois Indians, **June 19-July 10, 1754**.

Albigensian Crusade, proclaimed by Pope Innocent III [1161-June 16, 1216], **1208**;

crusaders under Simon de Montfort [c. 1160-June 25, 1218] defeated French nobles at Muret, **1213**; ended by Peace of Paris, **1229**.

Alcacovas, Treaty of, Castile gained control of Canary Islands, and Portugal gained West Africa, Guinea, and some ocean islands, **Mar. 6, 1460**.

Alcantara, battle of, Spanish army under duke of Alva invaded Portugal and defeated Portuguese army of peasants and townspeople near Tagus River, **Aug. 25, 1580**; Portugal became a realm of Spanish throne, until **1640**.

Alcantara, Order of, great military religious order, established Alcantara, Spain, **13th century**; fl. **13th-14th centuries**; prestige of order passed to Castilian crown, **15th century**.

Alcatraz, (The Rock), rocky island in San Francisco Bay used as U.S. military prison, **1859-1933**; used as federal prison for notorious criminals, **1933-63**.

Alcazarquivir, battle of, Moroccans defeated the Portuguese, **Aug. 4, 1578**.

Alcoholics Anonymous (AA), worldwide organization dedicated to curing alcoholics, organized by two former alcoholics in New York City, **June 10, 1935**.

Alcolea, battle of, rebel forces won decisive victory over Spanish royal army east of Cordova, causing Queen Isabella II [Oct. 10, 1830-Apr. 9, 1904] to flee to France, **Sept. 28, 1868**.

Aldie, battle of, Confederate cavalry under J.E.B.(Jeb) Stuart [Feb. 6, 1833-May 12, 1864] failed to drive back Union forces at Aldie, Va., **June 17, 1863**, during South's invasion of the North.

aldosterone, cortical hormone isolated,

1953, by Polish-Swiss chemist Tadeus Reichstein [1897-].

Aldrich Vreeland Currency Act, established National Monetary Commission that was the basis of the Federal Reserve System in U. S., **May 30, 1908**.

Alexandria, Mediterranean port in northern Egypt founded by Alexander the Great, **332 B.C.**; capital of the Ptolemies, **304-30 B.C.**; greatest center of Hellenistic and Jewish culture, **3rd-1st centuries B.C.**; center of Christian learning, **1st-3rd centuries**; its celebrated libraries destroyed in part by Theodosius I, **391**; declined after it fell to Arab Muslims, **642**.

Alexandria Government, Virginia state government established by Union supporters at Wheeling (now in West Virginia) after Virginia seceded from the Union, **Apr. 17, 1861**; government moved to Alexandria, Va., **June 20, 1863**; abolished, **1867**.

algebra, fundamental theorem of, proved, **1799**, by German mathematician Karl F. Gauss [1777-1855].

Algeciras Conference, diplomatic meeting at Algeciras, Spain, to settle conflicting interests of Germany, France, and other powers in Morocco, **Jan. 16-Apr. 7, 1906**.

Algeria, republic in northwest Africa, proclaimed its independence from France, **July 5, 1962**.

Algerian rebellion, Algerians fought French for independence, **Oct. 31, 1954-July 3, 1962**.

Algerine War, conflict between U.S. and Algeria over piracy in the Mediterranean, **1801-05**; dey of Algiers forced by Stephen Decatur [Jan. 5, 1779-Mar. 22, 1820] to renounce tribute by the U. S., **June 30, 1815**.

Alhambra, palace of the Moorish kings at Granada, Spain, built, **1230-1354**; mutilated, **1492**; restored after **1828**.

Alice in Wonderland, children's book, **1865**, about adventures of sensible girl in topsy-turvy world; by Lewis Carroll (pseud. of Charles Lutwidge Dodgson) [Jan. 27, 1832-Jan. 14, 1898]; sequel, *Through the Looking Glass*, **1872**; films: British, **1934**; U.S., **1951**.

Alien and Sedition Acts, U.S. congress authorized the President to deport "dangerous" aliens and to prohibit anti-government activity, **1798**; Alien Act, **June 25, 1798**; Sedition Act, **July 14, 1798**.

Alien Registration Act, U.S. Congress required all aliens living in U.S. to file personal and occupational record, **June 29, 1940**

Ali-Foreman fight, Muhammad Ali [Jan. 18, 1942—] knocked out George Foreman in eighth round in Kinshasa, Zaire, to win heavyweight boxing championship, **Oct. 30, 1974**; Ali regained World Boxing Association championship and defeated Leon Spinks [1954 -] in 15 rounds in New Orleans, **Sept. 15, 1978**.

Aliwal, battle of, British-Indian forces, under Sir Harry G. W. Smith [June 28, 1787-Oct. 12, 1860], won major victory over Sikhs in the Punjab, **Jan. 28, 1846**.

Aljubarrota, battle of, Portuguese army, aided by English archers, defeated Castilian-French army near Lisbon, assuring the independence of Portugal, **Aug. 14, 1385**.

alkali, chemical basis established, 1807, by English chemist Sir Humphry Davy [1778-1829].

alkaloid, concept introduced, **1806**, by German pharmacologist Friedrick W.A. Serturner [1783—1841].

Allatoona, battle of, Union troops

repulsed assault on fort by larger Confederate force at Allatoona, Ga., **Oct. 5, 1864**; about one third of the Union troops died.

Allia, battle of, Gauls inflicted heavy losses on the Romans, at Allia River, then sacked and burned Rome, **July 18, 390 B.C.**

Alliance for Progress, inter-American economic and social assistance program, announced by Pres. John F. Kennedy, **Mar. 13, 1961.**

All in the Family, TV situation comedy, **1971—79.**

All Saints' Day, Christian feast day, celebrated **November 1,** for all known and unknown saints; celebration fixed on November 1 date, **741,** by Pope Gregory III [c. 680—Nov., 741].

Almansa, battle of, Franco-Spanish force defeated Anglo-Portuguese army, southwest of Valencia, Spain, eliminating Portugal from any further part in the War of the Spanish Succession, **Apr. 25, 1707.**

Almohads, Berber Muslim dynasty, ruled Spain and Morocco, **12th—13th century;** ousted Almoravids, **1174;** defeated by Spanish and Portuguese, **1212;** replaced in Morocco by Merenids, **1269.**

Almoravids, Berber Muslim dynasty, ruled Spain and Morocco, **11th—12th century;** founded city of Marrakesh in Morocco, **1062;** aided Moors in stemming Christian reconquest of Spain, **1086;** lost control of Spain and Morocco to Almohads, **1174.**

Alouette, first Canadian spacecraft launched, **1962.**

alphabet, fixed series of letters for writing: Egyptian—24 letters, **c. 2000 B.C.;** proto-Sinaitic Semitic inscriptions—first phonetic alphabet, **c. 1900 B.C.;** Phoenician alphabet, **1600—1100 B.C.;** developed Greek script, **c. 800 B.C.;** Latin alphabet, **c. 500 B.C.**

Altamont, battle of, Confederate force under Gen. Joseph Wheeler [Sept. 10, 1836—Jan. 25, 1906] defeated Union force at Altamont, Tenn., **Aug. 30, 1862.**

Altamont Death Festival, unruly crowd at Rolling Stones concert at Altamont Speedway, Livermore, Calif., attacked by members of motorcycle gang Hell's Angels, **Dec. 6, 1969,** resulting in three deaths and many injuries.

alternator, high frequency, first transmission of human voice made possible, **1906;** invented by Swedish-American engineer Ernst F.W. Alexanderson [1878—1975].

aluminum, element, first isolated, **1825,** by Danish physicist Hans Christian Oersted [1777—1851].

aluminum cans, first used commercially, **1960,** by American manufacturers for food and beverages.

aluminum metal, first produced, **1854,** by French chemist Henri Etienne Saint-Claire Deville [1818—1881].

Amahl and the Night Visitors, first television opera, a Christmas story; broadcast premier, **December 24, 1951,** by Italian-U.S. composer Gian Carlo Menotti [July 7, 1911-]

Amalfi, early Italian maritime republic that rivaled Pisa, Venice, and Genoa, **10th-11th centuries.**

Amana Church Society, communal religious society originated in Germany, **17th century;** German emigrants settled near Buffalo, N.Y., **1842;** moved to settlements in east central Iowa, **1855;** became cooperative corporation, **1932.**

Amarillo (Texas), great rail center after **1887;** gas discovered, **1918;** oil discovered, **1921.**

Amateur Athletic Union, U.S., founded **Jan. 21, 1888.**

Amateur Hour, Major Bowes, early radio program, **1934-46,** often imitated on radio and television; originated by Major Edward Bowes [June 14, 1874-June 13, 1946]

Amazon River, world's second longest river, discovered by Spanish navigator Vicente Yanez Pinzon [c. 1460-c. 1524], **1500.**

Amboise, conspiracy of, French Huguenots and others attempted unsuccessfully to abduct French King Francis II [Jan. 19, 1544-Dec. 5, 1560] at the castle of Amboise and to seize power from the Guise family of France, **1560.**

America, discovery of, Norsemen (Vikings) reached coast of eastern Canada, **c. 1000;** Christopher Columbus [c. 1451-May 20, 1506] sighted and landed on island of San Salvador in the Bahamas, **Oct. 12, 1492.**

American Academy of Arts and Letters, organization established New York City, **1904.**

American Association for the Advancement of Science, founded and developed as a joint endeavor of U.S. and Canadian scientists, **Sept. 1848.**

American Ballet Theatre, ballet company, founded, New York City, **1940.**

American Bar Association (ABA), voluntary association of lawyers admitted to the bar in any state, established through efforts of Connecticut Bar Association, **Aug. 1878.**

American Cancer Society, U.S. organization formed, **1913.**

American Civil Liberties Union (ACLU), established by Jane Addams [Sept. 6, 1869-May 21, 1935], Helen Keller [June 27, 1880-June 1, 1968], Norman Thomas [Nov. 20, 1884- Dec. 19, 1968], and others, **1920.**

American Colonization Society, organized to transport free U.S. Negroes for settlement in Africa, **Dec. 1816-Jan. 1817;** purchased land in Africa that led to the founding of Liberia, **1822;** declined after **1840.**

American Dictionary of the English Language, An, authoritative American-English dictionary, by pioneer U.S. lexicographer Noah Webster [Oct. 16, 1758-May 28, 1843], **1828;** revised, **1841.**

American Federation of Labor-Congress of Industrial Organizations (AFL-CIO), federation of U.S. labor unions, formed by merger of AFL and CIO, **Dec. 5, 1955;** AFL organized and Samuel Gompers [Jan. 27, 1850-Dec. 13, 1924] elected president, **Dec. 8, 1886;** CIO established by John L. Lewis [Feb. 12, 1880-June 11, 1969], **Nov. 9, 1935.**

American Federation of Teachers (AFT), organization of teachers, established like a labor union, **1916;** negotiated unsuccessfully for a merger with the NEA, **1973-74.**

American Federation of Television and Radio Artists (AFTRA), union of broadcast performers (AFL-CIO), founded **August, 1937,** as AFRA (radio performers); "T" added, **1952,** after merger with Television Authority.

American Fur Company, chartered by John Jacob Astor [July 17, 1763-Mar. 29, 1848] to compete with Canadian fur-trading companies, **1808.**

American Humane Society, society for prevention of cruelty to animals formed, **Oct. 1877,** in Cleveland, Ohio.

American Indian Movement (AIM), organization of American Indians and supporters of Indian civil rights, **fl. 1970s—80s;** occupied village of Wounded Knee, S. Dak., alleging U.S. government's breach of Indian treaties, **Feb. 27—May 8, 1973.**

American in Paris, An, Broadway musical, **1928,** by U.S. composer George Gershwin [Sept. 26, 1898—July 11, 1937]; Academy Award-winning film, **1951.**

American Labor Party, organized to support the New Deal, **1936;** anti-Communist group broke away and formed Liberal Party, **1944;** voted out of existence by N.Y. state committee, **1956.**

American Language, The, pioneer study, **1919,** of the development of English in the United States, by U.S. critic, journalist, and editor, H(enry) L(ouis) Mencken [Sept. 12, 1880—Jan. 29, 1956]; *Supplement I,* **1945;** *Supplement II,* **1948;** fourth definitive edition, **1962.**

American Legion, founded as a national association of male and female war veterans in Paris, **Mar. 15, 1919.**

American Liberty League, conservative political organization formed to oppose the New Deal, **1934;** dissolved, **1940.**

American Party (Native American Party), U.S. political party established nationally by the merging of the "Know-Nothings" with a faction of Whigs, **1854.**

American Protective Association, powerful, secret anti-Catholic and anti-foreign organization founded in Clinton, Iowa, **Mar. 3, 1887.**

American Medical Association (AMA), founded in Philadelphia, **May 7, 1847.**

American Mercury, iconoclastic literary magazine, **1924—33.**

American Museum of Natural History, incorporated in New York City, **1869;** opened, **1877;** Hayden Planetarium completed and opened, **1935;** Roosevelt Memorial building, **1936.**

American Nazi Party (ANP), anti-Jewish American political party founded by Harold N. Arrowsmith, Jr., **Mar. 1959;** ANP chief George Lincoln Rockwell shot to death in Arlington, Va., **Aug. 25, 1967;** renamed National Socialist White People's Party, **late 1960s;** held well-publicized Nazi rally in Marquette Park, Chicago, **July 9, 1978.**

American Red Cross, organized by Clara Barton [Dec. 25, 1821—Apr. 12, 1912] to alleviate human suffering and to promote public health, **1881;** granted federal charter, **1900.**

American Revolution, struggle by which the Thirteen Colonies in North America gained independence from Britain, **1775—83;** fighting first at battles of Lexington and Concord, **Apr. 19, 1775;** Green Mountain Boys captured Fort Ticonderoga, **May 10, 1775;** pyrrhic British victory at Bunker Hill, **June 17, 1775;** adoption of Declaration of Independence, **July 4, 1776;** American victory at Saratoga, **Oct 17, 1777;** Continental Army survived winter at Valley Forge, **Dec. 1777—June 1778;** British surrendered at Yorktown, **Oct. 19, 1781;** British recognized independence of U.S. by treaty of Paris, **Sept. 3, 1783.**

American Society for the Advancement of Science, scientific society founded in Boston, Mass., **1847.**

American Society of Composers, Authors, and Publishers (ASCAP), established at Hotel Claridge, New York City, **Feb. 13, 1914.**

American Society for the Prevention of Cruelty to Animals (A.S.P.C.A.), founded by Henry Bergh [Aug. 29, 1811—Mar. 12, 1888], **Apr. 10, 1866.**

American Tragedy, An, vast, naturalistic novel, **1925,** by U.S. novelist Theodore Dreiser [Aug. 27, 1871—Dec. 28, 1945]; film version, *A Place in the Sun,* **1951.**

America's Cup, international sailing trophy, named for the *America,* schooner that defeated 14 British competitors in race around the Isle of Wight, **Aug. 22, 1851.**

americium, element No. 95, discovered, **1944,** by American physicist Glenn T. Seaborg [1912—].

Amiens, battle of, Allied armies inflicted heavy losses on German armies, marking turning point on the Western Front in WW I, **Aug. 8-11, 1918.**

Amiens, Treaty of, Britain made peace with France, Spain, Batavian Republic, ending French Revolutionary War, **Mar. 27, 1802.**

Amistad **incident,** Negroes aboard Spanish slave ship *Amistad* mutinied and were seized by U.S. warship off Long Island, 1839; U.S. Supreme Court declared Negroes free, **Mar. 9, 1841.**

ammonia synthesis, invented, **c. 1910**, by German chemist Fritz Haber [1868-1934].

Amnesty International, world-wide organization set up, **1965**, to seek immunity from prosecution for "criminals" and others during and after periods of war or civil disorder; awarded Nobel Prize for Peace, **1977**.

Amoco Cadiz, supertanker *Amoco Cadiz*, en route from Persian Gulf to Rotterdam, grounded in heavy gale off coast of northern Brittany, spilling her entire cargo of 223,000 tons of crude oil into the ocean, creating ecological disaster, **Mar. 16, 1978**.

amphibious warfare, combined use of land and sea forces for a military purpose, used by Athenians against Sicily, **415 B.C.**; used in Gallipoli campaign of WW I, **1915**; used by Allied forces invading Pacific islands in WW II **1943-45**; invading Italy and Sicily, **1943-44**; invading Normandy (D-day), **June 6, 1944**; used by United Nations forces invading Inchon in Korean War, **Sept. 15, 1950**.

Remains of Amphitheater of Nimes, France.

amphitheater, oldest extant, Pompeii, **82 B.C.**; largest, Colosseum, Rome, **75-80**; perfected style, amphitheater at Verona, **290**.

amplifier, feedback concept developed, **1912**, by American electronics engineer Edwin H. Armstrong [1890-1954].

amplifier, radio, patented, **1907**, by American radio pioneer Lee De Forest [1890-1961]

Amritsar massacre, troops under British order fired on and killed hundreds of Indian nationalists in Punjab, India, **Apr. 13, 1919**.

Amtrak, federally chartered National Railroad Passenger Corporation, began U.S. service, **May 1, 1971**.

amyl alcohol, discovered, **1849**, by English chemist Sir Edward Frankland [1825-1899].

amyl nitrite, discovered, **1844**, by French chemist Antoine J. Balard [1802-1876].

Anabaptists, Protestant sect that rejected infant baptism; formed as free believers' community, Zurich, **1525**; centered in Moravia as *"Moravian Brethren,"* **1526**; besieged and conquered while awaiting the Kingdom, Munster, Germany, **June 24, 1535**.

analytical geometry, introduced, **c. 1637**, by French philosopher and mathematician Rene Descartes [1596-1650].

analytical psychology, established, **1913**, by Swiss psychologist Carl Gustav Jung [1875-1962].

analytic mechanics, established, **1788**, by French mathematician and astronomer Joseph Louis Comte de Lagrange [1736-1813].

Anatomy Lesson, The, realistic painting by Rembrandt, **1632**, that insured the artist's fame and fortune.

anchor escapement (clock), invented, **c. 1666**, by English physicist Robert Hooke [1635-1703].

Ancon, Treaty of, restored peace between Peru and Chile during War of the Pacific; Peru ceded province of Tarapaca to Chile, **Oct. 20, 1883**.

Ancona **disaster**, Italian ocean liner *Ancona* sunk by torpedo from German submarine in WW I, **Nov. 9, 1915**; 272 persons died, including 27 Americans.

Andalusia, historic region in southern Spain, settled by Phoenicians, **11th century B.C.**; conquered by the Moors, **711**; seized (except for Granada) by Castile, **13th century**.

Anderson, Fort, battle of, 15 Union warships, commanded by Admiral David D. Porter [June 8, 1813-Feb. 13, 1891], and Union land troops forced Confederate army to abandon Fort Anderson, N.C., **Feb. 18, 1865**. *See Civil War, U.S.*

Andes survivors, ordeal of survival in Andes Mountains after airplane with 45 passengers crashed, bound from Uruguay to Chile. 16 stayed alive through human courage, prayers, and cannibalism until rescued, **Oct. 13-Dec. 23, 1972**.

Andrassy note, communique to signatories of 1856 Treaty of Paris, calling for Christian-Muslim commission to oversee establishment of religious freedom in Bosnia-Hercegovina; adopted by European powers but rejected by rebels, **Dec. 30, 1875.**

Andrea Doria and Stockholm collision, Italian luxury liner *Andrea Doria* and Swedish liner *Stockholm* collided in fog off Nantucket, Mass., sinking the *Doria*, **July 25, 1956.** 52 persons dead or unaccounted for.

Andromeda Nebula, first seen by telescope, **1612,** by German astronomer Simon Marius [1570-1624].

Andrussovo, Treaty of, ended 13-year war between Russia and Poland, which ceded Kiev, eastern Ukraine, and Smolensk, **Jan. 20, 1667.**

Angela Davis case, U.S. black militant Angela Davis [Jan. 26, 1944-] acquitted, **June 4, 1972,** on charges of murder, kidnapping, and conspiracy in connection with Soledad (Jackson Brothers) shootout at Marin County Courthouse, Calif., **Jan. 16, 1970,** in which one white guard was killed.

Angevin, two medieval dynasties originating in France; first dynasty founded by counts of Anjou, **10th century.** Geoffrey Plantagenet [Aug. 24, 1113-Sept 7, 1151] conquered Normandy, **1144;** England ruled by Angevin or Plantagenet kings, **1154-1399;** second dynasty founded when Charles I [1226-1285] of Naples gave Anjou in appanage to his brother, Count of Provence, **1246;** collateral line of second dynasty ruled kingdom of Naples, **1266-1486.**

Angkor Wat, great temple-complex established at ancient Khmer empire (Cambodia), **c. 1125-50;** destroyed by the Chams, **1177;** many buildings restored, **1900s.**

Anglicanism, doctrine and system of the Church of England and sister churches, established **1534,** with Act of Supremacy of King Henry VIII [June 2, 1491-Jan 28, 1547]; *Book of Common Prayer,* adopted **1549;** *Thirty-nine Articles,* **1563.**

Anglo-Egyptian Sudan, former condominium established by British and Egyptian agreement, **Jan. 19, 1899;** British ordered Egyptian forces out of Sudan, which was to be ruled separately, **Nov. 22, 1924;** condominium ended, **Jan. 1, 1956,** with Sudan as independent republic.

Anglo-Saxons, Germanic-speaking people (Angles from Schleswig, Jutes from Jutland, and Saxons from northern Gaul) who settled in England, **late 5th century.**

Angora (Ankara), battle of, about 800,000 Tatars, led by Mongol conquerer Tamerlane [c. 1336-1405], defeated Turkish army under Bajazet I (Beyazid I) [1347-1403] at Angora in central Asia Minor, **June 20, 1402.**

Angostura, Congress of, proclaimed the independence of Greater Colombia, to be constituted of New Granada, Venezuela, and Quito, with Simon Bolivar [July 24, 1783-Dec. 17, 1830] as president, **Dec. 17, 1819.**

angry young men, post World War II literary school in revolt against British class structure and values; representative books: *Look Back in Anger,* **1956** by John Osborne [Dec 12, 1929-]; *Lucky Jim,* **1954,** by Kingsley Amis [April 16, 1922-].

Animal Farm, stark, allegorical novel, **1945,** by English novelist, and critic George Orwell [June 25, 1903-Jan. 21, 1950].

animation, film technique used to produce a moving picture by photographing drawings in sequence, discovered **1882;** first animated film, *Gertie the Dinosaur,* **1909.**

Anna Karenina, novel, **1875-77,** depicting aristocratic life and tragedy of a love affair ending in suicide, by Russian writer Leo Tolstoy [Sept. 9, 1828-Nov. 20, 1910]; 15 film versions, **1910-1967.**

Annales Ecclesiastici, pioneer "scientific" history of the Catholic Church up to the year **1198,** published **1538-June 30, 1607,** in answer to the Protestant history, *Centuries of Magdeburg,* **1559-74.**

Annales Veteris et Novi Testament, treatise on the Bible **1650-54,** that fixed the beginning of the world at **4004 B.C.,** by the Anglican Archbishop of Armagh, James Ussher [Jan. 4, 1581-March 21, 1656].

Annapolis Convention, called by Virginia to discuss regulation of interstate commerce, resulted in the summoning of the Federal Constitutional Convention, **Sept. 11-14, 1786.**

Annie, Broadway musical, **1977,** based on comic strip *Little Orphan Annie;* won numerous awards, including Tony for best musical.

Annie Get Your Gun, Broadway musical, first produced, **1946**, based on life of sharpshooter Annie Oakley, by U.S. composer and lyricist Irving Berlin [May 11, 1888 -].

Another Country, novel, **1961**, about personal relationships between blacks and whites, by U.S. writer James Baldwin [Aug. 2, 1924-]; author's *The Fire Next Time*, **1963**, an angry indictment of society's treatment of blacks.

Anschluss, Hitler's Nazi German army invaded Austria, **Mar. 12, 1938**, and the *Anschluss* (political union) of Austria with Germany was proclaimed by Austrian Chancellor Arthur Seyss-Inquart [July 22, 1892-Oct. 16, 1946], **Mar. 13, 1938**; Austria incorporated into Germany (Reich) as new state, **Apr. 10, 1938**.

Antarctica, first circumnavigated by British navigator/whaler John Biscoe, **1830-32**; U.S. explorer Richard E. Byrd [Oct. 25, 1888-Mar. 11, 1957] established Little America, **1928-29**.

anthrax, life cycle discovered, **1876**, by German bacteriologist Robert Koch [1843-1910].

anthropology, modern, science developed, from **1886**, with efforts to confirm theory of evolution.

antibody, structure of, molecular structure determined, **1969**, by American biochemist Gerald M. Edelman [1929-] and English biochemist Rodney R. Porter [1917-].

Anti-Corn-Law League, organization that worked for repeal of English Corn Laws, founded by Richard Cobden [June 3, 1804-Apr. 2, 1865], **Sept. 24, 1838**.

Antietam (Sharpsburg), battle of, Confederates under Gen. Robert E. Lee [Jan. 19, 1807-Oct. 12, 1870] defeated by Union forces under Gen. George B. McClellan [Dec. 3,1826-Oct. 29, 1885], in what is said to be bloodiest day of U.S. Civil War, **Sept. 17, 1862**.

Anti-gag law, guaranteed U.S. federal employees the right to organize and to petition Congress individually and collectively, **Aug. 24, 1912**.

Antigone, Greek tragedy, **c. 441 B.C.**, about obligation to obey divine rather than human law, by Sophocles [c. 496—406 B.C.].

antihistamines, first discovered, **1937**, by Italian-Swiss pharmacologist Daniel Bovet [1907-]. First artificial antihistamines developed, **1942**, by French research biologist Bernard N. Halpern [1904-1978].

Anti-Masonic Party, U.S. political organization, began after disappearance of William Morgan [c. 1774-c. 1826] (allegedly murdered by Masons), **1826**; held first national nominating convention of any party, with first written party platform, **Sept. 1831**; absorbed by Whigs after **1836**.

Anti-Monopoly Party, U.S. political party, established **May 14, 1884**, that nominated former Union General Benjamin F. Butler [Nov. 5, 1818-Jan. 11, 1893] for U.S. President; merged with Greenback Party to form People's Party, **May 28, 1884**.

antimony, element No. 51; discovery credited, **c. 1450**, to German alchemist Basil Valentine [Fl. 15th century].

anti-Nebraska men, Democrats and Whigs who opposed repeal of Missouri Compromise and extension of slavery to the U.S. territories, **1854**.

Antioch, historic city in Turkey, seized by Christian Crusaders, **June 3, 1098**; sacked by Mamelukes, **1268**.

Antioch College, college, in Yellow Springs, Ohio, that pioneered early work-study program in U.S., **1921**.

antipolio vaccine (oral), accepted for licensing, **1960**, developed by American bacteriologist Albert B. Sabin [1906-].

antiproton, existence demonstrated, **1955**, by Italian-American physicist Emilio Segre [1905-] and American physicist Owen Chamberlain [1920-].

Anti-Saloon League, U.S. organization against the sale of alcoholic beverages, was founded as Ohio Anti-Saloon League, **1893**; merged with National Temperance League, **1950**.

antiseptic surgery, introduced, **c. 1860**, by English surgeon Lord Joseph Lister [1827-1912].

antitoxin, diphtheria, developed, **1890**, by German bacteriologist Emil Adolf von Behring [1854-1917].

Antony and Cleopatra, tragedy, **c. 1607**, about last days of Cleopatra, by English poet and dramatist William Shakespeare [Apr. 26, 1564-Apr. 23, 1616].

Antwerp, battles of, Spanish defeated Walloons and took city of Antwerp during Netherlands war of independence, **Nov. 4, 1576.** French captured city of Antwerp during the liberation of Belgium, **Nov.-Dec. 23, 1832**; German forces routed Belgians during great assault on Antwerp during WW I, **Sept. 28-Oct. 10, 1914.**

Anzio, Italian coastal town, where Allied troops landed in WW II to draw German forces from Cassino, **Jan. 1944.**

ANZUS Treaty, mutual defense pact signed by Australia, New Zealand, and U.S., **Sept. 1, 1951**.

Aoki-Kimberley, Treaty of, Japan and Britain agreed to abolish extra territoriality and make all occidentals subject to Japanese courts, **July 16, 1894**.

Apache Wars, series of conflicts between Apache Indians and U.S. troops and settlers in Arizona, New Mexico, Texas, and Oklahoma, **c. 1860-90**.

apartheid, government policy of segregating whites and nonwhites put into effect in the Republic of South Africa, **June 1949**; Group Areas Act, **Apr. 27, 1950**, assigned separate "homelands" to different racial groups.

Apocalypse, The, last book of the New Testament, probably written **c. 96**, also called the *Book of Revelation*, attributed to the Apostle John.

Apollo, Temple of, shrine at Delphi, Greece, built **c. 478 B.C.**; Apollo, god of prophecy and poetry, believed to deliver oracles through inspired priestess, from **c. 800 B.C.**; oracle fell silent, **390**, after edict of Christian Emperor Theodosius I [346-Jan. 17, 395].

Appian Way, famous Roman road built from Rome to Capua (later extended all the way to Brundisium), **312 B.C.**; new road, parallel to old, built from Rome to Albano, **1784**.

Appomattox Courthouse, site in Appomattox, Va., of the surrender of Confederate Gen. Robert E. Lee to Union Gen. Ulysses S. Grant [Apr. 27, 1822-July 23, 1885], ending U.S. Civil War, **Apr. 9, 1865**.

APRA (Alianza Popular Revolucionaria Americana) (Partido Aprista), political party in Peru, founded by Victor Raul Haya de la Torre [Feb. 3, 1895-], **1924**; outlawed, **1931-45**; legalized, **1945**; outlawed, **1948**; legalized, **1956**; outlawed, **1968**.

Aqaba (Akaba), Jordanian port on Gulf of Aqaba near Israeli port of Elat; trade center between Palestine and Syria, since **1000 B.C.**; taken by Saladin [c. 1138-Mar. 1193], **1187**; ceded to Trans-Jordan, **1924**.

Aqaba (Akaba), Gulf of, northern arm of Red Sea, blockaded by Arabs, **1949-56**, **1967**.

aqualung, coinvented, **1943**, by French marine explorers Emile Gagnan and Jacques-Yves Cousteau [1910-].

Arabia, peninsula in southwest Asia where Muhammad [570-June 8, 632] unified Arab tribes under Islam, **7th century**.

Arabic numerals, originated by Hindus, c. **200 B.C.**; adopted by Arabs, **800**; introduced into West, **13th century**; became standardized into modern numerical system, **mid-15th century**.

Arab-Israeli Wars, conflicts between Israel and Arab states; first, **May 14, 1948-Jan. 7, 1949**; second, **Oct. 29,-Nov. 6, 1956**; third (or Six-Day War), **June 5-10, 1967**; fourth (or Yom Kippur War), **Oct. 6, 1973-Jan. 18, 1974**.

Arab League, Arab states organized to resist the creation of the state of Israel, **1945**.

Arab Liberation Movement, political organization inaugurated to replace all political parties in Syria, **Oct. 24, 1952**.

Aramaeans, Semitic people who settled in Syria, c. **1900 B.C.**, bringing their language, Aramaic, with them.

Arausio, battle of, Gauls (Cimbri and Teutones) defeated Roman army on Rhone River in southern France, **105 B.C.**

Arbela, battle of, fought at Gaugamela, in ancient Assyria (now Iraq), where Alexander the Great defeated the Persians under Darius III [-330 B.C.], **331 B.C.**

Archimedes' principle, established, **3rd century B.C.** by Greek mathematician Archimedes [287-212 B.C.].

Archimedes screw, invented, **3rd century B.C.**, by Greek mathematician Archimedes [287-212 B.C.], to raise water from a lower to a higher elevation.

architectural acoustics, developed, **1895**, by American physicist Wallace Clement Ware Sabine [1868-1919].

Archive War, armed force sent by Pres. Samuel Houston [Mar. 2, 1793-July 26, 1863] failed to move government archives from Austin to Houston, **Sept. 1842**, thus keeping Austin as permanent capital of Texas.

Arch of Constantine, last important monument of Imperial Rome, built **315**, to celebrate triumph of the Emperor Constantine [c 280-Mar. 22, 337].

Triumphal Arch.— Arch of Constantine, Rome.

arc lights, invented, **1808**, by English chemist Sir Humphry Davy [1778-1829]. First commercial use of carbon arc lights was by the Paris Opera, **1844**.

arc (Moissan) furnace, developed, **1892**, by French chemist Henri Moissan [1852-1907].

Arcole, battle of, French forces under Napoleon I suffered heavy losses but drove main Austrian army out of village of Arcole, in northern Italy, **Nov. 15-17, 1796**.

Arctic, the, first explored by Vikings, c. **11th century**; by those seeking Northeast Passage and Northwest Passage, **16th-17th century**; various nations set up some 300 arctic stations for research purposes during International Geophysical Year, **1957-58**; U.S. nuclear-powered submarines have made successful voyages under the icecap, since **1958**.

Ardennes, wooded plateau in southeastern Belgium, northern Luxembourg, and northern France, site of heavy fighting in WW I,

1914-1918, and WW II, **1939-1945**.

Area Redevelopment Act (ADA), Pres. John F. Kennedy authorized, **May 1, 1962**, $394 million in federal aid to redevelop depressed areas in U.S.; program ended, **June 30, 1965**.

Argand lamp, invented, **1784**, by Swiss physicist Aime Argand [1755-1803].

Argentina, South American republic, declared its independence from Spanish rule, **July 9, 1806**; Argentine-Chilean boundary dispute settled, **1902**.

Arginusae, battle of, Athenian fleet, under Conon, won decisive victory over Spartan fleet off Arginusae, near Lesbos, **406 B.C.**

argon, discovered, **1892**, by English physicist John W. Strutt (Lord Rayleigh) [1842-1919]; identified, **1894**, by Scottish chemist William Ramsay [1852-1916]. Rayleigh was awarded Nobel prize in physics, **1904**.

Argonne, hilly wooded region in France, where French defeated Prussians at Valmy, **Sept. 20, 1792**; site of Allied victory drive (Meuse-Argonne sector), **Sept.-Nov. 1918**, in WW I.

Argos, city-state of ancient Greece that dominated Peloponnesus, **7th century B.C.**; rivaled Athens and Corinth, **6th century B.C.**, captured by Sparta, c. **494 B.C.**; fl. under Roman rule, after **146 B.C.**

Argus, U.S. war brigantine attacked and captured by British warship *Pelican* off English coast, **Aug. 14, 1813**.

arithmatic, fundamental theorem of, proved **1801** by German mathematician Karl F. Gauss [1777-1855].

Arizona, part of territory ceded to U.S. by Mexico, **1848**; admitted to the Union (U.S.) as 48th state, **Feb. 14, 1912**.

Arkansas, part of territory acquired by Louisiana Purchase, admitted to the Union (U.S.) as 25th state, **June 15, 1836**; seceded from the Union, **May 6, 1861**; readmitted, **June 22, 1868**.

Arlberg Tunnel, one of the world's longest RR tunnels (6.2 mi.), built in Austria on border between Tyrol and Vorarlberg, **1880-84**; opened, **Sept. 20, 1884**.

Arlington National Cemetery, established as a burial ground for U.S. war dead, on Potomac River, opposite Washington, D.C., **1864**.

Armada, Spanish, fleet of war vessels sent by Philip II [May 21, 1527-Sept. 13, 1598] of Spain against England; destroyed by English navy and battered by storms, **May-Aug., 1588**.

Armagnacs and Burgundians, opposing factions that fought for power in France, **15th century**; began open civil war, **1411**; became involved in Hundred Years' War, **1415**; Paris seized by Burgundians and Armagnacs massacred, **1418**; John the Fearless [May 28, 1371-Sept. 10, 1419] of Burgundy murdered by Armagnacs, **Sept. 10, 1419**.

Armenia, historic region and former kingdom in Asia Minor, conquered by Alexander the Great, **330 B.C.**; fell to the Romans, **69 B.C.**; became autonomous under native rulers, the Bagratids, **885-1046**; Little Armenia established in Cilicia, **1080**: Greater Armenia occupied by Mongol Tamerlane, **1386-94**; Russian Armenia made a Soviet republic, **1920**.

Armenian Church, established in Armenia, **302**, by St. Gregory the Illuminator [c. 240-332] rejected Christological definitions of the Council of Chalcedon, **451**; seceded from Byzantium and Rome, **491**.

Armory Show, exhibition at Sixty-Ninth Regiment Armory, New York City, **Feb. 15-March 15, 1913**; introduced avant-garde art to America.

Army, U.S. Department of the, created as one of the three security departments within the U.S. national military establishment, **July 25, 1947**.

Arnhem, battle of, Germans defeated British airborne troops in the Netherlands, **Sept. 19-28, 1944**.

Arnold, Benedict, court-martial of, Benedict Arnold [Jan. 14, 1741-June 14, 1801] reprimanded for improper behavior at court-martial in Morristown, N.J., **Dec. 23, 1779**.

Aroostock War, conflict between Maine farmers and New Brunswick lumbermen over territory on U.S.-Canadian border, **Jan.-Mar. 1839**.

Around-the-World Automobile Race, six cars (American, French, German, and Italian) raced from New York City to Paris by way of Alaska and Siberia, **Feb. 12-July 30, 1908**.

Around the World in 80 Days, novel, **1873**, by an originator of science fiction, French writer Jules Verne [Feb. 8, 1828-Mar. 24, 1905]; Academy Award-winning movie, **1956**, produced by Michael Todd [June 2, 1901-Mar. 22, 1958].

Arras, Treaty of, King Charles VII [Feb. 22, 1403-July 22, 1461] of France secured an alliance with Duke Philip the Good [June 13, 1396-June 15, 1467] of Burgundy against England, **1435**; King Louis XI [July 3, 1423-Aug. 30, 1483] of France signed agreement with Dutch representatives, **1482**, whereby France incorporated the duchy of Burgundy and held Artois and Franche-Comte as dowry of Margaret of Austria [1522-1586].

Arsacids (Arsacidae), ancient Parthian dynasty that ruled Persia, **c. 250 B.C.-A.D. 226**.

art deco, ornamental, artistic style stimulated by Exposition of Decorative Arts, Paris, **1925**.

Artemis, Temple of, huge temple dedicated to huntress and fertility goddess, Artemis, at Ephesus, Asia Minor, built **c. 560 B.C.**; one of seven wonders of ancient world; set on fire, **356 B.C.**; rebuilt **c. 356-236 B.C.**

Arthur Godfrey Time, long-running, radio talent show, **April 30, 1945-April 30, 1972**.

Arthurian legends, legendary chivalric stories of King Arthur, first mentioned in Welsh poem, *Gododin,* **c. 600**; in *History of the Kings of Britain,* **1147**, by Geoffrey of Monmouth [c. 1100-1154]; treated fully in compilation *Le Morte d'Arthur,* **1485**, by Sir Thomas Malory [c. 1415-Mar. 24, 1471].

Articles of Confederation, first constitution ratified by thirteen original states of U.S., **Mar. 1, 1781**; replaced by U.S. Constitution, **Mar. 4, 1789**.

artificial element, first produced, **1937**, by Italian-born U.S. physicist Emilio Segre [1905-]; called technetium, it was assigned No. 43 in the Periodic Table.

artificial heart, first used, **1966**, for left ventricle function during heart surgery, by U.S. surgeon Michael DeBakey [1908-]

artificial human heart, first implanted, **April 4, 1969**, by Argentine physician Domingo Liotta, [1924-], at Baylor University, Houston, Texas.

artificial kidney machine, invented, **1943**, by Dutch physician W. J. Kolff [1911-]

artificial respiration, principle of, first demonstrated, **1667**, by English scientist Robert Hooke [1635-1703].

Art Institute of Chicago, established in Grant Park, **1879**.

Art of the Fugue, nineteen-movement composition, written **1749**, published **1756**, left unfinished by German composer Johann Sebastian Bach [March 21, 1685-July 28, 1750].

Artois, battle of, battle of attrition, **May 9-June 18, 1915**, between French and German forces in France.

Art Students League of New York, independent art school, established **1875**.

Ascalon, battle of, Crusaders gained important victory over Saracens, **Aug. 19, 1099**; for a brief time, Muslim resistance to Christian occupation of Holy Land came to an end.

Asculum, battle of, Pyrrhus [c. 318-272 B.C.] of Epirus, with his mercenaries and elephants, defeated Romans in "Pyrrhic victory" at Apulia, Italy, **279 B.C.**

Ashanti Wars, series of conflicts between Ashanti tribal confederation and British for control of Ghana, West Africa; first war, **1822-31**; second, **1873-74**; third, **1893-94**.

Ashau Valley, North Vietnamese troops captured U.S. Green Beret camp at Ashau Valley after 72-hour siege, **Mar. 10, 1966**.

Ashcan School, school of American realistic painters of city life, formed **1908**.

Ashquelon (Ashkelon, Askelon, Ascalon, Eshkalon), biblical and historic city on Mediterranean, in Israel, conquered by Christian Crusaders, **1153**; captured by Richard I ("The Lion-Heart") [Sept. 8, 1157-Apr. 6, 1199], **1191**: sacked by Muslims, **1270**; modern Israeli city established, **1955**.

Asia Minor (or Anatolia), peninsula in Asia, roughly identical with Asiatic Turkey, settled by Hittites, **c. 1800 B.C.**; Greek coastal colonies established, **8th-7th century B.C.**; conquered by Persians, **6th century B.C.**; split into small states by Diadochi, **c. 300 B.C.**; reunified by Rome, **2nd century B.C.**; conquered by Ottoman Turks, **13th-15th century**.

Ask not what your county can do for you..., said by U.S. Pres. John F. Kennedy in his inaugural address, **Jan. 20, 1961**.

Aspern, battle of, great, indecisive battle, during Napoleonic Wars, between French and Austrians, **May 21-22, 1809**.

aspirin, production process discovered, **1859**, by German chemist Adolph Wilhelm Kolbe [1818-1884].

Aspromonte, battle of, Italian royal troops defeated rebels led by Giuseppe Garibaldi [July 4, 1807-June 2, 1882] in the southern Apennines; Garibaldi captured, **Aug. 29, 1862**.

Assandun (Ashingdon), battle of, Danes under Canute ("the Great") [c. 994-Nov. 12, 1035] defeated Saxons under Edmund II ("Ironside") [c. 989-Nov. 30, 1016] in southern England, **Oct. 18, 1016**.

Assassins, heterodox Islamic religious sect, **fl. 11th-13th century**.

Assaye, battle of, British-Indian force, under Gen. Arthur Wellesley (Duke of Wellington) [Apr. 29, 1769-Sept. 14, 1852], won costly but important victory over much larger Maratha army in Hyderabad, India, **Sept. 23, 1803**.

Assize of Arms, King Henry II [Mar. 25, 1133-July 6, 1189] of England made a freeman responsible, according to his income, for part of the defense of the realm, **1181**.

Assumption Bill, U.S. federal government assumed responsibility for the debts of the states, **July 26, 1790**.

Assyria, ancient empire in west Asia, originated around city of Ashur on upper Tigris River, **early 3rd millennium B.C.**; gained hegemony in region under Ashurnasirpal II [d. 860? B.C.], **c. 870 B.C.**; reached its peak under Assurbanipal [d. 626? B.C.], **c. 625 B.C.**; its capital, Nineveh, sacked by Babylonians, Medes, and Scythians, **612 B.C.**

ASSYRIAN PRIME MINISTER AND ROYAL OVERSEER.

astronomical observatory, first started, **1574**, by Danish astronomer Tycho Brahe [1546-1601], on island of Hveen (Ven), between Denmark and Sweden.

Aswan Dam, British completed building dam south of Aswan, on Nile River, to store irrigation water for Nile valley, **1902**; enlarged, **1934**.

Aswan High Dam, Egyptians, with Soviet financial aid, constructed dam south of

Aswan Dam, **1960-70**; dedicated to Egyptian Pres. Gamal Abdal Nasser [Jan. 15, 1918-Sept. 28, 1970], **1971**.

Atbara River, battle of, Anglo-Egyptian troops under Gen. Horatio H. Kitchener [June 24, 1850-June 5, 1916] soundly defeated larger Sudanese force (Mahdists); 6,000 Sudanese killed or captured, **Apr. 8, 1898**.

atheism, disbelief in God, espoused **c. 400 B.C.** by Greek philosopher Democritus [460?-370? B.C.].

Atheists, United World, U.S. organization founded to promote disbelief in God, **1970**, by Madalyn Murray O'Hair [Apr. 13, 1919-] principal in U.S. Supreme Court case, **1963**, that forbade prayer in the public schools.

Athens, fountainhead of Western civilization as the center of ancient Greek culture, **fl. 6th-5th centuries B.C.**; emerged as a power during Persian Wars, **500-449 B.C.**; Golden Age of Athens under Pericles, **5th century B.C.**; conquered by Sparta, **404 B.C.**; defeated by Macedonians at Chaeronea, **338 B.C.**; sacked by Romans, **86 B.C.**

Atlanta, battle of, Union forces under Gen. William T. Sherman [Feb. 8, 1820-Feb. 14, 1891] captured city of Atlanta, Ga., which was evacuated by Confederates under Gen. John B. Hood [June 1, 1831-Aug. 30, 1879], **Sept. 1-2, 1864**.

Atlantic, British White Star steamship *Atlantic* wrecked off Nova Scotia, **Apr. 1, 1873**; 547 persons perished.

Atlantic, battle of the, conflict between German submarines and allied merchant and warships during WW I, Germans instituted blockade of Britain, **Feb. 18, 1915**; Germans began attack on all ships in Atlantic, **Mar. 1, 1916**; Allies began moving ships in destroyer-escorted convoys to reduce heavy losses, **May 10, 1917**; conflict between Nazi Germany and Allies in Atlantic during WW II, British navy forced German pocket battleship *Graf Spee* to be scuttled, **Dec. 1939**; German battleship *Bismarck* sunk in North Atlantic, **May 1941**; allied destroyer-escorted convoys blunted German submarine menace, **1943**; German battle cruiser *Scharnhorst* sunk by British, **Dec. 26, 1943**; German battleship *Tirpitz* sunk, **Nov. 12, 1944**.

Atlantic cable, first successfully laid between North America and Europe, **1858**, by American financier Cyrus West Field [1819-1892]..

Atlantic Charter, basic Allied peace aims after WW II issued by British Prime Minister Winston Churchill [Nov. 30, 1874-Jan. 24, 1965] and U.S. Pres. Franklin D. Roosevelt [Jan. 30, 1882-Apr. 12, 1945], **Aug. 14, 1941**.

Atlantic Monthly, The, U.S. magazine of literature, art, society, and politics, founded **1857**.

atomic bomb (A bomb), first model exploded in desert near Alamogordo, New Mexico, **July 16, 1945**, using uranium-235 as a fissionable material. Used as a mass-destruction weapon at Hiroshima, Japan, **August 6, 1945**, and at Nagasaki, Japan, **Aug. 9, 1945**.

Atomic Energy Commission (AEC), U.S. government commission created by Atomic Energy Act, **Aug. 1, 1946**.

atomic heat law, described, **1819**, by French scientists Pierre Louis Dulong [1785-1838] and Alexis Therese Petit [1791-1820].

atomic nuclei, size and structure, determined, **c. 1960**, by American physicist Robert Hofstadter [1915-], using high-energy electron beam.

atomic particle reaction, first photographed, **1925**, by English physicist Lord Patrick M. Blackett [1897-1974], using Wilson cloud chamber.

atomic theory, idea that basic structure of universe is the atom; propounded, c. 450 B.C., by Greek philosopher Leucippus [5th century B.C.]; later expanded by Greek philosopher Democritus [5th century-4th century B.C.]; further developed, 1503, by English chemist John Dalton [1766-1844], with particular relevance for chemistry.

atomic transmutation, theory of, published, 1902, by British physicist Ernest Rutherford [1871-1937].

atomic weight values, established, 1894-1913, by American chemist Theodore W. Richards [1868-1928] for over 50 elements..

atom smasher, industrial, first designed and built, 1936, by American scientists at Westinghouse Electric Corporation.

atom, structure of, proposed, 1913, by Danish physicist Niels Bohr [1885-1962].

atonality, school of musical composition rejecting the major-minor tonal system; appeared 1907, in *Second Quartet*, written without key signature, by Austrian-U.S. composer Arnold Schoenberg [Sept. 13, 1874-July 13, 1961]; twelve-tone system adopted by Schoenberg, 1921.

Atonement, Day of (*Yom Kippur*), established as day of fasting and prayer, 5th century B.C.; observance centered on the synagogue since destruction of the Temple, 70.

Attica prison riot, 1200 inmates of Attica State Correctional Facility, Attica, N.Y., took over cell block and held 38 guards hostage, Sept. 9, 1971; on Gov. Nelson Rockefeller's orders, state police retook prison, Sept. 13, 1971, killing 28 inmates and 9 hostages.

ATP (adenosine triphosphate), theory of cell energy proposed, 1961, by English chemist Peter D. Mitchell [1920-].

Audubon Society, National, organization dedicated to the conservation of wildlife and the environment, established, 1905, in memory of John James Audubon [Apr. 26, 1785-Jan. 27, 1851.]

Auerstedt, battle of, French Field Marshal Louis Nicholas Davout [May 10, 1770-June 1, 1823] defeated the Prussians under Duke Charles [Sept. 3, 1757-June 14, 1828] of Brunswick, in East Germany, Oct. 14, 1806.

Aughrim (Aghrim), battle of, forces of William III [Nov. 4, 1650-Mar. 8, 1702] of England won victory over those of James II [Oct. 14, 1633-Sept. 6, 1701], July 12, 1691.

Augsburg, League of, defensive alliance formed by Holy Roman Emperor Leopold I [June 9, 1640-May 5, 1705] with Sweden, Spain, Bavaria, Palatinate, and other German states against Louis XIV [Sept. 5, 1638-Sept. 1, 1715] of France, 1686; transformed into the Grand Alliance, 1689.

Augsburg, Peace of, temporarily settled the religious conflicts arising from the Reformation within the Holy Roman Empire, 1555.

Augusta, Treaty of, peace treaty signed by Georgia's colonists with Creek and Cherokee Indians at Augusta, 1763, at the end of the French and Indian War.

Augustan Age, apogee of Latin literature, 27 B.C.-A.D. 14, coinciding with reign of Emperor Augustus.

Auray, battle of, English forces defeated French in Brittany, France, Sept. 29, 1364.

Austerlitz, battle of (battle of the Three Emperors), French forces under Emperor Napoleon I won great victory by defeating Russian and Austrian armies under Czar Alexander I and Emperor Francis II in Moravia (Czechoslovakia), Dec. 2, 1805.

Australia, Commonwealth of, British colonies of New South Wales, Victoria, Queensland, South Australia, West Australia, and Tasmania united by British parliament to become self-governing commonwealth, Jan. 1, 1901; Northern Territory added, 1911.

Australian Colonies Government Act, British parliament gave colonies in Australia rights of self-government, Aug. 1850.

Austria, republic in central Europe, occupied by German troops, **Mar. 12, 1938**; republic reestablished, **Dec. 19, 1945**; independence fully regained, **May 15, 1955**.

Austrian Succession, War of the, general European war brought on by succession of Maria Theresa [May 13, 1717-Nov. 29, 1780] of Austria to the Hapsburg lands by the Pragmatic Sanction, **1740-48**; Prussians defeated Austrians at Mollwitz, **Apr. 10, 1741**; English defeated French at Dettingen, **June 27, 1743**; Prussians defeated Austrians at Hohenfriedeberg, **June 4, 1745**; Prussia gained most of Silesia by treaty of Dresden, **Dec. 25, 1745**; war continued inconclusively until treaty of Aix-la-Chapelle, **Oct. 18, 1748**.

Austro-Hungarian Empire, former dual monarchy of central Europe established as a continuation of the Hapsburg Empire, **June 12, 1867-Nov. 3, 1918**.

Austro-Prussian War (Seven Weeks' War), Prussia, allied with Italy, battled Austria, allied with Bavaria, Saxony, and other smaller German states, in attempt to unify Germany under Prussian control, **June 15,-Aug. 23, 1866**; Prussians crushed Austrians at Sadowa, **July 3, ;** Austrians won victories against Italians at Custozza, **June 24**; Austrians destroyed Italian fleet off Lissa, **July 20**; ended by treaty of Prague, **Aug. 23**.

automobile differential gear, built, **1885**, by German engineer Karl Benz [1844-1929].

automobile engine (two-cycle), invented, **1879**, by German inventor Karl Benz [1844-1929].

automobile, gasoline, invented, **1855**, by German inventor Karl Benz [1844-1929].

automobile, gasoline powered, first successful run in U.S., **1894**, in Springfield, Mass.; patented, **1895**, by Charles E. Duryea [1861-1938].

automobile, gas-turbine, first commercially developed, **1963**, by American inventor George J. Huebner [1910-] and coworkers.

automobile, self-starter, patented, **1914**, by American inventor-industrialist Vincent Bendix [1881-1945]; manufactured **1924**.

automobile, steam-propelled, built, **1801**, by English inventor Richard Trevithick [1771-1833].

automobile (toy), invented, **c. 1680**, by English scientist Sir Isaac Newton [1642-1727]; experimental machine propelled by jet of steam.

autoplate, patented, **1903**, by American inventor Henry A. Wood [1886-1939]; made possible casting in metal of entire newspaper page.

Avars, mounted nomadic people who controlled the steppes of central Asia, **4th-5th centuries**; ravaged all of southern Russia, **late 6th century**; crushed by Charlemagne on lower Danube, **795-796**.

Avignonese Captivity ("Babylonian Captivity"), pope accepted French royal domination and moved the papacy to Avignon, France, **1309-77**.

Avogadro's law, proposed, **1811**, by Italian physicist Amedeo Avogadro [1776-1856].

Awami League, political organization established in East Pakistan (Bangladesh) and West Pakistan (Pakistan), **1949**; called for a federation of East and West Pakistan, **1966**.

Axe, War of the, conflict between British and Kaffirs (Bantus) in southern Africa, **1846-47**; British defeated Kaffirs and set up British Kaffraria, **1848**.

Axis Powers, originated with "Rome-Berlin axis" between Adolf Hitler [Apr. 20, 1889-Apr. 30, 1945] and Benito Mussolini [July 29, 1883-Apr. 28, 1945], **Oct. 1936**; became coalition of countries headed by Germany, Italy, and Japan, **1936-45**.

Axum (Aksum), kingdom of, ruled over northern Ethiopia and southwestern Arabia, **c. 1st-6th centuries**; became major center of Coptic Christianity, **4th century**.

Ayacucho (Candorcanqui), battle of,

Peruvians won important victory over Spanish royalists, **Dec. 9, 1824**, ensuring independence for Peru.

Aylesford, battle of, Jutes defeated Britons during Jutes' invasion of what is now Britain, **456**.

Azcapotzalco, battle of, Mexican revolutionary forces defeated Spanish loyalist troops, **1821**, during Mexico's War of Independence.

Azimghur, battle of, British infantry, aided by Sikh cavalry, routed and dispersed Dinapur rebels during Sepoy Rebellion, **Apr. 15, 1858**.

Aztec Empire, advanced Aztec Indian civilization in central Mexico, **fl. 15th-early 16th centuries**; fell before Spanish under Hernan Cortes [1485-Sept. 2, 1547], **1519-25**.

Babbitt, novel, **1922**, about conformist, booster American businessman whose name has become by-word for the type, by U.S. novelist Sinclair Lewis, Nobel Prize winner, **1930**.

Babington's conspiracy, Anthony B. Babington [Oct 1561-Sept. 20, 1586] and others plotted to murder Queen Elizabeth I and liberate Mary, Queen of Scots; leaders of plot executed, **Sept. 1586**.

Babi Yar, Nazis massacred at least 34,000 (some say over 100,000) Jews in a ravine near Kiev called Babi Yar, **Sept. 1941**.

Baby and Child Care, handbook on child-rearing, **1946**; largest selling paperback book ever; over 30 million copies sold, **1980**; by U.S. pediatrician Dr. Benjamin Spock [May 2, 1903-]

Babylonia, ancient Mesopotamian empire, centered on Babylon, **3rd-2nd millennia B.C.**; historically limited to first dynasty of Babylon under Hammurabi [c. 1792-50 B.C.] **c. 1792-50 B.C**; grew great and powerful under Nebuchadnezzar [d. 562 B.C.], **c. 605-562 B.C.**; conquered by Persians under Cyrus the Great, **538 B.C.**

Babylonian Captivity, 70-year-exile of the Jews in Babylon, from Nebuchadnezzar's capture of Jerusalem to rebuilding of the temple, **586-16 B.C.**

Babylonian Captivity of the Church, expression used to describe exile of popes at Avignon, France **1309-77**.

Babylonian Talmud, most important compilation of the Talmud; source of post-biblical Jewish law.

Baby Snooks Show, long-running radio show, **1938-51**, featuring U.S. singer and former Ziegfield Follies girl Fanny Brice [Oct. 29, 1891-May 29, 1951].

bacillus, a rod-shaped bacterium described, **1680**, by Dutch microscope-maker, Antony van Leeuwenhook [1632-1723].

Bacon's Rebellion, Nathaniel Bacon [Jan. 2, 1647-Oct. 18, 1676] led angry frontiersmen in short rebellion demanding governmental reforms in Virginia, **May 10-Oct. 18, 1676**.

Bactria, powerful ancient Greek kingdom in central Asia (now northern Afghanistan and eastern Iran), seized by Alexander the Great, **328 B.C.**; became independent, **240 B.C.**; declined after capture by nomadic Sakas, **130 B.C.**

bacteriolysins, demonstrated, **1895**, by Polish bacteriologist Richard F.J. Pfeiffer [1858-1945], while studying immune reactions to cholera vibrios.

Badajoz, battle of, British under Arthur Wellesley, Duke of Wellington [May 1, 1769-Sept. 14, 1852] stormed and seized fortress of Badajoz, held by French, Hessians, and Spanish during Napoleonic Wars, **Apr. 5, 1812**.

Bad Axe River, battle of, 1300 Illinois militia soundly defeated Sac and Fox Indians at mouth of Bad Axe River in southwestern Wisconsin, ending Black Hawk War, **Aug. 2, 1832**.

Baden, Treaty of, ended War of the Spanish Succession between France and Austria, the latter receiving the right bank of the Rhine; France retained Alsace, **Sept. 7, 1714**.

Baghdad (Bagdad), city on the Tigris River, founded **763**; great commercial center under caliph Harun-al-Rashid [c. 764-809] **786-809**; sacked by Mongols, **1258**; destroyed by Tamerlane, **1400**; became capital of Iraq, **1920**.

Baghdad Pact, Turkey and Iraq formed defensive alliance (Middle East Treaty Organization) at Baghdad, **Feb. 18, 1955**; joined by Britain, Pakistan, and Iran, **1955**; Iraq withdrew from pact, **Mar. 24, 1959**.

Bahamas, settled by English, **17th century**; haven for pirates, **17th-18th centuries**; haven for blockade runners in U.S. Civil War, **1861-65**; became independent nation, **July 10, 1973**.

Bahrain, Arab state on the Persian Gulf, proclaimed its independence from Britain, **Aug. 14, 1971**.

Bakelite, invented, **1909**, by Belgian-born U.S. chemist Leo Hendrick Baekeland [1863-1944].

Bakke case, U.S. Supreme Court ruled, **June 28, 1978**, that Alan Bakke [1940-] must be admitted to University of California Medical School at Davis.

Balaclava (Balaklava), battle of, British-French forces repulsed Russian assault and counterattacked with famous charge of the Light Brigade, **Oct. 25, 1854**.

Balfour Declaration, British Foreign Secretary Arthur J. Balfour [July 25, 1848-Mar. 19, 1930] declared British support for establishment of Jewish national homeland in Palestine, **Nov. 2, 1917**.

Balkan Entente, alliance formed by Yugoslavia, Greece, Turkey, and Rumania, **Feb. 9, 1934**, to protect their territorial integrity against Bulgarian intrusion.

Balkan Wars, conflicts fought for control of European territories of Ottoman Empire, **1912-13**; Serbia, Bulgaria, Montenegro, and Greece forced Turks out during first Balkan War, **Oct. 18, 1912-May 30, 1913**; Great Powers' Conference at London created Albania, cutting Serbia off from the sea, **1913**; Serbia, allied with Rumania, Greece, and Ottoman Empire, defeated and seized territory from Bulgaria during second Balkan War, **June 29-July 30, 1913**; Bulgaria lost territory to all by Treaty of Bucharest, **Aug. 10, 1913**.

ballet, art form in which costumed dancers perform to music; originated Italy, **c. 1490**; *ballet de cour* ("court ballet"), Paris, **1581**; Royal Academy of Dance founded, Paris, **1661**.

Ballet Russe, ballet company founded, **1901**, by Russian dance master Sergei Pavlovich Diaghilev [Mar. 31, 1872-Aug.

19, 1929], with dancers from old Imperial Ballet, St. Petersburg, established **1738**; brought Russian ballet to all Europe, **1911-29**.

balloon crossings, first trans-Atlantic balloon crossing, **Aug. 17, 1978**, by Americans Max Anderson, Ben Abruzzo, and Larry Newman; first nonstop trans-continental flight of U.S. completed by Anderson and his son, **May 15, 1980**; first trans-Pacific crossing completed by Newman, Abruzzo and two others, **Nov. 1981**.

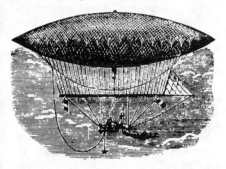

balloon flight, powered, introduced, **1852**, by French engineer Henri Giffard [1825-1882], who used a five horsepower steam engine to move a sausage-shaped balloon through the sky.

balloon tire, introduced, **1923**, by American rubber manufacturer, Harvey S. Firestone [1868-1938].

ball point pen, first practical model in U.S. developed, **1945**, by American manufacturer Milton Reynolds [1892-].

Baltic Pact, Baltic states of Lithuania, Latvia, and Estonia signed mutual agreement to defend their independence, **Sept. 12, 1934**, forming the Baltic bloc.

Baltimore Four, four members of Baltimore Interfaith Peace Mission poured blood on draft records at Baltimore's Selective Service headquarters, **Oct. 27, 1967**; found guilty of destroying government property, **Apr. 16, 1968**; sentenced to three to six years in prison, **May 24, 1968**.

Baltimore, (Maryland), Roman Catholic colony started by 2nd Lord Baltimore, **1632**; meeting place of Continental Congress, **1777**; disastrous fire destroyed much of city, **Feb. 7-8, 1904**.

Baltimore & Ohio Railroad (B&O), first public railroad in U.S. built between Baltimore and Ellicott's Mill, Md., **July 1829-May 1830**; extended to St. Louis, **1857**: merged with Chesapeake & Ohio, **1965**.

Baltimore Catechism, uniform textbook of doctrine for U.S. Catholics, **1885**; used until the Second Vatican Council, **1962-65**.

Baltimore, Councils of, series of national councils or synods, 3 plenary, **1852-84**, and 10 provincial, **1829-69**, by which the Catholic Church in the U.S. was organized and its discipline established.

Bandung Conference, 29 Asian and African nations met at Bandung, Indonesia, **Apr. 18-24, 1955**, to promote economic cooperation and their own self-determination.

Bank for International Settlements, established by European and U.S. bankers and diplomats at Basel, Switzerland, **1930**.

Banking Act of 1933, U.S. Congress corrected abuses that led to bank crises before stock market crash, strengthened bank supervision, use of credit, and created FDIC, **June 16, 1933**.

Bank of Canada, privately-owned, government-controlled central bank began operation, **Mar. 11, 1935**, according to Bank of Canada Act of **1934**.

Bank of England, founded by company of merchants headed by a Scotsman; lent English government £ 1.2 million in return for certain privileges, **July 27, 1694**.

Bank of North America, first bank in U.S. established at Philadelphia by Congress under Articles of Confederation, **Dec. 31, 1781**.

Bank of the United States, Federalists under Alexander Hamilton established central bank, **Dec. 12, 1791**; first Bank of the United States, **1791-1811**; second Bank of the United States, **1816-36**.

Bannister's mile run, British athlete Roger Bannister [Mar. 23, 1929-] became first man in history to run a mile in under four minutes (3:59.4), **May 6, 1954**, at Oxford, England.

Bannockburn, battle of, Scots led by Robert Bruce (Robert I) [July 11, 1274-June 7, 1329] defeated English forces under King Edward II [Apr. 25, 1284-Sept. 21, 1327] at Bannockburn moor, Scotland, **June 23-24, 1314**.

DICTIONARY OF DATES

Bantry Bay, battle of, French fleet checked English naval force off Ireland's s.w. coast, landing reinforcements to support counterrevolution of deposed James II against William and Mary, **May 11, 1689.**

Bantry Bay disaster, 512 persons killed when oil tanker blew up while unloading in Bantry Bay on Ireland's southwest coast, **Jan. 8, 1979.**

baptistery, Christian baptismal pool, **4th-14th centuries,** earliest example is baptistery of St. John Lateran, Rome, **4th century;** baptistery of Florence, **1100;** at Pisa, **c. 1300.**

Baptist Missionary Society, religious group founded, London, **October 2, 1792.**

Baptists, widespread Christian communion, founded, **1609,** on the basis of baptism of conscious believers; Baptist history in America began, **1639,** with settlement of Rhode Island by Roger Williams [c. 1603-Jan./Apr., 1683].

Barataria, pirates of, band of Louisiana outlaws led by Jean Laffite [178?-1825] that aided U.S. forces led by Gen. Andrew Jackson at New Orleans, **Jan. 8, 1815.**

Barbary pirates, Muslims from the states of Tripolitania, Algeria, Tunisia, and Morocco engaged in official piracy, forcing other nations to pay tribute to avoid raids on their ships, **c. 1550-1815;** U.S. opposition resulted in Algerine and Tripolitan Wars, **1800-15.**

barbed wire, first patented, **1874,** by American farmer-inventor Joseph F. Glidden [1813-1906].

Barber of Seville, The (Il Barbiere di Siviglia), romantic opera, Rome, **1816,** by Italian operatic composer Gioacchino (Antonio) Rossini [Feb. 29, 1792-Nov. 13, 1868].

Barcelona, Spanish city on Mediterranean conquered by Moors, **8th century;** conquered by Charlemagne, **801;** became independent under powerful counts of Barcelona, **9th-10th centuries;** fl. as trading and banking center, **12th-14th centuries;** center of Catalan revolt against Philip IV of Spain, **1640-52;** seat of Spanish loyalist government, **Oct. 1938-Jan. 26, 1939;** center of Spanish liberalism, since **1950s.**

Bar Cochba, revolt of, Jews, under Simon Bar Cochba (Bar Kokba) [d. 135], revolted against Roman rule, **132-35.**

Bardia, most strongly defended Italian position during British North African Campaign of WW II, **Dec. 1940-Feb. 1941;** British captured Bardia, **Nov. 1942.**

Bardo, Treaty of, regency of Tunis made a French protectorate, causing strong protests from Turkish government, Britain, and Italy, **May 12, 1881.**

Barebone's Parliament (Little Parliament), Cromwell established new council of state and a nominated British parliament of 140 members, **July 4, 1653.**

barium, element No. 56; discovered, **1808,** by English chemist Sir Humphry Davy [1778-1829]

Barnburners, radical, antislavery group in Democratic Party of New York, **1843-48;** at their convention in Utica, N.Y., nominated Martin Van Buren for U.S. President, **June 22, 1848;** united with Free-Soil Party at national convention, **Aug. 9, 1848.**

Barnet, battle of, Edward IV, of the House of York defeated and killed the Earl of Warwick of the House of Lancaster during the Wars of the Roses, **Apr. 14, 1471.**

Barnum & Bailey Circus, famous American circus known as *The Greatest Show on Earth* opened, **1871,** in Brooklyn, N.Y.; P.T. Barnum [July 5, 1810-Apr. 7, 1891] joined with rival James A. Bailey [July 4, 1847-Apr. 11, 1906] to form Barnum & Bailey, **1881;** purchased by Ringling Brothers, **1907,** to become Ringling Bros., Barnum & Bailey Circus, **1919;** Emmett Kelly [Dec. 8, 1898-Mar. 28, 1979] began 50-year circus clown career as *Weary Willy,* **1921;** performed last show under canvas tent, **July 16, 1956.**

barometer, invented, **1643**, by Italian mathematician and physicist Evangelista Torricelli [1608-1647].

Baron's War, struggle between King Henry III [1207-72] and barons in England, **1263-67**; barons led by Simon de Montfort [1208?-1265] won victory at Lewes, **May 14, 1264**; Montfort called Great Parliament, **1265**; Montfort defeated and killed at Evesham, **Aug. 4, 1265**.

baroque, movement or style in the arts, **1550-1750**.

Barren Hill, battle of, British forces of Gen. Howe failed to capture American patriots led by Lafayette at Barren Hill, Penn., **May 20, 1778**.

Barrier Treaty, Austria ceded to the Dutch a number of places on French border of the Austrian Netherlands, **Nov. 15, 1715**.

baseball, modern game of baseball originated in U.S. by Abner Doubleday [June 26, 1819-Jan. 26, 1893] at Cooperstown, N.Y., **1839**; Knickerbocker Baseball Club organized as first organized team, formed in New York, **1845**; professional National League established, **1876**; Western League reformed as American League to become second major professional league, **1900-1903**.

Baseball's Hall of Fame, shrine and museum commemorating baseball's great players founded in Cooperstown, N.Y., **1936**.

Basel, Council of, Roman Catholic Church council summoned to deal with Hussites, **1431-49**; drew up Compactata, **1433**.

Basel, Treaty of, Prussia, in conflict with Austria, withdrew from war with France and made peace, consenting to cession of left bank of Rhine River to France, **Mar. 5, 1795**.

basilica, large rectangular building with interior colonnade first built by Romans for public business, **184 B.C.**; form adopted by Christians for churches, **300s** on; construction began, Roman Basilica of St. John Lateran, **324**.

Basilica of St. Peter, largest of all Christian church buildings, erected in Vatican City, Rome, between **1506 and 1626**.

basketball, originated in U.S. by James Naismith [Nov. 6, 1861-Nov. 28, 1939] at YMCA college in Springfield, Mass., **1891**; National Invitation Tournament (NIT) established as annual postseason collegiate tournament, **1938**; National Collegiate Athletic Association (NCAA) championship begun, **1939**; professional National Basketball Association (NBA) established, **1949**; professional American Basketball Association (ABA) formed, **1967**.

Bassano, battle of, French forces of Napoleon I won great victory over Austrians at Bassano, Venetia, Italy, **Sept. 8, 1796**.

bassoon, largest and lowest of the woodwind instruments, invented, **c. 1600**.

Bastille, former French state prison in Paris, stormed and destroyed by mob, marking the beginning of the French Revolution, **July 14, 1789**.

Bastogne, battle of, U.S. troops successfully defended town of Bastogne, helping to halt German offensive in the Ardennes, **Dec. 20-26, 1944**.

Basutoland (Lesotho), former kingdom of the Basutos in South Africa annexed by British, **March 12, 1868**; granted independence as Lesotho, **Oct. 4, 1966**.

Bataan, battle of, U.S.-Filipino army, entrenched on Bataan peninsula in the Philippines, finally overwhelmed by Japanese forces in WW II, **Apr. 9, 1942**.

Bataan Death March, 35,000 U.S. and Filipino troops captured at Bataan in the Philippines, forced by Japanese to endure long, brutal "Death March" to prison camp near Cabanatuan, **Apr.-May 1942**; many thousands died.

Batavian Republic, United Provinces of the Netherlands reconstituted by the French during the French Revolutionary Wars **1795-1806**; transformed by Napoleon into the kingdom of Holland, **June 5, 1806**.

Bath, Order of the, English order of knighthood instituted by King Richard II and King Henry IV, **1399**; reinstituted by King George I as military order, **1725**; opened also to civilians, **1847**.

bathyscaphe, developed and first tested, **1948**, by Swiss ocean explorer Auguste Piccard [1884-1962].

Batoche, battle of, Canadian government forces defeated rebels, metis (French halfbreeds), under Louis Riel [1844-Nov. 16, 1885] at Batoche in central Saskatchewan, **May 12, 1885**.

Baton Rouge, La., city built as French fort, **1719**; captured by Union Admiral Farragut in U.S. Civil War, **May 1862**; Confederates failed to recapture it, **Aug. 1862**.

battery, electric, invented, **1800**, by Italian physicist Alessandro Volta [1745-1827].

Battle Hymn of the Republic, The, marching song of the North in U.S. Civil War, music composed **c. 1856**; words composed, **December 1861**, by Julia Ward Howe [May 27, 1819-Oct. 17, 1910].

***Battle of the Sexes* tennis match,** former Wimbledon champion Bobby Riggs [Feb. 25, 1918-] defeated by former Wimbledon champion Billie Jean King [Nov. 22, 1943-] in tennis "Match of the Century" at Houston Astrodome, **Sept. 20, 1973**.

Battleship Potemkin, The (Bronenosets Potemkin), classic film, **1925**, by Russian director and film theorist Sergei Eisenstein.

Bauhaus, German school of design; established Weimar, **1919**, it revolutionized development of modern architecture, especially through founder Walter Gropius [May 18, 1883-July 5, 1969].

Bautzen, battle of, great indecisive battle between French army under Napoleon I and Russo-Prussian army at Bautzen (East Germany) on Spree River; each side suffered 20,000 casualties, **May 20-21, 1813**.

Bavarian Succession, War of the, conflict between Austria and Prussia over claims to Lower Bavaria and Upper Palatinate, **1778-79**; ended with Congress of Teschen, **May 13, 1779**.

Bayonne Decree, Napoleon I of France ordered all U.S. ships entering French, Italian, and Hanseatic ports to be seized, **Apr. 17, 1808**.

Bay Psalm Book, oldest surviving book printed in British America, **1640**.

Bayreuth, city in northeast Bavaria, famous for annual music festivals; ruled by Hohenzollern family, **1248-1807**; residence of composer Richard Wagner, **1872-83**.

Baza, battle of, large Spanish army won important victory, capturing town of Baza in Granada province from the Moors, **Dec. 4, 1489**.

Beachy Head, battle of, French fleet defeated Anglo-Dutch fleet off southern coast of England, **July 10, 1690**.

Beagle, 235-ton naval ship on which naturalist Charles R. Darwin made five-year world cruise, **1831-36**.

Bean's Station, battle of, Confederates under Gen. James Longstreet [Jan. 8, 1821-Jan. 2, 1904] repulsed during attack on Union cavalry at Bean's Station, Tenn., **Dec. 14, 1863**.

Bear Flag Revolt, Californian settlers, headed by Capt. John C. Fremont [Jan. 21, 1813-July 13, 1890], revolted against Mexican rule and declared the Republic of California (Bear Flag Republic), **June 14, 1846**.

beat generation, U.S. socio-literary movement, from mid **1950s**, rejecting commercial and middle-class values.

Beatles, The, phenomenally successful rock music group, England, **1962-70**; symbol of 1960s subculture; members: George Harrison [Feb. 25, 1943-]; John Lennon [Oct. 9, 1940-Dec. 8, 1980]; Paul McCartney [June 18, 1942-]; Ringo Starr [July 7, 1940-]. Beatle films: *A Hard Day's Night*, **1964**; *Help!*, **1965**.

Beauge, battle of, one of the few defeats handed the English cavalry by the French in the Hundred Years' War, **Mar. 21, 1421**.

Beausejour, Fort, built by French in New Brunswick, Canada, **1751-55**; captured by British-American force, renamed Fort Cumberland, **1755**.

Beaver Dam, battle of, U.S. force from Niagara defeated by and surrendered to British and Indians at Beaver Dam, Ontario, **June 24, 1813**.

Beaver Dam Creek, battle of, Union forces repulsed fierce attack by Confederates under Gen. Ambrose P. Hill [Nov. 9, 1825-Apr. 2, 1865] during Peninsular campaign in Virginia, **June 26, 1862**. See **Civil War, U.S.**

Bechuanaland (Botswana), region in s. Africa made a British protectorate, **Sept. 30, 1885**; incorporated into Cape Colony, **Nov. 11, 1895**; granted full independence as Botswana, **Sept. 30, 1966**.

Becket, play, **1959**, about assassination of Thomas a Becket, **December 29, 1170**, by French dramatist Jean Anouilh.

Becket, assassination of, Thomas a Becket, Archbishop of Canterbury, stabbed to death by four knights of King Henry II of England, **Dec. 29, 1170**.

Beda Fomm, battle of, British-Australian forces won important victory during British North African Campaign, annihilating Italian Tenth Army and turning the tide of WW II in Africa, **Jan. -Feb. 1941**.

Beer Hall Putsch, National Socialist Party (Nazis), led by Adolf Hitler and Gen. Erich Ludendorff [Apr. 9, 1865-Dec. 20, 1937], failed to overthrow the Bavarian government at Munich, **Nov. 8-9, 1923**; *Mein Kampf* written by Hitler during nine months in prison, **1924**.

bees, communication of, discovered, **1923**, by Austrian-German zoologist Karl von Frisch [1886-].

Beggars of the Sea (Gueux), Dutch revolutionaries under William the Silent (William of Orange) who fought to drive Spanish out of the Netherlands, **1569-80**.

Beggar's Opera, The, dramatic satire, **1728**, on British upper-class and court life,

by poet John Gay [Sept. 16, 1685-Dec. 4, 1732]; opera, **1948**, by British composer Benjamin Britten [Nov. 22, 1913-Dec. 4, 1976].

Being and Nothingness (L'Etre et le Neant), philosophical treatise, **1943**, by French existentialist philosopher and writer Jean-Paul Sartre [June 21, 1905-Apr. 15, 1980].

Beirut, city on Mediterranean, ancient Phoenician trade center after **1500 B.C.**; site of famous Roman school of law, **3rd century**; seized by Arabs, **635**; part of the Latin Kingdom of Jerusalem, **1110-1291**; controlled by the Druses, after **1517**; captured by French in WW I, **1918**; became capital of Lebanon, **1920**.

bel canto, traditional Italian art of "beautiful singing," technique perfected, c. **1840**.

Belgian Congo, former Belgian colony in central Africa, established by Belgium's annexation of Congo Free State, **Oct. 18, 1908**; became independent as Republic of the Congo, **June 30, 1960**; renamed Zaire, **1971**.

Belgic Confession, The, Dutch Calvinistic confession of faith, **1561**; accepted by Synod of Dort, **1619**, as systematic expression of Calvinism for the Netherlands.

Belgrade, city grew around fort built by Celts, **3rd century B.C.**; controlled by Bulgars, who called it Beligrad ("white fortress") **9th-11th centuries**; became capital of Serbia, **12th century**; became main strategic fort of Ottoman Turks in Europe,

1521; stormed by Austrians, **1688, 1717, 1789**; held briefly by Austrians, **1717-39**; Turkish garrison withdrew from city, **1867**; capital of Yugoslavia, **1929**.

Belgrade, Treaty of, ended 3-year war between Austrians, Russians, and Turks; Austria ceded Belgrade to Turks; Russia agreed to raze forts and to build no fleet on Black Sea, **Sept. 18, 1739**.

Belleau Wood, battle of, U.S. forces, commanded by Gen. John J. Pershing [Sept. 13, 1860-July 15, 1948], defeated Germans in hard-fought, large-scale battle in Belleau Wood in n. France during WW I, **June 6-25, 1918**.

bell, electric, invented, **1831**, by American scientist Joseph Henry [1797-1878].

Belmont Stakes, annual American horse race for three-year-old thoroughbreds; first held at Jerome Park, N.J., **1867-89**; moved to Morris Park, N.Y., **1890-1905**; moved to Belmont Park, N.Y., **1906-present time**.

Bemis Heights, battle of, American revolutionary forces halted British redcoats under Gen. Burgoyne; Gen. Benedict Arnold led fierce counterattack against redcoats, **Oct. 7, 1777**.

Ben Day process, invented, **1879**, by American printer Benjamin Day [1838-1916] for shading in printed illustrations.

Benedictines, monastic order, founded **529**, at Monastery of Monte Cassino, Italy; spread throughout Europe, **c. 500-900**.

Benelux Economic Union, Belgium, Luxembourg, and the Netherlands signed treaty, **Dec. 2, 1958**, forming economic union; went into effect, **Nov. 1, 1960**.

Benevento, capital city of Lombard duchy, **11th-16th centuries**; under papal rule, **c. 1050-1860**; site of defeat of Manfred [1232?-66], King of Sicily, by Charles of Anjou [1227-85], **Feb. 26, 1266**.

Beneventum, battle of, Roman legionaries won important victory over Greeks, ending invasion of Italy by King Pyrrhus of Epirus, **275 B.C.**

Benin, nation in western Africa, gained its independence from France as Dahomey, **Aug. 1, 1960**, took its present name, **Nov. 30, 1975**.

Bennington, battle of, New England militiamen, aided by the Green Mountain Boys, routed Hessian-British force during Saratoga Campaign, **Aug. 14-16, 1777**.

Bentonville, battle of, Union army under Gen. Sherman forced Confederate army under Gen. Johnston to retreat at Bentonville, N.C., **Mar. 19-21, 1865**, during Sherman's march from Savannah north through the Carolinas.

Bent's Fort (Bent's Old Fort), famous, successful trading post established at fort on Arkansas River in present-day Colorado, **1833**; dominated trade on Santa Fe Trail's mountain branch, **c. 1835-45**; abandoned, **1852**; Bent's New Fort built further downstream, **1853**.

benzene ring, conceived, **1865**, by German chemist Friedrich A. Kekule [1829-1896].

Beowulf, Anglo-Saxon epic poem, from Norse legends; written down by anonymous poet, **c. 750**.

Berezina River, site of heroic crossing of Napoleon's Grand Army during its retreat from Russia; Napoleon saved his army despite great losses from Russian attack, **Nov. 26-29, 1812**.

Bergen, battles of, French forces won victory over European allies at Bergen, near Frankfurt, **Apr. 13, 1759**; French won victory over allies during French Revolutionary Wars, **Sept. 19** and **Oct. 2, 1799**.

Beria affair, Soviet Minister of Internal Security Lavrenti P. Beria [1899-Dec. 23, 1953] expelled from Communist Party, **July 10, 1953**, convicted secretly of treason with six others, and executed, **Dec. 23, 1953**.

Bering Sea dispute, dispute among U.S., Canada, and Britain over jurisdiction of the waters of the Bering Sea and pelagic seal hunting in the area, **1886-1911**; international tribunal decided against exclusive U.S. claim to waters outside three-mile limit, set season for sealing, **Aug. 15, 1893**; treaty by

U.S., Russia, Britain, and Japan ended pelagic sealing, **1911**.

berkelium, element No. 97; produced, **1949**, by American physicist Stanley G. Thompson and associates at University of California, Berkeley.

Berlin airlift, Soviet blockade of traffic between Berlin and West, **July 24, 1948** resulted in Western airlift of vital supplies through three air corridors to West Berlin; Soviet blockade ended, **May 12, 1949**; allied airlift ended after more than 277,000 flights, **Sept. 30, 1949**.

Berlin, battle of, Allied aerial bombardment and immense Soviet artillery barrage destroyed city of Berlin, Germany, which fell to Russians under Marshal Georgi Zhukov [1896-June 18, 1974] during end of WW II, **May 2, 1945**.

Berlin, Conference of, conference attended by all European nations and U.S., established freedom of navigation on Congo and Niger rivers, abolished slave trade, and recognized Belgian king's claim to Congo and Britain's to s. Nigeria, **Nov. 15, 1884-Feb. 26, 1885**.

Berlin, Congress of, European powers meet to revise Treaty of San Stefano; Rumania, Serbia, and Montenegro recognized as independent states; Bulgaria divided three ways; Bosnia and Hercegovina assigned to Austria-Hungary, **June 13-July 13, 1878**.

Berlin Decree, announcement of blockade of Britain and all her possessions in Europe by Napoleon I at Berlin, Prussia, **Nov. 21, 1806**.

Berlin, Treaty of, Austria ceded to Prussia all of Silesia except Teschen and present-day Czech Silesia, **July 28, 1742**.

Berlin Wall, 29 mile long concrete and wire barrier built by East German Communist government, **Aug. 1961**, to stop East Berliners defecting to the West.

Bermuda, small coral archipelago in Atlantic, first discovered by Span. navigator Juan de Bermudez, **1515**; uninhabited until group of English colonists led by Sir George Somers shipwrecked there, **1609**.

Bermuda Hundred (Virginia), historic fishing village founded, **1613**; Union Army of the James under Gen. Benjamin B. Butler retreated here after defeat on Drewry's

Bluff, **May 6-16, 1864**.

Bernoulli's principle, introduced, **1738**, by Swiss mathematician Daniel Bernoulli [1700-1782].

Bert Lance affair, Thomas B. ("Bert") Lance [June 3, 1931-], Director of U.S. Office of Management and Budget, criticized publicly for questionable banking practices prior to joining government, **Aug. 8, 1977**; resigned, **Sept. 21, 1977**.

beryllium, element No. 4; discovered in oxide form, **1798**, by French chemist Louis N. Vauquelin [1763-1829]; he called it glucina; metallic beryllium obtained **1828**, by German chemist Friedrich Wohler [1800-1882].

Bessemer process of steel making, patented, **1856**, by English engineer Henry Bessemer [1813-1898]; and patented **1857**, by American inventor William Kelly [1811-1888], who proved claim that he had developed same process independently, **1851**.

beta particles, suggested **1931** by Austrian-born physicist Wolfgang Pauli [1900-1958].

betatron, electron accelerator developed, **1940**, by American physicist Donald W. Kerst [1911-].

Bhagavad Gita, Hindu epic, c. 200 B.C., literally, "the song of the Lord"; describes nature of God.

Bhutan, kingdom in the Himalayas; became independent from Britain under India's protection, **1949**.

Biafra, eastern region of Nigeria, inhabited by the Ibos, proclaimed itself Republic of Biafra, **May 30, 1967**; war broke out between Nigeria and Biafra, **July 1967**; starving Biafra surrendered, **Jan. 12, 1970**, and pledged loyalty to Nigeria.

Bible, The, collection of sacred books written **c. 1000 B.C.-A.D. 100**, comprising Old and New Testaments.

Bibracte (Autun), Roman legions under Caesar routed large Helvetii army during Gallic Wars in present-day France, **58 B.C.**

Bicentennial, U.S., nationwide celebration of 200th anniversary of U.S. independence, **July 4, 1976**.

bicycle, first successful bicycle invented, **1839**, by Scottish blacksmith Kirkpatrick MacMillan [1810-1878]; improved, **1854**, by English inventor James Starley [1830-1881].

bicycle, direct drive, invented, **1861**, by French inventor Ernest Michaux.

bifocal lens, invented, **1780**, by American scientist-statesman Benjamin Franklin [1706-1790].

big-bang theory, first proposed, **1927**, by Belgian astrophysicist Georges E. Lemaitre [1894-1966].

Big Bertha bombardment, German heavy artillery guns shelled Paris from forest of Coucy, 75 miles away, during WW I, **Mar. 23-Aug. 19, 1918**.

Big Switch, mutual voluntary exchange of prisoners under terms of Korean War's armistice, completed, **Sept. 1953**.

Big Thompson River flood, flash flood killed 138 campers and others in Big Thompson Canyon, Loveland, Colo., **Aug. 1, 1976**.

Bilbao, battle of, Spanish Nationalist army attacked and captured Basque stronghold of Bilbao, thwarting Basque independence movement during Spanish Civil War, **June 11-19, 1937**.

Billie Sol Estes affair, Texas state court sentenced Texas financier and "wheeler-dealer" Billie Sol Estes [1925-] to eight years in prison, **Nov. 8, 1962**, for swindling Texas farmer; conviction overturned by U.S. Supreme Court, **June 7, 1965**, on grounds his televised criminal trial violated due process of 14th Amendment.

Billion Dollar Congress, the 51st U.S. Congress became first to make appropriations during peacetime in excess of one billion dollars, **1889-91**.

Bill of Rights, English, parliamentary statute established relationship between English monarchy and parliament and gave Englishmen certain inviolable civil and political rights, **Feb. 12, 1689**.

Bill of Rights, U.S., first 10 amendments to U.S. Constitution went into effect, approved by Congress and two thirds of states, **Dec. 15, 1792**.

binomial nomenclature for plants, advanced, **1576**, by French botanist Carolus (Charles) Clusius (de l'Ecluse) [1526-1609].

biplane (tail-first pusher), developed, **1906**, by Brazilian aviation pioneer Alberto Santos Dumont [1873-1932].

Birds of America, The, book of 435 engravings, in four volumes, published, **1827-38**, of birds of America; by U.S. ornithologist, naturalist and artist, John James Audubon (born Jean Rabine) [Apr. 26, 1785-Jan. 27, 1851].

Birds, The, comedy, **414 B.C.**, about a city in the clouds (cloud-cuckooland) cutting the gods off from the smoke of mortals' sacrifices, by Greek comic dramatist Aristophanes [c. 450-385 B.C.].

birth control clinic, first in U.S. established, **1916**, by American nurse and birth control pioneer Margaret Sanger [1883-1966].

birth control pill, first mass test, **1957**, directed by developers, American physicians Gregory Pincus [1903-1967] and John Rock [1890-].

Birth of a Nation, The, one of the first great movies, **1915**; objected to on extra-artistic grounds for favoring Ku Klux Klan; by pioneer U.S. director D(avid) W(ark) Griffith [Jan. 22, 1875-July 23, 1948].

Birth of Venus, tableau, **1484**, with *Primavera* (*Spring*), **1477**, painted by Renaissance painter Sandro Botticelli (born Alessandro di Filipepi) [1445-May 17, 1510].

Bishops' Wars, short campaigns of the Scots against King Charles I of England, **1639-40**; first war concluded, without battle, by pacification of Dunse, **June 18, 1639**; Scots won victory at Newburn on the Tyne in second war, **Aug. 28, 1640**; Charles I forced to sign Treaty of Ripon, **Oct. 26, 1640**.

Bismarck, German battleship *Bismarck* sank British battle cruiser *Hood* and damaged *Prince of Wales* off coast of Greenland, **May 24, 1941**; sunk by British 400 miles from Brest, France, in North Atlantic, **May 27, 1941**.

Bismarck Sea, battle of the, American and Australian planes sank four Japanese destroyers and eight transports in the Bismarck Sea, seriously curtailing Japan's ability to reinforce garrisons in the Pacific in WW II, **Mar. 2-5, 1943**.

black body radiation, proposed, **c. 1870**, by German physicist Gustav Robert Kirchoff [1824-1887], a step in development of the quantum theory.

Black Death, unusually virulent plague that devastated Europe and western Asia, **14th century**; began in Constantinople, **1334**.

Blackfriars Theatre, first private theater in London, **1576**.

Black Hawk War, conflict between U.S. settlers and Sac and Fox Indians under Chief Black Hawk [1767-Oct. 3, 1838], fought in Illinois and Wisconsin, **1831-32**; Black Hawk's warriors massacred settlers near Rock River, Ill., **Apr. 6, 1832**; Illinois militia wiped out Black Hawk's tribe at Bad Axe River, Wis., **Aug. 2, 1832**; Black Hawk's surrender ended war, **Aug. 27, 1832**.

black hole, proposed, **1798**, by French astronomer and mathematician Pierre Simon Laplace [1749-1827].

Black Hole of Calcutta, nawab of Bengal captured Calcutta, India, attacked British East India Company, and imprisoned 146 Englishmen in room 18' x 15' with two small windows for ventilation, **June 20, 1756**; 23 men survived and released, **June 21, 1756**.

Black Hundreds, Russian army restored order in provinces through violent punitive raids ("Black Hundreds") against insurgents and workers after 1905 Revolution, **Jan.-Mar. 1906**.

Black Muslims, U.S. black nationalist, religious movement established, **1930**, in Detroit; Elijah Muhammad (Elijah Poole) [Oct. 7, 1897-Feb. 25, 1975] became leader, **1934**, after mysterious disappearance of movement's founder Wali Farad; rival leader Malcolm X [May 19, 1925-Feb. 21, 1965] assassinated in Harlem, N.Y., **Feb. 21, 1965**.

Black Panthers, U.S. black militant organization established, **1966**, in Oakland, Calif.; involved in violent shoot-outs and confrontations with police, late **1960s**; split between violent and anti-violent factions in organization, **1972**.

Blackstock Hill, battle of, American revolutionaries under Thomas Sumter [1734-1832] defeated British raiders under Bannastre Tarleton [1754-1833] at Blackstock Hill, S.C., **Nov. 20, 1780.**

Black Warrior **incident**, U.S. merchant ship *Black Warrior* seized and confiscated by customs officials in Cuba, **May 1854,** resulting in brief international crisis between U.S. and Spain, which paid damages.

Black Watch (Royal Highlanders), Scottish infantry regiment first organized, **1739.**

Blackwood's Magazine, influential Scottish literary magazine, founded **1817.**

Bladensburg, battle of, American defeat at Bladensburg permitted British army to march on Washington, D.C., and set fire to the Capitol, White House, Navy yard, and other public and private buildings, **Aug. 24-25, 1814.**

Bland-Allison Act, U.S. Treasury required by congressional act, **Feb. 28, 1878,** to purchase $2-$4 million in silver each month to be made into silver dollars.

Bleeding Kansas, territory of Kansas terrorized by raids and civil war between pro- and anti-slavery groups, between Border Ruffians and Free State men (Jayhawkers), **1855-60.**

Blenheim, battle of, British-Austrian armies under duke of Marlborough and prince of Savoy defeated the French and Bavarians at village of Blenheim in present-day W. Germany in one of the most important battles of the War of the Spanish Succession, **Aug. 13, 1704.**

Blessing of the Bay, supposedly America's first seaworthy ship, *Blessing of the Bay*, built and launched, **July 4, 1631,** on Mystic River, Mass., for Gov. John Winthrop [Jan. 12, 1588-Mar. 26, 1649].

Blizzard of '88, immense winter storm paralyzed New York City and much of the Northeast; 400 persons died, **Mar. 11-14, 1888.**

Bloemfontein, battle of, British forces crushed Boers in the Orange Free State and stormed Boer capital-city of Bloemfontein in South Africa, **Mar. 31, 1900.** See **Boer War.**

Blois, Treaties of, German King Maximilian I invested King Louis XII of France with the duchy of Milan; Louis pledged Naples to Spain, **1504-1505.**

blood bank, storage place for whole blood first established, **1935**, at Mayo Clinic, Rochester, Minn..

blood-capillary action, circulatory regulating mechanism explained, **1919**, by Danish physiologist S. August Krogh [1874-1949].

blood circulation, speculated, **c. 1555**, by Italian botanist-physician Andrea Cesalpino [1519-1603], and, **1584**, by mystic Giordano Bruno [1548-1603]; demonstrated and established, **1628**, by English physician William Harvey [1578-1657].

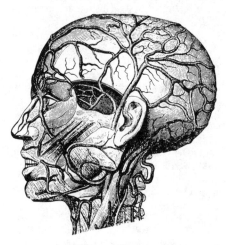

blood groups (ABO human), identified and classified, **1900**, by Austrian-American scientist Karl Landsteiner [1868-1943].

blood transfusion, first performed, **1665**, by English physician Richard Lower [1631-1691].

Bloody Sunday, Russian troops fired upon defenseless workers, led by a priest, who were proceeding to the palace to lay their demands before Czar Nicholas II [1868-1918]; set off 1905 Revolution in Russia, **Jan. 22, 1905.**

Bloomsbury Group, The, group of British intellectuals named for London district where they met, **1914-39**; group included economist John Maynard Keynes [June 5, 1883-Apr. 21, 1946]; biographer Lytton Strachey [Mar. 1, 1880-Jan. 21, 1932]; and novelist Virginia Woolf [Jan. 25, 1882-Mar. 28, 1941].

Blue Angel, The (Der Blaue Engel), German movie, **1930**, about degradation of a school teacher infatuated with a cafe singer; rocketed actress Marlene Dietrich [Dec. 21, 1901-] to instant stardom.

Blue Boy, The, painting, **1770**, typical of idealized "fancy pictures" of English landscape and portrait painter Thomas Gainsborough [bap. May 14, 1727-Aug. 2, 1788]; sold for $200,000, **1921**.

Blue Danube, The, waltz, **1867**, by Vienna's "Waltz King," Johann Strauss the Younger [Oct. 25, 1825-June 3, 1899].

Blue Lick, battle of, raids by the Indians and British from the Northwest across the Ohio River stopped by settlers at Blue Lick, Kentucky, **1782**.

Blue Lodges, secret order founded in Missouri, **c. 1854**, to help Southerners establish slavery in Kansas.

Blue Mosque, mosque, Istanbul, built, **1609-1616**, to be largest and finest in the world, with six minarets, cupola, and four half-domes..

Blues, slow kind of black American song, element in jazz, first written down, **1912**, by U.S. musician and composer W(illiam) C(hristopher) Handy [Nov. 16, 1873-March 28, 1958); composer's *St. Louis Blues*, **1914**.

B'nai B'rith, Jewish fraternal and service organization, founded, New York, **1843**.

Boat people, Vietnamese refugees fleeing,

1978, from Communist tyranny in Southeast Asia; turned back from over-crowded Asian nations; Pres. Carter ordered U.S. ships to pick up refugees, **July 8, 1978**.

Bobby Baker affair, Robert G. ("Bobby") Baker [1927?-] accused of using his position for personal financial gain, resigned as secretary of Democratic Senate Majority, **Oct. 1963**; Baker, despite support by friend, U.S. Pres. Lyndon B. Johnson, found guilty of "many gross improprieties" by Senate Ethics committee, **July 1964**; Baker indicted on charges of grand larceny and tax evasion, **Jan. 1966**, and imprisoned, **Ja...1971-June 1972**.

Bodleian Library, Oxford University library, opened **1602**, famous for rare books and manuscripts; began to receive copy of every book printed in England, **1610**; named after founder, Sir Thomas Bodley [Mar. 2, 1545-Jan. 28, 1613].

Body of Liberties, famous code of 100 laws, containing first sparks of colonial spirit for independence, adopted by General court of Massachusetts Bay Colony, **Dec. 1641**.

Boeotian League, confederacy of Greek city-states in ancient Boeotia dominated by Thebes, **7th-6th centuries B.C.**; broken up by Athens, **457 B.C.**

Boer-Basuto War, conflict between Boers of Orange Free State and South African Basutos, who were defeated and ceded much territory to Boers, **1865-66**.

Boer War (South African War), conflict between Great Britain and the Boer states (Transvaal and Orange Free State) in South Africa, **1899-1902**; Boer states declared war on British, **Oct. 12, 1899**; Boers, well equipped by Germany, besieged Mafeking, Kimberley, and Ladysmith, **1899-1900**; British captured Boer capital of Bloemfontein, **Mar. 31, 1900**; British, led by Horatio H. Kitchener [June 24, 1850-June 5, 1916] and others, occupied all major Boer cities, despite bloody Boer guerrilla warfare, **1901**; Boer submission formalized by Treaty of Vereeniging, **May 31, 1902**.

Boer-Zulu War, Zulu tribesmen massacred Boer immigrants (farmers and cattlemen) in Natal, South Africa, **Feb. 6, 1838**; Boers withstood attacks by 10,000 Zulus along Blood River, Natal, **Dec. 16, 1838**.

Boheme, La, romantic opera, produced

Turin, **Feb. 1, 1896**, by Italian operatic composer Giacomo Puccini [Dec. 22, 1858-Nov. 29, 1924].

Bolivia, country in South America, declared its independence, **Aug. 6, 1825**; joined Peru in the War of the Pacific against Chile, **1879-84**; defeated in war with Brazil, losing rich rubber-tree area on Acre River, **1903**; fought Paraguay in Chaco War, **1932-35**; suppressed guerrilla revolutionary movement of Che Guevara [June 14, 1928-Oct. 9, 1967], **1965-67**.

Bologna, University of, oldest university in the Western World, founded, **1119**; law faculty began, **1088**; medical faculty established, **1150**; earliest collection of university statutes, **1252**; modern university established, **1687**.

bolometer, invented, **1878**, by American scientist Samuel P. Langley [1834-1906].

Bolsheviks, Russians under leadership of Lenin split from Social Democratic Party, advocating revolution and a dictatorship of the proletariat, **1903**; overthrew Russian provisional government set up by Alexander Kerensky [Apr. 22, 1881-June 11, 1970], **Nov. 6, 1917**; Bolshevik Party renamed Communist Party, **Mar. 1918**.

Bolshoi Theater, oldest theater in the Soviet Union, founded, **1780**, as Petrovsky Theater; present building opened, **January 5, 1825**; rebuilt after fire, **1856**; home of Bolshoi Ballet.

book matches, invented, **1892**, by Ameri-can lawyer Joshua Pusey; sold patent, **1895**, to Diamond Match Company.

Boolean algebra, developed, **c. 1854**, by English mathematician George Boole [1815-1864].

Boomplaats, battle of, British suppressed Boer rebels, who claimed territory west of Natal, between Orange and Vaal rivers, **Aug. 29, 1848**.

Bonhomme Richard, rebuilt French ship *Bonhomme Richard*, commanded by John Paul Jones [July 6, 1747-July 18, 1792], defeated larger British warship *Serapis* in great naval battle off England's coast; Jones captured and boarded *Serapis* as his own ship burned and sank, **Sept. 23, 1779**.

Bonn, German city, residence of the electors of Cologne, **1238-1794**; destroyed during the War of the Grand Alliance, **1689**; annexed by France, **1798-1814**; made part of Prussia, **1815**; constitution for the Federal Republic of Germany drafted there, **1948-49**; made capital of West Germany, **1949**.

Bonus Army, veterans of WW I arrived in Washington, D.C., **May 29, 1932**, to demand cash payments of their bonus certificates; about 15,000 veterans camped near Capitol, **June, 1932**; most left after government provided money for their return home, **June 17, 1932**; U.S. troops under Gen. Douglas MacArthur forced remaining veterans to leave, **July 28-29, 1932**.

boogie-woogie, percussive style of jazz piano-playing with steady rhythmic bass, became popular **c. 1936**; boogie-woogie jazz concert, Carnegie Hall, New York, **1938**.

book, written or printed record of some length, books began **c. 3000 B.C.**, as clay tablets; writing on papyrus scrolls, from **500 B.C.**; codex, or book of leaves bound together, in use, from **300**.

Book of Common Prayer, official service book of the Church of England, **1549**, originally prepared by Archbishop Thomas Cranmer [July 2, 1489-March 21, 1556]; revision, **1662**, standard until **1928**; further revision of 1928 version widely criticized, **1979-80**.

Book of Mormon, religious book published, **1830**, believed to contain special divine revelation given to founder of Church of Jesus Christ of Latter Day Saints (*Mormons*), Joseph Smith [Dec. 23, 1805-June 27, 1844].

Book of the Dead, The, collection of ancient Egyptian mortuary texts, some dating back to Old Kingdom, **c. 3000 B.C.**; achieved final form in 26th Dynasty, **c. 600 B.C.**

Book-of-the-Month Club, began, **1926**.

Boonville (Booneville), battle of, Union troops defeated ill-equipped Confederate force at Boonville, Mo., **June 17, 1861**, thus preventing the secession of Missouri.

Bophuthatswana, second black African "homeland" for one of nine Bantu groups gained full independence from South African government, **Dec. 6, 1977**.

boranes (boron hydrides), structure and mechanism theory developed, **1954**, using X-ray diffraction analysis, by American chemist William N. Lipscomb [1919-].

Borgne, Lake, battle of, American squadron under Thomas ap Catesby Jones [Apr. 24, 1790-May 30, 1858] made heroic but unsuccessful effort to stop fleet carrying British army to New Orleans from crossing Lake Borgne, **Dec. 14, 1814**.

Borodino, battle of, Russian army under Field Marshal Mikhail I. G. Kutuzov [Sept. 16, 1745-Apr. 28, 1813] made unsuccessful heroic stand against Napoleon's Grand Army at village of Borodino, **Sept. 7, 1812**; Napoleon entered Moscow, **Sept. 14, 1812**.

boron, element No. 5; discovered, **1808**, by French chemists J. L. Gay-Lussac [1778-1850] and Louis J. Thenard [1777-1857].

Bosnia and Hercegovina, two regions placed under Austro-Hungarian administration, with Turkish overlordship, **1878**; annexed by Austria-Hungary, creating violent Serbian reaction, **1908**; annexed by Serbia, **1918**; became a major republic of Yugoslavia, **1946**.

Boston (Massachusetts), main colony founded by Massachusetts Bay Company, **Sept. 17, 1630**; Boston Latin School founded, **1635**; colonists killed at Boston Massacre, **Mar. 5, 1770**; Boston Tea Party in harbor, **Dec. 16, 1773**; site of battle of Bunker Hill, **June 17, 1775**; American patriots under George Washington captured Dorchester Heights, **Mar. 4, 1776**, commanding Boston and forcing the British under Gen. William Howe [Aug. 10, 1729-July 12, 1814] to evacuate the city, **Mar. 17, 1776**.

Boston Gazette, The, second newspaper in America, **1719-41**; merged, **1741**, with *The New England Weekly Journal*.

Boston Latin School, America's first secondary school and one of the oldest free public schools, established at Boston, Mass., **1635**; became coeducational, **1972**.

Boston Marathon, annual foot race from Hopkinton, Mass. to downtown Boston (26 mi. 385 yd.); first race, **1897**.

Boston Post Road, one of first roads in colonial America, completed **1672**.

Boston Public Library, oldest, free, tax-supported large municipal library in the U.S., established, **1852**.

Boston Strangler, notorious U.S. criminal who assaulted, robbed and killed 13 women in Boston area, **1962-64**; Albert Henry DeSalvo, self-confessed *Boston Strangler*, convicted of robbery and sex offenses, **Jan. 18, 1967**.

Bosworth Field, battle of, Henry, earl of Richmond, with French and Welsh support, defeated King Richard III, who was slain on battlefield; ended the Wars of the Roses, **Aug. 22, 1485**; Henry crowned as first Tudor king of England, Henry VII [Jan. 28, 1457-Apr. 21, 1509], **Oct. 30, 1485**.

Botswana, British protectorate of Bechuanaland in south-central Africa, became independent nation of Botswana, **Sept. 30, 1966**.

bottle making machine, automatic, invented, **c. 1900**, by American glassmaker Michael J. Owens [1859-1923].

Bounty **mutiny**, successful mutiny led by Christian Fletcher against Capt. William Bligh [Sept. 9, 1754-Dec. 7, 1817] of H.M.S. *Bounty*; Bligh and 18 others cast adrift in Pacific, **Apr. 28, 1789**.

Bourbons, cadet branch of Capetians, dynasty that ruled France, **1589-1792, 1815-48**; related royal family that ruled Spain, **1700-1931**; related royal family that ruled the Two Sicilies, **1759-1861**; related royal family that ruled Parma, **1748-1860**.

Bouvines, battle of, King Philip II of France defeated the combined forces of King John I of England, Holy Roman Emperor Otto IV [c. 1174-May 19, 1218], and the counts of Flanders, establishing the power of the French king, **July 27, 1214**.

Bowie knife, invented, **c. 1835**; credited to American soldier James Bowie [1796-1836].

Bowie-knife and Sheath.

Boxer Rebellion, Chinese uprising against increasing European settlements and interests in e. China, **1899-1901**; anti-foreign society called *I Ho Ch'uan* or, in English, the Boxers, formed, **1898**; Boxers besieged foreigners at Peking, **June-July 1900**; international force of British, French, Russian, German, Japanese, and U.S. troops lifted siege of Peking, **Aug. 1900**; China forced to pay indemnity of $333 million and to permit foreign troops in Peking, **1901**.

Boyaca, battle of, patriot army under Simon Bolivar [July 24, 1783-Dec. 17, 1830] defeated Spanish troops at Boyaca, throwing off Spanish rule in New Granada (Colombia) in South America, **Aug. 7, 1819**.

boyars, former aristocracy in Russia, **10th-17th centuries**; rank and title of boyar abolished by Peter I ("the Great") [June 9, 1672-Feb. 8, 1725], **c. 1685**.

Boyle's law, presented, **1662**, by British physicist Robert Boyle [1627-1691].

Boyne, battle of the, armies of King William III [Nov. 4, 1650-Mar. 8, 1702] overthrew Catholic forces of James II, who fled to France, **July 1, 1690**.

Boys' Clubs of America, national federation, organized **1906**.

Boy Scouts, organization of boys over 12 years old founded by Sir Robert Baden-Powell [Feb. 22, 1857-Jan. 8, 1941] in Britain, **1907**; Boy Scouts of America founded in Washington, D.C., **Feb. 8, 1910**.

Braganza, royal house descended from first duke of Braganza (Branca), ruled Portugal, **1640-1910**; ruled Brazil as independent empire, **1822-89**.

Brahmanism, religious system of Brahman caste in Hinduism, origins in the Vedas, compiled **c.1500 -900 B.C.**.

Braille printing, invented, **1829**, by French teacher of the blind Louis Braille [1809-1852].

brain and body scanner, first introduced in U.S., **1974**; designed by American radiologist Robert S. Ledley and colleagues at Georgetown University Hospital.

brake, disc, invented, **1902**, by English inventor F. Lanchester.

Brandy Station, battle of, (battle of Fleetwood Hill), greatest cavalry battle in U.S. history; Union and Confederate (latter under commander Jeb Stuart [Feb. 6, 1833-May 12, 1864] cavalries charged and countercharged in wild melee before Confederate infantry forced Union cavalry to withdraw, near Culpepper, Va., **June 9, 1863**.

Brandywine, battle of, British forces under Gen. William Howe [Aug. 10, 1729-July 12, 1814] defeated American Continental Army under Gen. George Washington along Brandywine Creek, near Chadds Ford, Penn., **Sept. 11, 1777**; British continued offensive and seized Philadelphia, **Sept. 27, 1777**.

Brave New World, satirical novel, **1932**, about a future scientific utopia, by English-U.S. novelist and essayist Aldous Huxley [July 26, 1894-Nov. 22, 1963]; author's *Brave New World Revisited*, **1958**.

Brazil, South American republic; proclaimed its independence from Portugal, **Sept. 7, 1822**.

Breda, battle of, fortress city of Breda in s. Netherlands surrendered after heroic six-month defense against Spanish during Dutch war for independence, **June 5, 1625**.

Breda, Declaration of, King Charles II [May 29, 1630-Feb. 6, 1685] of England and Scotland issued total amnesty to all, **Apr. 14, 1660**.

Breda, Treaties of, Anglo-Dutch war ended; English received New Netherlands and Delaware; Dutch, Surinam; France, Acadia; trade law modified in favor of the Dutch, **July 21, 1667**.

Breisach, German town on Rhine River captured by Bernhard of Saxe-Weimar, **Dec. 19, 1638**; ceded to France by Treaty of Westphalia, **Oct. 24, 1648**; ceded back to Holy Roman Empire by Treaty of Ryswick, **May 9, 1697**; ceded to former German state of Baden, **1805**.

Breitenfeld, battles of, during Thirty Years' War, Swedish army defeated Holy Roman Emperor's imperial forces at village of Breitenfeld, near Leipzig, **Sept. 18, 1631**; Swedes under Field Marshal Lennart Torstenson [Aug. 17, 1603-Apr. 7, 1651] again defeated imperial forces, **Nov. 2, 1642**.

Breslau (Wroclaw), city on Oder River made capital of duchy of Silesia, **1163**; member of Hanseatic League, **1368-1474**; became part of Hapsburg empire, **1526**; ceded to Prussia, **1742**; Poles replaced Germans as inhabitants of Breslau, **1945**, which is renamed Wroclaw.

Brest-Litovsk, Treaty of, Germany forced Russia to accept Ukraine's independence, to give up Poland and the Baltic states, and to cede Kars, Ardahan, and Batum to Turks, **Mar. 3, 1918**; armistice of WW I compelled Germany to renounce treaty, **Nov. 11, 1918**.

Bretigny, Treaty of, short truce during Hundred Years' War; France gave England 3 million gold crowns as ransom for King John II [1319-Apr. 8, 1364] and ceded much territory to England, **May 8, 1360**.

Breton Succession, War of the, part of the Hundred Years' War; John de Montfort recognized by France as ruler of Brittany after long war with several truces and after death of rival Charles of Blois, **1341-65**.

Bretton Woods Conference (United Nations Monetary and Financial Conference), delegates from 44 nations met at Bretton Woods, N.H., **July 1-22, 1944**, establishing International Monetary Fund for currency stabilization and International Bank for Reconstruction and Development.

Brice Cross Roads, battle of, Confederate cavalry under Gen. Nathan Forrest [July 13, 1821-Oct. 29, 1877] won decisive victory over Union troops at Brice Cross Roads, Miss., **June 10, 1864**.

Brier's Creek, battle of, British redcoats won victory over Americans under Gen. John Ashe [c. 1720-Oct. 1781] at Brier's Creek, Ga., **Mar. 3, 1778**, securing British control of Savannah and Georgia.

Bristoe Station, battles of, Union forces defeated the Confederates twice at Bristoe Station, Va., **Aug. 27, 1862; Oct. 14, 1863**.

Britain, battle of, series of battles fought between British and German aircraft over Great Britain during WW II, **Aug.-Oct. 1940**; Germans instigated heavy night bombing (blitz) of London and other English cities, **Sept. 7, 1940**.

British Columbia, Canadian province; coast first charted by Brit. navigator George Vancouver [June 22, 1757-May 10, 1798], **1792-94**.

British East Africa, former association of British dependencies in e. Africa, including Kenya, Tanganyika, Uganda, and Zanzibar, **c. 1880s-1960s**.

British Empire, sovereign states under the British crown; at its height included territories on all continents and comprised about one quarter of the world's population and area, **c. 1887-c. 1923**.

British Gazette, The, Sunday newspaper, **1780**; with *The Sunday Monitor*, **1780**, first Sunday paper to appear in London.

British Museum, British parliament established national museum for treasures in literature, art, and science, **1753**; first opened, **1759**; Elgin Marbles acquired by museum, **1816**.

British North America Act, British parliament united Quebec, Ontario, New Brunswick, and Nova Scotia in the Dominion of Canada; made English and French official languages in Canadian parliament and courts, **Mar. 29, 1867**.

British Open, prestigious annual golf tournament, inaugurated at Prestwick course in Scotland, **1860**.

Broad River, battle of, Americans under Gen. Sumter repulsed British regulars of Gen. Cornwallis at the Broad River, above Camden, S.C., **Nov. 12, 1780**.

bromine, element No. 35; discovered, **1826**, by French chemist Antoine J. Balard [1802-1876].

Bronze Age, prehistoric period, characterized by use of metal tools and weapons and artifacts in Egypt and Asia, by **2500 B.C.**

Brook Farm, utopian, communistic community established and run by George Ripley [Oct. 3, 1802-July 4, 1880] near West Roxbury, Mass., **1841-47**.

Brookings Institution, research organization, established **1927**, at Washington, D.C.

Brooklyn Bridge, world's first steel-wire suspension bridge, opened **May 24, 1883**, Brooklyn, N.Y.

Brotherhood of Sleeping Car Porters, railroad union, organized **1925**, by U.S. black labor leader A. Philip Randolph [Apr. 15, 1889-May 16, 1979].

Brothers Karamazov, The (Brat'ya

Karamazovy), novel, **1880** by Russian author Fyodor Mikhailovich Dostoyevsky [Nov. 11, 1821-Feb. 9, 1881].

Brownian motion, first described, **1827**, by Scottish botanist Robert Brown [1773-1858].

Brownsville Riot, black soldiers stationed at Fort Brown blamed for night gun raid on Brownsville, Tex., **Aug. 13, 1906**, resulted in dishonorable discharge of 167 blacks on order of Pres. Theodore Roosevelt.

Brown University, American institution of higher learning chartered as Rhode Island College at Warren, R.I., **1764**; moved to Providence, R.I., **1770**; renamed Brown, **1804**.

Bruce, famous Scottish family, descended from Norman duke, Robert de Brus [11th century], **11th century**; the 6th Robert the Bruce became claimant to Scottish throne, **1290**; the 8th Robert the Bruce [1274-1329] became king of Scotland as Robert I, **Mar. 27, 1306**; brother of Robert I, Edward Bruce [d. 1318], crowned king of Ireland, **1316**.

Brunkeberg, battle of, Swedish army won major victory over joint Danish-Norwegian army in s. Norway, ending Denmark's campaign to conquer Sweden, **Oct. 10, 1471**.

Brussels, capital of Belgium, seat of Spanish and later Austrian rulers of the Netherlands, **16th-18th centuries**; captured by the French in French Revolutionary War, **1792, 1794**; occupied by Germans in WW I, **1914-1918**, and WW II, **1939-45**.

bubble chamber, invented, **1955**, by U.S. physicist Donald A. Glaser [1926-]; world's largest bubble chamber successfully tested, **1969**, at Argonne National Laboratory, near Chicago.

Bucharest, Treaty of, Bulgaria stripped of its conquests in second Balkan War and forced to disarm; Greece, Rumania, and Serbia gained territory, **Aug. 10, 1913**.

Buchenwald, notorious Nazi concentration camp, opened **July 16, 1937**, at Buchenwald, s.w. East Germany, where about 57,000 prisoners (mostly Jews) died in gas chambers before U.S. troops liberated the camp, **Apr. 11, 1945**.

Buchlau conference, Russia agreed not to oppose Austria's annexation of Bosnia-Hercegovina in return for Austria's non-opposition to opening the Straits to Russian warships, **Sept 16, 1908**.

Buckingham Palace, 600-room palace built by the duke of Buckingham, **1703**; British monarch's residence in London, since **1837**.

Buckshot War, Pennsylvania militiamen, with arms loaded with buckshot, forced Anti-Masonic Party under Thaddeus Stevens [Apr. 4, 1792-Aug. 11, 1868] to allow Democratic members to be seated in state legislature at Harrisburg, Penn., **1838**.

Buddhism, religion, based on enlightenment achieved, India, **c. 528 B.C.**, by Gautama Buddha [c. 563-c. 486 B.C.].

Budget, Bureau of the, U.S. federal agency, created **June 10, 1921**

Buena Vista, battle of, U.S. troops under Gen. Zachary Taylor [Nov. 24, 1784-July 9, 1850] encountered Mexican army under Gen. Antonio Lopez de Santa Anna [Feb. 21, 1794-June 21, 1876] south of Saltillo, Mexico; Mexican army withdrew, **Feb. 22-23, 1847**.

Buenos Aires, capital of Argentina; founded by Pedro de Mendoza [1501?-1537], **1536**; made Argentine capital, **1862**.

Bulge, battle of the, last German offensive on Western Front during WW II, **Dec. 1944-Jan. 1945**; German surprise attack broke through American front in Belgian Ardennes region, creating a dent or "bulge"

in allied lines, **Dec. 16, 1944**; Americans successfully defended key junction at Bastogne to thwart German advance, **Dec. 20-26, 1944**; German offensive halted, **Jan. 16, 1945**.

Bull Moose Party (Progressive Party), U.S. political party begun by Republicans against Pres. Robert A. Taft [Sept. 8, 1889-July 31, 1953], **June 22, 1912**; nominated Theodore Roosevelt for president, **Aug. 7, 1912**; declined, after **1916**.

Bull Run, battles of, two important battles in n.e. Virginia during U.S. Civil War; Confederate resistance, with Gen. Thomas J. Jackson [Jan. 21, 1824-May 10, 1863] standing like a "stone wall," checked Union forces at first battle (or first battle of Manassas), **July 21, 1861**; Confederates under Gen. James Longstreet [Jan. 8, 1821-Jan. 2, 1904] defeated Union army under Gen. John Pope [Mar. 16, 1822-Sept. 23, 1892] at second battle [or second battle of Manassas), **Aug. 29-30, 1862**.

Bunker Hill, battle of, British troops under Gen. William Howe [Aug. 10, 1729-July 12, 1814] defeated American revolutionary forces at Breed's Hill, s.e. of Bunker Hill, outside Charlestown, Mass., **June 17, 1775**.

Bunsen burner, developed, **1850**, by German chemist Robert W. Bunsen [1811-1899].

Burgesses, House of, America's first legislative assembly, the House of Burgesses, met at Old Church, Jamestown, Va., **July 30, 1619**; last session of the Burgesses, **1774**.

Burkersdorf, battle of, Prussians defeated the Austrians during the Seven Years' War, **July 21, 1762.**

Burlingame Treaty, friendship treaty signed by U.S. and China, **1868,** encouraged Chinese immigration to U.S.

Burma, republic in southeast Asia; became independent, **Jan. 4, 1948.**

Burma Road, road, 700 miles long, from northern Burma to Yunnan province, China; built **1937-38.**

Burmese Wars, series of conflicts between Burmese and British over control of territory; first war, **1824-26;** ended by Treaty of Yandabo, **Feb. 24, 1826;** second war, **1852-53;** British annexed Pegu, **Jan. 20, 1853;** third war, **1885;** British gained complete control of Burma, **Jan. 1, 1886.**

Bursa, ancient Byzantine city captured by Ottoman Turks, **1326;** capital of Ottoman Empire, **1326-1402;** sacked by Mongols under Tamerlane, **1402.**

Burns and Allen, husband-and-wife comedy show that was successful on radio, **1932-49,** and television, **1950-58.**

Burnt Corn Creek, battle of, Creek Indians attacked white settlers in Alabama in the first battle of the Creek War, **July 27, 1813.**

Bursum Bill, U.S. congressional law to increase pensions to Civil War veterans and their widows vetoed by Pres. Warren G. Harding [Nov. 2, 1865-Aug. 2, 1923], **Jan. 3, 1923;** vetoed by Pres. Calvin Coolidge [July 4, 1872-Jan 5, 1933] **May 3, 1924.**

bushido, code of honor and conduct established in Japan, **c. 13th century;** put into writing, **16th century;** governed the conduct of the Samurai, **13th-19th centuries.**

Bushy Run, battle of, American colonial forces defeated a coalition of Indian tribes at end of French and Indian War, **Oct. 1763.**

Bussaco, battle of, British and Portuguese armies under duke of Wellington won important victory against French army near Coimbra and around Mt. Bussaco, w. central Portugal, **Sept. 27, 1810.**

Buxar (Baxar), battle of, British army, though greatly outnumbered, defeated native forces under nawab of Oudh, reestablishing British control over Bengal, **Oct. 23, 1764.**

Byland, battle of, Scottish forces attacked and routed English army at Byland, 20 mi. n. of York, compelling King Edward II [1284-1327] to recognize Scottish independence, **Oct. 14, 1322.**

Byrd Amendment, U.S. Congress passed, **Oct. 6, 1971,** amendment to weapons bill proposed by Sen. Harry F. Byrd [Dec. 20, 1914-] in order to allow U.S. to import Rhodesian chrome; implemented **Jan. 1, 1972;** repealed **1977.**

Byzantine Empire (Eastern Roman Empire), eastern portion of the later Roman Empire; centered at Constantinople, **395-1453.**

Byzantium, ancient city on the Bosporus, founded by Greeks, **667 B.C.;** captured by Romans, **196;** chosen by Emperor Constantine I as new capital of Roman Empire, **330.**

Cabinet of Dr. Caligari, The (Das Kabinett des Dr. Caligari), classic German expressionist film, **1919.**

Cabochien revolt, faction of Parisian tradespeople, led by skinner Simon Lecoustellier, called Caboche, seized Paris and passed radical reforms, **1413.**

Cade's rebellion, 30,000 Englishmen led by John (Jack) Cade [-d. July 12, 1450] marched on London to demand governmental reform, **May-July 1450.**

Cadiz, Spanish city and port on Atlantic where English fleet under Sir Francis Drake [c. 1540-Jan. 28, 1596] sank or captured about 30 Spanish ships, without loss of an English ship or man, **Apr. 29, 1587**; English forces under earl of Essex sacked the city, **1596**; became official Spanish center for New World trade, **1718**; successfully resisted French siege, **1810-12**; Spanish Cortes (parliament) issued famous liberal constitution at Cadiz, **Mar. 1812**.

cadmium, element No. 48; discovered, **1817**, by German chemist Friedrich Strohmeyer [1776-1835].

Caesar, assassination of, Julius Caesar, Roman emperor, killed by Gaius Cassius [- 42 B.C.], Marcus Brutus [85?-42 B.C.], and others in Senate chamber in Rome, **Mar. 15, 44 B.C.**

Caesarea Palestinae, ancient city in Palestine that was made capital of Herod the Great [73?-4 B.C.]; **30 B.C.**; site of massacre of Jewish citizens by the Romans, **66**.

Cahokia (Ill.), one of most important French trade centers in upper Mississippi River, **c. 1720-60**; seized by British, **1765**; seized by Americans, **1778**.

Cairo, city in Egypt; founded as Fustat by Fatimids, **969**; ruled by Mamelukes, **c. 1250-1517**; ruled by Ottoman Turks, **1517-1798**; controlled by British, **1882-1936**.

Cairo Conference, important meeting among U.S. Pres. F.D. Roosevelt, British Prime Minister Winston Churchill, Generalissimo Chiang Kai-Shek [Oct. 31, 1887-Apr. 5, 1975] at Cairo, Egypt, **Nov. 20, 1943**, planning future military strategy against Japan.

Cajamarca, site in Peru where Spanish conquistador Francisco Pizarro seized Inca chief Atahualpa, thwarting Inca Indians' ability to fight, **Nov. 16, 1532**.

Calais, major French seaport on Strait of Dover held by the English, **1347-1558**; English troops under King Edward III [Nov. 13, 1312-June 21, 1377] captured port after long siege during Hundred Years' War, **Sept. 4, 1346-Aug. 4, 1347**; England lost her toehold on the continent when French army under duc de Guise captured Calais, **Jan. 6, 1558**.

Calatafimi, battle of, Garibaldi and his "Thousand Redshirts" defeated the Neapolitans at Calatafimi, Sicily, **May 15, 1860**, and advanced on Palermo, which they seized, **May 27, 1860**.

calcium, element No. 20; discovered, **1808**, by English chemist Sir Humphry Davy [1778-1829].

calculating machine, invented, **1645**, by French mathematician Blaise Pascal [1623-1662].

calculus, discovered (differential), **1665**, and (integral), **1666**, by English mathematician Sir Isaac Newton [1642-1727]. Discovered independently, **c. 1676**, by German philosopher Gottfried Wilhelm Leibniz [1646-1716].

Calderon Bridge, battle of, Mexican revolutionaries suffered crushing defeat by Spanish royalist army at bridge of Calderon, near Guadalajara, during Mexican revolution against Spain, **Jan. 17, 1811**.

calendar, Gregorian, developed, **1603**, by Bavarian Jesuit astronomer Christopher Clavius [1538-1612] for Pope Gregory XIII's calendar reforms.

Cali disaster, seven dynamite trucks exploded in Cali, Colombia, destroying the city and killing approx. 1200 people, **Aug. 7, 1956**.

California, admitted to the Union (U.S.) as 31st state, **Sept. 9, 1850**.

California Gold Rush, discovery of gold at Sutter's Mill touched off great stampede to California by thousands of gold-rush miners ("the forty-niners"), **1849**.

californium, element No. 98; produced, **1950**, by American physicist Stanley G. Thompson and associates at University of California, Berkeley.

Callinicum, battle of, Byzantine army

under Belisarius defeated the Persians at Dara, **530**, but was defeated at Callinicum, **531**.

calliope, musical instrument, patented **Oct. 9, 1855**.

Calpulalpam, battle of, Mexican liberal army under Benito Juarez [Mar. 21, 1806-July 18, 1872] defeated conservatives at great battle 40 mi. n.e. of Mexico City, ending two-year civil war with Juarez in control of Mexico, **Dec. 22, 1860**.

Calvinists, followers of Protestant Christian religion developed **c. 1533-64**, by French-Swiss theologian John Calvin [July 10, 1509-May 27, 1564].

Cambodia, nation in southeast Asia; gained its independence from France, **1955**; became Khmer Republic, **Oct. 9, 1970**; became Democratic Kampuchea, **Jan. 8, 1979**.

Cambodian crisis, Pres. Richard M. Nixon announced U.S. troops would invade Cambodia to destroy enemy supply bases, **Apr. 30, 1970**, causing anti-war protests against this "escalation" of Vietnam War; U.S. Senate passed Cooper-Church Amendment, **June 30, 1970**, prohibiting use of U.S. troops in Cambodia.

Cambrai, battle of, British launched first massed tank assault in history against Germans in n. France; strong German counterattack, directed by Gen. Erich F.W. Ludendorff [Apr. 9, 1865-Dec. 20, 1937], forced British to withdraw with heavy losses, **Nov. 20-Dec. 4, 1917**.

Cambrai, League of, Holy Roman Emperor Maximilian I, King Louis XII of France, King Ferdinand V of Aragon, Pope Julius II, and several Italian states formed an alliance against Venice to halt its territorial expansion, **1508-10**; Venetian army defeated by French at Agnadello, **May 14, 1509**. Pope reconciled with Venice, **1510**.

Cambrai, Treaty of (Ladies' Peace), King Francis I paid indemnity to Holy Roman Emperor Charles V, but retained France and Burgundy; Charles held Italy, **Aug. 5, 1529**.

Cambria, German steamship; struck iceberg and sank in North Sea; 389 persons died, **Jan. 19, 1883**.

Cambridge University, one of Britain's principal seats of learning, founded **c. 1200**.

Camden, battle of, American militiamen led by Gen. Horatio Gates defeated by British redcoats at Camden, N.J.; one of most disastrous battles in U.S. history, **Aug. 16, 1780**.

camera (*Kodak*), invented, **1888**, by American inventor George Eastman [1854-1932].

camera, (*Kodak Instamatic*), introduced, **1963**, by Eastman Kodak Company; used film cartridges.

camera, Polaroid, invented, **1947**, by American inventor Edwin H. Land [1900-].

camera, telescopic, designed, **c. 1931**, by German engineer Bernhard V. Schmidt [1879-1935].

Cameroon, republic in Africa; gained its independence from France, **Jan. 1, 1960**.

camisards, French Protestants who revolted against French monarchy, **1702**; suppressed by force, **1705**.

Camorra, criminal association in Naples, Italy, and Sicily, used bribery, blackmail, and terrorism to gain influence, **c. 1830-1911**.

Camp Allegheny, battle of, Confederate troops forced Union troops to retreat at Camp Allegheny, W. Va., **Dec. 13, 1861**, in last important battle in West Virginia campaign.

Menachem Begin   Anwar Sadat

Camp David accord, preliminary "framework" for Mideast peace made by Prime Minister Menachem Begin [Aug. 16, 1913-] of Israel, Pres. Anwar el-Sadat [Dec. 25, 1918-Oct. 6, 1981] of Egypt, and U.S. Pres. Jimmy Carter during summit talks at Camp David, Md., **Sept. 5-17, 1978**; Israel and Egypt signed formal peace treaty, **Mar. 26, 1979**, ending 30 years of war and establishing diplomatic relations.

Camp Defiance, battle of, U.S. troops repulsed fierce attack by Creek Indians in Alabama, suffering heavy casualties, **Jan. 27, 1814**.

Campbell, Scottish noble family, **16th-18th centuries;** partly responsible for the massacre of the Macdonalds at Glencoe, **Feb. 13, 1692;** helped to suppress Jacobites, **1715**.

Campbell's Station, battle of, Union troops under Gen. Burnside forced back Confederates under Gen. Longstreet at Campbell's Station, Tenn., **Nov. 16, 1863,** reaching the fort at Knoxville.

Camperdown, battle of, British fleet won great naval battle against the Dutch fleet in North Sea off Camperdown in n. Netherlands, **Oct. 11, 1797**.

Campo Formio, Treaty of, Austria ceded Austrian Netherlands and left bank of Rhine River to France; Austria received most of Venetian republic (including Dalmatia), **Oct. 17, 1797**.

Canada Act, British parliament divided Canada at Ottawa River into Upper Canada (Ontario), mainly British and Protestant, and Lower Canada (Quebec), mainly French and Catholic, **June 10, 1791**.

Canada Company, English land company established, **1621,** by Sir William Alexander [1567?-1640] with grant of Nova Scotia and New Brunswick received from King James I.

Canada First movement, party in Canada formed to support country's nationalism and growth, **1867;** became political party known as Canadian National Association, **1874**.

Canadian Pacific Railway, privately-owned transcontinental railroad in Canada completed, linking Atlantic coast to Pacific coast, **Nov. 7, 1885**.

canal rays, discovered, **1886,** by German physicist Eugen Goldstein [1850-1930].

Canal Ring, corrupt group of politicians and contractors involved in repair contract work for Erie Canal, exposed by Gov. Samuel J. Tilden [Feb 9, 1814-Aug. 4, 1886], **1875**.

Candian War, Venetians lost control of Candia (Crete) after 24-year war with Ottoman Turks, **1645-69**.

Candide (Candide, ou L'Optimisme), philosophical novel, **1759,** by French writer Voltaire.

candlemas, traditional name of Christian feast of purification of Mary and presentation of Christ, since **542,** celebrated **February 2**.

Cannae, battle of, by brilliant military strategy, Hannibal led his Carthaginians to great victory over Roman troops at village of Cannae in s.e. Italy, **Aug. 3, 216 B.C.**

canned food, process devised, **1811,** by French chef Francois Appert [1750-1841].

canned strained baby food, introduced, **1929,** by American manufacturer Daniel F. Gerber [1898-1974].

canon law, body of Catholic ecclesiastical law, begun **325;** *Decretum of Gratian,* **1140,** basis of medieval code; present Catholic code issued, **May 27, 1917**.

Canossa, Italian village, site of penance done by Holy Roman Emperor Henry IV, standing barefoot in the snow, begging for forgiveness from Pope Gregory VII [c. 1020-May 25, 1085], **Jan. 21, 1077**.

cantata, composition for voices, developed Germany, **c. 1700**.

Canterbury Cathedral, cathedral church of England's principal see, begun **1070;** romanesque crypt survived fire, **1174;** rebuilt gothic cathedral, completed **1503**.

Canterbury Tales, The, 17,000-line English poem, **1387-1400**, in which more than 20 Canterbury pilgrims tell chivalric romances, folk tales, bawdy stories, moral tales, by English poet Geoffrey Chaucer [c. 1340-Oct. 25, 1400].

Canuck Letter, letter from Florida man, alleging Sen. Edmund S. Muskie [Mar. 28, 1914-] made derogatory remarks about blacks and "Cannocks" (sic) in Maine, published in *Manchester Union Leader*, **Feb. 24, 1972**; Muskie defended himself emotionally in public, **Feb. 26, 1972**, perhaps ruining his chances for Democratic presidential nomination.

Cape Colony, Dutch-held region in Africa annexed by British as Cape Colony, **1806**; Boers opposed British rule and made Great Trek north, **1835-36**; fighting at Mafeking and Kimberley during Boer War, **1899-1902**; became province of Union of South Africa, **1910**.

Cape of Good Hope (Cape Province), tip of Africa circumnavigated by a European for first time-Bartolomeu Dias [d. 1500], **Apr. 1488**; by Vasco da Gama [1460-Dec. 24, 1524], **Nov. 1497**.

Capetians, dynasty of French kings, founded by Hugh Capet [c. 938-Oct. 14, 996], **987-1328**.

Cape Verde, island nation off w. coast of Africa, gained its independence from Portugal, **July 5, 1975**.

capital, crowning architectural feature of a column; commonest types developed ancient Greece, were Doric, with convex block, **7th century B.C.**; Ionic, with scroll, **5th century B.C.**; Corinthian, with acanthus leaves, **4th century B.C.**

Capitol, seat of U.S. Congress, Washington, D.C., cornerstone laid, **1793**; rebuilt after War of 1812, **1818-30**; 288-foot dome and House and Senate wings added, **1851-65**.

Caporetto, battle of, German-Austrian artillery and troops won important month-long campaign against Italians in Julian Alps, **Oct 24-Nov. 12, 1917**.

capillary regulator mechanism, discovered, **1918**, by Danish physiologist Schack A. S. Krogh [1874-1949].

Capua, ancient city in Italy on Appian Way that opened its gates to Hannibal in second Punic War, **216 B.C.**; Roman legions recap-

tured city, many of whose senators were executed, **211 B.C.**; destroyed by Arabs, **841**.

Capuchin Order, (Friars Minor Capuchin), independent branch of Franciscan religious order, founded **1525**, by Matteo da Bascio [c. 1495-Aug. 6, 1552].

Carabobo, battle of, revolutionary force under Simon Bolivar, aided by British battalion, defeated Spanish royalist army at Carabobo in Venezuela, whose independence was secured, **June 24, 1821**.

Caracalla, Edict of, citizenship was extended by Roman Emperor Caracalla [188-217] to all free inhabitants of Roman Empire, **212**.

Carberry Hill, battle of, after the marriage of Mary, Queen of Scots [Dec. 7, 1542-Feb. 8, 1587] to James Bothwell [1536?-Apr. 4, 1578], **May 15, 1567**, the Scottish nobles rebelled and forced Mary's army to desert her at Carberry Hill, **June 15, 1567**; Mary was imprisoned at Lochleven Castle but escaped, **May 1568**.

carbohydrate chemistry, pioneered, from **1926**, by English chemist Walter N. Haworth [1883-1950].

carbon cycle, first proposed, **1840**, by German chemist Justus von Liebig [1803-1873].

carbon-14 dating, developed, **1947**, by American chemist Willard F. Libby [1908-1980].

carbon monoxide, first prepared, **1776**, by French chemist J. M. F. de Lassone [1717-1788]; method for detection invented, **1921**, by American chemist Charles R. Hoover [1885-1942].

carbon telephone transmitter, devised, **1876**, by American inventor Thomas A. Edison [1847-1931].

carborundum, an abrasive used for cutting and grinding hard materials; discovered, **1891**, by American inventor Edward G. Acheson [1856-1931].

carburetor, invented, **1876**, by German inventor Gottlieb Daimler [1834-1900].

carburetor, spray, invented, **1892**, by American inventor Charles E. Duryea [1861-1938].

car coupler, railroad, patented, **1873**, by American inventor Eli H. Janney [1831-1921].

cardiac catheterization, technique originated, **1929**, by German surgeon Werner Forssmann [1904-1979].

carding machine, invented, **1797**, by American inventor Amos Whittemore [1759-1828]; used for cotton and wool.

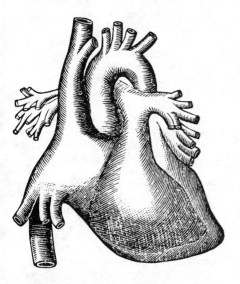

cardiology, medical specialty initiated **1818**, by French physician Jean N. Corvisart [1775-1821].

CARE (Cooperative for American Relief Everywhere), non-profit organization, formed **1945**; merged with Medical International Cooperation Organization (MEDICO), medical assistance program, **1958**.

Carlist Wars, Spanish forces of Isabella II [Oct. 10, 1830-Apr. 9, 1904] defeated the Carlists, supporters of pretender to the throne Don Carlos [Mar. 29, 1788-Mar. 10, 1855], in bloody civil war, **1836-39**; Spanish forces brutally suppressed the Carlists, supporters of Don Carlos' nephew, in second civil war, **1873-76**.

Carlsbad Decrees, resolutions made by German states convened by Metternich, providing strict press censorship and supervision of universities, **July 1819**.

Carlsbad Program, eight demands by Sudeten-German leader Konrad Henlein [May 6, 1898-1945] to Prague government to improve German-Czech relations in the Sudetenland, **Apr. 24, 1938**; unsuccessful talks between Prague government and Sudeten leader, **July-Aug. 1938**.

Carlson's Raiders, U.S. commando force led by Gen. Evans F. Carlson [Feb. 26, 1896-May 27, 1947] made famous raids on Makin Island, **Aug. 1942**, and on Guadalcanal, **Nov. 1942**, during WW II.

Carmathian revolt, Muslim rebels overran and devastated Arabia, Syria, and Iraq and seized the sacred Black Stone, **891-906**.

Carmelite Order, contemplative religious order, founded, Palestine, **c. 1155**; Discalced Carmelites, Spain, **1562-82**.

Carmen, novel of passion, **1847**, by French writer and historian Prosper Merimee [Sept. 28, 1803-Sept. 23, 1870]. Opera, **1875**, based on novel, by French composer Georges Bizet [Oct. 25, 1838-June 3, 1875].

Carnegie Corporation of New York, first U.S. foundation for scholarly and charitable causes, established, **Nov. 10, 1911**.

Carnegie Hall, New York City concert hall, opened, **1891**.

Caroline **affair**, U.S. steamship *Caroline* carrying supplies to Canadian rebels on Navy Island above Niagara Falls, set on fire by British and Canadian loyalists and sent over the falls, **Dec. 29, 1837**.

Caroline, Fort, French Huguenots established Fort Caroline at mouth of St. Johns River in present-day Florida, **1564**; Spanish from St. Augustine marched overland and seized Fort Caroline, which they renamed San Mateo, **Sept. 20, 1565**; French naval expedition captured San Mateo and hanged Spanish, **Apr. 6, 1568**.

Carolingians, Frankish dynasty, **751-843**; brought to its zenith by Emperor Charlemagne, **800**.

carpetbaggers, Northerners who went South after U.S. Civil War to make money and gain political power during Reconstruction, **1867-77**.

carpet loom, power-driven, devised, **1839**, by American inventor Erastus B. Bigelow [1814-1879].

carpet sweeper, patented, **1876**, by American inventor Melville R. Bissell.

Carrhae, battle of, by their archery, Parthians won victory against Roman legions at Carrhae in n. Mesopotamia, **53 B.C.**

carriage, steam, built, **1786**, by English inventor William Symington [1763-1831].

Carrickfergus, battle of, first defeat of a British warship by an American naval ship occurred off Carrickfergus, Northern Ireland, when privateer *Ranger*, commanded by John Paul Jones, defeated and captured British warship *Drake*, **Apr. 24, 1778**.

Carrizal, battle of, after Mexican bandits under Francisco ("Pancho") Villa [June 5, 1878-June 20, 1923] raided Columbus, N. Mex., **Mar. 9, 1916**, U.S. troops of Gen. John J. Pershing [Sept. 13, 1860-July 15, 1948] clashed with Mexicans at Carrizal, Mexico, **June 21, 1916**; Pershing's punitive expedition against Villa lasted until **Feb. 5, 1917**.

Cartagena pact, Britain, France, and Spain agreed to maintain status quo in Mediterranean and e. North Atlantic to stop any German encroachment, **May 16, 1907**.

Cartesianism, philosophical system, developed **1635-50**, by French rationalist philosopher and mathematician Rene Descartes [Mar. 31, 1596-Feb. 1, 1650.].

Carthage, ancient city-state in North Africa, founded by Phoenicians from Tyre, **9th century B.C.**; failed to conquer Sicily, **5th century B.C.**; defeated by Rome at Zama, **202 B.C.**; city destroyed by Scipio Africanus Minor, **146 B.C.**; capital of the Vandals, **439-533**; totally destroyed by Arabs, **698**.

Carthusian Order, strictest of Catholic contemplative religious orders, founded **1084**.

Casablanca, Moroccan city on Atlantic; site of Anfa, town destroyed by Portuguese,

1468; destroyed by earthquake, **1755**, rebuilt, **1757**; site of major Allied landing in WW II, **Nov. 8, 1942**; site of conference between Pres. Franklin Roosevelt, Prime Minister Winston Churchill, Gen. Charles de Gaulle, **Jan. 14-24, 1943**.

Casablanca affair, Franco-German tension increased when German consul gave refuge to deserters from French Foreign Legion at Casablanca, **Sept. 25, 1908**.

cash register, patented, **1879**, by American inventor James Ritty [1836-1918].

cash register (electric motor), invented, **c. 1905**, by American electrical engineer Charles F. Kettering [1876-1958].

Casilinum, ancient town in southern Italy became capital of Samnites, **5th century B.C.**; Roman infantry and mounted archers defeated Franks, ending Frankish invasion of Italy, **554**; citizens of nearby Capua moved to Casilinum and founded modern Capua, **9th century**.

Cassano d'Adda, town in northern Italy, site of French victory over imperial forces of Holy Roman Empire led by Prince of Savoy, during the War of the Spanish Succession, **Aug. 16, 1705**; site of Russian-Austrian victory over French army during French revolutionary wars, **Apr. 27, 1799**.

Cassino, town in central Italy where Allies broke German line of defense after four months of ground attacks in WW II, **Feb.-May 17, 1944**.

cast-iron, malleable, process patented, **1831**, by American inventor Seth Boyden [1788-1870].

Castelfidardo, battle of, Piedmontese (Sardinian) forces of Cavour decisively defeated the Papal army, **Sept. 18, 1860**, and advanced into the territory of Naples to join forces with Garibaldi.

Castelnaudary, battle of, Cardinal Richelieu [Sept. 9, 1585-Dec. 4, 1642] led French army in victory against rebel force in southern France, **Sept. 1, 1632**.

Castiglione delle Stiviere, town in Lombardy, Italy, where French army under Napoleon I won important victory against Austrians, **Aug. 5, 1796**.

Castillon, battle of, ended Hundred Years' War; English were defeated by French artillery fire and counterattacks, finally driving English from the Continent (with the exception of Calais in France), **July 17, 1453**.

Catalan Company, Grand, Spanish mercenaries hired by the Byzantine emperor to fight against the Turks, **1303**; besieged Constantinople, **1305-1307**; its leader Roger de Flor murdered, **1305**; controlled duchy of Athens, **1311-79**.

catalysis, process involving increasing speed of chemical reaction; research developed, **c. 1887**, by German physical chemist Wilhelm Ostwald [1853-1932].

catalytic converters (auto emissions control), installed, from **1975**, by U.S. automobile industry on most cars.

catapult, ship-mounted, first used, **c. 320 B.C.**, by Greek engineer and King of Macedonia Demetrius Poliorcetes [337-283 B.C.], to hurl 27-inch darts.

Catch-22, novel, **1961**, about absurdities of war; by U.S. novelist Joseph Heller [May 1, 1923-].

Catcher in the Rye, The, novel, **1951**, of precocious youth in revolt against empty, "phony" adult society, by U.S. writer J(erome) D(avid) Salinger [Jan. 1, 1919-].

Cateau-Cambresis, Treaty of, Spain gained hegemony over Milan, Naples, and Sicily; France restored Savoy to its duke; England ceded Calais to France, **Apr. 3, 1559**.

cathode rays, investigated, **1892**, by German physicist Philipp Lenard [1862-1947].

cathode ray tube, invented, **1875**, by English physicist Sir William Crookes [1832-1919].

cathode ray (wave theory), developed, **1892**, by German physicist Heinrich R. Hertz [1857-1894].

Catholic Church, title claimed by Western Church after schism with East, **1054**; by Roman Catholics since Protestant Reformation of **c. 1520-60**.

Catholic Emancipation Bill, British prime minister, duke of Wellington, alarmed at growing tension in Ireland, forced parliament to pass bill sponsored by Sir Robert Peel [Feb. 5, 1788-July 2, 1850], **Apr. 1829**.

Catholic Worker, The, penny newspaper, published from **1933**,, co-founded by Catholic convert Dorothy Day [Nov. 8, 1897-Nov. 29, 1980].

Cato Street conspiracy, British government discovered arsenal in Cato Street and arrested conspirators, led by Arthur Thistlewood [1770-May 1, 1820] who planned to assassinate cabinet members, **Feb. 23, 1820**.

Caudine Forks, battle of, Samnites ambushed and routed Roman army in narrow Apennine Mountain pass called Caudine Forks; Romans forced to march out under the yoke, a humiliation Rome never forgot, **321 B.C.**

Cavalier Parliament, first parliament of King Charles II of England; overwhelmingly royalist, **May 8, 1661,-Jan. 24, 1679**.

cavalier poets, English lyric poets, **1630-49**, associated with court of Charles I [Nov. 19, 1600-Jan. 30, 1649]; best-known cavalier poet: Robert Herrick [Aug. 1591-Oct. 15, 1674].

Cavalleria Rusticana (Rustic Chivalry), one-act opera, first produced, Rome, **May 17, 1890**, by Italian composer and conductor Pietro Mascagni [Dec. 7, 1863-Aug. 2, 1945].

cavity resonator, first constructed, **1937**, by American physicist William W. Hansen [1909-1949].

CBS Evening News, U.S. television news program, from **1962**, anchored by broadcast journalist Walter (Leland) Cronkite (Jr.), [Nov. 4, 1916-].

Cedar Creek, battle of, Union forces under Gen. Philip H. Sheridan [Mar. 6, 1831-Aug. 5, 1888] won important battle against Confederates under Gen. Jubal A. Early [Nov. 3, 1816-Mar. 2, 1894] at Cedar Creek in n. Virginia during U.S. Civil War, **Oct. 19, 1864**.

Cedar Mountain, battle of, Confederate

army under Gen. Jackson won victory over Union army under Gen. Nathaniel P. Banks [Jan. 30, 1816-Sept. 1, 1894] at Cedar Mountain, W. Va., **Aug. 9, 1862**.

Celles, furthest point of German armor advance in the Ardennes, halted by U.S. 2nd Armored Division during WW II, **Dec. 24-25, 1944**.

cello, tenor-bass stringed instrument of the violin family; developed, Italy, **1500-1600**.

cell structure, first detailed electronmicroscopy description published, **1945**, by Belgian-American biologist Albert Claude [1899-].

cell theory of life, advanced, **1839**, by German physiologist Theodore Schwann [1810-1882].

cellular chemistry, (proteins and nuclear substances) research published, **1880**, by German physiologist Albrecht Kossel [1853-1927].

celluloid film, patented, **1889**, by American inventor George Eastman [1854-1932].

cellulose, discovered, **1834**, by French chemist Anselme Payen [1795-1871].

Celts, ancient peoples who gained cultural and political domination in western and central Europe, **c. 1200-400 B.C.**

cement, hydraulic, rediscovered, **1756**, by English civil engineer John Smeaton [1724-1792]; forgotten since fall of Rome.

Censorship, Office of, former U.S. federal agency created, **Dec. 19, 1941**, to censor information passing between U.S. and foreign nations in WW II; abolished **Nov. 15, 1945**.

Censure, Resolutions of, U.S. Senate passed resolutions censuring Pres. Andrew Jackson for removing federal funds from the Bank of the United States and putting them in state banks ("pet banks"), **Mar. 28, 1834**; resolutions cancelled after long debate, **1837**.

census, first attempt to count persons regularly outside city areas occurred in French Canada, **1665**; first census in Britain, **1801**; census in Belgium established practice of careful analysis of data compiled, **1846**; U.S. Bureau of the Census, **1902**.

Census, U.S. Bureau of the, federal office established, **Mar. 6, 1902**, to become part of Dept. of Commerce.

cent, U.S. coin proposed by financier Robert Morris [Jan. 31, 1734-May 8, 1806] to be one-fourth of a grain of silver, **1781**; U.S. coin proposed by Thomas Jefferson, to be of copper, **1784**; coinage of copper cent pieces, began **1793**; U.S. cent pieces made of nickel, **1857**; cent pieces made of bronze, **1864**.

Central African Republic, nation in central Africa, proclaimed its independence from France, **Aug. 13, 1960**; became Central African Empire, **Dec. 4, 1976**; reverted to republic, **Sept. 20, 1979**.

Central American Common Market (CACM), trade organization formed by Guatemala, Honduras, Nicaragua, and San Salvador (later joined by Costa Rica), **Dec. 13, 1960**; Honduras rescinded its trade agreements with CACM, **1969**.

Central Intelligence Agency (CIA), independent U.S. federal agency established by National Security Act, **July 26, 1947**, replacing Office of Strategic Services.

Central Treaty Organization (CENTO), after Iraq withdrew from Baghdad pact, **Mar. 24, 1959**, Middle East Treaty Organi-

zation reformed as CENTO, **Aug. 19, 1959.**
centrifugal pump, invented, **1688**, by French physicist Denis Papin [1647-1712].
Century Illustrated Monthly Magazine, U.S. magazine, published **1881-1930.**
Century of Progress Exposition, public exhibition in honor of Chicago's 100th anniversary, held at Chicago, Ill., **May 27-Nov. 12, 1933.**
Century 21 Exposition, world's fair opened, **Apr. 21, 1962**, in Seattle, Wash.
cereal, flaked, first developed, **c. 1890**, by American surgeon John H. Kellogg [1852-1943].
Ceres, first asteroid to be discovered, **1801**, by Italian astronomer Giuseppe Piazzi [1746-1826]; rediscovered, **1802**, by German astronomer Heinrich Olbers [1758-1840], after becoming "lost" for a year..
cerium, element No. 58; discovered, **1803**, by Swedish chemist Jons J. Berzelius [1779-1848].
Cerro Gordo, battle of, U.S. forces under Gen. Winfield Scott [June 13, 1786-May 29, 1866] defeated Mexican army under Gen. Santa Anna at Cerro Gordo mountain pass, winning a decisive victory in Mexican War, **Apr. 17-18, 1847.**
cesium, element No. 55; discovered, **1860**, by German chemist Robert Bunsen [1811-1899] and German physicist Gustav Kirchhoff [1824-1887].
Cesme, battle of, Russian fleet destroyed entire Turkish fleet at Cesme, w. of Smyrna, in the Mediterranean, **July 5, 1770.**
Ceuta, port on Strait of Gibraltar, taken by Portuguese and became first permanent settlement as first European conquest in Africa, **1415**; seized by Spain, **1580**; withstood long siege by Moroccans under Sultan Ismail [1646?-1727], **1694-1720.**
Chaco War, conflict between Bolivia and Paraguay over region of Chaco Boreal, **1932-35**; more than 100,000 persons died in war before truce concluded, **June 14, 1935**; treaty signed, **July 21, 1938.**
Chad, republic in north-central Africa; proclaimed its independence from France, **Aug. 11, 1960.**
Chaeronea, battle of, one of the decisive battles of history; Macedonians under Philip II won overwhelming victory over citizen-soldier army of Athens and Thebes, ending the

freedom of the Greek city-states, **Sept. 1, 338 B.C.**
chain reactions, proposed as natural phenomena, **1918**, by German physical chemist Walther H. Nernst [1864-1941].
chain reactions, branched, theory developed, from **1920**, by Soviet physical chemist Nikolai N. Semenov [1896-].
Chalcedon, Council of, Fourth Ecumenical Council of the Catholic Church, held in Chalcedon, Asia Minor, **451**; decreed that Jesus Christ was true God and true man.
Chalchuapa, battle of, Salvadorean army defeated Guatemalan army led by Pres. Justo Rufino Barrios [c. 1835-Apr. 2, 1885] at Chalchuapa, El Salvador, **Apr. 2, 1885.**
Chaldiran, battle of, Ottoman Turks of Sultan Selim I [1467-Sept. 22, 1520] utterly defeated the Persians of Shah Ismail [July 17, 1487-1524], **Aug. 23, 1514.**
Chalons-sur-Marne, city in n. France, site of Romans' defeat of fierce Germanic tribesmen, the Alamanni, **366**; Romans, allied with Visigoths, fought successful pitched cavalry battle here against Huns under Attila [c. 406-453], checking Hun invasion of Gaul, **June 20, 451.**
chamber of commerce, Marseilles, France, *chambre de commerce* first organization to use name, **1599**; first British chamber of commerce on island of Jersey, **1768**; first U.S. chamber of commerce founded in New York City, **Apr. 5, 1768.**

chamber music, music for two to eight instrumental parts performed without a conductor, developed **c. 1600-1750**; trio sonatas, from **1700**; string quartets dominated, from **1755.**
Chambersburg (Pennsylvania), town

served as headquarters for abolitionist John Brown, **1859**; burned by Confederates, **July 30, 1864**.

Chamberlain-Hitler conferences, at Berchtesgaden, Bavaria, **Sept. 15, 1938**, Brit. Prime Minister Neville Chamberlain [Mar. 18, 1869-Nov. 9, 1940] and Ger. Chancellor Adolf Hitler discussed German annexation of Sudetenland in Czechoslovakia; at Godesberg, W. Germany, **Sept. 22-23, 1938**, discussed Hitler's demands for Sudetenland.

Champion's Hill (Baker's Creek), battle of, Union army under Gen. Ulysses S. Grant defeated Confederates under Gen. John C. Pemberton [Aug. 10, 1814-July 13, 1881], **May 16, 1863**.

Champlain, battle of Lake, one of most important naval battles in U.S. history; American flagship *Saratoga*, commanded by Thomas Macdonough [Dec. 31, 1783-Nov. 10, 1825], defeated larger British *Confiance*, compelling British forces to retreat to Canada, **Sept. 11, 1814**.

Chancellorsville, battle of, by brilliant strategy, Confederates led by Gen. Stonewall Jackson and Gen. Robert E. Lee [Jan. 19, 1807-Oct. 12, 1870] surprised and routed Union armies under Gen. Joseph Hooker [Nov. 13, 1814-Oct. 31, 1879] near Chancellorsville, Va., during U.S. Civil War, **May 2-4, 1863**.

Chantilly, battle of, Union army under Gen. John Pope [Mar. 16, 1822-Sept. 23, 1892] repulsed Confederates under Gen. Andrew Jackson [Jan. 21, 1824-May 10, 1863] during violent thunderstorm at Chantilly, Va., **Sept. 1, 1862**, with both sides suffering severe casualties.

Chappaquiddick incident, car driven by U.S. Sen. Edward M. Kennedy [Feb. 22, 1932-] plunged into water from bridge on Chappaquiddick Island, Martha's Vineyard, Mass.; Mary Jo Kopechne [1941-July 18, 1969] drowned in car, **July 18, 1969**.

Chapultepec, site of unsuccessful heroic Mexican stand against U.S. troops under Gen. Winfield Scott during Mexican War, **Sept. 12-13, 1847**.

Charabuco, battle of, revolutionary forces led by Gen. Jose de San Martin [Feb. 25, 1778-Aug. 17, 1850] and Bernardo O'Higgins [Aug. 20, 1778-Oct. 24, 1842] attacked and decisively defeated Spanish army at Chacabuco, n. of Santiago, securing independence for Chile, **Feb. 12, 1817**.

Charleroi, Belgian town where Germans defeated Allies in WW I, **Aug. 21-24, 1914**.

Charleston, S.C., English settled at Albermarle Point, nearby, **1670**; English moved settlement to Oyster Point and renamed it Charles Town, **1680**; scene of initial act of Civil War, the firing on Fort Sumter, **Apr. 12, 1861**; severe earthquake killed many and left many homeless, **Aug. 13, 1886**.

charmed quarks, new property of matter in theoretical particle, proposed, **1970**, by American physicist Sheldon L. Glashow [1932-].

Charter of Democracy speech, address delivered by Theodore Roosevelt at Columbus, Ohio, **Feb. 11, 1912**.

Charter Oak incident, when English governor of New England demanded Connecticut colonists surrender their charter, the document was stolen and hidden in an oak tree at Hartford, **1687**.

Chartism, workingman's movement in Britain advocating social and political reform, **1838-48**; voting by ballot, universal male suffrage, annual parliaments, and other reforms advocated in "People's Charter," **May 1838**; parliament rejected first Chartist petition, **May 13, 1839**; Chartist leaders arrested after riots, **July-Nov. 1839**; parliament rejected second Chartist petition, **May 3, 1842**; movement ended after failure to present third petition to parliament, **Apr. 1848**.

Chartres Cathedral, French gothic cathedral, especially admired for its carvings and stained glass; west front, **1134-50**; main cathedral begun, **1194**; south spire, **1160**; basically completed, **1260**.

Chateau Gaillard, famous castle built by Richard I ("the Lion-Heart") of England on the Seine River in France as an outpost against Philip II (Philip Augustus) [Aug. 21, 1165-July 14, 1223] of France, c. **1194-98**; besieged by Philip's French forces against English forces of King John (John Lackland) [Dec. 24, 1167-Oct. 19, 1216] **1203-1204**.

Chateaugay River, battle of the, about 1000 British and Indians defeated U.S. invading force of about 7,000 on the banks of the Chateaugay in Quebec, **Oct. 25, 1813**; U.S. abandoned plan to attack Montreal.

Chateau-Thierry, French village on Marne River where U.S. troops halted last German offensive in WW I, **June 1, 1918**.

Chattanooga Campaign, long military encounter between Union and Confederate forces near Chattanooga, Tenn., during U.S. Civil War, **Aug.-Nov. 1863**; Confederates under Gen. Braxton Bragg [Mar. 22, 1817-Sept. 27, 1876] routed Union forces at Chickamauga, **Sept. 19-20, 1863**; Gen. Bragg routed by Union Gen. Ulysses S. Grant [Apr. 27, 1822-July 23, 1885] at Chattanooga, **Nov. 25, 1863**.

Chaumont, Treaty of, Britain, Russia, Prussia, and Austria formed Quadruple Alliance at Chaumont, France, **Mar. 1, 1814**.

Chautauqua movement, adult education institution founded at Chautauqua, N.Y., **1874**.

Chauri Chaura affair, Indian peasants and nationalists killed 22 policemen at Chauri Chaura (United Provinces), **Feb. 4, 1922**; arrested and imprisoned Gandhi, **Mar. 10, 1922**, who had called a halt to civil disobedience.

Cheat Mountain, battle of, Gen. Robert E. Lee's first combat action in U.S. Civil War ended in drawn battle on Cheat Mountain in present-day West Virginia, **Feb. 15, 1861**.

chemical action kinetics, research published, **1926**, by English chemist Cyril Hinshelwood [1897-1967].

chemical bond of protein molecules, concept developed, c. **1939**, by American chemist Linus Pauling [1901-].

Cherbourg, battle of, allied forces during Normandy invasion captured port of Cherbourg, **June 27, 1944**.

Cherenkov radiation, effect explained, **1937**, by Russian physicists Ilya M. Frank [1908-] and Igor Y. Tamm [1895-1971].

Cheribon Agreement, Dutch recognized establishment of a United States of Indonesia under the Dutch crown, **Nov. 15, 1946**; Dutch recognized sovereignty of United States of Indonesia, **Dec. 27, 1947**.

Chernaia (Chernaya), battle of, Peidmontese troops of Comte di Cavour helped British and French win victory in Crimean War, **Jan. 26, 1855**.

Cherry Valley massacre, Indians led by Mohawk chief Joseph Brant [1742-1807] and aided by British loyalists massacred settlers at Cherry Valley, N.Y., **Nov. 11, 1778**.

Chesapeake affair, U.S. frigate *Chesapeake* fired upon and stopped by British warship *Leopard*, **June 1807**; *U.S.S. Chesapeake*, refitted and commanded by Captain James Lawrence [Oct. 1, 1781-June 1, 1813], defeated by *H.M.S. Shannon* in naval battle outside Boston harbor, **June 1, 1813**.

chess, first modern international chess tournament held in London, England, **1851**; title world champion first claimed by Wilhelm

Steinitz [May 14, 1836-Aug. 12, 1900] of Austria, **1866**; Paul C. Morphy [June 22, 1837-July 10, 1884] won first American chess championship at New York City, **Oct. 6, 1857**; Robert (Bobby) J. Fischer [Mar. 9, 1943-]became first American to win world chess championship, **1972**.

Chester (Penn)., site of landing of William Penn [Oct. 14, 1644-July 30, 1718] in America, **1682**; Penn renamed town and held first government assembly there, **May 1682**.

Cheyenne Wars, series of conflicts between U.S. troops and Cheyenne Indians in Colorado, Wyoming, and Montana, c. **1860-77**; U.S. troops massacred Cheyenne at Sand Creek, Colo., **Nov. 29, 1864**; Cheyenne joined with Sioux to massacre a segment of Gen. Custer's 7th Cavalry at Little Bighorn, **June 25, 1876**.

Chicago Eight, radical leaders accused of conspiracy to incite riots during 1968 National Democratic Convention in Chicago tried by federal jury, **Sept. 24, 1969-Feb. 18, 1970**; Black Panther leader Bobby G. Seale [1937-] sentenced to four years for contempt, **Nov. 5, 1969**; "Chicago Seven" found innocent, **Feb. 18, 1970**.

Chicago Fire, Great, most of city of Chicago destroyed by fire that killed more than 300 persons, left 100,000 homeless, and caused $200 million in property damage, **Oct. 8-9, 1871**.

Chickamauga, battle of, Confederates under Gen. James Longstreet [Jan. 8, 1821-Jan. 2, 1904] forced Union troops under Gen. William S. Rosecrans [Sept. 6, 1819-Mar. 11, 1898] to withdraw, though Union Gen. George H. Thomas [July 31, 1816-Mar. 28, 1870] stood firm, earning nickname "Rock of Chickamauga"; Confederates under Gen. Bragg won victory but failed to pursue, **Sept. 19-20, 1863**.

Chickasaw Bluffs, battle of, Union army under Gen. Sherman repulsed by Confederates near Vicksburg, **Dec. 27-29, 1862**, thwarting early attempt to split the Confederacy.

Chile, South American repubic; gained its independence from Spanish rule, **1818**; elected Salvador Allende Gossens first Marxist-Leninist president in a non-Communist country, **Sept. 4, 1970**.

Chilean earthquakes, great, area around Chillan, Chile, razed by violent quake; approx. 30,000 killed, **Jan. 24, 1939**; southern Chile rocked by quakes; approx. 6,000 killed, **May 21-30, 1960**.

China, Great Wall of, 2,484 mile long fortified wall, with watch towers, built by conscript labor, **221-210 B.C.**.

Chinese Civil War, (see Civil War, Chinese).

Chinese earthquakes, great, Shensi province devastated by deadliest quake in history; approx. 800,000 killed, **Jan. 24, 1556**; Kansu province rocked by severe earthquake; approx. 200,000 killed, **Dec. 16, 1920**; Tangshan and surrounding area devastated by second deadliest quake in history; approx. 700,000 killed, **July 28, 1976**.

Chinese Eastern Railway, Chino-Russian defense alliance granted Russia right to build and operate railway across northern Manchuria to connect with Trans-Siberian Railway, **June 3, 1896**.

Chinese Exclusion Act, U.S. banned immigration of Chinese laborers for 10 years, **May 6, 1882**; renewed as Geary Chinese Exclusion Act, **May 5, 1892**; renewed, **Apr. 29, 1902**.

Chinese floods, great, rebels destroyed seawall at Kaifeng, reputedly drowning approx. 300,000 Chinese, **1642**; Yellow River overflowed and killed hundreds of thousands, **1887**; Yangtze River overflowed and killed approx. 100,000, **1911**; millions left homeless, starved, or drowned in flood in Tientsin area, **1939**; floods in eastern and southern China left millions homeless, **Aug. 14, 1950**.

Chinese-Indian plague, great, bubonic plague swept through China and India, killing an estimated three million persons, **1898-1908**.

Chinese-Japanese Wars, conflict between China and Japan for possession of Korea, **1894-95**; ended by Treaty of Shimonoseki, **Apr. 17, 1895**; second war (undeclared) when Japan attacked and invaded China, merged with WW II, and ended with allied victory over Japan, **1937-45**.

Chinese Revolution, revolution led by Sun Yat-sen [Nov. 12, 1866-Mar. 12, 1925] overthrew Ch'ing dynasty (Manchus) and established republic in China, **Oct.-Dec. 1911**.

Ch'ing (Manchu) dynasty, last Chinese dynasty, founded by Manchus (Mongoloids). **1644-1912.**

Chippewa River, battle of, first battle of War of 1812, **July 5, 1814.**

chlorine, element No. 17; discovered, **1774,** by Swedish chemist Karl W. Scheele [1742-1786].

chloroform, introduced as an anesthetic, **1847,** by Scottish obstetrician Sir James Young Simpson [1811-1870].

chloromycetin (chloramphenicol), antibiotic developed, **1947,** by American inventor Mildred Rebstock, for Parke Davis Co.

chlorophyll research, pioneered, **1905,** by German organic chemist Richard Wilstatter [1872-1942].

Chola dynasty, famous ancient dynasty in s. India, noted for its conquest of present-day Sri Lanka and occupation of parts of Burma, Malaya, and Sumatra, **10th-12th centuries.**

cholesterol, structure of, determined, **c. 1930,** by German chemist Adolf Windaus [1876-1959]; research into its role in metabolism begun **1944** by German-American biochemist Konrad E. Bloch [1912-].

Chotusitz, battle of, Prussian army under Frederick II ("the Great") defeated the Austrians, **May 17, 1742.**

Chouans, peasants of France who rebelled against French revolutionary government, **1793;** so-called "Petite Chouannerie" lasted until **1815.**

Chremonidean War, conflict between confederation of Greek cities and King Antigonus II [320?-239 B.C.], **266-262 B.C.;** Antigonus captured Athens and restored Macedonian state, **262 B.C.**

Christian Brothers, Catholic religious orders of teaching brothers, variously founded, Rheims, France, **1680;** Waterford, Ireland, **1802;** Ploermel, France, **1817.**

Christianity, initially spread, c. **30-90,** by "apostles" chosen by Jesus Christ.

Christian Science, religious movement teaching healing through spiritual means (*Matt.* 9:1-8), founded, Boston, **1866;** first church organized there, **1879,** by U.S. religious leader Mary Baker Eddy [July 16, 1821-Dec. 3, 1910]; *Christian Science Monitor* published, from **1883.**

Christmas, popular English name for Christian Feast of the Nativity of Christ, celebrated **December 25,** since **336.**

Christmas Carol, A, Christmas story, **1843,** by English novelist Charles Dickens [Feb. 7, 1812-June 9, 1870].

chromatography, invented, **1906,** by Russian botanist Mikhail S. Tsvett [1872-1920]; partition, discovered, **1941,** by British biochemists, Richard L. M. Synge [1914-] and Archer J. P. Martin [1910-].

chromium, element No. 24; discovered, **1797,** by French chemist Louis N. Vauquelin [1763-1829].

chromium steel (Stellite), developed, **1910,** by American inventor Elwood Haynes [1857-1925].

chromoradiometer, invented, **1902,** by Austrian roentgenologist Guido Holzknecht [1872-1931].

chromosomes, investigated, **1913,** by American biologist Thomas H. Morgan [1866-1945].

Chronicles, books of the Old Testament written by "Chronicler," c.**400 B.C.;** final form, **350-300 B.C.**

chronograph, electromagnetic, invented,

DICTIONARY OF DATES

1844, by American scientist John Locke [1792-1856].

chronometer, developed, **1735**, by English horologist John Harrison, [1693-1776].

Chrysler's Field, battle of, American army under Gen. James Wilkinson [1757-Dec. 28, 1825] lost battle against British near St. Lawrence River, Quebec, **1813**.

Church of England, English Christian body organized under Archbishop of Canterbury: **594**, mission from Rome of St. Augustine of Canterbury [c. 550-May 26, 604]; **1534**, Royal Act of Supremacy; Synodical Government Measure for church government, **1969**.

Church of Scotland, Presbyterian Church (Kirk) established in Scotland, **1560**; efforts to make Kirk episcopal, **1584-1680**; Presbyterianism confirmed, **1690**; re-union of all Presbyterian Churches in Scotland under original name, **1929**.

Cibalae, battle of, Roman emperor Constantine I defeated rival co-emperor Licinius [250-325] **Oct. 8, 314**, who was forced to cede all his European territory except Thrace.

Ciceronian Age, age of classical Latin prose, last years of Roman Republic, **80-27 B.C.**; chief writers: Marcus Tullius Cicero [106-Dec. 7, 43 B.C.]; Gaius Julius Caesar; Gaius Sallustus Crispus (Sallust) [86-34 B.C.]

Cid, The (Le Cid), French classical tragedy, **1621**, about Spanish national hero, by French dramatist Pierre Corneille; revolutionized drama in the **17th century**.

Cid, The (Poema del Cid), Spanish epic poem, **c. 1140**, about exploits of national hero in Moorish wars *Cid Campeador* Rodrigo Diaz de Bivar [c. 1043-1099].

Cincinnati, Society of the, national patriotic organization founded **May 13, 1783**.

cinema (motion picture), first patented, **1888**, by French physician Jules Marey [1830-1904], as the "chronophograph" for studying the physiology of humans and animals; British inventor Eadweard James Muybridge [1830-1904] invented a "zoopraxiscope", in **1872**, to project moving pictures of animals on a screen.

cinemascope, film technique, invented, **1914-18**; adapted to film, **1927**; most U.S. movie theaters adopted, **1953**.

Cisalpine Republic, state and protectorate in Italy created by Napoleon through the union of Transpadane and Cispadane republics, **July 9, 1797**; renamed Italian Republic, **Aug. 2, 1802**; merged with Venetia to become Napoleon's kingdom of Italy, **Mar. 18, 1805**.

Cistercians, monks of Catholic order of Citeaux, reformed offshoot of Benedictines, founded, Burgundy, **1098**, by St. Robert of Molesme [c. 1027-April 29, 1110]; papal approval granted, **1100**.

Citizen Kane, film, **1941**, about private life of a press magnate.

City Center Joffrey Ballet, U.S. ballet company organized New York, **1966**, from R. Joffrey Ballet founded in, **1956**.

City Lights, film, **1931**, one of classic films of British-U.S. comedian Charlie Chaplin (Sir Charles Spencer Chaplin) [Apr. 16, 1889-Dec. 25, 1977].

Ciudad Real, city in central Spain, near which French won battle over Spanish in Peninsular War, **1809**; Spanish soldiers staged large revolt there, **Jan. 29, 1929**.

Civil Aeronautics Board, independent U.S. government agency, established **June 23, 1938**.

Civil Rights Acts, U.S. Congress granted citizenship to all persons born in U.S., except Indians, **Apr. 9, 1866**; gave Negroes equal rights in public places, **Mar. 1, 1875**; prohibited discrimination for reason of color, race, religion, or national origin in public places covered by interstate commerce, **July 2, 1964**; prohibited housing and real estate discrimination, **Apr. 11, 1968**.

Civil War, Chinese, conflict between Chi-

nese Communists of Mao Tse-tung [Dec. 26, 1893-Sept. 9, 1976] and Chinese Nationalists of Generalissimo Chiang Kai-shek [Oct. 31, 1887-Apr. 5, 1975] for control of China, **1946-49**; Communists seized Mukden (Shen-yang), annihilating Nationalists, **Nov. 1, 1948**; Peking fell to Communists, **Jan. 1949**; Chinese Communists proclaimed central people's government at their capital Peking, **Oct. 1, 1949**; Chinese Nationalist government established on Formosa (Taiwan), **Dec. 1949**.

Civil War, English, conflict between supporters of King Charles I [Nov. 19, 1600-Jan. 30, 1649] (royalists or Cavaliers) and the "parliamentarians" (Roundheads), **1642-48**; royalists defeated at Marston Moor, **July 2, 1644**; royalists again beaten at Naseby, **June 14, 1645**; invading Scottish army by Oliver Cromwell [Apr. 25, 1599-Sept. 3, 1658] at Preston, **Aug. 17-20, 1648**; Pride's Purge of parliament, **Dec. 6-7, 1648**, Charles I beheaded, **Jan. 30, 1649**.

Civil War, U.S., conflict between Northern states (Union) and Southern states (Confederacy), primarily over states' rights and slavery, **1861-65**; election of Abraham Lincoln [Feb. 12, 1809-Apr. 15, 1865] led to secession of Southern states, **1860-61**; Confederates fired on Fort Sumter, **Apr. 12, 1861**; Confederates won at Bull Run, **July 21, 1861**; Gen. Lee halted Gen. McClellan's Peninsular Campaign, **July 1862**; Gen. Lee's northern invasion halted at Antietam, **Sept. 17, 1862**; Admiral Farragut captured New Orleans for the Union, **Apr. 25, 1862**; *Monitor* and *Merrimack* fought drawn naval battle, **Mar. 9, 1862**;

Pres. Lincoln issued Emancipation Proclamation, **Jan. 1, 1863**; Confederates won victory at Chancellorsville, **May 2-4, 1863**; Confederates' second northern invasion stopped at Gettysburg, **July 1-3, 1863**; Union won major victory at Vicksburg, **May 7,-July 4, 1863**; Confederates checked at Chickamauga, **Sept. 20, 1863**; Gen. Grant forced Gen. Lee toward Richmond during Wilderness Campaign, **May-June 1864**; Union forces seized Atlanta, Ga., **Sept. 2, 1864**; Confederates evacuated their capital, Richmond, Va., **Apr. 3, 1865**; Gen. Lee surrendered to Gen. Grant at Appomattox Courthouse, ending U.S. Civil War, **Apr. 9, 1865**.

Civil Works Adminstration (CWA), U.S. Congress created, **Nov. 8, 1933**; dismantled, **Feb. 1934**, with Federal Emergency Relief Administration taking over operations.

Civilian Conservation Corps (CCC), U.S. Congress created, **Mar. 31, 1933**; abolished **1942**.

Clamshell Alliance, non-violent environmental organization; demonstrated at site of power plant in Seabrook, N.H., **Aug. 1976**; occupied site at Seabrook, **Apr. 30, 1977**.

Clarendon Code, series of repressive statutes enacted by the Cavalier Parliament, **1661-65**.

Clarendon, Constitutions of, articles issued by King Henry II to define church and state jurisdictions in England, **1164**.

clarinet, woodwind instrument invented, Germany, **1700**.

classicism, classical, movement or style in the arts, inspired by Greek models, **500-325 B.C.**, emphasizing simplicity, restraint, proportion and discipline; neo-classicism, from **1750**.

Clay-Liston fight, Cassius Clay (now Muhammad Ali) [Jan. 18, 1942-] knocked out Sonny Liston in seventh round in Miami Beach, Fla., to become heavyweight boxing champion, **Feb. 25, 1964**;.

Clayton-Bulwer Treaty, U.S. and Britain agreed to neutrality of any ship canal across

Central American isthmus, **Apr. 19, 1850**.

Clayton Compromise, U.S. Senate passed but House of Representatives rejected compromise bill to establish territories of Oregon, California, and New Mexico with antislavery governments, **July 27-28, 1848**.

Clermont, first commercially successful steamboat, launched **1807**, by American inventor Robert Fulton [1765-1815].

Clermont, battle of, French peasant uprising, (the *Jacquerie*), ended after French battled and massacred great mass of peasants near Clermont, n. of Paris, **1358**.

clipper ship, long, tall-masted sailing ship, with overhanging bow, built for fast transoceanic travel, **c. 1830-70**; Yankee clipper emerged with *Ann McKim*, launched from Baltimore, **1832**; one of last great British clippers, *Cutty Sark*, launched at Dunbarton, Scotland, **1869**.

clock, electric, first built, **1839**, by Swiss physicist Carl A. Steinheil [1801-1870].

clock, mechanical, one of earliest known tower clocks, begun **1362**, completed, **1370**, by German clockmaker Henry De Vick [fl. c. 1360] in what is now Palais de Justice, Paris.

clothes dryer, automatic, invented, **1938**, by American inventor J. Ross Moore.

cloud chamber, developed, **c. 1899**, for investigations in atomic physics, by Scottish physicist Charles T.R. Wilson [1869-1959].

Clouds, The, ancient comedy, **423 B.C.**, by Greek dramatist Aristophanes.

Cloyd's Mountain, battle of, Union army under Gen. George Crook [Sept. 23, 1829-Mar. 21, 1890] drove the Confederates back during raid on Virginia and Tennessee RR at Cloyd's Mountain, Va., **May 9, 1864**.

Cnidus (Cnidos), ancient Greek city, near where combined Athenian-Persian fleet won great naval victory over Spartan fleet under Pisander [d. 394 B.C.], **394 B.C.**.

Cnossos (Knossos), ancient city in n. Crete; center of Minoan civilization, **c. 3000-1000 B.C.**; destroyed by earthquake, **c. 1550 B.C.**; destroyed (after it was splendidly rebuilt) by Mycenaean invaders, **c. 1400 B.C.**

coal into gasoline, conversion first achieved, **1912**, by German chemist Friedrich Bergius [1884-1949].

coal-mining machine, patented, **1891**, by Belgian-American inventor Charles J. Van Depoele [1846-1892]; continuous machine invented, **1947**, by American inventor Harold F. Silver [1901-]

cobalt, element No. 27; discovered, **c. 1735**, by Swedish chemist Georg Brandt [1694-1768].

Coca-Cola, invented, **1886**, by American proprietary druggist John S. Pemberton [1835-1888] in Atlanta, Georgia.

cocaine, administered as a local anesthetic, **1884**, by Austrian-American ophthalmologist Carl Koller [1857-1944] in eye surgery.

cochlea, structure in the inner ear discovered, **1851**, by Italian histologist Marchese Alfonso Corti [1822-1888]; function of discovered, **1947**, by Hungarian-American physiologist Georg von Bekesy [1899-1972].

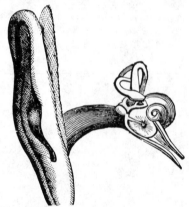

Cocoanut Grove fire, one of worst fires in U.S. history; night club in Boston burned, killing 492 people, **Nov. 28, 1942**.

Codex Alexandrinus, important early Bible manuscript, **5th century**.

Codex Amiatiuus, oldest extant manuscript of Latin Vulgate Bible, written, England, **c. 690-99**; in Florence's Laurentian Library, since **1782**.

coenzymes, discovered, **1923**, by English biochemist Sir Arthur Harden [1865-1940] and Swedish biochemist Hans von Euler-Chelpin [1873-1964].

Cognac, League of, alliance of the pope, Florence, France, Milan, and Venice against Holy Roman Emperor Charles V [Feb. 24, 1500-Sept. 21, 1558] and the Spaniards, **May 22, 1526**.

cogwheel railroad, world's first mountain-climbing train completed, **1869**.

Cold Harbor, battle of, Union forces under Gen. Ulysses S. Grant and Gen. George G. Meade [Dec. 31, 1815-Nov. 6, 1872] repulsed with horrible slaughter by smaller Confederate force under Gen. Robert E. Lee at Cold Harbor, 10 mi. from Richmond, Va., **June 3, 1864**.

Cold War, Soviet-American rivalry short of armed conflict introduced nationally in speech by Bernard M. Baruch [Aug. 19, 1870-June 20, 1965] before U.S. Senate committee, **Oct. 24, 1948**.

Colenso, battle of, British under Gen. Buller crushed by Boer forces at Colenso, **Dec. 15, 1899**, failing to cross Tugela River and advance on Ladysmith.

College de France, institution of higher learning, established, Paris, **1530**.

Colliers, U.S. magazine, published **1888-1957**.

Colline Gate, Roman legions under Lucius Cornelius Sulla [138-78 B.C.] defeated invading Samnites and anti-Sulla Romans at Colline Gate, **Nov. 82 B.C.**

collodion process (photography), invented, **1850**, by English photographer Frederick S. Archer [1813-1857].

Cologne Cathedral, Germany's largest and most imposing gothic cathedral, begun **1248**, completed, **1880**.

Colombo Plan, eight British Commonwealth countries adopted economic plan to aid India, Pakistan, Ceylon, Sarawak, and Borneo, **Nov. 28, 1950**.

Colorado, admitted to the Union (U.S.) as 38th state, **Aug. 1, 1876**.

color blindness, first detailed account, **1794**, by English chemist John Dalton [1766-1844].

color blindness, tests for, introduced, **1874**, by Swedish physiologist Alarik Frithiof Holmgren [1831-1897].

color copier, introduced, **1976**, by Xerox Corporation; machine, Xerox 6500, also reproduced texture.

colorimetric test method, developed, c. **1940**, by American biochemist Frederick C. Koch [1876-].

color photography, process of, invented, c. **1891**, by French physicist Gabriel Lippmann [1845-1921]; first color photo-graph produced by Scottish physicist James C. Maxwell [1831-1879].

color television, pioneered, **1928**, by Scottish inventor John L. Baird [1888-1946].

Colossians, Letter to the, letter (epistle) to the Church in Colossae, Asia Minor, c. **62**.

Colossus of Rhodes, erected in the harbor of Rhodes, **292-280 B.C.**; destroyed by earthquake, **224 B.C.**

Colt six-shooter revolver, patented, **1836**, by American inventor Samuel Colt [1814-1862].

Columbia University, American institution of higher learning founded as King's College in New York City, **1754**; King's College renamed Columbia College, **1784**; became a university, **1896**.

compass, gyroscopic, introduced, **1910**, by American engineer Elmer A. Sperry [1860-1930].

combine (harvesting, threshing, cleaning), invented **1911** by American inventor Benjamin Holt.

Comecon (Council for Mutual Economic Assistance), Communist nations formed organization, **Jan. 25, 1949**.

Comedie Francaise, French national theater, formed **1658**, from acting company established by Moliere, **1643**; merged with other companies and officially titled, **1681**.

comedy, drama with "happy ending," originated with Greek "old comedy," c. **465-400 B.C.**, which grew from fertility rites; Aristophanes's literary comedies called "middle comedy," c. **400-350 B.C.**; modern comedy developed from c. **1500**.

Comedy of Errors, The, play, **1592**, by William Shakespeare.

Cominate **(late Roman Empire)**, Roman period of decline and decay from Diocletian [245-316] to last Roman emperor, Romulus Augustulus [d. after 476], **284-476**.

Cominform (Communist Information Bureau), formed **Oct. 5, 1947**; expelled Yugoslavia because of hostility of Marshal Tito [May 7, 1892-May 4, 1980] to Soviet hegemony, **June 28, 1948**; dissolved **Apr. 17, 1956**.

Commandments, The Ten, divine precepts for human conduct, believed to have been delivered, **c. 1290 B.C.**

Commedia dell'Arte, dramatic form employing stock characters, such as Harlequin, flourished Italy, from **c. 1500**.

Commerce, U.S. Department of, federal department, established **Feb. 14, 1903**, as Dept. of Commerce and Labor; separate Labor Dept. established, **Mar. 4, 1913**.

Committee of Public Safety (Comite du salut public), French committee of nine (later 12) men including Robespierre and Georges Jacques Danton [Oct. 26, 1759-Apr. 5, 1794], who exercised ruthless, dictatorial power during French Revolution, **1793-94**.

Commodity Credit Corporation, U.S. federal agency, formed **Oct. 1933**.

Commodity Exchange Act, U.S. Congress regulated, **June 15, 1936**, trading on commodity futures markets; Commodity Exchange Authority, U.S. agency in Dept. of Agriculture, established to oversee trading, **1947**.

Common Cause, U.S. organization formed by John W. Gardner [Oct. 8, 1912-], **1970**.

Common Man's Charter, common social policy to bridge gap between rich and poor in Uganda, instituted by Pres. Milton Obote [1924-], **Oct. 8, 1969**.

Common Market (European Economic Community, EEC), customs union and

trading bloc formed by treaty among France, Belgium, Netherlands, Luxembourg, Italy, and W. Germany, **Mar. 25, 1957**; joined by Britain, Ireland, and Denmark, **1973**; joined by Greece, **Jan. 1, 1981**.

Common Sense, pamphlet, **1776**, by British-U.S. political philosopher and pamphleteer Thomas Paine.

Commonwealth, English republic set up after the beheading of Charles I, governed by Rump Parliament and army council headed by Lord Cromwell, **1649-60**.

Communards, members of the 1871 Commune of Paris who threw up barricades, shot hostages (including archbishop of Paris), and burned the Tuileries palace, city hall, and palace of justice during "Bloody Week, " **May 21-28, 1871**.

Communism, philosophical theory holding goods should be held in common, adumbrated, **370 B.C.**, in Plato's *Republic*; espoused, **1200s**, by followers of monk Joachim of Fiore [c. 1135-1202]; launched as modern political movement, **1848**.

Communist Manifesto, The, pamphlet, **1848**, by Friedrich Engels [Nov. 28, 1820-Aug. 5, 1895] and Karl Marx [May 5, 1818-Mar. 14, 1883].

Communist Party, Soviet, purged of all

opposition by Joseph Stalin, **1934-39**; old Bolshevik leaders Grigori E. Zinoviev [Sept. 11, 1883-Aug. 25, 1936], Lev. B. Kamenev [1883-Aug. 25, 1936], and 14 others tried as Trotskyists, confessed to charges, convicted, and executed, **Aug. 19-25, 1936**.

Comoro Islands, archipelago off east coast of Africa, declared its independence from France, **July 6, 1975**.

Compagnie des Indes (Company of the Indies), French credit corporation for development of overseas trade and colonies organized by John Law [1671-1729] in Paris, **1719**.

complementarity principle, proposed, **1927**, by Danish physicist Niels H. D. Bohr [1885-1962].

compression machine, invented, **1834**, by American inventor Jacob Perkins [1766—1849].

Compromise of 1850, eight resolutions introduced by Henry Clay [Apr. 22, 1777—June 29, 1852] in U.S. Congress to solve slavery question in the territories; five passed as separate bills, **Jan. 29, 1850**.

comptometer, invented, **1887**, by American inventor Dorr E. Felt [1862—1930].

computer, digital, first built, **1944**, by American mathematician Howard H. H. Aiken [1900—1973]; called *Mark I*; first automatic electronic computer (ENIAC) completed, **1946**, under direction of U.S. physicist John W. Mauchly [1907—1980].

computer, musical, digital synthesizer, invented, **1977**, by American scientist H. G. Alles at Bell Laboratories of American Telephone and Telegraph.

computerized axial tomography (CAT), diagnostic technique first introduced, **1973**.

concertina, free reed instrument with bellows and finger studs, patented, England, **1829**.

concerto, instrumental work, originating **c. 1600**.

Concorde (SST), first supersonic jet to exceed twice speed of sound, **1970**; U.S. Supreme Court lifted ban (because of noise level) on supersonic Concorde flights to JFK Airport, **Oct. 17, 1977**; Concorde began flights to JFK from London and Paris, **Nov. 22, 1977**.

condensation pump, high-vacuum, invented, **1916**, by American physical chemist Irving Langmuir [1881-1957].

condensed milk, method patented, **1856**, by U.S. inventor Gail Borden [1801-1874].

conditioned reflexes, studies of learned, reflexive acts pioneered, **c. 1890**, by Russian physiologist Ivan P. Pavlov [1849-1936].

Conestoga wagon, developed, **c. 1760**.

Confederate cruisers, raids by Confederate cruisers, notably the *Florida, Alabama*, and *Shenandoah*, inflicted serious damage on Union's merchant marine during U.S. Civil War, **1863-65**.

Confederate States of America (Confederacy), government in U.S. established by eleven southern states that seceded from the Union, **Feb. 4, 1861-Apr. 9, 1865**; Jefferson Davis [June 3, 1808-Dec. 6, 1889] elected president of Confederacy, **Feb. 9, 1861**; constitution adopted by Confederate Congress at Montgomery, Ala., **Mar. 11, 1861**; Confederate capital moved from Montgomery, Ala., to Richmond, Va., **May 21, 1861**; collapsed with Gen. Lee's surrender, **Apr. 9, 1865**.

Confederation of Koln (Cologne), 77 Hansa towns organized to prevent Denmark from breaking up the Hanseatic League and its trading monopoly, **Nov. 19, 1367**.

Confederation of the Rhine, confederation of German princes, including Bavaria, Baden, Saxony, Wurttemburg, and Westphalia, organized under French auspices with Napoleon as protector, **1806-13**

Confessing Church, The, German evangelical Churches openly opposed to Nazism, **1933-45**; organized by German Lutheran pastor Martin Niemoeller [Jan. 14, 1892-]; issued anti-Nazi Barmen Declaration, **1934**; issued *Declaration of (German) Guilt*, **1945**.

Confessions of Basel, two important Reformation confessions of faith, first issued, **1536**, second **1566**, Basel, Switzerland.

Confessions of St. Augustine, The, spiritual autobiography, **397-401**.

Confirmation, Christian sacrament believed to confer fullness of Holy Spirit, administered since apostolic times, **c. 65-85**;.

Confirmation of Charters, English barons and middle-class groups forced King Edward I [June 17, 1239-July 7, 1307] to reaffirm the Magna Carta, **1297**.

conformational analysis, independently developed, **1949**, by English organic chemist Derek H. Barton [1918-] and Norwegian chemist Odd Hassel [1897-].

Confucianism, traditional creed of China, one of several rival teachings during Chou dynasty, **1027-256 B.C.**; became orthodoxy during Han dynasty, **202 B.C.-220 A.D.**; based on teachings of Chinese philosopher Confucius [c. 551-487 B.C.].

Congo, country in w. central Africa, proclaimed its independence from France, **Aug. 15, 1960**; proclaimed a people's republic, Africa's first, **1970**; Congo's president assassinated by commando squad, **Mar. 18, 1977**; archbishop of Brazzaville assassinated, **Mar. 23, 1977**.

Congo Treaty, Britain signed agreement with King of the Belgians Leopold II [Apr. 9, 1835-Dec. 17, 1909], **May 12, 1894**.

Congregationalists, Christians affirming autonomy of local church congregation, arose, England, **c. 1550**; Toleration Act, **1689**, confirmed their right to exist; formed United Reformed Church with Presbyterians, **1972**.

Congregation for the Doctrine of the Faith, Roman office responsible for Catholic doctrine, began, **1542**, as Roman Inquisition; re-named *Holy Office*, **1908**; re-organized under present name, **1965**.

Congress, Confederate, provisional Confederate Congress, **Feb. 4, 1861-Feb. 17, 1862**; first Confederate Congress, **Feb. 18, 1862-Feb. 18, 1864**; second Confederate Congress, **May 2, 1864-Mar. 18, 1865**.

Congress of Racial Equality (CORE), U.S. civil rights organization, founded **1942**, by James L. Farmer [Jan. 12, 1920-] in Chicago; sponsored *Freedom Riders*, **1961**; sponsored massive civil rights march on Washington, D.C., **Aug. 28, 1963**.

Congressional Record, official publication of proceedings and debates of U.S. Congress, established **1873**.

conic sections, described, **c. 240 B.C.**, by Greek mathematician Apollonius [250-220 B.C.].

Conlon Report, U.S. study commissioned by Senate Foreign Relations Committee, released **Oct. 31, 1959**, urging "de facto recognition" of Communist China, establishing "two-Chinas policy."

Connecticut, one of Thirteen Colonies; ratified U.S. Constitution to become fifth state of the Union, **Jan. 9, 1788**.

Connecticut Compromise, Constitutional Convention of 1787 adopted proposal for bicameral U.S. Congress, **July 16, 1787**.

Constance, Council of, 16th ecumenical council of the Catholic Church, **1414-17**, that successfully healed Great Schism, **1378-1415**, but tried unsuccessfully to grant a council supreme Church authority.

Constantinople, named for Roman Emperor Constantine I as new capital of Roman Empire, **330**; capital of Byzantine Empire **395-1453**; capital of Ottoman Empire, **1453-1918**; officially renamed Istanbul, **1930**.

Constantinople, First Council of, 2nd ecumenical council of the Catholic Church, **381**, that united Church against Arianism and issued definitive Nicene Creed, ratifying Council of Nicaea, **325**.

Constantinople, Latin Empire of, feudal

empire formed in s. Balkan peninsula and Greek islands by Crusaders, **1204-61**.

Constantinople, Second and Third Councils of, 5th Catholic ecumenical council, **553**, that condemned Nestorianism; 6th Catholic ecumenical council, **680**, that settled Monothelite question, reaffirming Council of Chalcedon, **451**.

constant proportions, law of, discovered, **1799**, by French chemist Joseph L. Proust [1754-1826].

Constitution, (Old Ironsides), famous U.S. frigate launched, **1798**; defeated British warship *Guerriere* off Nova Scotia during War of 1812, **Aug.19, 1812**; defeated British frigate *Java* off Brazilian coast, **Dec. 29, 1812**; salvaged and rebuilt, **1833**; rebuilt again, **1877, 1925**.

Constitution, U.S., fundamental laws of U.S. drafted at Constitutional Convention, **Aug. 6,-Sept. 10, 1787**; submitted by Confederation Congress to states for ratification, **Sept. 28, 1787**; ratified by required number of states (nine), **June 21, 1788**; went into effect, superceding original U.S. charter, **Mar. 4, 1789**.

Constitutional Union Party, nominated John Bell [Feb. 1, 1797-Sept. 10, 1869] for U.S. president at national convention in Baltimore, **May 9, 1860**.

constructivism, movement in art, **1913-20**.

Consulate, government of France under three cousuls, after the Directoire, **Dec. 25, 1799-May 20, 1804**; Napoleon made consul for life, with right of appointing his successor, **Aug. 2, 1802**.

Consumer's League, National, organization formed in England, **1890**, to promote better conditions among workers; group founded in U.S. **1899**.

Consumers' Union, U.S. organization, established **1932**, at Mount Vernon, N.Y.

Continental Congress, legislative body of revolutionary American colonies and of U.S. under Articles of Confederation, **1774-89**; First Continental Congress at Philadelphia expressed colonial grievances against British policy and forbade importation of British goods, **Sept. 5-Oct. 26, 1774**; Second Continental Congress at Philadelphia created a Continental Army, with George Washington as commander-in-chief, **June 14-17, 1775**; Second Congress adopted Declaration of Independence, **July 4, 1776**; postwar Congress passed ordinance that set up Northwest Territory, **July 13, 1787**.

Continental Drift, theory originated, **1912**, by German geologist Alfred L. Wegener [1880-1930].

Continental money, paper money issued by Second Continental Congress, **June 1775**; depreciated in value until no further issues, after **1779**.

Continental System, scheme of economic warfare initiated by Napoleon I against Britain, **1806-12**; began with Berlin Decree, **Nov. 21, 1806**; intensified by Warsaw Decree, **1807**; further intensified by Milan Decree, **Dec. 17, 1807**; Britain retaliated with a blockade of Europe and a system of embargoes, after **1806**; Russia's refusal to conform to decrees resulted in Napoleon's disastrous Russian campaign of **1812**.

Contreras-Churubusco, battle of, U.S. forces routed large Mexican army, led by Gen. Santa Anna, at Contreras, and inflicted heavy losses on Mexican army at nearby Churubusco on same day, allowing Gen. Winfield Scott to advance on Mexico City, **Aug. 20, 1847**.

Conventicle Act, Cavalier Parliament forbade nonconformist (Puritan) religious meetings in England, **July 1664**.

Convention Parliament, 556 members of parliament elected without any restrictions in England, **Apr. 15-Dec. 29, 1660**; proclaimed Charles II king, **May 8, 1660**; summoned by advice of peers; offered English crown to William and Mary jointly, **Jan. 22, 1689-Jan. 27, 1690**.

conveyor belt, first used in production

assembly lines, **1913**, by automobile manufacturer Henry Ford [1861-1947].

Conway Bridge (suspension), constructed, **1826**, by English engineer Thomas Telford [1757-1834].

Conway Cabal, unsuccessful plot among American officers and congressmen to have Gen. Horatio Gates replace Gen. George Washington as commander-in-chief of Continental Army **1777-78**.

Coolidge tube, X-ray tube using tungsten filaments, developed, **1913**, by American physicist William D. Coolidge [1873-1975].

Copenhagen, Treaty of, Denmark surrendered to Sweden the southern part of Scandinavian peninsula but retained Trondheim and Bornholm, **June 6, 1660**.

Copernican system, advanced, **1543**, by Polish astonomer Nicolas Copernicus [1473-1543].

Coptic Church, Egyptian Christian Church claimed to have been founded, Alexandria, **c. 50-80**, by St. Mark.

copying lathe, invented, **1818**, by American inventor Thomas Blanchard [1788-1864]; involved principle of cutting irregular forms from patterns.

copyright, parliament passed first English copyright act, the basis of all future copyright laws, **1710**; Pres. Washington signed first U.S. copyright act to protect books, plays, and maps, **May 31, 1790**; U.S. Congress passed international copyright act to protect British, French, Belgian, and Swiss authors in U.S., **Mar. 4, 1891**; new U.S. copyright law took effect to protect authors, publishers, and composers under terms that

remained unchanged for the next 68 years, **July 1, 1909**; revised U.S. copyright law took effect, **Jan. 1, 1978**.

Coral Sea, battle of the, U.S. and Japanese aircraft carrier planes fought at long range, damaging and sinking each other's warships in s.w. Pacific; U.S. checked Japanese advance for the first time in WW II, **May 7-8, 1942**.

Corbett-Sullivan fight, big gloves used for first time in heavyweight boxing championship fight between James J. Corbett ("Gentleman Jim") [Sept. 1, 1866-Feb. 18, 1933] and John L. Sullivan [Oct, 15, 1858-Feb. 2, 1918]; Corbett won, **Sept. 7, 1892**.

cordite, smokeless powder used in propelling projectiles from guns, successfully developed, **1889**, by British chemists Sir Frederick August Abel [1827-1902] and Sir James Dewar [1842-1923].

Cordova (Cordoba), historic city in Spain, seat of wealthy, independent Omayyad emirate and later, Caliphate, **756-1031**; became subject to Seville, **1078**; conquered by Ferdinand III [1199-1252] of Castile, **1236**; sacked by French, **1808**.

Cordoba, Treaty of, Mexican revolutionary Agustin de Iturbide [Sept. 27, 1783-July 19, 1824] signed treaty with Spanish viceroy, establishing Mexico's independence, **Aug. 24, 1821**.

Corfu (Kerkira), island in Ionian Sea, Greece, where first recorded naval battle in history occurred, between Corfu and Corinth, **665 B.C.**; fought Corinth again in war over control of Epidamnus, **435-433 B.C.**; allied itself with Athens, **433 B.C.**; taken by Rome, **229 B.C.**; made part of Byzantine Empire, **336**; controlled by Venice, **1386-1797**; under British protection, **1815**, until ceded to Greece, **1864**.

Corfu incident, Italian officers murdered while trying to establish Greek-Albanian border, **Aug. 27, 1923**; Italy bombarded and occupied Corfu, **Aug. 31, 1923**; Greece's appeal to League of Nations brought Italy's withdrawal from Corfu, **Sept. 27, 1923**.

Corfu, Pact of, Serbian, Croatian, Slovenian, and Montenegrin delegates proposed single union under Serbian king, **July 20, 1917**.

Corinth (Korinthos), ancient Greek city-state in Peloponnesus; became important maritime power and colonizer under Periander [d. 585 B.C.] and his successors, **6th century B.C.**; rivaled Athens, **5th century B.C.**; conquered and destroyed by Romans, **146 B.C.**; restored by Julius Caesar, **46 B.C.**

Corinth, battles of, Union forces under Gen. Henry W. Halleck [Jan. 16, 1815-Jan. 9, 1872] seized Corinth, Miss., **May 30, 1862**; Confederates suffered heavy losses in unsuccessful attempt to seize Corinth from Unionists under Gen. William S. Rosecrans [Sept. 6, 1819-Mar. 11, 1898], **Oct. 4, 1862**.

Corinthian order, style of Greek architecture, **4th century B.C.**

Corinthians, Letters to, two letters (epistles), 7th and 8th books of the New Testament, written, **56-57**, by St. Paul the Apostle.

Corinthian War, conflict between Corinth, Athens, Thebes, and Argos on one side and Sparta on the other, **395-386 B.C.**

Coriolis force, determined, **c. 1840**, by French physicist Gaspard de Coriolis [1792-1843] to describe deviation of moving objects.

Cornerstone Speech, address in Savannah, Ga., delivered by Vice President of the Confederacy Alexander H. Stephens [1812-83] who declared the cornerstone of Confederacy to be the unequality of the Negro, **Mar. 21, 1861**.

Cornhill Magazine, The, periodical, founded **1860**.

Corn Laws, regulations restricting grain trade in England, especially the importation of grain, **c. 1361-1846**; Anti-Corn-Law League compelled British government to repeal corn laws, **June 6, 1846**.

Cornwallis' Code, Charles Cornwallis [Dec. 31, 1738-Oct. 5, 1805] introduced extensive judicial and administrative reforms as governor-general of India, **1793**.

coronagraph, invented, **1930**, by French astronomer Bernard F. Lyot [1897-1952].

Coronea, battles of, Boeotians defeated the Athenians, **447 B.C.**; Spartans defeated the allied Athenians, Corinthians, Thebans, and Argives, **394 B.C.**

Coronel, battle of, German fleet under Maximilian Johannes Maria Hubert, Graf von Spee [June 22, 1861-Dec. 8, 1914] defeated British fleet near Coronel, Chile, **Nov. 1, 1914**.

Corporation Act, Cavalier Parliament required all magistrates to take communion according to the Church of England and to abjure the Presbyterian covenant, **Nov. 20, 1661**.

Corregidor, battle of, historic fortified island of Corregidor at entrance to Manila Bay, in the Philippines, defended by 10,000 U.S.-Filipino troops under Gen. Jonathan M. Wainwright [Aug. 23, 1883-Sept. 2, 1953] until forced to surrender to Japanese in WW II, **May 6, 1942**; U.S. forces recaptured Corregidor, **Mar. 1945**.

Corsica, revolted successfully under leader Pasquale Paoli [1725-1807] against Genoese rule, **1755**; Genoa sold Corsica to France, **1768**; French defeated Paoli, **1769**; Paoli defeated French and united Corsica with British crown, **1794**; recovered by France, **1796**.

Corupedion, battle of, Syrians under Seleucus I [d. 280 B.C.] defeated Macedonians under Lysimachus [c. 355-281 B.C.] at Corupedion in ancient Lydia (w. Asia Minor), **281 B.C.**

cosmic rays, discovered, **1912**, by Austrian-American physicist Victor F. Hess [1883-1964], first photographed, **1932**, by English physicist Lord Patrick M. Blackett [1897-1974], using Wilson cloud chamber.

cosmic ray showers, detection of, coincidence method of detection devised, **1929**, by German physicist Walther Bothe [1891-1957].

cosmic state, first extraterrestrial radio

waves discovered, **1931**, by American electrical engineer Karl G. Jansky [1905-1950].

cosmology, geocentric, concept established, **c. 140**, by Greek astronomer Claudius Ptolemaeus (Ptolemy) [fl. 2nd century]; concept was dominant until **16th century**.

cosmology, heliocentric, developed, **c. 280 B.C.**, by Greek astronomer Aristarchus of Samos [310 B.C.-230 B.C].

Cossacks, famous peasant-cavalrymen of the Ukraine and other Russian regions, prominent in peasant revolts, **17th-18th centuries**; Don Cossacks made into special military caste, **1835**; fought against Bolsheviks in civil war, **1918-20**; Cossack communities collectivized, **1928-33**.

Costa Rica, Central American country; declared its independence as a republic, **1848**.

Cotton Bowl, major U.S. collegiate football game played each Jan. 1 at Dallas, Tex.; first Cotton Bowl game between Texas Christian and Marquette, **1937**.

cotton gin, patented, **1794**, by American inventor Eli Whitney [1765-1825].

cotton mill, first successful one in U.S. built, **1793**, by English-American technician Samuel Slater [1768-1835], in Pawtucket, Rhode Island.

cotton, mercerized, invented, **1850**, by British inventor John Mercer [1791-1866].

cotton picker, mechanical, devised, **c. 1927**, by American inventors John D. Rust [1892-1954] and Mack D. Rust [1900-1966].

Coulomb balance, devised, **c. 1784**, by French physicist Charles A. de Coulomb [1736-1806].

Coulomb's law, proposed, **1785**, by French physicist Charles Augustin de Coulomb [1736-1806].

counterpoint, contrasting musical part(s) added to one another to produce coherent texture; developed, Italy, **14th century**.

Counter-Reformation, Catholic revival following Protestant defections during the Reformation, **c. 1540-1650**; inspired especially by Council of Trent, **1545-63**.

Count of Monte Cristo, The (Le Comte de Monte Cristo), popular romance, **1844**, about comeback of falsely accused Edmond Dantes; by French adventure novelist Alexander Dumas *pere* (born Davy de la Pailleterie) [July 24, 1802-Dec. 5, 1870].

coupled tuned circuit (for radio reception and transmission), patented, **1902**, by American inventor John S. Stone [1869-1943].

Courier I, first active communications satellite launched, **1960**, by U.S. Army.

Court of Claims, U.S., Pres. Franklin Pierce enacted law setting up first Court of Claims for U.S. citizens, **Feb. 24, 1855**.

Courtrai (Kortrijk), Flemish burghers routed French mounted knights there in first *battle of the Spurs*, **July 11, 1302**.

Coutras, battle of, French Huguenots under Henri (later King Henry IV of France) defeated the Catholics, **Oct. 20, 1587**.

Covadonga, battle of, first victory of Spanish Christians over the Moslems, marking start of Christian reconquest of Spain, **718**.

covenant, an agreement, especially the agreement between God and Abraham and his descendents, **c. 2000 B.C.**; and at Sinai, **c. 1290 B.C.**-basis of Jewish religion.

covenanters, Scottish Presbyterians who bound themselves by oaths to resist royal efforts to restore Episcopalianism, **16th and 17th centuries**; King's Confession, **1581**, signed by most Scots; Presbyterianism finally accepted, **1689**.

Covent Garden, name of 3 successive theaters that have occupied the same site, Bow Street, London, since **1732**; second theater built, **1826**; burned, **1856**; present theater opened, **May 15, 1858**.

Covent Garden Market, London's monks of St. Peter's Abbey set up market on highway between London and Westminster, **1265**; began operations as London's produce and flower market, **1661**.

Cowpens, battle of, American revolutionary forces under Gen. Daniel Morgan [1736-July 6, 1802] won important victory at Cowpens, S.C., inflicting heavy losses on British, **Jan. 17, 1781.**

Coxey's Army, group of 500 unemployed men led by Jacob S. Coxey [Apr. 16, 1854-May 18, 1951] reached Washington, D.C., to demand public works programs for relief of unemployment, **Apr. 30, 1894;** Coxey arrested for trespassing at Capitol, **May 1, 1894,** and "army" disbanded.

Cracow (Krakow), University of, leading European center of learning founded by Casimir III ("the Great") [1310-70], **1364.**

crane, hydraulic, developed, **1845,** by English inventor William George Armstrong [1810-1900].

Crannon, battle of, Greek rebellion against Macedonian rule ended when Macedonian army under Antipater defeated rebel Greek forces; ended Lamian War, **322 B.C.**

Crater, battle of the, former Union coal miners tunneled 511 ft. under Confederate lines and planted huge powder bomb, which blew up, killing 278 Confederates and creating huge crater for Union forces to exploit, e. of Petersburg, Va., **July 30, 1864.**

Cravant (Crevant), battle of, English forces defeated the French at Cravant, France, **Aug. 1, 1423,** gaining renewed support for Henry VI [1421-71] of England as king of France.

Crecy, battle of, English longbows won victory for King Edward III over French crossbows of King Philip VI in France, during Hundred Years' War, **Aug. 26, 1346.**

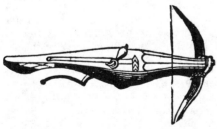

Credit-Anstalt, Austrian, major bank of Austria collapsed, **May 11, 1931,** marking the beginning of great economic depression and diplomatic crisis in central Europe.

Credit Mobilier of America scandal, federal investigation of Credit Mobilier of America, ended in censure of two congressmen for accepting bribes, **Sept. 1872-Feb. 18, 1873.**

Creed of the People of God, Catholic profession of faith, **June 29, 1968,** issued by Pope Paul VI, as authoritative modern statement of faith.

creed (credo), in Christianity, Apostle's Creed, from earliest times, text, **c. 390;** Nicene Creed, **325,** with additions, **381;** Athanasian Creed, **5th century.**

Creek War, conflict between Creek Indians and white settlers in Georgia, Alabama, and Florida, **1813-14;** more than 500 whites massacred at Fort Mims, **Aug. 30, 1813;** Creeks defeated at Horseshoe Bend, **Mar. 27, 1814.**

CREEP or CRP (Committee to Re-elect the President), Republican committee led by John N. Mitchell [Sept. 5, 1913-], Jeb. S. Magruder [Nov. 5, 1934-], Maurice H. Stans [Mar. 22, 1908-], E. Howard Hunt, Jr. [Oct. 9, 1918-], G. Gordon Liddy [Nov. 30, 1930-], and others established offices in Washington, D.C., **Mar. 1971,** to work for the reelection of Pres. Nixon.

Creole affair, Negro slaves aboard *Creole* seized ship to land at Nassau where British gave them sanctuary, **Oct. 27, 1841.**

Crepy (Crespy), Treaty of, ended two-year war in Netherlands between Holy Roman Emperor Charles V and Francis I of France, **Sept. 18, 1544.**

Crete, conquered by Romans, **68-67 B.C.;** conquered by Venice, **1204;** conquered by Turks, **1669;** fought over by Greece and Turkey, **1896-97;** joined Greece, **1913.**

Crime against Kansas speech, famous antislavery speech delivered by U.S. Sen. Charles Sumner [Jan. 6, 1811-Mar. 11, 1874] of Massachusetts in U.S. Senate, **May 19-20, 1856.**

Crime and Punishment (Prestupleniye i Nakazaniye), psychological novel, **1866,** by Russian novelist Fyodor Dostoyevsky; film, **1935.**

Crime of '73, coinage act passed by U.S. Congress, **Feb. 12, 1873.**

Crimean War, armed conflict between Russia and allied powers of Ottoman Empire, Britain, France, and Sardinia, **1853-56;** Russia occupied Turkish states of Moldavia and Walachia, precipitating declaration of war by Turks, **Oct. 23, 1853**; British defeated Russians at Balaclava, **Oct. 25, 1854**; Russians abandoned Sevastopol, **Sept. 11, 1855**; war ended by Congress of Paris, **Mar. 30, 1856**.

Crimisus River, battle of the, Greek force under Timoleon [d. after 337 B.C.] of Corinth defeated Carthaginian army in Sicily, **341 B.C.**, protecting Syracuse against tyrants.

Crittenden Compromise, Sen. John J. Crittenden [Sept. 10, 1787-July 26, 1863] proposed proslavery resolution to keep South in the Union, **Dec. 18, 1860**; rejected by Senate committee and Pres.-elect Lincoln, **Dec. 31, 1860**.

Croatia, historic region closely linked to kings of Hungary except when occupied by Turks, **1526-1699**; occupied by French **1809-13**; annexed by Austria, **1849-68**; joined to Serbia, **1918**; autonomy secured by Croatian nationalists, **1939**; became a major republic of Yugoslavia, **1946**.

Croix de Guerre, famous military decoration for bravery; instituted in France and Belgium, **1915**.

Cro-Magnon man, discovered, **1868**, by French archaeologist Edouard H. Lartet [1801-1871], in cave in France; skeletons of the cro-magnon date from **38,000 B.C.**

Crookes radiometer, invented, **1875**, by English physicist Sir William Crookes [1832-1919].

Crookes tube, vacuum tube invented, **1876**, by English physicist Sir William Crookes [1832-1919].

Cropredy Bridge, battle of, royalists of King Charles I defeated the parliamentarians led by Sir William Waller [1597?-Sept. 19, 1668] in s. England, **June 29, 1644**.

Cross Keys, battle of, inconclusive battle between Union and Confederate armies at Cross Keys, Va. during U.S. Civil War., **June 8, 1862**.

Cross of Gold **speech**, famous speech made by William Jennings Bryan, **July 10, 1896**, united free-silver Democrats, who nominated him for U.S. presidency, **July 11, 1896**.

Crown Point, (New York), historic site where French built strategic Fort St. Frederic to guard route from New York to Canada, **1731**; fort successfully resisted British

attacks, **1755-56**; fort blown up by French to prevent British takeover, **July 31, 1759**; British built Fort Amherst on site (renamed Fort Crown Point), **1759**; Green Mountain Boys captured fort at start of American Revolution, **May 12, 1775**; British General John Burgoyne [1722-Aug. 4, 1792] captured fort, **June 22, 1777**.

Crucifixion, execution of Jesus Christ under authority of Pontius Pilate, Roman Governor of Judaea, **26-36**, calculated to have occurred on **Friday, April 7, 30**.

Crusades, wars undertaken by European Christians to recover the Holy Land from the Muslims, **11th-13th centuries**; First Crusade, **1095-99**; Second, **1147-49**; Third, **1189-92**; Fourth, **1202-1204**; Children's Crusade, **1212**; Fifth, **1217-21**; Sixth, **1228-29**; Seventh, **1248-54**; Eighth, **1270**; Ninth, **1271-72**.

crystalloid, introduced, **1861**, by Scottish chemist Thomas Graham [1806-1869].

Crystal Palace, London exhibition hall constructed, **1851**; designed by English architect Sir Joseph Paxton [1801-1865].

Crystal Palace Exhibition, Great, international exhibition, first of its kind, held in Crystal Palace in Hyde Park, London, and sponsored by Prince Albert of Saxe-Coburg-Gotha [Aug. 26, 1819-Dec. 14, 1861], **May 1,-Oct. 15, 1851**.

crystals, atomic structure, analyzed, **1912**, by English physicists William H. Bragg [1862-1942] and his son William L. Bragg [1890-].

Ctesiphon, battle of, Roman army stormed ancient city of Ctesiphon, capital of Parthia, and captured thousands of Parthian soldiers and citizens, **197**; Parthian king made peace with Rome, which took over Ctesiphon, **198**.

Cuban missile crisis, U.S.-U.S.S.R. confrontation over installation of Soviet missile and bomber bases in Cuba, **Oct. 22-28, 1962**; Pres. Kennedy announced U.S. air and naval "quarantine" on arms shipments to Cuba, **Oct. 22**; Premier Khrushchev agreed to halt Soviet construction of bases and to remove missiles under U.N. supervision, **Oct. 28**.

Cuban refugees boat lift, Cuban government-aided boatlift of refugees, **Apr. 21-Sept. 26, 1980**, brought about 125,000 Cubans to U.S.

Cubism, movement in painting, began **c. 1907**, that reconstructed objects in geometric forms, breaking with traditional representational painting.

Cucuta, Congress of, South Americans drafted constitution for Greater Colombia, **Aug. 30, 1821**.

Culloden Moor, battle of, Jacobite rebellion, **1745**, ended when English forces under duke of Cumberland defeated Scottish Highlanders under Prince Charles Edward, who barely escaped with his life at Culloden Moor, Scotland, **Apr. 16, 1746**.

Culpepper's Rebellion, revolutionary government organized by John Culpepper [fl. 1678-80] in Carolina to protest arbitrary rule of English governor, **Dec. 3, 1677**.

cultivator, invented, **1820**, by American ironmaster Henry Burden [1791-1871].

Cultural Revolution, Chinese, program of Mao Tse-Tung against Communist Chinese leaders who had supported capitalistic ideals, **1966-69**.

Cumae, ancient city, earliest Greek colony in Italy, **c. 750 B.C.**; Syracusan fleet won important naval victory over Etruscan fleet off Cumae, **474 B.C.**

Cumberland Road (National Road), great highway of Western migration, first built from Cumberland, Md., to Wheeling, W. Va., **1811-18**; built westward through Ohio,

1825-33; reached Vandalia, Ill., **1840**.

Cunaxa, battle of, Greek mercenary army and Persian rebels suffered crushing defeat by superior Persian army led by Artaxerxes II at Cunaxa in Babylonia, **401 B.C.**

cuneiform, ancient Sumerian and Mesopotamian script writing, originated as picture-writing, **c. 3000 B.C.**; wedge-shaped "letters" by **2500 B.C.**; used only for astrological purposes, after **300 B.C.**; latest datable example, **75**.

Curacao, British cruiser *Curacao* sank after collision with liner *Queen Mary* off coast of England; 335 persons aboard cruiser died, **Oct. 2, 1942**.

curium, element No. 96; discovered, **1944**, by American chemist Glenn T. Seaborg [1912-] and associates at the Metallurgical Laboratory at the University of Chicago.

curling, sport of curling governed by rules first established at Royal Caledonia Curling Club, Scotland, **1838**.

Curzola, battle of, Genoa won naval victory over Venice, **1299**, gaining trading rights from Venetians and the Turks in Asia Minor.

Curzon Line, Poland's eastern border with Lithuania established by Allies, **Dec. 8, 1919**, depriving Poland of city of Vilna.

Custer's Last Stand, about 3500 Sioux and Cheyenne warriors under chiefs Sitting Bull [c. 1831-Dec. 15, 1890] and Crazy Horse [c. 1840-Sept. 15, 1877] massacred cavalry troops under Gen. George A. Custer [Dec. 5, 1839-June 25, 1876] at battle of Little Bighorn in s. Montana; U.S. army's worst defeat during long bloody Indian wars, **June 25, 1876.**

Custoza, battles of, Piedmontese (Sardinian) forces suffered disastrous defeat by Austrian army at Custoza, s.w. of Verona, Italy, **July 24, 1848**; battle resulted in armistice during Italian wars of independence, **Aug. 9, 1848**; Italian troops again lost battle against Austrians at Custoza, **June 24, 1866**; Austria, however, ceded Venice to Italy, **July 3, 1866.**

cyanamide process, (nitrogen fixation), invented, **1905**, by German chemists Adolph Frank [1834-1916] and Nikodem Caro [1871-1935].

cybernetics, explanation of, published, **1948**, by American mathematician Norbert Wiener [1894-1964].

cyclopropane, introduced as an anesthetic, **1929**, by Canadian pharmacologist George H. W. Lucas [1894-].

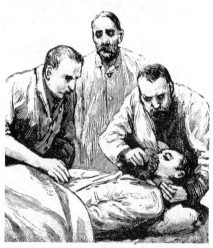

cyclotron (atom smasher), invented, **1930**, by American physicist Ernest Orlando Lawrence [1901-1958].

cynics, school of ancient philosophy, from **4th century B.C..**

Cynossema, battle of, Athenian fleet won decisive victory over the Lacedaemonian fleet, **411 B.C.**

Cynoscephalae, battles of, Theban cavalry and infantry attacks drove off Macedonians in Thessaly; great Theban general Pelopidas killed at the hour of victory, **364 B.C.**; Roman legions won major battle against Macedonians under Philip V [238-179 B.C.] of Macedon at Cynoscephalae, forcing Macedonians to withdraw entirely from Greece, **197 B.C.**

Cyprus, large island in Mediterranean, fell to the Turks, **1571**; came under British rule, **1878**; declared a British crown colony, **1925**; became independent nation, **Aug. 16, 1960.**

Cyrano de Bergerac, romantic, poetic cape-and-sword drama, **1897**, by French playwright Edmond Rostand.

Cyrene, ancient city in north Africa ruled by the Ptolemies, **c. 220-96 B.C.**; Jewish revolts against Roman rule severely punished by Emperor Trajan [Sept. 15?, 53-Aug, 8, 117], **115.**

Cyrillic Alphabet, alphabet used by Russians and some other Slavs; invention, **863.**

cystine, amino acid, discovered, **1810**, by English physician William Hyde Wollaston [1766-1828].

Cyzicus, ancient city in Turkey founded by Athenians, **756 B.C.**; rivaled Byzantium in commercial importance, **c. 3rd century B.C.-c. A.D. 4th century**; Athenian fleet sent by Alcibiades [c. 450-404 B.C.] defeated Spartan fleet off Cyzicus, maintaining Athenian supremacy at sea, **410 B.C.**; Roman army helped city withstand siege by Pontic army during third Mithridatic War, **74 B.C.**; plundered by Arabs on their approach to taking Constantinople, **675.**

Czechoslovakia, socialist republic established by Czech and Slovak patriots, **Oct. 28, 1918**; occupied by German Nazis, **Mar. 1939**; democratic reforms during Prague Spring, **1968**, brought Soviet invasion, **Aug. 20-21, 1968**; Alexander Dubcek [1921-], leader of the liberalization movement, was removed as Czech Communist Party leader, **Apr. 17, 1969.**

Dabney's Mills, battle of, Confederates repulsed Union troops at Dabney's Mills, Va., forcing their retreat to Hatcher's Run, **Feb. 6-7, 1865.**

Dachau, notorious Nazi concentration camp in Bavaria, West Germany, where thousands of Jews and others were imprisoned without trial, **1933-45.**

Dacron, invented, **1941**, by English inventors J. R. Whinfield [1901-1966] and J.T. Dickson; marketed in U.S., **1950**.

Dadaism, movement in the arts, **1916-22**, representing violent revolt against convention amid disillusionment following World War I.

daguerreotype, invented, **1839**, by French painter Louis J. M. Daguerre [1787-1851].

Dahomey War, French deposed king of Dahomey (Benin) and established protectorate; start of French expansion into Africa's interior, **1892-93**.

Daily Courant, The, first English daily newspaper, started, **March, 1702**; lasted until **1735**.

Daily News, The, English daily newspaper founded by English writer Charles Dickens, **1846**; became the News Chronicle, **1930**.

Daily Telegraph, The, first newspaper selling for a penny, founded, London, **1855**.

d'Alembert's Principle, published, **1743**, by French mathematician Jean le Rond d'Alembert [1717-1783], in his *Treatise on Dynamics*.

Dallas, television series, from **1978**; included most watched show in television history, **November 21, 1980**, to learn who shot detestable J.R. Ewing, played by U.S. actor Larry Hagman [1931-].

Damascus, reputedly oldest continuously inhabited city in the world, since before **2nd mil. B.C.**; made part of Assyrian empire, **732 B.C.**; conquered by Alexander the Great, **332 B.C.**; became Roman city under Pompey, **64 B.C.**; became Muslim city, **635**; seat of caliphate of the Omayyads, **661-750**; sacked by Mongols, **1260**, and by Tamerlane, **14th century**; ruled by Ottoman Turks, **1516-1918**; capital of a French Levant State under League of Nations mandate, **1920-41**; made Syrian capital.

Damascus Mosque, oldest surviving congregational mosque still in use, begun **707**, Damascus, Syria; includes converted Hellenistic buildings with minarets added.

dance, rhythmic bodily steps and movements, performed to music; Egyptian religious dances, **c. 5000 B.C.**; Chinese gymnastic dance, **2698 B.C.**; first formal European ballet, **1581**, Paris.

Dandridge, battle of, Confederates under Gen. James Longstreet forced Union troops to retreat at Dandridge, Tenn., **Jan. 17, 1864**.

Danegeld, money first paid by monks of Saint Denis in France, **845**; land tax first levied in England to buy off raiding Danes, **868**; collected by English ruler, until **12 century**.

Rose-window in North Transept of Abbey Church of Saint Denis, France.

Daniel, Book of, Old Testament book, written down, **c. 165 B.C.**, recounting life and prophecies of Jewish prophet and leader of

Babylonian Captivity, Daniel [c. 600-520 B.C.].

Danish invasions of Britain, Danish Norsemen invaded and maintained large army on island of Britain, **837-1016**; Danes made peace with Wessex King Edmund II (Ironside) [d. 1016] and Danish state set up in Britain under Canute [c. 995-1035], **1016-42**.

Danzig (Gdansk), important Baltic trading port of Hanseatic League, **13th century**; conquered by Teutonic Knights, **1308**; made autonomous Polish state, **1466**; ceded to Prussia in second partition of Poland, **1793**; free city, **1807-14**; restored to Prussia, **1814**; became free city again, **1919**; annexed by Nazi Germany, **Sept. 1, 1939**; taken by Russians, **Mar. 30, 1945**, and restored to Poland; site of riots by workers, **1970**, and strikes against Soviet domination, **1980**.

Darbytown Road, battles of, Union troops defeated Confederates at Darbytown Road, Va., during U.S. Civil War, **July 28, 1864**; Confederates won victory there, **Oct. 7, 1864**; Union troops won victory, **Oct. 13, 1864**.

Dark Ages, The, historical period from decay of classical culture, **c. 550**, to the beginning of medieval culture, **c. 1000**.

Dartmouth college, old American institution for higher learning founded by Congregationalists at Hanover, N.H., **1769**.

Dartmouth College case (*Dartmouth College v. Woodward*), U.S. Supreme court upheld the inviolability of private corporate charters under the Constitution.

Dartmoor Massacre, American sailors held prisoner during War of 1812 in Dartmoor Prison, Devonshire, England, massacred during attempted escape, **Apr. 6, 1815**.

Dartmoor Prison, famous prison built in Dartmoor, England, **1806-1809**; held French captives during later Napoleonic Wars and American captives in War of 1812, **1812-1815**, became civilian prison, **1850**.

Darwinism, philosophical theories, flourished, **1860-1930**, developed out of Charles Darwin's theory of organic evolution through natural selection of traits, as first described in Darwin's *Origin of Species*,

1859.

Daughters of Charity of St. Vincent de Paul, Catholic religious teaching order, founded, France, **1633**, by St. Louise de Marillac [Aug. 15, 1591-Mar. 15, 1660]; established, Maryland, **1809**, by St. Elizabeth Ann Seton [Aug. 28, 1774-Jan. 4, 1821], first U.S.-born saint, canonized, **1975**.

Dave Garroway Show, The, popular U.S. television variety show, appearing, **1949-71**, under various names, such as *Garroway at Large*, **1949-51**, *Wide, Wide World*, **1955-58**, featuring genial host, television personality Dave Garroway [July 13, 1913-], who was host of NBC *Today Show*, **1952-61**.

David Copperfield, novel, **1850**, about orphan boy who overcomes poverty and other obstacles to live happily ever after, by English author Charles Dickens; classic film, **1934**, based on Dickens' novel; featured as David, English actor Freddie Bartholomew (born Frederick Llewellyn) [Mar. 28, 1924-]; and, as Mr. Micawber, U.S. actor-comedian W. C. Fields (born William Claude Dukenfeld) [Jan. 29, 1880-Dec. 25, 1946].

David, bronze statue, **1433**, illustrating perfected technique of rendering human body in motion, by early Italian Renaissance sculptor Donatello (Donato de Niccolo di Betto Bardi) [1386-Dec. 13, 1466]; sculptor's marble *David*, **1408**; marble statue, **1501-4**, of biblical king carved larger than life from 14-foot block, by Italian Renaissance artist Michelangelo Buonarroti.

Davis Cup tournament, international team competition in men's tennis initiated by Dwight F. Davis [1879-1945], **1900**.

Dawson mine disaster, great explosion in coal mine at Dawson, N. Mex., killed 263 miners, **Oct. 22, 1913**.

Days of Our Lives, long-running television series, premiered, **November 8, 1965**.

Dawes Plan, comprehensive plan to reorganize Germany's finances prepared by international committee headed by Charles G. Dawes [Aug. 27, 1865-Apr. 23, 1951], went into effect, **Sept. 1, 1924**, with German reparation payments to Allies.

Dawes Severalty Act, U.S. Congress divided Indian territories among Indian families, with 160 acres per family, with land to be held in trust by U.S. government, **Feb. 8, 1887**.

daylight saving time, setting clocks one or more hours ahead of standard time to obtain more daylight at end of day established in U.S., **Mar. 31, 1918**; repealed **1919**; reestablished on year-round basis during WW II.

Dayton flood, great, heavy rainstorms devastated Miami Valley, Ohio, killing more than 400 persons, leaving about $100 million in property damage, **Mar. 21-26, 1913**.

DC-3, first airplane to make commercial air travel practical; developed, **1935**, by team of American aircraft engineers under direction of Donald W. Douglas, Sr. [1892-Feb. 1, 1981].

DDT insecticide, discovered, **1939**, by Swiss chemist Paul Mueller [1899-1965].

Dead End, film, **1937**, about slums as breeding places for crime; launched the popular "Dead End Kids" series.

Dead Sea Scrolls, documents dating from c. **100 B.C. to A.D. 100** and containing Hebrew and Aramaic biblical and liturgical writings, found in caves near Dead Sea, **1947-56**.

Dead Souls, realistic novel, **1842**, about swindler trading in dead serfs not yet reported to census, by Russian author Nikolai Vasilyevich Gogol [March 31, 1809-Feb. 21, 1852]; classic illustrations, 46 etchings, by Marc Chagall, **1949**.

Dearborn, Fort, on site of present-day Chicago; Americans abandoned fort during War of 1812 but were massacred by Potawatomi Indians (allied with British) on s. shore of Lake Michigan; Fort Dearborn was burned to the ground, **Aug. 1812**.

Death in Venice (Der Tod in Venedig), novella, **1913**, exploring the potentiality of decadence in the artistic life, by German author Thomas Mann, Nobel Prize-winner, **1929**; opera **1970**, by English composer Benjamin Britten.

Death of a President, The, definitive account, **1967**, by U.S. writer William Manchester [Apr. 1, 1922-], of assassination of U.S. President John F. Kennedy [May 29, 1917-Nov. 22, 1963]; first encouraged, then opposed, by Kennedy's widow.

Death of Marat, dramatic painting, **1793**, of Jean-Paul Marat [May 24, 1743-July 13, 1793], French revolutionary leader assassinated in bath, by neo-classical painter Jacques-Louis David.

Death of the Hired Man, The, poem, **1914**, in which farmer and wife debate taking in dying hired man who has returned to them, by U.S. poet Robert Frost [Mar. 26, 1874-Jan. 29, 1963].

Death of a Salesman, play, **1949**, intended as a modern tragedy of the common man, by U.S. playwright Arthur Miller.

decadents, school of poets and writers, c. **1880-1910**, that flaunted a fevered decadence and despair, included writers such as J. K. Huysmans and Oscar Wilde.

Decameron, The (Il Decamerone), 100 tales, **1351-53**, in classic Italian pre-Renaissance vernacular prose collection; by Giovanni Boccaccio [1313-Dec. 21, 1375].

Decembrist conspiracy, plot by Russian Decembrists, members of secret revolutionary societies, against Czar Nicholas I, crushed by artillery fire; police terrorism and revolutionary activity spread, **Dec. 26, 1825**.

decimal point, invented, **c. 1600**, by Scottish mathematician John Napier [1550-1617] in connection with his development of Napierian logarithms, which required long decimal fractions.

Declaration of Independence, historic document, drafted by Thomas Jefferson [Apr. 13, 1743-July 4, 1826], adopted without dissent by Second Continental Congress, declaring separation of Thirteen American Colonies from Britain and formation of the U.S., **July 4, 1776**.

Declaration of Rights, parliament defined its relationship with English monarchy as it offered the crown to William and Mary, **Feb. 13, 1689**.

Declaration of the Rights of Man and Citizen, historic French document, drafted by Emmanuel Sieyes [May 3, 1748-June 20, 1836] as preamble to French constitution, asserting equality of men and sovereignty of the people, **Aug. 26, 1789**.

Decline and Fall of the Roman Empire, The, history, **1776-88**, covering Roman Empire from Trajan [Sept. 15, 53-Aug. 8, 117] to fall of Constantinople, **1453**; a controversial treatment of Christianity, by British historian Edward Gibbon [Apr. 27, 1737-Jan. 16, 1794].

Decretum of Gratian, collection of ecclesiastical canons, or laws, **1140**; basis of medieval Catholic canon law; supplemented by papal decretals in years subsequent to **1234**.

Deep Throat, person whose identity was kept secret but who supplied Carl Bernstein [Feb. 14, 1944-] and Robert U. Woodward [Mar. 26, 1943-] with information that led to the Watergate Scandal, **1973**.

Deerslayer, The, novel, **1841**, one of *Leatherstocking Tales*, in which uncorrupted "natural man," frontiersman Natty Bumppo, is depicted, by U.S. novelist James Fenimore Cooper [Sept. 15, 1789-Sept. 14, 1851].

Defenestration of Prague, The, incident, **May 23, 1618**, in which Catholic imperial councillors were thrown by Protestants from window of Hradschin Palace, Prague, precipitating Thirty Years' War, **1618-48**.

Defense Day, nationwide celebration by more than 16 million Americans in more than 6500 locations in U.S., **Sept. 12, 1924**.

Defense, U.S. Department of, U.S. federal department created by National Security Act, **July 26, 1947**, unifying all armed services as National Military Establishment; adopted present name, **1949**.

Defense Plant Corporation, former U.S. federal corporation created **Aug. 1940**, to build plants to produce materials for WW II; dissolved **June 30, 1945**.

Defense Production Act, U.S. Congress gave President Truman, **Sept. 8, 1950**, authority to stabilize prices and wages.

Defense Transportation, Office of, former U.S. federal agency created by order of Pres. F. D. Roosevelt, **Dec. 18, 1941**, to coordinate and utilize effectively transportation in U.S. during WW II; dissolved **1949**.

Delaware, one of Thirteen Colonies, ratified U.S. Constitution to become first state of the Union, **Dec. 7, 1787**.

Delaware, crossing of the, American revolutionary troops led by Gen. George Washington crossed the icy Delaware River on Christmas night, **Dec. 25, 1776**, to make famous early morning raid on Hessians at Trenton, N.J.

Delaware Indians, Indian tribal group made famous treaty with William Penn, **Nov. 1682**; driven by Iroquois into Ohio, **1720**; defeated by Gen. Anthony Wayne, **Aug. 20, 1794.**

Delfthaven, small village in Holland from which Pilgrims left on board *Speedwell* for Southampton, England, **July 22, 1620.**

Delhi Pact, Gandhi discontinued civil disobedience, agreed to London Round Table Conference in return for British promise to release political prisoners not guilty of violence, **Mar. 4, 1931**; London Round Table Conference failed to accept Gandhi's program, **Sept. 7-Dec. 1, 1931**; India and Pakistan agreed to better treatment of their minorities, **Apr. 8, 1950.**

Delian League, confederation of Greek city-states led by Athens; first league opposed Persian kings, **478-404 B.C.**; second league, **378-338 B.C.**

Delium, ancient Greek town where Boeotians defeated the Athenians (including Socrates) in Peloponnesian War, **424 B.C.**

Delphi, Oracle of, ancient Greek sacred site near Mount Parnassus, from **1600 B.C.**; Temple of Apollo housing Oracle, built, **478 B.C.**; closed down by Christian Emperor Theodosius I, **390.**

Democracy in America, first outside, impartial and systematic study of American institutions, **1835**, considered a penetrating classic, by French historian Count Alexis de Tocqueville [July 29, 1805-Apr. 16, 1859].

Democratic Party, U.S. political party first known as Democratic Republican (or Republican) formed to oppose Federalist, **May 13, 1792**; took present name, **1828.**

Democratic Silver Convention, 1000 Democratic delegates at convention in Omaha, Neb., led by William Jennings Bryan [Mar. 19, 1860-July 26, 1925], adopted coinage plank of 16 to 1 silver-gold ratio, **June 21, 1894.**

Demoiselles d'Avignon, Les (Girls of Avignon), Cubist painting, **1906-07**, by seminal Spanish artist Pablo Picasso.

demotic writing, modified Egyptian hieroglyphic script, developed **5th century B.C.**; made writing possible for greater number of purposes; used, up to **452.**

Dempsey-Willard fight, Jack Dempsey [June 24, 1895-] knocked out Jess Willard in third round at Toledo, Ohio, to become heavyweight boxing champion, **July 4, 1919.**

Denain, battle of, French forces routed Austrians, who lost 8000 men (French lost only 500) at Denain in n. France; last important battle of the War of the Spanish Succession, **July 24, 1712.**

Denmark, Scandinavian country; became a constitutional monarchy, **1849**; occupied by German troops, **1940-45.**

Dennewitz, battle of, Prussians under Friedrich Wilhelm von Bulow [Feb. 16, 1755-Feb. 25, 1816] (Bulow von Dennewitz) won important victory over French under Michel Ney [Jan. 10, 1769-Dec. 7, 1815] at Dennewitz, near Berlin, **Sept. 6, 1813.**

dental plate, invented, **1817**, by American inventor Anthony A. Planston [1774-1837].

dental plate, rubber, invented, **1855**, by American inventor Charles Goodyear [1845-1921].

denture, patented, **1851**, by American dentist John Allen [1810-1892].

dephosphorizing of steel, process, patented **1877** by English chemists Percy C. Gilchrist [1851-1935] and Sidney G. Thomas [1850-1885].

Deportation Act, U.S. Congress authorized, **May 10, 1920**, deportation of aliens found guilty of sedition or of violation of any national security acts.

Depression, the, period of economic crisis, with bankruptcies, low production, and high unemployment, especially acute in U.S., **1930s.**

Derby, The, annual English horse race for

three-year-old colts and fillies at Epsom Downs, Surrey, England; instituted by 12th earl of Derby, **1779**.

dermatology, study of skin diseases, advanced, **1806**, by French physician Jean Louis Alibert [1768-1837].

De Re Diplomatica, treatise, **1681** by French Benedictine monk Jean Mabillon [Nov. 23, 1632-Dec. 27, 1707], laying down principles for studying historical documents; enhanced critical study of history.

desalination process (for sea water), development announced, **1952**, by American Research and Development Corp.

Descent of Man, The, treatise, **1871** by English naturalist Charles (Robert) Darwin [Feb. 12, 1809-Apr. 19, 1882].

Detroit, Michigan, French established fort and fur-trading post there called Ville d'etroit, **July 24, 1701**; captured by British, **1760**; U.S. control established, **1796**; territorial and state capital, **1805-47**; devastating race riots caused about $150 million in property damage, **July 23-30 1967**.

Dettingen, battle of, combined force of English, Hanoverians, and Hessians led by King George II [Nov. 10, 1683-Oct. 25, 1760] of England routed 28,000 French at Dettingen in n.w. Bavaria; last time a British king fought on battlefield, **June 27, 1743**.

deuterium, an isotope of hydrogen, discovered **1932** by American chemist Harold C. Urey [1893-Jan. 5, 1981].

Deuteronomy, fifth book of Old Testament, probably written down, **c. 698-643 B.C.**; reiterates Mosaic law and recounts death of Moses.

deuteron ray (in medicine), 190-million-volt ray tested, **1952**, as cancer weapon at University of California.

Devil's Dictionary, The, dictionary, **1906**, by U.S. writer and journalist Ambrose Bierce [July 24, 1842-c. 1914].

Devolution, War of, France invaded and overran Spanish Netherlands and Franche-Comte, but made peace with Spain when Netherlands formed Triple Alliance with England and Sweden, **1667-68**.

Devotia Moderna (modern devotion), spiritual movement, from **1380**, begun by Brethren of the Common Life; influenced both Reformation and Counter Reformation.

diabetes, honey-sweet taste of urine of dia-

betics noted, **c. 1665**, by English physician Thomas Willis [1621-1675].

Diadochi, Macedonian generals who succeeded Alexander the Great and fought each other for control of his empire, **323-281 B.C.**; Antipater [d. 319 B.C.] defeated Perdiccas [d. 321 B.C.] for the regency, **321 B.C.**; Antigonus I [382?-301 B.C.] and his son Demetrius I [337?-283 B.C.] were defeated at Ipsus, **301 B.C.**; Seleucus I [d. 280 B.C.] defeated Lysimachus [355?-281 B.C.] at Corupedion, **281 B.C.**

dialectical materialism, philosophical system that attempts to justify theory that history unfolds through class conflict in relation to means of production; presented in *Das Kapital*, **1867-95**, by Karl Marx.

Dialogues of the Carmelites (Dialogues des Carmelites), play, **1949**, by French writer Georges Bernanos [Feb. 20, 1888-July 4, 1948]; inspired opera, **1957**, by French composer Francis Poulenc [Jan. 7, 1899-Jan. 30, 1963].

dial telephone service, first transcontinental service begun, **1951**, in experiment at Englewood, New Jersey.

Dial, The, magazine published, New England, **1840-44**; organ of Transcendentalism; editor, **1840-42**, (Sarah) Margaret Fuller [May 10, 1810-July 19, 1850], early feminist and first U.S. newspaperwoman; editor, **1842-44**, philosopher, essayist, and poet Ralph Waldo Emerson; literary review,

1880-1929, founded Chicago; moved to New York, **1918**, and became radical journal of opinion; especially after **1920** published many important modern writers; editor, **1926-29**, U.S. poet Marianne Moore [Nov. 15, 1887-Feb. 5, 1972].

Diary of Anne Frank, The, diary of Jewish girl in family hiding from Nazis, **1942-44**, by Anne Frank [June 12, 1929-Mar., 1945]; published posthumously, the Netherlands, **1947**; in English, **1952**; play, based on book, **1955**.

Diary of Samuel Pepys, The, diary by English diarist and public figure of his day, Samuel Pepys [Feb. 23, 1633-May 26, 1703], deciphered and published, **1825**, contains vivid descriptions of English Restoration life, **1660-70**.

Diaspora, dispersion of Jewish people to other lands, begun **722 B.C.**, with Assyrian deportation of Jews from Palestine; continued, **597 B.C.**, with Babylonian deportation

diastase, first enzyme isolated, **1833**; achieved by French chemist Anselme Payen [1795-1871].

Dictionary of the English Language, monumental work, **1755**, standard English dictionary for more than a century, by English writer and literary figure Dr. Samuel Johnson [Sept. 18, 1709-Dec. 13, 1784].

Diels-Alder reaction, discovered, **1928**, by German organic chemists Otto Diels [1876-1954] and Kurt Alder [1902-1958].

Dienbienphu, battle of, last major battle between French and Vietminh forces of Ho Chi Minh [May 19, 1890-Sept. 3, 1969], **Mar. 13,-May 7, 1954**; about 50,000 Vietminh forces assaulted French military base of Dienbienphu, **Mar. 13, 1954**; French surrendered after 56-day siege; French domination of Vietnam ended, **May 7, 1954**.

diene synthesis, discovered, **1928**, by German chemists Kurt Alder, [1902-1958], and Otto Diels, [1876-1954].

Dieppe, French city on English Channel suffered severely from Anglo-Dutch naval bombardment, **1694**; allied amphibious commando raid against German-held Dieppe proved costly (Canadian forces alone suffered 900 killed, about 2000 captured) but provided valuable information later used by Allies in WW II, **Aug. 19, 1942**.

diesel electric locomotive, invented, **1924**, by American inventor Hermann Lemp.

Dies Irae (Day of Wrath), famous medieval hymn, **c. 1200**, vividly recounting "wrath" of Judgment Day.

diet, balanced, proposed as being essential to health, **c. 1920**, in research by English biochemist Frederich G. Hopkins [1861-1947] and Dutch physician Christiaan Eijkman [1858-1930].

Dieu et mon droit (God and my right), motto of sovereigns of England since **c. 1450**; said to have been password of King Richard I ("the Lion-hearted") at Battle of Gisors, **1198**.

differential analyzer, developed, **1928**, by American scientist Vannevar Bush [1890-1974]; forerunner of computer.

differential gear, invented, for farm machinery, **1870**, by Bavarian-American inventor Rudolf Eickemeyer [1831-1895].

digestion, gastric, demonstrated, **1803**, to be due to acidity of gastric juice by American physiologist John R. Young [1782-1804].

digestive process, described, **1833**, by American surgeon William Beaumont [1785-1853]; famous study made on patient with gun shot wound that left stomach exposed to outside.

Dilantin, (diphenylhydantoin), introduced, **1937,** by American neuropathologist Tracy Putnam [1894-]; first drug to control epileptic seizures, while allowing near-normal life.

Dingley Tariff Act, U.S. Congress passed high protective tariff, **July 7, 1897,** averaging almost 60 percent on value of imports.

Dinner at Eight, play, **1932,** portraying in episodes the multiple crises faced by characters who have been invited to the same dinner, by U.S. dramatists George S(imon) Kaufman [Nov. 16, 1899-June 2, 1961] and Edna Ferber [Aug. 15, 1885-Apr. 16, 1968]; film, **1933.**

Dionne quintuplets, Elzire Dionne gave birth to five identical daughters on a small farm in Ontario, Canada, **May 28, 1934.**

Dionysus, Theater of, arena in Athens, Greece, used for dramatic productions of Aeschylus, Sophocles, and Euripides, and others, from **c. 500 B.C.;** stone theater replaced wooden one, **c. 450 B.C.**

dioptrics of eye, work published, **1890,** by Swedish ophthalmologist Alvar Gullstrand [1862-1930].

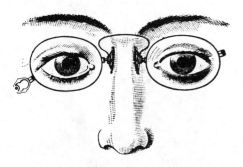

diphtheria, infectious agent discovered, **1883,** by German bacteriologist Theodor Albrecht Edwin Klebs [1834-1913]; because of parallel work in diphtheria by another German bacteriologist, Friedrich August Johann Loeffler [1852-1915], the disease agent sometimes is identified as the Klebs-Loeffler bacillus.

Diplomatic Appropriations Act, U.S. Congress created, **Mar. 1, 1893,** rank of ambassador for use by foreign countries that send ministers (ambassadors) to U.S.

Dirac electron theory, formulated, **1928,** by English physicist Paul A. Dirac [1902-].

direct current, discovered, **1799,** by Italian physicist Alessandro Giuseppe Volta [1745-1827], in the development of the principle of the electric battery.

directional radio antenna, invented, **1905,** by Italian inventor Guglielmo Marconi [1874-1937].

Directoire (Directory), five directors of French government, chosen by French legislative chambers, **Oct. 26, 1795-Nov. 9, 1799.**

Discalced Carmelites, Carmelite religious order with restored primitive rule, including being discalced (unshod); men reformed, **1579,** by St. John of the Cross (born Juan y Yepes y Alvarez) [June 24, 1542-Dec. 14, 1591]; women reformed, **1562-82,** by St. Theresa of Avila [Mar. 28, 1515-Oct. 4, 1582].

Disciples of Christ, religious body that originated within Presbyterianism, **c. 1812;** became separate communion, **1832;** congregationally organized around believers' Baptism and Lord's Supper; founder, Irish-born U.S. minister Alexander Campbell [Sept. 12, 1788-Mar. 4, 1866].

Discourse on Method (Discours de la Methode), philosophical treatise, **1637,** by French philosopher Rene Descartes.

Discourses, The (I Discorsi), treatise on political philosophy, **1519,** by Florentine writer Niccolo Machiavelli [May 3, 1469-June 22, 1527].

Discovery, English ship on which Henry Hudson's crew mutinied, **June 22, 1611,** setting Hudson and his son adrift to die.

disease, cellular basis of, first demonstrated, **1850,** by German pathologist Rudolf Virchow [1821-1902].

disinfectants, introduced, **1867,** by English surgeon Lord Joseph Lister [1827-1912].

Disneyland, television series, premiered, ABC, **October 27, 1954,** utilizing action-adventure segments, nature sequences, and animated characters of U.S. cartoonist and film producer Walt(er Elias) Disney [Dec. 5, 1901-Dec. 15, 1966]; from **1958,** on NBC, retitled Wonderful World of Disney; huge amusement park of the same name opened in Anaheim, Calif., **1955;** Walt Disney's World opened in Orlando, Fla., **1976.**

dispensary, first free dispensary in U.S. established, **1786,** by American physician Benjamin Rush [c. 1745-1813].

Displaced Persons Act, U.S. Pres. Truman authorized, **June 25, 1948,** admission to U.S. of 400,000 European displaced persons, including nonquota orphans.

dissection (of cadaver), for teaching medicine, initiated, **c. 1500,** by Italian anatomist Alessandro Achillini [1463-1512], at University of Bologna.

Dissertation on Roast Pig, A, essay, **1823,** explaining "accidental" discovery of process of cooking by tasting pig burned in fire, by English essayist Charles Lamb [Feb. 10, 1775-Dec. 27, 1834].

dissipative structures, theory of, developed, **1960s,** by Belgian chemist-physicist Ilya Prigogine [1917-].

Distinguished Flying Cross, U.S. military medal for heroism or outstanding achievement in aerial flight instituted by U.S. Congress, **July 2, 1926;** first medal given to Charles A. Lindbergh, **June 11, 1927.**

Distinguished Service Medal, U.S. military medal for outstanding meritorious service authorized for U.S. Army by Pres. Woodrow Wilson, **Mar. 7, 1918;** authorized for U.S. Navy, **Feb. 1919.**

Distinguished Service Order, British military decoration established by Queen Victoria for distinguished service in the United Kingdom, **Nov. 1886.**

Divine Comedy, The (La Divina Commedia), epic poem, **1307-21,** about poet's imaginary journey through hell, purgatory, and, finally, paradise, where he learns of divine love, by Italian poet Dante Alighieri; first printed, **1472.**

Dixie, popular song, **1859,** celebrating the "land of cotton," the American South, by U.S. songwriter Daniel Decatur Emmett [Oct. 29, 1815-June 28, 1904].

Dixiecrats **(States' Rights Democrats),** Southern Democrats opposed to Democratic Party's civil rights platform walked out of national convention at Philadelphia, **July 15, 1948,** and nominated Strom Thurmond [Dec. 5, 1902-] for U.S. President at Birmingham, Ala., convention, **July 1948.**

Djibouti, small republic in Africa, formerly Territory of Afars and Issas, gained independence from France, **June 27, 1977.**

DMZ (demilitarized zone), 2 1/2-mile-wide buffer zone between North and South Korea at 38th parallel established at end of Korean War, **July 27, 1953.**

DNA double-helix model, proposed, **1953,** by American biochemist James D. Watson [1928-] and English biochemist Francis C. Crick [1916-].

DNA polymerase, enzyme which catalyzes synthesis of DNA (deoxyribonucleic acid), first prepared, **1958,** by American biochemist Arthur Kornberg [1918-].

Doctor Doolittle, The Story of, children's novel, **1920,** first to feature Dr. Doolittle and his way with animals; followed by *The Voyages of Dr. Doolittle,* **1922,** and others in the series, by English-U.S. writer and illustrator Hugh Lofting [Jan. 14, 1886-Sept. 26, 1947].

Doctor Faustus, The Tragical History of, drama, **1588,** based on the Faust legend, of damnation resulting from overweening desire for knowledge, by Elizabethan dramatist Christopher Marlowe [Feb. 6, 1564-May 30, 1593].

Doctor Jekyll and Mr. Hyde, The Strange Case of, novel, **1886**, about dual personality of idealistic Dr. Jekyll who develops drug that transforms him into demonic Mr. Hyde; perceptive fictional study by Scottish writer Robert Louis Stevenson.

Doctors' Plot, alleged conspiracy by doctors to murder Soviet military leaders announced by *Pravda,* **Jan. 31, 1953**; initiated purge of Soviet Jews but ended with Joseph Stalin's death, **Mar. 5, 1953**.

Doctor Strangelove, film, **1963**, subtitled "How I Learned to Stop Worrying and Love the Bomb;" biting satire on nuclear holocaust, directed by Stanley Kubrick; starred English actor Peter Sellers [Sept. 8, 1925-July 24, 1980].

Doctor Zhivago, novel, **1957**, rejecting Soviet communistic society in favor of individualism and personalism; won Nobel Prize, **1958**—which was declined for Russian poet and author, Boris Leonidovich Pasternak [Feb. 10, 1890-May 30, 1960].

Dogger Bank crisis, crisis in Anglo-Russian relations, **Oct. 21, 1904**.

Doggett's Coat and Badge rowing race, one of the oldest annual sporting events originated in London, England, **1716**.

Dolce Vita, La, (the sweet (easy) life), film, **1960**, about gossip columnist in decadent modern Roman high society, by Italian director Federico Fellini [Jan. 20, 1920-].

dollar pocket watch, introduced, **1892**, by American merchant Robert H. Ingersoll [1859-1928].

Doll's House, A, realistic play, **1879**, in which sacrificing wife finally leaves "doll's house" (home) to make her way in the world, by "father of modern drama," Norwegian dramatist Henrik Ibsen [May 20, 1828-May 23, 1906].

dome, geodesic, developed, **c. 1940**, by American engineer-inventor Buckminster Fuller [1895-].

Dome of St. Peter's, world famous dome of world's largest church, designed, **1546**, by Italian Renaissance artist Michelangelo Buonarroti; completed, **1590**, by Italian architect Giacomo della Porta.

Dome of the Rock, The, mosque and Moslem shrine, Jerusalem, completed, **c. 690**; built in Jewish Temple area on rock from which the Prophet Mohammed [570-June 8, 632] believed to have ascended to heaven.

Domesday (Doomsday) Book, census and survey of most of England, **1086**; ordered compiled by William the Conqueror [c. 1028-Sept. 9, 1087]; used for tax assessments, until **1522**.

Dominican Order, Catholic religious order of "friars preachers," established, Toulouse, **c. 1215**; rule approved, Bologna, **1220-21**.

Dominion Companies Act, Canada established strong regulations to protect investors, shareholders, and creditors, **Oct. 1, 1934**.

Donation Lands, U.S. Congress gave persons who could bear arms one-quarter section of land in Florida on which to settle, **Aug. 4, 1842**; U.S. Congress gave settlers 160 to 640 acres in Oregon on which to settle, **Sept. 27, 1850**.

Donatism, Christian heresy, flourished, Africa, from **311**, holding that sacraments invalid if minister unworthy; condemned, Synod of Arles, **314**; repressed by state, **316-21**, **347-61**; Emperor definitively condemned, **411**.

Donauworth, historic Swabian town in Germany, became seat of dukes of upper Bavaria, **c. 1250**; adopted Reformation, **1555**; site of English victory (under duke of Marlborough) at cost of 5200 casualties over Bavarian-French force during the War of the Spanish Succession, **July 2, 1704**; town became part of Bavaria, **1714**.

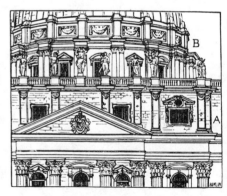

Attic of St. Peter's, Rome.
A, attic of the main edifice ; *B,* attic of the dome.

Don Carlos, opera, **1867**, about Spanish heir saved from being sacrificed for reasons of state, by Guiseppe Verdi; based on play, **1787**, by Friedrich von Schiller.

Don Giovanni, opera, **1787**, on Don Juan theme, in which famous libertine is escorted to hell by statue of man he murdered, composed by Wolfgang Amadeus Mozart.

Don Juan, legendary profligate and seducer of women, first appeared, **1630**, in play *El Burlador de Sevilla*, by Spanish dramatist Tirso de Molina (born Gabriel Tellez) [Oct., 1571-Mar. 12, 1648]; Moliere treated same theme in *Don Juan*, **1665**; English poet Lord Byron left his version, the epic satirical poem *Don Juan*, unfinished, **1819-24**.

Donner party, American emigrants on route to California trapped by snow in Sierra Nevada, half of whom survived by cannibalism, **Oct. 1846-Jan. 1847**.

Don Pacifico affair, British Foreign Minister (later Prime Minister) Viscount Palmerston [Oct. 20, 1784-Oct. 18, 1865] defended, in his greatest parliamentary speech, British seizure of Greek ships at Piraeus to force a settlement of claims by Don Pacifico, Moorish Jew and British citizen, and others against Greek government, **Jan.-June 1850**.

Doorn Kop, battle of, Boers forced Jameson and his men to surrender, **Jan. 2, 1895**, and turned them over to British for trial in England.

Don Quixote (El Ingenio Hidalgo, Don Quixote de la Mancha), novel, **1605-14**, about idealistic would-be chivalric hero who tilts with imaginary enemies in company of sage, realistic Sancho Panza, by Spanish writer Miguel de Cervantes (Saavedra) [Sept. 29, 1547-Apr. 23, 1616]. Opera, **1910**, by French composer Jules Massenet; one of many attempts to stage musically Cervantes' redoubtable Spanish knight: e.g., **1770**, by Antonio Salieri; **1833**, by Gaetano Donizetti. Series of famous lithographs, **1863**, illustrating Cervantes' masterpiece, by French lithographer Gustave Dore [Jan. 6, 1832-Jan. 23, 1883]. Classical Russian ballet, **1869**, based on Cervantes' hero; first choreographed and danced at Bolshoi Theater, **Dec. 26, 1869**, by pioneer French-Russian dancer and cho-

reographer Marius Petipa [Mar. 11, 1818-July 14, 1910].

Doppler principle, discovered, **1842**, by Austrian mathematician Christian Doppler [1805-1853].

Dornach, battle of, Swiss cantons defeated Germans of Holy Roman Empire at Dornach, south of Basel, virtually assuring independence for Switzerland, **July 22, 1499**.

Doric order, earliest style of Greek architecture, from **7th century B.C.**; perfected **c. 450 B.C.**; characterized by thick columns with molded, convex capitals; example: Temple of Poseidon, Sounion, **444-40 B.C.**

Dorylaeum, ancient Phrygian city in Asia Minor, important trading city of Rome, **c. 1st century B.C.-A.D. 2nd century**; site of Christian victory against Seljuk Turks during first Crusade, **July 1, 1097**; site of ambush of mounted Christian knights by Turkish bowmen, who decimated the Christian ranks during second Crusade, **Oct. 1147**.

Douai-Rheims Bible, Roman Catholic version of the Bible in English, translated by members of the English College at Douai, later at Rheims: New Testament published, **1582**; Old Testament, **1609**; Challoner revision, **1749-50**.

Double Eagle, 20-dollar gold piece authorized by U.S. Congress, **Mar. 1849**.

Double Eagle II, craft used by Max Anderson, Ben Abruzzo, and Larry Newman in first successful transatlantic balloon crossing, from Presque Isle, Maine, to field w. of Paris, **Aug. 11-17, 1978.**

Downs, battle of the ("Four Days Battle"), Dutch fleet under de Ruyter and Tromp defeated English fleet under Monck and Prince Rupert off Dunkirk, **June 11-14, 1666.**

Dracula, horror novel, **1897**, about Transylvanian vampire Count Dracula, by Irish writer Bram Stoker [1847-Apr. 20, 1912]. Film, **1931**, based on Bram Stoker's novel about vampire; immense success for actor who played Count Dracula, Hungarian-born Bela Lugosi (born B.L. Blasko) [Oct. 20, 1884-Aug. 16, 1956].

Dragnet, long-running television crime series, **1951-59, 1967-70**, dramatizing Los Angeles Police Department fight against crime; starred U.S. actor Jack Webb [Apr. 2, 1920-], who also did Dragnet radio show, **1949-51**, and movie, **1954**.

Dranesville, battle of, Confederates led by Jeb Stuart made unsuccessful surprise attack on Union forces at Dranesville, Va., **Dec. 20, 1861.**

Dreadnought, first "all-big-gun" battleship launched by British navy, revolutionizing world naval situation, **Feb. 10, 1906.**

dredge, steam, first built, **1803**, by American inventor Oliver Evans [1755-1819].

Dred Scott case, U.S. Supreme Court under Chief Justice Roger B. Taney [Mar. 17, 1777-Oct. 12, 1864] ruled that a Negro (Dred Scott [1795?-1858]) was not a U.S. citizen and had no standing in court; inflamed North-South slavery debate, **Mar. 6, 1857.**

Dresden, German city, residence of electors (later kings) of Saxony, **1485-1918**; center for baroque and rococo art and architecture, late **17th-18th century**; center of German romantic movement, late **18th-early 19th centuries**; center of German opera, late **19th-early 20th centuries**; severely damaged by British and U.S. bombs in WW II, **Feb. 1945.**

Dresden, Treaty of, Prussia retained Silesia and recognized Pragmatic Sanction of **1731**; Saxony (Austria) paid Prussia one million rix-dollars, **Dec. 25, 1745.**

Dreyfus affair, French Army Capt. Alfred Dreyfus [Oct. 19, 1859-July 11, 1935], wrongly convicted of treason and imprisoned, became center of political controversy in France, **1894-1906**; Dreyfus sent to Devil's Island in French Guiana, **Dec. 1894**; new trial divided France into anti-Dreyfusards (royalists, militarists, Catholics) and Dreyfusard (republicans, socialists, and anticlericalists) over innocence of the Alsatian Jew Dreyfus, **1898**; military court again found Dreyfus guilty, **Sept. 9, 1899**; world wide indignation led to French supreme court of appeals exoneration of Dreyfus, **1906.**

drop-hammer, invented, **1853**, by American mechanic Elisha K. Root [1808-1869].

drop shuttle boxes, (weft replenishing loom), invented, **1901**, by American inventor Horace Wyman [1827-1915].

drum, percussion instrument, consisting of skin stretched over frame, oldest and most widespread of instruments; modern forms developed from examples brought from the Orient by Western Crusaders, **1100s.**

Drury Lane Theatre, historic theater, London, built, **1812**, on site of two previous theaters, same name, built **1663** and **1674**.

Druses, hill people of Syria and Lebanon massacred the Christians, **1860s**; fought war against French control of Lebanon and Syria, **July 18, 1925-June 1927.**

Druzes, Eastern religious sect, offshot of

Islam, founded **c. 1010**, on belief in periodic manifestation of God in human form.

dry dock, floating, invented, **1838**, by American Theodore R. Timby [1822-1909].

Dry Wood Creek, battle of, Confederates won victory against Union Kansas forces at Dry Wood Creek, Mo., at beginning of U.S. Civil War, **Sept. 2, 1861**.

Dublin, University of (Trinity College), Queen Elizabeth I [Sept. 7, 1533-Mar. 23, 1603] founded university at Dublin, Ireland, **1591**.

Dubliners, collection of short stories, **1914**, dealing with ironies and complexities of Irish life; early work of Irish author James Joyce [Feb. 2, 1882-Jan. 13, 1941].

Duck Soup, film, **1933**, zany lampoon of war and diplomacy in imaginary Freedonia, starring the Marx Brothers.

Duke's laws, system of governing the English colony of New York (formerly New Netherlands) established by duke of York, **1664**, after Dutch relinquished control.

duma, former Russian national assembly created by czar's decree after **1905** Revolution and dissolved during Russian Revolution, **1906-17**.

Dumbarton Oaks Conference, U.S., U.S.S.R., Britain, and China agreed at conference in Washington, D.C., to proposals to set up United Nations, **Aug. 21,-Oct. 7, 1944**.

Dummer's (Lovewell's) War, conflict between British settlers and French Jesuit missionaries aided by Abenaki Indians in n. Maine; British accused French of encroach-

ment, **1722-25**.

Dunbar, battle of, 25,000 man Scottish army attacked English army under Oliver Cromwell, resulted in devastating defeat for Scottish Covenanters at Dunbar, Scotland, during English Civil War (10,000 Scots taken prisoner by English), **Sept. 3, 1650**.

Dunes, battle of the, combined English-French army led by great French Army Marshal Henri de la Tour d'Auvergne, Vicomte de Turenne [Sept. 11, 1611-July 27, 1675] won important victory over Spanish near Dunkirk, France, **June 14, 1658**.

Dunkirk, French port on North Sea, withstood strong Anglo-Dutch bombardment, **1694**; about 300,000 allied troops, cut off from retreat on land by German advance, evacuated from Dunkirk at start of WW II, **May 26,-June 4, 1940**.

Dunmore's War, Lord, Virginia governor, the earl of Dunmore, successfully waged war against Shawnee and Ottawa Indians, gaining control of Ohio River area, **Jan.-Oct. 1774**.

Dunning Tariff, Canada passed tariff revision, **May 2, 1930**, in response to Smoot-Hawley Tariff of U.S., giving British imports preferential treatment.

duplex telegraphy, practical system proposed, **1873**, by English mathematical physicist Oliver Heaviside [1850-1925].

Duquesne, Fort, strategic site (where Pittsburgh, Penn., now stands) seized and named by the French before arrival of Virginia militia under George Washington [Feb. 22, 1732-Dec. 14, 1799], **Apr. 17, 1754**; French withstood British attack under Gen. Braddock, **July 9, 1755**; British advance forced French to burn and abandon fort, **Nov. 25, 1758**; British rebuilt it and named it Fort Pitt, **1758**.

Durham Report, famous report by former governor of British North American provinces, proposing union of Upper and Lower Canada, **Feb. 11, 1839**.

Dutch War of Independence, seven Protestant provinces in the north (present-day Netherlands) rebelled against Spanish rule of King Philip II, declared their independence and finally gained it at the end of the Thirty Years' War, **1567-1648**.

Dutch Wars, conflicts between English and Dutch; first war, **1652-54**; Dutch gained control of English Channel, **Nov. 1652**; English fleet won victories off Portland, **Feb. 18-19, 1653**; off Gabbard's Shoal, **June 1653**; Dutch failed to break English blockade of Dutch coast, **July 31, 1653**; second war, **1664-67**; English won at Lowestoft, **June 13, 1665**; English fleet defeated at battle of Downs, **June 11-14, 1666**; ended by Treaty of Breda, **July 31, 1667**; third war mainly between French and Dutch, **1672-78**; Louis XIV overran s. Netherlands, **May 1672**; Dutch defeated English and French fleets at Southwold Bay, **June 7, 1672**; England made peace with Dutch, **1674**; French won victories at Seneff, **Aug. 8, 1674**; and at Sinzheim, **June 16, 1674**; ended by Treaties of Nijmegen, **1678-79**.

dye, synthetic, discovered, **1856**, by English chemist Sir William Henry Perkin [1838-1907].

Dying Swan, The, solo ballet, **1905**, to music from Saint-Saens' *Carnival of the Animals*, choreographed by Michel Fokine (Mikhail Mikhailovich) [Apr. 26, 1880-Aug. 22, 1942] for famous Russian prima ballerina Anna Pavlova [Jan. 31, 1882-Jan. 23, 1931]; most famous solo dance ever created.

dynamite, invented, **1866**, by Swedish scientist Alfred Bernhard Nobel [1833-1896].

dynamo, industrial, first perfected, **1872**, by Belgian electrician Zenobe T. Gramme [1826-1901].

dysprosium, element No. 66, discovered, **1886**, by French chemist Paul E. Lecoq de Boisbaudran [1873-1912].

Eagle, 10-dollar gold piece with U.S. national bird (eagle) stamped on it, authorized as legal tender, **1792**; first coined, **1794**; not coined, **1805-37**.

Earhart's trans-Atlantic flight, Amelia Earhart [July 24, 1898-July 2, 1937] became first woman to make solo flight across Atlantic, **May 20-21, 1932**, flying from Newfoundland to Ireland, 2026 miles in 13 1/2 hours.

Early Bird, launched, **1965**, from Cape Kennedy by Communications Satellite Corporation (COMSAT).

earth circumference, calculation of, earliest known, **c. 220 B.C.**, by Greek astronomer Eratosthenes [273-192 B.C.].

Earth Day, millions of Americans joined in anti-pollution demonstrations across U.S. to mark first Earth Day, **Apr. 22, 1980**.

earth scraper, land-leveling equipment invented, **1932**, by American manufacturer Robert G. LeTourneau [1888-].

East African Community, commercial and industrial union created by Tanzania, Uganda, and Kenya, **June 1967**, and inaugurated, **Dec. 1, 1967**.

Easter, Christian feast of the resurrection of Christ, from **c. 180**, celebrated first Sunday after first full moon of Spring; rule for this date fixed, Council of Nicaea, **325**.

Easter Oratorio, composition for chorus and orchestra, **1736**; by German composer Johann Sebastian Bach, composer's *Christmas Oratorio*, **1734**.

Eastern Orthodox Church, independent, self-governing Christian churches separated from Catholic Church since Great Schism, **1054**.

Easter Rebellion, Irish Republican Brotherhood's rebellion for Ireland's independence on Easter Sunday, suppressed by British after week of fighting, **Apr. 24-May 1, 1916**; British executed Irish leaders, including Sir Roger D. Casement [Sept. 1, 1864-Aug. 3, 1916], **Aug. 3, 1916**.

East India Company, British, mercantile association organized by Englishmen to carry on trade with the East Indies and Asia, **1600-1874**; parliamentary acts abolished its trade monopoly, **1813, 1833**.

East India Company, Dutch, mercantile association, chartered by Dutch government, monopolized trade in the East Indies; **1602-1798**.

East India Company, French, mercantile association organized by Frenchmen to compete with British trade in India, **1664-1769**; combined briefly with other French trading

companies to form Compaigne des Indes, **1719-23**.

East India Company, Ostend, mercantile company established by Holy Roman Emperor Charles VI [Oct. 1, 1685-Oct. 20, 1740] to rival English and Dutch East India Companies, **c. 1720-31**.

Eastland, Great Lakes excursion steamship *Eastland* capsized in port on Chicago River; 812 persons died, **July 24, 1915**.

East of Eden, novel, **1952**, retelling Cain and Abel story in California's Salinas Valley, by U.S. writer John (Ernst) Steinbeck [Feb. 27, 1902-Dec. 20, 1968]; Nobel Prize-winner, **1962**.

Ebionites, sect of Jewish Christians, **100-500**, that retained Mosaic law, believing Jesus was its fulfillment.

Ecclesiastes, Old Testament book written down, **c. 200 B.C.**, though ascribed to Solomon; expresses a pessimism that has led to doubt about its inspiration as true scripture.

Ecclesiastical History of the English People (Historia Ecclesiastica Gentis Anglorum), classic Latin history, **731**, covering British history from time of Caesar's invasion; indispensable source on invasion and conversion of Anglo-Saxons and for dates throughout period; by the Venerable Bede [672/3-May 25, 735].

Echmiadzin (Vagarshapat), town founded in Armenia, **6th century B.C.**; capital of Armenia, **2nd-4th centuries**; residence of the patriarch of the Armenian Catholic Church, since **1441**; took present-day name, **1945**.

Echo I, first passive communications satellite, launched, **1960**, by American scientists of NASA.

Ecnomus, battle of, Roman fleet won decisive naval victory against Carthaginian fleet off Cape Ecnomus, near Licata, Sicily, during first Punic War, **256 B.C.**

ecology, term devised, **1869**, by German zoologist Ernst Haeckel [1834-1919].

Economist, The, financial, political and literary review, founded, **1843**; reputation built especially during editorship, **1860-77**, of British critic and political writer Walter Bagehot [Feb. 3, 1826-Mar. 24, 1877].

Economy (Ambridge), former American communal settlement in Penn., established by Harmonists under George Rapp who sold

New Harmony, Ind., to Robert Owen and returned to Pittsburgh area, **1825**; ceased to exist, after **1906**.

Ecumenical Councils, synods recognized by entire Church; first so recognized: Council of Nicaea, **325**; 7 recognized by Eastern Orthodox Church, through Nicaea II, **787**; Catholic Church recognizes 14 more through Vatican II, **1962-65**.

Ecumenical Movement, The, movement promoting unity among Christian churches, begun, **1910**, Edinburgh, World Missionary Congress; developed through Faith and Order Conferences beginning, Lausanne, **1927**; World Council of Churches constitution ratified, Amsterdam, **August 22, 1948**.

Edda(s), The, mythological Norse poem, c. **850**; discovered, **1643**; *Elder Edda:* collection of 34 Norse and German mythological poems, **1194**; *Younger Edda:* Norse treatise on poetry, **c. 1225**.

Eddie Cantor Show, The, hugely popular radio show ran intermittently, from **September 13, 1931**, through Spring of **1950**.

Edessa (Urfa), ancient city of Mesopotamia, became center of Christianity, **3rd century**; major religious center of Byzantine Empire until captured by Arabs, **639**; captured by Crusaders, **1097**; recaptured by Muslims, **1144**; seized by Turks, **1637**.

Edge Act, U.S. Congress authorized, **Dec. 24, 1919**, nationally chartered U.S. corporations to engage in business abroad.

Edgehill, battle of, first major battle of

English Civil War; parliamentarians (Roundheads) and royalists (Cavaliers) fought bloody battle that ended in draw at Edgehill in Warwickshire, England, **Oct. 23, 1642**.

Edict of Milan, edict, **313**, issued under Emperor Constantine, by which legal personality of Christian churches recognized and all religions officially tolerated.

Edict of Nantes, royal decree, **1598**, ending French wars of religion and allowing Huguenots limited toleration; signed by King Henry IV (of Navarre) [Dec. 13, 1553-May 4, 1610]; revoked, **1685**, by King Louis XIV [Sept. 5, 1635-Sept. 1, 1715], precipitating Huguenot expatriation.

Edinburgh Festival, summer opera festival, founded, **1947**; world-famous for its notable performances.

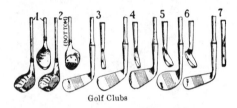

Golf Clubs

Edinburgh Golfers, Honorable Company of, oldest golfing club in the world established at Edinburgh, Scotland, **Mar. 1744**.

Edinburgh Review, The, influential Scottish literary and political periodical, published, **1802-1929**.

Edinburgh, Treaty of, English and Scots obtained French withdrawal from Scotland, **July 6, 1560**.

Edinburgh, University of, European institution of higher learning, founded, **1583**; became self-governing body, **1889**.

Edison Effect, that incandescent lamp could be used as valve admitting only negative electricity, discovered, **1883**, by American inventor Thomas A. Edison [1847-1931]; basis for vacuum tube.

Edsac, the first stored-program computer; built, **1949**, by British scientist Maurice V. Wilkes, at Cambridge University in England.

Ed Sullivan Show, The, early radio talk-and-variety show, **1932**, hosted by Ed Sullivan; introduced Jack Benny to radio, **March 29, 1932**. Television variety show, **1948-71**; guest stars introduced by stone-faced emcee Ed(ward) (Vincent) Sullivan [Sept. 28, 1902-Oct. 13, 1974].

Egypt, African country, declared an independent sovereign state by Britain, **Feb. 28, 1922**; constitution went into effect, **1923**; monarchy abolished and republic proclaimed, **June 18, 1953**.

Egyptian civilization, ancient, early agricultural community with knowledge of writing, government, art, and science, arose in Nile River valley, **c. 4000 B.C.**

Egyptian plague, great, epidemic of bubonic plague killed at least 800,000 persons in Egypt, **1792**.

Eichmann case, former Nazi SS leader Adolf Eichmann [Mar. 19, 1906-May 31, 1962] arrested by Israelis in Argentina, **May 22, 1960**; four-month trial of Eichmann before Israeli tribunal began in Jerusalem, **Apr. 11, 1961**; Eichmann sentenced to death for murder of millions of Jews in WW II, **Dec. 15, 1961**, and hanged, **May 31, 1962**.

Eiffel Tower, 620-foot-high cast-iron latticework structure in Paris, constructed, **1889**, for Universal Exposition, designed by French civil engineer Alexandre-Gustave Eiffel [Dec. 15, 1832-Dec. 28, 1923].

Eigerwand (Wall of the Ogre), notorious mile-high mountain face of the Eiger, in Bernese Alps of Switzerland, first climbed, **1938**.

18 Brumaire, Napoleon Bonaparte, supported by French army, overthrew the Directoire, **Nov. 9, 1799**; Napoleon established as first consul in the Consulate, **Dec. 25, 1799**.

Eighteenth Amendment to U.S. Constitution, ratified, **Jan. 29, 1919**, prohibited manufacture, transportation, and sale of alcoholic beverages and gave Congress powers of enforcement; repealed **Dec. 5, 1933**.

1812 Overture, festival overture, **1882**, written by Russian composer Peter Ilyich Tchaikovsky.

einsteinium, element no. 99; discovered, **1952**, by American physicist Albert Ghiorso [1915-] and coworkers.

Einstein photoelectric law, announced, **1905**, by German-American physicist Albert Einstein.

Eisenhower Doctrine, U.S. Congress approved, **Mar. 7, 1957**, Pres. Dwight D. Eisenhower's plan to prevent Communist aggression in Middle East.

El Bracito, battle of, Americans repulsed strong attack by 1100 Mexicans at El Bracito, N.M., **Dec. 24, 1846**.

Elbruz, Mt., highest mountain in Europe (18,481 ft.), in the Caucasus, first climbed by British expedition led by English explorer Douglas Freshfield [1845-1934], **1868**.

El Capitan, "impossible" perpendicular cliff (3,600 ft.) in Yosemite National Park, Calif., first climbed by Warren Harding [1924-] and Dean Caldwell [1943-], **Nov. 1970**.

Elders of Zion, Protocols of, fabricated document, first published, Russia, **1902**, purporting to describe Jewish plan for takeover of Western society; exposed as clumsy fabrication, **1919**; condemned in legal action, Berne, **1934-35**.

Eleatic School, school of ancient Greek philosophy, flourished, **c. 450 B.C.**

Electoral Count Act, U.S. Congress made each state responsible for its electoral votes, except in cases of fraud or states' indecision, **Feb. 3, 1887**.

Electra, Greek tragedy, **c. 414 B.C.**, by Sophocles; Euripides wrote his *Electra*, **413 B.C.**

electrical resonator, L.C. tuned circuit, developed, **c. 1889**, by Yugoslavian-American physicist Michael I. Pupin [1858-1935].

electrical units, absolute system of, developed, **1851**, by German physicist Wilhelm E. Weber [1804-1891] and German mathematician Karl F. Gauss [1777-1855].

electric-convulsive therapy, introduced, **1938**, by Italian physician Ugo Cerletti [1877-1963].

electric current flow, rule of, first described, **1820**, by French mathematician and physicist Andre Marie Ampere [1775-1836].

electric, generator, patented, **1880**, by Belgian-American inventor Charles J. Van Depoele [1846-1892].

electric relay, discovered, **1835**, by U.S. physicist Joseph Henry [1797-1878].

electrocardiograph, invented, **1900**, by Dutch physiologist Wilhelm Einthoven [1860-1927].

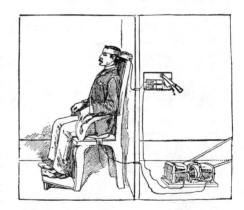

electrocution, first U.S. electrocution occurred, **Aug. 6, 1890**, at Auburn Prison, Auburn, N.Y.

electroencephalograph, invented, **1929**,

by German neurologist Johannes Hans Berger [1873-1941].

electrolysis, discovered, **1800,** by English chemist William Nicholson [1753-1815].

electrolytic method, (in manufacture of caustic soda and chlorine) invented **1886** by American chemist Hamilton Y. Castner [1859-1899].

electromagnet, invented, **1823,** by English electrician William Sturgeon [1783-1850].

electromagnetic waves, demonstrated, **1873,** by Scottish physicist James Clerk Maxwell [1831-1879].

electromagnetism, described as an electrical phenomena, **1820,** by Danish physicist Hans Christian Oersted [1777-1851].

electrometer, gold-leaf, invented, **1787,** by English scientist Abraham Bennet [1750-1799].

electron, term introduced, **1891,** by Irish physicist George J. Stoney [1826-1911]; existence first confirmed, **1897,** by English physicist Joseph J. Thomson [1856-1940].

electron activity, concept introduced, **1916,** by American chemist Gilbert N. Lewis [1875-1946] for explaining forces that hold atoms together in molecules.

electron-atom collision, laws formulated, **c. 1920,** by German physicist Gustav Hertz [1887-1975] and German-American physicist James Franck [1882-1964].

electron diffraction, (by crystals), discovered, **1927,** by American physicist Clinton J. Davisson [1881-1958] and independently by English physicist Sir George P. Thomson [1892-1975]; two shared Nobel Prize in physics, **1937,** for their discovery.

electron sharing, concept developed, **1916,** by American chemist Gilbert Newton Lewis [1875-1946] to explain organic compound binding.

electron transfer, concept introduced, **c. 1900,** by German chemist Richard Abegg [1869-1910].

electron tube, multi-grid, invented, **1913,** by American physical chemist Irving Langmuir [1881-1957].

electron wave mechanics, theory introduced, **1930,** by English physicist Paul A. Dirac [1902-].

electrophorus, device to accumulate weak electrical charges, designed, **1775,** by Italian physicist Alessandro Volta [1745-1827].

electroplating, process discovered, **1800,** by German physicist Johann W. Ritter [1776-1810].

electrostatic machine, first machine for producing electric charge; invented, **1672,** by German physicist Otto von Guericke [1602-1686].

elegy, poetic lament for the departed based on Greek classical models, developed, **c. 460-400 B.C.**.

element 104, synthesized, **1964,** by Russian theoretical physicist Dmitri I. Blokhintsev [1908-1979].

elevator, electric, patented, **1885,** by American engineer Schuyler S. Wheeler [1860-1923].

elevator, passenger, first in U.S. installed, **1859,** in Fifth Avenue Hotel, New York City.

elevator, steam-operated, patented, **1861,** by American inventor Elisha G. Otis [1811-1861].

Elgin Marbles, collection of classical Greek sculptures selected and shipped to London, **1803-12,** by British Ambassador to Turkey Lord Elgin (Thomas Bruce) [July 20, 1766-Nov. 14, 1841]; in British Museum since **1816**.

Elizabethan, era pertaining to 45-year reign, **1558-1603,** of Elizabeth I of England [Sept. 7, 1533-Mar. 23, 1603]; considered synonymous with English Renaissance.

Elizabethan Poor Laws, English government enacted measures to deal with widespread poverty, to regulate apprenticeships, and to levy taxes to support programs for the needy, **1563-1601.**

Elks, Benevolent and Protective Order of, fraternal and charitable society, founded **1868,** in New York City; opened to black males, as well as whites, **1973.**

Ellis Island, immigration station of U.S. opened, **Jan. 1, 1892** in New York harbor; fl. **1892-1943;** closed **Nov. 12, 1954,** after processing more than 20 million immigrants.

El Obeid, battle of, Mahdi forces utterly wiped out British-Egyptian army at El Obeid (Al Ubayyid) in central Sudan, **Nov. 5, 1883,** resulting in control of Sudan by the Mahdists, until early **1885.**

El Salvador, Central American republic, declared its independence from Spain, **Sept. 15, 1821;** part of confederation of Central American states until **1838;** torn by extremist violence, **1979-81.**

Elvira, Council of, Spanish ecclesiastical synod, **306;** passed first formal legislation requiring clerical celibacy; also enacted severe penalties for adultery and apostasy.

Ely, historic market town in central England, site of last resistance to William the Conqueror, **1071;** English barons and rebels subdued by forces of King Henry III, ending second Barons' War, **1267.**

Emancipation, Edict of, far-reaching measure by which Czar Alexander I liberated all Russian serfs, **Mar. 3, 1861.**

Emancipation Proclamation, edict issued by Pres. Abraham Lincoln that freed slaves in states in rebellion, **Jan. 1, 1863.**

Embargo Act, U.S. Congress passed retaliatory measure in response to British Orders in Council and Napoleon's Continental System, forbidding all international trade to and from U.S. ports, **Dec. 22, 1807;** repealed, **Mar. 1, 1809.**

embryology, study of prenatal development, recognized as a specialized branch of medicine, **c. 1830,** with work of Estonian biologist Karl Ernest von Baer [1792-1876].

embryonic development, organizer effect discovered, **1927,** by German biologist Hans Spemann [1869-1941].

embryonic germ layers, described, **c. 1770,** by German anatomist Caspar F.

Wolff [1733-1794].

Emesa (Hims), ancient city in central Syria, site of defeat of forces of Zenobia [d. after 272] of Palmyra by Romans under Emperor Aurelian [c. 212-75], **272;** Arabs captured town and renamed it Hims, **636.**

Emma, novel, **1816,** microcosmic social world by English novelist Jane Austin [Dec. 16, 1775-July 18, 1817].

Emmy Awards, annual awards conferred for outstanding television achievement, since **1949,** by National Academy of Television Arts and Sciences; first national telecast of awards, **Mar. 7, 1955.**

Emperor Concerto, piano concerto, **1809,** 5th work in this form by German composer Ludwig van Beethoven.

emphysema, first described, **c. 1819,** by French physician Rene Theophile Hyacinthe Laennec [1781-1826].

Empire State Building, elegantly designed skyscraper, long the world's tallest, begun **1929,** New York City; completed **1932.**

empiricism, philosophical theory, developed from **c. 1700,** holding that true knowledge is verifiable in experience; seminal work: *Essay Concerning Human Understanding,* **1690,** by British philosopher John Locke.

Emporia Gazette, The, small-town newspaper, **1895-1944,** published in Emporia, Kansas, that became internationally famous as representative of grass-roots opinion, mainly through efforts of its editor William Allen White [Feb. 10, 1868-Jan. 29, 1944].

Empress of Ireland, Canadian Pacific steamship *Empress of Ireland* sank after collision with collier (coal ship) in St. Lawrence River; 1024 persons died, **May 29, 1914.**

Ems Dispatch, Otto von Bismarck altered communication between Prussian king and French ambassador in such a manner as to make it appear their negotiations at Ems, Germany, had broken all relations, **July 13, 1870.**

emulsion gel, photographic, invented, **1878,** by American inventor George Eastman [1854-1932].

Enabling Act, National Socialists (Nazis), supported by the Nationalists, gained dictatorial control of German government, **Mar. 23, 1933.**

Enchiridion Symbolorum, standard manual of Catholic doctrine, first published, **1854**.

encyclopedia, reference book treating subjects in specialized articles; first modern example, Germany, **1630**; Chamber's *Cyclopedia*, England, **1728**; first medieval encyclopedia, *Etymologiae*, **623**, of Spanish late Church Father Isidore of Seville [c. 560-Apr. 4, 636].

Encyclopaedia Britannica, leading English-language encyclopedia, first published, Edinburgh, **1771**; 11th edition, edited Cambridge University, **1910-11**; current, 15th edition, edited United States, **1974**.

Encyclopedia (French) (L'Encyclopedie), 35-volume compendium of knowledge, **1751-77**, edited from rationalist point of view, upholding science and attacking "superstition".

English, language of England, developed, **c. 800-1100**, from Germanic dialects; French elements superimposed after Norman conquest, **1066**; modern English dates from **c. 1500**.

engine, Diesel, first successfully built in the U.S., **1897**, by French-born German mechanical engineer Rudolf Diesel [1858-1913].

engine, high-speed internal combustion, patented, **1887**, by German engineer Gottlieb Daimler [1834-1900].

engine, internal combustion, built, **1859**, by Belgian-born Jean Joseph Etienne Lenoir [1822-1900], using illuminating gas as a fuel; in **1860**, the engine was used to propel a small wagon which became the first gas-powered "horseless carriage." Two-cylinder engine patented in U.S. **1826**, by American inventor Samuel Morey [1762-1843].

engine, jet propulsion, first built and patented, **1937**, by English aeronautical engineer Sir Frank Whittle [1907-].

engine, outboard, invented, **1909**, by American inventor Ole Evinrude.

English Bible, the, English Protestant translations of the Bible: Middle English version, **c. 1380**, sponsored by John Wycliff [c. 1320-Dec. 31, 1384]; version, **1525-30**, by William Tyndale [c. 1492-Oct. 6, 1536]; King James version, **1611**; Revised Standard Version, **1952**; New English Bible **1961**.

English Channel swim, British Captain Matthew Webb [Jan. 18, 1848-July 24, 1883] swam across English Channel from Dover to Calais in 22 hours to become first to accomplish feat, **Aug. 25, 1875**; U.S. swimmer Gertrude Ederle [Oct. 23, 1906-] became first woman to swim English Channel, **Aug. 6, 1926**; Florence Chadwick [May, 1918-] became first woman to swim English Channel in both directions: France to England, **Aug. 20, 1950**, England to France, **Sept. 11, 1951**.

English Channel tunnel, England and France reached agreement to build RR tunnel under English Channel, **Feb. 6, 1964**; work begun, **1974**, but soon halted by lack of funds.

English Civil War, (see Civil War, English).

Enlightenment, age in European cultural history, **c. 1660-1800**, emphasizing belief in reason, science, and progress, skepticism in religion, and attacks against superstition.

Enola Gay, B-29 superfortress used by U.S. to drop atomic bomb on Hiroshima, **Aug. 6, 1945**.

Entebbe raid, Israeli airborne commandos freed 103 hostages held by pro-Palestinian hijackers on Air France plane at Entebbe Airport, Uganda, **July 4, 1976**.

Entente Cordiale, informal, friendly understanding established between the governments of Great Britain and France to resolve their colonial differences, **1904**.

environment chamber, controlled, developed, **1969**, by American physician, Robert E. Snell and American architectural engineer, John Everetts, Jr. to study effects of air pollution on health.

Environmental Protection Agency (EPA), independent U.S. government agency, established **Oct. 2, 1970**, with pollution-control functions.

enzyme-controlled reactions, study methods developed, from **late 1930s** by Australian chemist John Cornforth [1917-].

enzyme, fermentation of, discovered, **1896**, by German biochemist Eduard Buchner [1860-1917].

enzymes, oxidation, method of study developed, **1934**, by Swedish biochemist Axel H. Theorell [1903-].

enzymes, respiratory, investigated, **1928**, by German biochemist Otto H. Warburg [1883-1970].

enzyme (urease), first crystallized, **1926**, by American biochemist James B. Sumner [1887-1955]; first enzyme isolated in pure form.

ephemerides, published in U.S., **1792-1802**, by American pioneer astronomer Benjamin Banneker [1731-1806].

Ephesians, Letter to the, letter of St. Paul to Christians at Ephesus, Asia Minor, **c. 61-63**, 10th book of New Testament.

Ephesus, ancient Greek city and seaport of Ionia (w. Asia Minor); noted for its great temple of Artemis, **fl. c. 800-400 B.C.**; became important center of Christianity, **1st century**; sacked by Goths, **262**.

Ephesus, Council of, ecumenical council, **431**, held at Ephesus in Asia Minor; defined Mary as *Theotokos*, or "Mother of God."

epic, long narrative folk poem presenting adventures on heroic scale as in *Iliad* and *Odyssey*, written down, **c. 700 B.C.**, by leg-endary blind Greek poet Homer [fl. c. 850 B.C.]; Anglo-Saxon *Beowulf*, **c. 750**; French *Song of Roland*, **c. 1050**.

epic, literary, long narrative poem written in imitation of heroic folk epics, as Vergil's *Aeneid*, **19 B.C.**; Dante's *Divine Comedy*, **1307-21**; Milton's *Paradise Lost*, **1667**.

epic theater, dramatic style, originated, **1920s**, in German theater, combined loose epic (narrative) elements with conventional dramatic ones; realized especially in works of German dramatist Bertolt Brecht.

Epicureanism, philosophy taught in academy founded Athens, **c. 306 B.C.**, by Athenian philosopher Epicurus [341-270 B.C.].

Epiphany, Christian feast-day, celebrated, from **c. 180**, on **January 6**.

Epirus, ancient city on Ionian Sea in Greece, **fl. 3rd century B.C.**; sacked by Romans, **167 B.C.**

Epirus, despotate of, independent Greek state established at Epirus by member of Angelus family, **1204**; rivaled Greek empire of Nicaea until **c. 1246**; disappeared under Turkish control, **15th century**.

Episcopal (Anglican) Church (U.S.), first church, built Jamestown, Virginia, **1607**; established as autonomous, **1784**; has participated in Church of England Lambeth Conferences, since **1867**.

epistemology, branch of philosophy concerned with "theory of knowledge," what and how we know; established in *Theaetetus*, **c. 368 B.C.**, by Greek philosopher Plato.

E Pluribus Unum (one out of many), motto of the U.S. suggested by Benjamin Franklin, Thomas Jefferson, and John Adams,

Aug. 10, 1776; first appeared on U.S. coin in N.J., **1786**.

Equal Rights Amendment (ERA), U.S. Congress proposed, **Mar. 22, 1972**, amendment to Constitution to prohibit sex discrimination; ERA deadline ratification extended, until **June 30, 1982**, by U.S. Senate vote, **Oct. 8, 1978**.

Equal Rights Party, U.S. political party, established **1884**, by suffragettes who nominated first woman candidate, Belva A. Lockwood [Oct. 24, 1830-May 19, 1917], for U.S. presidency, **May 15, 1888**.

Equatorial Guinea, republic in Africa, formerly Spanish Guinea, gained its independence from Spain, **Oct. 12, 1968**.

equatorial sextant, patented, **1856**, by American surveyor-inventor William A. Burt [1792-1858].

Era of Good Feelings, period in U.S. history after decline of Federalist Party, **1817-23**.

Erastianism, ecclesiastical theory, formulated, **1568**, by Thomas Erastus (born Thomas Lieber) [Sept. 7, 1524-Dec. 31, 1583].

erbium, element No. 68; discovered, **1843**, by Swedish chemist Carl G. Mosander [1797-1858].

Erebus, Mt., best-known and very eruptive volcano in Antarctic (12,280 ft.), first climbed by British explorer-geologist, T. W. E. David, **May 5-10, 1908**.

Erechtheum, Athenian temple, built c. **421-406 B.C.**.

Caryatids.
Porch of the Erechtheum at Athens.

Erfurt, Congress of, Napoleon I and Czar Alexander I met at Erfurt to renew the Franco-Russian alliance, **Sept. 1808**.

Erfurt Program, German Social Democratic Party adopted strict Marxian program at Erfurt; marked triumph of Marxist doctrines over those of Lassalle, **1891**.

Erfurt, University of, leading European university in East Germany, **1392-1816**; attended by Martin Luther, **1501-1505**.

ergmetrine, isolated, **1935**, by English chemist Harold W. Dudley [1887-1935].

Erie Canal, U.S. waterway, opened, **1825**, connecting Albany and Buffalo (Hudson River to Lake Erie).

Erie, Lake, battle of, U.S. fleet commanded by Oliver Hazard Perry [Aug. 20, 1785-Aug. 23, 1819] defeated British fleet at Put-in Bay on Lake Erie, **Sept. 10, 1813**.

Erie Purchase, tract of land now in Erie County, known also as the "Triangle," purchased by the State of Pennsylvania, **1788**.

Eroica Symphony, "heroic" symphony, **1804**, Ludwig van Beethoven, dedicated to Napoleon but dedication cancelled when latter declared himself Emperor.

EROS, acronym for Earth Resources Observation Satellites; system initiated, **1966**, by U.S. government to be used for topographic mapping of earth surface.

Erzerum (Erzurum), Treaty of, ended war between Persia and Ottoman Empire; border reestablished, with no territorial changes, **1823**.

escalator, first installed, **1896**, by American inventor Jesse W. Reno [1861-1947] at Coney Island, New York.

Esch-Cummins (Transportation) Act, U.S. Congress released railroads from wartime government control, enabled them to raise rates, and created railway labor board to handle labor problems, **Feb. 28, 1920**.

E(scherichia) coli bacteria, common bacteria of human digestive tract discovered, **1885**, by German physician Theodore Escherich [1857-1911].

Esopus War, the, bloody conflict between Dutch settlers and Indians in and around Esopus (now Kingston), N.Y., **1658-64**.

ESP (extrasensory perception), study pioneered, **1934**, by American parapsychologist Joseph B. Rhine [1895-1980], at Duke University with Zener telepathy test.

Esperanto, international artificial language, proposed, **1887;** in use since first World International Esperanto Congress, **1905.**

Espionage Act, U.S. Congress provided, **June 15, 1917,** severe penalties for activities that impeded U.S. armed forces during WW I; broadened by Sedition Act, **May 16, 1918** to include verbal criticism of U.S.; "Red scare" led to U.S. deportation of 250 "anarchists," **Dec. 22, 1919.**

Essay Concerning Human Understanding, philosophical treatise, **1690,** by British philosopher and political writer John Locke.

Essenes, ancient Hebrew sect, flourished **c. 200 B.C-A.D. 100.**

essential oils, structure of, described, **1895,** by German organic chemist Otto Wallach [1847-1931].

Essex, famous American 32-gun frigate *Essex* defeated British 20-gun sloop-of-war *Alert* during War of 1812, **Aug. 13, 1812;** captured many British ships off west coast of South America, **1812-13;** surrendered after bloody battle against British 36-gun *Phoebe* and 22-gun *Cherub* off Valparaiso, Chile, **Mar. 28, 1814.**

Estates-General (States-General), French national assembly first summoned by King Philip IV, **1302;** collapsed, **1614;** reinstituted by King Louis XVI before French Revolution, **May 5, 1789-Sept. 30, 1791.**

Este, Italian noble family whose name derived from town of Este, ruled Ferrara, **1240-1597;** ruled Modena, **1288-1796.**

Esterhazy, Hungarian noble family supported Hapsburg rule and Holy Roman Empire, **c. 1680-1806.**

Esther, Book of, Old Testament book, believed to have been written down, **c. 300 B.C.**

estrone, hormone isolated, **1929,** by German chemist Adolph Butenandt [1903-].

Etaples, Peace of, England and France conclude agreement following war over France's annexation of Brittany, **Nov. 9, 1492.**

Ethandun (Edington), battle of, one of most decisive battles in English history; Saxons under Alfred the Great [849-Apr. 26, 899] defeated Danes, ensuring survival of Saxon kingdom of Wessex, which eventually overcame the Danish invaders, **878.**

ether theory, mathematically supported,

1952, by English physicist Paul A. Dirac [1902-].

ethics, branch of philosophy concerned with moral conduct, established as philosophical discipline, **c. 430-400 B.C.,** by insistent questioning of Greek philosopher Socrates; Aristotle's *Nicomachean Ethics,* first formal treatise on ethics, **c. 320 B.C.**

Ethiopia, nation in central Africa, established its independence by routing Italian invasion, **1896;** fascist Italy invaded it, **Oct. 3, 1935;** Emperor Haile Selassie of Ethiopia forced into exile, **May 1936;** British routed Italians and Selassie returned, **1941;** Selassie peacefully deposed, **Sept. 12, 1974;** abolished monarchy, **1975;** fought successfully to keep regions of Ogaden and Eritrea, **1977-78.**

ethyl gasoline, antiknock properties discovered, **1922,** by American chemist Thomas Midgley [1889-1944].

Etna (Aetna), Mt., volcanic eruption on coast of Sicily caused widespread destruction, killing approx. 20,000 persons, **1669.**

Eton College, largest and most well-known of the English public schools, founded by King Henry VI [1421-71], **1440.**

Eugene Onegin (Evgeni Onegin), romantic verse novel, **1831,** about Byronic hero, by Russian poet Alexander Pushkin; opera, **1879,** by Russian composer Peter Ilyich Tchaikovsky [May 7, 1840-Nov. 6, 1893].

eugenics, proposed, **1883,** by English anthropologist Francis Galton [1822-1911].

European Atomic Energy Community (Euratom), European nations formed, **Jan. 1, 1958,** organization to develop Europe's nuclear energy and coordinate nuclear research programs.

European Free Trade Association (EFTA), customs union and trading bloc, established, **May 3, 1960,** by Austria, Great Britain, Sweden, Norway, Denmark, Switzerland, and Portugal, the "outer seven" as opposed to "inner six" members of Common Market; joined by Iceland, **1970.**

europium, element No. 63; discovered, **1896,** by French chemist Eugene A. Demarcay [1852-1904].

Eurymedon, battle of, Greek expedition under Cimon [d. 449 B.C.] defeated Persian land and sea forces at mouth of Eurymedon River in Asia Minor, marking end of Persian-

Athenian conflict and linking Asia Minor to Delian League, **466 B.C.**

Eutaw Springs, battle of, British forces defeated the Americans under Gen. Nathanael Greene [Aug. 7, 1742-June 19, 1786], **Sept. 8, 1781.**

Evangelical and Reformed Church, The, union, officially constituted, Cleveland, Ohio, **1934,** between German Evangelical Church, founded **1840,** and German Reformed Church, organized independently, **1792;** combined with Congregationalists, **1961,** to form United Church of Christ.

Evangelicals, Christians claiming to base their teaching preeminently on the Gospels, hence from **c. 1517,** synonymous with Protestants; from **c. 1950** U.S. fundamentalists used term to distinguish themselves from "mainline" Protestants.

evaporated milk, invented, **1880,** by American inventor John B. Meyenberg.

Evening Post, The, first evening newspaper; first published, London, **1706.**

Everest, Mt., highest mountain in the world (29,028 ft.), on border of Tibet and Nepal, first climbed by Sir Edmund Hillary [July 20, 1919-] and Tenzing Norgay [1914-], members of British expedition, **May 29, 1953.**

Evergreen Review, The, literary quarterly, founded New York, **1957;** featuring avant-garde work.

Evesham, battle of, rebel army under earl of Leicester, Simon de Montfort [c. 1160-1218] trapped and massacred by knights of Prince Edward (later Edward I [1239-1307]), breaking the back of the English barons' rebellion in England; Montfort slain, **Aug. 4, 1265.**

Evita, small planet discovered, **1948,** by La Plata Institute, Argentina; named for Eva Peron; official recognition by Astronomical Commission; announced, **1951.**

evolutionism, philosophical theory stating that things develop according to natural laws: cosmic evolutionism, from Kant's theories, **1775;** organic evolutionism, from Darwin's theories, **1859.**

evolution, theory of, idea of natural selection was developed, **1858,** simultaneously but independently by English naturalists Alfred Russel Wallace [1823-1913] and Charles Robert Darwin [1809-1882].

exclusion principle, discovered, **1925,** by Austrian-born physicist Wolfgang Pauli [1900-1958].

Exile, The (Babylonian Captivity), period of Jewish exile, beginning **586 B.C.,** after Babylonian conquest of Jerusalem; return began after Persian conquest of Babylon, **539 B.C.**

existentialism, school of philosophy emphasizing importance of man's total experience; developed from **1920s,** especially in work of German philosophers Martin Heidegger [Sept. 26, 1889-May 26, 1976] and Karl Jaspers [Feb. 23, 1883-Feb. 26, 1969]; term coined by Kierkegaard, **c. 1845.**

Exodus, escape of ancient Hebrews from bondage in Egypt under leadership of Moses, **c. 1290 B.C.**

Exodus, second book of the Old Testament, written down, **c. 850-650 B.C.,** following Mosaic tradition.

Explorer I, first U.S. Earth satellite orbited, **1958,** by U.S. Army from Cape Canaveral, Fla.

exponential numbers, developed, **1594,** by Scottish mathematician John Napier [1550-1617].

Expo 67, world exposition at Montreal celebrated centennial of Canada's establishment as a dominion, **Apr.-Oct. 1967.**

expressionism, movement in literature and the arts, originated, **c. 1880,** dominant from **1910,** aiming to express innermost visions of artistic creator, often in startling, innovative ways.

eye bank, first established, **1944,** for corneal transplants at New York Hospital, New York City.

eyeglass lenses, designed to treat astigmatism, **c. 1827,** by English astonomer George Biddell Airy [1801-1892], to correct his own faulty vision.

Eylau (Bagrationovsk), battle of, French under Napoleon I and Russian-Prussian army fought bloody, indecisive battle in e. Prussia; 11,000 Russians killed; Napoleon's advance to Russian frontier halted, **Feb. 7-8, 1807**.

Ezekiel, Book of, Old Testament prophetic book containing prophecies delivered, from **593 B.C.**, while Prophet Ezekiel [677-570 B.C.] was in Babylonian exile.

Ezra, Book of, Old Testament book, written down, **c. 400 B.C.**.

Ezra Church, battle of, Confederate attack led by Gen. John B. Hood [June 1, 1831-Aug. 30, 1879] repulsed by Union forces at Ezra Church, Ga., **July 28, 1864**, during Gen. Sherman's march on Atlanta.

fable, story pointing moral through fictitious persons or talking animals, originated, **8th century B.C.**, with Greek poet Hesiod [c. 720 B.C.]; *Aesop's Fables*, **6th century B.C.**; medieval beast epic *Roman de Renard*, **1176**; *La Fontaine's Fables*, **1668**.

Fabian Society, influential socialist society established in Britain, **1884**; helped to establish Labour Party, **Feb. 1900**.

Faerie Queene, The, allegorical epic poem in 6 books, **1590-96**, celebrating chivalry as well as glory of Queen Elizabeth I, by English Elizabethan poet Edmund Spenser.

Fair Deal, domestic policies and programs of U.S. Pres. Truman, **1949**.

fairness doctrine, the, regulation governing radio-television broadcasting, established by U.S. Congress Radio Act, **1927**, and Communications Act, **1934** (as amended, **1959**), requiring reasonable broadcast time for public issues and chance to air opposing views.

Fair Oaks (Seven Pines), battle of, Union forces, reinforced by troops of Gen. Edwin V. Sumner [Jan. 30, 1797-Mar. 21, 1863], defeated the Confederates under Gen. Joseph E. Johnston [Feb. 3, 1807-Mar. 21, 1891] near Richmond, Va., **May 31-June 1, 1862**; Johnston was badly wounded.

fairy tale, popular tale, developed especially from **c. 1800**, in which hero or heroine "lives happily ever after" following fantastic or miraculous adventures; major European fairy-tale collections: Perrault's, **1697**; Grimm brothers', **1812-22**; Anderson's, **1835**.

Faisal (King of Iraq), assassination of, King Faisal [1935-July 14, 1958] of Iraq killed by rebels in Baghdad, **July 14, 1958**.

Faisal (King of Saudi Arabia), assassination of, King Faisal [1906?-Mar. 25, 1975] of Saudi Arabia murdered by his nephew, **Mar. 25, 1975**, who was publicly beheaded for crime, **June 18, 1975**.

Falkirk, battles of, English under King Edward I defeated the Scots under Sir William Wallace [1272?-1305] at Falkirk in what is said to be first battle in which the longbow was decisive, **July 22, 1298**; Scottish Highlanders led by Prince Charles Edward defeated English royalists during Jacobite uprising in Scotland, **Jan. 17, 1746**.

Fallen Timbers, battle of, U.S. forces under Gen. Anthony Wayne [Jan. 1, 1745-Dec. 15, 1796] defeated Indians in n.w. Ohio, helping to destroy Indian resistance in region, securing northwest frontier, and showing strength of new U.S. government, **Aug. 20, 1794**.

falling bodies, law of, demonstrated, **1590**, by Italian astronomer Galileo Galilei [1564-1642], at leaning tower of Pisa.

Fall, The (La Chute), novel, **1956**, by French writer and existentialist philosopher Albert Camus [Nov. 7, 1913-Jan. 4, 1960], Nobel Prize-winner, **1957**.

Family Compact, small, powerful group of men (mainly members of Church of

England) who controlled government of Upper Canada (Ontario), **c. 1795-1850**.

fan, electric, developed, **1882**, by American engineer Schuyler S. Wheeler [1860-1923].

Fantasia, film, **1940**, interpreting musical classics using animated cartoon techniques, collaboration between U.S. cartoonist, filmmaker, and entrepreneur Walt(er) (Elias) Disney [Dec. 5, 1901-Dec. 15, 1966] and U.S. conductor Leopold Stokowski [Apr. 18, 1882-Sept. 13, 1977].

Faraday, ship which laid Atlantic cable, **1874**; designed by German-British inventor Sir William Siemens [1823-1883].

Farber case, *New York Times* reporter Myron A. ("Barry") Farber ordered jailed, **Aug. 4, 1978**, for refusing to hand over files for defense use in murder trial and *Times* fined $5000 a day until files released; Farber freed by New Jersey Supreme Court, **Aug. 30, 1978**.

Far Eastern Triplice, Russia, Germany, and France formed investigative commission after Treaty of Shimonoseki, intervening in Japanese affairs and later Chinese, **Apr. 23, 1895**.

Farewell to Arms, A, novel, **1929**, by U.S. novelist Ernest Hemingway; Nobel Prize-winner, **1954**.

Farmer-Labor party, U.S. political party, formed **June 12, 1920**, by farm and labor representatives; dissolved after **1924**; reorganized, **1930s**, to support New Deal programs; merged with Minnesota Democratic Party, **1944**.

Farmer's Almanac, almanac, first published, **1793**, containing general-purpose information from colonial times to present; later called *Old Farmer's Almanac*.

farm tractor, gasoline engine, invented, **1892**, by American inventor John Froelich.

Farnese, Italian noble family of Rome, ruled Parma and Piacenza, **1545-1731**.

Fashoda crisis, Anglo-French diplomatic dispute over control of upper Nile River region, **1898**; Franco-Ethiopian force under Maj. Jean B. Marchand [Nov. 22, 1863-1934] seized village of Fashoda (Kodok) in s. Sudan, **July 10**; Anglo-Egyptian force under Gen. Horatio H. Kitchener claimed Fashoda, despite Marchand's presence, **Sept. 19**; fearing war, French government ordered Marchand to withdraw, **Nov. 3**; France yielded her claim to upper Nile, **Mar. 1899**.

Father Knows Best, television family situation comedy, **1954-63**; starred, U.S. actor Robert Young [Feb. 22, 1907-]; grew from radio series, same title, **1949-54**.

Fatima, Portuguese town, scene, **May 13, 1917**, of appearance of Blessed Virgin Mary to three children.

Fatimids (Fatimites), Arab dynasty in North Africa and Egypt, **909-1171**; sixth Fatimid caliph proclaimed himself a reincarnation of God, **1020**; dynasty ended when Saladin [c. 1138-Mar. 1193] entered Cairo, **1171**.

Fatti di Maggio, the, serious bread riots in Italy subdued by government troops after heavy loss of life; many socialists court-martialed, **May 3-8, 1898**.

Faust, drama based on the Faust legend; Part I published, **1808**, Part II, **1832**; by German literary figure Johann Wolfgang von Goethe. Opera, **1859**, by French composer Charles Gounod; *Damnation of Faust*, **1846**, by French composer Hector Berlioz-both works based on Goethe's *Faust*.

Fauvism, first artistic revolution of 20th century, **1899-1907**, exalting color over form; major exhibition, controversial Salon of Autumn Show, Paris, **1905**.

February Patent, new federal "constitution" issued by Emperor Franz Joseph, establishing a bicameral parliament that gave German bourgeoisie strong representation, **Feb. 1861**.

February Revolution, striking Russian workers at Petrograd (St. Petersburg) seized the capital, Russian troops mutinied, and duma established provisional government under Prince Georgi Y. Lvov [1861-1925] including Alexander Kerensky, (old-style calendar: Feb. 23-27) **Mar. 8-12, 1917**; Czar Nicholas II abdicated, **Mar. 15, 1917**.

Federal Bureau of Investigation (FBI), government division of U.S. Dept. of Justice created as Bureau of Investigation, **1908**; J. Edgar Hoover [Jan. 1, 1895-May 1, 1972] as FBI director, **1924-72**; adopted present name, **1935**.

Federal Communications Commission (FCC), independent U.S. federal agency, established **June 19, 1934**.

Federal Deposit Insurance Corporation (FDIC), U.S. Congress, created **June 16, 1933**, federal corporation to insure bank deposits.

Federal Election Campaign Act, U.S. Pres. Gerald R. Ford enacted law, **May 11, 1976**, limiting individual contributions to and primary spending of major-party presidential candidates.

Federal Emergency Relief Administration (FERA), U.S. Congress created, **May 12, 1933**, federal agency as part of New Deal program, with Harry L. Hopkins [Aug. 17, 1890-Jan. 29, 1946] as head.

Federal Firearms Act, U.S. Congress prohibited, **June 30, 1938**, interstate shipment of firearms and ammunition by unlicensed persons.

Federal Housing Adminstration (FHA), U.S. Congress created, **June 28, 1934**.

Federalist Papers, The, series of 85 articles on the American constitutional system published at regular intervals, **Oct. 1787-July 1788**, in New York press under pseudonym Publius (written by Alexander Hamilton, James Madison, and John Jay).

Federalist Party, political party, originally under leadership of Alexander Hamilton [Jan. 11, 1755-July 12, 1804] **1787-1830**; became minority party after War of 1812, opposed by New England Federalists at Hartford Convention, **Dec. 15, 1814-Jan. 4, 1815**.

Federal Power Commission (FPC), U.S. federal agency, established, **June 10, 1920**; reorganized as independent agency, **June 30, 1930**.

Federal Reserve System, central banking system of U.S. established by Federal Reserve Act, **Dec. 23, 1913**; began operation, **Nov. 1914**.

Federal Securities Act, U.S. Congress required that all new securities for sale be registered with Federal Trade Commission (FTC) and reliable information about securities be provided to investors, **May 27, 1933**.

Federal Trade Commission (FTC), U.S. Congress established, **Sept. 26, 1914**.

Federal Works Agency (FWA), U.S. federal agency formed by U.S. Pres. F. D. Roosevelt's consolidation of Public Buildings Administration, Public Roads Administration, Public Works Administration, Works Projects Administration, and U.S. Housing Authority, **July 1, 1939**; abolished, **1949**.

Fehrbellin, battle of, forces of William Frederick ("Great Elector") [Feb. 16, 1620-May 9, 1688] of Brandenburg won brilliant victory over Swedish forces of King Charles XI [Nov. 24, 1655-Apr. 5, 1697], **June 28, 1675**, ending Swedish reputation for military invincibility.

Fenian movement (Fenian Brotherhood,

Fenian Society, or Irish Republican Brotherhood), secret revolutionary society seeking Ireland's independence from Britain by force, organized in Ireland and U.S., **c. 1858**; many Fenians imprisoned after suspension of Habeas Corpus Act in Ireland, **1866**; Fenians in U.S. invaded Canada, **1866-70**.

fermium, element No. 100; discovered, **1953**, by American physicist Albert Ghiorso [1915-] and coworkers.

Ferris Wheel, invented, **1893**, by American engineer George W. G. Ferris [1858-1896].

ferronickle expansion, investigated, **1896**, by Swiss-French physicist Charles E. Guillaume [1861-1938].

fertilizer, superphosphate, first patented and manufactured, **1842**, by Irish physician James Murrat [1788-1871].

Feuillants, political club of supporters of constitutional monarchy during French Revolution, **1791**; suppressed by Jacobin Club, **1792**.

Fez, Treaty of, sultan of Morocco agreed to a French protectorate of Morocco, **Mar. 30, 1912**; Franco-Spanish agreement set up Spanish protectorate and international zone of Tangier in Morocco, **Nov. 27, 1912**.

Fibber McGee and Molly, radio comedy series, **1935-57**, featuring Fibber, with his crammed-full closet, foiled by wife, Molly.

fiber glass fabric, first developed and displayed, **1893**, at Columbian Exposition by American glass manufacturer Edward D. Libbey [1854-1925].

Fiddler on the Roof, musical, **1964**, holds record for second-longest Broadway run, 3242 performances, from **September 22, 1964**.

Fidelio, opera, first performed, Vienna, **Nov. 20, 1805**; only opera of Ludwig van Beethoven; composer's final version, **1814**.

Fifteen, The, Jacobites revolted under the earl of Mar, **Sept. 6, 1715-16**; Jacobite pretender to the throne fled to France, **Feb. 5, 1716**.

Fifteenth Amendment to U.S. Constitution, ratified, **Mar. 30, 1870**, prohibited any state to deny suffrage to anyone because of race, color, or previous condition of servitude.

Fifty-four Forty or Fight, famous political slogan adopted by supporters of James K. Polk [Nov. 2, 1795-June 15, 1849] and of American claims to Oregon territory to 54 40' parallel, **1844-48**.

Figaro, Le, Parisian daily newspaper, began publication, **1854**.

Fiji, archipelago island nation in southwest Pacific; gained its independence from Britain, **Oct. 10, 1970**.

file (tool), first machine-made file in U.S., **1864**, by American manufacturer William T. Nicholson [1834-1893].

filioque **(Latin, *and the Son*)**, Christian dogmatic formula, first added to Creed, Third Council of Toledo, **589**, expressing double procession of the Holy Spirit; not accepted by Orthodox Church and one cause of schism with West, **1054**.

film, paper-backed, first flexible film patented, **1884**, by American inventor George Eastman [1854-1932].

film projector, invented, **1895**, by American inventor Thomas A. Edison [1847-1931].

Finality Men, Northerners who accepted Compromise of 1850 as final settlement of slavery issue in U.S., **1850-61**.

fin-de-siecle, term used to describe period in literature and the arts, **c. 1880-1900**, characterized by preciousness and decadence; from French, "end of the century."

Finisterre Cape, battles of, British navy defeated French navy off Cape Finisterre on n.w. coast of Spain during the War of the Austrian Succession, giving Great Britain undisputed supremacy of the Atlantic, **Oct. 2, 1747**; British warships attacked and destroyed part of French-Spanish fleet off Cape Finisterre during Napoleonic Wars, **July 22, 1805**.

Finlandia, musical tone poem, **1899**, by Finnish composer Jean Sibelius [Dec. 8, 1865-Sept. 20, 1957].

Finnegans Wake, experimental novel, **1939**, by Irish writer James Joyce.

Firebird, The, ballet, **1910**, based on motifs from Russian fairy tales, music by Russian-U.S. composer Igor Stravinsky [June 17, 1882-Apr. 6, 1971]; originally choreographed, Paris, by Russian-U.S. choreographer-dancer Michel Fokine (born Mikhail Mikhailovich Fokine) [Apr. 26, 1880-Aug. 22, 1942].

fire engine, first in U.S. constructed, **1654**, by American ironmaker Joseph Jencks [1632-1717].

fire engine, steam, first practical one constructed, **1852**, for Cincinnati, Ohio by American inventor Alexander B. Latta [1821-1865].

fire engine system, electric, patented, **1885**, by American engineer Schuyler S. Wheeler [1860-1923].

Fireside Chats, friendly radio talks by Pres. Franklin D. Roosevelt to instill confidence in U.S. economy during the Depression and in U.S. war effort during WW II, **1933-45**.

Fireworks Music, The (Royal), suite for orchestra, **1749**, by German-English composer George Frederick Handel, written for celebration of cessation of hostilities between Britain and France, held in Green Park, London, **April 27, 1749**.

first folio, first published collection of Shakespeare's plays, **1623**, compiled by fellow actors; included all authentic plays except Pericles, **1608-09**; facsimile edition published, **1902**.

Fischer-Spassky match, Robert J. ("Bobby") Fischer [Mar. 9, 1943-] defeated Russian Boris Spassky [Jan. 30, 1937-] in chess match at Reykjavik, Iceland, **July-Sept. 1, 1972**, to become first American world chess champion; Fischer resigned title, **June 1974**, in dispute with rules of the International Federation of Chess.

Fisher's Hill, battle of, Union forces under Gen. Philip H. Sheridan [Mar. 6, 1831-Aug. 5, 1888] defeated Confederate army under Gen. Jubal A. Early in the Shenandoah Valley, **Sept. 19 and 21, 1864**.

fishing, largest freshwater catch of any type was 360 lb. white sturgeon on Snake River, Idaho, **Apr. 24, 1956**; largest catch (fresh- and saltwater) of any type was 2664 lb. white shark off Ceduna, Australia, **Apr. 21, 1959**.

Fishing Creek, battle of, British forces under Col. Banastre Tarleton routed American patriots at Fishing Creek, Ky., **Aug. 18, 1780**.

Fiume question, city of Fiume (Rijeka) on Adriatic claimed by Italy, **Apr. 14, 1919**; Italian compromise to make Fiume buffer state with Yugoslavia, **May 30, 1919**; Treaty of Rapallo made Fiume independent city, **Nov. 12, 1920**; Italian fascists seized control of Fiume, **Mar. 17, 1922**; Treaty of Rome gave Fiume to Italy and its suburb Susak to Yugoslavia, **Jan. 27, 1924**.

Five Classics, works in the Confucian canon, basis of traditional Chinese education: Books of Changes, **1400-1100 B.C.**; of Documents, **1027-256 B.C.**; of Odes, **600 B.C.**; of Rites, **1st century B.C.**; plus *Spring and Autumn Annals*, **722-481 B.C.**

Five Forks, battle of, Union forces under Gen. Sheridan won major victory over Confederate forces under Gen. George E. Pickett [Jan. 25, 1825-July 30, 1875] at crossroads near Dinwiddie Courthouse, Va.; Gen.

Lee's Confederate army placed in peril, **Apr. 1, 1865**.

Five-Mile Act, Cavalier Parliament forbade any nonconforming clergyman or teacher to come within 5 miles of a city, town, or any place where they had been a minister, **Oct. 1665**.

flag, U.S., Grand Union flag of 13 stripes, first U.S. flag, raised by Gen. Washington at Cambridge, Mass, **Jan. 2, 1776**; U.S. legend said Betsy Ross [Jan. 1, 1752-Jan. 30, 1836] made first American flag, **1776**; new flag with 13 stripes and 13 stars adopted by Continental Congress, **June 14, 1777**; contained 15 stripes and 15 stars, **1795-1818**; with 13 stripes and number of stars equal to number of U.S. states, since **1818**.

flagellants, medieval sectarians **c. 1260**, holding that wrath of God can be appeased only by public self-flagellation; public processions recurred during Black Death, **1348**; condemned as heretics, **1349**, by Pope Clement VI (born Pierre Roger) [c. 1291-Dec. 6, 1352].

flash spectroscopy, developed, from **1949**, by English chemists Ronald G. Norrish [1897-1978], George Porter [1920-] and German chemist Manfred Eigen [1927-].

flat iron, electric, patented, **1882**, by American inventor Henry W. Seeley of New York City.

Fledermaus, Die (The Bat), operetta, **1874**, by "waltz king," Austrian composer Johann Strauss, Jr.

Fleurus, battles of, Protestant armies defeated Spanish-Catholic forces at Fleurus in present-day Belgium, during Thirty Years' War, **Aug. 29, 1622**; by brilliant tactics, French forces under the duke of Luxembourg routed large allied army during the War of the Grand Alliance, **June 30, 1690**; French won decisive victory over Austrian forces, forcing Austria to evacuate its forces from the Netherlands, **June 26, 1794**.

Flight from Egypt, Moses led his Hebrew people out of bondage in Egypt to the edge of Canaan, **c. early 13th century B.C.**

flood-light system, first used, **1885**, to light Statue of Liberty; invented by American engineer James Wood [1856-1928].

Florence Cathedral, cathedral, called Duomo, begun, **1296**; dome, **1420-36**, a double-shelled vault designed by Filippo Brunelleschi; 269-foot-high campanile begun, **1334**, by Giotto; completed, **c.1358**; baptistery, adjacent to Florence Cathedral, noted for bronze-relief doors, cast **1403-24**, and **1425-52**, by Renaissance sculptor Lorenzo Ghiberti [1378-Dec. 1, 1455].

FLORENCE, (from San Miniato.)

Florence, Council of, 17th ecumenical council of the Catholic Church, **1438-45**, convened Ferrara, transferred to Florence, **1439**; decree of union with Orthodox Church signed, **July, 1439**; abrogated, **1472**, by Synod of Constantinople.

Florida, purchased from Spain for $5 million by treaty, **Feb. 22, 1819**; admitted to the Union as 27th state, **Mar. 3, 1845**; seceded from the Union, **Jan. 10, 1861**; readmitted to the Union, **June 25, 1868**.

fluorine, isolated, **1886**, by French chemist Henri Moissan [1852-1907].

Flushing Remonstrance, townspeople of Long Island settlement of Flushing issued declaration of religious tolerance to Peter

Stuyvesant [c. 1610-Feb. 1672], **Dec. 27, 1657**.

flying wing, patented, **1910**, by German airplane engineer Hugo Junkers [1859-1935].

FM (frequency modulation), radio broadcast technique developed, **1925**, by American elecronics engineer Edwin Howard Armstrong [1890-1954].

fodder conservation, methods discovered, from **1920**, by Finnish biochemist Artturi I. Virtanen [1895-].

foghorn, steam operated, invented, **1859**, by Canadian engineer Robert Foulis [1796-1866].

Focsani, battle of, Russian-Austrian army attacked and soundly defeated Ottoman Turks at Focsani in Moldavia (part of present-day Rumania), **Aug. 1, 1789**.

Folies-Bergere, Parisian music hall, opened, **1869**, featuring partially nude girls in lavish setting.

Fontainebleau Palace, French royal palace, built **1528-31**, in elegant mannerist style.

Fontainebleau, Treaty of, secret agreement between Napoleon and Spain to conquer and partition Portugal, **Oct. 27, 1807**.

Fontenoy, battle of, French army under Maurice de Saxe won great victory against combined British, Dutch, and Hanoverian army under the duke of Cumberland, **May 11, 1745**.

food, irradiated, first large-scale use of radioisotopes in irradiating bacon begun, **1966**, at Brookhaven National Laboratory for U.S.Army.

food preservation (glass jars), invented, **1804**, by French chef Francois Appert [?-c. 1840].

football, first intercollegiate football game played at New Brunswick, N.J., **1869**; Intercollegiate Football Association (composed of Columbia, Princeton, Rutgers, and Yale) standardized rules, **1873**.

Foraker act, U.S. Congress established, **Mar. 12, 1900**, civil government for newly acquired Puerto Rico, which became an unorganized territory with an appointive governor.

force bills, Pres. Jackson empowered to use army and navy to collect tariff objected to by South Carolina, **Mar. 2, 1833**; U.S. government enforced Fifteenth Amendment, penalizing those preventing citizens (especially Negroes) from voting, **May 31, 1870**; U.S. government declared acts of "armed combinations tantamount to rebellion" to deal with actions of the Ku Klux Klan; U.S. Pres. Grant empowered to suspend habeas corpus in lawless areas, **Apr. 20, 1871**.

Ford, attempted assassinations of, U.S. Pres. Gerald R. Ford [July 14, 1913-] escaped assassination attempt by Lynette Alice ("Squeaky") Fromme [1948-], member of Charles Manson "family," in Sacramento, Calif., **Sept. 5, 1975**; Ford escaped another attempt on his life made by Sara Jane Moore [Feb. 15, 1930-] in San Francisco, **Sept. 22, 1975**.

Fordney-McCumber Act, U.S. Congress raised duties on manufactured and farm products and introduced principle of flexible tariff for first time, **Sept. 21, 1922**.

Foreign Legion, French, volunteer regiment in French army created for pacification of Algeria, **1831**; reorganized, **1946**; headquarters moved from Algeria to southern France, **1962**.

Foreign Service, U.S., federal organization of agents, consuls, and diplomats in U.S., established when Congress combined the consular and diplomatic services under the Rogers Act, **1924**.

Fornovo (Taro), battle of, about 10,000

French troops of King Charles VIII defeated 40,000-man Italian army, **July 6, 1495,** ending Cisalpine military glory.

Forrestal, largest warship ever built, aircraft carrier U.S.S. *Forrestal* (almost 60,000 tons), launched at Newport News, Va., **Dec. 11, 1954.**

Forsyte Saga, The, series of novels, **1906-22**; work of British author John Galsworthy [Aug. 14, 1867-Jan. 31, 1933]; Nobel Prize-winner, **1932.** BBC television series, produced, London, **1967,** based on Galsworthy's novels; PBS-U.S. broadcast, **1969-70.**

Fort Astoria, site in Oregon of American fur-trading post established by John Jacob Astor [July 17, 1763-Mar. 29, 1848], **1811.**

Fort Stikine **explosion, great,** British cargo ship *Fort Stikine* carrying war explosives, sulfur, resin, fish, and cotton blew up in harbor of Bombay, India, killing more than 1000 persons and totally closing down the port; one of worst disasters of WW II, **Apr. 14, 1944.**

Fortune, U.S. magazine, founded, **1930,** dealing primarily with business, finance, and industry, established by U.S. publisher Henry R(obinson) Luce [Apr. 1, 1898-Feb. 28, 1967]

Fortune Bay incident, U.S. fishing ships attacked by Canadians at Fortune Bay, Newfoundland, in violation of U.S.-British treaty, **Jan. 1878.**

Fourty-five, the, Jacobites marched into Edinburgh and then into England, led by the Young Pretender Bonnie Prince Charlie, **1745-46.**

Forum, marketplace and civic center of ancient Roman towns: Roman Forum so functioned, from **c. 500 B.C.**; Temple of Saturn built there, **497 B.C.**; Temple of Castor and Pollux, **484 B.C.**

For Whom the Bell Tolls, novel, **1940,** about American idealist fighting on the Republican side in Spanish Civil War, by U.S. author Ernest Hemingway, Nobel Prize-winner, **1954.**

Foucault pendulum, experiment to prove Earth rotates on its axis, conducted, **1851,** by French physicist Jean Foucault [1819-1868].

Foundling Hospital, first true Renaissance building, Florence, **1419,** designed by Italian architect Filippo Brunelleschi.

foundling hospitals, first modern institution for unwanted children established in Milan, Italy, **787**; London Foundling Hospital founded by Thomas Coram [1668?-1751], **1739**; first U.S. foundling hospital, St. Vincent's Infant Asylum, founded by Roman Catholic nuns in Baltimore, **1856.**

Fountainhead, The, novel, **1943,** about American Nietzschean-style "superman" architect, by novelist and "objectivist" philosopher Ayn Rand.

Four Books, Chinese classics, basis of classical education from Sung Dynasty, **960-1279**; included *Analects, Great Learning, The Mean,* and *The Mencius*; used as basis for civil service examinations, until **1905.**

Fourdrinier machine, (papermaking) invented, **1799,** by French inventor Louis Robert.

Four Freedoms, in speech before U.S. Congress, **Jan. 6, 1941,** Pres. F. D. Roosevelt enumerated the *Four Freedoms* he felt should prevail in postwar world.

4-H Clubs, U.S. agricultural organizations for boys and girls from 9 to 19 years of age; first such club began in Macoupin County, Ill., **1900**; national organization established, **1914.**

400 Blows, The (Les Quatre Cents Coups), "new-wave," French film, **1959,** about twelve-year-old boy's wanderings in Paris, directed by Francois Truffaut.

Four Hundred, the, democracy of Athens was overthrown temporarily by oligarchy of

400 citizens, **July 411 B.C.**; deposed by moderates who established the so-called Government of the 5000, **Oct. 411 B.C.**

Fourmies, massacre of, French troops fired on crowd of laborers demonstrating for social reform and killed men, women, and children, **May 1, 1891.**

Four Seasons, The (Le Quattro Stagioni), 4 concerti grossi, c. **1720-23,** one for each season, by Italian baroque composer Antonio Vivaldi [c. 1675-July 28, 1741].

Fourteen Points, fourteen conditions for a just and lasting peace presented by U.S. Pres. Wilson in speech before Congress, **Jan. 8, 1918.**

Fourteenth Amendment to U.S. Constitution, ratified, **July 28, 1868,** granted citizenship to U.S. Negroes and nullified all state debts incurred during Civil War.

Four Year Plan, Nazi plan under Adolf Hitler initiated, **Oct. 19, 1936,** to make Germany self-sufficient and independent in the event of war.

Four-Year-Tenure Act, U.S. Congress set, **May 15, 1820,** four years as the term of most appointive officials in the federal government.

France, (see French Republics, French Revolution, Vichy Government.)

Franciscans, religious order of friars, founded, **1209,** by St. Francis of Assisi; rule of poverty, chastity and obedience, emphasizing poverty and dependence on alms; approved by Holy See, **1223.**

francium, element No. 87; discovered, **1939,** by French scientist Marguerite Perey.

Franco-Prussian War, armed conflict between France and Prussia, **July 19, 1870-Jan. 28, 1871;** Otto von Bismarck [Apr. 1, 1815-July 30, 1898] goaded France with Ems Dispatch, **July 13, 1870;** French routed at Sedan, **Sept. 1, 1870;** creation of German Empire proclaimed at Versailles, **Jan. 18, 1871;** Paris fell to Prussians, **Jan. 28, 1871;** formally ended by Treaty of Frankfurt, **May 21, 1871.**

Franklin, State of, independent state formed by settlers, **1784-88,** in region ceded to U.S. by North Carolina (present-day eastern Tennessee); adopted own constitution, **Nov. 1785.**

Frank, Manor of, a special territory with privilege of self-government granted by William Penn to Welsh settlers in Pennsylvania, **Mar. 20, 1682.**

Frankenhausen, battle of, armed forces from ruling houses of Brunswick, Saxony, and Hesse crushed great peasant revolt in Germany at Frankenhausen, **May 15, 1525.**

Frankenstein, horror novel, **1818,** about man who creates an artificial monster, by English writer Mary (Wollstonecraft) Shelley [Aug. 30, 1797-Feb. 1, 1851]. Horror film, **1931,** first of series depicting adventures of Frankenstein's monster, played by English-U.S. actor Boris Karloff [Nov. 23, 1887-Feb. 3, 1969]; sequels include *The Ghost of Frankenstein,* **1945.**

Frankfurt Parliament, national assembly of German states convened at Frankfurt to plan the unification of Germany, **May 18, 1848;** adopted federal constitution of German states, excluding Austria, and chose Frederick William IV [Oct. 15, 1795-Jan. 2, 1861] of Prussia as emperor (he refused crown), **Mar. 1849;** representatives withdrew from Frankfurt, and a "rump parliament" assembled at Stuttgart, **June 18, 1849.**

Frankfurt, Treaty of, ratified preliminary Treaty of Versailles, officially ending Franco-Prussian War, **May 21, 1871.**

Franklin stove, invented, c. **1740,** by American statesman-inventor Benjamin Franklin [1706-1790]; called "Pennsylvania Fireplace."

Franks, Germanic tribe that conquered Gaul, **5th century;** united under Clovis I [c. 466-511], **481;** kingdom of w. Franks became France and kingdom of e. Franks Germany after Treaty of Mersen, **870**.

Frastenz, battle of, Swiss confederation of cantons routed Swabian forces of Holy Roman Empire at Frastenz on disputed e. frontier with Austria, **Apr. 20, 1499**.

Frederiksborg, Treaty of, Denmark restored all its conquests in return for payment from Sweden; ducal and royal Schleswig united under Danish crown, **1720**.

Fredericksburg, battle of, Union army under Gen. Ambrose E. Burnside [May 23, 1824-Sept. 13, 1881] suffered overwhelming defeat by Confederates under Gen. James Longstreet at Fredericksburg, Va., **Dec. 13, 1862**.

Freedmen's Bureau, agency established by U.S. government to help newly freed Negroes in South after Civil War, **Mar. 3, 1865**.

free fall, explained, **c. 1658**, by Italian astronomer and physicist Galileo [1564-1642].

Freeman's Farm, battle of, American revolutionary forces, commanded by Gen. Horatio Gates [c. 1728-Apr. 10, 1806], checked British southward advance toward Albany, **Sept. 19, 1777**.

Freedom of Information Act (FOIA), U.S. law enacted by Congress, **July 1966**, to provide freer public access to government information; amended and strengthened, **Feb. 19, 1975**.

Freedom Riders, members and supporters of CORE who rode buses through the South to force integration on interstate bus lines, **1961**; attacked by mob in Birmingham, Ala., **May 14, 1961**.

Fredonian Rebellion, American settlers tried unsuccessfully to make Texas independent from Mexico and to establish state of Fredonia, **1826-27**.

Freemasonry, quasi-religious brotherhood, 1700s, grew out of guilds of masons, from **12th century**.

Freeport Doctrine, political doctrine of U.S. Sen. Stephen A. Douglas to reconcile his belief in territorial sovereignty with Dred Scott case decision, expressed during Lincoln-Douglas debate at Freeport, Ill., **Aug. 1858**.

Free Presbyterian Church of Ulster,

ultra-Protestant sect formed by Northern Irish religious and political leader Ian Paisley [Apr. 6, 1926-], **1951**; civil riots and street fighting between Protestants and Catholics in Londonderry and Belfast, **1966-69**, fomented in part by Paisley's nationalist Protestants.

Free-Soil Party, U.S. political party created to oppose extension of slavery in new territories acquired from Mexico, **1847**; merged into Republican Party, **1854**.

Freiberg, battle of, last battle of Seven Years' War; Prussians defeated Austrian-Saxon forces at Freiberg, southwest of Dresden, **Oct. 29, 1762**.

freight car, refrigerated, patented, **1868**, by American inventor William Davis [1812-1868].

French Academy (*Academie Francaise*), learned society of French literary notables, founded, **1635**, by Cardinal Richelieu [Sept. 9, 1585-Dec. 4, 1642].

French and Indian War, conflict waged in North America between British and French allied with the Indians, **1754-63**; British forces under Gen. Edward Braddock [1695-July 13, 1755] failed to take Fort Duquesne (Pittsburgh, Penn.), **July 9, 1755**; British seized Fort Louisbourg (Louisburg, Nova Scotia), **July 26, 1758**; British forced French out of Fort Duquesne, which they renamed Fort Pitt, **Nov. 25, 1758**; British Gen. Amherst seized Fort Carillon (Ticonderoga) from French, **July 26, 1759**; British defeated French at battle on Plains of Abraham and seized Quebec, **Sept. 18, 1759;** war ended by Treaty of Paris, **Feb. 10, 1763.**

French Community, political union of France with her overseas possessions (especially African) created by constitution of new Fifth French Republic, **Oct. 5, 1958;** states of French West Africa and French Equatorial Africa became independent, **1960.**

French Empire, the first, Napoleon Bonaparte (Napoleon I) made France the controlling nation of Europe until he was overthrown at Waterloo and abdicated, **May 20, 1804-June 22, 1815.**

French Republics, First French Republic after abolition of monarchy, **Sept. 21, 1792-1804,** followed by First Empire under Napoleon I, **1804-15;** Second Republic, **Feb. 24, 1848-52,** followed by Second Empire under Napoleon III, **1852-70;** Third Republic, **Sept. 4, 1870-1946;** Fourth Republic, **Oct. 13, 1946-58;** Fifth Republic, **Oct. 5, 1958-now,** with Charles de Gaulle [Nov. 22, 1890-Nov. 9, 1970] as president, **Dec. 21, 1958-Apr. 28, 1969.**

French Revolution, political upheaval in France that overthrew French monarchy, brought on French Revolutionary Wars, and ended at start of Napoleonic era, **1789-99;** Estates-General convened at Versailles to present grievances to crown, **May 5, 1789;** third estate proclaimed itself National Assembly, **June 17, 1789;** Paris mob stormed the Bastille, **July 14, 1789;** Assembly adopted the Declaration of the Rights of Man and Citizen, **Aug. 26, 1789;** King Louis XVI arrested at Varennes, **June 20-21, 1791;** Declaration of Pillnitz, **Aug. 27-1791;** French Revolutionary Wars began, **Apr. 20, 1792;** Swiss Guards massacred at Tuileries palace, **Aug. 10, 1792;** National Convention abolished French monarchy and set up First Republic, **Sept. 21, 1792;** King Louis XVI executed, **Jan. 21, 1793;** Robespierre triumphed during Reign of Terror over Girondists, **May 1793-Aug. 1794;** National Convention arrested and guillotined Robespierre, **July 27, 1794;** new French constitution created the Directoire, which ended with Napoleon Bonaparte's coup d'etat, **Oct. 26, 1795-Nov. 9, 1799.**

French Revolutionary Wars, general European conflict brought on by French Revolution and developed into French wars of conquest, **1792-1802;** Austrians and Prussians make Declaration of Pillnitz to restore French King Louis XVI, **Aug. 27, 1791;** French won battle of Jemappes, **Nov. 6, 1792;** King Louis XVI executed, **Jan. 21, 1793;** conterrevolutionaries routed out during Reign of Terror, **1793-94;** Napoleon's successful Italian campaign ended with Treaty of Campo Formio, **Oct. 17, 1797;** disunity between Austrians and Russians resulted in French victory at Zurich, **Sept. 1799;** Russians under Alexander V. Suvorov [Nov. 13, 1729-May 6, 1800] made epic retreat across Alps back to Russia, **Sept.-Oct. 1799;** Napoleon became First Consul, **Nov. 1799;** French army under Napoleon won at Marengo, **June 14, 1800;** French won at Hohenlinden, **Dec. 3, 1800;** peace Treaty of Luneville accepted by Austria, **Feb. 9, 1801;** British forced French to surrender in Egypt, **Aug. 1801;** British under Lord Nelson destroyed Danish fleet at Copenhagen, **Apr. 2, 1801;** warweary British accepted Treaty of Amiens, restoring all conquests to France, **Mar. 27, 1802.**

French Union, political union of France with her overseas possessions created by constitution of new Fourth French Republic **Oct. 13, 1946;** Vietnam, Laos, and Cambodia withdrew from Union, **1954;** Morocco and Tunisia became independent, **1958;** replaced by French Community, **Oct. 5, 1958.**

Freon, (low-boiling fluorine compounds) developed, **1930,** by American chemist Thomas Midgley [1889-1944] and coworkers.

Freudianism, theory of human behavior based on use of psychoanalysis and discovery of role of the unconscious mind, **1882— 1915,** by Austrian physician Sigmund Freud.

Friedland (Pravdinsk), battle of, French led by Napoleon I, aided by Poles, Saxons, Dutch, and Italians, won major victory over Russians along Alle River at Friedland in Prussia; 11,000 Russians killed, unknown thousands drowned in river, **June 14, 1807.**

Friends, Society of, religious body, called "Quakers," founded **c. 1652,** by English pacifist and anti-slavery religious leader George Fox [July, 1624-Jan. 13, 1691].

Friesland flood, great, more than 100,000 persons reputedly drowned in sea flood in Friesland, Holland, **1228.**

Fries's Rebellion (*Hot Water War*), armed Pennsylvania Germans, led by John Fries [1750?-1818], rebelled against federal property taxes, pouring scalding water on collectors and assessors before being suppressed, **Feb. 1799;** Fries, convicted of treason, pardoned by Pres. John Adams, **1800.**

frigate, steam, launched, **1815,** by American inventor Robert Fulton [1765-1815].

STEAM-FRIGATE OF 1850.

Frogs, The (Batrachoi), comedy, **405 B.C.,** by Greek dramatist Aristophanes.

Fronde, political party in France during minority of Louis XIV; opposed to Cardinal Mazarin and the court, **1648-53.**

Frontenac, Fort, British colonial forces in America surprised and captured French-held Fort Frontenac (Kingston, Ontario), **Aug. 27, 1758.**

fuel cell, biochemical, developed, **1961,** by American microbiologist Frederick D. Sisler [1916-1980].

fuel gas, process of manufacturing devised, **1869,** by American chemist Henry Wurtz [1828-1910].

Fuentes de Onoro, battle of, British army under Gen. Wellington won bloody battle against French under Marshal Andre

Massena [May 6, 1758-Apr. 4, 1817] at Fuentes de Onoro in w. Spain, **May 5, 1811.**

Fugger, House of, Swabian family of merchants and financiers prominent in Augsburg, Germany and central Europe, **15th-16th centuries;** Jakob Fugger ("Jakob the Rich") [1459-1525] lent huge sums to Holy Roman Emperor Maximilian I, **c. 1510;** richest family in Europe under Raimund Fugger [1489-1535] and Anton Fugger [1493-1560], **c. 1520-60.**

fugitive slave laws, enacted by U.S. government to provide for return of escaped Negro slaves to their respective states, **1793, 1850.**

fugue, polyphonic musical form, developed, **1700s.**

Fundamentalism, religious movement in Protestantism, from **c. 1890,** based on literal interpretation of the Bible in reaction to evolutionism and biblical criticism; Scopes trial about teaching evolution in schools, **1925.**

Funny Girl, musical, **1964,** about life of entertainer Fanny Brice, played by U.S. actress and singer Barbra Streisand [Apr. 24, 1942-].

furnace, electric, invented, **1861,** by German-British inventor Sir William Siemens [1823-1883]; patented, **1896,** by American inventor Edward G. Acheson [1856-1931].

furnace, hot air, invented, for use in homes, **1821,** by American inventor Zachariah Allen [1795-1882].

furnace, hot blast, developed, **1828**, by Scottish inventor James B. Neilson [1792-1865].

fusion power, first proposed, **c. 1930**, by American chemist William D. Harkins [1873-1951].

Fussen, Treaty of, Austria restored all conquered territory to Bavaria; elector of Bavaria renounced all pretensions to Austrian throne, **Apr. 22, 1745**.

Futurism, radical movement in literature and art, initiated, **1909**, advocating liberation from all restraints, formal or traditional; Cubist-Futurist manifesto, **1912**.

Gabon, republic in western Africa, gained its independence from France, **Aug. 17, 1960**.

Gabriel's Revolt, Negro slave revolt near Richmond, Va., incited by black known as "General Gabriel" and put down by state militia, **1800**.

Gacy case, worst mass slayings in U.S. history; John Wayne Gacy [1942-] arrested and charged with murder, **Dec. 22, 1978**; Gacy told police of committing murders between **Jan. 1972** and **Dec. 1978**, after 28 bodies of boys and young men found in crawlspace under his house, 3 others found in his garage, 4 in nearby river; Gacy convicted by jury of 33 counts of murder and of deviate sexual assault, **Mar. 12, 1980**, and **Mar. 13, 1980**, sentenced to die in electric chair.

gadolinium, element No. 64; discovered, **1880**, by Swiss chemist Charles de Marignac [1817-1894].

Gadsden Purchase, U. S. government bought southern parts of present-day New Mexico and Arizona from Mexico for $10 million, **Dec. 30, 1853**.

gag rule, rule to limit speech, discussion, or legislation, adopted by U. S. House of Representatives to table all antislavery petitions and motions, **May 26, 1836**.

Galatians, Letter to the, New Testament book, **c. 54**, epistle to Christians in Galatia, Asia Minor, by St. Paul the Apostle.

Gallican Confession, profession of faith, **1559**, issued by First National Synod of Protestants at Paris, drafted by John Calvin, containing central Calvinistic doctrines; ratified by Synod of La Rochelle, **1571**.

Galicia, historic region in Poland passed to Austria, **1772**; Polish inhabitants enjoyed limited autonomy, **1861-1918**; Poland wrested w. Galicia from Austria, e. Galicia incorporated into Ukraine, **1939**.

gall acids, steroid structure of, basic research conducted, **1912-1920**, by German chemist H. O. Wieland [1877-1957].

Gallic Wars, campaigns in Gaul by Julius Caesar during his two terms as proconsul, **58-51 B.C.**; Caesar pacified Belgica (roughly Belgium), **57 B.C.**; Caesar defeated the Britons (in present-day Britain), **54 B.C.**; Caesar defeated the Gauls led by Vercingetorix [d. 46 B.C.], **52 B.C.**

Gallic Wars, Commentaries on the, historical book, **c. 58-44 B.C.**; narrates campaigns, beginning **58 B.C.**, by which Gaul was made Roman; by Julius Caesar.

Gallipoli Campaign, expedition by the Allies during WW I to seize the Dardanelles and Bosporus straits and Constantinople and to open a route through Black Sea to Russia, **Apr. 1915-Jan. 1916**; Turks repulsed allied landing at Suvla, **Aug. 1915**; poor allied communications and stubborn Turkish resistance forced Allies to abandon campaign, **Jan. 9, 1916**.

gallium, element No. 31; discovered, **1875**, by French chemist Paul E. Lecoq de Boisbaudran [1873-1912].

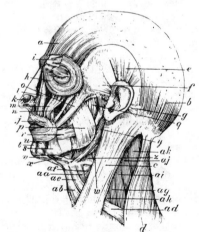

Muscles of Human Head, Face, and Neck.

galvanic electric impulses (in muscles), first investigated, **1771**, by Italian anatomist Luigi Galvani [1737-1798].

galvanometer, moving coil, first invented, **1836**, by English electrician William Sturgeon [1783-1850].

Galveston tidal wave, great, hurricane-swept waters from Gulf of Mexico inundated Galveston Island, Tex., killing approx. 6000 persons and causing more than $17 million in property damage, **Sept. 8, 1900**.

Gambia, republic in w. Africa, first made a British crown colony, **1843**; became an independent country within the British Commonwealth of Nations, **Feb. 18, 1965**; proclaimed itself a republic, **Apr. 24, 1970**.

games, theory of, advanced, **1944**, by Hungarian-American mathematician John von Neumann [1903-1957] and Austrian economist Oskar Morgenstern [1902-]; study founded early, **1920's** by French mathematician Felix E. Borel [1871-1956].

gamma globulin, complex antibody deciphered, **1969**, by U.S. physician Gerard M. Edelman [1929-].

Gandamak, Treaty of, British took control of the Khyber Pass for annual payment to emir of Afghanistan; all Afghan foreign relations to be conducted through British Indian government, **May 16, 1879**.

Gandhi, assassination of, Indian political leader Mohandas Karamchand Gandhi [Oct. 2, 1869-Jan. 30, 1948] shot to death by Nathuran Vinayak Godse in New Delhi, India, **Jan. 30, 1948**.

Gandhi's fasts, Gandhi's 'fast unto death'

in prison, ended when India's 'untouchables' gained larger number of representatives in government, **Sept. 20-26, 1932**; this and second fast by Gandhi **May 8-29, 1933**, aroused public against caste system in India.

garbage disposer, mechanical, invented, **1935**, by American inventor William Merrill.

Garfield, assassination of, U.S. President James A. Garfield [Nov. 19, 1831-Sept. 19, 1881] shot after only four months in office by Charles J. Guiteau [c. 1840-June 30, 1882], disappointed office seeker, **July 2, 1881**; Garfield died two and half months later, **Sept. 19**.

Gargantua and Pantagruel, four-volume Renaissance satire, published, **1534-52**, by French scholar and monk Francois Rabelais [c. 1490-Apr. 9, 1533].

Garigliano River, site near Cassino, central Italy, of Italian victory over French forces of King Louis XII, **Dec. 29, 1503**; great battleground during Allied drive on Rome in WW II, **Nov. 1943-May 1944**.

Garrisonians, fierce supporters of William Lloyd Garrison [Dec. 10, 1805-May 24, 1879], denouncing slavery and any government that favored it **c. 1830-65**.

Garter, Order of the, famous order of chivalry of royal foundation established by the English, **c. 1344**.

Garwood case, U.S. Marine Pfc. Robert Garwood [1946-], who spent 14 years behind enemy lines in Vietnam, court-martialed and convicted, **Feb. 5, 1981**, of collaborating with the Viet Cong; Garwood reduced to private, given a dishonorable discharge, and set free, **Feb. 13, 1981**.

gas engine, noncompression, patented, **1846**, by American inventor Stuart Perry [1814-1890].

gas engine, rotary-valve, first built, **1903**, by American inventor Elwood Haynes [1857-1925].

gases, concept introduced, **c. 1635**, by Flemish alchemist Jan B. van Helmont [1577-1644].

gases, inert, discovered, **1894, 1898**, by Scottish chemist William Ramsay [1852-1916].

gases, therapeutic use of, pioneered, **1792**, by English physician Thomas Beddoes [1760-1808].

gas gangrene, bacillus discovered, **1892**,

by American pathologist William H. Welch [1850-1934].

gas lights, introduced, **1792**, by British engineer William Murdock [1754-1839], using oil from coal; in **1802**, Murdock began installing gas lights for industry. Baltimore established the first gas company in the U.S., for purpose of lighting its streets, **1817**.

gas mantle, incandescent, patented, **1885**, by Austrian chemist Baron Carl Auer von Welsbach [1858-1929].

gas mask, prototype designed for use, **1915**, by Scottish scientist John S. Haldane [1860-1936].

gasoline, high-octane, invented, **1930**, by Russian chemist Vladimir N. Ipatieff [1867-1952].

Gastein, Convention of, Austria assumed administration of Holstein, Prussia that of Schleswig, **Aug. 14, 1865**.

Gazette of the United States, newspaper, founded, New York, **1789**; moved to Philadelphia and became daily, **1793**; later called *North American and United States Gazette* and published, until **1847**.

gazetteer, dictionary of place names, first one printed in English: *The Gazetteer's Interpreter: Being a Geographical Index*, **1703**.

Gazette, La, one of first Parisian newspapers, began publication, **1631**; published under name *La Gazette de France*, from **1752**.

Gaziantep (Aintab), ancient city (world's oldest, supposedly) founded in southern Turkey, **c. 3650 B.C.**

Geiger counter, prototype instrument developed, **1908**, by German physicist Hans Wilhelm Geiger [1882-1945].

Gelasian Sacramentary, The, Catholic liturgical book, **c. 780**.

gelatin (dessert), patented, **1845**, by American inventor Peter Cooper [1791-1883], adapted from **1682** discovery of gelatin manufacture by pressure cooker inventor Denis Papin.

Gembloux, battle of, Austrian forces of Don John [Feb. 24, 1547-Oct. 1, 1578] defeated the Dutch, then in revolt against Spanish rule in the Netherlands, **Jan. 1578**.

gene, artificial, first created, **1970**, by Indian-born U.S. enzymologist Har Gobind Khorana [1922-], at the University of Wisconsin.

gene, isolated, **1969**, by American scientist Jonathan Beckwith [1936-], at Harvard University.

General Accounting Office (GAO), U.S. federal, independent auditing office established by Budget and Accounting Act, **June 10, 1921**.

General Agreement on Tariffs and Trade (GATT), specialized UN agency, formed **1948**; 46 nations signed progressive tariff reductions over five-year period, **June 30, 1967**.

General Electric Theater, The, 'anthology' television drama series, **1951-63**; host and occasional star: future President Ronald (Wilson) Reagan [Feb. 6, 1911-].

General Magazine, The, pioneer magazine, published from January to June, **1741**, one of first in colonial America; founded by Benjamin Franklin.

General of the Army (*five-star general*), U.S. Congress created, **Dec. 15, 1944**.

General Services Administration (GSA), U.S. federal agency, established **July 1, 1949**; 18 GSA officials indicted on charges of fraud, bribery, and kickbacks, **Sept. 19, 1978**.

General Slocum, American excursion steamship caught fire and burned in East

River, New York City; 1030 persons died, **June 15, 1904**.

generator, high-frequency, invented, **1890**, by Yugoslavian-American inventor Nikola Tesla [1856-1943].

Genesis, first book of the Old Testament, written down, **c. 850-650 B.C.**, following Mosaic tradition.

genetic code, independent research, **c. 1961**, by American biochemists Marshall W. Nirenberg [1927-], Robert W. Holley [1922-], and India-born American H. Gobind Khorana [1922-].

genetic code (of DNA), concept proposed, **1954**, by Russian-American physicist George Gamow [1904-1968].

genetic transfer, announced successful, **1981**, by American scientists at USDA Agricultural Research Service, led by John D. Kemp and Timothy C. Hall.

Geneva Protocol, Assembly of League of Nations provided for peaceful settlement of international disputes, **Oct. 2, 1924**.

Genevan Catechism, compendium of Calvinist doctrine, issued, Geneva, **1537**; supplemented by question-and-answer catechism, **1542**.

Genoa, Conference of, international conference of 34 nations at Genoa, Italy, **Apr. 10-May 19, 1922**, discussed reconstruction of European finances after WW I.

Gentleman's Magazine, The, English periodical, founded **1731**; first publication to call itself a 'magazine'.

Gentlemen Prefer Blondes, novel, **1925**, by U.S. author Anita Loos [April 26, 1893- Aug. 18, 1981], written to entertain H. L. Mencken on a long train trip; play, **1926**; musical, **1949**, starred actress Carol Chan-

ning [Jan. 31, 1923-]; film, **1953**, starred Marilyn Monroe and Jane Russell.

genus-species plant names, established, **1736-1750**, by Swedish botanist, Carolus (Carl) Linnaeus (von Linne) [1707-1778].

geodesic dome, modern architectural construction, developed, **c. 1940**; invented by U.S. engineer, architect, and author R(ichard) Buckminster Fuller [July 12, 1895-].

geologic eras, developed, **1778**, by French naturalist George-Louis Leclerc Comte de Buffon [1707-1788] and included in his 44-volume *Natural History* encyclopedia.

geology, modern, developed, from **1795**, by Scottish geologist James Hutton [1726-1797].

geology, stratiographic, established, **1815**, by English geologist William Smith [1769-1839].

geometric principles, given systematic form in Greece, **c. 300 B.C.**, by Greek mathematician and teacher Euclid [fl. 4th century B.C.] in his 13-volume *The Elements of Geometry*.

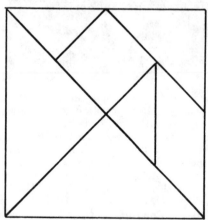

geometry, founded in Greece, **c. 575 B.C.**, by philosopher and scientist Thales [640-546 B.C.] at Miletus.

geometry, non-Euclidean, formulated, **1825-26**, by Russian mathematician Nikolai I. Lobachevski [1793-1856].

geometry of molecules, research published from **1939**, by German-Canadian physicist Gerhard Herzberg [1904-].

geometry (on curved surfaces), first systematic investigation, **1828**, by German mathematician Karl F. Gauss [1777-1855].

geometry, projective, originated, **c. 1485,** by Italian artist Leone B. Alberti [1404-1472].

Georgetown University, America's first Roman Catholic institution for higher learning founded by Jesuits at Washington, D.C., **1789.**

Georgia, one of Thirteen Colonies, ratified U.S. Constitution to become fourth state of the Union, **Jan. 2, 1788;** seceded from the Union, **Jan. 19, 1861;** readmitted to the Union, **July 15, 1870.**

German Confederation, loose confederation of German sovereign states established at the Congress of Vienna to protect "Germany" against its foreign enemies, 1815-66; briefly suspended when Frankfurt Parliament met, **1848-49.**

German Dictionary (Deutsches Worterbuch), definitive German dictionary, begun, **1852,** by German critics, collectors of folk tales, and philologists Jacob Ludwig Carl Grimm [Jan. 4, 1785-Sept. 20, 1863] and his brother Wilhelm Carl Grimm [Feb. 24, 1786-Dec. 16, 1859]; finally completed by a team of lexicographers, **1954.**

German East Africa, former German protectorate in eastern Africa organized by German East Africa Company and administered by German government, **1885-1916.**

German Empire, former empire of the German princes put together by Otto von Bismarck ("the Iron Chancellor") proclaimed in the Palace of Versailles, extending through WW I, **Jan. 18, 1871-June 28, 1919.**

germanium, element No. 32; discovered, **1886,** by German analytical chemist Clemens A. Winkler [1838-1904].

Germantown, battle of, American revolutionary forces under Gen. Washington unsuccessfully attacked British encampment at Germantown near Philadelphia, in last major battle before Americans camped for the winter at Valley Forge, **Oct. 4, 1777.**

Germany, divided into four zones after WW II, **May 8, 1945,** occupied by British, French, U.S., and Soviet forces; unsuccessful Soviet blockade of Berlin, **July 1948-May 1949;** divided into West Germany or Federal Republic of Germany, **May 8, 1949,** and East Germany or German Democratic Republic, **Oct. 7, 1949.**

germ-plasm continuity, theory of heredity, developed, **c. 1900,** by German zoologist August Weismann [1834-1914].

gerrymandering, device of reshaping a political district for one's advantage, introduced by Gov. Elbridge Gerry [July 17, 1744-Nov. 23, 1814] of Massachusetts, **1812.**

Gesta Regem Anglorum (Chronicle of the Kings of England), Latin history, written **1120-28,** covering history of England, between **449** and **1128,** by British monk and chronicler William of Malmesbury [Nov., c. 1090-c. 1143]; first printed, **1596.**

Gesta Romanorum (Deeds of the Romans), collection of medieval moralistic tales, written, late **1200s,** printed, **1473,** recounting valiant deeds supposedly carried out under various Roman emperors; influenced later writers, including Chaucer, and Shakespeare.

Getty kidnapping, J. Paul Getty III, grandson of the Texas oil billionaire, released by kidnappers in Italy; Getty family paid $2.8 million ransom, **Dec. 15, 1973.**

Gettysburg Address, immortal speech delivered by Pres. Abraham Lincoln at dedication of national cemetery at Gettysburg battlefield, **Nov. 19, 1863.**

Gettysburg, battle of, Union armies under Gen. George G. Meade [Dec. 31, 1815-Nov.

6, 1872] beat back Confederate assaults led by Gen. James Longstreet and Gen. George E. Pickett [Jan. 25, 1825-July 30, 1875] and won major Union victory at Gettysburg, Penn.; Gen. Robert E. Lee's Confederate army forced to retreat, ending Southerners' invasion of North, **July 1-3, 1863**.

Ghana, republic in western Africa, first made a British crown colony of the Gold Coast, **1874**; British Togoland incorporated into Ghana, **1956**; became independent country within the British Commonwealth of Nations, **Mar. 6, 1957**; became a republic, **July 1, 1960**.

Ghent Altarpiece, vast altarpiece, **1432**, dramatizing redemption of man in 20 panels, at once realistic and symbolic, by Flemish artist Jan van Eyck [c. 1395-July 9, 1441].

Ghent, Treaty of, U.S. and Britain made peace to end War of 1812; commissions established to settle border disputes in Northwest Territory, **Dec. 24, 1814**.

Giant, film, **1956**, based on novel by Edna Ferber, **1952**; starred Elizabeth Taylor and James Dean.

G.I. Bill of Rights (Servicemen's Readjustment Act), U.S. Congress provided, **June 22, 1944**, educational and other benefits for veterans returning from WW II; U.S. Congress provided similar benefits to Korean War veterans, **July 16, 1952**.

Gideons, International, Bible organization founded, **July 1, 1899**, in Boscobel, Wis., as Christian Men's Commercial Association of America; first Gideon Bible placed in Superior Hotel, Iron Mountain, Mont., **Nov. 1908**.

Gigi, novel, **1945**, about turn-of-the-century Paris schoolgirl taught coquettish arts by aunt and grandmother, by French novelist Colette. Film, **1958**, based on Colette's novel, with young heroine played by Leslie Caron, songs by Lerner and Loewe, directed by Vincente Minnelli [Feb. 28, 1910-].

gigue, lively dance in triple meter, normally formed last movement in baroque suites, **1650-1750**; from British "jig," popular dance that flourished, in **1500s**.

Gilgamesh, The Epic of, long, ancient Babylonian epic poem, **c. 1198 B.C.**, known from 12 tablets discovered at Nineveh, **1872**, chronicles rule of tyrannical demi-god; contains flood account similar to Biblical flood.

Gilmore execution, convicted murderer Gary Gilmore [1941?-Jan. 17, 1977] executed, **Jan. 17, 1977**, by Utah firing squad in first exercise of capital punishment in U.S., since **1967**.

Gioconda, La, painting, **c. 1503-06**, one of the world's most celebrated, immortalizing mysterious smile of *Mona Lisa* (other name of painting), by Italian Renaissance painter Leonardo da Vinci [1452-May 2, 1519]. Opera, **1876**, a romantic melodrama, work of Italian composer Amilcare Ponchielli [Aug. 31, 1834-Jan. 17, 1886]; includes *Dance of the Hours* ballet.

Giovanni Arnolfini and His Bride, painting, **1434**, executed in meticulous, realistic detail with every object symbolic of sacredness of marriage, by Flemish master Jan van Eyck.

Girl Scouts, U.S. organization for young girls organized as Camp Fire Girls, **Mar. 17, 1910**; organized on model of Britain's Girl Guides by Juliette Gordon Low [Oct. 31, 1860-Jan. 17, 1927] of Savannah, Ga., **Mar. 12, 1912**; World Association of Girl Guides and Girl Scouts, formed **1928**.

Girondists, members of moderate republican Gironde Party during French Revolution, **1791-93**; Jacobin extremists suppressed Girondists, **June 1793**.

Gizeh (Al Jizah), ancient city (one of

world's oldest) established near present-day Cairo in n. Egypt, **c. 2600 B.C.**

glacial ages, first described, **1840**, by Swiss-American naturalist Jean L. R. Agassiz [1807-1873].

Glasgow, University of, Scottish university established for the study of theology, canon, and civil law, **1451**.

glass blowing, introduced, **c. 1st century B.C.**, in Babylon.

Glassboro talks, U.S. Pres. Lyndon B. Johnson and Soviet Premier Aleksei N. Kosygin [Feb. 20, 1904-Dec. 18, 1980] held talks at Glassboro State College, N.J., **June 23 and 25, 1967**, concerning Mideast aggression and armaments.

glass, lead, developed, **1676**, by English glassmaker George Ravenscroft [1618-1681].

glass, mechanical pressing of, introduced, **1825**, in U.S. factories; apparatus devised by American inventor Enoch Robinson of New England Glass Works, Cambridge, Mass. (established 1818).

Glencoe massacre, Campbells of Scotland massacred Macdonald clan, causing years of feuding in the Highlands, **Feb. 13, 1692**.

Glen Grey Act, new native policy of self-government and land ownership inaugurated by South Africa Cape Colony, **Aug. 1894**.

glider, invented, **1891**, by German aeronautical engineer Otto Lilienthal [1848-1896].

Globe, circumnavigation of the, part of Spanish expedition under Ferdinand Magellan [1480-Apr. 27, 1521] completed first voyage around the world, **Sept. 20, 1519-Sept. 6, 1522**.

Globe, The, Elizabethan theater, built, **1599**, by English actor, Richard Burbage [c. 1567-Mar. 16, 1619]; housed Shakespeare's company, until burned, **1613**; rebuilt, **1614**; stood until **1644**.

Glorious First of June, British fleet under Admiral Richard Howe [Mar. 8, 1726-Aug. 5, 1799] defeated French fleet off Brittany during French Revolutionary Wars, **June 1, 1794**.

Glorious Revolution, events in England that resulted in the deposition of King James II and the accession of William and Mary to the throne, **1688-89**.

Gnosticism, ancient religious movements, **c. 100-200**, offering salvation by means of secret wisdom and a dualism of good and evil.

Gobelins, Manufacture nationale des, French tapestry factory that started as a dye works of the Gobelin brothers, **15th century**; tapestry works added by two Flemish weavers, **1601**; purchased by King Louis XIV, **1662**.

God Bless America, popular patriotic song, first performed, **November 11, 1939**, for which composer Irving Berlin received Congressional Gold Medal.

Godfather, The, novel, **1969**, about autocratic chieftain of crime organization; sold over 10 million copies, by U.S. author Mario Puzo [Oct. 15, 1920-]. Film, **1971**, based on Mario Puzo's best-selling novel about crime lord; Academy Awards for script; for direction by U.S. director Francis Ford Coppola; and for best actor by U.S. method-actor Marlon Brando [Apr. 3, 1924-].

God Save the King, British national anthem, possibly written, **1688**, author unknown; first public rendition, Drury Lane Theatre, **September 28, 1745**; became custom to greet king with it, **c. 1747-48**.

Godspell, musical, **1971**, semi-rock in style, based on life of Christ; film version, **1973**.

Godunov, House of, reigning family in Russia, under Boris Fyodorovich Godunov [c. 1551-Apr. 23, 1605], **1598-1605**.

Goettingen University, European institution of higher learning, founded, **1734**; became one of most famous and characteristic German universities.

Gold Democrats, members of Democratic Party who refused to support William Jennings Bryan and free silver, **1896**; established National Democratic Party and nominated separate presidential ticket, **Sept. 2-3, 1896.**

Golden Ass, The (Metamorphoses), prose romance, **c. 155**; only surviving Latin novel, by Latin writer Lucius Apuleius [c. 114- ?].

Golden Bough, The, 12-volume study of primitive magic and religion, **1890**, in which author attempted to document widespread myth of death and rebirth of gods, by pioneer Scottish anthropologist Sir James G(eorge) Frazer [Jan. 1,1854-May 7, 1941].

Golden Bull of Egar, Holy Roman Emperor Frederick II [1194-1250] declared his support of the pope against heretics, **1213**.

Golden Bull of Rimini, Holy Roman Emperor Frederick II organized the order of the Teutonic Knights as German, Christian missionaries, **1226**.

Golden Bull of 1356, most famous Golden Bull; Emperor Charles IV [1316-78] established rules for the selection of future emperors, changing the Holy Roman Empire from a monarchy to an aristocratic federation, **Dec. 26, 1356**; remained the constitution of the Holy Roman Empire, until **1816**.

Golden Bull of 1212, Holy Roman Emperor Frederick II decreed the right of the Bohemian nobles to elect their own ruler, **1212**.

Golden Bull of 1222, King Andrew II [d. 1235] of Hungary reluctantly exempted nobles and the church from taxes and gave other liberties to his subjects, **1222**.

Golden Calf, The, object of worship set up (Exodus 32) by Hebrews in the wilderness, **c. 1280 B.C.**; and at Bethel and Dan (I Kings) for 10 tribes, **c. 920 B.C.**, by Israelite King Jeroboam I [937-910 B.C.]; hence, any idol.

Golden Fleece, Order of the, famous order of chivalry of royal foundation established by the Burgundians, **1429**; became Hapsburg order, **1477**.

Golden Hind, English ship on which Francis Drake [c. 1540-Jan. 28, 1596] became first Englishman to make round-the-world voyage, **Dec. 13, 1577-Sept. 26, 1580.**

Golden Horde, fierce Mongol army under Batu Khan [d. 1255] that camped in golden tents and laid waste to eastern Europe, **13th century**.

Golden Legend, the (Aurea Legenda), compilation of lives of the saints, compiled, **c. 1275**, by Italian writer and prelate Jacopo da Voragine [1230-July 13/14, 1298]; first printed in English, **1483**, one of first books printed by William Caxton [c. 1422-1491].

Golden Spurs, Order of the, famous papal decoration for chivalry established by Pope Paul III [1468-1549], **1539**.

Golden Treasury, The, anthology, **1861**, of "best songs and lyrical poems in the English language;" popular collection of 16th to mid-19th century verse, compiled by English critic and anthologist Francis T(urner) Palgrave [Sept. 28, 1824-Oct. 24, 1897].

gold fillings (teeth), introduced, **c. 1850**, by American dentist Richard Arthur [1819-1880] in his Philadelphia practice.

Goldfinger, novel, **1959**, about sinister international operator who plans to rob gold from Fort Knox and who is thwarted by British secret agent 007 James Bond, by British writer Ian (Lancaster) Fleming [May 28, 1908-Aug. 12, 1964]; film, **1964**.

Gold Hoarding Act, U.S. Congress authorized, **Mar. 9, 1933**, the Secretary of the Treasury to call in all gold coins, certificates, and bullion, exchanging for them an equivalent amount of other U.S. currency or coin.

Gold Reserve Act, U.S. Congress authorized, **Jan. 30, 1934**, all gold called in and on deposit with federal reserve banks to be permanent gold reserve for outstanding U.S. paper money.

Goncourt Academy, French literary academy, established, **1896**, to award annual fiction prize, established by French writer Edmond de Goncourt [May 26, 1822-July 16, 1896], **1887-96**, with brother Jules de Goncourt [Dec. 17, 1830-June 20, 1870].

Gone with the Wind, novel, **1936**, about loves of fiery Southern belle Scarlett O'Hara in Civil War-ravaged South; only book by U.S. novelist Margaret Mitchell [1900-Aug. 16, 1949]; won Pulitzer Prize, **1937**. Film, **1939**, of Margaret Mitchell's novel, starred U.S. actor (William) Clark Gable [Feb. 1, 1901-Nov. 16, 1960]; and English actress Vivien Leigh (born Vivien

Hartley) [Nov. 5, 1913-July 8, 1967].

goniometer, invented, **1809**, by English physiologist William H. Wollaston [1766-1828]; device for measurement of crystals.

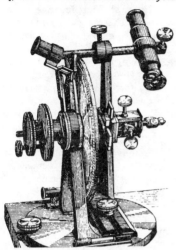

Gonzaga family, Italian noble family and patrons of the arts that ruled Mantua, **1328-1708**, Montferrat, **1536-1708**, and Guastalla, **1539-1746**.

Goodbye Mr. Chips, popular novel, **1934**, about life of an English schoolmaster; by English novelist James Hilton [Sept. 9, 1900-Dec. 20, 1954].

Good Earth, The, novel, **1931**, interpreting Chinese life to the West, by U.S. author Pearl S(ydenstricker) Buck [July 26, 1892-Mar. 6, 1973]; Nobel Prize-winner, **1938**.

Good-Neighbor Policy, U.S. policy adopted under the adminstration of Pres. F. D. Roosevelt, **1933-45**, to foster Pan-American political and economic cooperation and mutual hemispheric defense.

Good Soldier Schweik, The (Osudy Dobreho Vojaka Svejka za Svetove Valky), novel, **1920**, an epic satire, by Czech writer Jaroslav Hasek [Apr. 30, 1883-Jan. 3, 1923].

Gospels, first four New Testament books about life, deeds, and teachings of Jesus Christ, now believed written prior to **70**: Matthew, c. **45-60**; Mark, c. **40-60**; Luke, c. **57-60**; John, c. **40-65**.

Gotha, Almanach de, genealogical annual, published, since **1763**.

Gotha, Congress of, important socialist congress of German Social Democratic Party held at city of Gotha, East Germany, **May 1875**.

gothic, style of art and architecture that originated, France, c. **1100**, to give soaring, lofty expression to religious emotion; prevailed throughout Europe, **12th-15th centuries**.

gothic romance, type of English novel, popular from c. **1760**, featuring horror story set in gloomy, exotic location such as ruined castle or abbey: Walpole's *The Castle of Otranto*, **1764**; *The Mysteries of Udolpho*, **1794**, by Mrs. Ann Radcliffe [July 9, 1764-Feb.7, 1823].

gout, condition first explained, **1683**, by English physician Thomas Sydenham [1624-1689]..

Government of India Acts, Britain established, **Dec. 23, 1919**, provincial legislatures under "dyarchy" principle in India, with Indian ministers to share authority with appointed British ministers; protests by Gandhi led to conferences and new Govenment of India Act, **Aug. 2, 1935**, that gave more autonomy to Indian provincial governments.

Government of the 5000, 5000 of the wealthiest Athenians who deposed the Four Hundred and ruled temporarily, **Oct.-Dec. 411 B.C.**

Government Printing Office, U.S., largest printing plant in the world, created by act of Congress, **June 23, 1860**.

Graf Spee, first real naval battle of WW II; British heavy cruiser *Exeter* and light cruisers *Ajax* and *Achilles* inflicted heavy damage on heavier-gunned and faster German pocket battle ship *Graf Spee*, **Dec. 12, 1939**; German commander of *Graf Spee* scuttled battleship outside Montevideo harbor and committed suicide, **Dec. 17, 1939**.

Graham's law, established, **1831**, by Scottish physical chemist Thomas Graham [1805-1869].

grain binder, invented, **1850**, by American inventor John E. Heath.

grain-dressing machine, patented, **1768**, by Scottish millwright Andrew Meikle [1719-1811].

grain reaper, mechanical harvester, patented, **1833**, by American inventor Obed Hussey [1792-1860], one year before Cyrus McCormick reaper patented, **1834**.

gramicidin, bactericidal agent introduced, **1939**, by American bacteriologist Rene J. Dubois [1901-].

Grammy, award presented, since **1958**, by the National Academy for Recording Arts and Sciences for the best records during each year; given in 39 categories, since **1963**.

Gramophone, invented, **1887**, by German-American inventor Emile Berliner [1851-1929].

Granada, city in Andalusia, Spain; became capital of kingdom of Granada (last Moorish refuge in Spain), **1238**; fl. as great center of Moorish civilization, **13th-15th centuries**; conquered by Spaniards and united with kingdom of Castile, **Jan. 2, 1492**.

Grand Alliance, War of the (War of the League of Augsburg), conflict between France and a coalition of European countries, known as the League of Augsburg (as the Grand Alliance, after **1689**), **1688-97**; French support of counterrevolution in Ireland checked by English victory at Boyne, **July 1, 1690**; French won at Beachy Head, **July 10, 1690**; English won at La Hogue,

May 19-23, 1692; French won at Fleurus, **June 30, 1690**; at Neerwinden, **July 29, 1693**; and at Marsaglia, **Oct. 4, 1693**; end by Treaty of Ryswick, **Sept. 30, 1697**.

Grand National Steeplechase, Britain's famous steeplechase horse race first run at the Aintree course, Liverpool, England, **1839**.

Grand Old Opry, long-running, radio country- and western-music show, from **1925**.

Grand Old Party (GOP), Republican Party name first used by Republicans, **1880**.

Grand Pre, Treaty of, French settlers in Louisiana signed peace treaty with Choctaw Indians, **1750**.

Grand Remonstrance, English parliament called for religious and administrative reform and recited its grievances against King Charles I, **Dec. 1, 1641**.

Grand Slam of Golf, the winning of U.S. Amateur and Open and British Amateur and Open golf championships in one year, accomplished only once by Bobby Jones [Mar. 17, 1902-Dec. 18, 1971], **1930** (Grand Slam now considered winning of U.S. and British Open, the Masters, and the PGA championships in one year-a feat not yet done by anyone).

Grand Slam of Tennis, the winning of the U.S., Wimbledon, French, and Australian tennis singles championships in one year accomplished by Don Budge [June 13,

1915-], **1938**; by Maureen Connolly [Sept. 17, 1934-June 21, 1969], **1953**; by Rod Laver [Aug. 9, 1938-], **1962**, **1969**; by Margaret Smith Court [July 16, 1942-], **1970**.

Grand Teton, majestic mountain (13,766 ft.) in Teton Range, Wyoming, "classic" climb for mountaineers, first scaled, **1898**.

Grangers (Patrons of Husbandry), members of secret order of U.S. farmers organized in Washington, D.C., **Dec. 4, 1867**, to promote agricultural interests; railroad freight rates set in Illinois, Wisconsin, and Iowa by Granger laws, **1874**; Grangers turned from political activities to social, after **1876**.

Granicus (Kocabas) River, battle of, Macedonian army of 30,000 men led by Alexander the Great annihilated Persians and Greek mercenaries at mouth of Granicus River (Sea of Marmara), **334 B.C.**

Grantham, battle of, Roundheads under Cromwell won first victory over Cavaliers at Grantham, Lincolnshire, England, **Mar. 1643**.

Grapes of Wrath, The, novel, **1939**, recounting epic story of "Okie" dust-bowl farmers who go in search of field work in depression-ridden California, by John Steinbeck; Pulitzer Prize-winner, **1940**; Nobel Prize-winner, **1962**; film, **1940**, based on Steinbeck's novel; starred U.S. actor Henry Fonda, directed by U.S. director John Ford.

Gravelines, battle of, French forces defeated by Spanish, aided by guns of English squadron lying off French coast, during one of earliest land battles using naval gunfire, **July 13, 1558**.

Gravelotte, battle of, French army under Marshal Achille Bazaine [Feb. 13, 1811-Sept. 23, 1888] inflicted heavy losses on Prussian armies under Gen. Helmuth von Moltke [Oct. 26, 1800-Apr. 24, 1891] but failed to counterattack to win major battle during Franco-Prussian War, **Aug. 18, 1870**.

Great Awakening, religious revival that swept American colonies, **1740-50**, under impetus of preaching by Puritan divines such as Jonathan Edwards.

Great Dictator, The, film, **1940**, in which Charlie Chaplin played dual roles of mad European Dictator and ghetto barber.

Great Eastern **(steamship),** laid Atlantic telegraph cable, **1866**, built by English engineer Isambard K. Brunel [1806-1859].

Great Expectations, novel, **1861**, by English novelist Charles Dickens, in which a Victorian-era orphan overcomes adversity to find happiness.

Great Gatsby, The, novel, **1925**, of 1920s' *Jazz Age*, by U.S. novelist and short-story writer F(rancis) Scott (Key) Fitzgerald [Sept. 24, 1896-Dec. 21, 1940].

Great Illusion, The (La Grande Illusion), anti-war film, **1937**, starring German actor-director Erich von Stroheim (born Erich von Nordenwell) [Sept. 22, 1885-May 12, 1957]; by French director, Jean Renoir.

Great Leap Forward, Chinese program of Mao Tse-tung to decentralize the economy by establishing small, labor intensive industries run by local peasants throughout China, **1957-58**.

Great Schism, split between Eastern Orthodox and Western Catholic Churches, from **1054**; attempts to restore unity: Council of Lyons, **1272**, and Council of Florence, **1439**; anathemas of 1054 rescinded, **1965**.

Great Schism, (Schism of the West), split within Western Church, began, **1378**, when anti-pope was elected to oppose legitimate Pope Urban VI (born Bartolomeo Prignano) [c. 1318-Oct. 15, 1389]; schism ended with election, **1417**, of Pope Martin V (born Oddo Colonna) [1368-Feb. 20, 1431].

Great Society, national program to improve the quality of life for all Americans initiated by Pres. Lyndon B. Johnson in his state of union address, **Jan. 4, 1965**.

Great Train Robbery, film, **1903**, 11-minute drama of robbery and capture of outlaws; helped prove possibilities of medium.

Great Train Robbery, 11 armed holdup men stole £ 2.5 million (about $7 million) in currency from mail train in Cheddington, England, **Aug. 8, 1963**.

Great Wall of China, monumental defensive wall built between ancient Chinese empire and Mongolia by Ch'in dynasty, **246-209 B.C.**

Great Western **(steamship)**, launched, **1837**; built by English engineer Isambard K. Brunel [1806-1859]; after 16-day crossing, arrived in New York City, **Apr. 23, 1838**, establishing first transatlantic passenger steamship service between England and U.S.

Great White Fleet, U.S. naval fleet made world cruise on orders of Pres. Theodore Roosevelt to show off U.S. military strength, especially to Japan, **Dec. 16, 1907-Feb. 21, 1909**.

Greek Anthology, The, anthology of ancient Greek poems, songs, epigrams, epitaphs, etc., originally collected, **c. 60 B.C.**; standard collection of Greek poetry, from **5th century B.C.**, continuously added to, through **6th century**.

Greek Architecture (and Art), classical style that arose in Greece, **600s B.C.**, influencing subsequent art: Archaic Period, **c. 550-c. 450 B.C.**; Great Age, **c. 450-c. 323 B.C.**; Hellenistic Age, **c. 323- 146 B.C.** Early preclassical period, **900-700 B.C.**

Greek language, first recorded language of Western civilization, emerged, **c. 2000 B.C.**, with migration south of Greek-speaking peoples; Phoenician alphabet adopted, **c. 1000 B.C.**

Greek War of Independence, Greeks rebelled against Turkish rule and received assistance from European powers to gain autonomy for Greece, **1822-29**; European allies destroyed Egyptian fleet at Navarino, **Oct. 20, 1827**; Russia declared war on Turks, **Apr. 27, 1828**; Ottoman Empire accepted Treaty of Adrianople, **Sept. 14, 1829**.

Greenback-Labor Party, U.S. political party, formed **Feb. 22, 1878**, from fusion of laborers and greenback supporters; dissolved, after **1884**, with many members as Populists.

Greenback Party, U.S. political party, established **1874**, to promote currency growth; nominated Peter Cooper [Feb. 12, 1791-Apr. 4, 1883] for president, **May 18, 1876**.

Green Berets, U.S. Special Forces group established at Fort Bragg, N.C., **1952**; participated in counterinsurgency program in Vietnam, **1962-73**; seven Green Berets charged with killing double-agent, **Aug. 3, 1969**, but charges were dropped.

Greenland, largest island in the world, discovered by Eric the Red [fl. 10th century] who gave it its name, **c. 982**; came under Norway's rule, **1261**; came under Denmark's rule, **1815**.

Greensleeves, English folk song, first mentioned, **1580**; laments unrequited love for beautiful "Lady Greensleeves;" Ralph Vaughan Williams' orchestral *Fantasia on Greensleeves*, **1929**.

green revolution, pioneered **1944** by American agronomist Norman E. Borlaug [1914-]..

Greenville, Treaty of, U.S. government and 12 Indian tribes signed treaty differentiating Indian territory and territory open to white settlement in Northwest Territory, **Aug. 3, 1795.**

Gregorian calendar, introduced by Pope Gregory XIII [June 7, 1502-Apr. 10, 1585] to correct errors in Julian calendar, **1582;** adopted by Great Britain, **1752;** adopted by Russia and Greek orthodox countries, **1917;** adopted worldwide, by **1950.**

Gregorian Chant, traditional liturgical Latin plainsong of Western Church, first published, **c. 600,** in Antiphonar, by Pope St. Gregory the Great; in general use in Europe, **c. 750;** polyphonic singing began to replace, from **c. 1050.**

Gregorianum, Roman Jesuit University, founded, **1551,** as *Collegium Romanum,* by St. Ignatius Loyola (born Inigo de Onez y Loyola) [Dec. 24, 1491-July 31, 1556]; constituted university and endowed, **1582-84,** by Pope Gregory XIII (born Ugo Buoncompagni) [Jan. 1, 1502-Apr. 10, 1585].

Grenada, socialist island state in Caribbean, gained its independence from Britain, **Feb. 7, 1974.**

Grenoble, University of, one of world's most famous and oldest universities established at Grenoble, France, **1339.**

Grepon, most famous "unclimbable" pinnacle of the Chamonix *aiguilles* (or needles) near Mont Blanc, France, first scaled, **1881.**

Gresham's Law, economic principle that "bad money drives out good," attributed to English financier Sir Thomas Gresham [1519?-79], **c. 1560.**

Grimaldi dynasty, Italian family, founded **1017;** awarded territory of present-day Monaco, France, by Holy Roman Emperor, **1297;** Prince of Monaco Rainier III [May 31, 1923-] married American actress Grace Kelly [Nov. 12, 1929-], **Apr. 19, 1956.**

Grimm's Fairy Tales (Kinder- und Hausmarchen), collection of folk-fairy tales, **1812-15,** published by the brothers Jacob Ludwig Carl and Wilhelm Carl Grimm.

grinding machine, cylindrical, patented, **1904,** by American mechanical engineer Charles H. North [1851-1942].

Griswold, Fort, capture of, by British troops under Benedict Arnold, **Sept. 6, 1781,** in effort to turn attention from Cornwallis at Yorktown.

Grito de Dolores (Cry of Dolores), revolutionary document for racial equality and land redistribution issued by Mexican priest Miguel Hidalgo y Costilla [1753-1811], **Sept. 16, 1810,** igniting the Mexicans to revolt against Spanish rule.

Grochow, battle of, Polish patriots and Russian army of about 100,000 men fought savage battle at Grochow on right bank of Vistula River that ended in stalemate during Poland's rebellion against Russian control, **Feb. 20, 1831.**

Grossbeeren, battle of, Prussian force pushed back French attack at Grossbeeren, saving Berlin from French attack during Napoleonic Wars, **Aug. 23, 1813.**

Group Theater, theater company, **1929-41,** that supplied vigor to 1930s U.S. drama, producing works such as those of Clifford Odets, and William Saroyan.

Guadalcanal, battle of, U.S. troops made first large-scale invasion of Japanese-held island in WW II and conquered Guadalcanal after long, hard jungle warfare, **Aug. 7, 1942-Feb. 9, 1943.**

Guadalete (Rio Barbate), battle of, Arab-Berber army defeated Visigoths under Roderick [d. 713?], **711,** last Visigothic king in Spain, which fell to the Muslims.

Guadalupe Hidalgo, Treaty of, ended Mexican War; Mexico recognized Texas as U.S. possession, ceded most of present-day Southwest; U.S. paid Mexico $15 million and assumed Americans' claims against Mexico, **Mar. 10, 1848.**

Guam, island in w. Pacific belonged to Spain, **1521-1898;** captured by U.S. in Spanish-American War, **June 20, 1898;** governed by U.S. Dept. of the Navy, **1917-50,** before transferred to Dept. of the Interior; under Japanese control, **1941-44.**

Guardian, The, newspaper, begun, **1821,** as *Manchester Guardian;* organ of liberal opinion, assumed present title, **1959;** earlier periodical, same title, published, **March-October, 1713,** by Sir Richard Steele.

Guatemala, republic in Central America, site of the ancient Mayan civilization, **c. 1500 B.C.-A.D.1700;** conquered by Spanish, **1524;** established itself as republic, **1839;** devastating earthquake killed about 22,000 persons, **Feb. 4, 1976.**

Guernica, mural, **1937,** employing violent linear distortions to express horror of bombing of Guernica in Spanish Civil War, by Spanish painter Pablo Picasso.

Guggenheim Fellowships (John Simon Guggenheim Memorial Fellowships), annual awards in literature, music, and arts, from **1925.**

Guggenheim Museum, New York Museum, designed, **1945,** by U.S. architect Frank Lloyd Wright; opened, **1958;** 'Pop Art" show, **1963.**

Guide of the Perplexed, The (Dalalat al-Ha'irir), philosophico-theological synthesis, **c. 1190,** medieval summary of Jewish faith and practice, as harmonized with Bible and Aristotle, by Jewish philosopher and jurist Maimonides (Moses Ben Maimon) [Mar. 30, 1135-Dec. 13, 1204].

Guild Theatre, New York theater, opened, **April 13, 1925,** with Shaw's *Caesar and Cleopatra,* starring U.S. actress Helen Hayes (born Helen Brown) [Oct. 10, 1900-]; originally founded by Theatre Guild, became Anta Theatre, **1951.**

Guilford Courthouse, battle of, British redcoats under Gen. Cornwallis won pyrrhic victory over Carolina and Virginia militiamen under Gen. Nathanael Greene [Aug. 7, 1742-June 19, 1786] near Greensboro, N.C.; high British casualties forced Cornwallis back to Wilmington, N.C., **Mar. 15, 1781.**

guillotine, use proposed, **1789,** by French physician Joseph I. Guillotin [1738-1814], who is credited with invention.

Guinea, country in Africa, became independent republic after rejecting French constitution, **Oct. 2, 1958.**

Guinea-Bissau, republic in Africa, formerly Portuguese Guinea, waged guerrilla war, **1960-74,** against Portugal to gain its independence, **Sept. 10, 1974.**

Guinea Company, English merchants established company for trading in slaves to West Indies from Africa's coast of Guinea, **1588.**

guitar, plucked string instrument, primitive varieties developed as early as **1000 B.C.;** popular, early **1600s,** replacing lutes; first English manual on guitars published, **1758.**

Gujarat, region in India that became center of Jainism under the Hindu Anhilvada kingdom, **c. 755-1233.**

Gujrat, battle of, large Anglo-Indian army annihilated entire Sikh force at Gujrat, of Lahore, ending Anglo-Sikh war, with Punjab region under British control, **Feb. 22, 1849.**

Gulag Archipelago, The, three-volume

chronicle, **1973-78**, exposing the Soviet forced-labor system, by Russian author, Alexander Solzhenitsyn, Nobel Prize-winner, **1970**.

Gulliver's Travels, satire, **1726**, by English writer and clergyman Jonathan Swift [Nov. 30, 1667-Oct. 19, 1745].

Gumbinnen, battle of, Russian army invaded Prussia and won decisive victory over Germans at Gumbinnen, **Aug. 19-20, 1914**.

guncotton, discovered, **1845**, by German-Swiss chemist Christian F. Schoebein [1799-1868].

gun, Gatling, patented, **1862**, by American inventor Richard J. Gatling [1818-1903]; rapid-fire weapon.

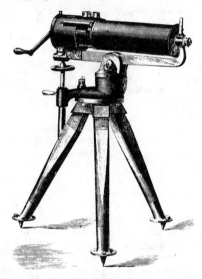

Gunnbjornsfjeld, Mt., highest mountain in the Arctic (12,139 ft.), first climbed, **1935**.

Gunpowder Plot, conspirators failed in their plan to blow up the houses of parliament, **Nov. 5, 1605**; conspirator Guy Fawkes [-] arrested in cellar of House of Lords, **Nov. 4, 1605**.

gun sight, telescopic, invented, **1891**, by American inventor Bradley A. Fiske [1854-1942].

Gunter's chain, invented, **1620**, by English mathematician Edmund Gunter [1581-1626].

Gunsmoke, long-running television Western, **1955-75**, featuring adventures of U.S. Marshall Matt Dillon in frontier Dodge City.

Gun War, conflict between British and Basutos, who refused to give up their guns, resulting in British making Basutoland a crown colony, **1880-81**. See **Basutoland**.

Gutenberg Bible, The, complete Bible in Latin, **1456**, Mainz, Germany; first book printed from movable type, published by German printer and inventor Johannes Gutenberg [c. 1398-Feb. 3, 1468].

Guys and Dolls, collection of stories, **1932**; slangy, humorous studies of Broadway and underworld characters, by U.S. newspaperman and writer (Alfred) Damon Runyon [Oct. 4, 1884-Dec. 10, 1946]. Broadway musical, **1950**, about Damon Runyon's gamblers; film version, **1955**, starred Marlon Brando and Frank Sinatra.

Guyana, republic in South America, formerly British Guiana, proclaimed its independence, **Feb. 23, 1970**; nationalized U.S. mining operation, **Jan. 1, 1975**; site of mass-suicide of People's Temple cult of Jim Jones, **Nov. 18, 1978**.

Gwalior, battle of, Anglo-Indian forces captured town of Gwalior in central India from rebel forces in hard-fought three-day battle, virtually ending Sepoy Rebellion, **June 17-19, 1858**.

gymnastics, Friedrich Ludwig Jahn [1778-1852] organized first gymnastic organization (*Turnverein*) in Berlin, Germany, **1811**; Charles Beck [Aug. 19, 1798-Mar. 19, 1866], a student of Jahn, established first U.S. "gymnasium" at Northampton, Mass., **1825**.

gyrocompass, invented, **1908**, by German engineer Hermann Anschutz-Kampfe [1872-1931]. U.S. inventor Elmer A. Sperry [Oct. 12, 1860-June 16, 1930] developed a gyrocompass that was demonstrated, **1911**, on the U.S. battleship *Delaware*.

gyroscope, invented, **c. 1817**, by German mathematician Johann Bohnenberger [1765-1831].

Haarlem, city in n. Holland sacked by Spanish during revolt of the Netherlands, **1573**; great center of Dutch painting, **16th-17th centuries**.

Habakkuk, Book of, Old Testament book, written, **c. 600 B.C.**, by minor prophet Habakkuk.

habanera, dance in moderate double time, emerged, **Spain, c. 1850**.

Habeas Corpus Act, parliament required English judges to issue upon request a writ of *habeas corpus*, directing the jailer to produce the body of the prisoner and to show cause for imprisonment, **May 27, 1679**.

Hadassah, women's Zionist organization, founded **1912**, by Henrietta Szold [Dec. 21, 1860-Feb. 13, 1945].

Hadrian's Wall, ancient Roman wall in n. England, built by Emperor Hadrian [Jan. 24, 76-July 10, 138], **c. 122-26**.

hafnium, element No. 72; discovered, **1923**, by Hungarian-Danish chemist Georg von Hevesy [1885-1966].

Haggai, Book of, Old Testament book recording prophecies delivered, **c. 520 B.C.**, by minor phophet Haggai, lamenting ruins of the Temple.

Hague Conferences, first international peace conference at The Hague called by Russia, changed some rules of war and set up Permanent Court of Arbitration, **May** 18-July 29, 1899; second international conference called by Russia, failed to limit armaments and to establish U.S.-sponsored world court, **June 15-Oct. 18, 1907**.

hahnium, element No. 105; first produced, **1970**, by American scientist Albert Ghiorso [1915-] and coworkers at University of California, Berkeley.

Haight-Asbury, area of San Francisco attracted "hippies" and "flower children," **c. 1966**; attracted dope pushers and petty criminals, and nicknamed "Hashbury," **1967**; site of violent riots, **1968**.

Hair, musical, **1967**, portraying 1960s lifestyle of "hippies" and dropouts; billed as "American tribal love-rock musical."

Haiti, w. third of island of Hispaniola, became French possession known as Saint Domingue, **1697**; declaration of independence by Toussaint L'Ouverture, **1801**; gained independence as nation of Haiti, **1804**; under U.S. customs receivership, **1905-41**; under direct U.S. rule, **1915-30**; under dictatorship of Francois ("Papa Doc") Duvalier [Apr. 14, 1907-Apr. 21, 1971], **Sept. 1957-Apr. 1971**.

Hale telescope, installed, **1948**, at Mount Palomar Observatory; conceived and developed by American astronomer George E. Hale [1868-1938].

Half Moon, famous, little Dutch vessel on which Henry Hudson explored river named after him, during his third voyage to America, **1609**.

half-tone negatives, cross-line screens on glass; devised, **1886**, by American inventor Frederic E. Ives [1856-1937].

half-tone process, patented, **1858**, by English pioneer in photography, W. H. Fox Talbot [1800-1877].

Haliartus, battle of, Boeotians and Thebans routed Spartan army under Lysander [d. 395 B.C.], who was killed, at Haliartus in Boeotia, **395 B.C.**

Halicarnassus Mausoleum, giant marble mausoleum, built, Greece, **353 B.C.**, to house tomb of King called Mausolus; word "mausoleum," derived from this structure.

Halidon Hill, battle of, English forces of Edward III [1312-77] defeated the Scots at Halidon HIll, near Berwick-upon-Tweed, **July 19, 1333**.

Halley's comet, return predicted, **1682**, by

English astronomer Edmund Halley [1656-1742]; designated time, **1758**, proved correct.

Hall of Fame, National Baseball, special building erected at Cooperstown, N.Y., to commemorate professional baseball's greatest figures, **1939**.

Hallmark Hall of Fame, long-running NBC television dramatic series, from **January, 1952**, that has featured 90-minute dramas by Shakespeare, Shaw, and Gilbert and Sullivan; on radio, **1948-55**.

Hamburg, allied with Lubeck to form the basis of the Hanseatic League, **1241**; destroyed by fire, **1842**; socialist republic, **1918-19**; heavily damaged by Allied bombs in WW II, **1943**.

Hamburger Hill, U.S. and South Vietnamese forces seized hill in A Shau Valley, **May 10, 1969**; bloody 10-day battle for that hill, with little strategic value, received much criticism in U.S.; hill abandoned by U.S., **May 28, 1969**.

Hamlet, William Shakespeare's tragedy, **1601**, about Hamlet, Prince of Denmark; opera, **1868**, by French composer Ambroise Thomas [Aug. 5, 1811-Feb. 12, 1896]; ballet, produced, London, **May 19, 1942**, by Sadler's Wells; employing Tchaikovsky's music to represent Shakespeare's theme; dancers included Prima Ballerina Dame Margot Fonteyn (born Margaret Hookham) [May 18, 1919-]; film, **1948**, produced and directed by Sir Laurence Olivier, who also played the prince; opera, **1968**, version of Shakespeare's play, by English composer Humphrey Searle [Aug. 26, 1915-].

Hammurabi's code, ancient system of laws

established by Hammurabi in Babylonia, **c. 1770 B.C.**

Hampton Court Conference, meeting, **1604**, between Anglican bishops and Puritan leaders presided over by King James I.

Hampton Court Palace, royal palace, begun, **1515**, in gothic style; additions, **1688-98**.

Hampton Roads Conference, peace conference between U.S. Pres. Abraham Lincoln and Confederate Vice Pres. Alexander H. Stephens and others aboard *River Queen* at Hampton Roads, Va., **Feb. 3, 1865**.

Hanafi Muslim takeover, gunmen of the Hanafi Muslim sect seized 134 hostages in three buildings in Washington, D.C., **Mar. 9, 1977**; hostages released, **Mar. 11, 1977**, and 12 Hanafis charged with armed kidnapping.

handkerchief, disposable, first introduced, **1924**, by Kimberly and Clark Company of Wisconsin.

Hanging Gardens of Babylon, series of planted terraces, constructed, **c.580 B.C.**, one of Seven Wonders of Ancient World; built by King Nebuchadnezzar [c. 605-562 B.C.].

Hanging Rock, battle of, American patriots surprised British forces, winning battle and strengthening patriots' effort in South Carolina during the American Revolution, **Aug. 6, 1780**.

Hanover, House of, royal, reigning family of Great Britain and Ireland from the accession of George I [Mar. 28, 1660-June 11, 1727] and ending with Queen Victoria [May 24, 1819-Jan. 22, 1901], **1714-1901**.

Hanseatic League, mercantile league of German town that banded together for mutual protection and trade advantages, **13th-15th centuries**; gained virtual trade monopoly in the Baltic and Scandinavia, **1370-1440**; league's last diet, **1669**.

Hansel and Gretel, opera, **1893**, based on Grimm's *Fairy Tales*, by German composer Engelbert Humperdinck [1854-1921]

Hanukkah, eight-day Jewish festival commemorating victory, **165 B.C.**, of Jewish leader Judas Maccabeus [?-160 B.C.].

Happy Days, popular ABC situation comedy, from **1974**, about teen-age life.

Hapsburg (Habsburg), House of, prominent German family that ruled Austria,

1282-1918; claimed Bohemia and Hungary, **1526**; Pragmatic Sanction, **Apr. 19, 1713**; end of male line, **1740**; line of Hapsburg-Lorraine began with Joseph II [Mar. 13, 1741-Feb. 20, 1790], **1765**; Hapsburg lands reorganized as Austro-Hungarian Empire, **June 12, 1867**.

Hard Cider Campaign, U.S. presidential campaign of Whig nominee William Henry Harrison [Feb. 9, 1773-Apr. 4, 1841], **1840**.

Harfleur, French town at mouth of Seine River, captured after prolonged siege by British under King Henry V during Hundred Years' War, **Aug. 19-Sept. 22, 1415**; French regained permanent possession of Harfleur, **1449**.

Harlem Globetrotters, well-known American Negro basketball team, noted for its artistic tricks, organized by Abe ("Little Caesar") Saperstein [1903-Mar. 15, 1966], **1927**.

Harlem Plains, battle of, British advance guard of Gen. William Howe won victory against Virginia-Connecticut militiamen at Harlem Plains, N.Y., during American Revolution, **Sept. 16, 1776**.

harmonica, small box wind instrument, played through holes on side; invented, Vienna, **1821**.

harmonica, glass, invented, **c. 1760**, by American scientist-statesman Benjamin Franklin [1706-1790].

harmonic analysis, discovered, **1822**, by French mathematician Baron Jean B. J. Fourier [1768-1830].

Harmony, former American communal settlement near Pittsburgh established by Harmony Society (religious German Separatists society) under George Rapp, **1803**; Harmonists led by Rapp moved to present-day Indiana and founded New Harmony, **1814**.

harp, stringed instrument on frame, played, from **c. 3000 B.C.**, in ancient Egypt and Mesopotamia; arrived in Europe, **c. 1050**; double-pedal harp invented, France, **1810**.

Harper's Bazaar, monthly U.S. women's magazine, established, **1867**, as a weekly; monthly, since **1901**.

Harpers Ferry, (W. Va.), with 21 followers, American abolitionist John Brown [May 9, 1800-Dec. 2, 1859] captured U.S. arsenal at Harpers Ferry with hopes of establishing abolitionist republic in Appalachians, **Oct. 16, 1859**; U.S. marines under Col. Robert E. Lee defeated Brown's small band, **Oct. 18, 1859**; Brown was tried, convicted, and hanged on charges of treason, **Dec. 2, 1859**.

Harper's Magazine, U.S. monthly, founded, **1850**, as *Harper's New Monthly Magazine*; purchased by nonprofit foundation to make continued publication possible, **1980**.

harpsichord, keyboard instrument, developed, **c. 1600**; flourished, **17th-18th centuries**.

Harriet Lane **incident**, U.S. revenue cutter *Harriet Lane* fired first shot from a ship in the Civil War when stopping a Southern cargo ship from entering harbor of Charleston, S.C., **Apr. 11, 1861**.

Harrow, English preparatory school, founded, **1572**.

Hartford, famous American battleship *Hartford*, used as Admiral David Farragut's flagship during U.S. Civil War and at battle of Mobile Bay, Ala., **Aug. 5, 1864**.

Hartford Convention, delegates from New England states expressed strong states' rights principles, debated New England secession; Federalist Party lost power, **Dec. 15-Jan. 4, 1815**.

Harvard University, institution of higher learning, founded as college, **1636**; oldest U.S. college, chartered, **1650**; named, **1639**, for English clergyman who first endowed it, John Harvard [Nov. 29, 1607-Sept. 14, 1638]; became a university, **1869**.

harvester rake (mechanical), patented, **1863**, by American inventor Samuel Johnston [1835-1911].

Hasidism, Jewish religious movement, originated Poland, **c. 1740**, emphasizing piety and devotion, rather than learning and dogma.

Hastings, battle of, Normans under William, duke of Normandy (William I, "the Conqueror") [c. 1028-Sept. 9, 1087] won famous victory over Anglo-Saxons under King Harold II [c. 1020-Oct. 14, 1066] at Hastings; King Harold killed in most important battle of Norman conquest of England, **Oct. 14, 1066**.

Hatt-i-humaioun, most important Turkish reform edict of 19th century, **Feb. 18, 1856**.

Hawaii, vast, panoramic "novel," **1959**, by U.S. writer James A(lbert) Michener [Feb. 3, 1907-].

Hawaii, former independent republic annexed to U.S. by joint resolution of Congress, **July 7, 1898**; organic act provided for complete territorial organization, making Hawaii an incorporated territory of U.S., **Apr. 30, 1900**; admitted to the Union (U.S.) as 50th state and first outside continental North America, **Aug. 21, 1959**.

Haw, battle of the, American forces under

Henry ("Light-Horse Harry") Lee [Jan. 29, 1756-Mar. 25, 1818] defeated loyalists near Haw River, N.C., **Feb. 25, 1781**.

Hawley-Smoot Tariff Act, highest protective tariff in U.S. history signed by Pres. Herbert C. Hoover [Aug. 10, 1874-Oct. 20, 1964], **June 17, 1930**, brought sharp decline in international trade.

Hay-Bunau-Varilla Treaty, U.S. signed treaty with new Republic of Panama, **Nov. 18, 1903**, giving U.S. lease on 10-mile strip of land across isthmus for $10 million and $250,000 annually.

Hayes-Tilden deadlock, electoral commission, created by U.S. Congress to resolve electoral vote deadlock in 1876 presidential election, **Jan. 29, 1877**; strict party vote, eight (Republicans) to seven (Democrats) elected Rutherford B. Hayes [Oct. 4, 1822-Jan. 17, 1893] U.S. President, **Mar. 2, 1877**.

Hay-Herran Treaty, U.S. Secretary of State John Hay [Oct. 8, 1838-July 1, 1905] and Colombia's foreign minister signed treaty, **Jan. 22, 1903**, leasing land across isthmus of Panama to U.S. for canal construction.

Haymarket Square riot, leftist laborers exploded bomb during demonstration at Haymarket Square, Chicago, inciting riot and use of force by police; 11 killed; 100 wounded, **May 4, 1886**; eight anarchists convicted of inciting violence, **Aug. 20, 1886**.

Haymarket Theatre, London theater, erected, **1720**; demolished and rebuilt, **1820**; since **1948**, one of leading British comedy theatres.

Hay-Pauncefote Treaty, U.S. and Britain signed new agreement, **Nov. 18, 1901**, repealing Clayton-Bulwer Treaty, that granted U.S. right to build and operate canal across isthmus of Panama.

Health and Human Services, U.S. Department of, federal executive department, formed **Mar. 30, 1953**, as U.S. Dept. of Health, Education, and Welfare; Mrs. Oveta Culp Hobby made first secretary, **Apr. 11, 1953**; adopted present name when separate U.S. Dept. of Education established, **1979**.

Hearst kidnapping, Patricia (Patty) Hearst [Feb. 20, 1954-], granddaughter of publisher William Randolph Hearst [Apr. 29, 1863-Aug. 14, 1951], kidnapped by Symbionese Liberation Army from her apartment, Berkeley, Calif., **Feb. 4, 1974**; Patty, facing bank robbery charges, apprehended by FBI in San Francisco, **Sept. 18, 1975**.

heart assistant, mechanical, flexible Silastic tube, first permanently implanted, **1966**, by American surgeon Adrian Kantrowitz [1918-].

heart auscultation, introduced, **1819**, by French physician Rene-Theophile H. Laennec [1781-1826].

heart, implant (artificial human), first by Argentine physician Domingo Liota [1924-] at Baylor University, Texas, **1969**.

heart-lung machine, invented, **1953**, by American surgeon John H. Gibbon [1903-].

heart muscle, electric charge of, first demonstrated, **1879**, by anatomist J. Burdon Sanderson [1829-1905].

heart transplant (human), first performed, **1967**, by South African physician Christiaan N. Barnard [1922-] at the University of Capetown. First in U.S. performed, **1967**, by American surgeon Adrian Kantrowitz [1918-].

Heavenfield, Northumbrians (Saxons) defeated Britons at Heavenfield near Hadrian's Roman Wall in n. England, **634**.

heavy gun sight, electric, patented, **1862**, by American inventor Theodore R. Timby [1822-1909]; adopted by U.S. government.

Hebrew Language, language of Hebrews, developed by **c. 2000 B.C.**, spoken by patriarchs migrating into Palestine; language of most of Old Testament; ceased to exist as spoken language, **c. 250 B.C.**; revived by State of Israel, **1948**.

Hebrew University, Israeli institution of higher learning, Jerusalem; foundation stones laid, **1918**; opened, **1925**.

Hebrews, Letter to the, New Testament book, **c. 67**.

Hegira, emigration from Mecca to Medina, **July 16, 622**, by the prophet Muhammad; traditional date for beginning of Muslim era.

Heidelberg, German city, residence of electors of Rhenish Palatinate, **1225-1720**.

Heidelberg University, important German institution of higher learning, founded, **1386**.

Heilsberg, battle of, French forces defeated the Prussians during the Napoleonic Wars, **June 10, 1807**.

Heisman Trophy, most prestigious American football award, first awarded, **1935**, in New York City.

Helgoland (Heligoland), strategic island in North Sea ceded to Britain by Denmark, **1814**; given to Germany in exchange for Zanzibar, **1890**; British destroyed German fortifications on island in one of largest known non-atomic blasts, **1947**.

helicopter, first successfully developed, **1937**, by German aviation engineer Heinrich Focke [1890-1979], using two rotors; first successful single rotor helicopter developed, **1939**, by Igor Sikorsky [1889-1972].

Heligoland Bight, battle of, first naval battle of WW I; British royal navy warships sank three German cruisers and one destroyer in the Heligoland Bight off n.w. coast of Germany, **Aug. 28, 1914**.

heliometer, invented, **1754**, by English optician John Dolland [1706-1761].

helium, element No. 2; discovered, **1895**, by Scottish chemist Sir William Ramsay [1852-1916].

helium, liquification of, device for liquification invented, **1934**, by Russian physicist Peter L. Kapitsa [1894-].

helium (on sun), discovered, **1868**, by English astronomer Sir Joseph N. Lockyer [1836-1921].

Hellenistic Age, period characterized by the spread of Greek culture and language throughout the Near East, began with Alexander the Great's conquests and ended with Rome's assimilation of Hellenistic culture, **c. 336-50 B.C.**

Hellespont (Dardanelles), 40-mil. long strait (1 mile wide at narrowest) connecting Aegean Sea with Sea of Marmara, crossed by Persian army under Xerxes I who used a bridge of boats, **c. 481 B.C.**; as did Alexander the Great, **334 B.C.**; closed by European powers to all but Turkish ships, **1841**; after Gallipoli campaign failed, Allies managed to pass through straits, (Bosporus and Dardanelles) **Nov. 1918**; straits internationalized by Treaty of Sevres, **Aug. 10, 1920**; straits restored to Turkey, **1923**; Turkey permitted to fortify straits, **1936**.

Hello, Dolly!, musical, opened **January 16, 1964**, about matchmaker, by U.S. composer-lyricist Jerry Herman [July 10, 1932-], directed by U.S. choreographer and director Gower Champion [June 22, 1921-Aug. 25, 1980]; film, **1969**; based on Thornton Wilder's play, *The Matchmaker*, **1954**.

Hell's Angels, famous U.S. motorcyle gang, first gained national attention, late **1950s**; prominent at West Coast rock concerts, **1960s**; attacked demonstrators at Oakland Moratorium Day, **Oct. 16, 1965**.

Helsinki accord, non-binding document dealing with European security, economics, and humanitarian matters, at Helsinki European Security Conference, **Aug. 1, 1975**.

Helvetic Republic, Swiss cantons occupied by the French and set up as a new republic with a central government, **1798-1803**; Bernese troops defeated French army at Laupen, **Mar. 5, 1798**; Bener Bernese defeated by French at Schauenberg on same day, **Mar. 5, 1798**; Five Forest Cantons (Catholic) accepted new republic, **Apr. 1798**; Geneva annexed to France, **Apr. 26, 1798**; Swiss cantons regained partial independence under terms of Napoleon's Act of Mediation, **Feb. 2, 1803**.

hemin, non-protein part of hemoglobin, synthesized, **1929**, by German chemist Hans Fischer [1881-1945].

hemoglobin, discovered, **1851**, by German physician Otto Funke [1828-1879]. Structure determined, **1960**, by Austrian-British chemist Max F. Perutz [1914-].

hemostatics, developed, **1733**, by English physiologist Stephen Hales [1677-1761].

Henry IV, two-part historical play, **1597-98**, by William Shakespeare; with *Henry V*, **1598-99**, chronicles transformation of profligate Prince Hal, companion of Falstaff, into Henry V [Aug. 9, 1387-Aug. 31, 1422], hero-king victor of Agincourt.

Henry VI, historical trilogy, **c. 1590-92**, dramatizing dark, violent events in years of incompetent King Henry VI [Dec. 6, 1421-May 21, 1471], by William Shakespeare.

Hepburn Act, U.S. Congress extended, **June 29, 1906**, Interstate Commerce Commission's powers over railroads, other carriers, and communications systems.

Hera, Temple of, Greek temple, **c. 900 B.C.**, oldest remaining monument from early period, Olympia, Greece.

Heraclea, ancient Greek city in s. Italy, site of defeat of Roman Legions by cavalry of King Pyrrhus [c. 318-272 B.C.] of Epirus, **280 B.C.**

Herculaneum, ancient Roman city completely buried by volcanic eruption of Mt. Vesuvius, **Aug. 24, 79**; discovery of ancient ruins, **1709**; excavations begun, **1927**.

Her (His) Majesty's Theatre, Haymarket, theater, established, **April 9, 1705**, as Queen's (then King's) Theatre; renamed again on accession of Queen Victoria, **1837**.

hereditary traits, demonstrated, **1885**, by German anatomist Rudolph A. von Kolliker [1817-1905] to be transmitted by a substance in the cell's nucleus.

Herero revolt, great, Germans suppressed by force revolt by Bantu-speaking Herero tribesmen in German South West Africa (Namibia), **1904-1908**.

Hermes, statue, **c. 343 B.C.**, by Greek sculptor Praxiteles [c. 390 B.C.-330 B.C.]; statue discovered, Olympia, Greece, **1875**.

Hero of Our Time (Geroi Nashevo Vremeni), novel, **1840**, about typical romantic hero, by Russian poet and novelist Mikhail (Yurevich) Lermontov [Oct. 15, 1814-July 27, 1841].

Herrenhausen, Treaty of, alliance among Britain, France and Russia in opposition to an agreement between Austria and Spain, **Sept. 23, 1725**.

Herrings, battle of the, English forces, barricaded behind barrels of herring fish, repulsed French attack at village of Rouvray near Orleans during Hundred Years' War, **Feb. 12, 1429**.

Herrin Riots, violent riots between striking United Mine Workers and strikebreakers, who mined coal secretly, near Herrin, Ill., resulted in 24 persons killed and many injured, **June 21, 1922**.

hertzian waves, demonstrated, **c. 1886**, by German physicist Heinrich R. Hertz [1857-1894].

Hessians, German soldiers from Hesse (state in W. Germany) hired by British to fight in American Revolution, **1776-80**; Americans led by Gen. Washington crossed Delaware River, surprised, and captured Hessian garrison in famous early morning raid at Trenton, N.J., **Dec. 26, 1776**.

Hexham, battle of, Yorkist army defeated the Lancastrians in Northumberland during the Wars of the Roses, **May 15, 1464**.

Hiawatha, narrative poem, **1855**, about Ojibway Indian who becomes leader of his people, by U.S. poet Henry Wadsworth Longfellow.

Hickey Plot, unsuccessful conspiracy by Thomas Hickey [?-June 27, 1776] to assassinate or hand over Gen. George Washington to the British, **June 1776**; Hickey hanged near Bowery Lane, N.Y., -first American soldier executed by military court order, **June 27, 1776**.

Hickory Pole Canvass, U.S. presidential campaign, **1828**, when Democrat Andrew Jackson, whose symbol was the hickory pole, won sweeping victory, **Dec. 3, 1828**.

hieroglyphics, ancient Egyptian writing, developed, **c. 3200 B.C.**; adapted to demotic script, **c. 700 B.C.**

higher-law doctrine, principle that "there is a higher law than the Constitution," expressed by U.S. Sen. William H. Seward [May 16, 1801-Oct. 10, 1872], leading abolitionist, of New York before the Senate, **Mar. 11, 1850**.

High Noon, film, **1952**, about marshall left alone to face vengeful outlaws; starred U.S. actor Gary Cooper (born Frank James Cooper) [May 7, 1901-May 13, 1961] and U.S. actress Grace Kelly (Princess Grace of Monaco) [Nov. 12, 1929-].

Himera, ancient Greek city on n. coast of Sicily where Gelon [d. 478 B.C.] of Syracuse defeated Carthaginians under Hamilcar [d. 480 B.C.], who was killed, **480 B.C.**; city destroyed by Carthaginians, **409 B.C.**

Hindenburg, German zeppelin (airship) *Hindenburg* exploded and burned at its tower mooring in Lakehurst, N.J.; 36 persons perished, **May 6, 1937**.

Hinduism, traditional religion of India, developed from **c. 3000 B.C.**; requires acceptance of Vedic scriptures, **1400-800 B.C.**, and *Upanishads*, from **800 B.C.**, and acceptance of Hindu social system.

Hiroshima, reportage, **1946**, a factual account of dropping of first atomic bomb on Japanese city of Hiroshima; told through interviews with six survivors, by U.S. writer John Hersey.

Hiss case, U.S. public official Alger Hiss [Nov. 11, 1904-], accused by Whittaker Chambers [Apr. 1, 1901-July 9, 1961] of spying for Soviet Union, **Aug. 1948**, found guilty of perjury, **Jan. 25, 1950**, and sentenced to prison for five years; released from prison, **Nov. 1954**.

histamine, synthesized, **1907**, by German chemist Adolf Windaus [1876-1959].

histidine, amino acid discovered, **1896**, by German physiologist Albrecht Kossel [1853-1927].

histology, study of living tissue; initiated, **c. 1800**, by French physician Marie F. X. Bichat [1771-1802].

Historiae Francorum (History of the Franks), history, **575-91**, chronicling in ten books history of Merovingian Franks, by chronicler and bishop St. Gregory of Tours [Nov. 30, 538-Nov. 17, 594].

Histories (Historiae), ancient historical work, **c. 110**, detailing Roman history from **69** to **96**, by Roman historian Cornelius Tacitus.

History of the English-Speaking Peoples, historical work in four volumes, completed, **1956**, detailing history of England and of lands colonized by England, by Sir Winston Churchill; Nobel Prize-winner, **1953**.

History of the Russian Revolution, history, **1932**, of events in which author played a significant role, by Communist leader and loser of power struggle Leon Trotsky (born Lev Davidovich Bronstein) [Oct. 25, 1879-Aug. 20, 1940].

H.M.S. Pinafore, comic opera, **1878**, by writing team of lyricist Sir William Gilbert [Nov. 18, 1836-May 19, 1911] and composer Sir Arthur Sullivan [May 13, 1842-Nov. 22, 1900].

Hittite Empire, ancient powerful federation of cities in Asia Minor and Syria under the Hittites, **fl. 1600-1200 B.C.**; destroyed by Thracians, Phrygians, and Assyrians, **c. 1200 B.C.**

Hobbit, the, romance, **1938**, about imaginary gnomelike creatures, by English philologist and writer J(ohn) R(onald) R(euel) Tolkien [Jan. 3, 1892-Sept. 2, 1973].

Hoboken fire, great, 326 persons killed when docks and steamship caught fire at Hoboken, N.J., causing $10 million in damage, **June 30, 1900**.

Hobkirk's Hill, battle of, misunderstanding of orders lost battle for Gen. Nathanael Greene's famous Maryland brigade at Hobkirk's Hill, near Camden, S.C., **Apr. 24, 1781**.

Hobson and *Wasp* collision, U.S. destroyer-minesweeper *Hobson* collided with U.S. aircraft carrier *Wasp* and sank during night maneuvers in the Atlantic; 176 persons perished, **Apr. 26, 1952**.

Hochstadt, battle of, French forces under General Jean Victor Moreau [Feb. 14, 1763-Sept. 2, 1813] defeated the Austrians during the French Revolutionary Wars, **June 19, 1800**.

Hochkirch, German village near Dresden where Austrians under Field Marshal Leopold Joseph Maria, Graf von Daun [1705-66] defeated Prussian army, **Oct. 14, 1758**; nearby site of Napoleon's defeat of Prussian-Russian army, **1813**.

Hoffman case, U.S. radical leader, Abbie Hoffman [1936-], co-founder (with Jerry Rubin) of the Youth International Party (Yippies) in the **1960s**, and one of the Chicago Seven defendants, **1967-73**; Hoffman arrested for selling cocaine, **Aug. 28, 1973**, but jumped bail on the charge; bench warrant issued for his arrest, **Apr. 16, 1974**; Hoffman surrendered 6 1/2 years later, **Sept. 1980**.

Hohenfriedeberg, battle of, well-disciplined Prussian army under Frederick II ("the

Great") routed larger Austrian-Saxon army at Hohenfriedeberg in s. Poland; one of Frederick's greatest military victories, **June 4, 1745.**

Hohenlinden, battle of, French army under Gen. Jean Moreau [Feb. 14, 1763-Sept. 2, 1813] won major victory over Austrians at Hohenlinden, e. of Munich, during French Revolutionary Wars, **Dec. 3, 1800.**

Hohenstaufens, German dynasty; emperors and German kings, **1138-1254**; Sicilian kings, **1194-1266.**

Hohenzollern, German dynasty; Prussian kings, **1701-1918**; German emperors, **1871-1918.**

hoisting and conveying machine, invented, **1879**, by American engineer Alexander E. Brown [1852-1911].

hole-punching machine (in steel), designed, **1848**, by Welsh inventor Richard Roberts [1789-1864].

Holland Land Company, company organized by Dutch bankers, **1796**; active in settlement of much of w. New York state, purchasing valuable lands from U.S. financier Robert Morris [Jan. 31, 1734-May 8, 1806],

1796-97; main office opened at Batavia, N.Y., **1801**; company's affairs in U.S. ended, **1846.**

Holland Tunnel, vehicular tunnel under Hudson River between New York and New Jersey; construction directed, **1919-1924**, by American engineer Clifford M. Holland [1883-1924].

Holmes-Ali fight, Larry Holmes [Nov. 3, 1949-] defeated Muhammad Ali by technical KO at Las Vegas, Nev., to retain World Boxing Council heavyweight crown, **Oct. 3, 1980.**

holmium, element No. 67, discovered, **1879**, by Swedish chemist Per T. Cleve [1840-1905].

Holy Family, The, painting, **1651**, one of three done during **1650-51**, depicting Jesus, Mary, and Joseph, by French classical painter Nicholas Poussin; brought record price of $3.6 million, London, **April 10, 1981.**

Holy Office, The, Roman congregation, established, **1542**, in connection with Inquisition, to safeguard faith and morals; reorganized, **1965**, and renamed *Sacred Congregation for the Doctrine of the Faith.*

Holy Year, Catholic jubilee year, instituted, **1300**, by Pope Boniface VIII (born Benedict Gaetani) [c. 1235-Oct. 11, 1303]; most recent Holy Year, **1975**, proclaimed by Pope Paul VI.

Holocaust, great Nazi purge of the Jews in Germany, Poland, and elsewhere in Europe, resulting in the killing of 6 million Jews, in death camps such as Auschwitz, Treblinka, Birkenau, and Majdanek, **1938-45.**

holography, lensless photography that produces realistic three-dimensional image; invented, **1948**, by Hungarian-British physicist Dennis Gabor [1900-1979].

Holy Alliance, emperors of Russia and Austria and king of Prussia formed alliance to preserve the social order according to Christian principles, **Sept. 26, 1815.**

Holy League, organization of French Catholics to suppress Protestants during the Huguenot Wars, **1576-98**; alliance formed by Pope Julius II with Venice, Spain, England, Swiss Confederation, and Holy Roman Emperor Maximilian I to expel King Louis XII of France from Italy, **1510-13.**

Holy Roman Empire, political empire in

central Europe, established as a kind of extension of the Western Roman Empire under the ecclesiastical rule of the pope, **962-1806**.

Homestead Act, U.S. Congress gave 160 acres of unoccupied public land to homesteaders for nominal fee after five years of residence, **May 20, 1862**.

Homestead strike, Pinkerton detectives, hired by management, and strikers at Carnegie steel mills in Homestead, Penn., fought bloody battle, in which 10 men were killed, **July 6, 1892**; Penn. state troopers ordered to Homestead, **July 9, 1892**, and remained there, until **Nov. 20, 1892**.

homeostasis, theory of, proposed, **1929**, by American physiologist Walter B. Cannon [1871-1945].

Honduras, republic in Central America, declared its independence from Spain, **1821**; part of confederation of Central American states, **1825-38**; became fully independent nation, **1838**.

Honduras-El Salvador war, Honduras' expulsion of 10,000 Salvadoran migrant workers precipitated invasion of Honduras by Salvadoran troops, **July 14, 1969**; ended by OAS-negotiated armistice, **July 18, 1969**, but border fighting continued for years.

Honkeiko Colliery mine disaster, world's worst mine disaster killed 1549 persons at Honkeiko coal mine, Manchuria, **Apr. 25, 1942**.

Hoover Commission, non-partisan group of U.S. business and professional experts, headed by former Pres. Herbert C. Hoover [Aug. 10, 1874-Oct. 20, 1964], created **July 7, 1947**, to examine government inefficiency and to recommend improvements; released series of final reports for changes, **Feb. 7, Feb. 17, Mar 21, Apr. 1, 1949**; more than half of commission's recommendations put into effect, **1949-55**.

Hoover Dam, U.S. Pres. Herbert Hoover authorized, **Dec. 21, 1928**, dam to be built on the Colorado River on the Arizona-Nevada boundary; built **1931-36**; named Boulder Dam, **1933-47**.

Hoover Institution on War, Revolution, and Peace, research organization, established **1919**, at Stanford University, Calif., as the Hoover War Library by Herbert C.

Hoover [Aug. 10, 1874-Oct. 20, 1964].

Hopetown, site on Orange River of first discovery of diamonds in South Africa, **1867**.

Horatio Alger stories, stories of poor boys who made good through honesty and industry, found in successive novels such as *Ragged Dick*, **1867**; *Luck and Pluck*, **1869**; *Tattered Tom*, **1871**, by U.S. writer Horatio Alger [Jan. 13, 1832-July 18, 1899].

Horatio Hornblower, British naval officer hero of popular novels, **1937-50**, whose career from midshipman to admiral in Napoleonic wars traced in, among others, *The Happy Return*, **1937**; *Lord Hornblower*, **1946**, by English novelist C(ecil) S(cott) Forester.

hormones, discovered, **1902**, by English physiologists Ernest H. Starling [1866-1927] and Sir William M. Bayliss [1860-1924]; role of pituitary hormone in diabetes first reported, **1930**, by Argentine physiologist Bernardo A. Houssay [1887-1971]; hormone implants, advocated, **1939**, by American physician George W. Thorn [1906-]; mechanics of, researched, from c. **1950**, by U.S. physiologist Earl W. Sutherland, Jr. [1915-].

Horseshoe Bend, battle of, U.S. militia under Gen. Andrew Jackson defeated Creek Indians under William Weatherford, also called Red Eagle, at the Horseshoe Bend of the Tallapoosa River in e. Alabama, **Mar. 27, 1814**.

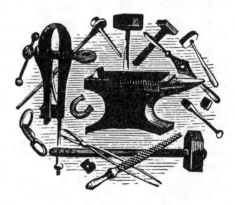

horseshoes, machine for making horseshoes invented, **1835**, by Scottish-American ironmaster Henry Burden [1791-1871].

Hosea, Book of, Old Testament book containing prophecies delivered, **c. 760-720 B.C.**.

Hospitallers, or Knights of St. John, medieval military religious order, founded, Jerusalem, **1099**, to help sick pilgrims; conquered and held Rhodes, **1310-1525**; ruled Malta, **1530-1798**.

hostage crisis, U.S., Iranian student militants seized U.S. embassy in Tehran, **Nov. 4, 1979**, holding Americans and others hostage, demanding return of Shah Muhammad Reza Pahlavi and his money; Iran halted oil shipments to U.S., **Nov. 12, 1979**; U.S. froze Iranian assets in U.S. banks, **Nov. 14, 1979**; Iran's Ayatollah Ruholla Khomeini [1901-] threatened to try hostages as spies; 18 women and black hostages released, **Nov. 19-22, 1979**; U.S. military mission to rescue hostages failed, **Apr. 24, 1980**; Shah Reza died in Cairo, **July 27, 1980**; U.S.-Algerian-Iran negotiations resulted in release of 52 American hostages, **Jan. 20, 1981**, with end to U.S. financial sanctions against Iran.

Hot Line, emergency 4,883-mile teletype cable system linking the White House with the Kremlin, since **Sept. 1, 1963**.

Hours, of the Duke of Berry, The (Belles Heures du Duc de Berry), medieval illuminated manuscript, **c. 1410-13**.

House Committee on Un-American Activities, U.S. Congress created, **May 26, 1938**, committee to investigate Communist, Nazi, Fascist organizations and other un-American groups.

House-Divided **speech**, address made by Abraham Lincoln at Illinois Republican state convention that nominated him for U.S. Senator, **June 16, 1858**, in which he said, "A house divided against itself cannot stand," referring to slavery controversy.

Houses of Parliament, extended Parliament buildings along the Thames, built, **1840-52**, in ornate neogothic style.

Hovercraft, air-cushioned boat introduced, **1959**, by English engineer Christopher S. Cockerell [1913-]; ferry service across English Channel began, **1968**.

Howes-Cutting Act, U.S. Congress provided transitional commonwealth for the Philippines, **Jan. 13, 1933**, with U.S. rights to military and naval bases and tariffs on Philippine products to U.S.; rejected by Philippine legislature, **Oct. 1933**.

Howdy Doody Show, The, television series, **1947-60**, one of earliest and most popular, featuring puppet Howdy Doody, animated by U.S. entertainer and ventriloquist "Buffalo" Bob Smith [1917-].

How to Win Friends and Influence People, popular guide, **1936**, followed by many subsequent editions, by self-help author Dale Carnegie [Nov. 24, 1888-Nov. 1, 1955].

Hsia, semi-legendary dynasty said to have ruled China, **c. 2205-c. 1766 B.C.** or **c. 1994-c. 1523 B.C.**

Huascaran avalanche, immense avalanche swept down Mt. Huascaran and buried village of Ranrahirca in w. central Peru; more than 3,000 killed, **Jan. 10, 1962**.

Hubbardton, battle of, British reinforcements won victory against American revolutionaries at Hubbardton, Vt., **July 7, 1777**, during Gen. Burgoyne's advance south from Canada.

Hubertusberg, Treaty of, signed by Austria and Prussia at end of Seven Years' War, **Feb. 15, 1763**.

Huckleberry Finn, The Adventures of, novel, **1884**, about adventures of an orphan and a runaway slave rafting down the Mississippi, by U.S. novelist Mark Twain.

Hudson's Bay Company, English merchants established fur-trading company in Hudson's Bay region, **1668**; chartered, **1670**; amalgamated with North West Company, **1821**; **fl. 1821-56**.

Hudson Review, literary quarterly, published, from **1948**, New York; has published works of writers such as Bellow, Eliot, Marianne Moore, and Pound.

Hudson River, Giovanni de Verrazano [c. 1485-c. 1528] was first European to sight present-day Hudson River, **1524**; explored by Henry Hudson [fl. 1607-11] for Dutch East India Company, **1609**; Hudson River linked to Great Lakes by Erie Canal, **1825**.

Hue, Treaty of, French established protectorates over Tonkin and Annam, **Aug. 25, 1883**.

Huesca, ancient fortress-town at foot of Pyrenees held by Moors, **8th-11th centuries**; Spanish stormed fortress and captured it, making town capital of kingdom of Aragon, **1096**.

Huguenot Wars (Wars of Religion), series of civil conflicts between Protestants (Huguenots) and Catholics in France, **1562-98**; first war, **1562-63**; second, **1567-68**; third, **1568-70**; fourth, **1572-73**; fifth **1574-76**; sixth, **1577**; seventh, **1580**; Edict of Nantes granted freedom of worship to Huguenots in France, **Apr. 15, 1598**; forced to flee France after its revocation, **1685**.

Hull House, one of first U.S. settlement houses for the poor, founded, **1889**, by Jane Addams [Sept. 6, 1869-May 21, 1935] in Chicago.

human mortality, law of, proposed, **1825**, by English mathematician Benjamin Gompertz [1779-1865]; known as Gompertz' law.

Humanae Vitae (Of Human Life), papal encyclical, issued, **July 29, 1968**, reaffirming traditional Roman Catholic Church moral condemnation of artificial contraception.

Human Comedy, The (La Comedie Humaine), title given to all his fiction,

1841, by French novelist Honore de Balzac.

Humani Generis, papal encyclical, issued **August 12, 1950**, warning about several modern theological trends.

humanism, philosophy and attitude glorifying human achievement that characterized the Renaissance; developed, from **c. 1453**, when fall of Constantinople brought Greek scholars and learning to Italy.

Humble Petition and Advice, new English constitution offered to and accepted by (with some changes) Lord Cromwell, who was also offered (but declined) the crown, **Mar.-May 1657**.

Humphrey-Hawkins Bill, U.S. Congress passed measure, **Oct. 15, 1978**, to reduce national unemployment to 4% and inflation to 3% by 1983; signed by U.S. Pres. James Earl ("Jimmy") Carter [Oct. 1, 1924-], **Oct. 27, 1978**.

Hunchback of Notre Dame, The (Notre Dame de Paris), novel, **1831**, about medieval life of great Parisian cathedral, featuring bell-ringer Quasimodo ("the hunchback"), by French writer Victor Hugo; film, **1939**, based on Hugo's romantic novel, starring as hunchback English actor Charles Laughton [July 1, 1899-Dec. 15, 1962]; film version, **1929**, starred U.S. actor Lon Chaney [Apr. 1, 1883-Aug. 26, 1930].

Hundred Days, Napoleon's, Napoleon returned to Paris from exile in Elba until he was defeated at Waterloo, **Mar. 20-June 28, 1815**.

Hundred Years' War, war between England and France, **1337-1453**; Edward III [1312-77] of England, proclaiming himself king of France, defeated French navy at Sluys, **June 24, 1340**; defeated French at Crecy, **Aug. 26, 1346**; England gained Calais and w. France by Treaty of Bretigny, **May 8, 1360**; France won back lost territory, by **1373**; Henry V of England defeated French knights at Agincourt, **Oct. 25, 1415**; Joan of Arc raised the English siege of Orleans, **May 7, 1429**; Charles VI of France made alliance with Burgundy by Treaty of Arras, **1435**; French reconquered rest of France, except Calais, **1436-53**.

Hungarian revolts, Hungarians rose up against Austrian rule but were suppressed by combined Austrian-Russian army, **1848-49**; Hungarian anti-communist revolt broke out at Budapest and throughout Hungary but was brutally suppressed by Soviet forces, **Oct. 23-Nov. 22, 1956**.

Hungarian Rhapsodies, 19 musical works, **1846-55**, utilizing Hungarian dances and melodies, by Hungarian composer Franz Liszt [Oct. 22, 1811-July 31, 1886].

Hungary, country in central Europe, became independent republic after collapse of Austria-Hungary monarchy, **1918**; brief Communist rule, **1919**, ended with Rumanian invasion, **Aug. 4, 1919**; reduced in size by Treaty of Trianon, **June 4, 1920**; joined Axis powers, **1941**; invaded by Russia, troops, **Oct. 1944**; signed armistice in Moscow, **Jan. 20, 1945**; its 1000-year-old monarchy abolished and republic established, **Feb. 1, 1946**; Soviets crushed Hungarian anti-Communist revolt, **Oct. 23, 1956**; U.S. returned to Hungary 977-year-old crown of St. Stephen, **Jan. 6, 1978**.

Hunkiar-Iskelesi, Treaty of, mutual defensive alliance between Ottoman Empire and Russia, which gained use of the Dardanelles closed to all other foreign warships, **July 8, 1833**.

Huns, barbarous, nomadic Asiatic people who invaded Europe, led by Attila [c. 406-53]; **4th-5th century**.

Huntley-Brinkley Report, The, NBC evening newscast, **1956-70**; premiered, **October 15, 1956**; famous for mutual "good night" spoken between two U.S. journalist anchormen Chet Huntley [Dec. 10, 1911-Mar. 20, 1974] and David (McClure) Brinkley [July 10, 1920-].

Huron Indians, confederation of four North American Indian tribes destroyed in war with Dutch-supported Iroquois Indians, **1648-49**.

Hurricane Agnes, eastern seaboard of U.S., from Fla. to N.Y., devastated by tropical storm Agnes; 134 killed; about $3 billion in damage, **June 10-20, 1972**.

Hurricane Camille, one of the most destructive tropical storms to hit U.S., swept through Miss., La., Ala., Va., and W. Va., leaving approx. 200 persons dead, **Aug. 17-22, 1969**.

Hurricane Carol, immense tropical storm struck Long Island, New York, and New England, leaving 68 persons dead and about $200 million in property damage, **Aug. 30-31, 1954**.

Hurricane Diane, U.S. eastern seaboard struck by violent tropical storm that caused serious floods in Northeast; approx. 400 persons killed and $2 billion in property damage, **Aug. 18-21, 1955**.

Hurricane Donna, immense tropical storm swept entire seaboard of U.S., from Fla. to New England, leaving 30 persons dead, **Sept. 4-13, 1960**.

Hurricane Fifi, violent hurricane struck n.

Honduras, killing 8000 persons, leaving 100,000 homeless, **Sept. 20, 1974**.

Hurricane Hazel, violent tropical storm struck e. seaboard of U.S. and into Canada, leaving 99 Americans and 249 Canadians dead and $100 million in property damage, **Oct. 15-16, 1954**.

Hurricane of '38, without warning, powerful tropical storm struck Long Island and s. New England, leaving approx. 600 dead and about $150 million in property damage, **Sept. 21, 1938**.

Hussites, followers of Czech religious reformer John Huss [1372-July 6, 1415], who were active **c. 1400-1425**; inflicted defeats on imperial forces; Huss condemned by Council of Constance and burned at stake, **1415**; toleration adopted, **1485**.

Hussite Wars, series of conflicts between Hussites (followers of John Huss) and Holy Roman Empire, **1419-36**; Hussites invaded Silesia, **1425-26**; invaded Franconia, **1429-30**; Hussite delegation accepted Compacta-ta, **1433**; radical Taborites routed at Lipany, during civil war, **1434**.

Hwai-Hai, battle of, one of great battles of modern history; Communist People's Liberation Army encircled and cut to pieces Nationalist army during 65-day battle in e. central China during Chinese Civil War, **Nov. 7, 1948-Jan. 12, 1949**.

Hyderabad, battle of, Indian army invaded former state of Hyderabad, **Sept. 13, 1948**, whose Muslim prince had wished to remain independent from India; Hyderabad surrendered, **Sept. 17, 1948**.

hydrocephalus, first described, **1758**, by Scottish physician Robert Whytt [1714-1766].

hydrogen, element No. 1; discovered, **1766**, by English chemist Henry Cavendish [1731-1810].

hydrogen bomb (Soviet), developed, **1952**, by Russian physicist Igor V. Kurchatov [1903-1960].

hydrogen bomb (U.S.), first developed by U.S. physicist Edward Teller and others, from **1949**; first thermonuclear test explosion, **1952**, by U.S. Atomic Energy Commission at Eniwetok Atoll in Pacific.

hydrogen from gas, method developed, **1909**, by German chemist Carl Bosch [1874-1940].

hydrogen (in sun's atmosphere), discovered, **1862**, by Swedish astronomer and physicist Anders J. Angstrom [1814-1874].

hydrogen peroxide, synthesized, **1818**, by French chemist Louis J. Thenard [1777-1857].

hydrogenated oils, process for synthesis discovered, **1897**, by French chemist Paul Sabatier [1854-1941].

hydrometer, invented, **1790**, by English chemist William Nicholson [1753-1815] for measuring density of water.

hydroplane, invented, **1911**, by American aviation pioneer Glenn H. Curtiss [1878-1930].

hymn, Christian song of praise of God (nonscriptural), first post-New-Testament example, **c. 200**; developed, from **c. 380**; introduced by Luther into Protestant services, from **c. 1520**; admitted to churches in English-speaking countries, **c. 1700**.

Hymns, book of hymns, **1707**, that revolutionized Protestant hymn-singing in the English language; included "O God, Our Help in Ages Past," by English hymn writer Isaac Watts [July 17, 1664-Nov. 25, 1748].

hyposulphite (sodium thiosulphate), use in fixing photographic image discovered, **c. 1819**, by English astronomer Sir John F. Herschel [1792-1871].

hypnotism, term introduced, **c. 1842**, by Scottish surgeon James Braid [1795-1860].

hysteresis, law of, first established, **1892**, by German-American mathematician, electrical engineer Charles P. Steinmetz [1866-1923].

I Am a Camera, play, **1951**, dramatization of Christopher Isherwood's *Berlin Stories*, by U.S. writer John Van Druten [June 1, 1901-Dec. 19, 1957]; made into musical *Cabaret*, **1966**.

Ibo, largest African tribe in s.e. Nigeria, played a major part in gaining Nigeria's independence from Britain, **1963**, thousands killed during political struggle in n. Nigeria, home of Hausa and Fulani tribes, **1966**; fled to Biafra, **1967**.

Iceland, island nation in North Atlantic, first settled by Norsemen, **c. 850-70**; drew up democratic constitution, **c. 930**; under Norwegian rule until Danes took control, **1483**; became fully independent republic, **June 17, 1944**.

ice-making machine, patented, **1851**, by American physician-inventor John Gorrie [1803-1855].

Ich bin ein Berliner (I am a Berliner), famous remark during speech by U.S. Pres. John F. Kennedy comparing free world and Communist world before Berlin Wall, W. Germany, **June 24, 1963**.

Iconoclastic Controversy, quarrel over veneration of icons that agitated Eastern Orthodox Church, **c. 725-842**; images ordered destroyed, **726**, by Emperor Leo III the Isaurian [675-June 18, 741]; degree of legitimate veneration of images defined, Second Council of Nicaea, **787**.

Idaho, admitted to the Union (U.S.) as 43rd state, **July 3, 1890**.

idealism, philosophical theory holding that ultimate reality consists of ideas, originated **c. 400 B.C.**, with Plato; school flourished in modern times especially in Germany, from **c. 1780**.

Idiot, The, novel, **1868**, attempting to portray a "good man;" Prince Myshkin (the "idiot"), however, brings bad luck to those he meets, by Russian novelist Fyodor Dostoyevsky.

Idylls of the King, series of poems, **1859-85**, about Arthurian legends, by English poet Alfred, Lord Tennyson.

I have a dream, famous statement first uttered by Rev. Martin Luther King, Jr. [Jan. 15, 1929-Apr. 4, 1968] to crowd of more than 200,000 blacks and whites at Lincoln Memorial, Washington, D.C., **Aug. 28, 1963**.

Iliad, Greek epic poem, written down, **c. 700 B.C.**, recounting last days of Trojan War, **c. 1200 B.C.**, attributed to poet, Homer, [fl. 8th century B.C.].

Illinois, formerly part of Northwest Territory, admitted to the Union (U.S.) as 21st state, **Dec. 3, 1818**.

Illuminati, The, masonic sect, founded, **1778**, to diffuse knowledge and humanistic ideals; they were ousted from Bavaria, **1784**; revived in Germany, **c. 1896**.

Illumination, art of decorating manuscripts with designs, pictures, and fine calligraphy; first known example: Egyptian *Book of the*

Dead, **800-600 B.C.**; best-known European example: *Hours of the Duke of Berry*, **c. 1410-13**.

Illyria (Illyricum), ancient kingdom in the Balkan peninsula conquered by Romans, **168-167 B.C.**; Roman territory of Illyricum split into provinces of Dalmatia and Pannonia, **9**; Napoleon revived name of Illyria, including much territory n. of Adriatic in the region, **1809**.

I Love Lucy, all-time popular television situation comedy, originally on CBS, **1951-57**, but still being syndicated; starred U.S. comedienne Lucille Ball [Aug. 6, 1911-] with one-time husband Cuban-born bandleader and actor Desi Arnaz [Mar. 2, 1917-].

image dissector tube, invented, **1927**, by American engineer Philo T. Farnsworth [1906-1971].

imagism, movement in English-U.S. poetry, **1910-20**, demanding direct treatment of object without rhetoric; U.S. expatriate poet Ezra Pound edited first imagist anthology, *Some Imagist Poets*, **1912**.

I'm Alone, The, Canadian registered rum-running ship, *The I'm Alone*, owned by U.S. citizens, sunk by U.S. Coast Guard about 200 miles off coast, **Mar. 22, 1929**, causing crisis in U.S.-Canadian relations.

Imitation of Christ, The, spiritual classic, **1418**; devotional book instructing Christian how to seek perfection by following Christ,

by monk and writer Thomas a Kempis [c. 1380-Aug. 8, 1471]; first English translation, **1503**.

immunity, investigated, **1895**, by Belgian bacteriologist Jules J. P. Bordet [1870-1961].

immunity (against transplanted tissue), theory developed, **c. 1950**, by Australian physician Sir F. Macfarlane Burnet [1899-] and British biologist Sir Peter B. Medawar [1915-].

immunology, mechanism of, specified, **1904**, by German bacteriologist Paul Ehrlich [1854-1915] and Russian biologist Elie Metchnikoff [1845-1916].

impressionism, artistic school, flourished, **c. 1860-1890**, especially in France.

Inca civilization, pre-Colombian Indian empire centered at Cuzco, Peru, founded **c. 1200**; reached its greatest extent and power under Huayna Capac [d. 1525], **1493-1525**; declined after Spanish conquest, **1533**.

Inchon, Korean port on Yellow Sea where U.S. forces made important amphibious landing during Korean War, **Sept. 15, 1950**; landing relieved pressure, allowing U.S. 8th Army to break out of Pusan perimeter, **Sept. 16, 1950**; U.S. forces linked up near Osan and South Korean capital of Seoul liberated from North Korean control, **Sept. 16, 1950**.

incubator, baby, developed, during **1930s**, by American pediatrician Charles C. Chapple [1903-1979].

incunabula, books printed before **c. 1500**.

Independence Hall, building constructed as State House, Philadelphia, **1731**; U.S. Declaration of Independence signed there, **July 4, 1776**.

Independence Party, U.S. political party, headed by William Randolph Hearst [Apr. 29, 1863-Aug. 14, 1951], nominated national ticket at Chicago, Ill., **July 27, 1908**.

Index Librorum Prohibitorum, list of books formerly forbidden reading for Roman Catholics, first issued, Rome, **1557**; list supervised by Congregation of the *Index*, **1571-1917**; *Index* abolished, **1966**, after Second Vatican Council.

India, country in Asia, became independent from British rule, **Aug. 15, 1947**; became republic, **Jan. 26, 1950**; fought Chinese in

Ladakh in Kashmir and on n.e. border, **Oct. 20-Nov. 21, 1962**; three-week war with Pakistan over Kashmir, **Aug. 1965**; two-week war with Pakistan in East Pakistan (Bangladesh) and Kashmir, **Dec. 1971**.

India Act, British parliament transferred control of government of India from British East India Company to the crown, **Aug. 2, 1858**.

Indiana, formerly part of Northwest Territory, admitted to the Union (U.S.) as 19th state, **Dec. 11, 1816**.

Indiana company, organization of colonial land speculators and Indian traders in upper Ohio River valley, **c. 1720**; absorbed into Grand Ohio Company, **1740s**.

Indian Affairs, Bureau of, established as part of U.S. War Dept., **1824**; combined with others to form Dept. of the Interior, **1849**.

Indianapolis 500, famous U.S. 500-mile auto race held annually during Memorial Day weekend at the Indianapolis Motor Speedway, first won by a Marmon Wasp, **May 30, 1911**.

Indian Councils Act (Morley-Minto reforms), British greatly increased Indian power in legislative councils of British India, with separate electorates for Muslims and other special groups, **May 25, 1909**.

Indian cyclones, great, Calcutta ruined and approx. 200,000 persons killed by cyclone followed by earthquake, **Oct. 7-11, 1737**; most of Calcutta destroyed and

approx. 70,000 killed, **Oct. 1, 1864**; Bakarganj, India, ruined and approx. 200,000 killed by cyclone followed by tidal wave, **Oct. 31, 1876**; city of Bombay hit and approx 100,000 killed by cyclone followed by tidal wave, **June 5, 1882**; Bengal, India, devastated and approx 40,000 killed, **Oct. 16, 1942**; more than 500,000 buildings leveled in India and Sri Lanka, **Nov. 23, 1978**.

Indian National Congress, political organization of India, established, **1885**, to gain British dominion status for India; militants led by Gandhi forced moderates out, **1917**, and began passive resistance program to achieve independence for India, **1919**; outlawed by British, **1942-45**; forced to accept Muslim League's demand for separate state of Pakistan, **1947**; became major party of India under Nehru, **1947-64**; led by Nehru's daughter, Indira Gandhi [Nov. 19, 1917-], **1966-77; 1980-**.

Indian Removal Act, Pres. Andrew Jackson authorized general resettlement of Indians to territories west of Mississippi River, **May 28, 1830**; about 60,000 Indians forced to move, **1830-43**.

Indian Walk, Delaware Indians granted land to Pennsylvanian settlers extending into the back country as far as a man could walk in a day and a half, **1737**.

indigo, synthesized, **1878**, by German chemist Adolph von Baeyer [1835-1917].

indium, element No. 49; discovered, **1863**, by German mineralogists Ferdinand Reich [1799-1882] and Hieronymus T. Richter [1824-1898].

individual psychology, established, **1911**, by Austrian ophthalmologist and psychiatrist, Alfred Adler [1870-1937].

Indochina, French, former federation of states formed by French in Asia, **1862-1954**; Cochin China became French colony, **June 5, 1862**; Tonkin and Annam made into French protectorates, **Aug. 25, 1883**; Cochin, Tonkin, Annam (together Vietnam), and Cambodia united to form French Union of Indochina, **1887**; Laos added to union, **1893**; Vietnamese fought French for independence, **1946-54**; French defeated decisively at Dienbienphu, **May 7, 1954**; French lost control of Indochina at Geneva Conference, **Apr.-July 1954**.

Indonesia, part of Malay archipelago in Asia, waged war, **1945-49,** to gain independence from Dutch rule, **Dec. 27, 1949.**

induction coil, invented, **1851,** by German inventor Heinrich Ruhmkorff [1803-1877].

inductive method, formalized, **1620,** by English philosopher Francis Bacon [1561-1626].

Industrial Congress, one of earliest U.S. labor unions, organized in New York City, **1845;** nominated candidates for president and vice president at Philadelphia, **1848;** declined, after **1856.**

Industrial Revolution, changes from an agricultural and handicraft society to machine and factory production c. **1750-1850,** started in England and later in other countries.

Industrial Workers of the World (IWW), revolutionary labor union, established **July 7, 1905,** in Chicago, aiming to overthrow capitalism; reached its peak with about 100,000 members, **1912;** declined, after **1917.**

infection, parasitic theory of, proposed, **1835,** by Italian scientist Agostino Bassi [1773-1856].

inferiority complex, concept introduced, **1918,** by Austrian psychiatrist Alfred Adler [1870-1937].

Informer, The, novel, **1925,** about the Irish revolution, by Irish author Liam O'Flaherty [1897-]. Film based on O'Flaherty's novel, **1935,** directed by U.S. director John Ford, starred U.S.-English actor Victor McLaglen [Dec. 11, 1883-Nov. 1959].

influenza bacillus, described, **1892,** by German bacteriologist Richard Friedrich Johannes Pfeiffer [1858-1945].

infinity, arithmetical concept introduced, **1874,** by Russian-German mathematician Georg Cantor [1845-1918].

Ingavi, battle of, Bolivian army defeated Peruvian army in pitched battle at Ingavi, south of La Paz, ending Peruvian invasion and Bolivian-Peruvian war, **Nov. 20, 1841.**

Ingersoll rock drill, patented, **1871,** by American inventor Simon Ingersoll [1818-1894].

In God We Trust, inscription appeared for first time on U.S. two-cent piece, **1864.**

inkblot test, introduced, **1921,** by Swiss psychiatrist Hermann Rorschach [1884-1922].

Inkerman, battle of, Russians failed to break British-French siege of Sevastopol at Inkerman and retreated, having lost 12,000 men, **Nov. 5, 1854.**

Inquisition, system instigated by the Roman Catholic Church for the discovery, examination, and punishment of heretics in central and south Europe, **13th-19th centuries;** began when Dominicans investigated the Albigenses in s. France, c. **1233.**

Inquisition, The, ecclesiastical court, established, **1235,** to inquire into doctrinal errors against Roman Catholic faith (then the state religion); heretics found guilty were delivered to secular arm for punishment.

Inquisition, The Spanish, ecclesiastical court, established, Spain, **1478,** at request of Spanish monarchs, to examine suspected heretics against official Roman Catholic faith; became synonym for cruelty under Grand Inquisitor Tomas de Torquemada [1420-Sept. 16, 1498]; abolished, **1808.**

Institut de France, national cultural institution of France established by the Directory, **1795,** after the five royal learned academies [French Academy (founded **1635**), Academie des Beaux-Arts (founded **1648**),

Academie des Inscriptions et Belles-Lettres (founded **1663**), Academie des Sciences (founded **1666**), and Academie des Sciences morales et politiques (founded **1795**)]; had been suppressed in **1793**; academies later restored within the Institut, by **1832**.

Insular cases, U.S. Supreme Court ruled, **May 27, 1901**, that territories acquired by U.S. during Spanish-American War were not part of U.S. and not foreign countries.

insulators, glass, first developed, c. **1840**, by American inventor and financier Ezra Cornell [1807-1874].

insulin, discovery first reported, **1922**, by Canadian physician Frederick G. Banting [1891-1941] and Canadian physiologist John J. Macleod [1876-1935]; molecular structure determined, **1955**, by British biochemist Frederick Sanger [1918-].

Insurance, first fire insurance company (Friendly Society for the Mutual Insurance of Houses Against Fire) in America established at Charleston, S.C., **1735**; first life insurance company (Presbyterian Ministers Fund) established at Philadelphia, **1759**; first mutual life insurance company (Mutual Life Insurance Company of New York) granted charter, **Apr. 12, 1842**; first accident insurance company (Travelers Insurance Company) established at Hartford, Conn., **1863**.

intelligence tests, point scale developed, **1918**, by American psychologist Robert M. Yerkes [1876-1956].

interchangeable parts, U.S. manufacture pioneered, c. **1800**, by American inventor Eli Whitney [1765-1825].

Intercolonial Railway, major Canadian government-owned and operated railroad opened, linking Ontario with Maritime Provinces of Canada, **1876**.

interferometer, invented, **1882**, by U.S. physicist Albert A. Michelson [1852-1931].

interferon, a natural substance produced by the body's infection defense system to block virus infections; identifed, in **1957**, by Scottish virologist Alick Isaacs [1921-1967].

interior environment, theory of, proposed, **1878**, by French physiologist Claude Bernard [1813-1887].

Interior, U.S. Department of the, federal executive department created as the Home Department, **Mar. 3, 1849**.

International Bureau of Weights and Measures, worldwide scientific organization, headquartered in Sevres, France, established, **1875**, to set standards for metric system.

International Copyright Act, U.S. Congress gave copyright protection to works of British, French, Swiss, and Belgian authors in U.S., **Mar. 4, 1891**.

International Labor Organization (ILO), special agency dealing with labor conditions, created by Treaty of Versailles, **June 28, 1919**, as part of League of Nations; became agency of United Nations, **1946**.

International Refugee Organization (IRO), former special agency of United Nations concerned with care and resettlement of refugees, established **Dec. 15, 1946**; superseded by United Nations High Commissioner for Refugees, **Jan. 1951**.

international style, style of architecture developed in U.S. and Europe, from c. **1910**; characterized by emphasis on function, eschewing decorative motifs.

International Trade Organization (ITO), special agency of United Nations to promote multilateral international trade and employment, established **Mar. 24, 1948**, by 53 countries at Havana, Cuba.

Internationale, The, song, composed, France, **1871**; official anthem of Communist movement ("Up, damned of the earth,...").

Interpretation of Dreams, The, epochal study of probing the unconscious mind through free-association techniques, **1900,** by Austrian physician Sigmund Freud.

Interstate Commerce Commission (ICC), U.S. Congress enacted, **Feb. 8, 1887,** Interstate Commerce Act, setting up federal commission to regulate transportation and commerce beyond state borders.

Intolerable Acts (Coercive Acts), name given by American patriots to five acts passed by British parliament as reprisals against Americans for Boston Tea Party, **1774;** first act, Boston Port Bill, closed Boston harbor until East India Company was paid for destroyed tea, **Mar. 31, 1774;** second and third acts increased Crown's power over Massachusetts courts and charter, **May 20, 1774;** fourth, Quebec Act, called "intolerable," **May 30, 1774;** fifth, new Quartering Act, forced Massachusetts residents to house and feed British troops, **June 2, 1774.**

introversion-extraversion, personality traits first conceptualized, **1921,** by Swiss psychoanalyst Carl Gustav Jung [1875-1962].

iodine, element No. 53; discovered, **1811,** by French chemist Bernard Courtois [1777-1838].

iodoform, discovered, **1822,** by French chemist George S. Serullas [1774-1832].

Ionia, ancient Greek region in w. Asia Minor and coastal Aegean Islands, **fl. c. 1000-500 B.C.**

Ionic Architecture.—Temple of Wingless Victory, on the Acropolis of Athens.

Ionic order, Greek style of architecture, developed from **c. 450-400 B.C.;** characterized by tapered columns with graceful, spiral volute capitals; used on Erechtheum, Athens, **421-405 B.C.**

ionic solutions, theory of, developed, **1923,** by Dutch-American physical chemist Peter J. Debye [1884-1966].

ions, concept introduced, **1887,** by Swedish chemist Svante August Arrhenius [1859-1927].

Iowa, part of territory acquired by Louisiana Purchase, admitted to the Union (U.S.) as 30th state, **Dec. 28, 1846.**

ipecac, discovered, **1649,** by Dutch physician Gulielmus Le Pois (Piso) [1611-1678].

Iphigenia in Aulis (Iphigeneia he en Aulidi), tragedy, **405 B.C.,** by Greek dramatist Euripides; tragedy, **1679,** based on Euripides' tragedy, by French playwright Jean Racine; opera, **1772,** with often performed overture, by Christoph Gluck.

Iphigenia in Tauris (Iphigeneia he en Taurois), tragedy, **c. 414-12 B.C.,** by Greek dramatist Euripides; opera, **1779,** by Christoph Gluck; play, **1787,** by German writer Johann Wolfgang von Goethe.

Ipiranga, Grito de (Cry of Ipiranga), famous declaration of Brazilian independence made by Dom Pedro (later Emperor Pedro I [Oct. 12, 1798-Sept. 24, 1834] at little Ipiranga (Ypiranga) River in Brazil, **Sept. 7, 1822.**

Ipsus, battle of, Macedonians under Antigonus I [382?-301 B.C.] defeated and killed by other Diadochi at village of Ipsus in Asia Minor, resulting in dissolution of Alexander the Great's old empire beyond recovery, **301 B.C.**

IQ test, Stanford-Binet, first constructed in France, **1905,** by French psychologist Alfred Binet [1857-1911] and revised in U.S., **1916,** by American psychologist Lewis M. Terman [1877-1956] of Stanford University.

iridium, element No. 77; discovered, **1804,** by English chemist Smithson Tennant [1761-1815].

Irish Free State, British parliament enacted law, **Dec. 23, 1920,** establishing separate parliaments for Ulster (Northern Ireland) and Catholic Ireland, which became Irish Free State, **Dec. 6, 1922;** adopted new constitution, **Dec. 29, 1937**, establishing sovereign state of Eire (Ireland) within British Commonwealth of Nations; proclaimed as Republic of Ireland, **Apr. 18, 1949**, withdrawing from Commonwealth and claiming jurisdiction over six Ulster counties (Northern Ireland).

Irish Land Question, great problem of land ownership and agrarian reform in Ireland under British rule, **19th century**; Catholic Emancipation underscored miserable Irish tenantry, **1829**; great Irish famine increased Irish hatred for British, **1840s**; Gladstone's Land Act helped Irish against arbitrary eviction, **Aug. 1, 1870**; Irish gained fair rent, fixity of tenure, and freedom from sale by Land Act, **Aug. 1881**; solved by Wyndham Act, **1903**.

Irish Renaissance, outburst of Irish creativity, **c. 1890-1930**, in literature and the theater, that led to fame of Yeats, Synge, O'Casey, and others.

Irish Republican Army (IRA), nationalist organization to integrate all of Ireland organized by Michael Collins [1890-Aug. 22, 1922] after Easter Rebellion, **1916**; formally constituted, **Mar. 1922**; outlawed by Irish governments after WW II; made devastating bomb attacks in Belfast, London, and Ulster border regions, **1950s**; split into militant "provisional" wing and peaceful moderates, **1969**; Dublin government began imprisonment of militant members **1972**, who began terrorist activities in Great Britain.

Iron Age, period of industrial development that began with the general use of iron, ear-

ly as **4000 B.C.**; began in ancient Greece, c. **1000 B.C.**

Iron Cross, famous military decoration in the shape of a Maltese cross, awarded for bravery, instituted in Germany, **1813**; revived, **1939**.

Iron Guard, fascistic, nationalistic, anti-Semitic group formed by Cornelia Codreanu [c. 1899-Nov. 30, 1938] in Rumania, **1924**; banned **1933**; Iron Guardists and Codreanu arrested and imprisoned, **Apr. 1938**; disappeared, after **1945**.

iron lung (Drinker Respirator), first introduced, **1928**, by American inventor Philip Drinker [1887-].

iron, malleable, process patented, **1762**, by English inventor John Roebuck [1718-1794].

Iron Mask, Man in the, mysterious French prisoner (maybe Count Mattioli kidnapped by King Louis XIV) condemned to wear a black velvet (not iron) mask at all times imprisoned at chateau of Pignerol, **1662**; brought to Bastille, **1698**; died at age 63 in the Bastille, **1703**.

Iroquois Confederation (Five Nations), tight knit Indian confederation of five tribes: Mohawk, Oneida, Onondaga, Cayuga, and Seneca, **c. 1570-1779**; Tuscarora Indians joined confederation to form the "Six Nations," **c. 1722**; colonial expedition defeated Indians aided by British loyalists at Newtown (near Elmira, N.Y.), breaking up the confederation, **Aug. 29, 1779**.

Irwinsville, Ga., site of the capture of Jefferson Davis, President of the Confederate States of America, **May 10, 1865**.

Isaiah, Book of, Old Testament book recording prophecies from **c. 740 B.C.**; bulk of book goes back to Prophet Isaiah [c. 760-680 B.C.].

Isandhlwana, battle of, Zulus under Cetewayo [c. 1836-84] crushed the British in the Zulu War, **Jan. 22, 1879**.

Isfahan (Esfahan), city in central Iran, suffered massacres by Tamerlane, **1387**, and by Ghalzai Afghans, **1723**; occupied by Russian forces in WW I, **1916**.

Isly River, battle of, French infantry and cavalry routed native Moroccan and Algerian armies during large-scale battle along Isly River in Morocco, strengthening French control of Algeria, **Aug. 14, 1844**.

Isonzo, battles of the, Italians and Austrians fought 11 successive battles along a 60-mi.-front on the Isonzo River during WW I, **1915-17**; first battle, **June 23,-July 7, 1915**; second, **July 18,-Aug. 3, 1915**; third, **Oct. 18-Nov. 3, 1915**; fourth, **Nov. 10,-Dec. 2, 1915**; fifth, **Mar. 9-17, 1916**; sixth, **Aug. 6-17, 1916**; seventh, **Sept. 14-17, 1916**; eighth, **Oct. 10-12, 1916**; ninth, **Nov. 1-4, 1916**; tenth, **May 12-June 8, 1917**; eleventh, **Aug. 19-Sept. 12, 1917.**

isostasy, theory developed, **1892,** by American geologist Clarence E. Dutton [1841-1912].

isotope, term coined, **1912,** by English chemist Frederick Soddy [1877-1956].

Israel, republic on Mediterranean's coast, declared a sovereign state, **May 14, 1848.**

Issus, battle of, Macedonian army under Alexander the Great won major victory against Persian forces of Darius III [d. 330 B.C.] at village of Issus in Asia Minor; Alexander continued his invasion of Persian Empire, desiring to unite entire civilized world into one immense empire under his leadership, **Oct. 333 B.C.**

Issy (Jassy), Treaty of, Russia secured control of Crimea from Turks, **Jan. 9, 1792.**

Isthmian Games, athletic contests held in ancient Corinth; similar to Olympic Games but with added amusements, **c. 581-146 B.C.; 44-20 B.C.**

Italian earthquake of '80, worst earthquake in 65 years devastated southern Italy, leaving more than 4000 persons dead and 200,000 homeless, **Nov. 24, 1980.**

Italian-Turkish War, Italians declared war on Turkey, which accepted peace terms before any battle was fought; Italy gained possession of Tripoli and Cyrenaica (and later the Dodecanese Islands), **Sept. 29, 1911-Oct. 8 ,1912.**

Italian Wars, great European powers, especially France and Spain, fought over control of small independent states of Italy, **1494-1529**; France occupied Milan, Genoa, and (jointly with Spain) Naples, **1499-1504**; League of Cambrai won campaign against Venice, **1509**; Swiss expelled French from Lombardy, **1510-13**; French defeated Venetians at Agnadello, **May 14, 1509**; French defeated Swiss and Milanese at Marignano, **Sept. 13-14, 1515**; French renounced all claims in Italy by Treaty of Madrid, **Jan. 15, 1526**; ended by Treaty of Cambrai, **Aug. 5, 1529.**

Italy, unification achieved formally with declaration of Victor Emmanuel as King, **Mar. 17, 1861**; fascist leader Benito Mussolini took over government at King's request, **Oct. 28, 1922**; fascism overthrown, **1943**; became a republic, **June 10, 1946.**

Ituzaingo, battle of, combined army of Argentines and Uruguayans decisively defeated army of Brazilians ensuring final independence for Uruguay from Brazil, **Feb. 20, 1827.**

Ivanhoe, novel, **1819,** about adventures of young knight and girls in days of Richard the Lion-Hearted, by Scottish writer Sir Walter Scott.

Ivory Coast, republic in w. Africa, gained its independence from France, **Aug. 7, 1960.**

Iwo Jima, volcanic island in Pacific captured from Japanese at great cost by U.S. Marines, **Feb. 19-Mar. 16, 1945**; American flag raised on Mt. Suribachi, Iwo Jima, **Feb. 23, 1945.**

Jabberwocky, mock heroic ballad, **1872,** in *Through the Looking Glass,* by English author Lewis Carroll.

J'Accuse (I Accuse), letter published in French newspaper *l'Aurore,* **Jan. 13, 1898,** addressed to President of France accusing war ministry of injustices in Dreyfus case, by French novelist Emile Zola.

Jack Armstrong, the All-American Boy, long-running juvenile U.S. radio adventure series, **1933-51**; last program broadcast, **June 28, 1951**.

Jack Benny Program, The, situation comedy series, on radio, **1932-55**; on television, **1955-65**.

Jackie Gleason Show, The, series of popular television shows, **1949-70**, appearing sometimes under variant names (*Life of Riley*, **1949-50**; *The Honeymooners*, **1955-56**), featuring U.S. comedian Jackie Gleason [Feb. 26, 1916-].

Jack Paar Show, comedy variety show, on radio, **1947**; on television, **1952-56, 1962-73**; featured personality of pioneer U.S. "talk-show" emcee Jack Paar [May 1, 1918-]; who hosted NBC's *Tonight Show*, **1957-62**.

Jackson State tragedy, violent demonstrations at all-black Jackson State College, Jackson, Miss., led to two blacks killed and 11 wounded during shooting by state highway police, **May 14, 1970**.

Jacobean Age, period in English literature, **1603-25**, succeeding Elizabethan Age, so named from King James I's reign.

Jacobin Club, society of violent radical democrats in France during revolution, **1789-94**.

Jacobite Church, Monophysite church of Syria and Iraq, established, **543**.

Jacobites, supporters of James II of England, after his abdication in **1688**, and of any of his descendants, **1688-1807**.

Jacquerie, violent revolt by French peasants against nobles, repressed by Charles II of Navarre, **1358**, who massacred thousands in retaliation.

Jadar River, battle of the, Austrian offensive, repulsed by Serbians in WW I, **Aug. 17-21, 1914**, forcing Austrians to withdraw from Serbia.

Jagello (Jagiello), dynasty that ruled Lithuania and Poland, **1386-1572**; ruled Hungary, **1440-44**, **1490-1526**; ruled Bohemia, **1471-1526**.

Jainism, Indian religion, founded, c. **500 B.C.**.

Jalula, battle of, Arab Saracens defeated the Persians, **637**, seizing control of much territory in the Near East.

Jamaica, Caribbean nation, became independent republic, **Aug. 6, 1962**.

Jamaica Race Track, one of most famous horse race tracks, opened **Apr. 27, 1903**, in Long Island, N.Y.

James gang, band of American outlaws led by Jesse James [Sept. 5, 1847-Apr. 3, 1882] and his brother Frank left trail of bank and train robberies and murders in Midwest, **1866-76**.

James, Letter of, New Testament book, probably written between **45** and **60**.

Jameson's Raid, British colonial administrator Leander Starr Jameson [1853-1917] led famous, ill-timed raid into Boer colony of Transvaal in an effort to trigger uprising by foreigners against Pres. Stephanus J. P. Kruger [Oct. 10, 1825-July 14, 1904], **Dec. 29, 1895-Jan. 2, 1896**; Jameson forced to surrender to Boers (who handed him over to British for trial) at Doorn Kop, **Jan. 2, 1896**.

Jamestown, Va., first permanent English settlement in North America established by London Company at mouth of James River in Virginia, **May 14, 1607**; colony nearly destroyed by severe winter ("starving time"), **1609-10**; tobacco first cultivated there by John Rolfe [1586-1622], **1612**.

Jane Eyre, novel, **1847**, about orphan turned governess, by English novelist Charlotte Bronte [Apr. 21, 1816-Mar. 31, 1855]. Film, **1944**, adaptation of Bronte novel, screenplay written by Aldous Huxley.

Janissaries, elite soldiers' corp of the Ottoman army, established by Sultan Murad I Orkhan [1288?-1362?], **14th century**; massacred in their barracks by Spahis under orders of Sultan Mahmud II [1784?-1839], **June 16, 1826**.

Jankau, battle of, Swedish forces under Field Marshal Lennart Torstenson [Aug. 17, 1603-Apr. 7, 1651] outmaneuvered Austrian army and inflicted heavy casualties on Bavarian cavalry at Jankau, southeast of Prague, **Mar. 6, 1645**.

Jansenism, theological school resembling Calvinism, persistent sect among French Catholics, **c. 1650-1750**; based on *Augustinus*, **1640**, by Bishop Cornelius Jansen [Nov. 3, 1585-May 6, 1638]; key tenets rejected, **1713**, in *Unigenitus*, issued by Pope Clement XI (born Giovanni Francesco Albani) [July 23, 1649-Mar. 19, 1721].

January Revolution, Poles revolted unsuccessfully against Russian rule in Poland; Polish autonomy abolished; program of "Russification" began, **Jan. 1863-May 1864**.

Japan, according to legend founded by Emperor Jimmu, **660 B.C.**; central power held by successive families of shoguns, **1192-1867**; opened to U.S. trade by Commodore Matthew C. Perry, **1854**; power recovered by Emperor Meiji, **1868**; fought with China, gaining Taiwan, **1894-95**; war with Russia, **1904-05**; annexed Korea, **1910**; took Manchuria, **1931**; and started war with China, **1932**; launched war against U.S. by attack on Pearl Harbor, **Dec 7, 1941**; surrendered, **Aug. 14, 1945**; adopted new constitution (in which emperor gave up divinity), **May 3, 1947**; agreed to resume relations with mainland China, **Sept 29, 1972**, severing relations with Taiwan; signed friendship treaty with China, **1978**.

Japanese earthquake, great, one-third of Tokyo and most of Yokohama destroyed by violent earthquake that killed approx. 143,000, **Sept. 1, 1923**.

Jasmund, battle of, first major sea battle in Swedish-Danish war; Danish squadron of ships soundly defeated Swedish fleet off Jasmund peninsula, **May 25, 1676**.

jasperware, invented and developed, **1773-1780**, by English potter Josiah Wedgwood [1730-1797].

Java man, prehistoric species of man who appeared on Earth **c. 500,000 years ago**.

Javanese revolts, widespread revolt by Javanese suppressed by Dutch on island of Java; Dutch conquered island's interior, **1825-30**; Dutch successfully put down Javanese uprisings, **1849, 1888**.

Java Sea, battle of the, Japanese forces defeated Allies in w. Pacific, **Feb. 1942**.

Jay's Treaty, Britain promised to withdraw from U.S. Northwest's military posts, gave U.S. unrestricted travel on Mississippi, but failed to stop British interference with neutral U.S. ships, **Nov. 19, 1794**.

jazz, type of music that emerged, **c. 1900**, around New Orleans; term in use from, **c. 1915**.

jazz age, period in U.S. cultural history, **1920-29**, in which post World War I euphoria combined with popularity of jazz music; ended with stock-market crash, **1929**.

Jazz Singer, The, first talking picture, **1927**, starred U.S. singer-actor Al Jolson (born Asa Yoelson) [May 26, 1886-Oct. 23, 1950].

jeep, first mass-produced, **1940**, in U.S. for armed forces.

Jefferson's Manual, parliamentary rules compiled by Thomas Jefferson as U.S. Vice President presiding over the Senate, **1797-1801**.

Jefferson, Territory of, independent (but illegal) territorial government created by settlers, **1859-61**, in Pikes Peak region of w.

Kansas Territory (present-day Colorado); adopted own constitution, **Oct. 24, 1859**; ceased after Congress created Territory of Colorado, **Feb. 28, 1861**.

Jeffries-Fitzsimmons fight, James J. Jeffries [1875-1953] defeated Robert Fitzsimmons [1863-1918] to win heavyweight boxing championship at Coney Island, N.Y., **June 9, 1899**; Jeffries retired undefeated, **Mar. 1905**; returned, **1910**, and fought for title, losing to Jack Johnson.

Jehovah's Witnesses, sect, founded, **1871**; doctrines based on teachings of U.S. religious leader Charles T. Russel [Feb. 16, 1852-Oct. 31, 1916].

Jemappes, battle of, sudden French attack won important victory over Austrian army at Jemappes in present-day Belgium, **Nov. 6, 1792**.

Jena, battle of, French army under Napoleon I suffered heavy losses but won major battle against Prussian and Saxon armies at Jena, allowing Napoleon to begin northward advance on Berlin, **Oct. 14, 1806**.

Jena, University of, German institution of higher learning, founded **1558**.

Jenkin's Ear, War of, conflict between Britain and Spain over colonial trade, **1739-41**; name of war derived from claim by British shipmaster that his ear had been cut off by Spaniards, **1731**; merged with the War of the Austrian Succession in Europe, **1740-48**.

Jeremiah, Book of, Old Testament prophetic book, substantially written, **604 B.C.**, with later additions, by Hebrew prophet Jeremiah [c. 650-585 B.C.]; whose name has become synonymous with righteous denunciation; prophecies probably re-edited, **c. 537 B.C.**

Jericho, ancient city in Palestine, where excavations in early **1900s** showed settlement there, perhaps from **c. 8000 B.C.**

Jerusalem, city that King David made his capital after capturing it from Jebusites, **c. 1000 B.C.**; taken by the Babylonians, **586 B.C.**, who destroyed the Temple; capital of the Maccabees, **2nd-1st century B.C.**; Second Temple destroyed by Roman emperor Titus [39-81], **70**; site of revolt of Bar Kokba, **132-35**; became Roman pagan shrine called Aelia Capitolina, **135**; captured by Muslims, **637**, who made it chief shrine after Mecca; conquered by the Crusaders, **1099**; retaken by Muslims led by Saladin, **1187**; captured by British forces, **1917**; capital of British-held mandate of Palestine, **1922-48**; Jordan annexed Old City, **Apr. 1949**; Israel annexed Old City, **June 1967**.

Jesuits, members of Catholic religious order, founded Paris, **1534**, by St. Ignatius Loyola, under name, Society of Jesus; spread everywhere, notable in education; suppressed by papacy for political reasons, **1773**; restored, **1814**.

Jesus Christ, Superstar, rock opera, **1970**, depicting life of Jesus, by British song-writing team, lyricist Tim Rice and composer Andrew Lloyd-Webber.

Jesus Movement, religious movement, popular in U.S., from **1971**.

Jewish Chronicle, The, oldest extant Jewish periodical, founded, London, **1841**.

Jewish Defense League (JDL), militant organization to combat antisemitism established as Jewish Defense Corps in New York City, **June 1968**.

Jewish State, The (Der Judenstaat), treatise, **1896**, laying philosophical foundations for Jewish state, later realized in founding of Israel, **May 15, 1948**, by Zionist theorist and leader Theodor Herzl [May 2, 1860-July 3, 1904].

Jidda (Jedda), battle of, Wahabis under Ibn Saud [c. 1880-Nov. 9, 1953] captured last Hejaz stronghold, Jidda, after year-long siege, **Dec. 23, 1925**; Ibn Saud proclaimed himself king of Hejaz and Nejd (Saudi Arabia), **Jan. 8, 1926**.

jig, English popular dance, flourished from **c. 1550**; forerunner of baroque art-music *gigue*.

Jim Crow laws, statutes passed by Southern states and cities that served to segregate and discriminate against Negroes, **1880s-1940s**; U.S. Supreme Court ordered Univ. of Texas to admit Negro to its law school, **1950**; U.S. Supreme Court declared separate racial facilities to be unconstitutional, **1954**.

Jimmy Durante Show, The, comedy variety programs, on radio, **1943-50**; on television, **1952-57**; revolved around personality of rasp-voiced U.S. vaudeville-style singer and comedian Jimmy Durante [Feb. 10, 1893-Jan. 29, 1980].

jitterbug, one of several fast dances performed to jazz music, popular from **c. 1945**.

Joan Little case, Joan Little [1954-], serving 10-year prison term, fled from Beaufort County Jail, N. C., **Aug. 27, 1974**, after murdering white guard she later accused of forcing her to have sexual intercourse; widely publicized trial in Raleigh, N. C., ended in jury's acquittal of Miss Little of second degree murder, **July 14-Aug. 15, 1975**; Miss Little fled minimum security prison in N. C., **Oct. 15, 1977**; caught in New York City, **Dec. 7, 1977**; and returned to prison after U.S. Supreme Court refused to block her extradition, **June 5, 1978**.

Jockey Club, British club established at Newmarket, England, to organize and supervise all horse racing affairs, **1750**; American club formed to oversee turf affairs, especially horse race gambling, **1894**.

Joel, Book of, Old Testament book, probably written, **c. 400 B.C.**.

Johannesburg, major city of the Rand in South Africa, founded as a gold mining settlement, **Sept. 1886**.

John Birch Society, right-wing, anti-Communist society organization, founded **Dec. 1958**, in honor of U.S. intelligence officer John Birch [?-Aug. 25, 1945], first American casualty of the "Cold War."

John, Gospel According to, fourth New Testament book, now believed written, c. **40-65**, by John, Apostle of Jesus, or member of his school.

John, Letters of, three New Testament

books, possibly written, c. **60-65**, by Apostle John or member of his school.

John F. Kennedy (JFK) International Airport, world's largest commercial airport, New York City, dedicated, **July 31, 1948**, as Idlewild International Airport; renamed JFK, **1963**.

Johnny Belinda, film, **1948**, about deaf-mute farm girl befriended by sensitive doctor, performance as girl by U.S. actress Jane Wyman (born Sarah Jane Fulks) [Jan. 4, 1914-].

Johnny Carson Show, The, television variety series, **1953-58**, that under various names featured television personality and emcee Johnny Carson [Oct. 23, 1925-]; host of NBC *Tonight Show*, from **1962**.

Johns Hopkins University, U.S. institution of higher learning, opened Baltimore, **1876**.

Johnson-Burns fight, Jack Johnson [Mar. 31, 1878-June 10, 1946] defeated Tommy Burns [1881-1955] in Sydney, Australia, to become first black to hold world heavyweight boxing title, **Dec. 26, 1908**.

Johnstown flood, about 2,200 killed during legendary deluge at Johnstown, Pa., **May 31, 1889**.

Jonah, Book of, Old Testament book written after c. **538 B.C.**.

Jonestown mass suicide, more than 900 members of the People's Temple, American socialist-religious commune in Jonestown, Guyana, committed suicide by drinking cyanide poison on orders from their leader James Warren ("Jim") Jones [May 13, 1931-Nov. 18, 1978], **Nov. 18, 1978**.

Josephinism, anti-Catholic movement, **1781-90**; instituted by so-called Edict of Toleration, **1781**, of Emperor Joseph II [Mar. 13, 1741-Feb. 20, 1790].

Joshua, Book of, sixth book of Old Testament, written in present form, **c. 800 B.C.**, based on materials going back to, **1250-1225 B.C.**

Joule's law, first established, **1840**, by English physicist James P. Joule [1818-1889].

Journal des Savants, first literary periodical, founded Paris, **1665**.

Judaism, historic monotheistic faith of Jewish people, instituted, **c. 1800 B.C.**, through God's covenant with Abraham [fl. 1800 B.C.?] confirmed, with Moses, Mt. Sinai, **c. 1290 B.C.**; name from Southern Palestinian kingdom that ended with Babylonian Captivity, **586 B.C.**

Jude the Obscure, novel, **1895**, depiction of divorce and living together outside marriage—all culminating in tragedy, by English novelist and poet Thomas Hardy.

Judges, Book of, Old Testament historical book, covering period of Judges in Israel, **c. 1225-1025 B.C.**; probably written down in present form, **c. 600-550 B.C.**

Judgment of Paris, painting, **1529**, with goddesses in hats and Paris in medieval armor, by German painter Lucas Cranach the Elder; painting, **1639**, by Flemish baroque artist Peter Paul Rubens; painting, **1914**, mythological study in impressionistic mode; by French impressionist Pierre-Auguste Renoir [Feb. 25, 1840-Dec. 3, 1919]; classical treatment, same theme, **1754**, by Francois Boucher.

Jugend, German art magazine, first appeared, Munich, **1896**, promoting *Jugendstil*, or *art nouveau*, popular, beginning **c. 1893**.

Jugurthine War, king of Numidia, Jugurtha [c. 156-104 B.C.], was defeated by the Romans through treachery, **111-105 B.C.**

Jules et Jim, film, **1961**, in which woman, played by French actress Jeanne Moreau, loves two friends in way that eventually defeats both, by French director Francois Truffaut [Feb. 6, 1932-].

Julian calendar, system of astronomical dating introduced by Julius Caesar [July 12, 100 B.C.-Mar. 15, 44 B.C.], **46 B.C.**; used in Christian world, until **16th century**.

Julius Caesar, tragedy, **c. 1599**, by William Shakespeare, based on historical conspiracy against Julius Caesar, includes Antony's funeral oration. Film, **1953**, directed by Joseph L. Mankiewiecz, with performances as Cassius, by British actor Sir John Gielgud [Apr. 14, 1904-], Brutus, by British actor James Mason [May 15, 1909-] and Marc Antony, by U.S. actor Marlon Brando.

July Revolution, French revolt that overthrew government of King Charles X [Oct. 9, 1757-Nov. 6, 1836] and established the July Monarchy under duc d'Orleans, proclaimed as King Louis Philippe, **July 28-30, 1830**.

June Bug, first U.S. award-winning racing plane, built, **1908**, by American aviation pioneer Glenn H. Curtiss [1878-1930].

Jungfrau, majestic, high mountain in Bernese Alps of Switzerland (13,642 ft.), first climbed, **1811**.

Jungle Books, The, animal stories for children, **1894-95**, centered around the boy Mowgli, raised by a wolf in the Indian jungle, by British author Rudyard Kipling.

Junin, battle of, revolutionary forces under Simon Bolivar and Antonio Jose de Sucre [Feb. 3, 1795-June 4, 1830] won important victory against Spanish royalist forces at village of Junin, central Peru, **Aug. 6, 1824**.

Junto, the, humanitarian society, that opposed slavery and other "evils", established by Benjamin Franklin [Jan. 17, 1706-Apr. 17, 1790] at Philadelphia, **1727**.

Jupiter Symphony, symphony, **1788**, in C major; symphonic work composed by Wolfgang Amadeus Mozart, No. 41 (K551).

Justice, U.S. Department of, U.S. Congress created department under direction of Attorney General, **June 22, 1870**.

Justinian Code (*Corpus Juris Civilis***),** Byzantine Emperor Justinian issued comprehensive revision of Roman law, comprised of the Codex, the Digest or Pandects, and the Institutes, **529-35**; issued fourth part, the Novellae, **535-65**.

Just So Stories, animal stories for children, **1902**, written and illustrated by British writer Rudyard Kipling.

Jutland (Skagerrak), battle of, only major naval battle between British and Germans in WW I, **May 31-June 1, 1916**.

Kabul, Afghan city that Babur [1483-1530] made capital of Mogul Empire, **1504-26**; captured by Nadir Shah [1688-1747] of Persia, **1738**; became Afghan capital, **1773**; occupied by British during Afghan Wars, **1839, 1879**.

Kadesh, ancient city in Syria, site of great indecisive battle between Egyptians under Ramses II [d. 1225 B.C.] and Hittites that ended in peace treaty, **1288 B.C.**

Kaffir War, British defeated Kaffirs in new war, annexing all of Kaffraria and extending their authority to the northeast in s. Africa, **1877-78**.

Kaifeng (K'ai-feng), Chinese capital of the Five Dynasties, as Pienliang, **906-59**; capital of n. Sung dynasty, **960-1127**; captured by invading Mongols, **13th century**; Chinese Communists stormed Nationalist-held Kaifeng, seizing huge amounts of military supplies during Chinese Civil War, **June 19, 1948**.

kaleidoscope, invented, **1816**, by Scottish physicist David Brewster [1781-1868].

Kalisch, Treaty of, Prussia and Russia formed offensive and defensive alliance against Napoleon I of France and extended invitation to Britain and Austria to join, **Feb. 28, 1813**.

Kalisz (Kalisch), Peace of, Poles recognized Teutonic Knights' possession of Pomerelia (e. Pomerania), in return for aid against the Lithuanians, **1343**.

Kalka River, battle of the, Mongols under Subotai (Subutai) [1172?-1245], chief of staff of Genghis Khan, defeated Russian army at Kalka River, **1223**.

Kalmar Union, Queen Margaret I [1353-Oct. 28, 1412] of Denmark combined the three crowns of Denmark, Sweden, and Norway, **July 20, 1397**; Sweden left union, **1523**; union of Denmark and Norway lasted, until **1814**.

Kalmar War, indecisive conflict between Denmark and Sweden, **1611-13**; Danes besieged Kalmar, Sweden, **Apr. 4, 1611**; war ended with Peace of Knaeroed, **Jan. 20, 1613**.

Kanagawa, Treaty of, U.S. Commodore Matthew C. Perry [Apr. 10, 1794-Mar. 4, 1858] signed treaty with Japan, establishing limited U.S.-Japanese trade and U.S. consulate in Japan, **Mar. 31, 1854**.

Kandurcha, unknown site in steppes of Russia, where Mongol conqueror Tamerlane won major battle, involving more than 100,000 horsemen, against rival Mongol Golden Horde, **1391**.

Kanpur (Cawnpore), Mahrattas under Nana Sahib [b. c. 1821] massacred the British garrison and colony at Kanpur in India during Sepoy Rebellion, **June 26-July 15, 1857**; British infantry and cavalry defeated Indian-Mahratta rebels in savage assault on Kanpur, **Dec. 6, 1857**.

Kansas, part of territory acquired by Louisiana Purchase, admitted to the Union (U.S.) as 34th state, **Jan. 29, 1861**.

Kansas-Missouri flood, great, one of most severe floods in U.S. history left 200,000 persons homeless, 41 dead, and over $1 billion in property damage in Kansas and Missouri, **July 2-19, 1951**.

Kansas-Nebraska Act, repealed Missouri Compromise; all U.S. states and territories free to choose on question of slavery; territories of Kansas and Nebraska formed, **May 26, 1854**.

Kappel, battle of, Swiss Catholic cantons defeated Zurich, **Oct. 11, 1531**, at Kappel, where Huldrych Zwingli [Jan. 1, 1484-Oct. 11, 1531] was killed.

Kapp Putsch, right-wing German group led by Wolfgang Kapp [July 24, 1858-July 12, 1922], seized government buildings in Berlin, Germany, **Mar. 13, 1920**, in attempt to restore monarchy; revolt collapsed, **Mar. 17, 1920**, as a result of general strike and lack of army support.

Kardis, Treaty of, Sweden and Russia reestablished the status quo before the war of 1655-60, **June 21, 1661**.

Karlowitz, Treaty of, marked start of decline of Ottoman Empire; **Jan. 26, 1699**.

Karmathians (Carmathians), mysterious Muslim sect conquered Arabia, early **10th century**; stole black stone from Kaaba, **930**, keeping it 10 years; disappeared, **11th century**.

Karnak, Temple of, great Temple of Egyptian god Amon, constructed, Karnak, upper Nile, from **1530 B.C.**

Kars, ancient fortress-city, capital of Armenian state, **9th-10th century**; totally destroyed by Mongol conqueror Tamerlane, **1386**; rebuilt by Ottoman Turks, c. **1550**; seized by Russians, **1828, 1855, 1877**; ceded to Russia at Congress of Berlin, **June 13-July 13, 1878**; U.S.S.R.-Turkish peace treaty returned city to Turkey, **1921**.

Kashmir, former princely Hindu state until taken by Muslims, **14th century**; became part of Mogul Empire, **1586**; pacified by British, **1846**; divided between India and Pakistan, **1949**.

Katanga (Shaba), province of Katanga under leadership of Moise K. Tshombe [Nov. 10, 1919-June 29, 1969] proclaimed itself independent from Congo (Zaire), **July 1960**; UN-Congolese forces ended Katanga's secession from Congo, **Jan. 15, 1963**.

Kazan, city on Volga River became capital of great Tatar khanate, **1445**; conquered and sacked by Ivan IV ("the Terrible"), **1552**.

Kellogg-Briand Pact (Pact of Paris), U.S. Secretary of State Frank B. Kellogg [Dec. 22, 1857-Dec. 21, 1937] and French Foreign Minister Aristide Briand [Mar. 28, 1862-Mar. 7, 1932] negotiated antiwar pact, agreeing to arbitration to settle international differences, **Aug. 27, 1928**.

Kells, Book of, artistic Gospel manuscript, c. **800**.

Kennedy assassination, U.S. Pres. John F. Kennedy, riding in motorcade, shot and pronounced dead at 1:00 P.M. in Dallas, Tex., **Nov. 22, 1963**; Lee Harvey Oswald [Oct. 18, 1939-Nov. 24, 1963], accused assassin of Kennedy, shot and killed by Jack Ruby [c. 1911-Jan. 3, 1967] in Dallas Municipal Building, **Nov. 24, 1963**; Ruby convicted of murder and sentenced to death, **Mar. 14, 1964**, died of cancer and blood clot, **Jan. 3, 1967**; Warren Commission established, **Nov. 29, 1963**, to investigate Kennedy's death.

Kennedy Center for the Performing Arts, landmark cultural center, Washington, D.C., constructed, **1964**.

Kennedy-Nixon debates, famous series of four TV debates between U.S. Vice Pres. Richard M. Nixon and his Democratic challenger for the presidency, Sen. John F. Kennedy, **Sept. 26, Oct. 7, Oct. 13, Oct. 21, 1960**.

Kennesaw Mountain, battle of, Confederate troops won victory over Union troops of Gen. William T. Sherman in Georgia, **June 27, 1864**.

Kenny method, treatment for poliomyelitis first demonstrated in U.S., **1940,** by Australian nurse Elizabeth Kenny [1884-1952].

Kent, kingdom of, kingdom established by Jutes in modern county of Kent, England, **mid-400s;** Aethelbert [d. 616] of Kent received Christian missionaries from pope, **597,** and became first Christian king in Anglo-Saxon England; subjugated and split up by neighboring Wessex and Mercia, **8th century;** conquered by Wessex, **825,** and made part of that kingdom.

Kent State University slayings, four students at Kent State University in Ohio shot to death by National Guardsmen, **May 4, 1970,** during protest against U.S. incursion into Cambodia.

Kentucky, formerly part of Virginia, admitted to the Union (U.S.) as 15th state, **June 1, 1792**.

Kentucky Derby, the, annual American horse race for three-year-old thoroughbreds; first held at Churchill Downs, Louisville, Ky., **May 17, 1875**.

Kenya, country in Africa, became independent republic, free from British rule, **Dec. 12, 1963;** ordered Asians with Kenyan passports to leave, **1972**.

Kerner Report, Pres. Johnson's Kerner Commission (National Advisory Committee on Civil Disorders) released report, **Feb. 29, 1968,** citing "white racism" as major reason for civil disorders and black violence in U.S.

kerosene, refining process invented, **c. 1846,** by Canadian geologist Abraham Gesner [1797-1864]; derived originally from coal, then, in **1854,** from oil.

Kettle Creek, battle of, American revolutionaries defeated loyalists at Kettle Creek, Ga. during the American Revolution, **Feb. 14, 1779**.

Khartoum, city in Sudan, at Blue Nile and White Nile rivers, where Mahdi massacred British garrison under Gen. Charles G. Gordon [Jan. 28, 1833-Jan. 26, 1885], **Jan. 26, 1885;** recaptured by British under H. H. Kitchener, **Sept. 2, 1898**.

Khilafat movement, Mohandas K. Gandhi organized movement to unite India's Hindus and Muslims to protest allied treatment of Turks after WW I, **1920**.

Khmer Empire, ancient Indo-Chinese kingdom established by Khmers (Cambodians) in present-day Cambodia and Laos, **6th century;** golden age of Khmer civilization with capital at Angkor, noted for great sculpture and architecture, **889-1434;** Thais captured Angkor, **1434**.

Khorezm (Khwarazm), ancient empire in central Asia around Caspian and Aral seas, **fl. 12th-13th centuries;** conquered by Genghis Khan, **1221;** became independent Uzbek state known as khanate of Khiva, **16th century**.

***Khufu,* Pyramid of (or *Cheops*),** oldest and largest of the Pyramids at Gizeh, Egypt, built, **2650 B.C.,** out of some 2,300,000 blocks of stone, each averaging more than two tons in weight.

Khyber Pass, ancient route between Kabul and Peshawar, held by British during second Anglo-Afghan War, **1879**.

Kiel mutiny, German naval crews refused at Kiel, West Germany, to put to sea near end of WW I, **Oct. 28, 1918;** mutiny spread to Hamburg, Lubeck, and Bremen.

Kiel, Treaty of, Denmark ceded Norway to Sweden, which ceded w. Pomerania and Rugen to Denmark; peace made between Denmark and Great Britain, **Jan. 14, 1814**.

Kiev, city in Ukraine that was capital of medieval Russia until devastated by Mongols, **1240**; controlled by Lithuania, **14th century** and Poland, after **1569**; Ukrainian Cossacks ousted Polish and made independent state, **1648-54**; united to Russia, **1654**; became capital of Ukraine, **Jan. 1918**; occupied by German, White Russian, Polish, and Soviet troops during Russian civil war, **1918-20**; devastated by Germans in WW II.

Kilimanjaro, highest mountain in Africa (19,340 ft.), first climbed by Hans Meyer [1858-July 5, 1929], member of British-German expedition, **1889**.

Killdeer Mountain, battle of, Sioux Indians defeated by skillful use of artillery and cavalry by U.S. troops during Sioux Indian Wars in the Badlands, **July 28, 1864**.

Killiecrankie, battle of, Jacobite Scottish Highlanders routed large English government army, **July 27, 1689**.

Kilpatrick's Raid, Union cavalry expedition led by Gen. Hugh J. Kilpatrick [1836-81] that destroyed Confederate bridges and railroads and caused much damage near Richmond, Va., **Feb. 25-Mar 4, 1864**.

Kim, novel, **1901**; portrait of British India, by British author Rudyard Kipling; Nobel laureate, **1907**.

kinematoscope, invented, **1861**, by American inventor Coleman Sellers.

kinescope, television receiver invented, **1924**, by Russian-American physicist Vladimir K. Zworykin [1889-].

kinetoscope, patented, **1891**, by American inventor Thomas A. Edison [1847-1931].

King and I, The, musical, opened, **March 29, 1951**; Rodgers-and-Hart creation that starred actress Gertrude Lawrence (born Alexandra Dagmar Laurence-Klasen) [July 4, 1898-Sept. 6, 1952] and Yul Brynner [July 11, 1920-].

King David Hotel, site of one of modern history's first massive terrorist attacks with Jewish Irgun bombing of King David Hotel, Jerusalem, **July 22, 1946**.

King George's War, conflict between Britain and France over colonial control in North America, **1744-48**; New Englanders led by William Pepperrell [June 27, 1696-July 6, 1759] and backed by British fleet seized French stronghold, Fort Louisbourg, Nova Scotia, **June 16, 1745**; Treaty of Aix-la-Chapelle ended war, with Fort Louisbourg returned to France, **Oct. 18, 1748**.

King James Bible, English version of the Bible, **1611**, commissioned by James I of Great Britain [June 19, 1566-Mar. 27, 1625].

King Kong, film, **1933**; starred U.S. actor Bruce Cabot [1905-May 3, 1972] and actress Fay Wray [Sept. 10, 1907-].

King Lear, tragedy, **c. 1605**, by William Shakespeare.

King Philip's War, conflict between Indians led by Philip [d. Aug. 12, 1676] and New England colonists, **1675-76**; Indians surrendered, but at extremely, bloody, ruinous cost to colonists, **Aug. 28, 1676**.

King assassination, U.S. civil rights leader Martin Luther King, Jr. assassinated in Memphis, Tenn., **Apr. 4, 1968**; large-scale race riots erupted in 125 U.S. cities, **Apr. 4-14, 1968**; ex-convict James Earl Ray arrested in London for King's murder, **June 8, 1968**; Ray pleaded guilty to murder and sentenced to 99 years in prison, **Mar. 10, 1969**.

Kings, Books of, Old Testament historical books narrating events from accession of

Solomon, **c. 970 B.C.**, to Babylonian Exile, **586 B.C.**; probably completed in present form, **c. 550 B.C.**

Kings Mountain, battle of, American patriots and frontiersmen won resounding victory over loyalists on Kings Mountain, S.C., near border of N.C.; Gen. Cornwallis gave up plan to invade North Carolina during American Revolution, **Oct. 7, 1780**.

King William's War, conflict between Britain and France over colonial possessions in North America, corresponded with the War of Grand Alliance in Europe, **1689-97**. See **Grand Alliance, War of the; Queen Anne's War**.

Kiribati, former Gilbert Island in South Pacific, became independent nation after 87 years of British rule, **July 12, 1979**.

Kitchen Debate, U.S. Vice Pres. Richard M. Nixon [Jan. 9, 1913-] engaged in much-publicized debate with Soviet Premier Nikita Khrushchev [Apr. 17, 1894-Sept. 11, 1971] in the kitchen exhibit at American Exhibition in Moscow, **July 24, 1959**.

Kiwanis International, U.S. service organization of community business and professional men, founded **1915**, in Detroit, Mich.

Klondike gold rush, gold deposits discovered on Bonanza Creek, a tributary of Klondike, in Yukon Territory, **Aug. 1896**; stampede to Klondike by thousands of U.S. gold seekers, **1897-98**.

klystron, component of radar sets; developed, **1941**, by American physicist William W. Hansen [1909-1949].

Knights Hospitalers (Knights of St. John or Knights of Malta), military-religious order established to care for pilgrims in the Holy Land, **c. 1113**; order moved to Cyprus, **1291**; conquered Rhodes, **1308-10**; heroically defended Rhodes against the Turks, **1480-1522**; given a home on the island of Malta by Holy Roman Emperor Charles V [Feb. 24, 1500-Sept. 21, 1558], **1530**; helped stop Turks at Lepanto, **Oct. 7, 1571**; order dissolved after Napoleon's capture of Malta, **1798**.

Knights of Columbus, international fraternal benefit organization of Catholic men, founded **1882**, New Haven, Conn.

Knights of Labor, U.S. labor union established secretly, **1869**, at Philadelphia, Penn.; reached its peak, **1886**, with more than 700,000 members; defunct, after **1900**.

Knights of St. Crispin, U.S. shoe industry union, founded **Mar. 7, 1867**, to protect members against cheaper competition; became largest trade union in U.S., **c. 1870**; went out of existence, **1878**, with members joining the Knights of Labor.

Knights of the Golden Circle, secret order of Northerners sympathetic to the South before and during U.S. Civil War, made up of Copperheads, **1854-64**; reorganized as Order of American Knights, **1863**; reorganized as Order of the Sons of Liberty, with Clement L. Vallandigham [July 29, 1820-June 17, 1871] as commander, **1864**.

Knights of the White Camellia, U.S. secret organization advocating "white supremacy," established in Louisiana, **1867**.

Knights Templars, military-religious order established by the Crusaders for protection of pilgrims and defense of the Latin kingdom of Jerusalem, **1119**; **fl. 12th-13th centuries**; accused of many crimes and persecuted by king of France, Philip IV [1268-Nov. 29, 1314], **1308-14**; completely destroyed, **1314**.

Knights' War, knights under Franz von Sickingen waged war against the ecclesiastical princes in Germany, **1522**; Sickingen besieged at Landstuhl and forced to surrender, **1523**.

knitting machine, circular, invented,

1816, by French-British inventor, Sir Marc I. Brunel [1769-1849]; called *tricoteur*.

knitting machine, flat, successfully designed and patented, **1863**, by American clergyman and inventor Isaac W. Lamb [1840-1906].

Knossos, site of ancient pre-Hellenic palace of King Minos, Crete, built **c. 2000 B.C.**; rebuilt progressively more splendidly until suddenly destroyed, **c. 1400 B.C.**

Know-Nothing Party, unofficial political organization in U.S. formed to combat "foreign" influence and to uphold American view, **c. 1843**; evolved into Native American Party, **1845**; dissolved into American Party, **1854**.

Knoxville, Tenn., capital of U.S. territory south of Ohio River, **1792-96**; occupied during U.S. Civil War by Union forces under Gen. Burnside, who successfully withstood Confederate attack under Gen. Longstreet, **Nov. 29, 1863**.

Koblenz (Coblenz), city at cross of Rhine and Moselle rivers, annexed by France, **1798**; taken by Prussia, **1815**; occupied by allied forces after WW I, **1919-29**.

Koge Bight, battle of, Danish fleet won naval battle against Swedish fleet, sinking or capturing 11 Swedish warships, in Koge Bight, south of Copenhagen, **June 30, 1677**.

Kolin, battle of, Austrian forces of Marshal Daun defeated the Prussians of Frederick II ("the Great") in Bohemia, **June 18, 1757**.

Konigsberg and Marienberg, treaties of, Sweden and Brandenburg partitioned Poland between them following their victory over the Poles at Warsaw, **July 28-30, 1656**.

Kon-Tiki **expedition**, Thor Heyerdahl with five companions sailed in balsa raft (*Kon-Tiki*) 4300 miles across Pacific from Peru to Tuamotu Islands, **1947**, to prove first Polynesians were from South America.

Kootenay, Fort, first post on the Columbia River founded by Canadian explorer and fur trader David Thompson [Apr. 30, 1770-Feb. 10, 1857] for the North West Company, **1807**.

Koran, The, sacred book of Islam, believed revealed to Prophet Mohammed **c. 610**; dictated from **c. 625**; definitive text of 114 chapters compiled by Caliphs succeeding prophet, **c. 650**; first English translation, **1734**.

Korea, 600-mile peninsula jutting into the Sea of Japan, unified into a kingdom under Silla dynasty, **7th century**; occupied by Mongols, **1231-60**; called the Hermit kingdom, became vassal state of China, **early 1600s**; annexed by Japan as Chosun, **1910**; divided into occupation zones, Soviet north of and U.S. south of 38th parallel, **July 1945**; Democratic People's Republic of Korea (North Korea) established, **May 1, 1948**; Republic of Korea (South Korea) established, **Aug. 15, 1948**.

Koreagate, U.S. government scandal disclosed, **Apr.-Sept. 1977**, involving millions of dollars spent by Korean agent, Tongsun Park [1935-], to buy influence with U.S. officials; Park indicted by U.S. Justice Dept., **Sept. 8, 1977**; three California Democratic congressmen reprimanded by Senate Ethics Committee, **Oct. 13, 1978**.

Korean War, conflict between North and South Korea, **June 25, 1950-June 27, 1953**; North Korean army crossed 38th parallel and invaded South Korea, **June 25, 1950**; UN authorized U.S. and other nations to send military aid, **June 27, 1950**; UN forces broke out of Pusan perimeter, **Sept. 16, 1950**; UN forces under Gen. Douglas MacArthur [Jan. 26, 1880-Apr. 5, 1964] drove North Koreans to Yalu River, **Nov. 24, 1950**; North Korean-Communist Chinese forced UN forces back to 38th parallel, **Jan. 1951**; Gen. MacArthur replaced by Gen. Matthew B. Ridgway [Mar. 3, 1895-], **Apr. 10, 1951**; negotiations for cease-fire began at Panmunjom, **July 10, 1951**; armistice signed, **July 27, 1953**.

Kossovo, battle of, Turks under Sultan Murad I [1326?-1389] defeated allied Christian army at Kossovo Field, **Aug. 27, 1389**.

Koufax's perfect game, Sandy Koufax [Dec. 30, 1935-] of Los Angeles Dodgers pitched perfect baseball game (no one got to first base) against Chicago Cubs, winning 1-0, **Sept. 9, 1965**.

Krakatoa, volcanic island between Java and Sumatra exploded, killing approx. 36,000, **Aug. 26-28, 1883**.

Krebs (citric acid) cycle, discovered, **1937**, by German-British biochemist Sir

Hans A. Krebs [1900-] to explain sugar metabolism.

Krefeld (Crefeld), battle of, aggressive, well-disciplined Prussian troops defeated much larger French army in Rhine region during Seven Years' War, **June 23, 1758.**

Kremlin, historic walled-fortress section of Moscow, built, from **c. 1450,** containing some 20 palaces and churches; residence of Czars, to **1712;** seat of Soviet government, from **1917.**

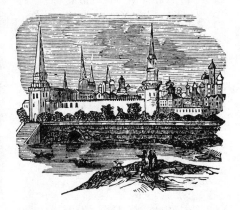

Kronstadt mutiny, Russian sailors mutinied at Kronstadt, **Feb. 23, 1921,** protesting food shortages, pay, and conditions; violently suppressed by Communists, **Mar. 17, 1921.**

krypton, element No. 36; discovered, **1898,** by Scottish chemist Sir William Ramsay [1852-1916] and English chemist Morris W. Travers [1872-1961].

K2 (Mt. Godwin-Austen), second highest mountain in the world (28,250 ft.), in Karakorum range, first climbed by Italian expedition led by Ardito Desio [1897-], **Aug. 4, 1954.**

Ku Klux Klan, secret society opposing Negro rights established in South, **1865;** secret anti-Negro, anti-Catholic, and anti-Jewish society established in Georgia, **1915.**

Kulikovo, battle of, first Russian victory over Mongolian Tatars; Russian army led by grand duke of Moscow, Demetrius Donskoi [1350-89], decisively defeated Mongol horde at Kulikovo, **Sept. 8, 1380.**

Kulturkampf, religious political movement, inaugurated, **1871,** to bring Catholic Church under control of Prussian state; organized

by German Chancellor Otto von Bismarck [Apr. 1, 1815-July 30, 1898]; failure acknowledged, **c. 1878.**

Kunersdorf, battle of, Frederick II ("the Great") of Prussia suffered his most crushing defeat when Austrian-Russian army of 90,000 men overwhelmed Prussian army of 50,000 men, **Aug. 12, 1759.**

Kursk, historic city in European Russia, ruined by Mongol horde, **1240;** became Moscovite fortress, **1586;** site of one of largest tank battles in history, between Russians and Germans in WW II, **July 5-13, 1943.**

Kutchuk-Kainardji, Treaty of, ended Russia's war with Turks; Russia secured right of passage in Turkish waters and to make pilgrimages to Holy Sepulchre, **July 21, 1774.**

Kuwait, small state at northern end of Persian Gulf, became independent nation, **June 1961,** ending status as British protectorate, since **1897.**

kymography, invented, **1847,** by German physician Carl F. Ludwig [1816-1895].

Kyoto, capital of Japan, **794-1868.**

Labor, U.S. Department of, U.S. federal department created, **June 27, 1884,** as U.S. Bureau of Labor in the Department of the Interior; gained separate department status, **Mar. 4, 1913.**

Labor Reform Party, minor U.S. political party, formed **1869,** from National Labor Union; nominated presidential candidate, **Feb. 22, 1872.**

Labor's NonPartisan League, former organization to unite labor for political action, established **Aug. 10, 1936.**

La Bourgogne **and** *Cromartyshire* **collision,** French steamship *La Bourgogne* and British sailing ship *Cromartyshire* collided near Sable Island, off Nova Scotia; 560 persons drowned, **July 4, 1898.**

Labour Party, British political party established by trade unions and socialist groups, **Feb. 1900;** James Ramsay MacDonald [Oct. 12, 1866-Nov. 9, 1937] became first Labour prime minister of Britain, **1924;** Clement Richard Attlee [Jan. 3, 1883-Oct. 8, 1967] became prime minister in Labour's first majority government, **1945.**

Laconia Company, colonial land company formed, **1631,** to settle parts of present-day New Hampshire.

lacrosse, sport first played by North American Indians, **16th-18th centuries**; adopted and named lacrosse by French settlers, **18th century**; Montreal Lacrosse Club organized, **1856**; Canadian parliament made lacrosse national game of Canada, **1867**.

Lade, battle of, Persians won decisive naval victory over Greek fleet of 353 Samian, Chian, and Lesbian galleys off island of Lade, that permitted Persians to crush Ionian revolt at Miletus, **494 B.C.**

Ladies' Home Journal, popular magazine, founded, **1883**.

Lady Chatterley's Lover, novel, **1928**; by English novelist D(avid) H(erbert) Lawrence [Sept. 11, 1883-Mar. 2, 1930]; ban on book lifted in U.S. **1959**, in Britain, **1960**.

Lady of the Camelias, The (La Dame aux Camelias), play, **1852**, from novel, **1848**, by Alexandre Dumas *fils*; formed basis of Verdi's opera, *La Traviata*, **1853**, and movie *Camille*, **1936**, featuring Swedish-American actress Greta Garbo.

Lady of the Lake, British ship bound from England to Quebec struck iceberg in North Atlantic; 215 persons perished, **May 11, 1833**.

Ladysmith, town in Natal, South Africa, where British forces were under heavy, 119-day siege by Boers during Boer War, until relieved by British reinforcements, **Nov. 1899-Feb. 1900**.

LaFollette Seamen's Act, U.S. Congress, established **Mar. 4, 1915**, regulations on wages, conditions, and crew-sizes on U.S. merchant ships.

La Fontaine's Fables, satiric verse stories, **1668-94**, endowing animals with human characteristics; by French writer Jean de La Fontaine [July 8, 1621-Apr. 13, 1695].

La France (airship), developed, **1884**, by French inventors Charles Renard [1847-1905] and Arthur Krebs [1847-1935].

La Hogue, battle of, British and Dutch fleet pursued and destroyed French ships at La Hogue off the coast of France, **May 19-23, 1692**.

Laibach, Congress of, international conference to complete discussions of the Congress of Troppau, **Jan. 26-May 12, 1821**.

Laing's Nek, battles of, Boer forces defeated the British at Laing's Nek in the Transvaal, **Jan. 28, 1881**; Boers crushed the British at Laing's Nek, **Oct. 12, 1899**, in their drive towards Natal and the sea.

Lake Poets, group of romantic poets that flourished from **c. 1800-1830**, included Coleridge, Shelley, and Wordsworth.

Lamentabili, Decree of the Holy See, issued **July 3, 1907**, in which St. Pius X (born Giuseppe Sarto) [June 2, 1835-Aug. 20, 1914] formally condemned as contrary to Catholic doctrine 65 propositions derived from theological "Modernism."

Lamentation of Christ, fresco, **c. 1305**, Arena Chapel, Padua, one of first Western paintings in which the women and disciples lamenting Christ's crucifixion come through as individuals, by Florentine painter Giotto.

Lamentations of Jeremiah, Old Testament book lamenting destruction of Jerusalem by Babylonians, **586 B.C.**, traditionally ascribed to Prophet Jeremiah; certainly written under his influence, **586-538 B.C.**

Lamian War, confederate Greek city-states led by Lamia waged war against Macedonians under Antipater [d. 319 B.C.] in central Greece, **323-22 B.C.**; Antipater defeated Greeks, at Crannon, near Larisa, **322 B.C.**

lamp, Davy, invented, **1815**, by English chemist Sir Humphry Davy [1778-1829] as a miner's safety light.

lamp, Doebereiner, invented, **1812**, by German chemist Johann W. Doebereiner [1780-1849].

lamp, incandescent, first made practical, **1879**, by American inventor Thomas A. Edison [1847-1931].

lamp, mercury vapor, invented, **1912**, by American scientist and inventor Peter C. Hewitt [1861-1921].

lamp, neon, invented, **1911**, by French inventor Georges Claude [1871-1960].

Lancashire Witch, constructed, **1828**, by English engineer Robert Stephenson [1803-1859].

Lancefield system, technique for bacterial classification established, **1944**, by Rebecca C. Lancefield [1895-1981].

Landeshut, forces of Holy Roman Empire held onto Silesian fortress of Landeshut, virtually destroying entire Prussian army during assault on fortress in Seven Years' War, **June 23, 1760**.

Landrum-Griffin Act (Labor-Management Reporting and Disclosure Act), U.S. Congress authorized, **Sept. 14, 1959**, regulation of internal union affairs and bill of rights to protect union members against abuses by officials.

Landshut, German city, became residence of dukes of Bavaria-Landshut, **1255**; heavily damaged during Thirty Years' War, **1618-48**; Austrians defeated Prussians at Landshut, **June 23, 1760**; Napoleon overwhelmed Austrians there, **Apr. 19, 1809**.

Langensalza, town in East Gemany, seat of Teutonic Knights, **13th century**; annexed by Prussia, **1815**; site of Prussian victory over Hanoverians during Seven Weeks' War between Prussia and Austria, **June 27, 1866**.

Lansing-Ishii Agreement, U.S. granted Japan "special interests" in China, provided Japan accepted Open Door Policy and territorial integrity of China, **Nov. 2, 1917**; terminated **Apr. 14, 1923**.

lanthanum, element No. 57; discovered, **1839**, by Swedish chemist Carl G. Mosander [1797-1858].

Laocoon, marble sculpture of Greek Hellenistic period, **38 B.C.**, depicting Laocoon and sons being strangled by serpents; discovered, Rome, **1506**.

Laos, nation in Southeast Asia, became constitutional monarchy under French, **July 19, 1949**; torn by civil war instigated by Pathet Lao and others, **1953-75**; Pathet Lao's People's Democratic Republic proclaimed, **Dec. 3, 1975**, with help from Communist North Vietnam.

La Rochelle, battle of, Castilian fleet defeated English fleet off La Rochelle on the Bay of Biscay, **June 23, 1372**, restoring domination of the (English) Channel to France.

Larousse **dictionaries**, French "family" of dictionaries: 15-volume comprehensive *Grand Larousse*, **1877-90**; 20th-century counterpart, **1927-33**, with supplement, **1954**; perennial Nouveau Petit Larousse Illustre, first published, **1924**.

Larsen's perfect game, Don Larsen [Aug. 7, 1929-] of the New York Yankees pitched only perfect game in World Series history against Brooklyn Dodgers in Yankee Stadium, retiring 27 batters in a row, **Oct. 8, 1956**.

laryngoscope, invented, c. **1885**, by Spanish voice teacher Manuel Garcia [1805-1906].

La Scala, opera house, Milan, Italy, opened, **1778**; Arturo Toscanini [Mar. 25, 1867-Jan. 16, 1957] music director from **1898**.

Lascaux Cave Paintings, prehistoric cave

paintings at Lascaux, France, discovered, **1940**; renderings of bison, horses, and other animals possibly date back to **20,000 B.C.**

laser, acronym for light amplification by stimulated emission of radiation; patented, **1960**, by American physicists Arthur L. Schawlow [1921-] and Charles H. Townes [1915-].

Lassie, long-running television series, **1954-75**.

Last Judgment, The, frescos, begun, **1305**, completed, **1309-10**, Arena Chapel, Padua, by Florentine artist Giotto; frescos on lives of Christ, and *Sts. Joachim and Anne*, same chapel, **1305-06**. Altarpiece painting, Danzig, **1472-73**, graceful, meticulous painting by German-born member of Flemish school, Hans Memling (or Memlinc) [c. 1430-Aug. 11, 1494]. Fresco, **1536-41**, on altar wall of Rome's Sistine Chapel, by Italian Renaissance painter Michelangelo Buonarroti.

Last of the Mohicans, The, adventure novel, **1826**, about colonial frontier war around Lake Champlain, by U.S. novelist James Fenimore Cooper.

Last Supper, The, mosaic, **c. 550**, first extant representation of Christ's last meal with apostles; in Byzantine Church of St. Appollinore in Classe, Ravenna, Italy. Fresco, **1445-50**, St. Apollonia, Florence, by early Renaissance painter who introduced naturalism and perspective into religious scenes, Andrea del Castagno (born Andrea di Bartolo de Simone) [c. 1421-Aug. 19, 1457]. Painting, **1467**, central panel of St. Peter altarpiece, Louvain, Belgium; model for interior perspective, by Dutch painter Dirk Bouts. Painting, **1495-98**, cov-

ers entire wall of convent of Santa Maria delle Grazie, Milan, depicting Christ and the apostles, by Italian Renaissance painter Leonardo da Vinci.

Las Vegas Hilton Hotel fire, eight persons died and 300 injured in fire at 2783-room Las Vegas Hilton, largest hotel in the U.S., **Feb. 10, 1981**.

Lateran Basilica, The (San Giovanni in Laterano), cathedral of Rome, built, from **c. 1365**, after fire destroyed earlier basilica, **1360**; facade completed, **1734**.

Lateran Councils, five ecumenical councils, held, Lateran Palace, Rome, **12th to 16th centuries**: First, **1123**; Second, **1139**; Third, **1179**; Fourth, **1215**; Fifth, **1512-17**; decided ecclesiastical questions of the times.

Lateran Treaty, agreement signed between kingdom of Italy and the Holy See, which was granted rule over the new sovereign state of Vatican City, **Feb. 11, 1929**.

lathe, engine driven, developed, **1805**, by English mechanical engineer Henry Maudslay [1771-1831].

Latin American Free Trade Association (LAFTA), Argentina, Brazil, Chile, Mexico, Paraguay, Peru, and Uruguay formed union to reduce tariffs and increase reciprocal trade, **1960**; LAFTA and Central American Common Market to form Latin American common market, planned at meeting of 19 Latin American presidents at Punta del Este, Uruguay, **Apr. 12-14, 1967**; Andean

Group (Bolivia, Chile, Colombia, and Ecuador) became subregional association in LAFTA **May 26, 1969**.

Latrocinium ("Robber Council"), false Church council, held, Ephesus, Asia Minor, **449**, acquitting leader of Monophysite heresy; decision reversed by true Council of Chalcedon, **451**.

Latter Day Saints, official name of Mormon Church, founded, New York, **1830**, by Joseph Smith; led west to establish Salt Lake City, **1846-47**, by Smith successor Brigham Young [June 1, 1801-Aug. 29, 1877].

Laufeld, battle of, French army under Marshal de Saxe [1696-1750] defeated British and Dutch army of the duke of Cumberland, **July 2, 1747**.

laughing gas (nitrous oxide), anesthetic properties discovered, **c. 1800**, by English chemist Sir Humphry Davy [1778-1829].

Launcelot, or the Knight of the Cart, Arthurian verse legend, **1170**, about most famous Round Table Knight and lover Guinevere, by medieval French poet Chretien de Troyes [fl. 1160-90].

launderette, first U.S. established, **1934**, by American inventor J. F. Cantrell in Fort Worth, Texas.

Laurel and Hardy, television series, from **1948**, presenting films (and excerpts) out of more than 200 movies made, from **1926**, by U.S. film comedy team Stan Laurel [June 16, 1890-Feb. 23, 1965] and Oliver Hardy [Jan. 18, 1892-Aug. 7, 1957].

Lausanne, Conference of, first conference of the modern Christian ecumenical movement, **1927**, aiming to restore Christian unity.

Lausanne, Conference of, refusal of Turkish leader Kemal Ataturk [1881-Nov. 10, 1938] to accept Treaty of Sevres compelled Allies to negotiate new treaty, restoring e. Thrace, the Straits, and Smyrna to Turkey, **July 24, 1923**.

lawn mower, power, invented, **c. 1915**, by American inventor Ransom E. Olds [1864-1950].

Lawrence of Arabia, film, **1962**, that explores adventures of World War I British Arab "guerrilla" leader and writer T(homas) E(dward) Lawrence [Aug. 15, 1888-May 19, 1935], starred Irish actor Peter O'Toole [Aug. 2, 1932-].

Lawrence, sack of, proslavery Border Ruffians sacked Lawrence, Kansas, causing great Northern abolitionist sentiment, **May 21, 1856**.

lawrencium, element No. 103; discovered, **1961**, by American physicist Albert Ghiorso [1915-] and coworkers.

lay, poetic form developed by French troubadours, from **c. 1200**.

lead, desilverizing, process, developed **1829** by English assay-master Hugh L. Pattinson [1796-1858].

League of the Lion (Knights' League), Bohemian knights and lords organized to fight the towns for power in Bohemia, **1378-89**.

League of Nations, former international organization created at Paris Peace Conference, **Jan. 25, 1919**; League of Nations Covenant, drafted **Feb. 3-14, 1919**; fell apart after Munich Pact, **1938**; dissolved itself, **1946**, and transferred its services to the United Nations.

League of Women Voters, U.S. voluntary organization to aid women in public affairs, organized, **1920**, in Chicago as a branch of the National American Suffrage Association; accepted men as full members, **1974**.

Leaning Tower of Pisa, campanile of Pisa cathedral, 180 feet in height, built, **1174**.

Leavenworth, Fort, U.S. military post constructed near Leavenworth, Kan., to protect Santa Fe Trail, **1827**; oldest U.S. military prison established at fort, **1874**.

Leaves of Grass, book of poems, first published, **1855**, comprising poems written by U.S. free-verse poet Walt Whitman; volume augmented every few years until final edition, **1892**.

Lebanon, country at eastern end of the Mediterranean, ruled by Christian military government under Turkish sovereignty, **1864-1914**; administered as independent state under French mandate, **1920-41**; gained full independence, **Nov. 26, 1941**; civil war between Christians and Muslims, with U.S. troops sent, **May-Oct. 1958**; Lebanese raids into Israel brought Israeli invasion, **Mar. 14, 1978**; Syrian troops and weapons in Lebanon resulted in Israeli threat to wage war, **May 1981**.

Lechfeld, plain in Bavaria, site of crushing defeat of Magyars by German mail-clad army, assembled by Otto I ("the Great") [912-73], **955**.

Lecompton Constitution, slavery approved in Kansas territory when Free State men refused to vote at convention, **Dec. 21, 1857**; constitution rejected, **Jan. 4, 1858**.

Legal Tender Act, U.S. Congress authorized, **Feb. 25, 1862**, issue of greenbacks without any reserve or specie basis; declared unconstitutional by Supreme Court, **Feb. 7, 1870**; declared constitutional, **May 1, 1871**.

Legion of Honor, French, famous order of merit, military or civil, instituted in France by Napoleon Bonaparte when he was first consul, **May 19, 1802**.

Legnano, battle of, first major victory of infantry over feudal cavalry in Middle Ages; Lombard League infantrymen defeated mounted German knights of Holy Roman Emperor Frederick I (Frederick Barbarossa) [c. 1125-90] at Legnano, northwest of Milan, **May 29, 1176**.

Leiden (Leyden), Dutch city, prominent during revolt of the Netherlands against Spanish rule, **16th century**; Beggars of the Sea relieved Spanish siege of Leiden, **1574**; home of English Pilgrims before they sailed to America, **c. 1610-20**.

Leipzig, battle of (*battle of the Nations*), about 355,000 troops (Austrians, Russians, and Prussians) launched continual attacks against about 175,000 French troops under Napoleon at Leipzig; 38,000 French killed; Napoleon retreated, followed by allied armies, **Oct. 18-19, 1813**.

MARTIN LUTHER

Leipzig, Disputation of, ecclesiastical debate, **June 27 to July 16, 1519**, that helped jell Protestant Reformation; Martin Luther asserted Church ecumenical councils had erred while debating with Catholic theologian Johann von Eck.

Leipzig, University of, established when German scholars withdrew from Charles University (University of Prague), **1409**; renamed Karl Marx University, **1953**.

Leisler's Rebellion, German merchant Jacob Leisler, proclaiming the new Protestant English sovereigns William and Mary, [1640-May 1691] seized power in New York until forced to surrender by new English governor, **June 12, 1689-Mar. 29, 1691**.

Lelantine War, city of Chalcis (Khalkis) defeated Eretria and took possession of the rich Lelantine plain in ancient Euboea, **c. 570 B.C.**

Lemanic Republic, Swiss canton of Vaud organized by the French, who freed it from Bernese rule, **Jan. 23, 1798**.

Le Mans, battle of, well-trained Prussian army overwhelmed larger French army at Le Mans, southwest of Paris, during Franco-Prussian War, **Jan. 10-12, 1871.**

Lemberg, battles of, Russian forces seized Lemberg (Lvov) in the Ukraine, **Sept. 8-12, 1914,** compelling the Austrians to abandon Galicia; Germans and Austrians retook Lemberg and other cities in Galicia, **July 18-28, 1917.**

Lend-Lease Act, U.S. Congress authorized President, **Mar. 11, 1941,** to lend, lease, sell, or transfer war materiel to any nations he considered vital to the defense of U.S.; Lend-Lease Administration formed, **Oct. 1941;** Pres. Truman announced end of lend-lease aid, **Aug. 21, 1945,** which totaled about $50 billion.

Lenin Peace Prize, Soviet award given to citizens of any country in the world who have contributed to peace among nations; established in Moscow, **June 23, 1925;** called Stalin Peace Prize, **1935-56.**

lens, anastigmatic, invented, **1890,** by German mathematical optician Paul Rudolph [1858-1941].

Lens, battle of, last major battle of Thirty Years' War; French army surprised and totally defeated Austrian-Spanish army at Lens in France, **Aug. 2, 1648.**

lens, camera, improved, **1865,** by German-American inventor Joseph Zentmayer [1826-1888].

Leoben, Peace of, France and Austria signed armistice at Leoben in Austria to con-

clude Napoleon's successful Italian campaign, **Apr. 18, 1797.**

Leopold-Loeb case, in the "Crime of the Century," Nathan Leopold, Jr. [c. 1905-Aug. 30, 1971] and Richard Loeb [c. 1906-Jan. 28, 1936] kidnapped and later murdered in cold blood 14-year-old Bobby Franks in Chicago, **May 22, 1924;** lawyer Clarence Darrow saved them from the death penalty during sensational trial, **1924.**

Lepanto, battle of, fleet of the Holy League (mainly 200 Spanish, Venetian, and papal ships) virtually destroyed Turkish fleet during bloody naval battle off Lepanto, Greece, **Oct. 7, 1571.**

Lesotho, country surrounded by South Africa, formerly British Basutoland, became independent republic and kingdom, **Oct. 4, 1966.**

Leticia dispute, territory of Leticia in Amazon basin claimed by Peru and Colombia, **1932-34,** threatening war; League of Nations mediation brought final settlement, **Nov. 2, 1934,** with Leticia awarded to Colombia.

leucine, amino acid discovered, **1818,** by French chemist Joseph L. Proust [1754-1826].

Leuctra, battle of, by brilliant military tactics, Thebans under Epaminondas [d. 362 B.C.] defeated the Spartans at village of Leuctra, Greece, **371 B.C.**

leukemia, first described, independently, **1845,** by German pathologist Rudolf Virchow [1821-1902] and by English physician John Hughes Bennett [1812-1875].

Leuthen, battle of, by skillful use of infantry, artillery, and cavalry, Prussians under Frederick II ("the Great") won clear-cut victory over Austrians at Leuthen on Oder River, **Dec. 5, 1757.**

Levant Trading Company, English import-export company established in London for East Indian spice trade with Turkey, **1578.**

Levellers, English religious and political party, **1640-1660,** advocating abolition of monarchy and total religious freedom; name first mentioned, **1647;** died out after Restoration of English monarchy, **1660.**

lever escapement (clock), devised, c. **1756,** by English inventor Thomas Mudge [1717-1794].

Lever House, skyscraper, **1952,** by Skidmore, Owings and Merrill firm headed by U.S. architect Louis Skidmore [Apr. 8, 1897-Sept. 27, 1962].

Leviathan, philosophical treatise, **1651**, by English philosopher Thomas Hobbes [Apr. 5, 1588-Dec. 4, 1679].

Leviticus, Book of, third Old Testament book consisting of legislation traditionally ascribed to Moses and dating back to **c. 1280 B.C.**, book probably edited in present form, **c. 586-538 B.C.**

Lexington and Concord, battles of, opening military engagements of American Revolution; British regulars forced American minutemen to withdraw at Lexington, Mass., continued to Concord, Mass., fought Americans again, and retreated back to Boston, **Apr. 19, 1775**.

Leyte, island in the Philippines, site of first major U.S. amphibious landing in campaign to retake Japanese-held Philippine Islands, **Oct. 20, 1944**, preceding battle of Leyte Gulf.

Leyte Gulf, battle of, U.S. naval forces under Admiral William F. Halsey, Jr. [Oct. 30, 1882-Aug. 16, 1959] defeated Japanese naval forces at Leyte Gulf in the Philippines during greatest sea battle of all time, **Oct. 23-26, 1944**.

L'Humanite, French newspaper founded, **1904**, as voice of Socialism, later became Communist daily.

Liaoyang, battle of, Japanese forces managed to check large-scale offensive by 100,000-man Russian army at Liaoyang, south of Mukden in Manchuria, in first great land battle of Russo-Japanese War, **Aug. 25-Sept. 3, 1904**.

liberalism, political philosophy originally emphasizing belief in liberty, term first employed in English, **1816**; origins of philosophy in Locke's *Two Treatises of Government*, **1690**; from **c. 1920**, term reflects growing emphasis on economic freedom; religious philosophy, popular from **c. 1850**.

Liberal Republican Party, U.S. political party of Republicans discontented with Pres. Grant's Reconstruction policies and government corruption, nominated New York newspaper editor Horace Greeley [Feb. 3, 1811-Nov. 29, 1872] for U.S. President at national convention in Cincinnati, Ohio, **May 1, 1872**.

Liberator, The, journal, published, **1831-65**, advocating emancipation of black slaves, edited by U.S. abolitionist and pacifist William Lloyd Garrison [Dec. 12, 1805-May 24, 1879].

Liberia, colony in w. Africa founded by American Colonization Society for freed U.S. slaves, **1822**; declared a republic, **July 26, 1847**.

Liberty, sloop *Liberty* owned by John Hancock [Jan. 12, 1737-Oct. 8, 1793] seized by British customs officials for non-payment of duty on wine imports into American colonies; officials assaulted by colonists, **June 10, 1768**.

Liberty Bell, bell in Independence Hall, Philadelphia, first cast in London, **1752**; recast, Philadelphia, **1753**; cracked, **1835**, tolling for death of U.S. Chief Justice John Marshall [Sept. 24, 1755-July 6, 1835].

Liberty, On, philosophical treatise, **1859**, examining liberty, by British utilitarian philosopher and economist John Stuart Mill [May 20, 1806-May 8, 1873].

Liberty or Death speech, Patrick Henry gave immortal speech before Virginia assembly at Richmond, uttering "...give me liberty or give me death" in opposition to Britain's arbitrary rule, **Mar. 23, 1775**.

Liberty Party, U.S. political party established by abolitionists led by James G. Birney [Feb. 4, 1792-Nov. 25, 1857], **1839**; merged with antislavery Democrats and Whigs to form Free-Soil Party, **1847**.

Liberty, Statue of, colossal statue-monument, dedicated, **1886**, in entrance to New York harbor.

Liberty Tree, two distinct trees; one on which Bostonians hanged colonial administrator Andrew Oliver [1706-74] in effigy, **Aug. 1765**; one under which patriots in Charleston held meetings, cut down and burned by British, **1780**.

libido, term introduced, **1914**, by Austrian psychiatrist Sigmund Freud [1856-1939].

Library of Congress, U.S. national library at Washington, D.C., established by Congress, **1800**; books destroyed by fire ignited by British in War of 1812, **Aug. 24-25, 1814**; Jefferson donated his library, **1815**; books again destroyed by fire, **Dec. 24, 1851**; act of Congress, **1870**, mandated copies of all books copyrighted to be sent to Library of Congress.

Libya, country on northeast coast of Africa, became constitutional monarchy, **Jan. 2, 1952**; taken over by military junta led by Muammar el-Qaddafi [1942-] who declared it a socialist state, **1969**; warred with Egypt, **July 21-24, 1977**; sent soldiers to help Idi Amin of Uganda, **1979**.

Lidice, Czech village in central Bohemia, razed by Germans who killed all the men and deported women and children, **June 6, 1942**.

Liechtenstein, principality between Austria and Switzerland, created as a fief of the Holy Roman Empire, **1719**; joined German Confederation, **1815**; became independent principality, **1866**; disbanded its army and became neutral, **1868**.

Lied, Lieder, German art song(s); form developed from **c. 1814**, by German composers such as Schubert, Schumann, Brahms, and Wolf; origin of form, German *Minnesinger* and *Meistersinger* songs, **1250-1550**.

Liege, city in Belgium, whose guild workers and bishop's officials created tribunal of 22 persons, Peace of Twenty-two, to govern, **1373-1792**; Charles the Bold of Burgundy abolished citizens' communal liberties, **1467**, and sacked the city, **1468**, after it rose in revolt; seized by Germans in WW I,

Aug. 17, 1914 and in WW II, **May 12, 1940**; liberated by Allies, **May, 1944**.

Liegnitz, battles of, German and Polish infantry, aided by Teutonic Knights, defeated by Mongol horse archers and swordsmen at Wahlstatt, near Liegnitz (Legnica), during Mongol invasion of Europe, **Apr. 9, 1241**; Prussian army of Frederick II ("the Great") inflicted heavy losses on Austrian army at Liegnitz during Seven Years' War, **Aug. 15, 1760**.

Life, magazine, founded, **1936**, that pioneered photo journalism, published by Henry R. Luce; suspended publication **1971**; revived, **1978**.

Life of Samuel Johnson, LL.D., biography, **1791**, portrait of English man of letters, by Scottish writer James Boswell [Oct. 29, 1740-May 19, 1795].

Full-length portrait of Dr. Johnson, in the dress worn by him in his journey to the Hebrides.

Life on the Mississippi, autobiographical memoir, **1883**, describing life of Mississippi-riverboat pilot and life on the river, by American author Mark Twain.

Life with Father, humorous sketches, **1935**, about eccentric, domineering father, by U.S. essayist Clarence (Shepherd) Day (Jr.) [Nov. 18, 1874-Dec. 28, 1935]; Broadway play, **1939**, by writing team of Howard Lindsay and Russel Crouse.

Light Brigade, charge of the (see Balaclava, battle of).

lighting, coal-gas, first developed, **1792**, by Scottish inventor William Murdock [1754-1839].

lighting, electric, first demonstrated for homes, **1858**, by American inventor Moses G. Farmer [1820-1893]; first installed on railroad train, the Overland Ltd. of Chicago and Northwestern Railroad, **1905**.

lightning, man-made, accomplished in laboratory, **1921**, by German-American mathematician, electrical engineer Charles P. Steinmetz [1865-1923].

lightning, electrical nature proved, **1752**, by American statesman and scientist, Benjamin Franklin, [1706-1790] in experiment with kite.

Ligny, battle of, French forces of Napoleon I defeated Prussians, **June 16, 1815**, at village of Ligny in central Belgium.

Lima, Declaration of, declaration of 21 countries at Pan-American Conference in Lima, Peru, reaffirmed sovereignty of states in Western Hemisphere and determination to defend themselves against possible fascistic, foreign intervention, **Dec. 24, 1938**.

Lima, University of, institution of higher learning, founded, **1551**; one of oldest in Western hemisphere.

Limelight, film, **1952**, about aging comedian who helps young ballerina to stardom; last American film of Charlie Chaplin; debut of actress Claire Bloom [Feb. 15, 1931-].

limelight, invented, **1825**, by Irish inventor Thomas Drummond [1797-1840].

limerick, five-line rhymed facetious jingle, first appeared, **1820**; popularized, **1846**, in *Book of Nonsense*, by English poet Edward Lear [May 12, 1812-Jan. 29, 1888].

Limerick, last stronghold of Jacobites in Ireland, captured by English royalists, ending Irish rebellion against English rule, **Oct. 3, 1691**.

Lincoln, assassination of, U.S. President Abraham Lincoln [Feb. 12, 1809-Apr. 15, 1865] shot at Ford's Theatre, Washington, D.C., by John Wilkes Booth [May 10, 1838-Apr. 26, 1865], an actor; first U.S. president assassinated, **Apr. 14, 1865**; Lincoln died next day, **Apr. 15**.

Lincoln Center for the Performing Arts, New York City cultural center, built, **1959**.

Lincoln-Douglas debates, seven debates between Abraham Lincoln and Stephen A. Douglas [Apr. 23, 1813-June 3, 1861] during Illinois campaign for U.S. Senate seat; Lincoln lost but gained national prominence, **Aug. 21-Oct. 15, 1858**.

Lincoln's Second Inaugural Address, including the memorable words, "with malice toward none," **Mar. 4, 1865**.

Lindbergh kidnapping, Charles A. Lindbergh, Jr., 20-month-old son of aviator Charles A. Lindbergh [Feb. 4, 1902-Aug. 26, 1974], kidnapped from his parents' home, Hopewell, N.J., **Mar. 1, 1932**; baby found dead, **May 12, 1932**; German-American Bruno Richard Hauptmann [1899-Apr. 3, 1936], convicted of the murder, electrocuted in prison, Trenton, N.J., **Apr. 3, 1936**.

Lindbergh's transatlantic flight, Charles A. Lindbergh [Feb. 4, 1902-Aug. 26, 1974] made first solo nonstop flight across Atlantic in monoplane *Spirit of St. Louis*, **May 20-21, 1927**, flying New York to Paris, 3600 miles in 33 1/2 hours.

linotype, patented, **1884**, by German-American inventor Ottmar Mergenthaler

[1854-1899]; eliminated need to handset type; first commercial use, **1886**, by *New York Tribune*.

liquid helium, wave theory developed, **c. 1941**, by Soviet physicist Lev. D. Landau [1908-1968].

Lisbon earthquakes, great, some 30,000 killed by quake in Lisbon, Portugal, **Jan. 26, 1531**; 10,000-30,000 killed during quake accompanied by fire and flood of Tagus River, **Nov. 1, 1755**.

Lisbon, University of, one of world's first important universities established at Lisbon, Portugal, **1290**; transferred to Coimbra, **1537**; reestablished at Lisbon, **1911**.

Liston-Patterson fight, Sonny Liston [May 8, 1917?-Dec. 28, 1970] knocked out Floyd Patterson in first round in Chicago to become heavyweight boxing champion, **Sept. 25, 1962**; Liston again knocked out Patterson in first round in Las Vegas, Nev., to retain title, **July 22, 1963**.

lithium, element No. 3; discovered, **1817**, by Swedish chemist J. A. Arfvedson [1792-1841].

lithography, invented, **1796**, by German inventor Aloys Senefelder [1771-1834].

lithography, color, invented, **1826**, by German inventor Aloys Senefelder [1771-1834].

Little America, U.S. exploration and scientific base on Ross Ice Shelf in Antarctica, established by explorer Richard E. Byrd [Oct. 25, 1888-Mar. 11, 1957], **1929**.

Little Assembly, UN committee with representatives from each UN country, created **Nov. 15, 1947**, to resolve problems that may arise between sessions of the General Assembly.

Little Entente, defensive alliance formed by Czechoslovakia, Rumania, and Yugoslavia, **1920-21**; ended when Czechoslovakia was disjointed by Munich Pact, **1938**.

Little Foxes, The, play, **1939**, depicting new breed of ruthless, modern Southerners, by U.S. playwright and memoirist Lillian Hellman [June 20, 1905-]; successfully revived, **May 7, 1981**, with actress Elizabeth Taylor in her first Broadway appearance. Film, **1941**, based on Hellman play, starring actress Bette Davis and British actor Herbert Marshall [May 23, 1890-Jan. 22, 1966].

Little House on the Prairie, juvenile novel, **1935**, one of series about pioneer Ingalls family settling Minnesota frontier, by U.S. writer Laura Ingalls Wilder [Feb. 7, 1867-Jan. 10, 1957]; made into television series, beginning **Sept. 11, 1974**.

Little League Baseball, youth baseball program throughout the world originated in Williamsport, Penn., **1939**; first Little League World Series held at Max M. Brown Memorial Park (now Original Little League Field), **1947**.

Little Lord Fauntleroy, children's story, **1886**, about American heir to English title who wins back birthright, by English-born U.S. children's writer Frances Hodgson Burnett [Nov. 24, 1849-Oct. 29, 1924].

Little Rock Central High School, National Guardsmen and U.S. paratroopers, on orders from Pres. Eisenhower, enforced federal integration law that permitted nine Negroes to enroll at Central High School, Little Rock, Ark., **Sept. 25, 1957**; Arkansas Gov. Orval E. Faubus [Jan. 7, 1910-] failed to shut down city public schools which reopened to Negroes under police guard, **Aug. 12, 1959**.

Little Women, novel for young people, **1868**, about fortunes of several sisters, by U.S. writer Louisa May Alcott [Nov. 29, 1832-Mar. 6, 1888]; film version, **1933**, directed by George Cukor with Katharine Hepburn and Joan Bennett; remade, **1949**, with Elizabeth Taylor and June Allyson (born Ella Geisman) [Oct. 7, 1923-].

Litvinov Protocol, U.S.S.R., Poland, Rumania, Latvia, and Estonia signed agreement, **Feb. 9, 1929**, renouncing war.

Livonian Knights (Brothers of the Sword), German military-religious order established by the bishop of Riga to christianize the Baltic area, **c. 1202**; conquered Courland (s. Latvia) and Livonia (Estonia) but were defeated by Lithuanians at Siauliai, **1236**; united with Teutonic Knights, **1237-1525**.

Livonian War, struggle among Poland, Russia, and Sweden for Livonia (present-day Estonia and n. Latvia), **1557-71**.

Lizzie Borden case, stepmother and father of spinster Lizzie Borden [July 19, 1860-June 1, 1927] murdered with an axe or meat cleaver (Lizzie Borden acquitted, but believed to be guilty), **Aug. 4, 1892**.

Lloyd-La Follette Act, U.S. Congress allowed, **Aug. 24, 1912**, federal employees to form unions, provided union did not strike against government.

Lobositz, battle of, Prussians under Frederick II ("the Great") claimed victory over Austrians, though battle was not conclusive, **Oct. 1, 1756**.

lobotomy (prefrontal), surgical technique introduced, **1935**, by Portuguese neurologist Antonio Caetano Moniz [1874-1955].

Locarno Treaties, Britain, France, Germany, Italy, Belgium, Poland, and Czechoslovakia signed series of treaties of mutual guarantee and arbitration, **Oct. 5-16, 1925**.

lock, cylinder, patented, **1861**, by American locksmith Linus Yale [1821-1868].

Lockheed Aircraft scandal, former Japanese Prime Minister Kakuei Tanaka [May 4, 1918-] indicted for accepting $1.6 million bribe from U.S. corporation, Lockheed Aircraft, **July 28, 1976**; Prince Bernhard of the Netherlands, charged with involvement in scandal, resigned all military and business posts, **Aug. 26, 1976**; Lockheed payments to foreign nationals to win aircraft contracts revealed to reach $38 million, **May 26, 1977**.

locomotive, first U.S., designed and built, **1830**, by American manufacturer Peter Cooper [1791-1883] for Baltimore and Ohio Railroad.

locomotive, electric, invented, **1887**, by American Stephen D. Field [1846-1913] and Bavarian-American Rudolf Eickemeyer [1831-1895].

locomotive, gearless electric, patented, **1894**, by Belgian-American inventor Charles J. Van Depoele [1846-1892].

locomotive, steam, first U.S. built, **1825**,

by American inventor John Stevens [1749-1838].

Lodz, battles of, German armies drove the Russians back during bloody battle in mud and snow in central Poland, **Nov. 16-Dec. 6, 1918**; Russians captured city of Lodz, **Jan. 19, 1945**, forcing the Germans to give up the Vistula defense line.

loganberry, developed, **c. 1881**, by American horticulturist James H. Logan [1841-1928].

Logan, Mt., highest mountain in Canada (19,850 ft.), first climbed by Canadian-American expedition, **June 23, 1925**.

logarithms, invented, **c. 1590**, by Scottish mathematician John Napier [1550-1617].

Lohengrin, opera, composed to original libretto, **1846-48**, produced **1850**, on knightly theme set in 10th-century Germany, by German opera composer-librettist Richard Wagner [May 22, 1813-Feb. 13, 1883]; based on German epic, **1285**.

Lolita, novel, **1958**, modern tale of middle-aged professor's uncontrollable passion for 12-year-old "nymphet," by Russian-U.S. author Vladimir Nabokov.

Lollards, 14th-century religious movement, reached height in decade following death of leader John Wycliff, **1384**.

Lombards, Germanic people who established a kingdom in n. Italy, **6th century**.

Lombardy became center of the kingdom of the Lombards, **569**.

London Conferences, major European powers helped establish Greece as independent principality; set up armistice between Dutch and Belgians, **1830-31**; helped prepare separation treaty Dutch-Belgian, **1839**; split Luxembourg and Limburg between Dutch and Belgian crowns,

1838-39; settled Denmark's claim to Schleswig-Holstein, **1852**; issued Declaration of London, international maritime law, **1908-1909**; failed to established worldwide economic stabilization agreements, **1933**.

London Daily Express, London newspaper, first appeared, **1896**; rivaled *London Daily Mail*.

London Daily Mail, newspaper, first published, **1896**, pioneering sensational news coverage.

Londonderry, battle of, Irish Catholic army (Jacobites) laid siege to English Protestant town of Londonderry, resisting Glorious Revolution; Irish abandoned 105-day siege after British received reinforcements and supplies, **Apr. 17-July 30, 1689**.

London, Great Fire of, four-fifths of London burned to the ground, **Sept. 2-6, 1666**.

London Naval Conference, assembly of 10 major naval powers adopted Declaration of London, international maritime code of law, **1908-1909**.

London plagues, great, outbreak of bubonic plague killed c. 30,000 persons in London, England, **1407**; bubonic plague killed thousands more in London, **1499-1500**; epidemic of bubonic plague killed more than 33,000 persons in London, **1603**; another outbreak of bubonic plague killed approx. 41,000 in London, **1625**; last great outbreak of bubonic plague; at least 65,000 died in London and other surrounding English towns, **1665**.

London Round Table Conference, Gandhi as sole representative of Indian National Congress at conference in London, which ended without acceptance of Gandhi's representation of religious and other minorities in government, **Sept. 7-Dec. 1, 1931**; Gandhi resumed civil disobedience and was arrested, **Jan. 4, 1932**.

London's Brixton riots, worst racial violence in England in 50 years as about 500 black youths, joined by some whites, wrecked trucks, cars, and shops in Brixton area of London, **Apr. 10-13, 1981**.

London Stock Exchange, world's first true stock exchange founded in London, England, **1698**.

Lone Ranger, The, long-running show, on radio, **1933-55**, on television, **1949-65**.

Long Convention, Missouri's long constitutional convention unseated state officials seeking secession from Union, **1861**, and acted as state legislature, until **Sept. 1864**.

Long Day's Journey into Night, play, **1956**, a domestic tragedy, by U.S. dramatist Eugene O'Neill, Nobel Prize-winner, **1936**.

long division, invented, **1624**, by English mathematician Henry Briggs [1556-1631].

Long Island, battle of, American forces under Gen. George Washington, besieged by British under Gen. William Howe, withdrew from Brooklyn Heights, Long Island, and moved north at start of American Revolution, **Aug. 27-30, 1776**.

Long March, incredible 6000-mi. march made by Chinese Communists (90,000-man Red Army) under Mao Tse-tung across high mountains and treacherous rivers from Kiangsi to Shensi province, with Kuomintang army of Chiang Kai-shek in pursuit, **Oct. 1934-Oct. 1935**.

Long Parliament, fifth parliament of King Charles I of England that became known as Rump Parliament after Pride's Purge and that dissolved itself by its own consent, **Nov. 3, 1640-Mar. 16, 1660**.

long (Pennsylvania) rifle, German colonists introduced the long rifle in Pennsylvania, **1710-20**; gunsmiths added improvements, lengthening bore and lubricating more parts, **1730-40**.

Look Back in Anger, play, first performed, London, **May 8, 1956**, recounting frustrations of young man fed up with modern life, by British playwright John Osborne.

Look Homeward, Angel, novel, **1929**, semi-autobiographical celebration of life, youth, love and America, by U.S. novelist Thomas (Clayton) Wolfe [Oct. 3, 1900-Sept. 15, 1938].

Lookout Mountain, battle of, an important military engagement at the battle of Chattanooga in which Confederates under Gen. Braxton Bragg gave up key position on Lookout Mountain, south of Chattanooga, **Nov. 24, 1863**.

loom, automatic, invented, **1894**, by American inventor James H. Northrop.

loom, dobby, first U.S. invented, **1879**, by American inventor Horace Wyman [1827-1915].

loom, Jacquard, apparatus with punched cards for producing figured weaving devised, **1804**, by French inventor Joseph M. Jacquard [1752-1834].

loom, pile-fabric, invented, **1872**, by American inventor Horace Wyman [1827-1915].

loom, power, invented, **1785**, by English inventor Edmund Cartwright [1743-1823].

loom-box, device invented, **1871**, by American inventor Horace Wyman [1827-1915].

Lopez expedition, Spanish refugees and American Southerners led by Gen. Narciso Lopez [?-Sept. 1, 1851] sailed to Cuba, failed to incite uprising of Cubans against Spain, **Aug. 11-12, 1851**; 51 Americans executed in Havana, **Aug. 16, 1851**; mob destroyed Spanish consulate at New Orleans, **Aug. 21, 1851**.

Lord Jim, novel, **1900**, by Polish-English novelist Joseph Conrad (born Joseph Teodor Konrad Korzeniowski) [Dec. 3, 1857-Aug. 3, 1924].

Lord of the Flies, novel, **1955**, about reversion to savagery of group of boys stranded on paradisal island after airplane crash, by English novelist William (Gerald) Golding [Sept. 19, 1911-].

Lord of the Rings, The, trilogy, **1954-56**, romance in invented world, Middle Earth; includes: *The Fellowship of the Ring*, **1954**; *The Two Towers*, **1954**; *The Return of the King*, **1955**, by English writer J. R. R. Tolkien.

Lost Dauphin, titular King Louis XVII

[1785-June 8, 1795] of France, whose "uncertain" death created numerous pretenders to French throne, died in revolutionary French prison (the Temple), **June 8, 1795**.

lost generation, term referring to literary generation affected by World War I, **1914-18**, coined by Gertrude Stein in conversation with Hemingway.

Lost Horizon, novel, **1933**, about mythical land of Shangri-La, by popular English novelist James Hilton; made into film, **1937**, with British actor Ronald Colman [Feb. 9, 1891-May 19, 1958].

Lost Weekend, The, film, **1945**, realistic portrayal of horrors of alcoholism, starred Welsh-U.S. actor Ray(mond) (Alton) Milland [Jan. 3, 1908-].

Lotharingia, ancient kingdom of Lothair I [795-855] and his second son, established by Treaty of Verdun, **843**.

Loudon Hill, battle of, Scots under Robert I, self-proclaimed king of Scotland, repulsed English mounted knights at Loudon Hill in Ayr County; England soon abandoned its renewed war with Scotland, **1307**.

Louisbourg (Louisburg), Fort, great stone fortress built by the French on Cape Breton Island, Nova Scotia, as its "Gibraltar in America" to guard entrance to St. Lawrence River **1720-40**; small group of New Englanders aided by English ships captured stronghold, **June 16, 1745**; British forces under Gen. Jeffrey Amherst [Jan. 29, 1717-Aug. 3, 1797] captured fort and ruined it, **July 26, 1758**.

Louis-Braddock fight, Joe Louis [May 13, 1914-Apr. 12, 1981] knocked out Jim Braddock in eighth round in Chicago to win heavyweight boxing championship, **June 22, 1937**; Louis successfully defended his title 25 times, **1937-48**; Louis retired as champion, **Mar. 1, 1949**.

Louisiana, part of territory acquired by Louisiana Purchase, admitted to the Union (U.S.) as 18th state, **Apr. 8, 1812**; seceded from the Union, **Jan. 26, 1861**; readmitted to the Union, **June 25, 1868**.

Louisiana Purchase, U.S. bought from France for $15 million the Louisiana Territory (more than 500 million acres), doubling the area of U.S., **Apr. 30, 1803**.

Louvre, French royal palace, built on 7th century royal site, **c. 1180**; totally rebuilt, from **1546**; transformed into art museum, **1793**.

The Victory of Samothrace, in the Louvre Museum.

Love Canal disaster, U.S. Environmental Protection Agency released study, **May 16, 1980**, showing chromosome damage to residents of Love Canal area, Niagara Falls, N.Y.; serious health emergency declared by Pres. Jimmy Carter, **May 21, 1980**.

Love Me Tender, film, **1956**, that introduced with title song to nationwide audience

1950s and 1960s rock-and-roll star, U.S. singer-actor Elvis Presley [Jan. 8, 1935-Aug. 16, 1977].

Love song of J. Alfred Prufrock, The, poem, **1915**, monolog of a fearful, futile man, expressing sterility of modern life, by U.S.-British poet T.S. Eliot.

Love Story, novel, **1970**; romantic tale of Harvard man who marries poor girl, by Yale classics professor Erich Segal [June 16, 1937-]; film, **1970**, made from Erich Segal's novel, starring as young lovers Ryan O'Neal [Apr. 20, 1941-] and Ali MacGraw [Apr. 1, 1939-].

Lowell-Moody machinery, (for cotton cloth manufacture) first began operation, **1814**, in Waltham, Mass.; developed by American inventor Paul Moody [1779-1831] and American textile manufacturer Francis C. Lowell [1775-1817].

Lowestoft, battle of, English fleet of 150 ships under duke of York (later James II) won major naval battle against Dutch fleet off Lowestoft in North Sea, **June 13, 1665**.

Lubeck, acquired hegemony over the Baltic trade and headed the Hanseatic League, **13th-15th centuries**; sacked by French, **1803**; free Hanseatic city, **1815-1937**.

Lubeck, Treaty of, ended fighting between Holy Roman Empire and Denmark, which agreed not to interfere in German affairs, **May 22, 1629**.

Lublin, Union of, Lithuania and Poland merged, **July 1, 1569**.

Lucknow Pact, agreement by Indian National Congress and All India Muslim

League, **1921**, giving Muslim minority more seats in British India's legislature.

Lugdunum (Lyons), battle of, Pannonian legions under Septimius Severus [146-211] won decisive battle against legions of Britain and Gaul; Severus, as Roman emperor, returned to Rome in triumph, **197**.

Luke, Gospel According to, third book of New Testament about life and message of Jesus, now believed to have been written **c. 57-60**, by Luke, disciple of Paul.

Lumumba, assassination of, ex-Premier Patrice Lumumba [July 2, 1925-Jan. 17, 1961] of Congo killed in Katanga province, **Jan. 17, 1961**.

lunar landing, achieved, **July 20, 1969**, by U.S. Apollo 11 astronaut crew of Neil Armstrong [1930-] and Edwin Aldrin [1930-]. Armstrong was first to set foot on moon.

lunar orbital flight, first, launched, **December 21, 1968**, with U.S. Apollo 8 astronaut crew of Frank Borman [1928-], James Lovell [1928-], and William Anders [1931-]; returned to Earth, **December 27, 1968**.

lunar topography studies, pioneered, **1647**, by Polish astronomer Johannes Howelcke [1611-1687].

Luncheon on the Grass (Le Dejeuner sur l'Herbe), painting, **1863**, exhibiting nude women picnicking with decorously clad gentlemen, by impressionist painter Edouart Manet.

Lundy's Lane, battle of, fiercest land battle of War of 1812, in which Americans under Gen. Winfield Scott led attack against British position at Lundy's Lane, w. of Niagara Falls, **July 25, 1814**.

Luneville, Treaty of, Holy Roman Empire practically destroyed by treaty between France and Austria, confirming and supplementing the Treaty of Campo Formio, **Feb. 9, 1801**.

Lunik I (Mechta), first man-made planet launched, **1959**, by Soviet scientists.

Lusitania, British Cunard Line steamship *Lusitania* torpedoed by German submarine without warning and sank off coast of Ireland; 1195 persons died (128 Americans); aroused U.S. sentiment against Germany, **May 7, 1915**.

lute, plucked stringed instrument with pear-shaped body, appearing on Mesopotamian

figurines from **c. 2000 B.C.**; on Persian and Indian figures, **800 B.C.**; introduced into Europe, **c. 1250**; height of popularity, **1500-1700**.

lutetium, element No. 71; discovered, **1906**, by French chemist Georges Urbain [1872-1938].

Lutheranism, major Christian denomination, from **1517**, first Lutherans in America, **1623**, from Holland.

Lutzen, battle of, Swedish forces of Gustavus II ("Lion of the North") [Dec. 9, 1594-Nov. 16, 1632] defeated forces of Holy Roman Empire under Gen. Count Albrecht von Wallenstein [Sept. 24, 1583-Feb. 25, 1634] at Lutzen during Thirty Years' War; Gustavus II killed, **Nov. 16, 1632**.

Luxembourg, country in w. Europe, ruled by House of Luxembourg, after **1060**; became Grand Duchy, **1815**; western part annexed by Belgium, **1839**; eastern part became neutral territory, **1867**; occupied by German troops, **1914-18, 1940-44**.

Luzon, largest and most important Philippine island, where Filipinos revolted against Spanish rule, **1896**; taken over by U.S. after Spanish-American War, **1898**; Filipinos revolted against U.S. rule, **1899-1902**; invaded by Japanese in WW II, **Dec. 10, 1941**; recovered by Allies, **Jan.-Feb. 1945**.

Lvov, city in w. Ukraine, founded by a prince of Galicia, **c. 1250**; major trade center on Vienna-Kiev route, **13th-15th centu-**

ries; seized by the Poles, **1340s**; by the Turks, **1672**; by the Swedes, **1704**; annexed to Russia, **1939**; most of 100,000 Jewish inhabitants killed during German occupation, **1941-44**.

Lyceum, philosophical school, founded, **c. 335 B.C.**, on banks of Ilissus in Greece, near grove where Aristotle lectured and walked.

Lydia, ancient wealthy kingdom in w. Asia Minor, **7th-6th century B.C.**; first use of coined money in the world by Lydian rulers, **7th century B.C.**; absorbed into Persian Empire, **c. 546 B.C.**

Lydians, succeeded Hittites in central Asia Minor; noted for their trading and wealth, **fl. 6th century, B.C.**

Lynchburg, battle of, Confederate army under Gen. Jubal A. Early [Nov. 3, 1816-Mar. 2, 1894] forced Union army to retreat at Lynchburg, Va., **June 1864**, allowing Early to march through Shenandoah Valley, **July 2-13, 1864**, to raid Washington, D.C.

Lyons, Councils of, 13th and 14th ecumenical councils, **1245 and 1274**.

lysine, amino acid discovered, **1889**, by German chemist Edmund Drechsel [1843-1897].

Lysistrata, comedy, **411 B.C.** by Greek dramatist Aristophanes.

Lys River, battle of the, German forces broke through British front at Lys River, along Franco-Belgian border, **Apr. 9-29, 1918**.

Lytton Report, League of Nations commission recommended establishment of an autonomous government in Manchuria under Chinese sovereignty, **Oct. 2, 1932**; adopted by League of Nations, except Japan, **Feb. 25, 1933**; Japan's withdrawal from League of Nations, **May 27, 1933**, initiated collapse of that structure.

M, film, **1931**, legendary crime movie that starred U.S.-Hungarian actor Peter Lorre [June 26, 1904-Mar 23, 1964] as a deranged child murderer; first sound film by German-U.S. director Fritz Lang [Dec. 12, 1890- Aug. 2, 1976]

Maastricht, Dutch city seized by Spanish, **1579**, who massacred many citizens during Netherlands war of independence; recovered by Dutch, **1632**; seized by French, **June 30, 1673; 1794**.

Macbeth, tragedy, **c. 1606**, about "vaulting ambition" which leads to murder of the king by his subject, Macbeth, by William Shakespeare.

Maccabees, Books of, Old Testament books, probably written, **c. 100 B.C.**, about Jewish War of Independence under Maccabee family and related historical, moral and religious items.

Macedon, kingdom of, ancient kingdom of the Balkan region, **fl. 4th century B.C.**; became first Roman province (Macedonia), **146 B.C.**

Macedonian Wars, conflicts between Macedon and Rome; first war, **215-205 B.C.**; second, **200-197 B.C.**; Philip V [238-179 B.C.] king of Macedon defeated at Cynoscephalae, **197 B.C.**; third, **171-168 B.C.**; King Perseus [212?-166 B.C.] king of Macedon defeated at Pydna, **168 B.C.**; fourth, **149-148 B.C.**

Machine gun, invented, **1883**, by American-English engineer Sir Hiram S. Maxim [1840-1916].

Machine-spun yarn, developed, **1768**, by Sir Richard Arkwright [1732-1792] in Nottingham, England.

Machine tooling, numerically controlled, invented, **1952**, by American inventor Frank Stuelen.

Machine tools, electrical discharge, invented, **1943**, by Russian inventors B. R. and N. I. Lazarenko.

mackintosh, waterproofing invented, **1823**, by Scottish chemist Charles Macintosh [1766-1843].

Mackle kidnapping, Barbara Jane Mackle [1948-], daughter of wealthy businessman, kidnapped from motel, Atlanta, Ga., **Dec. 17, 1968**; Barbara found buried alive in coffin-like box after her father paid $500,000 ransom, **Dec. 20, 1968**.

Macon's Bill No. 2, U.S. Congress authorized president to reopen trade with France and Britain and to renew Non-Intercourse Act with either country before Mar. 3, 1811, if need be, **May 1, 1810**.

macromolecules, research pioneered, **1940**, by German chemist Hermann Staudinger [1881-1956].

Madagascar, world's fourth-largest island, taken over in part by French, **1885**; occupied by British during WW II, **1942-43**; became autonomous French republic as Malagasy Republic, **Oct. 1958**; became completely independent nation, **June 25, 1960**.

Madame Bovary, novel, **1856**, about the folly, adultery and suicide of a provincial Norman bourgeois woman, by French stylist Gustave Flaubert.

Madama Butterfly, romantic opera, **1904**, set in Japan, by Italian composer Giacomo Puccini.

Maddox, U.S. destroyer *Maddox* attacked by North Vietnamese torpedo boats in international waters, **Aug. 2, 1964**; attacked again by North Vietnamese, **Aug. 4, 1964**, serving as a pretext for retaliation by U.S.

aircraft against North Vietnamese oil and naval installations.

Madonna and Child, relief terracotta with polychrome glaze, **c.1455-60**, a rendering of Madonna and child, by Florentine artist Luca della Robbia [1400-Feb., 1482]; series of paintings, **1493-97**, exhibiting sweet, almost prettified style of Madonna that became hallmark of Perugino.

Madonna of the Chair (Madonna della Sedia), painting, **1514-15**, one of series of Madonnas done by classical Italian Renaissance painter Raphael.

Madonna of the Rocks, painting, **1494**, by Italian Renaissance painter Leonardo da Vinci.

Madonna with Angels, painting, **1490**, one of several devoted to the Madonna, by Florentine painter Sandro Botticelli.

Madras, city on Bay of Bengal, India, near site of martyrdom of Thomas the Apostle, **68**; became important English trading center, **c. 1650**; seized by French under Joseph Francois Dupleix [Jan. 1, 1697-Nov. 10, 1763], **Sept. 21, 1746**; recovered by British through Treaty of Aix-la-Chapelle, **Oct. 28, 1748**.

Madrid, Treaty of, Jan. 14, 1526, King Francis I of France renounced his Italian claims and ceded Burgundy.

madrigal, irregular verse form, originated, Italy, **c. 1340**, with Petrarch (Francesco Petrarca); popular, England, **16th century**; renaissance vocal music developed according to set metrical verse forms, from **c. 1340** in Italy; flourished, **1500s**, in low countries; and in England, **1580-1620**.

Mafeking, battle, British at Mafeking (on Bechuanaland border of Transvaal) thwarted 217-day siege by Boers during Boer War, **Oct. 13, 1899-May 17, 1900**.

Mafia incident, mob lynched 11 Italian immigrants, allegedly members of secret criminal society, indicted for murder of Irish chief of police in New Orleans, **Mar. 1891**; international crises in which Italy and U.S. both recalled their ambassadors, **Mar. 31, 1891**; U.S. offered $25,000 indemnity for the deaths, **Apr. 12, 1892**, and Italy accepted.

Magdala, Ethiopian capital stormed and destroyed by British expeditionary force led by Robert C. Napier [Dec. 6, 1810-Jan. 14,

1890], who rescued British prisoners, **Apr. 13, 1868**.

Magdeburg hemispheres, first used, **1654**, by German physicist Otto von Geuricke [1602-1686] to demonstrate the power of a vacuum.

Magenta, battle of, French and Piedmontese (Sardinian) forces defeated Austrian forces at Magenta, Lombardy, **June 4, 1859**, opening the route to Milan.

Maghreb (Maghrib), region in North Africa, united politically under Arab rule, **c. 714-56**; united under the Almohads, **1159-1229**.

Magic Flute, The (Die Zauberflote), opera, first produced, Vienna, **1791**; last opera by Austrian composer Wolfgang Amadeus Mozart.

Magic Mountain, The (Der Zauberberg), symbolic novel, **1924**, by German novelist Thomas Mann, Nobel Prize-winner, **1929**.

Maginot Line, supposed impregnable system of fortifications built along France's border, **1925-35**; flanked by German forces at start of WW II, **May 1940**.

Magna Carta (Magna Charta), great charter of English liberties signed by King John [Dec. 24, 1167-Oct. 19, 1216] on demand by the English barons, **June 19, 1215**.

Magnesia, battle of, 13,000-man Roman army under Scipio Africanus Major and his brother defeated Syrian forces under Antiochus III ("the Great") near Smyrna, Asia Minor, **190 B.C.**

magnesium, element No. 12; discovered, **1808**, by English chemist Sir Humphry Davy [1778-1829].

magnetic force, experimentally demonstrated, **1600**, by English physician and physicist William Gilbert [1540-1603].

magnetic materials, interaction of, theories developed, from **1930's**, by French physicist Louis E. F. Neel [1904-].

magnetic moment of protons, measured, **1933**, by German-American physicist Otto Stern [1888-1969].

magnetic North Pole, discovered, **c. 1905**, by Norwegian explorer Roald Amundsen [1872-1928].

magnetic-resonance technique, developed, **1934**, by Italian-American physicist Enrico Fermi [1901-1954].

magnetic units, Gauss', developed, **1832**, by German mathematician, Karl F. Gauss [1777-1855].

magneto-electric machine, first practical, working model of generator constructed, **1831**, by French instrument maker Hippolyte Pixii [1808-1835].

magnetohydrodynamics, founded, **1965**, by Swedish physicist Hannes O. Alfven [1908-].

magnetosphere, discovered, **1958**, by U.S. physicist James Van Allen [1914-].

Magnificat in D, notable musical setting of Magnificat, **1723**, by German composer Johann Sebastian Bach.

Magyars, nomadic people who settled in present-day Hungary, **9th century**; checked by Otto I ("the Great") at Lechfeld, **955**.

Mahabharata, epic poem of India completed c. **350**.

Maine, formerly part of Massachusetts, admitted to the Union (U.S.) as 23rd state, **Mar. 15, 1820**.

Maine, U.S. battleship *Maine* blown up in Havana harbor, Cuba, **Feb. 15, 1898**.

Main Street, novel, **1920**, about provincialism of small-town America that established reputation of Sinclair Lewis; Nobel laureate, **1930**.

Mainz, Diet of, great medieval pageant at which the sons of Holy Roman Emperor Frederick I (Frederick Barbarossa) [c. 1125-90] were knighted before a huge concourse, **1184**.

Maipo River, battle of, Chilean patriots commanded by Jose de San Martin won major battle against Spanish royalist troops south of Santiago; victory secured independence for Chile, **Apr. 5, 1818**.

Majuba Hill, battle of, Transvaal Boers under Petrus Jacobus Joubert [Jan. 20, 1831-Mar. 27, 1900] routed British forces at Majuba Hill, e. Natal, South Africa, **Feb. 27, 1881**.

Malachi, Book of, Old Testament prophetic book, written about **460 B.C.**.

Malaga, important seaport in Andalusia, Spain, founded by Phoenicians, **12th century B.C.**; captured by Muslims, **711**, and made part of Moorish kingdom of Granada until seized by Ferdinand of Aragon, **1487**; captured by Spanish rebels in Spanish Civil War, **Feb. 8, 1937**.

malaria, transmission by mosquitoes first suggested, **1717**, by Italian physician Giovanni Maria Lancisi [1654-1720]; determined true, **1898**, by English physician Ronald Ross [1857-1932].

Malawi, country in Africa, formerly Nyasaland, gained independence from British rule, **July 6, 1964**; became independent republic, **July 6, 1966**.

Malaysia, nation as constitutional monarchy, formed by federation of Malaya, Singapore, Sabah, and Sarawak, **Sept. 16, 1963**; Singapore withdrew, **Aug. 9, 1965**.

Malcolm X, assassination of, militant black leader Malcolm X [May 19, 1925-Feb. 21, 1965] shot and killed in public auditorium in New York City, **Feb. 21, 1965**.

Maldives, group of islands in Indian Ocean, came under British protection, **1887**; gained independence, **July 26, 1965**; became independent republic, **Nov. 11, 1968**.

Malenkov and Molotov ouster, Soviet Communist leaders Georgi M. Malenkov [Jan. 8, 1902-] and Vyacheslav M. Molotov [Mar. 9, 1890-] expelled from Central Committee, **July 3, 1957**.

Mali, country in w. Africa, first became a French colony, **1904**; Federation of Mali formed as a union of Sudan and Senegal, **June 20, 1960**; Senegal withdrew from federation, **Aug. 20, 1960**; Sudanese Republic renamed Mali, **Sept. 22, 1960**; devastated by sub-Sahara drought, **1969-74, 1977-78**.

Malplaquet, battle of, English and Holy Roman Empire forces, led by duke of Marlborough and prince of Savoy, won major victory over French forces in bloodiest battle of the War of the Spanish Succession, **Sept. 11, 1709**.

Malta, five islands in the Mediterranean, gained independence from British, **Sept. 21, 1964**; became a republic, **Dec. 13, 1974**; end of 179 years of British military on Malta, **Apr. 1, 1979**.

Maltese Falcon, The, detective novel **1930**, by Dashiell Hammett [Mar. 27, 1894-Jan. 10, 1961]; film, **1941**, adaptation of Dashiell Hammett mystery novel, with Humphrey Bogart as Sam Spade.

Malvern Hill, battle of, Union forces under Gen. McClellan repulsed Confederate assaults, in some of bloodiest fighting of U.S. Civil War, on Malvern Hill, near bank of James River, Va., **July 1, 1862**.

Managua earthquake, worst earthquake in Nicaraguan history leveled city of Managua, killing approx. 12,000, **Dec. 22-23, 1972**.

Man and Superman, philosophical play, **1905**, by British playwright George Bernard Shaw, Nobel Prize-winner, **1925**.

Mandingo Empire, large native kingdom established by Mandingos in Africa, **11th-15th centuries**; brilliant Mandingo culture centered at Timbuktu, **14th century**; conquered by Songhoy Empire, **c. 1500**; replaced in Niger by Bambara kingdoms of Segu and Kaarta, **1670**.

manganese, element No. 25; discovered, **1774**, by Swedish chemist Karl W. Scheele [1742-1786].

manganese steel, invented, **1882**, by English metallurgist Sir Robert Hadfield [1858-1940].

Manhattan, U.S. ice-breaking oil tanker SS **Manhattan** became first commercial ship to voyage through the Northwest Passage, **Sept. 14, 1969**; ship's journey from Chester, Penn., to Point Barrow, Alaska, **Aug. 24-Sept. 21, 1969**, proved feasibility of transporting crude oil by sea from North Slope to U.S.

MANIAC, first computer used for weather

research tested successfully, **1950**; designed from **c. 1944** by Hungarian-American mathematician John Von Neumann [1903-1957].

Manichaeism, dualistic religion, flourished **250-600**, founded Persia, **c. 240**, by religious leader Mani (also Manes or Manichaeus) [Apr. 24, 216-274?].

Manila Bay, battle of, American fleet under Admiral George Dewey [Dec. 26, 1837-Jan. 16, 1917] destroyed entire Spanish fleet at Manila Bay in Philippines, without loss of one U.S. ship, **May 1, 1898**.

Manitoba, Canadian province, which Hudson's Bay Company first acquired by charter as part of Rupert's Land, **1670**; Red River Settlement established by Scotsman Thomas Selkirk [1771-1820], **1812**; site of Red River rebellions under Louis Riel [1844-85], **1869-70, 1884-85**; became province of Canada, **July 15, 1870**.

Mann (White Slave Traffic) Act, U.S. Congress prohibited interstate transportation of women for immoral purposes, **June 25, 1910**.

Mann-Elkins Act, U.S. Congress strengthened powers of Interstate Commerce Commission over railroads and placed telegraph, telephone, and cable companies under ICC jurisdiction, **June 18, 1910**.

Mannerheim Line, Finnish fortification line across the Karelian Isthmus, n. of Leningrad, planned and built by Carl G. Mannerheim as defense against U.S.S.R., **1930s**; breached by Soviets in Russo-Finnish War, **Mar. 1940**, and dismantled.

mannerism, style in art, **c. 1520-1600**, between high Renaissance and baroque.

mansard roof, roof with double slope, designed, **c. 1640**, by French architect Francois Mansart.

Man's Fate (La Condition Humaine), novel, **1933**, by French novelist and art historian Andre Malraux [Nov. 3, 1901-Nov. 23, 1977].

Mansfield Park, novel, **1814**, by English novelist of manners Jane Austen.

Manson murder case, Charles M. Manson [Nov. 12, 1934] and three members of his hippie cult family convicted, **Jan. 26, 1971**, of 1969 murders of actress Sharon Tate [1943-Aug. 10, 1969] and six others.

Mantinea, ancient Greek city, the site of the Theban victory over Sparta, **362 B.C.**

Mantua, Italian city in Lombardy, fl. under Gonzaga family rule, **1328-1708**; annexed by Hapsburg Austria, **1708**; captured by French under Napoleon I, **Feb. 2, 1797**; retaken by Austria, **1815**; part of Italy, **1866**.

Manzikert, battle of, Seljuk Turks led by Alp Arslan [1029-72] won brilliant victory over Byzantine army under Emperor Romanus IV [d. 1072] at Armenian village of Manzikert; Turks gained complete control of Asia Minor, **1071**.

Maori-British wars, guerrilla-type conflicts between New Zealand natives (Maoris) and British colonists over control of territory, **1843-70**; British "peacefully" suppressed Maori uprising, **1843-48**; British and Australians forcefully suppressed second Maori uprising, confiscating much Maori land, **1860-70**.

Ma Perkins, long-running daytime radio serial, **1933-60**, featuring homespun philosophy of Ma Perkins; 7,065 episodes broadcast, last one on **November 24, 1960**.

Maranhao Company, Portuguese monopolistic trading company established in Brazil, **c. 1682-1710**.

marathon, foot race of 26 mi. 385 yd., so-called from the run of Pheidippides [fl.490 B.C.]; long-distance foot race included in Olympic Games, **1896**.

Marathon, battle of, Athenians, and Plataean citizen-soldiers under Greek general Miltiades [d. 489 B.C.] repulsed first major assault by Persian army, temporarily halting military encroachments from Asia Minor, **Sept. 12, 490 B.C.**

marble-sawing mill, patented, **1794**, by American inventor Robert Fulton [1765-1815].

Marburg, University of, university, founded Hesse, Germany, **1527**; first Protestant university established in Europe.

Marbury v. Madison, U.S. Supreme Court, through Chief Justice John Marshall [Sept. 24, 1755-July 6, 1835], voided an act of Congress for first time, establishing the principle of judicial review, **Feb. 24, 1803**.

March Laws **(Ten Points of Deak)**, reform program of Hungarian politician Ferencz Deak [Oct. 17,1803-Jan. 29, 1876] united liberal groups that sought autonomous government for Hungary, independence from Hapsburg rule, **1847**.

March of Dimes, The, U.S. organization, formed **1938**, to finance research to fight poliomyelitis.

March of Time, The, best-known radio news documentary, begun, **March 6, 1931**, in conjunction with Movietone newsreels, same title; last programs, **1945**; *March of Time Through the Years*, on television, utilizing newsreels, **1956**.

Marciano-Walcott fight, Rocky Marciano [Sept. 1, 1923-Aug. 31, 1969] knocked out Joe Walcott in 13th round in Philadelphia to win heavyweight boxing championship, **Sept. 23, 1952**; Marciano successfully defended his title six times, **1953-55**; Marciano retired undefeated, **Apr. 27, 1956**.

Marcionites, early Christian sect, founded Rome, **c. 140**; founder, Marcion [c. 100-c. 160], excommunicated by Church of Rome, **144**.

Marco Polo, journeys of, Venetian adventurer Marco Polo [1254-1324] with his father and uncle journeyed eastward to Kublai Khan's court at Cambuluc (now Peiking), **1271-75**; made journey back to Venice, **1292-95**.

Marcusean revolution, utopian philosopher Herbert Marcuse [July 19, 1898-July 29, 1979] advocated violent social revolution for man to rid himself of oppressive, materialistic, modern culture and to find freedom, **c. mid-1960s**.

Marengo, battle of, French under Napoleon won brilliant battle at village of Marengo in n. Italy, during French Revolutionary Wars, **June 14, 1800**.

Mareth Line, British 8th Army forced German forces under Field Marshal Rommel to give up defensive position along Mareth Line in Tunisia, **Mar. 16-30, 1943**.

Marists, Catholic religious order, founded Lyons, **1824**; missionary order to Pacific islands; approved by Pope, **1836**.

Mark, Gospel According to, second book of New Testament; now believed to have possibly been written, **c. 40-60**; attributed to Mark, disciple of Peter.

Mark I, first modern digital computer completed, **1944**, by American mathematician-inventor Howard H. Aiken [1900-1973].

Marne, battles of the, Allies under French Army Marshal Joseph Jacques Joffre [Jan. 12, 1852-Jan. 3, 1931] and others stopped German advance on Paris at the Marne River; Germany failed to win quickly WW I according to Schlieffen Plan, **Sept. 6-9, 1914**; Allies again halted Germans at the Marne during last great German offensive of WW I, **July 1918**.

Maronites, Lebanese Christians, in communion with Roman Catholic Church, since **1182**.

Marprelate controversy, Elizabethan pamphlet war, **1588-90**, in which Church of England attacked by Puritans in pamphlets.

Marriage of Figaro, The (Le Nozze di Figaro), lyrical comic opera, **1786**, written to an Italian libretto by Austrian composer Wolfgang Amadeus Mozart.

Mars, moons of, *Phobos* and *Deimos*; discovered, **1877**, by American astronomer Asaph Hall [1829-1907].

Marsaglia, battle of, well-trained French army routed allied army of Spanish, English, and Austrian troops at Marsaglia, near the Po River, **Oct. 4, 1693**.

Marseillaise, The (La Marseillaise), hymn of the French Revolution and national anthem of France, words and music composed, **April 24, 1792**, by French army captain and writer Claude Joseph Rouget de Lisle [May 10, 1760-June 26, 1836].

Marshall Plan (European Recovery Program), economic plan to rebuild European countries devastated by WW II proposed by U.S. Secretary of State George C. Marshall at Harvard commencement, **June 5, 1947**; Committee of European Economic Cooperation (minus Soviet Union and its satellites), formed **July 12, 1947**, to determine Europe's needs; U.S. Congress voted funds for program, **Apr. 3, 1948**; more than $12 billion in aid given before program completed, **1952**.

Mars-la-Tour, battle of, Prussians repulsed fierce attempts by French to break through their lines, **Aug. 16**, and **18, 1870**.

Marston Moor, battle of, parliamentarians (Roundheads) of Oliver Cromwell won first major victory of English Civil War, defeating the royalists (Cavaliers) at Marston Moor, near York, England, **July 2, 1644**.

Marxism, philosophy based on economic determinism and dialectical materialism, formulated principally by Karl Marx in the *Communist Manifesto*, **1848**, and *Capital*, **1867-94**.

Marxist First International, radical faction of French trade unions organized during liberal government in Paris, **1869**; supported Communards against Versailles government, **1871**.

Maryland, one of Thirteen Colonies, ratified U.S. Constitution to become seventh state of the Union, **Apr. 28, 1788**.

Mary Margaret McBride Show, The, long-running radio talk-and interview-show, **1934-54**, featured U.S. commentator and personality Mary Margaret McBride [Nov. 16, 1899-Apr. 7, 1976]; on television, **1948**.

Masada, stronghold, one mile west of Dead Sea, where, **73**, 960 zealots held out against Romans and finally committed mass suicide to avoid capture; site extensively excavated, **1963-65**.

maser, developed, **1953**, by American physicist Charles H. Townes [1915-].

M.A.S.H., television situation comedy, from **1972**, about army field hospital, stars U.S.

actor Alan Alda [Jan. 28, 1936-]; U.S. actress Loretta Swit [Nov. 4, ?-].

Mason-Dixon line, boundary between Pennsylvania and Maryland, surveyed by Englishmen Charles Mason [1730-87] and Jeremiah Dixon [fl. 1763-67], **1763-67**; became boundary between free and slave states before U.S. Civil War, **c. 1790-1860**.

Masons, Free and Accepted (Freemasons), largest secret fraternal society in the world, believed to have arisen from English and Scottish stonemasons in Middle Ages, **14th century**; Mother Grand Lodge of Freemasons established in London, **1717**; first lodge in U.S. established in Philadelphia, **1730**.

masque, form of dramatic court spectacle with music, dance, dialogue and lavish decorations that flourished, **1600-50**.

Massachusetts, one of Thirteen Colonies, ratified U.S. Constitution to become sixth state of the Union, **Feb. 6, 1788**.

Massachusetts Bay Company, English chartered company founded Massachusetts Bay Colony at present site of Boston as political and religious refuge, **1630**.

Massacre Hill, Sioux Indians under Chief Crazy Horse and Red Cloud surrounded and massacred U.S. troops on a height later called Massacre Hill in n. Wyoming, **Dec. 21, 1866**.

mass spectrograph, invented, **1919**, by English physicist Francis W. Aston [1877-1945].

Masterpiece Theater, television dramatic series, from **1971**.

Masters, the, prestigious annual men's golf tournament held at the Augusta National Golf Club, Augusta, Ga., since **1934**.

Matabele, Bantu-speaking tribesmen led by King Lobengula [c. 1833-Jan. 23, 1894], defeated in war with British South Africa Company, **1893**.

Matapan, battle of, British navy won important victory over Italian navy off Cape Matapan in the Greek Peloponnesus, during WW II, **Mar. 28, 1941**.

match, friction, invented, **1827**, by English druggist John Walker [1781-1859].

materialism, philosophical theory holding that ultimate reality consists of material particles, first formulated, **c. 400 B.C.**, by Greek philosopher Democritus; most consistently maintained in modern times, from **1629**, by English philosopher Thomas Hobbes.

matrix (quantum) mechanics, discovered, **1924**, by German physicist Werner Heisenberg [1901-1976].

Matterhorn, majestic mountain (14,701 ft. high) in the Alps near Zermatt, Switzerland, first climbed by Edward Whymper [Apr. 27, 1840-Sept. 16, 1911], **July 14, 1865**.

Matthew, Gospel According to, first book of New Testament, now believed to have been written, **c. 40-60**, attributed in an Aramaic version to apostle of Jesus, Matthew (Levi).

Mau Mau Uprising, secret organization, Mau Mau, led by Kikiyu tribesmen, began terrorist movement against white settlers in Kenya, **Oct. 20, 1952**; suspected Mau Mau leader Jomo Kenyatta [c. 1894-Aug. 22, 1978] imprisoned by British, **1952-59**, then exiled, until **Aug. 21, 1961**; Mau Mau finally crushed by British troops, **1956**.

Mauritania, country in n.w. Africa, first organized as a territory by French, **1904**; became independent Islamic republic, **Nov. 28, 1960**; annexed s. part of former Spanish Sahara (Western Sahara), **1976**; relinquished its claim to s. part of Spanish Sahara to Morocco, **1980**.

Mauritius, small island nation in the Indian Ocean, settled by Dutch, **1638**; captured by French, **1721**; ceded to British by Treaty of Paris, **May 30, 1814**; gained independence, **Mar. 12, 1968**.

Maurya, ancient Indian dynasty, **325-c.**

183 B.C., founded by Chandragupta (Sandraçottus) [d. c. 298 B.C.]; whose grandson Asoka [d. 232 B.C.] united present-day India and Afghanistan under one rule and substituted Buddhism for Hinduism as state religion, c. 250 B.C.

Maxen, battle of, Prussian army of 12,000 men, surrounded by Austrian army of 42,000 men, failed to break out and surrendered during Seven Years' War, **Nov. 20, 1759.**

Mayaguez, Cambodian forces captured U.S. merchant ship *Mayaguez* in Gulf of Siam, **May 12, 1975;** U.S. planes and marines attacked Tang Island and freed ship and crew, **May 14-15, 1975.**

Mayan civilization, advanced pre-Columbian Indian empire on the Yucatan peninsula and in n. Guatemala, founded c. **1500 B.C.;** fl. **200-800;** disintegrated after Spanish conquest, c. **1500-46.**

Mayflower, English ship on which Pilgrims (Separatists) sailed from Plymouth, England, to America, **Sept. 16-Nov. 19, 1620.**

Mayflower Compact, Pilgrims drafted and signed social contract, first basis of government in New England, on board *Mayflower,* **Nov. 11, 1620.**

May Fourth Movement, first mass protest in modern China, instigated by 5000 Chinese students in Peking, **May 4, 1919.**

McArthur's Raid, American mounted men under Gen. Duncan McArthur [1772-1839] made daring raid into Canada to divert attention of British during the War of 1812, **Oct. 25-Nov. 17, 1814.**

McCarran Act (Internal Security Act), U.S. Congress overrode Pres. Truman's veto, **Sept. 23, 1950,** to establish tight control of U.S. Communists during national emergencies and to prohibit entry to U.S. of members of totalitarian groups.

McCarran-Walter Act (Immigration and Nationality Act), U.S. Congress overrode Pres. Truman's veto **June 27, 1952,** to tighten law on admission, exclusion, and deportation of aliens dangerous to U.S. national security and to abolish racial restriction on immigration.

McClure's Magazine, U.S. literary and "reform" magazine, **1893-1929,** that published major authors of the day.

McFadden Act, U.S. Congress allowed, **Feb. 25, 1927,** state and national banks to consolidate and the latter could engage in investment banking.

McGill University, Canadian institution of higher learning, chartered, Montreal, **1821,** opened, **1829.**

McKinley, assassination of, U.S. President William McKinley [Jan. 29, 1843-Sept. 14, 1901] shot (at Pan-American Exposition at Buffalo, N.Y.), by anarchist Leon F. Czolgosz [1873-Oct. 29, 1901], **Sept. 6, 1901;** McKinley died eight days later, **Sept. 14.**

McKinley, Mt., highest mountain in North America (20,320 ft.), in s. central Alaska, first climbed by Alaskan explorer Hudson Stuck [Nov.11, 1863-Oct. 10, 1920], member of Canadian-American expedition, **June 7, 1913.**

McKinley Tariff Act, U.S. Congress raised tariffs to new highs to protect industry, **Oct. 1, 1890.**

McMahon Line, border line, established **1941,** between India and Tibet; Chinese invasion of Tibet, **Oct. 1950,** led to Chinese control, **May 1951;** McMahon Line not accepted by China, **Apr. 26, 1960,** as India-China border; border war between China and India, **Oct. 20-Nov. 22, 1962.**

Mecklenburg Declaration of Independence, alleged document of independence from British rule, proclaimed at Charlotte, N.C. by inhabitants of Mecklenburg, **May 20, 1775.**

Medal of Freedom, America's highest civilian award, established to recognize meritorious service to nation, **1945;** expanded to

Presidential Medal of Freedom by Pres. John F. Kennedy, **1963**.

Medal of Honor, Congressional, highest U.S. military award, for exceptional heroism in action, authorized by U.S. Congress, **July 12, 1862**.

Medea, tragedy, **431 B.C.**, in which Medea, abandoned by Jason, kills her children and is transformed into witch, by Greek tragedian Euripides.

Medicare, medical-hospital insurance plan for the aged, funded by Social Security, proposed by U.S. Pres. Kennedy, **Feb. 21, 1963**; signed by Pres. Lyndon B. Johnson [Aug. 27, 1908-Jan. 22, 1973], **July 30, 1965**; went into effect, **July 1, 1966**.

Medici, Florentine family of bankers and statesmen prominent in the Italian Renaissance, **15th-16th centuries**.

medicine, homeopathic, system established, **c. 1810**, by German physician Christian

Friedrich Samuel Hahnemann [1755-1843].

Meditations, philosophical work, written, **c. 170**, expression of ancient Stoic philosophy, by Roman Emperor Marcus Aurelius.

medium is the message, the, expression popularized in book of that name, **1967**, and other books, of Canadian writer and media theorist Marshall McLuhan.

Meerut conspiracy case, British Indian government arrested 31 Communist leaders for sedition, **Mar. 15, 1929**; trial lasted four years and gained nationalists' sympathy.

Meet the Press, prototype public affairs news and interview show, on radio, **1945-47**, on television, from **1947**.

Megalopolis, ancient city of Greece, founded as headquarters of the anti-Spartan Arcadian League, **c. 370 B.C.**

Megiddo, ancient city in Palestine, inhabited, **c. 3500-450 B.C.**; Egyptians under Thutmose III [d. 1436 B.C.] defeated Syrians at battle of Megiddo, **c. 1468 B.C.**; Josiah, [d. 609 B.C.] died there fighting Egyptians and Assyrians, **609 B.C.**; site of successful British offensive under Gen. Edmund Allenby [Apr. 23, 1861-May 14, 1936] against Turks and Germans in WW I, **Sept. 1918**.

MHD (magnetohydrodynamics) power plant, first experimental plant began producing electricity, **1977**, near Moscow, Russia.

Meiji, reign of Emperor Mutsuhito [Nov. 3, 1852-July 30, 1912] in Japan; period of great reform, **1868-1912**; feudalism abolished, **Aug. 29, 1871**; emperor gained power by new constitution, **Feb. 11, 1889**.

Melitene, battle of, Byzantine army of Emperor Justinian defeated the Persians in central Asia Minor, **576**, in last battle between them.

Meloria, battle of, Genoa won naval victory over Pisa off Meloria, **1284**, marking Pisa's decline and Genoa's rise to power in the Mediterranean.

Melos (Milo or Milos), island in the Aegean Sea, center of early Aegean civilization, early **3rd mil. B.C.**; conquered by Athenians who massacred inhabitants, **416 B.C.**; Venus of Milo discovered there, **1820**.

Memel Territory, former Prussian region on Baltic Sea placed under League of Nations-sponsored French administration,

1919; Lithuanians forced French garrison to evacuate from Memel, **Jan. 11, 1923**; *Memel Statute* signed by Britain, France, Italy, and Japan made territory autonomous within Lithuania, **May 8, 1924**; Nazis seized Memel, **Mar. 23, 1939**; Soviets restored territory to Lithuania, **1945**.

Memphis, capital of Old Kingdom of ancient Egypt, **c. 3200-2200 B.C.**

Mendel's laws, (of inheritance), formulated, **1865**, by Austrian botanist Gregor Mendel [1822-1884].

mendelevium, element no. 101; discovered, **1955**, by American physicist Albert Ghiorso [1915-] and coworkers.

Mennonites, Christian community, founded, **1536**, among Anabaptists at Munster by Dutch religious leader Menno Simons [1492-Jan. 13, 1559].

Mensheviks, conservative Russians of Social Democratic Party, led by Georgi Plekhanov [Dec. 11, 1856-May 30, 1918] and opposed to Bolsheviks, **1903-17**; helped establish Kerensky's provisional government, **Mar. 12, 1917**; "liquidated" by Communist Party, **1918**.

Mercator projection, system developed, **1568**, by Flemish geographer Gerardus (Gerhard Kremer) Mercator [1512-1594].

Mercer, Fort, siege of, British reinforcements helped Gen. William Howe capture Fort Mercer, **Oct.-Nov. 1777**.

Merchant of Venice, The, comedy, **c. 1595**, by William Shakespeare; includes Portia's speech on "the quality of mercy."

Mercia, kingdom of, kingdom established by Angles in present-day Midlands of England, **c. 500**; fl. under rule of kings Aethelbald [d. A.D. 757] and Offa [d. A.D. 796], **8th century**; taken over by invading Danes, **874**.

mercurochrome, germicide introduced, **1919**, by American urologist Hugh H. Young [1870-1945].

Mer, La (The Sea), three symphonic sketches, **1903-05**, by French composer Claude Debussy.

Merode Altarpiece, The, altarpiece, **c. 1425-28**, centering on Annunciation scene, by Flemish painter Robert Campin [1378-Apr. 26, 1444].

Merovingians, first Frankish dynasty founded by Clovis I and named after semi-legendary Frankish chieftain Meroveus, **c. 500-751**.

Merry Widow, The (Die Lustige Witwe), operetta, **1905**, about turn-of-the-century continental high life, by Hungarian composer Franz Lehar [Apr. 30, 1870-Oct. 24, 1948].

Mersen, Treaty of, divided Lotharingia empire between Charles II (the Bald) [June 13, 823-Oct. 6, 877] of the West Franks (France) and Louis the German [c. 804-Aug. 28, 876] of the East Franks (Germany), **Aug. 9, 870**.

Merv, ancient city in central Asia, in Turkmenistan, major center of Islamic learning, **651-1157**; city totally destroyed by Mongols, **1221**; conquered by Russians, **1884**.

Merz, artistic movement, variation of dadaism, founded, Germany, **1920**.

Mesabi iron range, discovered, **1844**, by U.S. government surveyors headed by American surveyor-inventor William A. Burt [1792-1858].

Mesolithic Age, prehistoric period that marked the period of transition between the Old Stone Age and New Stone Age, **c. 10,000-5000 B.C.**

Mesolongion (Missolonghi), Greek port, stronghold of Greek rebels during Greek War of Independence, **1822-27**; Lord Byron, supporter of Greek independence, died there, **Apr. 19, 1824**; fell to Ottoman Turks, **Apr. 23, 1826**.

meson, suggested, **1935**, by Japanese physicist Hideki Yukawa [1907-], as involved in binding force of atomic nucleus; existence as secondary products of cosmic rays confirmed experimentally, **1938**, by American physicist Carl D. Anderson [1905-].

Mesopotamia, "cradle of civilization." where supposedly arose the first agricultural communities, **c. 4000 B.C.**

Messene, ancient city of Greece, founded and built by Theban army under Epaminondas [d. 362 B.C.], **c. 370 B.C.**

messenger RNA, discovered, **1961**, by French biologist Francois Jacob [1920-] and French biochemist Jacques L. Monod [1910-1976] as substance that builds enzymes.

Messenian Wars, series of conflicts between Messenians and Spartans in the Peloponnesus; first war, **c. 736-16 B.C.**; second, **c. 650-30 B.C.**; third, **464-59 B.C.**

Messiah, The, oratorio, first performed, Dublin, **April 13, 1742**, by George Frederick Handel; revised and published, **1767**.

Messina, city in Sicily, founded by Greeks who named it Zancle, late **8th century B.C.**; captured by mainland Italians from Rhegium **5th century B.C.**, who renamed it Messina; seized by Rome in first Punic War, **264 B.C.**; rebelled against Bourbon rule, **1774-78**; captured by Red Shirts of Garibaldi, **July 1860**; most of city destroyed by great earthquake, **Dec. 28, 1908**; taken by Allies during Sicilian campaign of WW II, **Aug. 17, 1943**.

metal construction, (in aircraft), first used, **1915**, by German airplane engineer Hugo Junkers [1859-1935] to produce J.1 monoplane.

metal-planing machine, designed, **1817**, by Welsh inventor Richard Roberts [1789-1864].

metallocene compounds, developed, from **1951**, by German chemist Ernst O. Fischer [1918-] and English chemist Geoffrey Wilkinson [1921-].

Metamorphoses, poetic rendering of legends about the history of the world, **5**, by Roman poet Ovid.

metaphysical poets, school of English poets, **c. 1620-50**.

metaphysics, science of being, fundamental branch of philosophy, begun systematically, **c. 475 B.C.**, by Greek philosopher Parmenides; name coined, **c. 340-320 B.C.**, by editors of Aristotle's *Metaphysics*.

Metaurus River, battle of, one of most decisive battles of history; Carthaginian army under Hannibal's brother Hasdrubal [d. 207 B.C.] defeated by Romans under Caius Claudius Nero [fl. 216-201 B.C.], **207 B.C.**

meter, introduced, as standard of measurement, **1795**, by French National Convention.

Methodism, religious system that grew from Anglican association founded, **1729**, by English theologian and religious leader John Wesley [June 17, 1703-Mar. 2, 1791].

Method, The, acting style, developed by the Group Theater, **1930s**, and Actor's Studio, since **1947**; also called *Stanislavski Method*, after originator, Konstantin Stanislavski [Jan. 7, 1863-Aug. 7, 1938].

Metonic cycle, discovered, **432 B.C.**, by Greek astronomer Meton [c. 460 B.C.-d.?].

metronome, invented, **1816**, by German

musician-inventor Johann N. Maelzel [1772-1838].

Metropolitan Museum of Art, largest U.S. art museum, incorporated, New York City, **1870**; moved into present Central Park building, frequently enlarged, **1880**.

Metropolitan Opera, U.S. opera company, founded, New York, **1883**; opera house at Broadway and 39th, **1893** to **1966**; since **1966**, at Lincoln Center for the Performing Arts.

Metz, battle of, French army of about 170,000 men surrendered at fortress of Metz on the Moselle River after prolonged siege by Prussian army during Franco-Prussian War, **Oct. 27, 1870**.

Mexican War, conflict between U.S. and Mexico over boundaries and Mexican annexation of Texas, **1846-48**; Mexicans invaded Texas, **Apr. 25, 1846**; U.S. declared war, **May 13, 1846**; California came under U.S. rule, **July 1846**; U.S. troops under Gen. Taylor forced Mexicans to withdraw at Buena Vista, **Feb. 22, 1847**; U.S. troops under Gen. Scott seized Veracruz, **Mar. 27, 1847**; U.S. troops entered Mexico City, **Sept. 14, 1847**; ended by Treaty of Guadalupe Hidalgo, **Mar. 10, 1848**.

Mexico, country in Central America, conquered by the Spanish under Hernando Cortes [1485-Sept. 2, 1547], **1519-21**; ruled by Spain for 300 years until Mexicans

revolted, **Sept. 16, 1810**, and won independence, **Sept. 27, 1821**; Agustin de Iturbide [1783-1824] as emperor of Mexico, **1822-23**; lost territory of Texas, **1836**; defeated by U.S. in Mexican War, **1846-48**; Austrian Archduke Maximilian [July 6, 1832-June 19, 1867] crowned emperor of Mexico by conservatives, aided by French troops, **Apr. 10, 1864**; Maximilian forced to abdicate by liberals under Juarez, **May 14, 1867**; Maximilian executed, **June 19, 1867**; torn by political-military strife until new constitution brought social reform, **Feb. 5, 1917**.

MGM Grand Hotel fire, second worst hotel fire in U.S. history killed 83 persons and injured more than 500 others at Las Vegas, Nev., **Nov. 21, 1980**.

Micah, Book of, Old Testament book, 6th of minor prophets, probably written down, **c. 731 B.C.**

Michigan, formerly part of Northwest Territory, admitted to the Union as 26th state, **Jan. 26, 1837**.

Michigan, University of, first U.S. state university, founded, Detroit, **1817**; moved to Ann Arbor, **1837**.

Mickey Mouse Club, The, children's television variety series, **1955-59** and from **1977**, featuring music, cartoons, guests and numerous Walt Disney adventure serials.

microanalysis, (of organic substances), method invented, **1911**, by Austrian chemist Fritz Pregl [1869-1930] using precise balance.

micrometer, invented, **1636**, by English astronomer William Gascoigne [1612-1644].

microphone, invented, **1877**, by German-American inventor Emile Berliner [1851-1929], using loose-contact, telephone transmitter.

microscope, first manufactured in U.S., **1847**, by American optical instrument maker Charles A. Spencer [1813-1881].

microscope, compound, principle of, commonly attributed, **c. 1604**, to Dutch spectacle maker Zachoria Jansen [1588-1678].

microscope, dioptric achromatic, invented, **1827**, by Italian optician Giovanni B. Amici [1786-1863].

microwave, radio-relay channel, opened, **1953**, between U.S. and Canada.

Middle Kingdom, second main era of ancient Egyptian civilization; centered at Thebes; founded by XI and XII dynasties, **c. 2100-1800 B.C.**

midnight judiciary, Federalist judges, marshals, and clerks appointed by U.S. Pres. John Adams [Oct. 30, 1735-July 4, 1826] during his last days in office, **Feb. 27-Mar. 3, 1801.**

Midsummer Night's Dream, A, romantic comedy, **c. 1594,** by William Shakespeare.

Midway, battle of, one of most decisive battles of WW II; allied dive bombers destroyed three Japanese aircraft carriers, crippling the Japanese navy and making possible allied counter offensive in the Pacific, **June 4, 1942.**

Migratory Bird Act, U.S. Congress enforced, **July 3, 1918,** treaty between U.S. and Great Britain, **Aug. 16, 1916,** that protected migratory birds; upheld by U.S. Supreme Court, **1920.**

Mikado, The, comic operetta, **1885,** a political satire and comic love story, by British operetta writers Gilbert and Sullivan.

Milan Decree, Napoleon enforced Continental System and strengthened Berlin Decree, authorizing French warships and privateers to capture neutral ships sailing from British ports or from territory occupied by British forces, **Dec. 17, 1807.**

Milan, Edict of, agreement between Roman emperors, **313,** to recognize legal personality of Catholic Church.

Milazzo, battle of, Red Shirts led by Garibaldi defeated Neapolitans (Bourbons) at Milazzo, **July 20, 1860,** forcing them to evacuate from Sicily.

Milesian School, world's earliest philosophical school, originating, Miletus, Greece, and flourishing **600-550 B.C..**

Miletus, ancient seaport of Ionia (w. Asia Minor); settled by Greeks, **c. 1000 B.C.**

Milky Way, dimensions determined, **1918,** by American astronomer Harlow Shapley [1885-1972].

mill (for fine grinding), patented, **1870,** by American paint manufacturer John W. Masury [1820-1895].

milling machine, invented, **1818,** by American inventor Eli Whitney [1765-1825].

Milner Commission, British commission investigated native uprisings in Egypt and problems of governing, **Dec. 7-Mar. 6, 1920;** Milner Report proposed Egyptian independence with guaranties for British concerns, **Dec. 9, 1920.**

Milton Berle Show, The, television variety show, **1948-67,** of television's first superstar, U.S. comedian and personality Milton Berle, "Uncle Miltie" [July 12, 1908-]; on radio, **1939-49.**

mime, form of drama in which actors tell story by gestures, originated, Sicily, **400s B.C.;** popular in Italy with Commedia dell' Arte, **1500s;** popularized since **1950s** by French mime and actor, Marcel Marceau [Mar. 22, 1923-].

Mimeograph, invented, **June, 1875,** by American Thomas A. Edison [1847-1932].

mimicry (in animal coloration), established, **1861,** by English naturalist Henry W. Bates [1825-1892].

Mims, Fort, Creek Indians led by William Weatherford [1780?-1824], called Red Eagle, attacked Fort Mims on the Alabama River, killing more than 500 whites in the garrison and enraging white frontiersmen to take revenge, **Aug. 30, 1813.**

Minden, battle of, British and Hanoverian foot soldiers and horsemen soundly defeated French at Minden in Germany, ending last serious French threat to Hanover and to Prussia in the Seven Years' War, **Aug. 1, 1759.**

Mineralogy, first textbook, *De Re Metallica,* published, **1556,** by German physician Georgius Agricola (Georg Bauer) [1494-1555].

Ming dynasty, last native Chinese dynasty,

noted for its scholarly and artistic achievements, ruled empire that stretched from Burma to Korea, **1368-1644**.

Minisink massacre, Indians and renegades led by Joseph Brant [1742-1807], Mohawk Indian chief, raided village of Minisink, N. Y., massacring many inhabitants, **July 19, 1779**.

Minnesota, carved out of Northwest Territory and territory acquired by Louisiana Purchase, admitted to the Union (U.S.) as 32nd state, **May 11, 1858**.

Minoan civilization, advanced Bronze Age civilization on the island of Crete, **fl. 3000-1100 B.C.**

Minseito, Japanese political party (identified with Mitsubishi financial interests,) founded as the Kaishinto (progressive) party, **1882**; dissolved and reformed into the Shimpoto party, **1884**; joined with the Jiyuto party to form the Kenseito, **1898**; (rivaled Seiyukai party, 1927-32;) dissolved with all Japanese parties, **1940**; reformed gradually to join with Democrats to form Liberal-Democratic party, **1955**.

Minsk, battle of, German *Panzers* enveloped Russian forces near city of Minsk in WW II; about 300,000 Russians killed or captured, **June 27-July 2, 1941**.

minstrel show, theatrical spectacle, popular **1850-1910**; first organized, **1843**, by Daniel D. Emmett, author of *Dixie*.

minuet, French dance, introduced into Lou-

is XIV's court, **c. 1650**; inspiration for classical sonata and symphonic movements, from **c. 1700**.

miracle plays, medieval dramas presenting miracles of the Virgin Mary or the saints, **1200-1500**; originated in France; adapted in England.

mirs, Russian peasant communes established by Edict of Emancipation to distribute land among peasants according to size of family, **1861-1917**.

Misanthrope, The (Le Misanthrope), satiric comedy, **1666**; by French comic dramatist Moliere.

Miserable Ones, The (Les Miserables), panoramic novel, **1862**, about contrasts of wealth and poverty in 19th-century France, by Victor Hugo.

Miser, The (L'Avare), "bitter" comedy of human greed, **1668**, by French comic dramatist Moliere.

Miss America contest, annual competition among beautiful, talented young women at Atlantic City, N.J.; first held, **1921**.

Missa Solemnis, mass in D, **1818-23**, chorale work (Opus 123) of German composer Ludwig van Beethoven; introduced, Vienna, **May 8, 1824**.

missile, intercontinental ballistic, (U.S.), first-full-range test firing announced, **1958**, by American government.

missile, intercontinental ballistic (U.S.S.R.), announced, **1957**, successfully tested by Soviet Union.

missile, Polaris, first successful underwater firing of ballistic missile, **1960**, launched from nuclear submarine, *George Washington*.

Missionary Ridge, battle of, Union troops under Gen. Ulysses S. Grant assaulted and captured Confederate-held Missionary Ridge during battle of Chattanooga in U.S. Civil War, **Nov. 25, 1863**.

Mississippi, formerly Georgia territory, admitted to the Union (U.S.) as 20th state, **Dec. 10, 1817**; seceded from the Union, **Jan. 9, 1861**; readmitted to the Union, **Feb. 23, 1870**; plagued by violent racial problems, **1960s**.

Mississippi River, Hernando De Soto [c. 1499-May 21, 1542] was first European to discover the Mississippi, **May 1541**; Jacques Marquette [June 1, 1637-May 18,

1675] and Louis Jolliet [Sept. 21, 1645-May, 1700] reported first accurate data on river's course, **1673**; Robert Cavelier, Sieur de La Salle [Nov. 21, 1643-Mar. 19, 1687] led first expedition down river to Gulf of Mexico, **1681-82**; U.S. acquired river as part of Louisiana Purchase, **1803**.

Mississippi Scheme, plan by John Law [Apr. 21, 1671-Mar. 21, 1729] for commercial exploitation and colonization of Mississippi River valley and other French regions in America, **1717-20**.

Missouri, part of territory acquired by Louisiana Purchase, admitted to the Union (U.S.) as 24th state, **Aug. 10, 1821**.

Missouri Compromise, measures passed by U.S. Congress to deal with extension of slavery into new territory, **Mar. 3, 1820**.

Mister Roberts, play, **1948**, about adventures of World War II Navy cargo-ship crew, by Joshua Logan and Thomas (Orlo) Heggen [Dec. 23, 1919-May 19, 1949]; film, **1955**; television series, **1967-75**.

Mitchell, Billy, court-martial of, U.S. Army Air Corps General William ("Billy") Mitchell [Dec. 29, 1879-Feb. 19, 1936] found guilty of insubordination during his court-martial in Washington, D.C., **Oct.-Nov. 1925**.

Mithradatic Wars, series of conflicts between the king of Pontus, Mithradates VI [c. 131-63 B.C.], and Rome; first war, **88-84 B.C.**; second, **83-81 B.C.**; third, **74-63 B.C.**

Mithraism, ancient cult of sun-god, flourished **100 B.C.-A.D. 300**; introduced into Rome, **67 B.C.**; popular among Roman soldiers; superseded by Christianity, 4th century.

Mitsui, powerful trading and banking house established in Japan, **1673**.

Mobile Bay, battle of, Union warships under Admiral David G. Farragut [July 5, 1801-Aug. 14, 1870] won naval battle against Confederate ironclad *Tennessee* and other wooden ships in Mobile Bay, Ala..

Mobius band, invented, **c. 1850**, by German mathematician August Ferdinand Mobius [1790-1868].

Moby Dick, novel of good and evil, **1851**, about whaling captain's frenzied pursuit of white whale, Moby Dick, by U.S. novelist Herman Melville.

Modernism, intellectual movement within Catholic Church, **c. 1880-1910**, formally condemned by Pope St. Pius X in *Lamentabili*, **July 3, 1907**.

Modern Language Association (MLA), U.S. organization formed to promote scholarship, especially in languages, **1883**.

Modern Times, individualistic utopian community founded and run by Josiah Warren [1799-1874] on 700 acres in the center of Long Island, N.Y., **1851-57**.

Modern Times, film, **1936**, satire on the machine age, last silent film by Charlie Chaplin.

Modified Mercalli Scale, (measurement of earthquake intensity) used from **1931**; devised by Italian geologist Giuseppe Mercalli [1850-1914].

Modoc War, U.S. troops fought series of battles against Modoc Indians encamped in lava beds near Tule Lake, Calif., finally defeating them, **1872-73**.

Mogul Empire, Muslim empire in India, founded by Babur (Baber) [1483-1530], **c. 1526**; reached its greatest extent under Emperor Aurangzeb [1618-1707], **c. 1682**; survived in part, until **1857**.

Mohacs, battle of, 200,000-man Turkish army of Sultan Sulayman I ("the Magnificent") massacred about 30,000 Hungarians led by King Louis II [1506-Aug. 29, 1526] at Mohacs on the Danube, **Aug. 29, 1526**.

Mohs scale, (of mineral hardness) established, **c. 1822**, by German mineralogist Friedrich Mohs [1773-1839].

Molasses Act, British parliament placed high duties on rum, molasses, and sugar imported from French and Spanish West Indies to colonies, **May 17, 1733**.

molecular structure, coordination theory, announced, **1893**, by Swiss chemist Alfred Werner [1866-1919].

molecules chemical formulas proposed, **1803**, by English chemist John Dalton [1766-1844] to explain atomic composition of molecules..

Mollwitz, battle of, Prussian infantry of Frederick II ("the Great") won major victory over Austrian cavalry at Mollwitz, in present-day southwest Poland, **Apr. 10, 1741**.

Molly Maguires, secret organization of Irish-Americans, derived from Ancient Order of Hibernians in Ireland, fought for social and industrial reform in Scranton coalmining district of Pennsylvania, **c. 1865-75**.

molybdenum, element No. 42, discovered, **1778**, by Swedish chemist Karl W. Scheele [1742-1786].

Monaco, tiny principality on French Mediterranean coast, belonging to House of Grimaldi, since **1297**; annexed to France, **1793**; became part of kingdom of Sardinia, **1815**; became French protectorate, **1861**; treaty gave France veto over succession to throne of Monaco, **1918**; Monaco to become autonomous state under French protection if throne is vacant, according to treaty, **July 17, 1919**.

Mona Lisa (see Gioconda, La).

monasticism, religious, founded, Egypt, **A.D. c. 305**, by hermit St. Antony [c. 251-Jan. 17, 356]; Benedictine Rule, basis for Western monasticism, **c. 540**.

Moncontour, battle of, Catholics defeated the Huguenots at Moncontour, France, **1569**, resulting in peace of St. Germain with amnesty granted to Huguenots, **Aug. 8, 1570**.

Mongrel Tariff Act, U.S. Congress removed excise taxes from everything except tobacco and liquor and instituted unsystematic protective tariff increases, **Mar. 3, 1883**.

Mongol Empire, created by the conquests and wars of Mongol leader Genghis Khan [1167?-1227] in central Asia, **c. 1213-24**; divided into four khanates, **c. 1260**.

Mongolia, landlocked country in n. central Asia, reached its peak under Genghis Khan and his successors, **13th century**; declared its independence from Chinese rule, **1911**; communist government formed, **July 11, 1921**.

monism, philosophical theory that nature of universe is one, first expounded, **c. 475 B.C.**, by Greek philosopher Parmenides; maintained most consistently in modern times from **c. 1807**, by German philosopher G.F.W. Hegel.

Monitor **and** *Merrimack*, Union ironclad *Monitor* and Confederate frigate *Merrimack* engaged in four-hour drawn naval battle—the first engagement ever between ironclad ships—at Hampton Roads, Va., during U.S. Civil War, **Mar. 9, 1862**; *Merrimack* destroyed by Confederates on purpose during Union attack on Norfolk, **May 9, 1862**; *Monitor* sank in heavy gale off Cape Hatteras, **Dec. 1862**.

BATTLE BETWEEN THE " MONITOR " AND " MERRIMAC " IN HAMPTON ROADS.

Monk's Corner, American communications outpost seized by British forces sent by Gen. Henry Clinton [1738-Dec. 11, 1795], thus encircling Charlestown, Mass., **Apr. 14, 1780**.

Monmouth, battle of, American Gen. Charles Lee [1731-Oct. 2, 1782] ordered surprise retreat during attack on British at village of Monmouth Courthouse (Freehold, N.J.); arrival of Gen. George Washington and Baron von Steuben checked nearly-successful British counterattack on Lee's troops (Lee later court-martialed and suspended); British forces escaped, **June 28, 1778**.

Monocacy Bridge, battle of, Confederate army under Gen. Jubal A. Early defeated Union army at Monocacy Bridge, Md., **July 9, 1864**.

monomolecular films, (on a surface) studied, **c. 1930**, by American physical chemist Irving Langmuir [1881-1957].

Monongah mine disaster, coal mines in Monongah, W. Va., exploded; one of deadliest coal mine accidents, with 361 miners killed, **Dec. 6, 1907**.

monoplane, first successfully developed, **1909**, by French engineer Louis Bleriot [1872-1936].

monoplane, *Grasshopper*, constructed, **1909**, by Brazilian aeronaut Alberto Santos Dumont [1873-1932].

monotheism, belief in one God, affirmed in *Deuteronomy* (6:4), probably written, **c. 698-643 B.C.**, based on Mosaic traditions from **c. 1290-1280 B.C.**; non-existence of other gods clearly affirmed, **c. 750 B.C.**, by Prophet Amos (Chapters 1 and 2).

monotype machine, patented, **1887**, by American lawyer-inventor Tolbert Lanston [1844-1913].

Monroe Doctrine, U.S. foreign policy doctrine in Western Hemisphere, formulated by Pres. James Monroe [Apr. 28, 1758-July 4, 1831], stated no European colonization or interference in the Americas, **Dec. 2, 1823**.

Mons, battle of, first battle of WW I between Germans and British, **Aug. 23, 1914**, who were forced to fall back with the French.

Mons-en-Pevele, battle of, French forces defeated the Flemings in Flanders, **Aug. 18, 1304**.

Mons Graupius, Roman legions fiercely and bloodily repulsed Caledonian uprising against Roman military rule at Mons Graupius (probably Mt. Killiecrankie in Scotland), ending all organized resistance to Roman rule in Britain for nearly 300 years, **84**.

Montana, formerly territory included in Louisiana Purchase and Oregon Territory, admitted to the Union (U.S.) as 41st state, **Nov. 8, 1889**.

Montanism, early Christian sect, established, **c. 156-57**, Phrygia, Asia Minor, by Asiatic prophet Montanus; first pentecostal sect in Christian history; condemned by Eastern Synods before **200**.

Mont Blanc, highest mountain in the Alps (15,771 ft.), on French-Italian border, first climbed by Michel Gabriel Paccard and Jacques Balmat, members of French expedition, **Aug. 7, 1786**.

Mont Blanc and Imo collision, French ammunition ship *Mont Blanc* and Belgian relief steamship *Imo* collided and exploded in Halifax harbor, Nova Scotia, causing fire to engulf one square mile of Halifax; approx. 1400 persons died, **Dec. 6, 1917**.

Montebello, battle of, French army of Napoleon Bonaparte defeated the Austrians, **June 6, 1800**.

Monte Cassino, principal monastery of Benedictine order, founded, **c. 529**; destroyed by invaders, **585**, **884**, and **1046**, but always rebuilt; destroyed by allied bombs, **1944**, but rebuilt and rededicated by Pope Paul VI, **October 24, 1964**.

Monterey convention, Californians adopted territorial constitution prohibiting slavery and requested admission to the Union, **Sept. 1-Oct. 13, 1849**.

Monterrey, battle of, U.S. army under Gen. Zachary Taylor [Nov. 24, 1784-July 9, 1850] besieged Mexican city of Monterrey during Mexican War, forcing Mexican forces to surrender, **Sept. 20-24, 1846**.

Montpellier, University of, founded by Cardinal Conrad and confirmed by papal bull, **1289**; attended by Rabelais, **c. 1500**; university suppressed during French Revolution, **c. 1790s**; reestablished as a university, **1896**.

Montreal, group of French priests, nuns, and settlers founded Ville Marie de Montreal in Canada, **1641**; briefly occupied by

American troops during American Revolution, **1775-76**; opening of Lachine Canal made water travel to Great Lakes possible, **1825**; capital of United Canada, **1844-49**.

Mooney case, U.S. labor leader Thomas J. Mooney [1882-Mar. 6, 1942] sentenced to hang, **1917**, as participant in bomb-killings during Preparedness Day Parade in San Francisco, **July 22, 1916**; Mooney's sentence commuted to life imprisonment by U.S. Pres. Wilson, **1918**; Mooney became *cause celebre* because of confessions of perjured testimony until he was pardoned by the governor of California, **Jan. 7, 1939**.

Moonlight Sonata, piano sonata, **1801**, 14th sonata (Opus 27) composed by German composer Ludwig van Beethoven.

Moonstone, The, novel, **1868**, mystery, by English novelist (William) Wilkie Collins [Jan. 8, 1824-Sept. 23, 1889].

Moore's Creek, battle of, inspiring victory by Southern militiamen against British loyalists at Moore's Creek, N.C., at start of American Revolution **Feb. 17, 1776**.

Moplahs uprising, Muslim peasants revolted against Hindu landlords in the Malabar region of India, **Aug. 1921**, despite Gandhi's call for non-violence between Muslims and Hindus.

morality plays, late medieval pageant-dramas, **1400-1500**, performed on church porches with abstract personifications.

Moral Rearmanent, movement for moral reawakening through fellowship, public confession and purity, founded, **1921**, as Oxford Group Movement, by U.S. evangelist Frank (Nathan) Buchman [June 4, 1875-Aug. 7, 1961]; renamed, **1939**.

Morat (Murten), battle of, Swiss pikemen defeated Burgundians led by Charles the Bold at Morat in w. Switzerland, **1476**.

Morgarten, battle of, about 1500 Swiss infantrymen ambushed and methodically cut to pieces 15,000-man Austrian army as it advanced through Morgarten Pass in Switzerland, **Nov. 15, 1315**.

Moriscos, revolt of, Moriscos (Christian Moors suspected of retaining the faith of Islam] revolted unsuccessfully against Spanish Inquisition and restrictive legislation, **1568-71**; expulsion of Moriscos from Spain, **1609**.

Mormons, popular name for members of Church of Jesus Christ of Latter Day Saints, founded, New York, **1830**, by Joseph Smith; migrated west under Brigham Young to found Salt Lake City, **1846-47**.

Moroccan crisis, German emperor declared at Tangier Germany's support of Morocco's independence, upsetting French designs for a protectorate, **Mar. 31, 1905**; arrival of German warship *Panther* at Agadir speeded Franco-German agreement about Morocco, **July 1, 1911**.

Morocco, country in Africa, site of powerful Berber empire that ruled region and much of Spain, **11th-12th centuries**; divided into French and Spanish zones, **1904**; gained independence from France, **Mar. 2, 1956**, from Spain, **Apr. 7, 1956**; international zone of Tangier made part of Morocco, **Oct. 29, 1956**; annexed two-thirds of former Spanish Sahara (Western Sahara), **Apr. 14, 1976**; acquired Mauritania's claim to Western Sahara, **1980**.

morphine, isolated, **1805**, by German pharmacologist Friedrick Wilhelm Adam Serturner [1783-1841].

Morrill Tariff Act, U.S. Congress enacted law to protect industry, with duties on specific imports, **May 10, 1860**.

Morristown mutiny, Gen. Washington's soldiers demanded greater rations and overdue pay after very severe winter encampment at Morristown, N.J.; subdued by Pennsylvania regulars, **May 5, 1780**.

Morse telegraph, caveat filed in patent office, **1837**, by American inventor Samuel F. B. Morse [1791-1872].

Morte d'Arthur, The, first published collection and literary rendering in English of Arthurian tales, **1469**, by English writer, Sir Thomas Malory.

Mortimer's Cross, battle of, Yorkist forces under Edward, duke of York (later Edward IV), won decisive victory over Lancastrians at Mortimer's Cross near Leominster in England, **Feb. 2, 1461**.

Mortlack, Scots halted Danish invasion of Scotland, winning pitched battle at Mortlack; victory laid foundation for unification of Scots into a nation, **1010**.

Mortmain, Statute of, King Edward I [1239-1307] of England prohibited a landholder from giving his lands to the church to escape taxation, without royal consent, **1291**.

Mosaic law, Ten Commandments, criminal code, and liturgical law given by God through Moses [c. 1350?-1250?B.C.] to the Hebrews, c. early **13th century B.C.**

mosaic mouse, achieved, **1978**, by Yale University researchers Clement L. Markert and Robert M. Petters.

Moscow Art Theater, theater, founded, **1898**, to produce artistic plays regardless of commercial popularity, by Russian actor and director Konstantin Stanislavski.

Moscow fire, great, Russian patriots or French looters started fire that burned nearly all of Moscow to the ground; helped to force Napoleon's retreat from Russia, **Sept. 10-14, 1812**.

Moscow, University of, first Russian university, founded, **1755**.

Moses, statue, **1515-16**, by Italian Renaissance artist Michelangelo Buonarroti.

Moslem Brotherhood (Ikhwan al-Muslimin) political-religious society, established, Egypt, **1929**, based on principal that Koran provides guidance on all subjects in public and private life; dissolved by Egyptian government, **1955**.

Mossbauer effect, discovered, **1958**, by German physicist Rudolf L.Mossbauer [1929], as phenomenon caused by emission and absorption of gamma rays by crystals.

motet, chorale works based on Latin sacred text, composed, **1220-1750**.

Mother Goose (Contes de Ma Mere L'Oye), collection of traditional children's fairy tales, published, **1697**, by French writer and critic Charles Perrault; English translation, **1729**.

motion picture camera, patented, **1889**, by English photographer William Friese-Green [1855-1921].

motion pictures, introduced in U.S., **1896**, by inventor Thomas A(lva) Edison [Feb. 11, 1847-Oct. 18, 1931]; who invented basic techniques; first feature film: *The Great Train Robbery*, **1903**; first Hollywood studio, **1908**.

motor, electric, invented, **1831**, by American physicist Joseph Henry [1797-1878].

motor scooter, invented, **1919**, by English inventor Greville Bradshaw.

motorcycle, invented, **1885**, by German engineer Gottlieb Daimler [1834-1900].

Moulin de la Galette, La, painting, **1876**, rendition of Sunday throng in popular Parisian dance hall, by French impressionist painter Pierre-Auguste Renoir.

Mountain, the (Montagnards), French radicals whose seats were the highest on left side of French National Assembly and Convention, **1791-94**; the Mountain's Jacobin and Cordelier members ruled France, **1793-94**.

Mountain Meadows massacre, Indians under Mormon fanatic John D. Lee [fl. mid-1800s] killed about 140 emigrants bound for California at Mountain Meadows, Utah, **Sept. 11, 1857**.

mountains, roots of, theory developed, **1889**, by American geologist Clarence E. Dutton [1841-1912].

Mount Holyoke College, first college in U.S. intended specifically for women, established as Mount Holyoke Female Seminary, **1837**; took present name, **1893**.

Mourning Becomes Electra, trilogy of plays, **1931**, based on Aeschylus' *Oresteia* but in U.S. Civil War setting; by U.S. playwright Eugene O'Neill.

moving cable system and gripping device, invented for San Francisco cable cars, **1871**, and installed, **1873**, by English-American engineer Andrew S. Hallidie [1836-1900].

mower, agricultural, patented, **1857**, by American inventor Ephraim Ball [1812-1872]; first two-wheeled hinged bar mower.

Mowing machine, invented, **1810**, by American inventor Peter Gaillard.

Mozambique, country on east coast of Africa, gained independence from Portugal after almost 500 years of colonial rule, **June 25, 1975**; closed border with Rhodesia (Zimbabwe), **Mar. 3, 1976**.

Mrs. Dalloway, novel, **1925**, in which lives and pasts of society woman and insane man are revealed through interior monologue, by English novelist and essayist Virginia Woolf.

Mt. St. Helens, volcano in s.w. Washington state erupted, **May 18, 1980**, hurling ash 12-mi. high, reducing peak from 9677 ft. to 8300 ft. high, and creating 2-mi. wide crater.

muckraking, movement in U.S. journalism, **1895-1915**, intended to expose abuses and corruption in government and society, term coined, **1906**, by President Theodore Roosevelt [Oct. 17, 1858-Jan. 6, 1919].

Mudki, battle of, about 30,000 Sikh rebels made surprise attack on 12,000 British-Indian troops at Mudki in Punjab; British won victory with heavy casualties in her first war against the Sikhs, **Dec. 18, 1845**.

Muhlberg, battle of, forces of Holy Roman Emperor Charles V defeated those of the Schmalkaldic League, **Apr. 24, 1547**.

Muhldorf, battle of, Louis of Bavaria (later Holy Roman Emperor Louis IV [1287?-1347] defeated and captured his rival Frederick the Handsome [1286?-1330], **Sept. 28, 1322**.

Mukden Incident, alleged railway explosion at Mukden, **Sept. 18, 1931**, used by Japanese as excuse to occupy Manchuria, to seize Kirin, **Sept. 21, 1931**, and three e. provinces, **Feb. 1932**, from Chinese.

Mukden (Shen-yang), Chinese city captured by Japanese after 15-day siege during Russo-Japanese War, **Mar. 10, 1905**; Mukden Incident allowed Japanese to occupy city and begin the occupation of all Manchuria, **Sept. 18, 1931**; Chinese Communists annihilated Nationalists during 10-month siege of city, which fell to Communists on **Nov. 1, 1948**.

Munchengratz, battle of, Prussian army of 140,000 men overpowered Austrians at Munchengratz (Mnichovo Hradiste) near Prague at outbreak of Austro-Prussian War (Seven Weeks' War), **June 28, 1866**.

Munich, became capital of the kingdom of Bavaria, **1806**; developed into artistic and cultural center under Bavarian kings, referred to as a "modern Athens," **19th century**; site of Hitler's "beer-hall putsch," **Nov. 8, 1923**.

Munich's Olympic village, raid on, eight Arabs, members of Black September group, invaded Olympic village in Munich, Germany, killing 11 Israeli athletes, **Sept. 5, 1972**.

Munich Pact, Adolf Hitler [Apr. 20, 1889-Apr. 30, 1945] of Germany, Benito Mussolini [July 29, 1883-Apr. 28, 1945], of Italy, Neville Chamberlain [Mar. 18, 1869-Nov. 9, 1940] of Britain, and Edouard Daladier [June 18, 1884-Oct. 10, 1970] of France signed agreement, **Sept. 29-30, 1938**, at Munich, permitting immediate German occupation of Sudetenland and Czech military fortifications to keep peace in Europe.

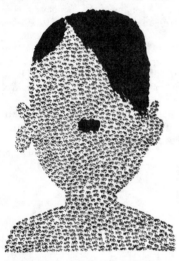

Muret, battle of, French nobles of the north under Simon de Montfort decisively defeated nobles of the south at Muret, **1215**, ending resistance and independence of Albigenses (Catharist heretics).

Mursa, battle of, Roman legions under Constantius II [317-61] defeated those under Flavius Popilius Magnentius [d. 353] at Mursa, near the juncture of the Danube and Dave, **Sept. 28, 351**; Constantius became sole Roman emperor.

Murzsteg program, Russian-Austrian program, approved by major European powers, provided for administrative, judicial, and financial reform of Macedonia, **Oct. 2, 1903**.

Muscovy Company (Russia Company), first major English joint-stock trading company, established for trading and exploration in Russia and Asia, **1555-1615**.

Musuem of Modern Art, art museum devoted to modern art, founded, New York, **1929**; moved into own building **1939**; expanded, **1964**.

Muslim League, political organization to protect rights of Muslims in India, founded by Aga Khan III [Nov. 2, 1877-July 11, 1957], **1906**; demanded establishment of separate Muslim state (Pakistan), **1930s**; became major political party of newly formed Pakistan, **1947**; defunct, **1958-62**, while martial law existed in Pakistan; reformed into two separate groups: Convention Muslim League and Council Muslim League, **1962**; Convention Muslim League, ceased **1969**; Council Muslim League, ceased **1970**.

Mussolini's *March on Rome*, Italian fascists, backed by nationalists, led by Benito Mussolini, occupied Rome, **Oct. 28, 1922**; King Victor Emmanuel III [Nov 11, 1869-Dec. 28, 1947] permitted Mussolini to form cabinet of fascists and nationalists, **Oct. 31, 1922**; Mussolini granted dictatorial powers, **Nov. 25, 1922**.

Mutiny on the Bounty, historical novel, **1932**, based on revolt of crew of *H.M.S.*

Bounty against Captain Bligh, by Charles (Bernard) Nordhoff [Feb. 1, 1887-Apr. 11, 1947] and James Norman Hall [Apr. 22, 1887-July 5, 1951].

Mycale, battle of, combined Greek-Ionian attack totally destroyed 60,000-man Persian army on Cape Mycale in Asia Minor, ending for certain peril of Persian domination of Greece, **479 B.C.**

Mycenaean civilization, advanced civilization centered around ancient Greek city of Mycenae, **fl. 1400-1200 B.C.**

My Fair Lady, musical comedy, opened, **March 15, 1956**, based on Shaw's *Pygmalion*, by Lerner-Loewe writing team; performances by English actors Rex Harrison (born Reginald Carey) [Mar. 5, 1908-] and Julie Andrews. Film, **1964**, based on Lerner-Loewe musical, with Rex Harrison and U.S. actress Audrey Hepburn (born Audrey Hepburn-Ruston) [May 4, 1929-].

Mylae, battle of, ancient Rome's first sea victory halted Carthage's planned invasion of Italy; by brilliant naval tactics, Roman galleys defeated large Carthaginian fleet at Mylae (Milazzo), w. of Messina, during first Punic War, **260 B.C.**

My Lai massacre, Co. C., 1st Batt., 20th Inf. attacked Viet Cong village of My Lai in South Vietnam, massacring more than 100 unarmed men, women, and children, **Mar. 16, 1968**.

My Little Chickadee, film, **1940**, burlesque of life in the Old West, with U.S. actor W.C. Fields and U.S. actress Mae West [Aug. 17, 1893-Nov. 22, 1980].

Mysore Wars, British East India Company fought native Muslim state of Mysore (Karnataka) in India; first war, **1767-69**; second **1780-84**; British won at Porto Novo, **July 1, 1781**; third, **1790-92**; British captured fortress-capital Seringapatam, **Mar. 19, 1792**; fourth, **1799**; British again took Seringapatam, **May 4, 1799**.

Mytilene, battles of, Athenians suppressed rebellion at Mytilene on the island of Lesbos, **427 B.C.**; Athenian fleet commanded by Conon [c. 460-c. 390 B.C.] defeated off Mytilene, **406 B.C.**

Myton, battle of, (*the chapter of Myton*), Scottish force, sent by King Robert I to raid Yorkshire, routed English force, hastily assembled by archbishop of York and con-

taining many monks and priests, at Myton, near Swale River, **Sept. 20, 1319**.

myxedema, condition demonstrated, **1883**, after thyroidectomy by Swiss surgeon Emil T. Kocher [1841-1917].

Nahum, Book of, Old Testament book, written between **663-612 B.C.**.

nail-making machine, invented, **1786**, by American inventor Ezekiel (Jesse) Reed.

nail-making process, from cold iron devised **1777**, by American forgemaster Jeremiah Wilkinson [1741-1831].

Naked and the Dead, The, novel, **1948**, about World War II by U.S. novelist Norman Mailer [Jan. 31, 1923 -]

Nakht, Tomb of, Egyptian tomb, **c. 1450 B.C.**, containing best preserved Egyptian tomb paintings.

Namibia (South-West Africa), country in Africa, site of British, Dutch, and German missionary activity, **1800s**; became German protectorate, **1884**; conquered by South Africa, **1915**; named Namibia by UN, **1968**; UN condemned South Africa's "illegal" rule of country, **Dec. 1969**; UN plan for independence of Namibia by the end of 1978 rejected by South Africa, **Sept. 20, 1978**; South-West Africa People's Organization (SWAPO), increased guerrilla war to force independence, **1978-80**.

Nancy, battle of, Swiss foot soldiers routed Burgundian army at Nancy, capital of Lorraine, ending the power of Burgundy, **Jan. 5, 1477**.

Nanking, historic Chinese city on Yangtze River; capital of Ming dynasty, **1368-1421**; occupied by insurgents during Taiping Rebellion, **1853-64**; Sun Yat-sen [Nov. 12, 1866-Mar. 12, 1925] made Nanking his capital, **1912**; capital of Chinese Nationalist government, **1928-37, 1945-49**.

Nanking, Treaty of, Britain won first Opium War; Chinese ports of Canton, Amoy, Foochow, Ningpo, and Shanghai opened to foreign trade, **Aug. 29, 1842**.

Nantes, Edict of, decree, **April 13, 1598**, establishing qualified religious toleration for French Huguenots (Protestants); issued by French King Henry IV (Henry of Navarre) [Dec. 13, 1553-May 14, 1610]; revoked, **Oct. 18, 1685**, by Louis XIV, causing Huguenot exodus from France.

Napoleonic Wars, wars waged by or against France under Napoleon Bonaparte (Napoleon I), **1803-15**; Napoleon won victory at Austerlitz, **Dec. 2, 1805**; Napoleon defeated at Jena, **Oct. 14, 1806**; British won naval victory at Trafalgar, **Oct. 21, 1805**; Russians defeated at Friedland, **June 14, 1807**; Napoleon controlled Continent by Treaties of Tilsit, **July 7-9, 1807**; Napoleon led French Grand Army in attack on Russia and entered Moscow, **Sept. 14, 1812**; Moscow fire and harsh Russian winter forced Napoleon to retreat, **Oct. 19, 1812**, Grand Army devastated at Berezina, **Nov. 26-29, 1812**; Napoleon suffered major defeat at Leipzig, **Oct. 18-19, 1813**; in the face of allied advance, Napoleon abdicated, **Apr. 11, 1814**; Napoleon left exile on Elba and, rallying the French, entered Paris to begin Hundred Days rule, **Mar. 20-June 28, 1815**; Napoleon defeated decisively at Waterloo, **June 18, 1815**; Napoleon abdicated again, **June 22, 1815**; Napoleon, as prisoner of war, exiled by British to island of St. Helena in s. Atlantic, where he died, **May 5, 1821**.

Narva, battle of, Swedish forces under

Charles XII won first great battle of Great Northern War, defeating Russian forces of Peter I at Narva in present-day Estonia, **Nov. 30, 1700**.

Naseby, battle of, parliamentarians (Roundheads) of Oliver Cromwell defeated decisively royalists (Cavaliers) of King Charles I at Naseby in central England, **June 14, 1645**.

Nashville, battle of, Union army under Gen. George H. Thomas [July 31, 1816-Mar. 28, 1870] won major victory in U.S. Civil War, defeating Confederates under Gen. John B. Hood [June 1, 1831-Aug. 30, 1879] at Nashville, Tenn., **Dec. 15-16, 1864**.

Nashville Convention, delegates from nine Southern states convened at Nashville, Tenn., to consider slavery issue, **June, Nov. 1850**.

National Academy of Science, U.S. private organization chartered by Congress, **Mar. 3, 1863**.

National Association for the Advancement of Colored People (NAACP), organization to promote legal and political rights of U.S. Negroes, founded **May, 1910**.

National Conference of Christians and Jews, U.S. organization, founded **1926**.

National Football League (NFL), professional football association formed from American Professional Football Association, **1922**; merged with All-America Conference, **1949**; merged with professional rival, American Football League, **1970**.

National Gallery of Art, U.S. national art museum, opened, **1941**, Washington, D.C..

National Hockey League (NHL), conference of U.S. and Canadian professional hockey teams organized first with Canadian teams, **1917**; Boston became first U.S. city to join league, **1924**; league expanded to 21 teams, **1979**.

National Labor Relations Board (NLRR), established, **July 5, 1935**, by Wagner Act.

National Progressive Republican League, established by Sen. Robert M. La Follette [June 14, 1855-June 18, 1925] of Wisconsin, **Jan. 21, 1911**, to promote popular government and to pass progressive legislation.

National Recovery Administration (NRA), federal bureau created by National Industrial Recovery Act, **June 13, 1933**, to stimulate industrial recovery and employment during the Depression; U.S. Supreme Court voided NRA's compulsory fair-practice codes, **May 27, 1935**; ceased operations, **Jan. 1, 1936**.

National Republican Party, former U.S. political party established to oppose Andrew Jackson and his party, **1828**; merged with other groups into Whig Party, **1836**.

National Review, The, weekly journal of opinion, founded **1955**.

National Socialist German Workers' Party (National Socialist Party or Nazi Party), German political party, founded **1919**; led by Adolf Hitler, **1920-45**; party's fascistic program of National Socialism dominant in Germany, **1933-45**.

National Women's Conference, 1422 delegates to first National Women's Conference in Houston, Tex, **Nov. 19-21, 1977**.

Nation, The, U.S. weekly journal of opinion, founded **1865**.

Native American Party, anti-Catholic, anti-Irish minor U.S. political party, established, **1845**; nominated Gen. Zachary Taylor for U.S. President at Philadelphia convention, **Sept. 1847**; evolved into Know-Nothing Party, **c. 1853**.

natural gas, first well in U.S. established, **1821**, at Fredonia, New York.

naturalism, movement in literature, fl. **1880-1940**, that sought to depict reality as objectively and dispassionately as science does.

natural selection, theory proposed, **1859**, by English naturalist Charles Darwin [1809-1882].

Nauru, tiny island nation in Pacific, became independent republic, **Jan, 31, 1968**.

Nautical Almanac, first published, **1767**, by English astronomer Nevil Maskelyne [1732-1811].

Nautilus, first U.S. atomic-powered submarine launched, **1954**, by U.S. Navy at Groton, Conn.

Navaho (Navajo) Indians, nomadic North American Indians living in Southwest fought whites until Kit Carson [Dec. 24, 1809-May 23, 1868] subdued them, **1863-64**; many Navahos imprisoned at Fort Sumner, N.M., **1864-68**.

Navarino, battle of, Europeans intervened in Greek war of independence from Ottoman Empire; allied fleet (English, French, and Russian) destroyed entire Egyptian fleet at Navarino (Pylos) after Ottoman Turks refused to accept armistice in the war, thus ending Egypt's part in the war; last pitched battle between wooden sailing ships, **Oct. 20, 1827**.

Navigation Act, first British, forbade importation of goods into England except in English vessels, **Oct. 9, 1651**.

navigation, study of, established, **1421**, by Portuguese prince Henry the Navigator [1394-1460] at his Sagres home.

Navy, U.S. Department of the, Congress established Navy Department, **May 3,**

1798; united with War and Air Force departments under single secretary of U.S. Cabinet rank, **July 25, 1947**.

Naxos, battle of, Athenian fleet won decisive victory over Lacedaemonian fleet near island of Naxos, **376 B.C.**, restoring Athenian supremacy of the sea.

Nazi Blood Purge, 77 persons, many members of the Nazi Party, executed for allegedly plotting against Hitler and his regime, **June 30, 1933**.

Neanderthal man, discovered, **1856**, skull identified, **1858**, by German scientist D. Schaaffhausen [1816-1893].

Nebraska, part of territory acquired by Louisiana Purchase, admitted to the Union (U.S.) as 37th state, **Mar. 1, 1867**.

nebular hypothesis, proposed, **1796**, by French astronomer Marquis Pierre Simon de Laplace [1749-1827].

Necessity, Fort, entrenched camp at Great Meadows (Uniontown, Penn.) where Virginia militiamen under George Washington were defeated by French forces from nearby Fort Duquesne, **July 4, 1754**.

Neerwinden, battles of, French won important victory over English, Dutch, German, and Spanish forces at village of Neerwinden during the War of the Grand Alliance, **July 29, 1693**; Austrians halted and then resoundingly defeated French at Neerwinden during French Revolutionary Wars, then drove French out of Brussels and the Austrian Netherlands, **Mar. 18, 1793**.

Nefertiti, painted limestone bust, **c. 1360 B.C.**, of Nefertiti, Pharaoh Ikhnaton's queen.

negative-positive process, (in photography) patented, **1841**, by English pioneer W.H. Fox Talbot [1800-1877].

Negro College Fund, United, U.S. charitable organization established, **1944**.

Nehemiah, Book of, Old Testament book, written down, **c. 400 B.C.**.

Nehru Report, conference at Lucknow, headed by Jawaharlal Nehru [Nov. 14, 1889-May 27, 1964], adopted report proposing constitution to give India dominion status with a representative government, **Aug. 28, 1928**.

Nelidov scheme, Russian government adopted plan to send expeditionary force to seize Constantinople and the straits if British intervened in Armenian massacres in Anatolia (Ottoman Empire), **Aug. 1896**.

Neoclassicism, movement in literature, **c. 1660-1780**; sought traditional classic values of form, balance, and discipline; style of painting and sculpture that flourished, **c. 1780-1830**.

neodymium, element No. 60: discovered, **1885**, by Austrian chemist Baron Carl Auer von Welsbach [1858-1929].

neo-Guelphs, Italians seeking a confederation of states under the presidency of the pope, opposing the republicanism of Mazzini, led by Vincenzo Gioberti [1801-52], **1843-52**.

neomycin, antibiotic developed, **1949**, by American inventor Selman A. Waksman [1888-1973].

neon, element No. 10; discovered, **1898**, by Scottish chemist Sir William Ramsay [1852-1916], and English chemist Morris W. Travers [1872-1961].

Neon, battle of, Boeotians defeated the Phocians in central Greece, **354 B.C.**, ending with the victory of Philip II [382-336 B.C.] of Macedon over Phocia, **346 B.C.**

Neoplatonism, school of philosophy, articulated, Rome, **c. 244**.

Nepal, country in central Asia astride the Himalayas, first unified as a Hindu kingdom, **c. 1770**; British established residency at Katmandu, **1816**; became independent, **1923**; proclaimed a constitutional monarchy, **1951**.

Neptune, planet, existence predicted, **1845,** by English astronomer John C. Adams, [1819-1892]; first observed, **1846,** by German astronomer Johann G. Galle, [1812-1910]. Satellites discovered, **1846,** by English astronomer William Lassell [1799-1880] at Greenwich Observatory.

neptunium, element No. 93; discovered, **1940,** by American chemist Edwin M. McMillan [1907-] and American physical chemist Philip H. Abelson [1913-].

Nerchinsk, Treaty of, first Russian treaty with China; Russia withdrew from Amur region, **1689.**

nerve fibers, research on functional variation published, **1937,** by American physiologists Joseph Erlanger [1874-1965] and Herbert S. Gasser [1888-1963].

nerve impulse, chemical transmission discovered, **1934,** by English physician Sir Henry H. Dale [1875-1968] and German physician Otto Loewi [1873-1961].

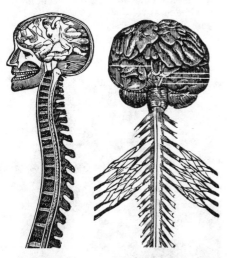

nerve impulse, transmission of, chemical basis discovered, **1952,** by English physiologists Andrew F. Huxley [1917-], Alan L. Hodgkin [1914-] and Australian physiologist Sir John C. Eccles [1903-].

nervous system structure, tissue of the nervous system identified by new staining technique, begun, **1870,** by Italian neurologist Camillo Golgi [1844-1926], and used by Spanish histologist Santiago Ramon y Cajal [1852-1934].

Nestorians, Christians condemned by Council of Ephesus, **431;** Nestorian Church flourished, Asia, **433-1295;** most churches destroyed in Mongol invasions, **c. 1400.**

Netherlands, Austrian and Spanish, part of the Low Countries controlled by the House of Hapsburg, **1482-1794;** ceded to France, **1797;** incorporated into the kingdom of the Netherlands, **1815;** former Austrian Netherlands rebelled against Dutch rule and declared Belgian independence, **Aug. 25-Oct. 4, 1830;** Netherlands recognized Belgium as independent nation **Apr. 19, 1839.**

Neuilly, Treaty of, peace treaty signed by Bulgaria with Allies after WW I, **Nov. 27, 1919.**

neuron, function of, discovered, **1928,** by English physiologists Edgar D. Adrian, [1889-], and Sir Charles Sherrington, [1857-1952].

Neutrality Act, U.S., Congress prohibited enlistment of U.S. citizens in service of foreign countries and forbade U.S. ports to supply war vessels of belligerent nations, **June 5, 1791;** forbade U.S. citizens to travel on ships of belligerent nations and gave U.S. president power to declare embargo on arms to belligerent nations, **Aug. 31, 1935;** revised, **Nov. 4, 1939,** to allow "cash and carry" sale of arms to belligerent nations; amended, **Nov. 13, 1941,** to permit arming of U.S. merchant ships.

neutron bomb, secret U.S. nuclear weapon publicly revealed, **Apr. 7, 1978,** when Pres. Carter announced deferment of its production.

neutron bombardment, (of uranium) pioneered, **1933,** by Italian-American physicist Enrico Fermi [1901-1954]; first production of transuranium elements.

Nevada, part of territory ceded to U.S. by Mexico, **1848;** admitted to the Union as 36th state, **Oct. 31, 1864.**

Neville's Cross, battle of, English forces halted Scottish invasion of England, **Oct. 17, 1346.**

New Amsterdam (New York City), Dutch founded settlement at tip of Manhattan, **1625;** Dutch administrator Peter Minuit [1580-June 1638] supposedly bought Manhattan island from Indians for about $24 worth of trinkets, **1626;** English captured town from Dutch, **Sept. 8, 1664**; renamed New York, **Oct. 4. 1664**.

NEW YORK IN 1664.

Newark race riot, New Jersey state police and National Guardsmen put down 6-day race riot in Newark's black ghetto, **July 12-17, 1967**.

New Brunswick, Canadian province, first visited by John Cabot, **1497**; British gained control by Treaty of Utrecht, **Apr. 11, 1713**; became separate colony, **1784**; entered into confederation with other provinces to form Canada, **July 1, 1867**.

Newbury, battles of, forces of King Charles I and parliamentary forces fought indecisive battle at Newbury, central England, **Sept. 20, 1643**; second indecisive battle at Newbury fought during English Civil War, **Oct. 27, 1644**.

New Deal, political, economic, and social reform legislation enacted under the administration of U. S. Pres. Franklin D. Roosevelt [Jan. 30, 1882-Apr. 12, 1945], **1933-45**.

New England Confederation, colonies of New Haven, Connecticut, Massachusetts Bay, and Plymouth united as New England Confederation for common defense against Indians and Dutch expansion from Hudson River valley, **May 19, 1643**.

New England Primer, The, textbook, first published, **c. 1727**, to teach alphabet and rudiments of reading.

Newfoundland, Canadian island and province, first discovered by John Cabot, **1497**; claimed by England, **1583**; French claims to it ended by Treaty of Utrecht, **Apr. 11, 1713**; refused entry into dominion of Canada, **1890s**; became province of Canada, **Mar. 31, 1949**.

New Granada, former viceroyalty created and ruled by the Spanish in South America, **1717-1819**; called Greater Colombia, **1819-30**; renamed Republic of New Granada after Venezuela and Ecuador seceded

1830; renamed Republic of Colombia, **1886**; Panama seceded, **1903**.

New Hampshire, one of Thirteen Colonies, ratified U.S. Constitution to become ninth state of the Union and to put (unofficially) Constitution into effect, **June 21, 1788**.

New Harmony, settlement on Wabash River, Ind., founded by Harmony Society under George Rapp [Nov. 1, 1757-Aug. 7, 1847], **1814**; utopian collectivist community established at New Harmony by Robert Owen [May 14, 1771-Nov. 17, 1858], **1825**.

New Jersey, one of Thirteen Colonies, ratified U.S. Constitution to become third state of the Union, **Dec. 18, 1787**.

New Kingdom (Empire), third main era of ancient Egyptian civilization, **c. 1580-1085 B.C.**

New Mexico, part of territory ceded to U.S. by Mexico, **1848**; admitted to the Union as 47th state, **Jan. 6, 1912**.

New Mexico prison riot, 400 over-crowded inmates at New Mexico penitentiary at Santa Fe went on 36-hour rampage of murder and vandalism, **Feb. 2-3, 1980**.

New Netherland, territory in Hudson River region granted by Holland's government to Dutch East India Company for settlement in America, **1621**; first permanent Dutch settlement at Fort Orange (Albany, N.Y.), **1624**; chief Dutch settlement established at New Amsterdam (New York City), **1625**;

territory taken by English, who split it into New York and New Jersey.

New Orleans, (La.), French settlers from Canada founded city of New Orleans, **1718**; became part of U.S. with Louisiana Purchase, **1803**; Andrew Jackson [Mar. 15, 1767-June 8, 1845] defeated British at New Orleans, **Jan. 8, 1815**; jazz originated in New Orleans, late **19th century**.

New Orleans, battles of, about 5000 Americans, including expert Kentucky and Tennessee riflemen, led by Gen. Andrew Jackson defeated British at New Orleans, forcing British to retreat to their ships to learn the War of 1812 had ended two weeks earlier, **Jan 8, 1815**; Union fleet under Admiral David Farragut attacked and annihilated Confederate fleet, forcing the surrender of New Orleans during U.S. Civil War, **Apr. 24-25, 1862**.

New Republic, The, weekly journal of opinion, founded **1914**.

New Spain, former viceroyalty created and ruled by Spain in s. North America, **1535-1821**; Mexico proclaimed independence, **Feb. 24, 1821**.

newspaper folding machine, high speed, developed, **1875**, by American inventor Richard M. Hoe [1812-1886].

New Testament, The, Christian portion of the Bible, comprising 27 books now believed written, **c. 47-68**.

New Wave, The (*La Nouvelle Vague***),** movement in French films, prose, and theater, **1955-65**, aiming to present art without moral judgments.

New York, one of Thirteen Colonies, rati-fied U.S. Constitution to become 11th state of the Union, **July 26, 1788**.

New York City, first capital of U.S., **1789-90**; city's politics dominated by Tammany and the Tweed Ring, led by William Marcy Tweed [Apr. 3, 1823-Apr. 12, 1878].

New York City Ballet, distinguished ballet company, founded **1934**, under name American Ballet; known as Ballet Society, **1946-48**; received present name, **1948**.

New York City fires, great, more than 700 buildings destroyed in fire throughout city, **Dec. 16, 1835**; Conway's Theater in Brooklyn burned down and killed approx. 300 persons, **Dec. 5, 1876**; Triangle Shirtwaist Factory burned down and killed 145 persons, **Mar. 25, 1911**; 12 firemen killed in sudden collapse of burning New York City building, **Oct. 17, 1966**.

New York City Opera, opera company, founded **Feb. 1944**, City Center, New York.

New Yorker, The, U.S. magazine, founded **1925**, aiming to embody ideals of sophistication and wit.

New York Herald Tribune, U.S. newspaper, founded **1924**, with merger of *Herald,* founded **1835**, and *Tribune,* founded **1841**; suspended publication, **1964**, except for Paris edition, which continues.

New York State Barge Canal, large waterway system improving the Erie Canal, completed linking Great Lakes with Hudson River and Lake Champlain, **1918**.

New York Stock Exchange, largest U.S. stock exchange organized at Merchants Coffee House, New York City, **May 17, 1792**; opened for trading for first time, **1825**.

New York Times, The, premier U.S. newspaper, founded **1851**, as newspaper of depth and record; purchased **1896**, by U.S. publisher Adolph S. Ochs [Mar. 12, 1858-Apr 8, 1935].

New York World's Fairs, held at Flushing Meadows, Queens, New York City, **1939-40**; held at Flushing Meadows, **Apr. 22, 1964-Oct. 17, 1965**.

New York Yacht Club, America's first and oldest continuously existing yacht club, **July 29, 1844**; Hundred-Guinea Cup trophy presented to New York Yacht Club became the America's Cup, **1857**.

New Zealand, island nation in South Pacific, first discovered and named by Abel Tasman [c. 1603-Oct. 1659], **1642**; explored by Capt. James Cook, **1769-70**; annexed by Britain, **Jan. 22, 1840**; British suppressed the Maoris, **1870**; achieved dominion status, **1907**.

New Zealand Company, powerful colonizing company founded in England, **May, 1839**; established first British colony in New Zealand, at Wellington, **Jan. 1840**; signed Treaty of Waitangi with Maoris, **Feb. 6, 1840**; company dissolved, **1851**.

Niagara Falls, N.Y., hydroelectric plant, designed and constructed **1886** to **1896**, by American electrical and mechanical engineer John L. Harper [1873-1924].

Niagara, Fort, British, allied with Iroquois Indians, besieged and captured French-held Fort Niagara, **June-July 25, 1759**.

Nibelungenlied, The, medieval German epic poem, written, **c. 1190-1200**, in four-line stanzas; celebrates exploits of warrior Siegfried and courtship of Queen Brunhild of Iceland; utilized for his operas by German composer Richard Wagner.

Nicaea, Council of, first ecumenical council, convened **325**, Asia Minor; issued original version of Nicene Creed; seventh ecumenical council, **787**, assembled to deal with Iconoclastic controversy; declared veneration (not worship) of images legitimate.

Nicaragua, country in Central America, won its independence from Spain, **1821**; became independent republic, **1838**; U.S. Marines occupied country to keep order, **1912-25, 1926-33**; civil war instigated by Sandinistas resulted in overthrow of government of Gen. Anastasio Somoza-Debayle, **May 29-July 17, 1979**.

Nicene Creed, Catholic creed basically formulated by Council of Nicaea, **325**, with additions by Council of Constantinople, **381**.

Nicholson's Nek, battle of, Boer forces of Gen. Petrus Joubert won victory over British at Nicholson's Nek in South Africa, **Oct. 30, 1899**.

nickel, element No. 28, discovered, **1751**, by Swedish mineralogist Axel F. Cronstedt [1722-1765].

nickel, U.S. five-cent piece issued by authorization of Congress, **May 16, 1866**.

Nicopolis, battle of, Ottoman Turks of Sultan Bayezid I [c. 1360-Mar. 1403] defeated forces of Sigismund [Feb. 15, 1368-Dec. 9, 1437] of Hungary (later Holy Roman Emperor) in Asia Minor, **Sept. 28, 1396**, ending European crusade against the Turks.

nicotine, synthesized, **1903**, by Swiss chemist Ame Pictet [1857-1937].

nicotinic acid, isolated, **1913**, by German scientist Casimir Funk [1884-1967].

Niger, country in s. central Africa, established first as French colony, **1901-22**; declared its independence, **Aug. 3, 1960**; Sahel region devastated by drought and famine, **1969-74**.

Nigeria, country in Africa, exploited by Portuguese and British slave-traders, **15th-16th centuries**; Lagos annexed by British, **1861**, who took full control of country, by **1914**; became independent, **Oct. 1, 1960**; became a republic, **Oct. 1, 1963**; civil war with secessionist east region (Biafra), **July 1967-Jan. 15, 1970**.

Night Watch, The, painting, **1642**, by Dutch painter, Rembrandt.

nihilism, political philosophy, **1850-80**, advocating "annihilation" of God, right and civilization in order to acheive one's own happiness; principal exponent: Russian anarchist Mikhail Bakunin [May 30, 1814-July 1, 1876].

Nijmegen, Treaties of, ended the Dutch war of King Louis XIV of France, **1678-79**; signed by France and Holland, **Aug. 10, 1678**; by France and Spain, **Sept. 17, 1678**; by France, Sweden and Holy Roman Emperor, **Feb. 5, 1679**; by Sweden and Holland, **Oct. 12, 1679**; by France and Denmark (at Fontainebleau), **Sept. 2, 1679**; by Sweden and Denmark (at Lund), **Sept. 26, 1679**.

Nika rebellion, Emperor Justinian [483-Nov. 14, 565] crushed popular uprising against the government at Constantinople, **532**.

Nike of Samothrace, sculpture, **c. 190 B.C.**, of winged goddess of victory.

Nile River, longest river in the world (4160 mi. long); source of Blue Nile discovered by Scottish explorer James Bruce [Dec. 14, 1730-Apr. 27, 1794] as Lake Tana, **1770**; source of White Nile discovered by British explorer John Speke [May 4, 1827-Sept. 18, 1864] as Lake Victoria and Ripon Falls, **1862**.

1984, novel, **1949**, stark, bitter satire of totalitarian regimes that impose on world, by English writer George Orwell.

Nineteenth Amendment to U.S. Constitution, ratified, **Aug. 26, 1920**, gave women the right to vote.

9 Thermidor, French National Convention, fearing the Reign of Terror might turn against it, arrested the leader Robespierre and had him guillotined, **July 27, 1794**.

95 Theses, original document of the Protestant Reformation, nailed to church door, Wittenberg, Germany, **Oct. 31, 1517**, by Martin Luther.

Nineveh, capital of ancient Assyria, **fl. 7th century B.C.**; sacked by a coalition of Babylonians, Medes, and Scythians, **612 B.C.**

niobium, element No. 41; discovered, **1801**, by English chemist Charles Hatchett [c. 1765-1847].

Nipkow Disk, (mechanical television scanning device) invented **1884**, by German inventor Paul G. Nipkow [1860-1940].

nitrogen, element No. 7; discovered, **1772**, by Scottish chemist Daniel Rutherford [1749-1819].

nobelium, element no. 102; discovered, **1958**, by American physicist Albert Ghiorso [1915-] and coworkers.

Nobel Prize, annual award, since **1901**, for outstanding achievement, given in physics, chemistry, physiology or medicine, literature, and work for peace; first memorial prize in economics awarded, **1969**.

noctovision, demonstrated, **1925**, by Scottish television pioneer John L. Baird [1888-1946].

Nome, (Alas.), gold first discovered at Nome, Alaska, by party of Swedes, **Sept. 1898**; beach gold discovered, **July 1899**, resulting in wild gold rush, until **1903**.

nominalism, philosophical theory, articulated from **c. 1110**, by Peter Abelard; developed, **c. 1315**, by William of Ockham.

non-Euclidean geometry, discovered, **1823**, by Hungarian mathematician Johann Bolyai [1801-1860].

Non-Intercourse Act, Pres. Jefferson repealed Embargo Act and renewed trade with all countries except France and Britain, **Mar. 1, 1809**.

noradrenaline, isolated, **1946**, by Swedish chemist Ulf Svante von Euler [1905-].

Nordic Council, Denmark, Norway, and Sweden formed council to discuss common social, economic, and cultural matters, **Feb. 12, 1953**; joined by Finland, **1955**; established Nordic Cultural Foundation, **1967**.

Nordlingen, battles of, Holy Roman Empire gained dominant position in Thirty Years' War after imperial forces defeated Swedes at Nordlingen in Bavaria, **Sept. 5-6, 1634**; Bavarian-Austrian army of Holy Roman Empire suffered defeat by French army during second battle of Thirty Years' War at Nordlingen, **Aug. 3, 1645**.

Nore mutiny, British government used force to suppress serious mutiny by British sailors demanding better treatment, **June 30, 1797**.

Norma, opera, **1831**, by Italian *bel canto* composer Vincenzo Bellini.

Norman Conquest, subjugation of England by French Normans under William the Conqueror [c. 1028-Sept. 9, 1087] after the battle of Hastings, **1066-c. 1154**.

Normandie, great French ocean liner *Normandie* burned and capsized at New York pier, **Feb. 10, 1942**.

Normandy invasion (Operation Overlord), WW II Allied invasion of Normandy, France, directed by Gen. Dwight D. Eisenhower, and Field Marshal Bernard L. Montgomery, began on D-day, **June 6, 1944**; U.S. forces established beachheads at Utah Beach and Omaha Beach, with British on three beaches, Gold, Juno, and Sword, **June 12**.

North Americans, antislavery faction split from Know-Nothing Party and nominated John C. Fremont [Jan. 21, 1813-July 13, 1890] for U.S. President, **June 2, 1856**; Fremont won Republican nomination, **June 17, 1856**.

Northampton, Treaty of, England formally acknowledged Scottish independence and recognized Robert Bruce (Robert I) [July 11, 1274-June 7, 1329] as King of Scotland, **May 4, 1328**.

North Atlantic Treaty Organization (NATO), defensive alliance established, **Apr. 4, 1949**, by U.S., Canada, Britain, France, Belgium, the Netherlands, Norway, Denmark, Iceland, Italy, Luxembourg, and Portugal; joined by Turkey and Greece, **1952**; joined by West Germany, **1955**.

North Carolina, one of Thirteen Colonies, ratified U.S. Constitution to become 12th state of the Union, **Nov. 21, 1789**; seceded from the Union, **May 21, 1861**; readmitted to the Union, **June 25, 1868**.

North Dakota, part of territory acquired by Louisiana Purchase, admitted to the Union (U.S.) as 39th state, **Nov. 2, 1889**.

Northeast blackout, the great, massive electric failure at generating plant near Niagara Falls caused blackout in New York, most of New England, parts of New Jersey, Pennsylvania, Ontario, and Quebec for up to 13 hours, **Nov. 9-10, 1965**.

Northeast Passage, water route from Atlantic to Pacific along n. Europe and Asia sought by Dutch navigator Willem Barents [c. 1550-June 20, 1597], **1594-97**; first successful navigation of passage by Nils A. E. Nordenskjold [1832-1901] of Sweden, **1878-79**.

Northern Campaign, Nationalists under Chiang Kai-shek, successor to Sun Yat-sen, marched northward to begin unification of China under Kuomintang, which held the south, **July-Oct. 1926**; Chiang seized Wuchang, **Oct. 10, 1926**; Kuomintang government established at Nanking, **1928**.

Northern Ireland, British province of Northern Ireland created by British parliament, **Dec. 23, 1920**; civil rights protests by Catholics in Londonderry, **Oct. 5, 1968**, led to widespread violence between Protestants and Catholics in Northern Ireland, **1968-69**; British suspended Northern Ireland's government, **Mar. 30, 1972**, and imposed British rule; Protestant-Catholic coalition government formed, **Nov. 1973**; general strike by militant Protestants overthrew government, **May 1974**, which British took control of; bombings and shooting by "provisional" IRA killed more than 2000 persons in Northern Ireland's sectarian war through **1980**.

Northern War, Great, general European conflict, caused by Sweden's neighbors' desires to break Swedish supremacy in the Baltic, **1700-21**; Swedes defeated Russians at Narva, **Nov. 30, 1700**; Swedes badly defeated at Poltava, **July 8, 1709**; Russians forced to conclude Treaty of Pruth with Turks, **July 21, 1711**; Sweden made peace with all allies except Russia, **1720**; Sweden made peace with Russia by Treaty of Nystad, **Sept 10, 1721**.

North German Confederation, alliance under Prussian leadership formed by 22 German sovereign states n. of Main River; replaced German Confederation, **1867-71**; replaced by the German Empire, **Jan. 18, 1871**.

North Pole, northernmost end of the Earth, first reached by U.S. explorer Robert E. Peary [May 6, 1856-Feb. 20, 1920], and his black aide Matthew A. Henson [1866-Mar. 9, 1955], **Apr. 6, 1909**.

North Sea flood, great, storms accompanied by floods ruined North Sea coastal areas, especially the Netherlands; approx. 2,000 killed, **Jan 31-Feb. 1, 1953**.

Northwest Conspiracy, Copperheads' scheme to have states in U.S. Northwest secede from the Union, exposed during Civil War, **June 1864**.

Northwest Ordinance (Ordinance of 1787), Congress under Articles of Confederation established government for west territories and created Northwest Territory, **July 13, 1787**.

Northwest Passage, water route from Atlantic to Pacific along n. North America sought by British navigator Martin Frobisher [1535-Nov. 22, 1594], **1576-78**; sought by Henry Hudson, **1610-11**; first transit of passage by Norwegian explorer Roald

Amundsen, **1903-1906**; icebreaking super-tanker *Manhattan* became first commercial ship through passage, **1969**.

Northwest Territories (Canada), Canadian region, first opened up to exploration by Henry Hudson, **1610**; known as Rupert's Land until ceded to Canada by Hudson's Bay Company, **1870**; present-day boundaries established, **1912**.

Northwest Territory (Old Northwest) U.S., first national territory of U.S., created when awarded to U.S. by Britain (Treaty of Paris), **Sept. 3, 1783**; Northwest Ordinance set up laws to govern territory, **July 13, 1787**; Grand Ohio Company established early settlements in territory, **1748-76**.

Norway, Scandinavian country united with Denmark, **1381-1814**; united with Sweden, **1814-1905**; invaded by Germans in WW II, **Apr. 9, 1940**; liberated by Allies, **May 8, 1945**; large oilfields discovered in North Sea, **1968, 1974, 1979**.

Notium, battle of, Peloponnesian fleet under Lysander destroyed Athenian fleet off Notium in Asia Minor, **407 B.C.**

Notre Dame de Paris, cathedral, Paris, built **1163-1250**, consecrated, **1182**.

nova, name established, **1572**, by Danish astronomer Tycho Brahe [1546-1601] for exploding stars. Flare of nova, later called Tycho's star, observed, **Nov. 11, 1572**, the first recorded in Europe since Greek astronomer Hipparchus noted an apparent nova in the constellation of Scorpio, **134 B.C.**

Novara, battles of, Swiss-Italian force defeated French at Novara, Italy, **June 6, 1513**; Austrians defeated Piedmontese (Sardinians) at Novara, **Apr. 8, 1821**; Austrians led by Field Marshal Joseph Wenzel

Radetzky [Nov. 2, 1766-Jan. 5, 1858] defeated Piedmontese forces of Charles Albert (of Sardinia) [Oct. 1798-July 28, 1849] at Novara, **Mar. 23, 1849**.

Nova Scotia, Canadian province, first settled by French who called it Acadia, **1605**; English fought French for control, **17th century**; ceded to England by Treaty of Utrecht, **Apr. 11, 1713**; Cape Breton Island made part of colony, **1763-84, 1840**; entered into confederation with other provinces to form Canada, **July 1, 1867**.

novel, fictional narrative in prose, telling story and analyzing character, **c. 1750**.

November Revolution, Polish nationalists revolted unsuccessfully against Russian rule in Poland, **Nov. 1830-31**; Russian army defeated Poles at Ostroleka, **May 26, 1831**; Russians retook Warsaw, **Sept. 8, 1831**.

Novgorod, old city on Volkhov River, where, according to legend, Rurik [d. 879], with a band of Varangians, (Vikings) founded the Russian state, **862**; became capital of independent Russian republic (Sovereign Great Novgorod), **1136**; became one of four major trade centers of Hanseatic League, **13th century**; center of Russian art, culture, and commerce, **14th century**; taken over by Muscovites, **1478**; laid waste by Ivan IV ("the Terrible") [Aug. 25, 1530-Mar. 17, 1584], who abolished its liberties, **1570**; severely damaged during German occupation in WW II, **1939-1945**.

Noyon, Treaty of, Austria, faced with problems in Spain and Germany and eager for allies against the Turks, concluded treaty with France, **Aug. 13, 1516**.

nuclear accelerator, developed, **1929**, by English physicist Sir John Douglas Cockcroft [1897-1967]; in **1932**, device was first to split nuclei of atoms.

nuclear chain reaction, first man-made, **1942**, at Stagg Field, University of Chicago, by team of scientists organized under name, Manhattan Engineering District.

nuclear explosion, first underground test set off, **1957**, by Atomic Energy Commission in Nevada.

nuclear fission, first paper published, **1939**, by Austrian-Swedish physicist Lise Meitner [1878-1968] and Austrian-British physicist Otto Frisch [1904-].

nuclear fission, measurement of, release

of energy first measured, **1939**, by American physicist John R. Dunning [1907-1975].

nuclear isomers, discovered, **1921**, by German physicist Otto Hahn [1879-1968].

nuclear particle multiplets, classification introduced, **1953**, by American physicist Murray Gell-Mann [1929-].

nuclear power generator, (in space) first developed and launched, **1961**, by U.S. Atomic Energy Commission.

nuclear power station (civilian), world's first, Calder Hall, began operation, **1956**, in Cumberland, England; in U.S., first station, in Shippingport, Pa., began operation, **1957**.

nuclear resonance absorption, method measuring magnetic fields of atomic nuclei discovered **c. 1950** by Swiss-American physicist Felix Bloch [1905-] and, independently, by American physicist Edward M. Purcell [1912-].

nuclear shell, structure of, theory proposed, **1949**, by German-American physicist Marie Goeppert-Mayer [1906-1972] and German physicist J. Hans D. Jensen [1905-].

nucleic acid synthesis, mechanism discovered, **1955**, by Spanish-American biochemist Severo Ochoa [1905-].

nucleotides, researched and synthesized, from **1940**, by British biochemist Alexander Todd [1907-]. For his work on cell composition, Todd shared Nobel Prize in chemistry, **1957**.

Nullification, Ordinance of, South Carolina declared U.S. tariff laws null and void, strongly applying the principle of states' rights, **Nov. 27, 1832**; revoked, **Mar. 15, 1833**.

Numbers, Book of, fourth Old Testament book, probably written down, **c. 698-43 B.C.**, based on traditional Mosaic materials going back to **c. 1290 B.C.**.

number theory, advanced, **1801**, by German mathematician Karl F. Gauss [1777-1855] with publication of *Disquisitiones Arithmeticae*.

numerical aperture, (for lens openings) introduced, **c. 1875** by German physicist and mathematician Ernst Abbe **1840-1905**.

Nuremberg Laws, laws depriving Jews of German citizenship and prohibiting intermarriage with Jews, enacted by Nazi Party at Nuremberg, Germany, **Sept. 15, 1935**.

Nuremberg trials, series of trials for war crimes conducted by International Military Tribunal at Nuremberg, Germany, **Nov. 21, 1945- Sept. 30, 1946**; 22 Nazis found guilty, 11 sentenced to death by hanging, **Oct. 1, 1946**; Herman W. Goering [Jan. 12, 1893-Oct. 15, 1946] committed suicide in prison two hours before his hanging, **Oct. 15, 1946**. See **World War II**.

Nutcracker Man, hominid skull fragments with stone tools found in Tanzania's Olduvai Gorge by British anthropologist Louis S. B. Leakey [Aug. 7, 1903-Oct. 1, 1972], **1959**, suggested existence of ape-man 1,750,000 years ago.

Nutcracker, The (Le Casse-Noisette), ballet, **1892**, choreographed by Marius Petipa to a story by E.T.A. Hoffmann; music by Peter Ilyich Tchaikovsky; popular orchestral suite, adapted from **1892**.

nutrient deficiencies, causal role in disease maintained by Hippocratic physicians, **5 B.C.-3 B.C.**; accepted in Galenic medicine, **2-c. 1650**; deficiency specific to particular disease noted by English physician James Lind [1716-1794], who suggested it in relation to scurvy; experimentally-produced deficiencies achieved, **c. 1897**, by Dutch scientist, Christian Eijkman [1858-1930].

nylon, invented, **c. 1935**, by American chemist Wallace Hume Carothers [1869-

1937]; patented, **1937**; patent assigned to du Pont Company.

nylon stockings, first marketed, **1940** by Du Pont.

Nyon Agreement, European powers established system of patrol zones to deal with piracy of Spanish Civil War in Mediterranean, **Sept. 14, 1937**.

Nystad, Treaty of, Sweden ceded to Russia, Livonia, Estonia, Ingermanland, Karelia, and some Baltic islands but retained Finland, **Sept. 10, 1721**.

Obadiah, Book of, Old Testament book, written **c. 400 B.C.**, foretelling destruction of Edom for its unbrotherly attitude; 4th book of minor prophets.

Oberammergau, Passion Play of, German play, performed by Oberammergau villagers every ten years; begun **1633**, as vow of villagers' ancestors to escape plague; performances in decimal years, from **1670**.

Oberlin College, Ohio coeducational institution, founded **1833**, first college to admit black students, **1835**, and first to award degrees to women, **1837**.

oboe, conical pipe wind instrument with double reed, evolved from double-reed instruments documented in Sumeria, **c. 2800 B.C.**; modern European instruments developed from, especially in France, from **c. 1600**.

Ocala Platform, farmers meeting at Ocala, Fla., demanded abolition of national banks, low rates of interest for loans, free coinage of silver, low tariffs, graduated income tax, **Dec. 8, 1890**.

Ockham's razor, rule of thought that forbids unnecessarily complicated thought processes in philosophizing, formulated, **c. 1320**, by English nominalist philosopher William of Ockham.

October Diploma, document issued by Austrian Emperor Franz Joseph established federal constitution recognizing autonomy for various Hapsburg possessions, **Oct. 20, 1860**.

October Manifesto, document issued by Czar Nicholas II, granting civil liberties and a representative duma to be elected democratically in Russia, **Oct. 30, 1905**. Octobrist Party formed to support manifesto, **Nov. 1905**.

October Revolution, Bolsheviks staged coup, led by Leon Trotsky [Oct. 26, 1879-Aug. 20, 1940], captured Russian government buildings and palace at Petrograd (St. Petersburg), and set up a dictatorship of the proletariat, (old-style calendar **Oct. 24-25**) **Nov. 6-7, 1917**.

ocular dioptrics, investigated, **1900**, by Swedish ophthalmologist Alivar Gullstrand [1862-1930].

Odd Fellows, Independent Order of, secret society, first originated in England, **1745**; first U.S. lodge began at Baltimore, **Apr. 26, 1819**.

ode, poetic form, with formal stanza structure and elevation of tone; first odes written, **c. 600 B.C.**, by Greek poetess Sappho [fl. c. 600 B.C.]; and Greek poet Pindar [518/522-438 B.C.].

Ode on a Grecian Urn, poem, **1819**, by English romantic poet John Keats.

Oder-Neisse Line, border between Germany and Poland established along Oder and Neisse rivers, **Feb. 1945**; recognized by E. Germany as permanent border, **1950**; recognized by W. Germany, **Aug. 12, 1970**, signing treaty with U.S.S.R. recognizing inviolability of all post-WW II European borders.

Ode to a Nightingale, poem, **1819**, contrasting immortality of nightingale's song with transience of existence, by English romantic poet John Keats.

Ode to the West Wind, The, poem, **1820**, by English romantic poet Percy Bysshe Shelley celebrating nature.

Odyssey, Greek epic poem, written down, **c. 700 B.C.**, from traditional material attributed to legendary blind poet Homer, **c. 850 B.C.**, about adventures of Odysseus returning from Trojan War.

Oedipus complex, attachment to a parent of the opposite sex, described, **1900**, in *The Interpretation of Dreams*, by Austrian physician Sigmund Freud.

Oedipus Rex, Greek tragedy, **c. 450 B.C..**

Office of Strategic Services (OSS), former secret U.S. federal agency established, **1942**, to obtain information about enemy nations and to sabotage their war potential; abolished **1945**.

Of Human Bondage, novel, **1915**, about young man's struggle for independence, by British writer W. Somerset Maugham.

Of Mice and Men, novelette, **1937**, about grotesque, tragic friendship between migrant workers, by U.S. writer John Steinbeck.

Ohio, formerly part of Northwest Territory, admitted to the Union (U.S.) as 17th state, **Feb. 19, 1803**.

Ohio and Erie Canal, former important waterway, especially for development of Cleveland, Akron, and Columbus, built, linking Lake Erie and Ohio River, **1825-32**.

Ohio-Indiana river flood, great, Ohio and Indiana rivers overflowed and killed 730 persons, **Mar. 25-27, 1913**.

Ohio State Penitentiary fire, 318 prisoners died in fire that broke out in large prison at Columbus, Ohio; one of largest prison fires in history, **Apr. 21, 1930**.

Ohio, USS, U.S. Navy's mightiest under-

water vessel and first Trident submarine, *USS Ohio*, launched at Groton, Conn., **June 17, 1981**.

Ohm's law, announced, **1827**, by German physicist Georg S. Ohm [1787-1854].

oil drilling, first commercial in U.S. introduced, **1859**, by American oil industry pioneer Edwin L. Drake [1819-1880]; struck oil at Titusville, Pennsylvania.

oil refining, pioneered in U.S., **c. 1850**, by American industrialist Samuel M. Kier [1813-1874].

Ojibwa (Chippewa) Indians, North American Indian tribe fought Iroquois Indians to take control of peninsula between Lakes Huron and Erie, **c. 1740s**; ceded most of their lands on Lake Erie, **1805,**; ceded lands in Ohio by peace treaty, **1816**.

O.K. Corral, gunfight at the, Wyatt Earp [1848-Jan. 13, 1929], his brother Virgil, and Doc Holliday killed Clanton gang and McLowery brothers in gun battle at O.K. Corral, Tombstone, Ariz., **Oct. 26, 1881**.

Okeechobee, Lake, tropical storm caused lake to overflow; 2000 killed in s. Florida, **Sept. 6-20, 1928**.

Okinawa, island in w. Pacific, site of last great U.S. amphibious assault in WW II, **Apr. 1, 1945**; about 13,000 U.S. troops killed and 40,000 wounded before Okinawa surrendered, **June 21, 1945**.

Okinawa, battle of, last and largest land battle in Pacific during WW II; U.S. Marines and Army forces under overall command of Admiral Chester Nimitz [Feb. 24, 1885-Feb. 20, 1966] made last great amphibious assault, fought and won bloody battle against Japanese on island of Okinawa; Japanese *kamikaze* heavily damaged offshore naval forces, **Apr. 1-June 28, 1945**.

Oklahoma, part of territory acquired by Louisiana Purchase, admitted to the Union as 46th state, **Nov. 16, 1907**.

Oklahoma, musical comedy, New York, **March 31, 1943**, by writing team of Rodgers and Hammerstein.

Oklahoma land rush, wild stampede by more than 40,000 persons to stake claims on Oklahoma (Indian) Territory, began **Apr. 22, 1889**, resulted in establishment of city of Guthrie and Oklahoma City in 24 hours; second stampede to Oklahoma, **Sept. 16, 1893**.

Oklahoma Territory, last territory in continental U.S. created by Congress, **May 2, 1890**.

Old Folks at Home, popular ballad, **1851**, by U.S. songwriter Stephen Collins Foster.

Old Kingdom, first main era of ancient Egyptian civilization; centered at Memphis; comprised of dynasties I-VI, **c. 3200-2200 B.C.**

Old Man and the Sea, The, novelette, **1952**, about struggle of aged fisherman with sea marlin, by U.S. author Ernest Hemingway; Pulitzer Prize-winner, **1953**, Nobel Prize-winner, **1954**.

Old Testament, The, first part of Bible: collection of books believed to contain God's revelation, written between **c. 900 B.C.** and **c. 70**, in Hebrew (except for brief passages in Aramaic).

Old Vic, Royal Victoria Hall, London, opened as theater, **1818**; became music hall, **1871**; became home of famous Shakespeare company, **1914**; damaged in World War II; re-opened, **1944**, at new location.

Oliva, Treaty of, Poland's John Casimir abandoned his claim to Swedish throne and ceded Livonia to Sweden, **May 3, 1660**.

Oliver Twist, novel, **1838**, depicting poverty and crime in the workhouse world of 19th-century London, by English novelist Charles Dickens.

Olmutz (Olomouc), ancient city in central Czechoslovakia, where Wenceslaus I [d. 1253], king of Bohemia, checked Mongol invasion of Batu Kahn [d. 1255], grandson of Genghis Khan, **1241**; ruled by Sweden, **1642-50**; Treaty of Olmutz restored German Confederation under Austrian leadership, dissolved German Union under Prussia, **Nov. 29, 1850**; Prussia endured "humiliation of Olmutz" until it defeated Austria, **1866**.

Olympian Zeus, colossal statue of Zeus, Olympia, Greece, sculpted, **c. 450-40 B.C.**, by Greek sculptor Phidias [500 B.C.-430 B.C.]; one of seven wonders of ancient world; moved to Constantinople, 5th century; destroyed in fire there, **476**.

Olympian Zeus, Temple of, Greek temple, Athens, begun **c. 500 B.C.**, to rival Ionian temples; completed more than 600 years later, **c. 130**, on orders of Roman Emperor Hadrian [Jan 24, 76-July 10, 138].

Olympic Games, athletic competitions initiated at Olympia in ancient Greece, where first Olympiad began, **776 B.C.**; discontinued by Emperor Theodosius I ("the Great) [346-95] of Rome, **c. 390**; modern revival of Olympic Games at Athens, **1896**.

Oman, sultanate of s.e. Arabian peninsula, formerly called Muscat and Oman, controlled by Portugal, **1508-1659**; most powerful state in Arabia, controlling Zanzibar and much of Persian and Pakistani coasts, early **1800s**; lost Zanzibar, **1856**; confirmed ties with Britain, **1951**; British suppressed tribal revolt, **1957**; discovered oil, **1964**.

Omayyads (Umayyads), Arabian dynasty of caliphs, ruled at Damascus, **661-750**; ruled in south Spain, **776-1031**; climax of dynasty during reign of al-Mansur [914-1002], **10th century**.

Omdurman, battle of, Anglo-Egyptian army under Gen. Horatio H. Kitchener [June 24, 1850-June 5, 1916] won major victory over Mahdists and Sudanese dervishes at Omdurman, marking end to Mahdist state in Sudan and British control, **Sept. 2, 1898**.

One Day in the Life of Ivan Denisovich, novel about Soviet forced-labor camps, **1962**, by Russian author Alexander Solzhenitsyn.

Onin War, conflict between two great feudal war lords for control of w. Japan, **1467-77**.

Ontario, Canadian province, first visited by Champlain, **1615**, region became part of Quebec, **1774**; became known as Upper Canada, **1791**; dominated by Family Compact, **c. 1795-1850**; entered into confederation with other provinces to form Canada, **July 1, 1867**.

On the Waterfront, film, **1954**, featured Marlon Brando; directed by Elia Kazan

(born Elia Kazanjoglous) [Sept. 7, 1909-].

ontology, science of being, branch of philosophy, term coined, **1647**.

open-hearth steel manufacture, developed, **1861**, by German-born English inventor Sir William Siemans [1823-1883].

Open Skies, U.S. proposal made at Geneva Summit Talks, **July 1955**, to allow U.S. and U.S.S.R. aerial reconnaissance of each other's military installations.

opera, drama set to music, common dramatic form in ancient Greece, **400s B.C.**; first opera in modern times, *Dafne*, **1597**, by Italian composer Jacopo Peri.

Operation Big Lift, U.S. 2nd Armored Division airlifted from Texas to W. Germany in 63 hours, **Oct 24, 1963**, to demonstrate speed with which U.S. could send ground forces to Europe.

operetta, musical play in lighter vein, originated, **c. 1840**, with Viennese composer Franz von Suppe (born Francesco Suppe-Pemelli) [Apr. 18, 1819-May 21, 1895].

ophthalmoscope, device for viewing interior of eye, invented, **1851**, by German physiologist Hermann L. F. von Helmholtz [1821-1894].

Opium Wars, conflict between Britain and China over Chinese trade restrictions, especially ban on import of opium, **1839-42**; first war ended by Treaty of Nanking, **Aug. 29, 1842**; British and French conducted second war to open Chinese ports, **1856-58**; ended by Treaties of Tientsin, **June 26-29, 1858**.

Oppenheimer affair, U.S. physicist Robert J. Oppenheimer [Apr. 22, 1904-Feb. 18, 1967], accused of being Soviet agent, had top-secret U.S. security clearance lifted, **Dec. 1953**; vindicated in part when Pres. Lyndon B. Johnson gave him Fermi Award, **1963**.

optical pumping, method of studying Herzian resonances in atoms; research published, **1951**, by French physicist Alfred Kastler [1902-].

optical scanning device, electrical, developed for commercial use, **1969**, by Cybertek, Inc., New York, as remote-control identifier of causes of disease.

Oran, battles of, British naval ships sunk French fleet stationed at Oran, n. Algeria, to prevent takeover by Germans, **July 3,**

1940; Anglo-American forces overran French Vichy garrison at Oran during North African Campaign, **Nov. 11, 1942**.

Orange Bowl, major U.S. collegiate football game played each Jan. 1 at Miami, Fla.; first Orange Bowl game between Miami and Manhattan, **1933**.

Orange Free State, British annexed region in e. central South Africa as the Orange River Sovereignty, **1848**; British granted Orange River Sovereignty independence as Orange Free State under Boer rule, **1854**; British again annexed the region and formed Orange River Colony, **1900**; colony granted self-government, **1907**; became founding province of the Union of South Africa, **1910**.

Orangemen, members of Loyal Orange Institution (Protestant Irish society) founded in Ulster (Northern Ireland), **1795**; **fl. 19th-20th centuries**.

Oranges, War of the, conflict between Spain and Portugal; Spain sought to break Portuguese-British alliance, **Feb.-Sept. 1801**; Portugal renounced treaties with Britain, **Sept. 29, 1801**.

Oratorians, congregation of Catholic priests who live in community without special vows fostering religious works of all kinds; founded Rome, **1564**, by Florentine St. Philip Neri [July 21, 1515-May 26, 1595]; founded in England, **1848**, by John Henry Newman.

oratorio, narrative or dramatic work, usually sacred, with soloists, choruses and orchestras, originated, Italy, **c. 1600**; e.g.; Carissimi's *Jeptha*, **1650**; Handel's *Messiah*, **1742**.

Oratory, On (De Oratore), classic Latin treatise, **55 B.C.**, on style of oratory, by Roman philosopher, writer, statesman, and orator Cicero.

orbit of comet, calculated, **1680**, in Colonial America by Boston merchant-mathematician Thomas Brattle [1658-1713].

orbits of heavenly bodies, method of determining calculated, **1801**, by German mathematician Karl F. Gauss [1777-1855].

orbits of Venus and Mercury, plotted, **1769**, by American astronomer-mathematician David Rittenhouse [1732-1796].

orchid, florist variety discovered, **1873**, by Belgian botanist and horticulturist Jean J. Linden [1817-1898].

Oregon, formerly territory included in Oregon Territory, admitted to the Union as 33rd state, **Feb. 14, 1859**.

Oregon Treaty, boundary between U.S. and British Northwest Territory in Canada fixed at 49th parallel, **June 15, 1846**.

Oresteia, tragic Greek trilogy, **458 B.C.**, recounting story of royal house of Mycenae, by earliest Athenian tragedian, Aeschylus [525-456 B.C.].

Orestes, Greek tragedy, **408 B.C.**, by Greek tragic playwright, Euripides.

organ, keyboard instrument played through pipes on wind chest, primitive form, invented, Greece, **c. 250 B.C.**; developed, Europe, from **c. 800**; modern double keyboard instrument with stops, from **c. 1450**; electricity replaced bellows, **1915**.

organic compounds, produced with ultraviolet light, **1971**, in simulated Martian environment by American scientists at Jet Propulsion Laboratory in Pasadena, California.

Organization for European Economic Cooperation (OEEC), formed European nations at Paris, **Apr. 16, 1948**; replaced by Organization for Economic Cooperation and Development (OECD), **Dec. 14, 1960**.

Organization of African Unity (OAU), 30 African countries formed union at Addis Ababa, Ethiopia, **May 25, 1963**, to promote common interests.

Organization of American States (OAS), international body established at ninth Pan-

American conference at Bogota to promote economic development and hemispheric solidarity, **Apr. 30, 1948**.

Organization of Central American States, established by Guatemala, Honduras, Nicaragua, El Salvador, and Costa Rica to promote economic integration and solve problems, **Oct. 14, 1951**.

Organization of Petroleum Exporting Countries, (OPEC), group of oil-producing nations formed by Venezuelan initiative, **Nov. 14, 1960**; contained 13 members, **1980**.

Origin of Species, The, treatise, **1859**, by English naturalist Charles Darwin.

Origins of Totalitarianism, The, philosophico-historical study, **1951**, of totalitarianism as man's amoral effort to create his own reality, by German-U.S. philosopher and scholar Hannah Arendt.

Oriskany, battle of, American column of 800 militiamen under Gen. Nicholas Herkimer [1728-Aug. 6, 1777], seeking to relieve Fort Stanwix, ambushed and driven back by British and Mohawk Indians; Herkimer was killed, along with 250 Americans, **Aug. 6, 1777**.

Orizaba, highest mountain in Mexico and third highest in North America (18,700 ft.), first climbed, **1848**.

Orleans, battle of, small French army led by 17-year-old girl, Joan of Arc [c. 1412-May 30, 1431], defeated English in desperate fight at Orleans, the turning point in the Hundred Years' War, **May 7, 1429**.

ornithopter, designed, **c. 365 B.C.**, by Greek scientist Archytas of Tarentum [400 B.C.-350 B.C.]; machine designed to fly by flapping of its wings

orthodontia, established, **c. 1885**, by American pioneer orthodontist Edward H Angle, [1885-1930].

Oslo Agreements, Netherlands, Belgium, and Luxembourg (Oslo powers) agreed on tariffs, **Dec. 22, 1930**; at Ouchy Convention they reduced tariffs, **July 19, 1932**; their trade agreements ended **July 1, 1938**.

osmium, element No. 76; discovered, **1803**, by English chemist Smithson Tennant [1761-1815].

osmosis, phenomenon first reported, **1748**, by French abbott and physicist Jean Antoine Nollet [1700-1770]. Process introduced, **1827**, by French chemist Rene Dutrochet [1776-1847].

osmotic pressure, described, **1877**, by German scientist Wilhelm F. Pfeffer [1845-1920], with terminology and system for measuring force of osmosis.

osmotic pressure (in plants), discovered, **c. 1880**, by Dutch botanist Hugo De Vries [1848-1935].

Ostend Manifesto, document drafted by U.S. ministers to Britain, France, and Spain at Ostend, Belgium, implying U.S. might consider seizing Cuba by force if Spain refused to sell, **Oct. 18, 1854**.

Ostia, ancient city of Italy, established by Etruscans, **8th century B.C.**; rivaled Puteoli as major Roman port, **1st century B.C.-A.D. 3rd century**.

Ostpolitik, W. German foreign policy to improve relations with European countries, while maintaining strong ties to the West, since **c. 1966**; W. German Chancellor Willy Brandt [Dec. 18, 1913-] signed non-aggression treaties with U.S.S.R., **Aug. 12, 1970**, Poland, **Dec. 7, 1970**, and E. Germany, **Dec. 1972**.

Oswego, Fort, French expedition laid siege to, forced the surrender of, British-held Fort

Oswego at end of Lake Ontario during French and Indian War, **Aug. 11-14, 1756**.

Othello, Elizabethan tragedy, **1604-5**, about the effects of jealousy: Othello's, concerning his wife, Desdemona; and the malicious Iago's, of his rival Cassio, by William Shakespeare. Film, **1952**, adaptation of Shakespeare play, scripted, directed, and produced by Orson Welles.

Ouchy (Lausanne), Treaty of, agreement ended war between Italy and Ottoman Empire, which abandoned sovereignty of Tripoli and again received possession of Dodecanese Islands, **Oct. 18, 1912**.

Oudenarde, battle of, English, Dutch, and German troops under duke of Marlborough and prince of Savoy won important victory over French force at Oudenarde; allies' initiative restored in Flanders during the War of the Spanish Succession, **July 11, 1708**.

Our Town, play, **1938**, about New England town employing garrulous Yankee as "chorus", by U.S. writer Thornton Wilder; author's *The Skin of Our Teeth*, **1942**.

Outline of History, The, one-volume history of the world, **1920**, by English novelist, historian, and Socialist H.G. Wells.

oven, microwave, first developed, **1945**, by American radio engineer and inventor Percy L. Spencer [1894-]. Model for use in homes introduced, **1967**, by Amana Refrigeration, Inc.; the Amana Radarange.

overture, instrumental composition intended as introduction, used with operas, oratorios, etc., from **c. 1607**, beginning with Monteverdi's *Orfeo*.

ovonic switch, semi-conductor with memory, produced, **1969**, by Energy Conservation Devices, Inc., Troy, Mich.

Oxford English Dictionary, dictionary, published between **1884** and **1928**, produced by Oxford scholars providing quotations to illustrate meaning of words.

Oxford Gazette, The, newspaper, first issued Oxford, **1665**; first real newspaper, rather than newsletter, ever published.

Oxford Movement, The, movement among Oxford Christian scholars, begun **1833**, with John Keble's sermon against government suppression of bishoprics; *Tracts for the Times*, produced, **1833-41**, under leadership of Newman; movement diffused when Newman became Catholic, **Oct. 9, 1845**.

Oxford, University of, educational institution founded **1167**, by students migrating from Paris; University College, founded **1249**, Balliol, **1263**, Merton, **1264**; incorporated by Act of **1571**.

oxygen, element No. 8; discovered, **c. 1774**, by Swedish apothecary Carl Scheele [1742-1786]; independently discovered shortly afterward by English chemist Joseph Priestly [1733-1804]; each published his discovery, **1775**.

oxygen, liquification of, achieved, **1883**, by Polish physicist Zygmunt von Wroblewski [1845-1888].

oxy-hydrogen, blowpipe, devised, **1801**, by American chemist Robert Hare [1781-1858].

Oyster War, most lengthy local conflict in American history, between Virginia and Maryland oyster and crab fishermen on Potomac River, **1632-1980s**; King Charles I of England granted Lord Baltimore as s. boundary "further bank" of Potomac River down to Chesapeake Bay, **1632**.

ozone layer, first tested, **1958**, by U.S. scientists for possible harmful effects caused by high-altitude flights of jet aircraft and nuclear weapons tests.

Paardeberg, battle of, British brigades under Gen. Kitchener, with help of steady artillery fire, forced Boer army of 4000 men to surrender; first major British victory in Boer War, **Feb. 18-27, 1900**.

pacemaker, (for heart) introduced, **1930**, by American physician Albert S. Hyman [1894-].

Pacem in Terris (Peace on Earth), papal encyclical letter, dated **April 11, 1963**.

Pacific Ocean, sighted by a European for the first time by Vasco Nunez de Balboa [c. 1475-Jan. 1519], **Sept. 29, 1513**.

Pacific scandal, Canada's conservative government resigned, accused of accepting campaign funds in return for promise to aid private company build intercontinental railroad, **Nov. 1873**.

Pacific, War of the, conflict between Chile and alliance of Peru and Bolivia over territory, **1879-84**; Bolivia forbade Chile to mine nitrate in Atacama province, **Feb. 1879**; Chile seized Atacama, Tarapaca, Tacna, and Arica, **1879-80**; Chile and Peru signed peace Treaty of Ancon, **Oct. 20, 1883**; Chile and Bolivia signed truce at Valparaiso, **Apr. 4, 1884**; Chile officially acquired Atacama (Antofagasta), **1904**.

packet ship, steamship with sails that rivaled clipper ship, **c. 1830-1900**.

THE CLERMONT.

(The first steam-packet in the world)

Padua, University of, established by teachers and students who fled from Bologna, **1222**; established first anatomy hall in Europe, **1594**; Galileo taught at university, **1592-1610**.

Pagliacci, I (The Clowns), opera, **1892**, by Italian composer Ruggiero Leoncavallo [Mar. 8, 1858-Aug. 19, 1919].

Pahlavi dynasty, Persian (Iranian) dynasty founded by Reza Shah Pahlavi (Reza Khan) [Mar. 16, 1878-July 26, 1944], **Dec. 13, 1925**, who had engineered successful coup, **Feb. 21, 1921**; Reza Shah renamed Persia Iran, **Mar. 21, 1935**; Reza Shah abdicated,

Sept. 16, 1941, to his son Muhammad Reza Pahlavi [Oct. 26, 1919-July 27, 1980], who was deposed and forced into exile, **Jan. 16, 1979**.

Pakistan, country in Asia, established as separate British state, **1947**; fought undeclared war with India, **1948-49**; became a republic, **Mar. 23, 1956**; defeated in war with India, resulting in new nation of Bangladesh (East Pakistan), **Mar. 25, 1971-Dec. 16, 1971**; peace agreement with India, **July 3, 1972**; became federal Islamic republic under new constitution, **Apr. 10, 1973**; first elections under civilian rule, **Mar. 7, 1977**; military coup, **July 5, 1977**.

Pakistani cyclone, East, immense cyclone from Bay of Bengal, deadliest on record, killed approx. 300,000 persons, **Nov. 13, 1970**.

Palatinate, two historic German regions (Rhenish or Lower Palatinate and Upper Palatinate) acquired by Bavarian Wittelsbach dynasty, **1214**; Rhenish Palatinate devastated by French during the War of the Grand Alliance, **1688-89**; palatine lands w. of the Rhine conquered by France, **1790s**; administered by Bavaria, **1837-1945**.

Palestine Liberation Organization

(PLO), established at Arab summit, **May 28-June 2, 1964**; Popular Front for the Liberation of Palestine, terrorist wing of PLO, hijacked its first Israeli airliner, **July 23, 1968**; Yasir Arafat [1929-], head of Al Fatah, became chairman of PLO, **Feb. 4, 1969**; recognized by United Nations, **Oct. 14, 1974**.

palladium, element No. 46; discovered, **1803**, by English physiologist William Hyde Wollaston [1766-1828].

Palo Alto, battle of, U.S. army under Gen. Zachary Taylor won first battle of Mexican War at Palo Alto, near Brownsville, Tex., **May 8, 1846**.

Panama, country in Central America, became part of Colombia after declaring independence from Spain, **1821**; proclaimed its independence from Colombia, **Nov. 3, 1903**; granted use, occupation, and control of Panama Canal Zone to U.S., **Nov 18, 1903**; concluded treaties with U.S. to take full control of canal by the end of 1999, **June 16, 1978**.

Panama Canal, waterway across isthmus of Panama built, **1904-14**, by U.S. on territory leased, **Nov. 18, 1903**, from the Republic of Panama; project headed by George W. Goethals [June 29, 1858-Jan. 21, 1928], **Apr. 1, 1907**; U.S. paid Colombia $25 million in damages, **1921**; U.S. annuity to Panama raised to $1.93 million, **1955**; U.S. and Panama signed treaty, **Sept. 7, 1977**, giving Panama full control of canal by the end of 1999.

Panama Canal Company (Compagnie du Canal Interoceanique), French company under Ferdinand de Lesseps granted rights by Colombia to build canal across isthmus of Panama, **May 18, 1878**; company began construction, **Jan. 1, 1880**; company failed, **1889**; second company formed, **1894**; failed, **1899**.

Panama Canal locks, designed, **1906-1914**, by American civil engineer Henry Goldmark [1857-1941].

Pan-American Conference, first International Conference of American States, met at Washington, D. C., **Oct. 2, 1889-Apr. 19, 1890**.

Pan-American Games, amateur athletic competitions held every four years, since **1951**.

Pan-American Union, international agency formed as the Commercial Bureau of the American Republics at first Pan-American Conference, **Apr. 14, 1890**; adopted present name, **1910**.

Panay **incident**, U.S. gunboat *Panay* sunk by Japanese in Yangtse River, China, **Dec. 12, 1937**; caused increased tension between U.S. and Japan, which apologized **Dec. 14, 1937**, and paid reparations.

Panic of 1907, run on Knickerbocker Trust Co. of New York City began, **Oct. 21, 1907**, until bank's reserves gone, forcing other banks to close, **Oct. 23, 1907**.

Panic of '73, banking house of Jay Cooke & Co., involved in financing Northern Pacific RR, failed **Sept. 18, 1873**.

Panipat, strategic town between Afghanistan and India, site of Moguls' great victory over Afghans, ending Lodi dynasty, **Apr. 20, 1526**; Mogul army under Akbar ("the Great") [1542-1605] repulsed elephant-led attack by Hindus at Panipat, reestablishing Mogul Empire, **Nov. 5, 1556**; Afghans won bloody battle over Mahrattas and Sikhs at Panipat, **Jan. 14, 1761**.

Panormus, battle of, Roman legions defeated invading Carthaginians at Panormus (Palermo, Italy), **251 B.C.**

Pan-Slav congress, first, assembly at Prague proclaimed the unity of the Slavic peoples, **June 1848**.

Pantheon, church, Rome, built, **125**, as spacious, domed Roman rotunda.

Pantheon, national shrine, Paris, since **1791**, locus of remains of those France wished most to honor.

paper, invented, **c. 105**, by Chinese court official Tsai Lun [c. 50-c.118].

paper chromatography, first described, **1850**, by German chemist Friedlieb F. Runge [1795-1867] in his work, *Farbenchemie*.

paper-making machine, constructed, **1798**, by French inventor Nicholas L. Robert [1761-1829].

Pap smear test, devised, **1928**, by Greek-American physician George N. Papanicolaou [1883-1962].

Papua New Guinea, attained its independence, from Australian-held UN trusteeship, **Sept. 16, 1975**.

parachute, invented, **1797**, by French

inventor Andre-Jacques Garnerin [1769—1823]; first descent was from balloon.

Paradise Lost, epic poem, **1667**, by English poet John Milton; sequel, *Paradise Regained*, **1671**.

Paraguay, country in s. central South America, declared its independence from Spanish rule, **1811**; lost half its population and much territory in the War of the Triple Alliance, **1865—70**; fought Bolivia in Chaco War, **1932—35**.

parasites, malarial, discovered, **1880**, in blood cells by French surgeon Charles L.A. Laveran [1845—1922].

Paris, Commune of, revolutionary government established in Paris during French Revolution, **1792—95**; instigated the storming of the Tuileries and arrest of King Louis XVI, **Aug. 10, 1792**; government established at Paris in opposition to French government at Versailles after Franco-Prussian War, **Mar.—May 1871**; Versailles troops entered Paris and defeated the *Communards*, **May 28, 1871**.

Paris, Congress of, conference by major European powers to negotiate peace after Crimean War, **Mar. 30, 1856**.

Paris Review, The, quarterly literary journal, founded **1953**.

Paris, Treaties of, signed by France, England, and Spain, ended Seven Years' War, **Feb. 10, 1763**; Great Britain recognized U.S. independence and effected a large-scale peace settlement with France and Spain, **Sept. 3, 1783**; signed by France and the allies (Great Britain, Russia, Austria, and Prussia) after the first abdication of Napoleon I, **May 30, 1814**; signed by France and the allies after Napoleon's defeat at Waterloo, **Nov. 20, 1815**.

Paris, University of, founded in Paris, France, **c. 1155**.

parity conservation law, (in nuclear physics) disproved, **c. 1950**, by Chinese-American physicists Chen Ning Yang [1922-] and Tsung Dao Lee [1926-].

parking meter, invented, **1935**, by American inventor Calton C. Magee.

Parsifal, long musical drama, **1882**, composed by German composer Richard Wagner.

Parthenon, Greek temple, Acropolis, Athens, built between **447** and **432 B.C.**.

particle accelerator, invented, **1931**, by American physicist Robert J. Van de Graaff [1901—1967].

Partisan Review, American literary magazine, founded **1934**.

Passion play, **c. 1200—c. 1600**; Oberammergau modern passion play, from **1633**, villagers have performed passion play each decade.

pasteurization, process invented, **1860**, by French chemist Louis Pasteur [1822—1895].

Patay, battle of, Orleanist French army of Joan of Arc pursued and routed English forces at Patay during Hundred Years' War, **June 18, 1429**.

patent leather, first manufactured in U.S., **1818**, by American inventor Seth Boyden, at Newark, N.J.

Patent Office, U.S., federal agency enacted first patent law in U.S., **Apr. 10, 1790**; Congress created permanent U.S. Patent Office, **1836**.

Pathet Lao, pro-Communist Laotian nationalists, formed **1951**, in North Vietnam; invaded Laos with Viet Minh forces, **Feb. 1, 1954**, and established government in n. Laos; gained control of half of Laos, **May 1961**; part of coalition government, **Sept. 1973**; took control of government, **May 1975**.

Pathetique Sonata, piano sonata, **1799**; written by German composer Ludwig van Beethoven (Opus 13).

pathology, modern, generally considered founded, **1761**, by Italian physician Giovanni-Battista Morgagni [1682—1771] with his publication, *De sedibus et causis morborum*.

Patterson-Johansson fights, Swede Ingemar Johansson knocked out Floyd Patterson in third round in New York City to win heavyweight boxing championship, **June 26, 1959**; Patterson knocked out Johansson in fifth round in New York City to become first heavyweight in boxing history to regain title, **June 20, 1960**.

Patterson-Moore fight, Floyd Patterson [Jan. 4, 1935-] knocked out Archie Moore [Dec. 13, 1913-] in fifth round in Chicago to become heavyweight boxing champion, **Nov. 30, 1956**.

Patton, film, **1970**, about career of controversial U.S. World War II general, George S(mith) Patton, Jr. [Nov. 11, 1885—Dec. 21, 1945].

Paulists, popular name for U.S. Catholic Missionary Society of St. Paul the Apostle, founded, New York, **1858**.

Paul Revere's Ride, poem, **1860**, celebrating Paul Revere's [Jan. 1, 1735—May 10, 1818]; ride, by Henry W. Longfellow.

Paulus Hook, capture of, from British by Americans during American Revolution, **Aug. 18, 1779**.

Pavia, battle of, Spanish-Italian-German army defeated French forces under Francis I, **Feb. 24, 1525**, who was captured, and forced to renounce Italian claims by Treaty of Madrid, **Jan. 14, 1526**.

Pavia, University of, its 9th-century law school became a famous university, **1361**.

Pawnbroker, The, film, **1964**, powerful study of man embittered by Nazi concentration camps.

Pax Romana **(Roman peace)**, Augustus Caesar (Octavian) ushered in two centuries of relative peace; marked by cultural achievements and prosperity, **27 B.C.—A.D. 180**.

Payne-Aldrich Tariff Act, U.S. Congress passed, **Aug. 5, 1909**, tariff, less protectionist than McKinley Tariff of 1890 and Dingley Tariff of 1897.

PCBs (polychlorinated biphenyls), production halted, **1979**, by rule of U.S. Environmental Protection Agency.

Peace Corps, U.S. government agency to help underdeveloped countries established, **Mar. 1, 1961**, by Pres. John F. Kennedy [May 29, 1917—Nov. 22, 1963]; joined with ACTION, U.S. federal agency to coordinate all volunteer programs, **1971**.

Pea Ridge (Elkhorn Tavern), battle of, Union forces won first decisive victory w. of Mississippi during U.S. Civil War, **Mar. 6—8, 1862**.

Pearl Harbor, Japanese carrier-based planes attacked, without warning (at 7:55 A.M. local time) U.S. Pacific fleet at Pearl Harbor, Oahu island, Hawaii, **Dec. 7, 1941**; U.S. declared war on Japan, **Dec. 8, 1941**.

Peasants' Revolt, English farm and city workers and proletarians under Wat Tyler [?—June 15, 1381] revolted against repressive wages, poll tax, and landlords' manorial rights, **June 1381**; rebels captured Tower of London, **June 14**; Tyler murdered, **June 15, 1381**.

Peasants' War, revolt of the peasants in central and s. Germany, **1524—26**; peasants' forces crushed by the army of the Swabian League, **1525**.

Peel Commission, British government commission investigated conflict between Arabs and Jews in Palestine, **Oct. 1936— Jan. 1937**; commission's report recommended partition of Palestine into Jewish, Arab, and British states, **July 8, 1937**; report adopted by Zionists, **Aug. 2, 1937**, but not Arabs.

Peking, Edict of, China forbade the importation of opium, **1796**.

Peking man, prehistoric species of man who appeared on Earth at same time as Java man, **c. 500,000** years ago.

Pelee, Mt., volcanic eruption of Mt. Pelee wiped out entire city of St. Pierre on island of Martinique, West Indies, killing approx. 40,000, **May 8, 1902**.

Peloponnesian League, confederation of Greek city-states dominated by Sparta; rivaled first Delian League, **c. 560-404 B.C.**

Peloponnesian War, struggle for power in ancient Greece between Athens and Sparta, **431-404 B.C.**; Spartans captured Athenian cities, including Olynthus and Amphipolis, **424 B.C.**; Athens suffered heavy loss during expedition against Syracuse, **413 B.C.**; Alcibiades [c. 450—404 B.C.] destroyed Spartan fleet at Cyzicus, **410 B.C.**; new Spartan fleet under Lysander wiped out Athenian navy at Aegospotamos, **405 B.C.**; Athens capitulated, **404 B.C.**

Peltier thermoelectric effect, discovered, **1834**, by French physicist Jean C. A. Peltier [1785—1845].

P.E.N., international association of poets, playwrights, editors, essayists, and novelists, founded London, **1921**.

Pendleton Act, U.S. Congress reformed civil service, setting up Civil Service Commission and testing system for civil service appointees, **Jan. 16, 1883**.

pendulum, first designed, **1657**, by Dutch scientist Christian Huygens [1629—1695].

pendulum, gridiron, invented, **1726**, by English clockmaker John Harrison [1693—1776].

pendulum, isochronous property of, discovered, **1581**, by Italian physicist Galileo Galilei [1564—1642].

pendulum, mercury-vial, invented, **1711**, by English mechanician George Graham [1673—1751].

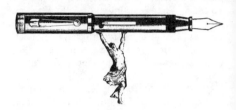

pen, fountain, patented, **1884**, by American inventor Lewis E. Waterman [1837—1901].

pencil, mechanical, invented, **1915**, by Japanese engineer Tokuji Hayakawa.

penicillin, discovered, **1928**, by British bacteriologist Sir Alexander Fleming [1881—1935]; became therapeutically feasible antibiotic, **1943**.

Peninsular Campaign, military campaign in U.S. Civil War, in which Union forces under Gen. George McClellan failed to capture Richmond, Va., by way of peninsula between York and James rivers, **Apr.— July 1862**.

Peninsular War, military engagements fought between French and British, aided by Spanish and Portuguese, on Iberian Peninsula during Napoleonic Wars, **1808—14**; British defeated French at Vimeiro, **Aug. 21, 1808**; French under Napoleon seized Madrid, **Dec. 3, 1808**; French defeated at Talavera, **July 27—29, 1809**; French defeated at Fuentes de Onoro, **May 5, 1811**; British routed French at Vitoria, **June 21, 1813**; war ended on news of Napoleon's abdication, **Apr. 12, 1814**.

Pennsylvania, one of Thirteen Colonies, ratified U.S. Constitution to become second state of the Union, **Dec. 12, 1787**.

Pennsylvania, University of, first founded as a charity school, **1740**; school turned into an academy by Benjamin Franklin [Jan. 17, 1706—Apr. 17, 1790], **1751**; academy chartered as college, **1755**; College of Philadelphia joined to form first U.S. university, **1791**; established first U.S. business school (Wharton School of Finance and Commerce), **1881**.

Pennsylvania Coal Tax, U.S. Supreme Court upheld right of states to levy tax on goods before such goods enter interstate commerce, **Nov 27, 1922**.

Pennsylvania Railroad, U.S. company established single-track line from Philadelphia to Pittsburgh, **1854**; expanded between East Coast and Mississippi, **1870—80**; merged with New York Central RR to form Penn Central, **1968**.

Penruddock uprising, Cromwell crushed royalist uprising against Puritan government at Salisbury and divided England into 12 military districts, **Mar.—May 1655**.

Pentagon Papers, publication of U.S. top secret government study of U.S. involvement in Southeast Asia begun in *New York Times*, **June 13, 1971**; *Times'* right to publish articles on papers upheld by U.S. Supreme Court, **June 30, 1971**; Daniel Ellsberg [Apr. 7, 1931-], government official who leaked papers to *Times*, arraigned on charges of possession of secret documents, **June 28, 1971**; federal judge dropped all charges against Ellsberg, **May 11, 1973**.

Pentateuch, The, name used to designate first five books of Old Testament, written down, between **850—43 B.C.**.

Pentland Hills, battle of, English royalist army routed Scots at Pentland Hills in Scotland, crushing revolt by Scottish Covenanters, **Nov. 28, 1666**.

Pepsi-Cola, invented, **1893**, by American druggist Caleb B. Brabham in New Bern, North Carolina.

Pequot War, settlers in Connecticut River valley defeated Pequot Indians, avenging murder of English trader by Pequots, **1636-37**.

perfusion pump, early artificial heart mechanism invented, **1936**, by French-American surgeon Alexis Carrel [1873-

1944] with American aviator Charles A. Lindbergh [1902-1974].

Pergamum (Pergamon, Pergamus, Pergamos), ancient city in Asia Minor, great center of Hellenistic civilization, **3rd-2nd century B.C.**, noted for its large library and splendid sculpture; Attalus I [d. 197 B.C.] defeated Galatians and established kingdom, **230 B.C.**; King Attalus III [d. 133 B.C.] bequeathed kingdom of Pergamum to Rome, **133 B.C.**

periodic law, (in chemistry) developed independently, **1869**, by Russian chemist Dmitri Mendeleev [1834-1907] and in **1863** (published **1870**) by German chemist Julius Lothar Meyer [1830-1895].

peripatetic school, school of philosophy, founded **c. 335 B.C.**, by Greek philosopher Aristotle.

periscope, invented, **1865**, by German optician Adolph Steinheil [1832-1893].

pernicious anemia, therapy (liver extract treatment) discovered, **1926**, by American physicians George R. Minot [1855-1950], William P. Murphy [1892-], and George H. Whipple [1878-1976].

Peronista Party (Peronistas), Col. Juan D. Peron [Oct. 8, 1895-July 1, 1974] elected president of Argentina, **Feb. 24, 1946**, and his supporters, the Peronista Party, gained control of assembly, **Dec. 5, 1948**; dictatorial regime under Peron and his wife Eva ("Evita") Duarte de Peron [May 7, 1919-July 26, 1952] until overthrown by military coup, **Sept. 19, 1955**; Peron, after 18 year exile, reelected president, **Sept. 23, 1973**, and was succeeded by his third wife, Maria Estela (Isabel) Martinez de Peron [Feb. 6, 1931-], **July 1, 1974**, who became Western Hemisphere's first woman head of state until ousted by military junta, **Mar. 24, 1976**.

perpetual motion, "explained," **c. 590 B.C.**, by Greek mathematician and philosopher Anaximander [611 B.C.-547 B.C.].

Perry Como Show, The, television musical variety show, **1948-63**.

Perry Mason, fictional detective, created, **1932**, in *The Case of the Velvet Claws*, by U.S. mystery novelist Erle Stanley Gardner [July 17, 1889-May 11, 1970].

Persian Wars, series of conflicts between Greek city-states and Persian Empire, **500-**

449 B.C.; Persians suppressed revolt of Greek Ionian states, **494 B.C.**; Persians failed to annex all of Greece when storm crippled Persian fleet, **492 B.C.**; Athenians stopped Persians at Marathon, **Sept. 12, 490 B.C.**; Spartans held off Persian army at Thermopylae, **480 B.C.**; Persian fleet defeated at Salamis, **480 B.C.**; Athenian-Spartan army won at Plataea, **479 B.C.**; Greek-Ionian navy routed Persians at Mycale, **479 B.C.**

personality psychology, theory established, **1937**, by American psychologist Gordon W. Allport [1897-1967].

Person to Person, pioneer television interview show, **1953-61**; through most of its life program hosted by U.S. broadcast journalist Edward R(oscoe) Murrow [Apr. 25, 1908-Apr. 27, 1965].

Peru, country on w. coast of South America, proclaimed its independence from Spain, **July 28, 1821**; achieved its independence after defeat of Spanish at Ayacucho, **Dec. 9, 1824**; joined Bolivia in unsuccessful War of the Pacific against Chile, **1879-84**; dispute with Chile over Tacna-Arica, **1883-1929**.

Perusia (Perugia), battle of, Roman forces of Octavian defeated those of Marc Anthony's wife Fulvia [d. 40 B.C.] at Perusia, **40 B.C.**.

Peruvian earthquakes, great, Peru and Ecuador both rocked by violent quakes; approx. 25,000 killed, **Aug. 13-15, 1868**; north Peru devastated by quake; approx. 65, 000 killed, **May 31, 1970**.

Peshtigo fire, great, more than one million acres of forest and approx 1800 persons killed in fire that totally destroyed the community of Peshtigo, Wis., **Oct. 8-9, 1871**.

Pestalozzi's school, Swiss educational reformer Johann Heinrich Pestalozzi [Jan. 12, 1746-Feb. 17, 1827] conducted his experimental elementary school at Burgdorf, Switzerland, **1799-1804**; transferred to Yverdon, **1805-25**.

Peter and the Wolf, symphonic fairy tale, **1936**, by Russian composer Sergei Prokofiev; produced as ballet, **1940**, New York.

Peterloo massacre (Manchester massacre), public disturbance **Aug. 16, 1819**, by about 60,000, petitioning for repeal of England's corn laws and reform of parliament, charged by cavalry.

Peter Pan, whimsical children's drama, **1904**, by Scottish playwright Sir James M. Barrie.

Petersburg, battle of, long military battle at Petersburg, Va., during U.S. Civil War, **June 15, 1864-Apr. 3, 1865**.

Peterwardein, battle of, Holy Roman Empire forces defeated Turkish forces at Peterwardein on Danube River, **Aug. 5, 1716**.

petroleum, first shown to be mixture of hydrocarbons, **1855**, by American chemist Benjamin Silliman [1816-1885].

Petropolis, Treaty of, Bolivia ceded rich rubber-producing district of Acre to Brazil in return for rail and water outlets eastward, **Nov. 17, 1903**.

Peyton Place, best-selling novel, **1956**, by U.S. writer Grace Metalious [Sept. 8, 1924-Feb. 25, 1964]; made into popular television series, **1964-69**.

PGA championship, annual golf tournament, inaugurated by Professional Golfers Association at Siwanoy course in Bronxville, N.Y., **Apr. 10, 1916**.

Phaedo, philosophical dialogue, **c. 380 B.C.**, by Greek philosopher Plato.

phagocytes, (in immunity), announced, **1887**, by Russian physiologist Elie Metchnikoff [1845-1916].

Phantom of the Opera, The, film, **1925**, classic silent thriller; memorable Lon Chaney role; remade, with sound, **1943**; remade again, **1962**.

Pharisees, ancient Jewish school or party, founded, **c. 425 B.C.**, in time of Second Temple.

Pharos, ancient lighthouse, built, **c. 250 B.C.**, for Port of Alexandria, Egypt; one of ancient Seven Wonders of the World; destroyed in Roman invasion, **47 B.C.**

Pharsalus (Pharsalia), battle of, by brilliant tactics, Julius Caesar's legions routed Pompey's cavalry at Pharsalus in Thessaly, Greece, **Aug. 9, 48 B.C.**

phasotron, frequency modulated cyclotron, proposed, **1945,** by Soviet physicist Vladimir I. Veksler [1907-1966].

Phedre, French tragedy, **1677,** a drama by Jean Racine, based on *Euripides*.

phenol, structure of, theory developed, **1956,** by English organic chemist, Derek H.R. Barton [1918-].

Phenomenology, modern school of philosophy, flourished, **1900-50**; leading exponent: Austrian philosopher Edmund Husserl [Apr. 8, 1859-Apr. 26, 1938]

Phi Beta Kappa, oldest U.S. Greek-letter society established, **Dec. 5, 1776,** at College of William and Mary, Williamsburg, Va.; became honorary society for students with high academic standing, **1831.**

Philadelphia, (Penn.), city founded as Quaker colony by William Penn [Oct. 14, 1644-July 30, 1718], **Oct. 27, 1862**; seat of Continental Congress, **1774-89**; capital of U.S., **1790-1800.**

Philadelphia, College of, first professional medical school in America founded at Philadelphia, Penn., **1765**; affiliated with Benjamin Franklin's university to become the renamed University of Pennsylvania, **1791.**

Philadelphia-Lancaster Turnpike, one of America's first successful toll roads built between Philadelphia and Lancaster, Penn., **1792-94.**

Philadelphia Story, The, by U.S. playwright Philip Barry [June 18, 1896-Dec. 3, 1949]; film, **1940** with memorable roles by Katharine Hepburn, Cary Grant, James Stewart, and Ruth Hussey [Oct. 30, 1917-].

Philadelphia Zoological Gardens, first public zoo opened in U.S., **1874.**

Philemon, Letter of Paul to, New Testament book, probably written, Rome, **62.**

Philhellenism, strong European movement in Germany, France, Great Britian and Switzerland in support of Greek war of independence against Turkish control, **1821-30.**

Philippi, battles of, Roman legions under Octavian (Augustus Caesar) and Anthony defeated legions of Brutus and Cassius at Philippi in Macedonia, **Oct. 27, 42 B.C.**; Union forces routed Confederates at Philippi in present-day West Virginia in first land battle of U.S. Civil War, **June 3, 1861.**

Philippine Government Act, U.S. Congress declared, **July 1, 1902,** Philippine Islands an unorganized territory, setting up a commission to govern it.

Philippines, island nation off southeast coast of Asia, achieved complete independence, **July 4, 1946.**

Philippolis (Plodiv), former capital of Eastern Rumelia, **1878-85**; annexed by Bulgaria after revolt, **Sept. 18, 1885.**

Philippopolis, battle of, Franks defeated the Bulgars at Philippopolis, **1208.**

Phillipians, Letter to the, New Testament book, probably written, Rome, **63,** by St. Paul while a prisoner.

Philomelion, battle of, Byzantine cavalry overpowered Seljuk Turkish bowmen at Philomelion (Aksehir) in central Asia Minor, **1116.**

Philosophes, French Enlightenment thinkers, flourished **1720-1800,** who believed reason ought to be supreme guide in human affairs.

Phoenicia, ancient territory in e. Mediterranean, centered around Tyre and Sidon, **3rd-2nd mil. B.C.**; centered at Crete, **c. 2000-1250 B.C.**; sent navigators, traders, and explorers possibly around Africa, **7th century B.C.**

Phoenix, world's first seagoing steamboat

launched, **1809**, by American inventor John Stevens [1749-1838].

phonograph, invented, **1877**, by American inventor Thomas A. Edison [1847-1931].

phonograph, electric, developed, **1929**, by American engineer H.C. Harrison of Western Electric Co.

phonograph records, flat, invented, **1887**, by German-American inventor Emile Berliner [1851-1929].

phosphorus, element No. 15; discovered, **1669**, by German chemist Hennig Brand [fl c. 1670].

phosphorus matches, invented, **1852**, by English industrial chemist Arthur Albright [1811-1900].

photocell, first practical photocell constructed, **1895**, by German physicists Julius Elster [1854-1920] and Hans F. Geitel [1855-1923].

photocopy machine, invented, **1900**, by French inventor Rene Graffin.

photoelectric cell, first practical model developed, **1904**, by German physicists Julius Elster [1854-1920] and Hans F. Geitel [1855-1923].

photoelectric effect, discovered, **1905**, by German physicist Albert Einstein [1879-1955].

photo-etching, (metal plate), patented, **1852**, by English pioneer in photography W.H. Fox Talbot [1800-1877].

photograph, (on pewter), first successful use of bitumen coated pewter, **1826**, by French physicist Joseph N. Niepce [1765-1833].

photography, Kirlian, discovered, **1939**, by Russian electrician, Semyon D. Kirlian; developed with wife, Valentina C. Kirlian; process introduced in U.S., late **1960s.**

photograph (on paper), first retained on sensitized paper, c. **1790**, by English physicist Thomas Wedgwood [1771-1805].

photographic dry plates, process perfected, **1880**, by American inventor George Eastman [1854-1932].

photographic film, patented, **1898**, by American inventor Hannibal W. Goodwin [1822-1900].

photographic flash, first used, **1851**, by English pioneer in photography W.H. Fox Talbot [1800-1877]; utilized electric sparks.

photographic paper, sensitized, invented, **1898**, by American chemist Leo H. Baekeland [1863-1944].

photography, high-speed strobe flash, equipment developed, c. **1960**, by American engineer Harold E. Edgerton [1903-].

photography, subatomic particle, method devised, **1946**, by British physicist Cecil B. Powell [1903-1969].

photon, discovered and named, **1905**, by German-American physicist Albert Einstein.

photosynthesis, principle discovered, c. **1950**, by American biochemist Melvin Calvin [1911-].

phototypesetting machine, invented, **1945**, by American inventors E. G. Klingberg, Fritz Stadelmann, and H.R. Freund.

phrenology, theory advanced, **1800**, by German anatomist Franz J. Gall [1758-1828].

Phrygia, ancient kingdom of central Asia Minor inhabited by the Phrygians, c. **1000-700 B.C.**; overrun by Lydians, Gauls, and Romans, after **700 B.C.**

pH value, measure of acidity devised, **1909**, by Danish biochemist Soren P.L. Sorensen [1868-1939].

physics, high pressure, pioneering work published, **1931**, by American physicist Percy W. Bridgeman [1882-1961].

piano, keyboard instrument utilizing hammers that strike strings, invented, **1711**, by Italian harpsichord maker Bartolomeo Cristofori [May 4, 1665-Jan. 27, 1731], who produced instrument with four-octave range, **1720**.

Pichincha, battle of, revolutionary army under Antonio Jose de Sucre [Feb. 3, 1795-June 4, 1830] won major battle against Spanish royalists at Pichincha, assuring the independence of Ecuador, **May 24, 1822**.

Pickett's charge, Gen. George E. Pickett's Confederate division made famous charge, on Union center on Cemetery Hill during battle of Gettysburg, which ended in annihilation for his division, **July 3, 1863**. See **Gettysburg, battle of.**

picture press, two revolution, invented, **1867**, by American press manufacturer Andrew Campbell [1821-1890].

Pickwick Papers, novel, **1836-37**, by Victorian English novelist Charles Dickens.

Pictures at an Exhibition, collection of impressionistic "pictures" for piano, **1874**, by Russian composer Modest Mussorgsky.

Piers Plowman, epic morality poem, c. **1362-87**, pre-Chaucerian English poet William Langland [c. 1330-c. 1400].

Pieta, world-famous statue, **1497-99**, of dead Christ in Virgin Mary's arms; early work that made reputation of Italian Renaissance master Michelangelo Buonarotti; damaged by crazed man, **1972**.

Pig War, economic conflict between Serbia and Austria over tariffs. especially on pigs and other food, **1905-1907**.

Pikes Peak, discovered by and named after U.S. explorer Zebulon M. Pike [Jan. 5, 1779-Apr. 27, 1813], **1806**.

piledriver, steam, invented, **1845**, by Scottish engineer James Naysmyth [1808-1890].

Pilgrim's Progress, allegory, **1678**, by English preacher and author John Bunyan.

Pillnitz, Declaration of, Holy Roman Emperor Leopold II and Frederick William II of Prussia called on European powers to help restore Louis XVI to French throne, **Aug. 27, 1791**.

Pilsen (Plzen), old city in Bohemia, stronghold of Catholicism during Hussite Wars, **15th century**; Austrian army captured city, thwarting Catholic plans to take Prague during Thirty Years' War, **Nov. 1-2, 1618**; seized by Germany and made German armament center in WW II, **1939-45**.

pi-meson, discovered, **1947**, by British physicist Cecil F. Powell [1903-1969].

Pinckney Draught, Charles Pinckney [Oct. 26, 1757-Oct. 29, 1824] submitted plan for U.S. Constitution that had considerable effect on final draft by Confederation Congress; exact provisions unknown, **1787**.

ping-pong diplomacy, U.S. policy to establish friendly foreign relations with mainland China, began at world table tennis championships in Japan, **Apr. 6, 1971**, and continued at exhibitions in Peking, **Apr. 13, 1971**.

Pinkham Vegetable Compound, (patent medicine) first produced, **1875**, by American reformer Lydia E. Pinkham [1819-1883].

pin-making machine, invented, **1824**, by American inventor L. W. Wright.

pin-making machine, rotary, patented, **1841**, by American physician-inventor John I. Howe [1793-1876].

Pinocchio, The Adventures of (Le Avventure di Pinocchio), children's story, **1883**, by Italian writer Carlo Collodi (pseud. of Carlo Lorenzini) [Nov. 24, 1826-Oct. 26, 1890]; film, **1940**, a Walt Disney production.

Piqua, Council of, Christopher Gist, agent for the Grand Ohio Company, made peace with the Miami Indians in the Scioto River valley, **1751**.

Pirates of Penzance, The, comic opera, **1878**, perennially popular work by English opera-writing team Gilbert and Sullivan.

Pirot, battles of, Bulgarians defeated Serbians at Pirot, Serbia, **Nov. 27, 1885**, but Austrian intervention forced Bulgarians to make peace, **Mar. 3, 1886**; Bulgarians seized Pirot during WW I, **Oct. 28, 1915**.

piston pump, flexible (fire engine), patented, **1817**, by American inventor Samuel F. B. Morse [1791-1872].

pitch (in sound), standardization first proposed, **c. 1700**, by French physicist Joseph Sauveur [1653-1716].

Pithecanthropus erectus, discovered, **1892**, by Dutch physician-paleontologist Eugene Du Bois [1858-1940].

Plague, The (La Peste), novel, **1947**, by French writer and philosopher Albert Camus; Nobel laureate, **1957**.

planetary distances, relationships of, numerically described, **1766**, by German mathematician Johann D. Titius [1729-1796], according to the size of individual planet's orbit.

planetary motion, Kepler's laws of, announced, **1609** and **1619**, by German astronomer Johannes Kepler [1571-1630].

planetary motions, earliest explanation, **c. 370 B.C.**, by Greek scholar Eudoxus [c. 409-353 B.C.].

Planned Parenthood Federation of America, U.S. non-profit organization established, **1916**.

Plantagenets, Angevin dynasty of English kings from the accession of Henry II [Mar. 25, 1133-July 6, 1189] to the House of Tudor, **1154-1485**.

GEOFFREY PLANTAGENET

plant cells, first described, **1665**, by English scientist Robert Hooke [1635-1703].

plant name classification, first proposed, **1583**, by Italian botanist Andrea Cesalpino [1519-1603].

plants, sex of, first explained, **c. 1730**, by Swedish botanist Carolus Linnaeus [1707-1778].

plasma torch, invented, **1958**, by American engineer Merle L. Thorpe [1930-].

plasmolysis, study introduced, **c. 1885**, by Dutch botanist Hugo De Vries [1848-1935].

Plassey, battle of, British under Robert Clive [Sept. 29, 1725-Nov. 22, 1774] won major victory over army of nawab of Bengal, assuring British control of n.e. India and making Clive master of Bengal, **June 23, 1757**.

Plata, Rio de la, large estuary between Argentina and Uruguay discovered by Amerigo Vespucci, **c. 1501**; explored by Ferdinand Magellan, **1520**; first Spanish settlement on its banks at Buenos Aires, established by Pedro de Mendoza [c. 1487-1537], **1536**; viceroyalty established by Spanish, **1776**.

Plataea, battles of, Greeks under Pausanias [d. c. 470 B.C.] won major victory over Persians at Plataea in s. Boeotia, **479 B.C.**; Spartans besieged and forced Plataean-Athenian force to surrender during Peloponnesian War, **429-27 B.C.**

platinum, element No. 78; discovered, **1735**, by Spanish scientist Don Antonio de Ulloa; discovered independently, **1741**, by English metallurgist Charles Wood.

Platt Amendment, U.S. Congress informed Cuba, **Mar. 2, 1901**, that U.S. troops would not be withdrawn until new Cuban constitution was amended; Cuba became unofficial protectorate of U.S., **June 12, 1901**; U.S. troops withdrew from Cuba, **May 20, 1902**; abrogated **May 29, 1934**.

Plattsburgh, battle of, American fleet under Thomas Macdonough won decisive battle against British on Lake Champlain near Plattsburgh, N.Y., **Sept. 11, 1814**.

Pleasant Hill, battle of, Confederate troops tried unsuccessfully to halt the advance of Union troops of Gen. Nathaniel P. Banks [Jan. 30, 1816- Sept. 1, 1894] at Pleasant Hill, La., **Apr. 9, 1864**.

Plei Me, battle of, U.S.-South Vietnamese

forces held off massive assault by Viet Cong and North Vietnamese troops at Plei Me near Cambodian border during Vietnam War, **Oct. 19-27, 1965**.

Pleven (Plevna), battle of, Russian-Rumanian forces besieged Turkish-held fortress of Pleven; Turkish breakout failed and Ottoman Turks surrendered, **July 20-Dec. 11, 1877**.

Plough and the Stars, The, play, **1926**, about struggle of leader of Dublin Rebellion of 1915-16, by Irish-Renaissance playwright Sean O'Casey.

plow, cast-iron, first U.S. patented, **1797**, by American inventor Charles Newbold, of Burlington, N.J.; improved version, patented, **1819**, by American inventor Jethro Wood [1774-1834].

plow, moldboard, invented, **1793**, by American statesman-scientist Thomas Jefferson [1743-1826].

plow, steel moldboard, first developed, **1846**, by American inventor John Deere [1804-1886].

Pluto (planet), discovered, **1930**, by U.S. astronomer Clyde W. Tombaugh [1906-].

plutonium, element No. 94, discovered, **1940**, by American chemist Glenn T. Seaborg [1912-] and American physicist Edwin M. McMillan [1907-].

Plymouth Colony, settlement established by Pilgrims on coast at present-day Plymouth, Mass., **Dec. 26, 1620**; made peace treaty with Wampanoag Indians that lasted for 50 years, **1621**; joined New England Confederation, **1643**; joined other colonies to form royal colony of Massachusetts, **1691**.

Plymouth Rock, landing place of the Pilgrims of the *Mayflower* in Plymouth harbor, **Dec. 21, 1620**.

pneumatic caisson, developed, **c. 1867**, by American engineer James B. Eads [1820-1887].

pneumatic hammer, patented, **1890**, by American inventor Charles B. King.

pneumatic tire, automobile, developed, **1895**, by French inventors Andre Michelin [1853-1931], and Edouard Michelin [1859-1940].

pneumatic tire, bicycle, invented, **c. 1887**, by Scottish veterinary surgeon John B. Dunlop [1840-1921].

pneumatic tire, carriage, patented, **1845**, by English inventor Robert W. Thomson [1822-1873]; used on horse-drawn carriage.

Poetics, treatise, written, **c. 335-322 B.C.**, by Greek philosopher Aristotle; first printed as separate treatise, **1536**; influential for modern drama.

Poetry: A Magazine of Verse, American literary magazine, founded, Chicago, **1912**.

pogroms, violent attacks or massacres of the Jews in Russia, **1881-82**; **1903-21**; in Germany and Poland when Hitler came to power, **1933-45**.

Point Pleasant, battle of, one of bloodiest battles fought in Indian wars east of Mississippi; Virginian frontiersmen routed Shawnees at Point Pleasant in present-day West Virginia; Indian power in west colonial territory broken, **Oct. 9, 1774**.

poisoning, lead, first published account, **1735**, by American physician Thomas Cadwalader [1707-1799].

Poitiers, battle of, English longbowmen under Edward, the Black Prince [1330-76] slaughtered French knights at Poitiers during Hundred Years' War; King John II [1319-64] of France captured, **Sept. 17, 1356**.

Poland, Partitions of, three successive partitions that eliminated Poland from the map; first partition among Austria, Russia, and Prussia, **Aug. 5, 1772**; second between Russia and Prussia, **Jan. 23, 1793**; third among Austria, Russia, and Prussia, **Oct. 24, 1795**.

polar-front, theory developed, from **1919**, by Norwegian meteorologist Jacob Bjerknes [1897-].

polarization (of light), discovered, **1811**, by French physicist Dominique Francois Jean Arago [1786-1853].

polarography, invented, **c. 1950**, by Polish chemist Iaroslav Heyrovsky [1890-1967]; electrochemical method of analysis.

Polaroid lens, invented, **1932**, by American inventor Edwin H. Land [1909-].

Polianov, Treaty of, ended two-year Russian-Polish war, **1634**.

polio virus, technique for growing the virus discovered, **1948**, by American microbiologists John F. Enders [1897-], Frederick C. Robbins [1916-] and American physician Thomas H. Weller [1915-].

polio vaccine, (see Salk polio vaccine).

Polish National Uprising, Poles led by Thaddeus Kosciuszko [Feb. 12, 1746-Oct. 15, 1817] rebelled unsuccessfully against Prussian and Russian domination, **Mar. 24, 1794**.

Polish revolt against Russia, great, revolt by Polish patriots against Russian rule of Czar Nicholas I [May 18, 1868-July 17, 1918], crushed at Warsaw, **Feb. 20 -Sept. 8, 1831**.

Polish Succession, War of the, general European war over ascendancy to Polish throne, sought by Stanislaus I [Oct. 20, 1677-Feb. 23, 1766], **1733-35**; Spanish troops seized Naples and Sicily, **1734**; truce obtained through dynastic reshuffle, **1735**.

Politics, eight-book treatise, written down, **c. 340-20 B.C.**, by ancient Greek philosopher Aristotle.

Polka, dance in quick double meter, with characteristic rhythms, originated **c. 1830**, in Bohemia.

Pollentia, battle of, Romans under Flavius Stilicho [d. 408] forced Visigoths under Alaric [c. 370-410] to retreat on Easter day, **Mar. 29, 403**.

Polonaise, Polish national dance of formal, stately character, with music in triple meter; originated, **1600s**; form perfected, **c. 1800**; developed especially from **c. 1835**.

Poltava, battle of, Russian army of Peter I ("the Great") defeated Swedish army of Charles XII at Poltava in the Ukraine; one of most decisive battles of history, ending Swedish military power forever and beginning Russian strength in e. Europe, **July 8, 1709**.

Polyeucte, tragedy, **1641**, by French tragic dramatist Pierre Corneille.

polygraph (lie detector), invented, **1921**, by Canadian-American John A. Larson [1892-].

polymer research, statistical method developed from **1930s**, by American chemist Paul J. Flory [1910-].

Pomp and Circumstance, five concert marches for orchestra, first four composed, **1901-07**, fifth, **1930**, by English composer Sir Edward Elgar.

Pompeii, ancient Roman city buried by volcanic eruption of Mt. Vesuvius, **Aug. 24, 79**; discovery of ancient ruins, **1748**.

Pondicherry, battle of, British and sepoy troops forced French-held garrison at Pondicherry on India coast to surrender during Seven Years' War, **Jan. 10, 1761**.

Pontiac's Rebellion (Pontiac's Conspiracy), Indians in Ohio-Great Lakes region, led by Ottawa chief Pontiac [c. 1720-Apr. 20, 1769] destroyed British forts and settlements, protesting British ownership of Indian lands, **1763-66**; Pontiac made peace and accepted British rule, **July 25, 1766**.

Pony Express, U.S. mail carried by riders on ponies from St. Joseph, Mo., to Sacramento, Calif., **Apr. 1860-Oct. 1861**.

Poor People's Campaign, U.S. civil rights campaign, **May-June 1968**.

Poor Richard's Almanac, composite

name given almanacs issued, **1732-57**, by Benjamin Franklin.

pop art, school of U.S. artists, flourished **1960-70**, noted for meticulous recreation of "artificial" environment of mass-produced objects, advertising, etc..

Popham Colony, two English ships, the *Gift of God* and the *Mary and John*, led by George Popham [c. 1550-1608], landed at the mouth of Sagadahoc (now Kennebec) River, Me., to establish colony, **Aug. 19, 1607**; Popham died that winter and colony abandoned, summer **1608**.

Popish Plot, the, Jesuit-guided plan to assassinate King Charles II of England; fabricated by Titus Oates [1649-July 12, 1705], **Sept. 1678**.

Popular Unity Party, Salvador Allende Gossens [July 26, 1908-Sept. 11, 1973], head of Popular Unity Party, supported by Socialist-Communist coalition, elected president of Chile, **Oct. 24, 1970**, to become first Marxist elected head of state in Western Hemisphere; Allende died during successful military coup, **Sept. 11, 1973**.

Populist (People's) Party, U.S. political party formed, **May 19, 1891**, by farmers and others in Cincinnati, Ohio; nominated James B. Weaver [June 12, 1833-Feb. 6, 1912] for presidency, **July 4, 1892**; party dissolved, after **1896**.

Porgy and Bess, opera, **1935**, by U.S. composer George Gershwin.

Port Arthur (Lu-shun), Russian naval base at tip of Liao-tung peninsula (China) attacked without warning by Japanese, precipitating Russo-Japanese War, **Feb. 8, 1904**; city of Port Arthur passed to Japan by Treaty of Portsmouth, **Sept. 5, 1905**; China took control again, **1955**.

Port Gibson, battle of, advance guard of Gen. Ulysses S. Grant's Union army forced Confederates to retreat during campaign near Vicksburg, Miss., **May 1, 1863**.

Port Hudson, siege of, Union army under Gen. Nathaniel P. Banks [Jan 30, 1816-Sept. 1, 1894], aided by fleet of Admiral David G. Farragut, failed to capture Confederate-held Fort Hudson, La., **Mar. 14, 1863**; Banks failed again, **May 21** and **June 13, 1863**; Confederates at fort surrendered, **July 9, 1863**, with the Union taking control of the Mississippi.

Portland cement, developed, **1824**, by English inventor Joseph Aspdin [1779-1855].

Portobelo (Porto Bello), seaport in Panama, believed impregnable but sacked by English buccaneer Sir Henry Morgan [1635-Aug. 25, 1688], **1688**; captured by English Admiral Edward Vernon [Nov. 12, 1684-Oct. 30, 1757] during War of Jenkin's Ear, **Nov. 22, 1739**.

Portrait of a Lady, novel, **1881**, by U.S.-British novelist Henry James.

Portrait of the Artist as a Young Man, autobiographical novel, **1916**, first major work of Irish expatriate writer James Joyce.

Port Republic, battle of, Confederate army of Gen. Thomas Jackson defeated Union army, burned bridges to halt Union pursuit, and marched to join Gen. Robert E. Lee at Richmond, **June 9, 1862**.

Port Royal (Annapolis Royal), first permanent French colony in Canada established by Pierre du Gua, Sieur de Monts [c. 1560-c. 1630] at Port Royal in Nova Scotia, **1604**; fought over by French and English (town changed hands five times), **1605-1710**; New Englanders captured Port Royal and renamed it Annapolis Royal in honor of Queen Anne, **1710**.

Portsmouth, Treaty of, U.S. Pres. Theodore Roosevelt [Oct. 17, 1858-Jan. 6, 1919] helped end Russo-Japanese War at Portsmouth, N.H., **Sept. 5, 1905**.

positivism, philosophical movement developed from c. **1830**.

positron, discovered **1932**, by U.S. physicist Carl David Anderson [1905-].

Possessed, The (Besy), novel, **1871-72**, by Fyodor Dostoyevsky.

postage meter, first patented, **1902**, by American inventor Arthur H. Pitney [1871-1933]; further developed with American manufacturer Walter H. Bowes [1882-1957]; first U.S. metered mail system, **1920**.

postimpressionism, school of painting, **1890-1910**.

Post Office Department, U.S., Congress organized federal Post Office in U.S., **1795**; federal department created as part of U.S. government, **1829**; airmail service instituted, **1918**.

potassium, element No. 19; discovered, **1807**, by English chemist Sir Humphry Davy [1778-1829].

Potato Famine, Great, blight killed potato crops throughout Europe, especially in Ireland, **1845-48**.

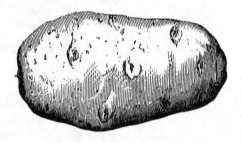

Potato War, campaign during the War of the Bavarian Succession, **1778-79**.

Potawatami (Pottawatomi) Indians, North American tribe living on w. shores of Lake Michigan helped conquer the Illinois Indians, **c. 1765**; took part in the battle of Fallen Timbers, **Aug. 20, 1794**; signed Treaty of Greenville, **Aug. 3, 1795**; many moved to Indian Territory (Oklahoma), **1868**, and became known as Citizen Potawatami.

Potosi silver mines, one of the world's most fabulous sources of silver discovered in s. Bolivia in the high Andes, **1545**.

Pottawatomie Creek massacre, abolitionist John Brown [May 9, 1800-Dec. 2, 1859], with four sons and three others, massacred five proslavery settlers at Pottawatomie Creek, Kans., in retaliation for sack of Lawrence, **May 24, 1856**.

powder, smokeless, invented, **1887**, by French engineer Paul M. Vieille [1854-1934]; adopted by French army.

Powell case, U.S. Representative Adam Clayton Powell, Jr. [Nov. 29, 1908-Apr. 4, 1972] excluded from Congress for alleged misuse of government funds, **Mar. 1, 1967**; Powell reelected in special New York election, **Apr. 11, 1967**; U.S. House voted to reseat him, **Jan. 3, 1969**.

power reactor, gas-cooled, first in U.S. constructed, **1966**, for Philadelphia Electric Co. at Peach Bottom, Pa.

power station, electric, first major station in U.S. developed, **1822**, by American inventor Thomas Edison [1847-1931], at Pearl Street in New York.

Powhatan Confederacy, confederation of about 30 Indian groups in Tidewater area, Va., under chief Powhatan [d. 1618], **17th century**; attacked English colonists, **1622**; resulting in violent English reprisals; ceded much territory, **1646**; ceased to exist after Treaty of Albany, **1722**.

Poynings' law, English privy council must assent to the calling of the Irish parliament and to its laws, enacted by Sir Edward Poynings [1459-1521], **Dec. 1494**; repealed **1782**.

Poznan riot, Polish worker's strike at Poznan for better socio-economic conditions, **June 18, 1956**, spread to other cities in Poland; led to Wladyslaw Gomulka [Feb. 6, 1905-] as first secretary of Polish Communist Party, **Oct. 21, 1956**.

Prague, defenestration of, Protestant Czech nobles threw Bohemian governors from a window in Hradcany Castle, Prague, to protest imperial interference with Czech liberties, **May 23, 1618**.

Prague Spring, Czechoslovakia's Communist government at Prague under Alexander Dubcek, introduced further "democratization" into everyday life, **Apr.-June 1968**.

Prague, Treaty of, resolved difference between Holy Roman Empire and Saxony, which received Lusatia, **May 30, 1635**.

Prague, University of (Charles University), oldest and most important university in central Europe, founded by Holy Roman Emperor Charles IV, **1348**.

Pragmatic Sanction, Holy Roman Emperor Charles VI changed Hapsburg family law, enabling females to succeed to the Austrian possessions, **Apr. 19, 1713**; confirmed by the Treaty of Aix-la-Chapelle, **Oct. 18, 1748.**

praseodymium, element No. 59; discovered, **1885,** by Austrian chemist Baron Carl Auer von Welsbach [1858-1929].

Preakness Stakes, annual American horse race for three-year-old thoroughbreds; first held at Pimlico racetrack, Baltimore, Md., **May 1873.**

pregnancy test, introduced, **1928,** by German obstetricians Selmar Aschheim [1878-1965] and Bernhardt Zondek [1891-]; proved more reliable than test developed by Swiss physiologist Emil Abderhalden [1877-1950], **1912.**

Pre-Raphaelite Brotherhood, association of British painters, from **1848,** inspired by simplicity of Italian painters before Raphael.

Presbyterians, Christian communion in which churches governed by presbyters, developed, from **c. 1560,** especially in Scotland; World Alliance of Reformed and Presbyterian Churches, founded Geneva, **1875.**

Presidential Succession Act, congressional act signed by Pres. Truman, **July 18, 1947.**

pressure cooker, invented, **1679,** by French physicist Denis Papin [1647-1712].

Preston, battles of, invading Scottish army routed by Cromwellian army at Preston in n. England, stopping all resistance against rule of Oliver Cromwell, **Aug. 17-20, 1648;** Jacobites crushed by English royalists at Preston, **Nov. 14, 1715,** See **Civil War, English.**

Prestonpans, battle of, Scottish Highlander Jacobite army routed English royalists at Prestonpans, **Sept. 21, 1745.**

Pretoria, capital of the Transvaal until seized by British in Boer War, **1860-June 5, 1899;** became administrative capital of Union of South Africa, **1910.**

Prevesa, battle of, Ottoman Turks won naval victory over Venetians, **Sept. 1538,** leading to peace treaty with Venice, **1540.**

Pride and Prejudice, novel, **1813,** by English novelist of manners Jane Austen.

Pride's Purge, Thomas Pride [d. 1658], by orders of army council, forcibly expelled Presbyterian members from parliament on grounds they were royalists, **Dec. 6-7, 1648.**

Prince Edward Island, Canadian island and province, first visited by Cartier, **1534;** annexed to Nova Scotia, **1763;** became separate British colony, **1769;** became province of Canada, **July 1, 1873.**

Prince of Wales **and** *Repulse,* **sinking of,** Japanese bombers and torpedo bombers attacked and sank British battleship *Prince of Wales* and battle cruiser *Repulse* in South China Sea, **Dec. 10, 1941.**

Prince, The, (Il Principe), philosophical treatise on statecraft, **1517,** by Italian writer Niccolo Machiavelli.

Princeton, battle of, American revolutionary forces of Gen. George Washington won victory over British during early morning surprise attack at Princeton, N.J., **Jan. 3, 1777.**

Princeton University, old American university chartered, **1746,** by Presbyterian ministers as the College of New Jersey at Elizabethtown; moved to Princeton, N.J., **1756;** became university known as Princeton University, **1896.**

printing, color, first produced, **1457,** by German printers Johann Fust [c. 1400-c. 1466] and Peter Schoeffer [c. 1425-c. 1502].

printing machine (hand), patented, **1843,** by American inventor Charles Thurber [1803-1886]; forerunner of typewriter.

printing press, invented, **c. 1439,** by German printer Johannes Gutenberg [1396-1468].

printing press, cylinder, sheet-fed, invented, **1814,** by German inventor Friedrich Konig [1774-1833].

printing press (hand), *Columbian,* first American, invented, **1817,** by American inventor George E. Clymer [1754-1834].

printing press, web, invented, **1865,** by American printer William Bullock [1813-1867].

procaine (Novocain), introduced as an anesthetic, **1905,** by German surgeon Heinrich F.Braun [1862-1934].

Proclamation of Amnesty and Reconstruction, Pres. Lincoln offered pardon to all Southerners who took loyalty oath, and plan of reconstruction, **Dec. 8, 1863.**

proctoscope, invented, **1877,** by German surgeon Max Nitze [1848-1906].

Profiles in Courage, essays, **1956,** by future President John F. Kennedy; Pulitzer Prize-winner in history, **1957;** dramatized in television series, **1964-65.**

progesterone, hormone isolated, **1934,** by German chemist Adolph Butenandt [1903-].

Progressive Party, three different U.S. political parties; first, also known as Bull Moose Party, nominated Theodore Roosevelt for president, **Aug. 7, 1912;** second called for social and economic reform and nominated Sen. Robert M. La Follette [June 14, 1855-June 18, 1925] for president, **July 4, 1924;** third, made up of Democrats against Pres. Harry S. Truman [May 8, 1884-Dec. 26, 1972], nominated Henry A. Wallace [Oct. 7, 1888-Nov. 18, 1965] for president, **July 24, 1948.**

Prohibition, prevention of the manufacture and sale of liquor in U.S., **1919-33;** Volstead Act forbade liquor traffic, **Oct. 28, 1919;** ended by Twenty-first Amendment, **Dec. 5, 1933.**

Prohibition Party, minor U.S. political party organized **Sept. 1, 1869;** fielded presidential candidates, since **1872.**

Prometheus Bound (Prometheus Desmotes), Greek tragedy, **c. 490-460 B.C.,** by Athenian tragedian Aeschylus.

Prometheus Unbound, lyrical drama, **1820,** by English poet Percy Bysshe Shelley.

promethium, element No. 61; discovered, **1947,** by American scientists at Oak Ridge nuclear research laboratory.

Proposition 13, initiative to cut property taxes in California by 57% to limit government spending, co-sponsored by Howard A. Jarvis [1902-], adopted by 65% majority of state voters, **June 6, 1978.**

protactinium, element No. 91; discovered independently, **1917,** by Austrian-Swedish physicist Lise Meitner [1878-1968] and German physicist Otto Hahan [1879-1968].

Protectorate, English government under the rule of the Cromwells, **1653-59;** Oliver Cromwell as Lord Protector of the Commonwealth of England, Scotland, and Ireland, **Dec. 16, 1653-Sept. 3, 1658;** Richard Cromwell, Oliver's son, Lord Protector, **Sept. 3, 1658-May 25, 1659.**

protein, composition of, first explained, **1882,** by German chemist Emil Fischer [1852-1919].

Protestant Episcopal Church, U.S. branch of Anglican Communion, first service held in America at Jamestown, **1607;** first bishop consecrated in America, **1784,** Samuel Seabury [Nov. 30, 1729-Feb. 25, 1796]; independent Communion with own episcopate, from **1789.**

Protestantism, system of Christian faith and practice based on Reformation principles, developed, from **1517**, by Martin Luther and followers and successors; name from "*protestatio*" of reforming members of Diet of Speyer, **1529**.

Protestant Union (Evangelical League), German Protestant states formed defensive alliance against Holy Roman Empire's attempt to restore all former church lands taken by Protestant princes after 1552, **1608-21**.

Proverbs, Book of, Old Testament book, compilation of traditional materials, completed, **c. 300 B.C.**.

Providence, (R.I), colonists from Massachusetts Bay Colony led by Roger Williams [c. 1603-Mar. 1683] established Rhode Island Colony at Providence, **June 1636**; site of Dorr's Rebellion, **Apr. 18, 1842**.

proximity fuse, invented, **c. 1942**, by American physicist James A. Van Allen [1914-] as weapon that utilized reflected radio waves to explode anti-aircraft shell.

Prussian revolt, Prussians, supported by the Poles, battled against the oppressive rule of the Teutonic Knights, **1454**.

Pruth, Treaty of, Ottoman Turks forced Russia's Peter the Great to cede Azov and to allow Charles XII to return to Sweden, **July 21, 1711**.

Psalms, Book of, Old Testament book, collection of some 150 songs in praise of God used in Israelite public worship; compiled by **c. 515 B.C.**.

psalter, common name for psalms translated into vernaculars, often set to music; best-known example: *Geneva Psalter*, published in French, **1562**; English version published, **1564**; Dutch version, **1566**.

Psycho, film, **1960**, about homicidal psychopath operating motel; technically accomplished Alfred Hitchcock film.

psi/J particle, discovered independently, **1974**, by American physicists Burton Richter [1931-] and Samuel C.C. Ting [1936-].

psychoanalysis, method of probing unconcious mind; developed, **1882-1915**, by Austrian physician and thinker Sigmund Freud.

psychology, feminine, pioneered, **c. 1937**, by Norwegian-Dutch psychoanalyst Karen Horney [1885-1952].

psychology laboratory, experimental, first established, **1879**, by German physiologist and psychologist Wilhelm Wundt [1832-1920] in Leipzig.

psychology of set, concept, established, **1904**, by German psychologist Narziss Kaspar Ach [1871-1946].

PTA (Parent Teachers Association), U.S. national organization formed, **1897**.

pterodactyl, extinct flying reptile, discovered, **1871**, by American paleontologist Othniel C. Marsh [1831-1899].

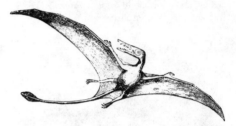

Ptolemies, dynasty of kings of ancient Macedonia and Egypt, **305-30 B.C.**

Public Works Administration, federal agency created by National Recovery Act, **June 16, 1933**, to oversee construction of public works and to make loans to states for similar projects; ceased operations, **Jan. 1, 1947**.

puddling iron furnace, invented, **1784**, by English ironmaster Henry Cort [1740-1800].

Puebla, battle of, Mexican liberal forces defeated French troops and Mexican conservatives at Puebla, central Mexico, **May 5, 1862**.

Pueblo **incident**, North Korean patrol boats captured U.S. intelligence ship *Pueblo* in Sea of Japan, **Jan. 23, 1968**; ship's crew of 83 men subjected to torture during captivity but released, **Dec. 22, 1968**.

Pulitzer Prizes, annual awards, given each May, for outstanding achievement in American journalism, letters, and music; first awarded, **May 1917**.

pulley, invented, **c. 365 B.C.**, by Greek scientist Archytas of Tarentum [400-350 B.C.].

Pullman Palace Car, U.S. manufacturer George Pullman [Mar. 3, 1831-Oct. 19, 1897] introduced first "palace" sleeping car, "The Pioneer," **1865**; introduced first combined sleeping and restaurant car,

1867; first chair car, 1875; first vestibule car, 1887.

Pullman strike, workers at Pullman Palace Car Company in Chicago struck amid much violence, **May 11, 1894;** American Railway Union leader Eugene V. Debs [Nov. 5, 1855-Oct. 20, 1926] ordered sympathy strike, **June 26, 1894;** Pres. Cleveland ordered U.S. troops to Chicago, **July 3, 1894;** Debs indicted for criminal conspiracy and contempt of court, **July 17, 1894;** U.S. troops withdrawn from Chicago, **July 20, 1894;** strike officially ended, **Aug. 3, 1894,** with nothing accomplished.

pulsars, first detected, **1967,** and reported, **1968,** by English astronomers Anthony Hewish [1924-] and Sir Martin Ryle [1918-].

pulse watch, introduced, **1707,** by English physician Sir John Floyer [1649-1734].

Pultusk, battles of, Swedish army of Charles XII crushed Saxon-Polish-Russian forces of Peter I ("the Great"), **May 1, 1703;** inconclusive battle between French under Napoleon and allied Prussians and Russians, **Dec. 26, 1806.**

pump-oxygenator, introduced, **1953,** by American surgeon John H. Gibbon [1903-].

Punch, magazine, published London, from **1841.**

punch card tabulation, invented, **c. 1886,** by American engineer Herman Hollerith [1860-1929], with card holes to represent number code manipulated by machine, patented, **1889.**

Punic Wars, struggles between Rome and Carthage for control of the Mediterranean area; first war, **264-41 B.C.;** Carthaginians under Hannibal [247-183 B.C.] seized Saguntum in Spain, **219 B.C.;** second war (Hannibalic War), **218-201 B.C.;** Hannibal won victories at Ticinus and Trebbia, **218 B.C.;** Hannibal's great victory at Cannae, **Aug. 3, 216 B.C,;** Romans won at Metaurus, **207 B.C.;** Hannibal lost at Zama, **202 B.C.;** third war, **149-46 B.C.;** Carthage razed by Scipio Africanus Minor [c. 185-129 B.C.], **146 B.C.**

Punjab, historic region divided between India and Pakistan on the basis of concentrations of Muslim and Hindu populations, **1947.**

pupil-light reflex, (of eye) discovered, **1751,** by Scottish physician Robert Whytt [1714-1766].

Pure Food and Drug Act, U.S. Congress authorized statement of contents on package labels and forbade sale of adulterated food or drugs, **June 30, 1906;** Federal Food, Drug, and Cosmetic Act strengthened government control over misbanding and false advertising, **June 24, 1938.**

purine, (derivatives of) synthesized, **1898,** by German organic chemist Emil Fischer [1852-1919].

Puritans, extreme Protestant party in England, developed from **c. 1570;** condemned by Queen Elizabeth, **1583** and **1593;** "Puritan Revolution," **1642,** led to temporary triumph reversed by Restoration, **1660.**

Purple Heart, the, decoration first known as the Badge of Military Merit, established by Gen. George Washington at Newburgh, N.Y., **Apr. 7, 1782;** fell in disuse but revived by U.S. War Department as award for soldiers wounded in action or cited for bravery, **Feb. 22, 1932.**

Pusan perimeter, North Koreans drove U.S. 8th Army and South Korean forces back to perimeter around key port of Pusan in Korea; U.S. Army Gen. Walton H.Walker [Dec. 3, 1899-Dec. 23, 1950] checked enemy penetration, **Aug.-Sept. 1950.**

Puteoli, ancient city of s. Italy, founded by Greeks, **c. 520 B.C.;** became famous and very wealthy as Rome's port of entry for Eastern trade, **1st century B.C.-A.D. 3rd century;** destroyed by Germanic raiders, **5th century.**

Pydna, ancient Macedonian town, near which Romans under Aemilius Paullus [c.

229-160 B.C.] defeated Macedonians under King Perseus [c. 212-166 B.C.]; kingdom of Macedon ended, **June 22, 168 B.C.**

Pygmalion, Greek legend of sculptor falling in love with his own statue, told in Ovid's *Metamorphoses*, **5**; retold many times, e.g., in *Earthly Paradises*, **1868-70** by William Morris [Mar. 24, 1834-Oct. 1, 1896]; play **1913**, by George Bernard Shaw; Lerner-Loewe musical, *My Fair Lady*, **1956.**

Pyle Massacre, the, British troops led by Col. Pyle slaughtered during surprise attack by American revolutionaries led by Henry Lee in North Carolina, **Mar. 2, 1781.**

pyramids, designed, **c. 2960 B.C.** by Egyptian physician and architect Imhotep [c. 2980-2950 B.C.] for Pharaoh Zoser [c. 2980-2950 B.C.]

Pyramids, battle of, French under Napoleon defeated Egyptian Mamelukes, allowing Napoleon to seize Cairo during French Revolutionary Wars, **July 21-22, 1798.**

Pyramid, Step, of King Zoser, The, pyramid, Sakkara, Egypt, **c. 2750 B.C..**

Pyramids, The (the Great Pyramids), three massive pyramids at Gizeh, near Cairo, Egypt, built, **2723-2563 B.C.**; one of ancient Seven Wonders of the World.

Pyrenees, Treaty of, Franco-Spanish border was fixed at the Pyrenees; Spain ceded parts of Flanders and Roussillon to France, **Nov. 7, 1659.**

pyrometer, developed, **1780,** by English potter Josiah Wedgwood [1730-1795] for measuring high kiln temperatures.

Qairawan Mosque, mosque, built **670,** Qairawan, Tunisia.

Qait Bey Mosque, mosque, built, Cairo, Egypt, **1436-80.**

Qatar, small state on Persian Gulf, declared itself independent of Britain, **Sept. 1, 1971.**

quadrant, invented, **1730,** by American mathematician Thomas Godfrey [1704-1749]; quadrant, reflecting, invented, **1731,** by English mathematician John Hadley [1682-1744].

quadrille, classical "square" dance, introduced into court of Napoleon I, **c. 1803**; imported into Britain, **1816.**

Quadruple Alliance, Britain, France, Netherlands, and Austria formed alliance to counteract the attempts of Philip V [Dec. 19, 1683-July 9, 1746] of Spain to overturn the peace settlements after the War of the Spanish Succession, **Aug. 2, 1718**; Britain, Russia, Prussia, and Austria formed alliance to reinforce coalition against Napoleon I, **Mar. 1814.**

Quakers, members of Society of Friends, founded, **c. 1652,** by English pacifist and anti-slavery religious leader George Fox.

quantum electrodynamics, theory won Nobel prize in physics, **1965,** for Japanese physicist Sin-Itiro Tomonaga [1906-1979]. Concurrent research done by American physicists Richard P. Feynman [1918-] and Julian S. Schwinger [1918-].

quantum mechanics, mathematical formulas developed, **c. 1920,** by German-British physicist Max Born [1882-1970] for motion and position of electrons.

quantum theory, developed, **1900,** by German physicist Max Planck [1858-1947].

quark, type of subatomic particle; existence postulated, **1961,** by American physicist Murray Gell-Mann [1929-].

Quartering Act, British parliament required American colonists to provide food and lodging for British troops, **Mar. 24, 1765**; discontinued, **Apr. 12, 1770.**

Quarterly Review, The, famous British literary periodical, founded **1809,** as rival to *Edinburgh Review.*

quartz crystals, electromechanical effects first studied, **c. 1880,** by French chemists Pierre Curie [1859-1906] and Marie Curie [1867-1934].

quaternions, discovered, **1843,** by Irish

mathematician Sir William R. Hamilton [1805-1865].

Quatre Bras, battle of, British forces under duke of Wellington defeated French under Marshal Michel Ney [Jan. 10, 1769-Dec. 7, 1815], **June 16, 1815.**

Quebec, Canadian province, first visited by Cartier on the Gaspe peninsula, **1634;** British gained control of region from France after French and Indian War, **1763;** became known as Lower Canada, **1791;** dominated by Chateau Clique, **c. 1795-1850;** entered into confederation with other provinces to form Canada, **July 1, 1867.**

Quebec, city in Canada became capital of New France, **1663;** after losing battle on Plains of Abraham, French surrendered city to British, **Sept. 18, 1759;** Americans failed to capture city during American Revolution, **1775-76;** twice capital of United Provinces of Canada, **1851-55, 1859-65.**

Quebec Act, British parliament established strong Crown-controlled government in Canada and extended Canadian border southward to Ohio River, **May 30, 1774.**

Quebec Convention, representatives of Canadian provinces drafted resolutions for act of confederation, **Oct. 10-28, 1864.**

Queen Anne's War, Britain and France carried on European War of the Spanish Succession in North America, **1702-13;** French with Indian allies massacred men, women, and children at Deerfield, Mass., **Feb. 29, 1704;** British captured Port Royal and Acadia (Nova Scotia), **1710;** Treaty of Utrecht granted Britain possession of Acadia, Newfoundland, and Hudson Bay, **Apr. 11, 1713.**

Queen Mary, turbine-powered British steamship made maiden voyage across Atlantic from England to New York, **June 1936,** as largest liner afloat.

Queensbury Rules, the 8th marquis of Queensbury devised code of boxing rules that called for gloved contests, **1865;** became standard boxing rules, **1889.**

Queen's Plate, oldest horse racing stake event in North America, first run in province of Quebec, Canada, **1836.**

Queenston Heights, battle of, American offensive against British Canada in War of 1812 failed at Queenston Heights in s. Ontario, **Oct. 13, 1812.**

Queretaro, city in central Mexico where Hidalgo y Costilla [May 8, 1753-July 31, 1811] planned conspiracy that led to Mexican revolution against Spain, **1810;** Mexicans under Gen. Mariano Escobedo [Jan. 12, 1827-May 22, 1902] defeated French-Mexican forces of Emperor Maximilian, **May 14, 1867.**

Quiberon Bay, battle of, British fleet under Admiral Edward Hawke [1705-Oct 17, 1781] defeated French fleet at Quiberon Bay, Brittany, France, **Nov. 20, 1759,** capturing five ships and running others ashore.

Quintuple Alliance, Quadruple Alliance joined by France, **1818.**

Quisling affair, Vidkun Quisling [July 18, 1887-Oct. 24, 1945] helped Germany conquer Norway, **Apr. 30, 1940,** made virtual dictator of Norway by Germans, **Feb. 1, 1942,** convicted of high treason, **Sept. 10, 1945,** and shot, **Oct. 24, 1945.**

Quiz Kids, The, broadcast quiz show, on radio, **1940-53,** on television, **1952-56.**

Qumran, biblical archeological site, locus of ancient religious community, destroyed, **c. 68,** by Romans; Dead Sea Scrolls, ancient manuscripts, discovered in caves there, **1947.**

Raab, battle of, French forces under Gen. Eugene de Beauharnais [1781-1824], defeated the Austrians at Raab or Raba River on Austria-Hungary border, **June 14, 1809.** See **Napoleonic Wars.**

Racconigi agreement, Russia and Italy signed accord to maintain status quo in Balkans, **Oct. 24, 1909.**

race for the sea, major German offensive

DICTIONARY OF DATES

at start of WW I toward English Channel and North Sea, **Oct.-Nov. 1914**; Germans captured Ghent, **Oct. 11**, Lille, **Oct. 12**, Bruges, **Oct. 14**, Ostend, **Oct. 15**; Germans halted by Belgian flooding of Yser district, **Oct. 18-Nov. 30, 1914**; Germans failed to take Ypres, **Oct. 30-Nov. 24, 1914**. See **Ypres, battles of.**

radar, acronym for radio detection and ranging; patented, **1935**, by Scottish physicist Sir Robert A. Watson-Watt [1892-1973]; airborne, first demonstrated, **1937**, by Scottish physicist Sir Robert Watson-Watt [1892-1973]; racons (radar beacons), first demonstrated, **1938**, by Scottish physicist Sir Robert Watson-Watt [1892-1973].

radar (development), ionosphere measured, **1925**, using radio-pulse technique by American physicists Gregory Breit [1899-] and Merle A. Tuve [1901-].

radar (origin), first discovery of "beat" method of detection, **1922**, by American scientists A. Hoyt Taylor and Leo C. Young.

radioactive isotopes, produced, **1934**, by French physicists Frederic Joliot-Curie [1900-1958] and Irene Joliot-Curie [1897-1956].

radioactive tracers, discovered, **1923**, by Hungarian-Danish chemist Georg von Hevesy [1885-1966] in study of biological processes with radioactive isotope of lead.

radioactivity, discovered, **1896**, by French physicists Henri Becquerel [1852-1908], Pierre Curie [1859-1906], and Marie Curie [1867-1934] from compound containing uranium.

radioactivity alarm clock, demonstrated, **1951**, by U.S. Navy.

radio-controlled ship model, patented and built, **1898**, by Yugoslavian-American inventor Nikola Tesla [1856-1943]; forerunner of remote-controlled craft.

radio control of moving objects, pioneered, **1910**, by American inventor John H. Hammond [1888-1965].

radio emission from galaxy, first discovered, **1932**, by American radio engineer Karl G. Jansky [1905-1950].

radio-frequency spectra (of atomic particles), investigated, from **1934**, by American physicist Isador I. Rabi [1898-].

radioimmunoassay techniques, (for peptide hormones) developed, from **1950**, by

American medical physicist Rosalyn S. Yalow [1921-], French-British physiologist Roger Guillemin [1924-], and Polish-American physiologist Andrew V. Schally [1926-].

radioisotope battery, installed, **1964**, to power lighthouse in Chesapeake Bay.

radiomagnetic detector, invented, **1902**, by Italian inventor Guglielmo Marconi [1874-1937].

radio receiver cascade tuning, invented, **1913**, by Swedish-American electrical engineer Ernst F. W. Alexanderson [1878-1975].

radio receiver, heterodyne, invented, **1913**, by American inventor Reginald A. Fessenden [1868-1932].

radio station (experimental), first developed, **1908**, by Danish electrical engineer Valdemar Poulsen [1869-1942].

radiotelephone, invented, **1906**, by American inventor Lee De Forest [1873-1961].

radio transmitter triode modulation, invented, **1914**, by Swedish-American electrical engineer Ernst F. W. Alexanderson [1878-1975].

radio-tube oscillator, invented, **1915**, by American inventor Lee De Forest [1873-1961].

radio tuner, invented, **1916**, by Swedish American electrical engineer Ernest F. W. Alexanderson [1873-1975].

radium, element No. 88, isolated, **1898**, by French physicists Pierre Curie [1859-1906], and Marie Curie [1867-1934].

radon (radon isotope), element No. 86; discovered, **1900**, by German physicist Friedrich E. Dorn [1848-1916].

radon (thoron isotope), element No. 86; discovered, **1899**, by British physicist Ernest Rutherford [1871-1937].

Ra **expedition,** Thor Heyerdahl [Oct. 6, 1914-] with seven companions sailed in papyrus boat *Ra II* from Morocco to Barbados, **May 17-July 12, 1980**.

ragtime, jazz-type music, flourished, **1890-1920**.

railroad accidents, great, train ran through open switch near Beloeil, Canada, killing 90 persons, **June 29, 1864**; iron bridge collapse derailed train at Ashtabula, Ohio, killing 92 persons, **Dec. 29, 1876**; train wreck at Eden, Colo., killing 96 persons, **Aug. 7, 1904**; avalanche swept two trains into canyon near Wellington, Wash., killing 96 persons, **Mar. 1, 1910**; three trains crashed near Gretna, Scotland, killing 227 persons, **May 22, 1915**; troop train derailed near mouth of Mt. Cenis tunnel, France, killing 550 persons in worst disaster in railroad history, **Dec. 12, 1917**; Italian train stalled in tunnel near Salerno, Italy, and 521 persons suffocated to death, **Mar. 2, 1944**; two trains of Burlington Railroad collided near Naperville, Ill., killing 47 persons, **Apr. 25, 1946**; Danzig-Warsaw express derailed in Nowy Dwor, Poland, killing 200 persons, **Oct. 22, 1949**; Long Island commuter train crashed into rear of another at Richmond Hill, N.Y., killing 79 persons, **Nov 22, 1950**; two express trains crashed into commuter train at Harrow-Wealdstone, England, killing 112 persons, **Oct. 8, 1952**; two Japanese trains crashed into derailed freight train near Yokohama, killing 162 persons, **Nov. 9, 1963**; express and commuter trains collided near Buenos Aires, killing 236 persons, **Feb. 4, 1970**; two Illinois commuter trains collided at Chicago, killing 45 persons, **Oct. 30, 1972**.

railroad bridge, first constructed, **1865**, over Mississippi River between Rock Island, Ill., and Davenport, Iowa.

railroad car coupler, invented, **1868**, by American inventor Eli H. Janney [1831-1912].

railroad spikes, hook-head, machine for making them invented, **1836**, by Scottish-American Henry Burden [1791-1871].

railway, electric, patented, **1883**, by Belgian-American inventor Charles J. Van Depoele [1846-1892].

railway post office and mail-car, invented, **1862**, by American postmaster William A. Davis [1809-1875].

rainmaking (cloud-seeding), first successful man-made precipitation, **1946**, by American physicists Vincent J. Schaeffer [1906-] and Bernard Vonnegut [1914-].

Raisin River Massacre, successful British-Indian surprise attack on Kentuckians along Raisin River, Mich., ended in massacre of wounded after battle, **Jan. 22, 1813**.

rake for grain reaper, automatic device invented, **1852**, by American inventor Jearum Atkins [c. 1840-c. 1880].

Rake's Progress, The, series of eight paintings, **c. 1735**.

Raman effect, discovered, **1928**, by Indian physicist Sir Chandrasekhara Venkata Raman [1888-1970], proving that visible light changes wavelengths when scattered.

Ramayana, epic poem dating back to **500 B.C.**, with *Mahabharata*, **c. 350**, one epic of India in 24,000 stanzas; about Rama, an incarnation of god Vishnu.

Rambouillet Decree, Napoleon I of France ordered all U.S. ships in French ports to be seized and confiscated, **Mar. 23, 1810**.

Ramillies, battle of, British, Dutch, and Danish forces led by duke of Marlborough won brilliant victory against French, **May 23, 1706**.

ramjet engine, invented, **1913**, by French inventor Rene Lorin.

Rancagua, battle of, Spanish government forces defeated revolutionary force of Bernardo O'Higgins at Rancagua, reestablishing royal government at Santiago, Chile, **Oct. 1, 1814**.

Rand, the (Witwatersrand), region in s. Transvaal where gold was first discovered in South Africa, **1886**.

range finder, stereoscopic device, developed, **1899**, by German inventor Carl Pulfrich [1858-1928].

Rapallo, Treaty of, Italy and Yugoslavia agreed to make Fiume an independent state, Dalmatia given to Yugoslavia, except for Zara, **Nov. 12, 1920**; Fiume given to Italy, **1924**.

Rape of the Sabine Women, painting, **1624**, mythological work exhibiting teeming movement and attention to detail, by founder of French classicism Nicolas Poussin.

Raphia (Rafa), battle of, Ptolemy IV (Ptolemy Philopator) [244?-203 B.C.], king of Egypt, defeated Antiochus III ("the Great") [d. 187 B.C.], king of Syria, at Raphia on Egyptian border, **217 B.C.,** and peace was made between them.

Ras Shamra tablets, cuneiform tablets, discovered, **1929,** written, **c. 1300 B.C.,** in ancient Ugaritic.

Rastatt, Treaty of, ended War of the Spanish Succession between France and Austria, which took possession of Spanish Netherlands, Naples, Milan, and Sardinia, **Mar. 6, 1714.**

Rathmines, battle of, Roundhead army defeated royalist-Catholic army at Rathmines, south of Dublin, during English Civil War, **Aug. 2, 1649.**

Ratisbon Conference, The, religious conference, **April 27-May 22, 1541;** after failure, Reformation became permanent.

Ravenna, capital of Western Roman Empire, **402-476;** captured by Lombards, **751;** ceded to the pope, **756,** by Pepin the Short [c. 714-68].

Ravenspur, battle of, Flemish and German mercenaries aided Yorkists to overpower Lancastrians at Ravenspur in Yorkshire, England, and march into London, **Mar. 1471.**

Rawalpindi, Treaty of, ended third Afghan War; British recognized Afghan independence for first time, **Aug. 8, 1919.**

rayon, invented, **1884,** by French chemist Louis M. Chardonnet [1839-1924].

rayon, acetate, invented, **1895,** by British inventor Charles F. Cross [1855-1935].

rayon, viscose, discovered and patented, **1892,** by English industrial chemist Charles F. Cross [1855-1935] and collaborators.

RCA 501 computer, first all-transistorized, introduced, **1959,** by Radio Corporation of America.

Reader's Digest, The, U.S. magazine published, from **1922.**

Reagan assassination attempt, U.S. Pres. Ronald Reagan and three others wounded in Washington D.C., by shots allegedly fired by John W. Hinckley, Jr. [1956-], **Mar. 30, 1981.**

reagents, Grignard, discovered, **1900,** by French chemist Victor Grignard [1871-1935], leading to development of magnesium-linked synthetic compounds.

realism, philosophical school inaugurated **c. 335 B.C.,** by Aristotle; masterful exponent, from **c. 1250;** medieval philosopher St. Thomas Aquinas [c. 1224-Mar. 7, 1274]. Literary trend, aiming to render faithfully real life; from **c. 1720** in England; from **c. 1850** in France; from **c. 1880** in U.S.; led to naturalism.

Reciprocity Treaty, U.S. and Canada agreed to offshore fishing rights and duty-free entry of agricultural products, **June 5, 1854;** abrogated by U.S., **Mar. 17, 1866.**

Reconstruction, U.S. government ran restoration program in the South after Civil War, **1867-77;** first Reconstruction Act passed, **Mar. 2, 1867.**

Reconstruction Finance Corporation (RFC), former U.S. government agency established, **Jan. 22, 1932,** with Charles G. Dawes [Aug. 27, 1865-Apr. 23, 1951] as head, to advance loans during the Depression; joined other agencies to form Federal Loan Agency, **1939;** reinstituted, **1947;** abolished **1957.**

records, long-playing (LP), developed, **1948,** by American inventor Peter C. Goldmark [1906-1977].

records, wax cylinder, invented, **1888**, by American inventor Thomas A. Edison [1847-1931].

Recovery, Fort, 2000 U.S. government militiamen suffered disastrous defeat by large force of Indians at Fort Recovery in Northwest Territory, **Nov. 4, 1791**.

rectifier, vacuum tube for converting alternating current to direct current, developed, **1904**, by English electrical engineer John Fleming [1849-1945].

Red Badge of Courage, The, novel, **1895**, a psychological study of fear, by U.S. author Stephen Crane; film, **1951**, John Huston-directed version brought to screen real-life U.S. war hero and actor Audie Murphy [June 20, 1924-May 28, 1971].

red blood cells, (erythrocytes), first described, **1665**, by Italian physician Marcello Malpighi [1628-94].

Red Cross, international organization for the care of the sick and wounded in war established, **1864**, in Geneva, Switzerland; Clara Barton [Dec. 25, 1821-Apr. 12, 1912] organized, **1881**, American Red Cross at Washington, D.C.

Redemptorists, Catholic religious order, founded Italy, **1732**, for active missionary work among poor and heathen; papal approval, **1749**.

Red Guards, Chinese students and youths organized by Mao Tse-Tung at start of Cultural Revolution, **Apr. 1966**, to rid China of "old ideas" and dissidents; great rally of hundreds of thousands of Red Guards in Peking, **Aug. 18, 1966**; uncontrolled mobs of Red Guards attacked peasants and Chinese officials, **1967**, until ordered to desist by Mao. See **Cultural Revolution**.

Red Hand Commandos, paramilitary Prot-

estant group opposed to union of Northern Ireland and Irish Republic, formed **1972**; outlawed **1973**; allegedly shot Catholic nationalist leader Bernadette Devlin (McAliskey) [Apr. 23, 1947-] and her husband, **Jan. 16, 1980**.

Red River Rebellion, French halfbreeds called metis led by Louis Riel, established provisional government at Fort Garry (Winnipeg), claiming Dominion government's takeover of their land rights, **Nov. 1869**; government troops dispersed rebels without bloodshed; Riel escaped, **Mar. 1870**; Riel's second rebellion ended in failure at Batoche, **May 12, 1885**; Riel executed, **Nov. 16, 1885**.

red shift, (shift toward red end of spectrum of light from stars moving away from earth), discovered, **1868**, by English astronomer Sir William Huggins [1824-1910].

Red Shirts, the, Giuseppe Garibaldi [July 4, 1807-June 2, 1882] with his thousand volunteers, *the Red Shirts*, conquered the island of Sicily in a spectacular campaign, crossed the straits, and conquered Naples, **May-Sept. 1860**.

Reformation, movement to reform Catholic Church that ended in establishment of Reformed (Protestant) Churches, launched, **Oct. 31, 1517**, by Luther's posting of 95 theses; declaration of independence of German Reformed Church, Augsburg, **1530**.

reflector, parabolic, first constructed, **1938**, by American Grote Reber, in Wheaton, Illinois.

Reform Bills, major measures that liberalized representation in British parliament's House of Commons, **19th century**; Whigs' ministry redistributed seats in interest of bigger communities by Reform Bill of 1832, **Mar. 23, 1832**; Benjamin Disraeli [Dec. 21, 1804-Apr. 19, 1881] gave vote to workingmen in the towns, doubling the electorate by Reform Bill of 1867, **Aug. 15, 1867**; William Gladstone [Dec. 29, 1809-May 19, 1898] ended distinctions between county and borough votes, reduced rural qualifications, adding more voters to rolls, by Reform Bill of 1884, **Dec. 1884**.

Reform Judaism, religious movement, originated, Germany, **c. 1800**.

Reform Party, political party led by William Lyon Mackenzie [Mar. 12, 1795-Aug.

28, 1861] in Upper Canada and by Louis J. Papineau [Oct. 1786-Sept. 23, 1871] in Lower Canada, **c. 1820-50.**

Reform, War of, Mexican civil war between conservatives and liberals led by Benito Juarez, **1858-61;** liberals seized conservative capital, Mexico City, **Dec. 1860;** Mexican government under Juarez suspended payment on foreign debt, **July 17, 1861;** France, Britain, and Spain occupied Veracruz to protect interests, **Dec. 17, 1861.**

refraction of light, double, discovered, **1669,** by Danish mathematician Rasmus Bartholin [1625-1698].

refrigerator, invented, **1913,** by American inventor A. H. Goss.

Refugee Relief Act, U.S. Pres. Eisenhower permitted, **Aug. 7, 1953,** entry into U.S. of 214,000 victims of Communist persecution.

refuse-derived fuel, one of earliest resource recovery systems; began operation **1971** at Franklin, Ohio.

Reich, German government, First Reich from establishment of Holy Roman Empire to its downfall, **962-1806;** Second Reich encompassed German Empire and Weimar Republic, **1871-1933;** Third Reich under Nazi dictatorship of Adolf Hitler, **1933-45.**

Reichsbank, German national bank, founded **Jan. 1876.**

Reichstag, lower assembly of federal parliament of Germany, **1871-1945;** dissolved and new elections held when Hitler became Chancellor, **Jan. 30, 1933;** partly destroyed by fire that Hitler accused Communists of having set, **Feb. 27, 1933;** passed Enabling Act giving Hitler dictatorial powers, **Mar. 23, 1933.**

Reichstag fire, Nazis under Hitler accused Communists of setting fire to Reichstag building in Berlin, **Feb. 27, 1933;** Ger. Pres. von Hindenburg suspended freedom of speech and assembly; Nazis, with Nationalists' support, gained more control of government in Reichstag elections, **Mar. 5, 1933.** See **Enabling Act.**

Reid's yellow dent, variety of corn, bred, **c. 1880,** by American agriculturalist James L. Reid [1844-1910].

Reign of Terror, period at end of French Revolution, when the Mountain under Maximilien Francois Marie Isidore de Robespierre [May 6, 1758-July 28, 1794] and the dictatorial Committee of Public Safety routed out counterrevolutionaries and guillotined thousands, including Louis XVI and Marie Antoinette [Nov. 2, 1755-Oct. 16, 1793], **May 1793-Aug. 1794.**

relativity, special theory of, announced, **1905,** by German-American physicist Albert Einstein [1879-1955], in his *Special Theory of Relativity,* completed **1915,** with his *General Theory.*

Remagen, battle of, U.S. 9th Armored Division captured Ludendorff bridge over Rhine River at Remagen, opening way for allied advance into Germany during WW II, **Mar. 7, 1945.**

Remembrance of Things Past, semi-autobiographical fictional masterpiece in seven volumes, published **1913-27,** by French novelist Marcel Proust [July 10, 1871-Nov. 18, 1922].

REM studies, pioneered, **1953,** by American physiologists, Eugene Aserinsky and Nathaniel Kleitman.

Renaissance, period of "rebirth" in Western cultural history between medieval and modern periods: in Italy, **c. 1380-1580**; Flanders, **c. 1440-1570**; Germany, **c. 1490-1600**; England, **1500-1600**.

Reo motor car, first constructed, **1904**, by American inventor Ransom E. Olds [1864-1950].

Republican Party, U.S. political party formed at Jackson, Mich., to oppose the extension of slavery, **Feb. 28, 1854**.

Republic of New Africa (RNA), separate black nation within the U.S. to consist of Alabama, Mississippi, Georgia, South Carolina, and Louisiana, proposed at National Black Government Conference in Detroit, **Apr. 1968**; RNA members presented to U.S. State Dept. demand for $200 billion in "reparations" due black Americans, **May 1969**; RNA conference in Washington, D.C., to form official government structure, **Aug. 1969**.

Republic, On the (De Re Publica), six-book Latin treatise, **54-51 B.C.**, on political philosophy, by Roman orator, prose master, and statesman Cicero.

Republic, The, philosophical dialogue, **375 B.C.**, in which Socrates guides thought towards meaning of justice and of ideal state, by ancient Greek philosopher, Plato.

Resaca, battle of, one of first battles fought by Gen. William T. Sherman's Union army during his march through Georgia; Sherman forced Confederates to retreat, **May 14-15, 1864**.

Resaca de la Palma, battle of, U.S. forces under Gen. Zachary Taylor routed Mexican troops in valley of Resaca de la Palma in second battle of Mexican War, **May 9, 1846**. See **Palo Alto, battle of**.

Resht, Treaty of, Persia acquired many cities formerly occupied or claimed by Turks or Russians, **1732**.

resonant-cavity magnetron, invented, **1939**, by British physicist Henry Boot [1917-] and British biophysicist John T. Randall [1905-].

resonator, sound wave analysis, invented, **1875**, by American inventor Thomas A. Edison [1847-1931].

Restoration, reestablishment of monarchy in England, **1660**; Charles II proclaimed king, **May 8, 1660**; Charles II entered London, **May 29, 1660**.

Resurrection, painting, **c. 1463**; noted for "mathematical" arrangement of figures, by Italian Renaissance painter Piero della Francesca.

Resurrection City, camp of civil rights activists near Washington Monument, Washington, D.C., **May-June 1968**, following Poor People's March on Washington led by Rev. Ralph Abernathy [Mar. 11, 1926-], **May 2, 1968**.

Resurrection Symphony, symphony, completed, **1894**, No. 2, in C minor, of nine composed by Austrian composer Gustav Mahler [July 7, 1860-May 18, 1911].

Return of the Native, The, novel, **1878**, by English novelist and poet Thomas Hardy.

Reval, battle of, Danes defeated army of Germans (Danes went on to take present-day Estonia), **1219**.

Revelation to John, The, New Testament book, also called Apocalypse, generally believed written under Neronian persecutions, **c. 68**, by a John believed to be Jesus' apostle.

reverse transcriptase, viral enzyme; existence demonstrated, **1970**, by U.S. microbiologist David Baltimore [1938-] and U.S. molecular biologists Howard M. Temin [1934-] and Renato Dulbecco [1914-].

Revised Standard Version, English translation of Bible, commissioned, **1870**, by Convocation of Canterbury; published,

1881-85; variant edition published, U.S., **1901**.

Revolutionary Republican calendar, calendar instituted by first French republic with the 12 months of Vendemiaire, Brumaire, Frimaire, Nivose, Pluviose, Ventose, Germinal, Floreal, Prairial, Messidor, Thermidor, Fructidor, **Oct. 5, 1793-Dec. 31, 1805**.

Rheims Cathedral, gothic cathedral, begun, **1211**, completed, **1481**, on site of coronation of French kings, since **496**; perfect cruciform plan; western facade damaged, **1914-18**; restored, **1927**.

Rheinfelden, battle of, Protestant German-French army under Bernhard of Saxe-Weimar [Aug 16, 1604-July 18, 1639] overwhelmed Holy Roman Empire troops, **Mar. 3, 1638**.

rhenium, element No. 75; discovered, **1925**, by German chemists Walter K. Noddack [1893-] and Ida Tacke Noddack [1896-].

Rhode Island, one of Thirteen Colonies, ratified U.S. Constitution to become 13th state of the Union, **May 29, 1790**.

Rhodes, Aegean island that flourished as commercial power and center of Greek culture, **4th-3rd century B.C.**; Colossus of Rhodes built in harbor, **292-80 B.C.**; sacked by Romans, **43 B.C.**; defended by Knights Hospitalers against Ottoman Turks, **c. 1475-1523**.

Rhodesia, British South African Company of Cecil Rhodes [July 5, 1853-Mar. 26, 1902] defeated Ndebele tribesmen and took over territory in s. Africa, **1893**; territory became self-governing British Crown Colony, **Sept. 12, 1923**; proclaimed unilateral declaration of independence, **Nov. 11, 1965**; became a republic, **Mar. 2, 1970**; became nation of Zimbabwe, **Apr. 18, 1980**.

rhodium, atomic No. 45; discovered, **1803**, by English physiologist William Hyde Wollaston [1766-1828].

ribonuclease, structure determined, **1960**, by American biochemists Christian B. Anfinsen [1916-], Stanford Moore [1913-], and William H. Stein [1911-1980].

ribosomes, function discovered, **1956**, by Romanian-American physiologist George E. Palade [1912-].

Richard III, play, **c. 1594**, about hunchbacked Duke of Gloucester who connives to secure throne of England; history play by William Shakespeare. Film, **1955**, based on Shakespeare's play; produced, directed, and acted by Laurence Olivier.

Richter scale, devised as measurement of earthquake magnitude, **1935**, by American seismologist, Charles F. Richter [1900-], California Institute of Technology.

Ried, Treaty of, Austria made alliance with Bavaria, which withdrew from Confederation of the Rhine and joined to fight Napoleon, **Oct. 8, 1813**.

Riff War, Riff tribes led by Abd el-Krim [1882?-1936] defeated Spanish army at Anual, Morocco, **July 21, 1921**; Riffs drove Spanish back to Tetuan, **1924**; combined Franco-Spanish army forced Abd el-Krim to surrender, **May 26, 1926**, ending war.

rifle, automatic, produced, **1918**, by American designer of firearms John M Browning [1855?-1926].

rifle, breech-loading, invented, **1851**, by American inventor Edward Maynard [1813-1891].

rifle, semiautomatic (M-1), developed, **1930**, by Canadian-American gun designer John C. Garand [1888-1974], for U.S. Army.

Riga, battles of, Swedish army of King Gustavus II seized city of Riga, Latvia, from Poles, **1621**; German forces defeated Russian-Latvian forces at battle of Riga during WW I, **Sept. 3-5, 1917**.

Rights of Man, The, political treatise by Thomas Paine, **1791-92**, defending French Revolution and its principles from attacks on them by Edmund Burke.

Rigoletto, opera, **1851**, about court jester whose daughter is seduced by his master, by Italian operatic composer Giuseppe Verdi.

ring flyer (cotton-spinning machine), patented, **1830**, by American inventor James Bogardus [1800-1874].

Ringgold Gap, battle of, Union forces under Gen. Joseph Hooker suffered terrible loss against Confederates under Patrick R. Cleburne [1828-64] at Ringgold Gap, Ga., **Nov. 27, 1863**.

Ring of the Nibelung, cycle of four operas, **1853-74**, including *The Rhinegold*, **1853-54**, *The Valkyrie*, **1854-56**, *Siegfried*, **1856-71**, and *Twilight of the Gods*, **1869-74**, by German operatic composer Richard Wagner.

Ring Theater fire, great, more than 850 Europeans killed in fire at Ring Theater, Vienna, Austria, **Dec. 8, 1881**.

ring winding for dynamo, invented, **1860**, by Italian physicist Antonio Pacinotti [1841-1912]; independently discovered, **1870**, by Belgian electrician Zenobe T. Gramme [1826-1901].

Rio Branco Law, Brazilian law freed state and crown slaves and stipulated children of all slaves to be free, **1871**; Brazilian parliament abolished slavery, **May 13, 1888**.

Ripon, Treaty of, signed, **1640**; concluded Bishop's Wars.

Rip Van Winkle, tale, **1819**, by U.S. writer Washington Irving.

Risorgimento, movement for the cultural liberation and unification of Italy, **c. 1750-1870**; Austrians suppressed widespread revolts throughout Italy, **1848-49**; Napoleon III promised Camillo Benso, conte di Cavour [Aug. 10, 1810-June 6, 1861] French military aid at Plombieres, **July 20, 1858**; king-

dom of Italy proclaimed, **Mar. 17, 1861**; Papal States annexed by Italy, **Oct. 2, 1870**.

Rite of Spring, The (Le Sacre du Printemps), 20th-century ballet, produced Paris, **May 29, 1913**; created scandal by dissonances and bold rhythms, by innovative Russian-French-U.S. composer Igor Stravinsky.

Rivals, The, drama, **1775**, by Irish-English Restoration dramatist Richard Brinsley Sheridan, includes famous character Mrs. Malaprop.

Roanoke Island colony (lost colony), Sir Walter Raleigh [1552?-Oct. 29, 1618] dispatched English colonists that landed on Roanoke Island, N.C., **Aug. 1585**; first colonists returned to England because of severe hardships, **1586**; Raleigh's second group of colonists landed at Roanoke, **1587**; Virginia Dare [Aug. 18, 1587-c. 1587] born at colony to become first English child born in North America, **Aug. 18, 1587**; entire Roanoke Island colony vanished, disappearance noted, **1591**.

Robinson Crusoe, novel, **1719-20**, about English sailor marooned on desert island; by English novelist Daniel Defoe.

Rock around the Clock, song, **1955**, by U.S. singer, songwriter and guitarist, Bill Haley (born William John Clifton Haley) [Mar., 1927-Feb. 9, 1981].

Rockefeller Foundation, philanthropic institution established by John D. Rockefeller [July 9, 1839-May 23, 1937] who donated $100 million, **May 14, 1913**.

rocket engine flight, achieved, **1928**, by American physicist Robert H. Goddard [1882-1945].

rocket propellants, developed, **1943**, by American chemist Bryce L. Crawford [1914-].

rocket, recoilless, pioneered, **1916**, by American physicist Robert H. Goddard [1882-1945].

rocket theory, proposed, **1895**, by Russian physicist Konstantin E. Tsiolkovsky [1857-1935].

rock 'n' roll, type of music popular from **c. 1955**; developed from combination of hillbilly and Negro music; characterized by triplet beat in four-four time.

Rocky Mountain, battle of, American

patriots under Thomas Sumter made heroic, but unsuccessful, attempt to seize strategic Rocky Mountain, S.C., held by the British, **July 30, 1780**.

Rocky Mountain spotted fever, transmission by ticks established, **1906**, by American pathologist Howard T. Ricketts [1871-1910].

rococo, florid, ornate style in art and decoration, flourished, **c. 1710-50**, that dominated Europe in era of Louis XV.

Rocroi, battle of, French troops under Louis II de Bourbon, ("the Great Conde") encircled and killed almost to a man entire Spanish army at Rocroi in n. France; turning point in Spanish military history, **May 19, 1643**.

Rodeo, ballet, first produced, **Oct. 16, 1942**; choreographed by Agnes DeMille to music by Aaron Copland.

roentgenkymography, introduced, **1916**, by American physician August W. Crane [1868-1937].

roentgen rays, official name of X-rays, adopted, **1896**, at a meeting of the Wurzburg (Germany) Physico-Medical Society when Munich physicist, Wilhelm Conrad von Roentgen [1845-1923], first explained his discovery.

roentgen stereoscopy, invented, **1896**, by Austrian physicist Ernst Mach [1838-1916].

roller-bearing, devised, **1892**, by American inventor John W. Hyatt [1837-1920].

Romance of Helen Trent, The, long-running U.S. daytime radio serial, **1933-60**.

Romance of The Rose (Roman de la Rose), medieval allegorical romance expounding nature of love; first 4,058 lines written, **c. 1240**, treat ideal courtly love, by Guillaume de Lorris [c 1210-1250]; last 18,000 lines written, **c. 1290**, treat love realistically, by Jean (Clopinel) de Meung [c. 1260-c 1315].

Roman Empire, empire of ancient Rome, established by Augustus Caesar and ended with Theodosius I ("the Great") [346?-95], when it split into Eastern and Western Roman Empire, **27 B.C.-A.D. 395**.

Roman Empire, fall of the, Goths under Odoacer (Odovacar) [c. 435-93] dethroned western Roman Emperor Romulus Augustulus at Ravenna, **Aug. 28, 476**.

romanesque, style of architecture and art, flourished, **c. 900-1200**, characterized by rounded arches and abundance of arcades; superseded by gothic style, **c. 1200**.

Romans, Letter to the, New Testament book, epistle of St. Paul, written, **c. 57-58**, Corinth.

romanticism, movement in the arts, began second half of the **1800s**, emphasizing emotion and imagination over reason and restraint; opposed to classicism; English romanticism, **1780-1830**; French, **1820-1850**; U.S., **1830-1860**.

Rome, traditionally said to be founded by Romulus, **753 B.C.**; sacked by Gauls, **390 B.C.**; burned during reign of Nero [37-68], **64**; sacked by Visigoths, **Aug. 14 (or 24), 410**; sacked by Vandals, **June 2-16, 455**.

Rome-Berlin Axis, Italo-German accord reached by Mussolini and Hitler, **Oct. 25, 1936**, to strengthen their positions with respect to France and Great Britain. See **World War II**.

Romeo and Juliet, early tragedy, **c. 1596**, by William Shakespeare; dramatic symphony, **1839**, for soloists, chorus, and orchestra, Opus 17 by French composer Hector Berlioz; symphonic poem (fantasy overture), **1869**, by Russian composer Peter Ilyich Tchaikovsky; opera, **1867**, inspired by Shakespeare's play, by French composer Charles Gounod; opera, *I Capuleti e i*

Montecchi, **1830**, by Italian composer Vincenzo Bellini; ballet, **1938**, by Russian composer Sergei Prokoviev.

Roncesvalles, mountain pass in Pyrenees where mountain Basques ambushed and massacred rear guard of Charlemagne's Christian Frankish army; Roland [d. 778], great French hero, died, **778**.

Room of One's Own, A, critical essay, **1929**, early feminist work by English writer Virginia Woolf.

Roosebeke (Rozebeke), battle of, French forces won victory against Flemings in present-day Belgium, **Nov. 27, 1382**, crushing further revolt in Flanders with severity.

Root and Branch Bill, radical petition of parliament to abolish bishops, on which moderate Puritans split with radical Presbyterians in England, **Dec. 11, 1640**.

Roots, autobiographical work, **1977**, by U.S. author Alex Haley [Aug. 11, 1921-]; special Pulitzer citation, **1977**. Television series, **Jan. 23-30, 1977**, dramatization of Haley's book.

ropeway, Hallidie, developed, **1867**, by English-American engineer Andrew S. Hallidie [1836-1900].

Rorke's Drift, 140 British troops successfully resisted assault by 4000 Zulus at Rorke's Drift in n. Natal, **Jan. 22-23, 1879**.

Rosa Americana (Wood's money), mixed metal coins resembling brass, issued by Great Britain for her American colonies, **1722**.

Rose Bowl, major U.S. collegiate football game played each Jan. 1 at Pasadena, Calif.; first Rose Bowl football game between Michigan and Stanford, **Jan. 1, 1902**.

Rosebud River, battle of, Sioux and Cheyenne Indians under Chief Crazy Horse [c. 1840-Sept. 1877] inflicted heavy casualties on U.S. Army columns under Gen. George Crook [Sept. 23, 1829-Mar. 21, 1890] on Rosebud River in Montana, **June 17, 1876**.

Rose Marie, operetta, **1924**, romance about mounties set in Canadian Rockies; music by Czech-U.S. composer (Charles) Rudolph Friml [Dec. 7, 1879-Nov. 12, 1972]; young Oscar Hammerstein II collaborated on lyrics; film, **1936**, one of series of operettas filmed by U.S. singing-acting team Nelson Eddy [1901-Mar. 6, 1967] and Jeanette MacDonald [June 18, 1907- Jan. 14, 1965].

Rosencrantz and Guildenstern Are Dead, play, first performed, Edinburgh, **Aug. 24, 1966**, by English playwright Tom Stoppard [July 3, 1937-].

Rosenkavalier, Der, (The Knight of the Rose), opera, first produced, Dresden. **Jan. 26, 1911**, composed by Richard Strauss with original libretto by Hugo von Hofmannsthal.

Rosen-Nishi Agreement, Russia and Japan agreed not to interfere in Korean internal affairs, but Japan gained control in economic matters, **Apr. 25, 1898**.

Roses, Wars of the, struggle for the throne of England between the houses of Lancaster (red-rose badge) and York (white-rose badge), **1455-85**; Yorkists captured Henry VI at Northampton, **July 10, 1460**; Yorkists defeated at Wakefield, **Dec. 30, 1460**; Lancastrians defeated at Mortimer's Cross, **Feb. 2, 1461**; at Towton Field, **Mar. 29, 1461**; Richard III [Oct 2, 1452-Aug. 22, 1485] defeated and killed by Lancastrian claimant Henry Tudor (later Henry VII) at Bosworth Field, **Aug. 22, 1485**.

Rosetta Stone, carved stone, discovered, Rosetta, Egypt, **1799**, by French expedition; deciphered, **1821**, by French scholar Jean Francois Champollion [Dec. 23, 1790-Mar. 4, 1832].

Rosicrucians, mystical secret societies, founded **c. 1614**; literature still circulates but societies extinct from **c. 1900**.

Rossbach, battle of, by skillful maneuvers, Prussian army under Frederick II ("the Great") won spectacular victory over French and Holy Roman Empire forces at village of Rossbach, **Nov. 5, 1757**.

Rotary International, first Rotary Club for businessmen, founded **1905**, in Chicago;

National Association of Rotary Clubs, formed **1910**; adopted present name, **1922**.

Rouen Cathedral, 26 impressionist paintings, **1892-95**, by French artist Claude Monet.

Rough Riders, 1st Regiment of U.S. Cavalry Volunteers, organized **Apr. 22, 1898**, under command of Col. Leonard Wood [Oct. 9, 1860-Aug. 7, 1927] and Lt. Col. Theodore Roosevelt [Oct. 17, 1858-Jan. 6, 1919]; took part in famous charge up Kettle Hill (San Juan Hill) in Spanish-American War, **July 1, 1898**.

Rover Boys series, popular boys' books, published from **1899**; mass-produced by literary syndicate established by Edward Stratemeyer [Oct. 4, 1862-May 10, 1930].

Rowlatt Acts, two British anti-sedition laws allowed officials to intern agitators without trials and judges to try cases without juries in India, **Mar. 18, 1919**; Mohandas K. Gandhi [Oct. 2, 1869-Jan. 30, 1948] organized pacifist resistance campaign in response. See **Amritsar Massacre**.

Royal African Company, British trading company that sold African Negroes as slaves in the West Indies, **1672-1750**.

Royal Ballet, The, name given by royal charter, **Oct. 31, 1956**, to former Sadler's Wells Ballet, London; latter began as Academy of Choreographic Art. **1926**; moved to newly built Sadler's Wells Theater, **Jan., 1931**.

Royal Canadian Mounted Police, constabulary organized as Northwest Mounted Police, **Aug. 30, 1873**.

Royal Pavilion, Brighton, structure, Brighton, England, built from **1815**,.

Roy Rogers Show, The, modern U.S. western broadcast show, on radio **1944-52**, on television, **1951-64**.

Royal Scots, oldest regular regiment in the British army established in Scotland, **1633**.

Royal Society, The, still-existing association, founded London, **1660**.

Royal Titles Act, parliament declared Queen Victoria *Empress of India*, **Apr. 1876**.

R-S system for stereoisomers, developed, **1950s**, by Yugoslavian-Swiss chemist Vladimir Prelog [1906-].

rubber, latex foam, invented, **1928**, by English scientists at Dunlop Rubber Co., Birmingham, England; team headed by E. A. Murphy.

rubber shredder, invented, **1820**, by English inventor Thomas Hancock.

rubber, synthetic, invented, **1891**, by British inventor Sir William A. Tilden [1842-1926].

rubber, synthetic (Koroseal), invented, **1926**, by American chemist Waldo L. Semon [1898-].

rubber, synthetic (Neoprene), developed, c. **1930**, by Belgian-born American chemist Julius Arthur Nieuwland [1878-1936].

rubber, synthetic (Thiokol), invented, **1926**, by American inventor J.C. Patrick.

Rubicon, small stream that divided Gaul from Italy; Julius Caesar crossed in defiance of the Roman senate, **49 B.C.**

rubidium, element No. 37; discovered, **1861**, by German chemist Robert Bunsen [1811-1899] and German physicist Gustav Kirchhoff [1824-1887].

Rudy Vallee Show, The, radio music and talent show, **1929-43**.

Rugby School, one of England's great public schools founded, **1567**; rugby football originated at the school, **1823**.

Ruhr pocket, allied armies directed by Gen. Omar N. Bradley [Feb. 12, 1893-Apr. 8, 1981] advancing into Germany encircled Nazi Panzer and 15th armies in Ruhr industrial center and forced the surrender of 317,000 German soldiers and 30 generals —largest Nazi mass surrender in WW II, **Apr. 1-18, 1945.**

rule of electric current flow, first described, **1820,** by French mathematician Andre M. Ampere [1775-1836]

Rumelia, huge Bulgarian state divided by Congress of Berlin into n. Bulgaria under nominal Turkish control and s. Bulgaria, Eastern Rumelia, and autonomous province, **1878;** Eastern Rumelia annexed by Bulgaria, **1885,** Serbia failed to gain Eastern Rumelia in war with Bulgaria, **1886.**

Rump Parliament, legislative remnant of Long Parliament established after Pride's Purge, **Dec. 7, 1648-Mar. 16, 1660;** voted that King Charles I of England be brought to trial, **Dec. 13, 1648;** passed resolve that legislative power resided solely in Commons, **Jan. 6, 1649.**

Rum Rebellion, British army officers rebelled in New South Wales, captured William Bligh, and forced him to be removed as governor, **Jan. 26, 1808.**

runes, ancient Germanic characters, probably first used by East Goths, **c. 300.**

Runnymede, meadow-site in Surrey, England, where King John signed the Magna Carta, **June 19, 1215.**

Rurik, House of, reigning family in Russia, founded by Viking conqueror Rurik [d. 879], **862?-1598.**

Rush-Bagot Agreement, Britain and U.S. agreed to limit naval forces on the Great Lakes; demilitarization of Canadian border began, **Apr. 28-29, 1817.**

Russian-American Company, Russian fur-trading company organized and given monopoly rights in Russian America (including Alaska and Aleutian Islands) by czarist government, **1799;** established permanent settlement at Sitka, **1799;** dissolved after sale of Alaska to U.S., **1867.**

Russian famines, great, political disorder and drought caused widespread famine in Russia, **1891-92;** drought and economic collapse caused peasant uprisings and great famine, **1921-22;** bad government agrarian policy, drought caused famine, **1932-33.**

Russian peasant rebellions, great, czar suppressed uprising led by Don Cossacks under Stenka Razin [d. 1671], **1670-71;**

Czarina Catherine II ("the Great") suppressed peasant-Cossack uprising under Emelian Ivanovich Pugachev [d.1775], **1773-75.**

Russian-Polish War of 1920, unresolved boundaries between Russia and Poland resulted in war between the two, **Apr. 25-Oct. 12, 1920;** Poles invaded and seized Kiev, **May 7;** Bolsheviks drove Poles out of Kiev, **June 11,** and Vilna, **July 15;** Poles and Bolsheviks signed truce at Riga, **Oct. 12;** Treaty of Riga, **Mar. 18, 1921,** established borders between the two countries.

Russian Revolution, violent revolution in Russia, overthrowing government of Czar Nicholas II and establishing the power of the Bolsheviks (Communist Party), **1917;** February Revolution forced czar to abdicate, **Mar. 15, 1917;** October Revolution enabled Bolsheviks under leadership of Vladimir I. Lenin [May 4, 1870-Jan. 21, 1924] to seize power at Petrograd (St. Petersburg, now Leningrad), **Nov. 7, 1917.**

Russo-Finnish War, conflict between U.S.S.R. and Finland over demilitarization of Mannerheim Line and islands in Gulf of Finland, **Nov. 30, 1939-Mar. 12, 1940;** Finns, though ably led by Field Marshal Carl G. Mannerheim [June 4, 1867-Jan. 27, 1951], forced to sign peace treaty **Mar. 12, 1940,** ceding to U.S.S.R. the Karelian Isthmus, city of Viborg (Viipuri), and some border areas; war resumed between U.S.S.R. and Finland, **June 1941** as part of WW II. See **Mannerheim Line.**

Russo-Japanese War, armed conflict between Russia and Japan over control of Manchuria and Korea, **1904-1905;** without warning, Japan attacked Russian fleet at Port Arthur, **Feb. 8, 1904;** Japanese won victory at Mukden, **Mar. 1905;** Japanese destroyed Russian fleet at Tsushima Strait, **May 27-28, 1905;** ended by Treaty of Portsmouth, **Sept. 5, 1905.**

Rust cotton picker (mechanical), invented, **1928,** by American inventors John D. Rust [1892-1954] and Mack D. Rust [1900-1966].

Rutgers University, old American institution of higher learning chartered as Queen's College at New Brunswick, N.J., **1766;** Queen's College renamed Rutgers College, **1825;** became a university, **1924.**

Ruth, Book of, Old Testament book, written, c. **450-350 B.C.**.

ruthenium, element No. 44; discovered, **1844**, by Russian chemist Karl K. Klaus [1796-1864].

Rwanda, small country in central Africa, gained its independence, **July 1, 1962**, ending Belgian UN trusteeship.

Ryder Cup matches, prestigious biennial men's professional golf tournament between British and U.S. teams, inaugurated at Worcester, Mass., **1927**.

Rye House Plot, Whigs, angry at increased Tory power extended by King Charles II of England, conspired to assassinate the king, **June 1683**.

Ryswick, Treaty of, ended War of the Grand Alliance; France surrendered to Spain all conquests made, since **1679**; independence of Savoy recognized; William III [Nov. 4, 1650-Mar. 8, 1702] recognized as king of England, **Sept. 30, 1697**.

Saalfeld, battle of, French army defeated Prussian army under duke of Brunswick at Saalfeld, e. Germany, during Napoleonic Wars, **Oct. 10, 1806**.

Saarland, region made autonomous Saar Territory by Treaty of Versailles, **1919**; its coal fields exploited by France until region voted for reunion with Germany, **Jan. 13, 1935**; site of heavy fighting in WW II, **1944-45**; gained autonomous government, **1947**; economic union with France rejected by referendum, **Oct. 1955**; became W. German state of Saarland, **Jan. 1, 1957**.

saccharin, discovered, **1879**, by American chemist Ira Remsen [1846-1927].

Sacco-Vanzetti case, two aliens, anarchist Nicola Sacco [Apr. 22, 1891-Aug. 23, 1927] and Bartolomeo Vanzetti [July 11, 1888-Aug. 23, 1927], convicted, **July 14, 1921**, of murder and robbery of paymaster in South Braintree, Mass., **Apr. 15, 1920**; both denied their guilt; international protests preceded and followed their conviction and execution, **Aug 23, 1927**.

Sackets Harbor, important naval base on Lake Ontario, where U.S. forces successfully defended themselves against British expeditionary force during War of 1812, **May 28-29, 1813**.

Sacred and Profane Love, painting, **c. 1515**, by Venetian Renaissance painter Titian.

Sadler's Wells Ballet, ballet company, London, founded **1926**, as Academy of Choreographic Art; moved to new Sadler's Wells Theatre, **Jan. 1931**, hence name; renamed Royal Ballet by royal charter, **Oct. 31, 1956**.

Sadler's Wells Theatre, famous London theater, built, **1765**; rebuilt, **1931**; damaged in World War II, but reopened, **1945**.

Sadowa (Sadova), battle of, using the needle gun, Prussians won important victory during Austro-Prussian (Seven Weeks' War) at Sadowa, e. of Prague, forcing larger Austrian army to withdraw, **July 3, 1866**.

safety fuse (for explosives), patented, **1831**, by English inventor William Bickford [1774-1834].

safety match, invented, **1855**, by Swedish inventor J.E. Lundstrom.

safety pin, patented, **1849**, by American inventor Walter Hunt [1796-1859].

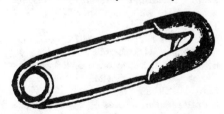

safety razor, invented, **c. 1895**, by American inventor King Camp Gillette [1855-1932]; first with disposable blades.

Saguntum (Sagunto), Roman town in e.

Spain besieged and captured by Carthaginians under Hannibal, **219-18 B.C.**; reconquered by Romans, **214 B.C.**

Saint Albans, battles of, Yorkists defeated Lancastrians at Saint Albans, e. central England, during the Wars of the Roses, **May 22, 1455**; Lancastrians won second battle at Saint Albans, **Feb. 17, 1461**. See **Roses, Wars of the**.

St Andrews, Royal and Ancient Golf Club of, golfers established first beginnings of club at St. Andrews, Scotland, **1552**; formally established with rules of golf, **1754**.

Saintes, Les, battle of, British fleet under Admiral George Rodney [Feb. 13, 1718-May 23, 1792] defeated French fleet under Francois Joseph Paul, comte de Grasse [Sept. 13, 1722-Jan. 11, 1788] at Les Saintes, **Apr. 12, 1782**.

Saint-Germain, Treaty of, Austria signed peace treaty with Allies after WW I, **Sept. 10, 1919**.

Saint Louis Blues, song, **1914**, by "father of the blues," U.S. composer W. C. Handy.

Saint-Mihiel, battle of, U.S. forces drove Germans back at Saint Mihiel, n.e. France, **Sept. 13, 1918**.

Saint-Quentin, battles of, Spanish-English force defeated French at Saint-Quentin, n. France, **Aug. 10, 1557**; Germans used heavy gas attack to take Saint-Quentin in WW I, **Mar 21, 1918**; British recaptured it, **Oct. 1, 1918**.

Saint Vincent, Cape, battles of, British warships under Admiral George Rodney attacked and captured Spanish warships and supply convoy off Cape Saint Vincent on s.w. coast of Portugal, **Jan. 16, 1780**; British fleet under Admiral John Jervis [Jan. 9, 1735-Mar. 14, 1823] defeated larger Spanish fleet off Cape Saint Vincent; Horatio Nelson led attack, **Feb. 14, 1797**.

Saipan, volcanic island in w. Pacific mandated to Japan by League of Nations, **1920**; besieged and captured by U.S. troops during WW II, **June 15-July 9, 1944**.

Salamanca, battle of, British, Portuguese, and Spanish forces under Gen. Wellington won major battle against French army at Salamanca, n.w. of Madrid, during Napoleonic Wars, **July 22, 1812**.

Salamis, battle of, Athenian fleet led by Themistocles [c. 524-460 B.C.] attacked and defeated Persian fleet of Xerxes [c. 519-465 B.C.] off island of Salamis in Saronic Gulf in first decisive naval battle of history, **480 B.C.**

Salary Grab Act, U.S. Congress doubled salary of president, and raised those of Supreme Court justices, the cabinet, and congressmen, **Mar. 3, 1873**; repealed **1874**, except for salaries of president and justices.

Salem, (Mass.), colony founded by English members of Massachusetts Bay Company, **Sept. 6, 1628**; site of witchcraft trials, **1692**; Nathaniel Hawthorne as surveyor oversaw port of Salem, **1846-49**.

Salem witchcraft trials, many women accused of witchcraft by children and clergymen and brought to trial at Salem, Mass. (many convicted and later hanged), **Oct. 1692**.

Salerno, battle of, allied amphibious assault at Salerno, Italy, resulted in fierce, but unsuccessful, German counterattack during WW II, **Sept. 9-16, 1943**.

Salisbury Cathedral, English gothic cathedral, begun **1220**, completed **1266**; spire, built between **1334** and **1350**, highest in England.

Salk antipolio vaccine, developed, **1954**, by American physician Jonas E. Salk [1914-], reported successful, **1955**.

Salonica (Salonika or Saloniki) campaigns, allied force at Salonica tried to establish blockade of neutral Greece, **1915**; Allies established rival Greek government under Eleutherios Venizelos [Aug 23, 1864-Mar. 18, 1936] at Salonica, **1916**; Greek king abdicated and Greece joined Allies, **June 1917**; new allied offensive forced Bulgaria to surrender, **Sept. 30, 1918**; Allies took Serbia, **Nov. 1, 1918**; Allies captured Rumania, **Nov. 10, 1918**.

Salt Lake City, capital of Mormon community established by Brigham Young [June 1, 1801-Aug. 29 1877], **1847**; gigantic Mormon Temple built there, **1853-93**.

salt manufacturing process, first patent in American colonies issued to Samuel Winslow of Massachusetts, **1641**.

Salt March, Mohandas K. Gandhi led Indians on 200-mi. march to Gujarat coast to extract salt from the sea in protest against government's salt tax, **Mar. 12-Apr. 6, 1930**; Gandhi arrested and imprisoned, **May 5, 1930**; Gandhi released, **Jan. 26, 1931**, and began talks with government.

Salvation Army, international Christian organization on semi-military lines founded by William Booth [Apr 10, 1829-Aug. 20, 1912] as London mission, **1865**; adopted present name, **1878**; first U.S. branch organized in Pennsylvania, **1880**; Evangeline C. Booth [Dec. 25, 1865-July 17, 1950] headed U.S. Salvation Army, **1904-34**.

Samaria, ancient capital of kingdom of Israel captured by Assyrians, **721 B.C.**; rebuilt by Herod the Great [73?-4 B.C.].

samarium, element No. 62; discovered, **1879**, by French chemist Paul E. Lecoq de Boisbaudran [1873-1912].

Samarkand, oldest city in central Asia, founded **4th mil. B.C.**; conquered by Alexander the Great, **329 B.C.**; sacked by Genghis Khan, **1220**; capital of Tamerlane's Mongol empire, **14th century**; fell under Russian control, **1868**.

Samnite Wars, conflicts between Romans and Samnites in ancient Italy; first war, **343-41 B.C.**; second, **c. 326-304 B.C.**; third, **298-90 B.C.**; Samnites crushed by Roman General Lucius Cornelius Sulla [138-78 B.C.], **82 B.C.**

Samoa, volcanic islands in South Pacific discovered by Dutch, **1722**; U.S.-Samoan treaty, **Jan. 17, 1878**, permitted U.S. naval station at Pago Pago; U.S., Germany, and Britain signed Samoan treaty, **Dec. 2, 1899**, partitioning Samoa between U.S. and Germany; New Zealand captured German Samoan Islands, **1914**, which became, **1962**, independent nation of Western Samoa.

Samoa, Western, island group in s. Pacific, became independent nation, **Jan. 1, 1962**.

Samos, Agean island off w. Asia Minor, colonized by Ionian Greeks, **c. 1000 B.C.**; fl. under Polycrates [d. c. 522 B.C.], **6th century B.C.**

Samosata (Samsat), ancient city on Euphrates River, founded as capital of Commagene kingdom, **c. 150 B.C.**; captured by Romans, **72**; captured by Arabs, **c. 660**; site of Byzantine defeat of Muslims, **873**.

Samuel, Books of, Old Testament books, written, **c. 700 B.C.**

Sanctuary, novel, **1931**, by U.S. novelist William Faulkner.

Sand Creek massacre, U.S. troops swept down on unsuspecting Cheyenne and Arapahoe village at Sand Creek, Colo., **Nov. 29, 1864**.

Sandinista civil war, Marxist Sandinista guerrillas fought to overthrow Somoza family rule in Nicaragua, **1970s**; strike against Somoza government led to civil war at Matagalpa, **Aug. 25, 1978**; Sandinistas began major offensive, **May 29, 1979**, that resulted in the resignation of Anastasio Somoza-Debayle [Dec. 5, 1925-Sept. 17, 1980], **July 17, 1979**.

Sand River Convention, British government recognized Boers' independence in the Transvaal, **Jan. 17, 1852**.

Sands, death of Bobby, Bobby Sands [1954-May 5, 1981], IRA Catholic militant prisoner in Maze Prison, died on 66th day of hunger strike, touching off riots and battles in Northern Ireland between police and Catholics, **May 5, 1981**; second IRA hunger striker, Francis Hughes [1956-May 12, 1981] died on 59th day in Maze Prison, **May 12, 1981**, igniting more violence; third hunger striker Raymond McCreesh [1957-May 21, 1981]; died on 61st day in Maze Prison, **May 21, 1981**; fourth hunger striker Patrick O'Hara [1957-May 22, 1981] died in Maze Prison, **May 22, 1981.**

Sandusky, capture of, Indians attacked and killed traders and soldiers in fort at Sandusky, Ohio, **May 16, 1763.**

Sandwich glass, first mass production of glassware, **1825,** by American glass manufacturer Deming Jarves [1790-1869] at Sandwich Glass Co., Mass.

Sandwich Islands, former name of Hawaiian Islands first discovered by English explorer Capt. James Cook [Oct 27, 1728-Feb. 14, 1779] who named them for the earl of Sandwich, **Jan. 18, 1778;** U.S. recognized Hawaiian independence, **Dec. 19, 1842;** Lydia Liluokalani [Sept. 2, 1838-Nov. 11, 1917] became queen, **Jan. 20, 1891;** republic of Hawaii declared, **July 4, 1894.**

San Francisco Conference, delegates from 50 nations drafted United Nations Charter at San Francisco, **Apr. 25-June 26, 1945;** charter ratified, **Oct. 24, 1945,** United Nations Day. See **United Nations.**

San Francisco earthquake, violent earthquake, accompanied by fire, killing approx. 700, **Apr. 18-19, 1906.**

San Ildefonso, Treaty of, Spain aligned itself with France in the war against Britain, **Aug. 19, 1796;** France secured Louisiana Territory and promised to enlarge Parma for Spain, **Oct. 1, 1800.**

San Jacinto, battle of, final and decisive battle of Texas revolution; Texans under Gen. Samuel Houston [Mar. 2, 1793-July 26, 1863] defeated Mexicans under Gen. Santa Anna on San Jacinto River, **Apr. 21, 1836.**

San Juan, Juan Ponce de Leon established Spanish colony near present-day San Juan, Puerto Rico, **1508;** often attacked by English pirates, **1595;** sacked by Dutch, **1625;** occupied by U.S. troops during Spanish-American War, **1898.**

San Juan Hill, battle of, U.S. cavalry including the Rough Riders under Lt. Col. Theodore Roosevelt [Oct. 17, 1858-Jan. 6, 1919] assaulted and overran both Kettle and San Juan hills in Cuba during Spanish-American War, **July 1, 1898.**

San Lorenzo, Treaty of (Pinckney Treaty), Spain recognized U.S. southern and western borders and right of navigation on Mississippi, **Oct. 27, 1795.**

San Marcos, National University of, oldest university in South America founded at Lima, Peru, **1551.**

San Marino, oldest republic in the world, founded, **c. 350;** formed customs union with Italy, **1862.**

San Remo, Conference of, representatives of Britain, France, Italy, Greece, Belgium, and Japan at San Remo, Italy, **Apr. 19-26, 1920,** discussed ratification of Treaty of Versailles, peace treaty with Turkey, and Class A Mandates in Middle East. See **Sevres, Treaty of; Versailles, Treaty of.**

San Stefano, Treaty of, Russia forced Ottoman Empire to cede part of Armenia, to recognize the independence of Rumania, Serbia, and Montenegro, and to make Bulgaria an autonomous principality, **Mar. 3, 1878.**

Santa Cruz de Tenerife, battle of, British warships under Admiral Robert Blake [Aug. 1599-Aug 17, 1657] sank 16 Spanish warships and destroyed city of Santa Cruz de Tenerife in Canary Islands, **Apr. 20, 1657.**

Santa Fe Trail, important route, from Franklin (later Independence), Mo., to Santa Fe, N. Mex., **1821-80.**

Santa Sophia, basilica, built, Constantinople, **532-37;** converted to mosque by Turks, **1453.**

Santiago de Cuba, battle of, U.S. fleet blockaded and destroyed Spanish fleet in Santiago's harbor, **July 3, 1898.**

Santo Domingo, former Spanish colony on island of Hispaniola discovered by Columbus, **1492;** city of Santo Domingo (oldest continuously inhabited settlement in Western Hemisphere) founded, **1496;** island's w. part (Saint-Domingue, now Haiti) ceded to France, **1697;** Haitian band under Francois

Toussaint L' Ouverture [1749-1803] ousted Spanish and French and freed slaves, **1801**; island united as republic of Haiti, **1822**; Santo Domingo (Dominican Republic) gained its independence through revolution, **Feb. 27, 1844**.

Sao Tome and Principe, two volcanic islands off w. central African coast, became independent of Portugal, **July 12, 1975**.

Saragossa (Zaragoza), battles of, Moors defeated Charlemagne's forces at Saragossa, n.e. Spain, **778**; Austrians defeated Spanish under King Philip V, **1709**; Spanish made heroic defense of Saragossa, **1808-1809**, against French, but capitulated, **Feb. 21, 1809**.

Sarajevo, former capital of Bosnia and Hercegovina where Archduke Francis Ferdinand of Austria was assassinated, **June 28, 1914**.

Saratoga Campaign, British plan to split American colonies along Hudson River halted near present-day Saratoga Springs, N.Y., **June-Oct. 1777**; American forces prevented British breakthrough at Freeman's Farm, **Sept. 19, 1777**; British second attempt to break through failed at Bemis Heights, **Oct. 7, 1777**; Americans won first great victory of American Revolution when Gen. John Burgoyne [1722-Aug. 4, 1792] surrendered, **Oct. 17, 1777**.

Sardinia, kingdom of, established under rule of duke of Savoy, **1720**; Liguria added, **1815**; Lombardy added, **1859**; kingdom annexed Parma, Modena, Bologna, Marche, and n. part of Papal States, **1860**; annexed the Two Sicilies, **1861**; became kingdom of Italy, **Mar. 17, 1861**.

Sardis, ancient capital of Lydia, political and cultural center of Asia Minor, **c. 650-546 B.C.**; King Croesus [d. c. 546 B.C.] defeated and captured by Cyrus the Great of Persia [d. 529 B.C.], **546 B.C.**; captured by Ionians in Persian War, **499 B.C.**; destroyed by Tamerlane, **14th century**.

Saskatchewan, became part of Northwest Territories, **1869**, became a province of Canada, **Sept. 1, 1905**.

Satsuma Rebellion, last serious internal rebellion against Meiji restoration in Japan; imperial forces crushed Satsuma warriors, **Jan.-Sept. 1877**.

Saturday Evening Post, U.S. magazine, first appeared, Philadelphia, **Aug. 18, 1821**.

Saturday Night Massacre, resignation of U.S. Atty. Gen. Elliot L. Richardson [July 20, 1920-]; his deputy William D. Ruckelshaus [July 24, 1932-] and Special Watergate Prosecutor Archibald Cox [May 17, 1912-] fired by U.S. Pres. Richard M. Nixon, **Oct. 20, 1973**, when Cox threatened to sue Nixon to have White House tapes handed over to Judge John J. Sirica [Mar. 19, 1904-]; Leon Jaworski [Sept. 19, 1905-] named to replace Cox, **Nov. 1, 1973**. See **Watergate scandal**.

Saturday Review, The, weekly literary magazine, founded **1924**.

Saturn (planet), satellite, discovered, **1848**, by English astronomer William Lassell [1799-1880].

Saturn launcher series, developed from, **1960**, at George C. Marshall Space Flight Center; directed by German-American rocket pioneer Wernher von Braun [1912-1977].

Savannah, (Ga.), city founded by James Oglethorpe [Dec. 22, 1696-July 1, 1785] as refuge for English debtors in the colony of Georgia, **Feb. 12, 1733**; seized by British during American Revolution, **Dec. 29, 1778**; Union forces under Gen. Sherman seized city, **Dec. 21, 1864**.

saw, circular, invented, **1777**, by English inventor Samuel Miller.

Saxa Rubra, battle of, Constantine's Roman soldiers and horsemen won great victory at Saxa Rubra near Rome, massacring legions of Valerius Maxentius [d. 312] at Milvian Bridge, **312**.

Saxon Confession, The, authoritative Protestant profession of faith, **1551**.

Scala, La, opera house, Milan, Italy, built, **1778**.

scandium, element No. 21; discovered, **1879**, by Swedish chemist Lars F. Nilson [1840-1899].

scarlet fever, first described accurately, **1533**, by Italian anatomist Giovanni Filippo Ingrassias [1510-1580].

Scapa Flow, body of water off n. Scotland where the German fleet was scuttled by its crew, **June 21, 1919**.

Scarlet Letter, The, novel, **1850**, about adulteress in Puritan New England, by U.S. novelist and short-story writer Nathaniel Hawthorne.

Scheherazade, orchestral suite, **1888**, based on *The Arabian Nights*, by Russian composer Nikolai Rimsky-Korsakov.

Schick test, discovered, **1913**, by Hungarian-American pediatrician Bela Schick [1877-1967].

Schism, Great, split in the Roman Catholic Church, **1378-1417**; the cardinals, alienated by Pope Urban VI [1318?-89], chose Robert of Geneva (Antipope Clement VII [d. 1394], who established himself at Avignon, **1378**; ended at Council of Constance, **1417**.

schizophrenia, term introduced, **1911**, by Swiss psychiatrist Eugene Bleuler [1857-1939].

schizophrenia, psychogenic theory, proposed, **1907**, by Swiss psychoanalyst, Carl G. Jung [1875-1962].

Schleswig-Holstein, two duchies inherited by king of Denmark, **1460**; subdivided, **1500s**; reunited under king of Denmark, **1773**; warfare between Danish nationalists and German nationalists over duchies, **1848-50**; annexed by Prussia, **1866**; plebiscite restored n. Schleswig to Denmark, **1920**; made state within British occupation zone after WW II, **1946**; joined West Germany, **1949**.

Schlieffen Plan, German military plan devised by Alfred Schlieffen [Feb. 28, 1833-Jan. 4, 1913] for invasion of Belgium, Holland, and France in WW I, **1914-15**; variation of plan used by Germans at start of WW II, **May-June 1940**.

Schmalkaldic League, German Protestant princes formed alliance to oppose Holy Roman Emperor Charles V, who sought to stamp out Lutheranism, **Dec. 31, 1530**.

Schmalkaldic War, Holy Roman Emperor Charles V sought to crush the Schmalkaldic League and to restore the unity of the Church, **1546-47**; Imperial troops won at Muhlberg.

Schmeling-Sharkey fight, Max Schmeling [Sept. 28, 1905-] of Germany defeated Jack Sharkey in New York City to win heavyweight boxing championship of the world, **June 12, 1930**.

scholasticism, philosophy of medieval schools, developed, from **c. 1070**, by St. Anselm of Canterbury.

Schonbrunn, Peace of, Napoleon imposed peace on Austria, **Oct. 14, 1809**.

School for Scandal, The, play, **1777**, by Irish-English Restoration dramatist Richard Brinsley Sheridan.

Schuman Plan, plan for integration of Western European coal and steel industries proposed by French Foreign Minister Robert Schuman [June 29, 1886-Sept. 4, 1963], **May 9, 1950**; France, W. Germany, Italy, Netherlands, Belgium, and Luxembourg formed European Coal and Steel Community embodying Schuman Plan, **1952**.

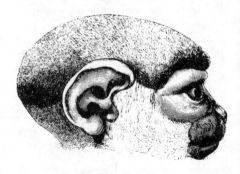

Scopes Trial (*monkey case*), Tennessee schoolteacher John T. Scopes [1900-Oct. 21, 1970] arrested, **May 5, 1925**, for violating state law forbidding the teaching of evolution; Scopes, defended by Clarence S. Darrow [Apr. 18, 1857-Mar. 13, 1938], tried, **July 10-21, 1925**, convicted, and fined $100; William Jennings Bryan, one of prosecuting attorneys, died suddenly, **July 26, 1925**.

Scotism, system of scholastic philosophy, developed, **c. 1290-1307**, by Franciscan schoolman John Duns Scotus, affirming primacy of will and love of God.

Scottish Covenanters' revolt, Presbyterians in Scotland defended their beliefs against the Anglicans in England, **17th century**; Covenanters fought in Bishops' Wars, **1639-40**; fought in English Civil War, **1642-48**; subdued by Cromwell's conquest of Scotland, **1650-51**; crushed by royalist army at Pentland Hills, **Nov. 28, 1666**; crushed by duke of Monmouth at Bothwell Bridge, **June 22, 1679**; ended by Glorious Revolution, **1688-89**.

Scottsboro Boys, jury at Scottsboro, Ala., found nine black youths guilty, **Apr. 9, 1931**, after three-day trial, on charges of having raped two white women aboard a railroad frieght car, **Mar. 25, 1931**; last survivor of *Scottsboro Boys* pardoned, **Oct. 27, 1976**.

Screwtape Letters, The, popular theological work, **1942**, by British Christian scholar and writer C. S. Lewis.

screw thread machine, patented, **1798**, by American inventor David Wilkinson [1771-1852]; incorporated slide rest; adopted by U.S. government in firearms manufacture.

screw threads, standard, system proposed, **1864**, by American machine-tool builder William Sellers [1824-1905].

Scythian culture, nomadic and warlike Scythians grew powerful north of the Black Sea and traded with the Greeks, **fl. 7th-4th century B.C.**

Seagram Building, skyscraper, **1956-57**, New York, by German-U.S. architect Ludwig Mies van der Rohe [Mar. 27, 1886-Aug. 17, 1969].

Sea Wolf, The, novel, **1904**, by U.S. novelist and short-story writer Jack London..

Second Sex, The (Le Deuxieme Sexe), treatise, **1949**, by French writer and existentialist philosopher Simone de Beauvoir.

Secret Service, U.S., law enforcement agency of U.S. Dept. of the Treasury, established to investigate and prevent currency counterfeiting, **1865**; charged with protecting U.S. president, **1901**.

Sedan, battle of, Prussian armies won decisive victory of Franco-Prussian War, overwhelming French at Sedan in n. France and forcing Napoleon III [Apr. 20, 1808-Jan. 9, 1873] to surrender, **Sept. 1, 1870**.

seismograph, built **132**, by Chinese astronomer Chang Heng [?-132]; designed, **1855**, by Italian physicist Luigi Palmieri [1809-76].

seismograph, developed, **1931**, by American scientist Hugo Benioff [1899-]

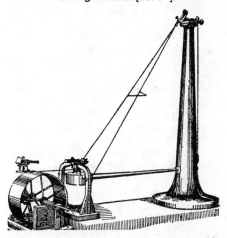

Seiyukai, Japanese political party identified with Mitsui financial interests, founded from the Jiyuto party, **1900**; most powerful party in Japan, **1900-21**; dissolved with all Japanese parties, **1940**; reappeared to be absorbed into Liberal-Democratic party, late **1950s**.

selective service, U.S., national military draft began in U.S. Civil War, **July 13-16, 1863**; Selective Service Act, **May 18, 1917**, required all men 21-30 years old to register; Selective Training and Service Act, **Sept. 14, 1940**, authorized first U.S. peacetime draft; more than 10 million U.S. men inducted into armed forces, **1940-47**; U.S. abolished draft, **1973**, in favor of all-volunteer army.

selenium, element No. 34, discovered, **1818**, by Swedish chemist Jons J. Berzelius [1779-1848].

DICTIONARY OF DATES

Seleucids, dynasty of kings that ruled ancient Syria, **312-64 B.C.**

Seljuk Turks, conquered and reigned over large part of central and western Asia, **11th-13th centuries**; defeated Byzantine emperor at Manzikert, **1071**; involved in struggle with Christians and Egyptian Mamelukes during the Crusades, **11th-13th centuries**; Seljuk states overrun by Mongols and Turks (Tatars) led by Genghis Khan and his successors, **13th century**.

Sellasia, battle of, Spartan army under Cleomenes II [c. 260-219 B.C.] decisively defeated by Achaean League, allied with Antigonus III [d. 221 B.C.], **222 or 221 B.C.**

Selma to Montgomery, Ala., march, led by Martin Luther King, Jr. [Jan. 15, 1929-Apr. 4, 1968] to protest discrimination against Negroes, **Mar. 21-25, 1968**.

Seminole War, conflict between U.S. troops and Seminole Indians in Florida, **1835-42**; Seminoles forced to evacuate their lands and move westward, **1842**.

Sempach, site in central Switzerland where Swiss won decisive victory over Austrians, **July 9, 1386**.

Seneffe (Seneff), battles of, French under Louis II de Bourbon ("the Great Conde") won great victory over Dutch at Seneffe in present-day Belgium, **Aug. 8, 1674**; French defeated Austrians during French Revolutionary Wars, **1794**.

Senegal, country on African coast, first taken by the French, **1840**; made a French colony, **1904**; became part of the Federation of Mali with Sudan, **June 20, 1960**; withdrew from federation as independent republic, **Aug. 20, 1960**; devastated by drought and famine, **1969-74, 1978**.

Senlis, Treaty of, Charles VIII [June 30, 1470-Apr. 7, 1498] of France ceded Franche-Comte and Artois to Austria, **May 23, 1493**.

Senta (Zenta), battle of, Holy Roman Empire army under Eugene, Prince of Savoy [1663-1736], inflicted crushing defeat on Turkish army at Senta, n.w. of Belgrade, **Sept. 11, 1697**.

Sentinum, battle of, Romans won great victory over Samnites and Gauls at Sentinum (Sassoferrato) near Adriatic Sea during Samnite Wars, **295 B.C.**

Sepeia, battle of, Spartan army under Cleomenes I [d. c. 489 B.C.] won decisive victory over Argive (Argos) army, establishing undisputed supremacy in the Peloponnesus, **494 B.C.**

Sepoy Rebellion (Indian Mutiny), rebellion of native Indian soldiers (sepoys) in Bengal army of British East India Company developed into general rebellion against British rule in India, **1857-58**; sepoys besieged and seized Kanpur (Cawnpore), **June 26-July 15, 1857**; British troops recaptured Delhi, **Sept. 1857**; and recaptured Lucknow, **Mar. 1858**; sepoys defeated at Gwalior, **June 17-19, 1858**.

September Laws, repressive measures, enacted by French government of Louis Philippe to bring radical movement under control, **Sept. 1835**.

Septinsular Republic, Ionian Islands seized from the French and organized as a republic under Turkish protection and Russian guarantee, **Oct. 22, 1799**; Russians left the islands, **1807**.

Serbs, Croats, and Slovenes, Kingdom of the, proclaimed by Serbians, Croatians, Slovenes, and Montenegrins, **Dec. 4, 1918**; became Yugoslavia, **Oct. 3, 1929**. See **Corfu, Pact of.**

Seringapatam, fortress-capital of Mysore, India, captured by British, **Mar. 19, 1792**; again British captured Seringapatam, killed Tipu Sahib [1749-May 4, 1799], sultan of Mysore, and established British rule in s. India, **May 4, 1799**.

serum therapy, developed, **1890**, by German bacteriologist Emil A. von Behring [1854-1917].

Sesame Street, made its debut, **1969**.

Sevastopol, battle of, fortress-city of Sevastopol abandoned by Russians after long siege by British-French-Turkish force; Crimean War virtually ended, **Oct. 17, 1854-Sept. 11, 1855**.

Seven Days battles, week-long Confederate counter-offensive near Richmond, Va., ending Peninsular Campaign in U.S. Civil War, **June 26,-July 2, 1862**; Confederates severely defeated at battle of Mechanicsville, **June 26, 1862**; Confederates broke Union resistance at Gaine's Mill, **June 27, 1862**; Confederates under Gen. Lee failed to stop Union drive at Savage's Station, **June 29, 1862**; Confederates failed at

Frayser's Farm, **June 30, 1862**; Union forces checked Confederates at Malvern Hill, **July 1, 1862**; Union forces under Gen. McClellan withdrew; Gen. Lee had saved Confederate capital of Richmond, **July 2, 1862**.

Seventeenth Amendment to U.S. Constitution, ratified, **May 31, 1913**, established direct popular election of U.S. senators.

Seventh Day Adventists, Christian communion, founded **1844**; name adopted, **1864**.

Seven Wonders of the World, The,: Colossus, Rhodes, **c. 250-25 B.C.**; Hanging Gardens of Babylon, **c. 580 B.C.**; Mausoleum, Halicarnassus, **350 B.C.**; Phidias' Olympian Zeus, **c. 460 B.C.**; Pharos, Alexandria, **c. 250 B.C.**; Pyramids, Egypt, **2750-2563 B.C.**; Temple of Artemis, Ephesus, **c. 560 B.C.**

Seven Years' War, worldwide conflict fought between, on the one side, Austria, France, Russia, Saxony, Sweden, and, on the other side, Prussia, England, and Hanover, **1756-63**; Prussians won great victories at Rossbach, **Nov. 5, 1757**; at Leuthen, **Dec. 5, 1757**; Prussians badly beaten at Kunersdorf, **Aug. 11, 1759**; English won victories at Krefeld, **June 1758**; at Louisburg (in America), **July 26, 1758**; at Plassey (in India), **June 23, 1757**; ended by treaties at Paris and Hubertusburg, **Feb. 1763**.

Seville, Treaty of, Britain and France agreed to Spanish succession in the Italian duchies, **Nov. 9, 1729**.

Sevres, Treaty of, Turks signed peace treaty with Allies after WW I, **Aug. 10, 1920**.

sewing machine, patented, **1830**, by French inventor Barthelemy Thimonnier [1793-1854]. Patented, **1846**, by American inventor Elias Howe [1819-1867].

sewing machine, commercial, patented, **1851**, by American inventor Isaac M. Singer [1811-1875].

Seychelles, archipelago in the Indian Ocean, captured from France by Britain, **1810**; ruled as part of Mauritius, after **1814**; became separate British Crown Colony, **1903**; proclaimed its independence, **June 29, 1976**.

Shakers, religious sect, Quaker offshoot, founded England, **1747**; settled in New York State, **1774**.

Shangri-La, operation, U.S. bombers under Col. James H. Doolittle [Dec. 14, 1896-], launched from carrier *Hornet*, made first U.S. bombing raid on Tokyo during WW II, **Apr. 18, 1942**.

shaver, electric, first patented, **1923**, by American inventor Jacob Schick.

Shays's Rebellion, farmers led by Daniel Shays [c. 1747-Sept. 29, 1825] rose in arms against merchants and lawyers in w. Massachusetts, **Jan. 25, 1787**.

Sheridan's Ride, swift rush by Union forces under Gen. Philip H. Sheridan [Mar. 6, 1831-Aug. 1888] from Winchester to Cedar Creek, Va. to counterattack and win victory against the Confederates, **Oct. 19, 1864**. See **Cedar Creek, battle of**.

Sherlock Holmes, fictional detective introduced by English author Sir Arthur Conan Doyle [May 22, 1859-July 7, 1930] in *A Study in Scarlet*, **1887**; appeared in, among others, *The Hound of the Baskervilles*, **1902**, and *The Return of Sherlock Holmes*, **1904**.

Sherman Adams incident, assistant to President Eisenhower, Sherman Adams [Jan. 8, 1899-], denied charges of accepting gifts from Boston industrialist for political influence, **June 17, 1958**; Adams resigned, **Sept. 22, 1958**.

Sherman Antitrust Act, U.S. government and federal courts gained authority by congressional act, **July 2, 1890**, to prevent restraint of interstate or foreign commerce in effort to check monopolies, "trusts"; used by U.S. Supreme Court to dissolve Northern Securities Company, **Mar. 14, 1904**; supplemented by Clayton Antitrust Act, **Oct. 15, 1914**.

Sherman's March to the Sea, Union army under Gen. William T. Sherman burned Atlanta, Ga., and marched to Savannah, devastating the countryside, cutting the South in half during U.S. Civil War, **Nov. 14-Dec. 10, 1864**.

Shiloh, battle of, one of greatest and bloodiest battles of U.S. Civil War, **Apr. 6-7, 1862**.

Shimabara uprising, Christianity wiped out in Japan, **1637-38**.

Shimonoseki, Treaty of, Japan forced China to recognize the independence of Korea, to cede Formosa, the Pescadores Islands, and Liaotung peninsula to Japan, and to pay a large indemnity, **Apr. 17, 1895**.

Shipka Pass, battle of, Russo-Bulgarian army defeated Turks at Shipka Pass in the Balkans in central Bulgaria, **Jan. 1878**.

shogun, hereditary military dictators who ruled Japan, **c. 1185-1868**; overthrown to bring Meiji restoration, **1868**.

shrapnel shell, invented, **1803**, by English artillery officer Henry Shrapnel [1761-1842]; first used at Surinam, **1804**.

Shrewsbury, battle of, English forces of Henry IV defeated the Percys (dukes and earls of Northumberland) led by Henry Percy (Hotspur) [1364-July 23, 1403] at Shrewsbury, w. England, **July 23, 1403**.

Shrine, (Ancient Arabic Order of the Nobles of the Mystic Shrine) secret fraternal order established in the U.S., **1872**.

Sian (Hsi-an), ancient city founded (one of world's oldest) in Wei River valley, China, c. **2200 B.C.**; capital as Hsien-yang of Ch'in dynasty, **255-206 B.C.**; center of Buddhist, Muslim and Nestorian Christian missionary activity, **7th-10th centuries**.

Sicilian Vespers, rebellion staged by Sicilians against French-Angevin control of Sicily, **Mar. 30, 1282**.

Sid Caesar Show, The (Your Show of Shows, Caesar's Hour), U.S. television comedy-variety shows, **1949-58, 1963-64**, presenting zany humor of U.S., Emmy-winner, **1965**, comedian Sid Caesar [Sept. 8, 1922-]

side-chain theory, (of immunity) first announced, **1904**, by German bacteriologist Paul Ehrlich [1854-1915].

Sidon, one of the great seaports of ancient Phoenicia that colonized Tyre, c. **2800 B.C.**; became famous for its purple dyes and glassware, after **1000 B.C.**

Siena, University of, one of world's first universities established at the rich art city of Siena, Italy, **1247**.

Sierra Club, U.S. organization established, **1892**, by John Muir [Apr. 21, 1838-Dec. 24, 1914].

Sierra Leone, country in Africa, established as haven for freed slaves from Britain, **1787**; became British Crown Colony, **1808**, gained independence in the British Commonwealth of Nations, **Apr. 27, 1961**; became a republic, **Apr. 19, 1971**.

Silent Don, The, novel, **1940**, four-volume model of "socialist realism," by Russian writer Mikhail Alexandrovich Sholokhov [May 24, 1905-]; first volume, *And Quiet Flows the Don*, **1928**; Sholokhov Nobel Prize-winner, **1965**.

Silent Night (Stille Nacht), Christmas carol, first performed, Austria, **1818**.

Silesian Wars, conflicts between Prussia and Austria over control of Silesia, as part of the general War of the Austrian Succession; first war, **1740-42**; Prussians won Mollwitz, **Apr. 18, 1741**; ended by Treaty of Berlin, **July 28, 1742**; second war, **1744-45**; Prussians won at Hohenfriedberg, **June 4, 1745**; and at Soor, **Sept. 30, 1745**; ended by Treaty of Dresden, **Dec. 25, 1745**.

silicon, element No. 14; discovered, **1823**, by Swedish chemist Jons J. Berzelius [1779-1848]. Research developed, **1904**, by English chemist Frederic S. Kipping [1863-1949]; led to use of silicones in industry.

silicon carbide, discovered, **1891**, by American inventor Edward G. Acheson [1856-1931].

silicon transistor, first practical introduced, **1954**, by Texas Instruments, Inc.

Silistra, battles of, Russians defeated Ottoman Turks at Silistra in n.e. Bulgaria, **1809**; German-Bulgarian forces defeated Rumanians at Silistra, **Sept. 10, 1916**.

Singapore, small island nation off s. tip of Malay peninsula, site of trading post founded by British East India Company, **1819**; made part of the British Straits Settlements, **1826**; became separate British Crown Colony, **Apr. 1, 1946**; joined Malaya, Sabah, and Sarawak in the federation of Malaysia, **Sept. 16, 1963**; withdrew from

federation and proclaimed itself an independent republic, **Aug. 9, 1965**.

Singspiel (Sing-Play), type of German music drama, from **c. 1700**.

Sinn Fein, Irish political society organized to achieve Ireland's independence from Britain, **1905**; grew after British crushed Easter Rebellion in Ireland, **Apr. 24-May 1, 1916**; organized Irish parliament called Dail Eireann and declared Irish independence, **Jan. 21, 1919**; Britain created separate parliaments for Northern and Southern Ireland, **Dec. 23, 1920**; Britain granted Southern Ireland dominion status as Irish Free State, **Dec. 6, 1921**; Eamon De Valera [Oct. 14, 1882-Aug. 29, 1975] resigned as head of Sinn Fein, **Mar. 11, 1926**.

Sinope, battle of, Russian fleet sent by Czar Nicholas I totally destroyed Turkish fleet at port of Sinope on Black Sea, **Nov. 30, 1853**.

Sinzheim, battle of, French army under Turenne routed combined Spanish-Brandenburg-Holy Roman Empire force and laid waste to the Palatinate, **June 16, 1674**.

Sioux Wars, conflicts between Sioux Indians and U.S. troops and settlers west of Mississippi River, **c. 1850-77**; Sioux uprising caused by Sand Creek massacre, **Nov. 29, 1864**; Sioux abandoned Bozeman Trail and accepted reservation in Dakota territory by Treaty of Fort Laramie, **Apr. 29, 1868**; white gold rush renewed wars, with major Sioux victory at Little Bighorn, **June 25, 1876**; Sioux crushed by U.S. troops on Wolf Mountain, **Jan. 7, 1877**.

siren, invented, **1822**, by German physicist Thomas J. Seebeck [1770-1831].

Sistine Chapel, chapel in papal Vatican palace, begun, **1473**, completed, **Oct. 27, 1481**; ceiling, **1508-12**, painted by Italian artist Michelangelo Buonarroti.

Sitva-Torok, Treaty of, Turks signed first peace treaty outside Constantinople; Austrians abandoned Transylvania and ceased paying tribute for their part in Hungary, **Nov. 11, 1606**.

Sixteenth Amendment to U.S. Constitution, ratified, **Feb 25, 1913**, authorized U.S. Congress to establish the income tax.

skating, figure, invented by American Jackson Haines [1840-1876], **1860s**; America's first national figure skating tournament held in New Haven, Conn., **1914**; Sonja Henie [Apr. 8, 1912-Oct. 12, 1969] won women's figure skating gold medal in winter Olympic Games, **1928, 1932, 1936**; Dick Button [July 18, 1929-] won men's figure skating gold medal in winter Olympic Games, **1948, 1952**.

skating, roller, first roller skates introduced at masquerade party in Soho Square, London, **1760**; roller skating introduced in U.S. by New York inventor James L. Plimpton, who patented the four-wheeled roller skate, **1863**; spectator sport called roller derby gained prominence in U.S. after WW II, **fl. 1950s-60s**.

Skinner box, invented, **1938**, by American psychologist B.F. Skinner [1904-].

Skopje earthquake, large quake killed more than 1100 persons in Skopje, Yugoslavia, **July 26, 1963**.

skyscraper, erected in Chicago, **1884**, by American architect William LeBaron Jenny [1832-1907]. The Home Insurance Building.

Slankamen, battle of, army of Holy Roman Empire routed larger Turkish army at Slankamen, n.w. of Belgrade, **Aug. 19, 1691**.

slide rule, invented, **c. 1630**, by English mathematician William Oughtred [1575-1660].

Slivnitza, battle of, Bulgarians won decisive victory over Serbians at Slivnitza, **Nov. 17, 1885**, allowing them to invade Serbia. See **Pirot, battles of**.

Slovik, Eddie, court-martial of, U.S.

army private Eddie D. Slovik [1920-Jan. 1945] convicted of desertion, **Nov. 11, 1944**; Slovik killed by firing squad in France, **Jan. 1945**.

Sluys (Sluis), battle of, English fleet of King Edward III defeated French fleet of Philip VI off Sluys, Netherlands, in first major battle of Hundred Years' War, **June 24, 1340**.

smelting oven (glass manufacture), invented, **1856**, by German scientist Friedrich Siemens [1826-1904].

smelting process, introduced in Colorado, **1868**, by American metallurgist Nathaniel P. Hill [1832-1900].

Smith Act (Alien Registration Act), U.S. Congress required, **June 29, 1940**, registration and fingerprinting of all aliens.

Smithsonian Institution, institution, founded, **1846**, Washington D.C..

Smolensk, battles of, Russians lost heroic battle against French forces of Napoleon I, **Aug. 17, 1812**; Germans captured or killed more than 100,000 Russians, winning city of Smolensk during WW II, **July 16-Aug. 6, 1941**.

Snow White and the Seven Dwarfs, film, **1938**, first full-length animated cartoon film by Walt Disney.

Soap Box Derby, international race for youngsters 10 to 15 years old, held each August, first held at Dayton, Ohio, **1934**; since then, held at Akron, Ohio.

Sobraon, battle of, British-Indian forces under Sir Hugh Gough [Nov. 3, 1779-Mar. 2, 1869] and others decisively defeated the Sikhs in the Punjab, **Feb. 10, 1846**. See **Aliwal, battle of**.

soccer, popular sport under the name football in England, **12th century-present**; adopted by other countries, **18th century**.

Social Contract, The (Le Contrat

Social), philosophical treatise, **1762**, by French philosopher Jean-Jacques Rousseau.

Social Democratic Party, British, members of British parliament established first new political party in Great Britain in 80 years, **Mar. 26, 1981**.

Socialist Labor Party, U.S. political party, formed, **1876**, as Workingmen's Party by socialists in New York City; adopted name, **1877**; organized its own labor union, **1896**; declined, after **1899**.

Socialist Party, U.S. political party, formed **1898**, as Social Democratic Party; adopted present name, **1901**; nominated Eugene V. Debs [Nov. 5, 1855-Oct. 20, 1926] five times for U.S. President, **1900-20**; nominated Norman M. Thomas [Nov. 20, 1884-Dec. 19, 1968] six times for U.S. President, **1928-48**.

Socialist Revolutionary Party, former Russian agrarian party established, **1901**, by Populist groups; won majority in short-lived constituent assembly, **Jan. 1918**; suppressed by Bolsheviks (Communists), **1922**.

Social Security, U.S. government old-age, disability, and unemployment insurance program instituted by Social Security Act, **Aug. 14, 1935**.

sodium, element No. 11; isolated, **1807**, by English chemist Sir Humphry Davy [1778-1829] by passing an electric current through molten soda.

Soissons, battle of, Salian Franks under Clovis I [c. 466-511] defeated rival Frankish-Roman force at Soissons, firmly establishing Merovingian dynasty, **486**.

Sokoto, former capital of a Fulani-Muslim empire of w. Africa, **c. 1810-1903**; fell to British troops, **1903**.

solar battery, developed, **1954**, by American scientists at Bell Laboratories of American Telephone and Telegraph.

solar compass, invented, **1836**, by American surveyor-inventor William A. Burt [1792-1858], to offset magnetic attraction.

solar furnace, world's first built, **1921**, in Jena, Germany.

solar rays, infrared, discovered , **1800**, by German-English astronomer William Herschel [1738-1822].

solar spectrum, dark lines in, discovered, **1802**, by English physicist William H. Wollaston [1766-1826], and independently,

1814, by German physicist Joseph von Fraunhofer [1787-1826].

Solemn League and Covenant, agreement signed by members of parliament, pledging religious reform and acceptance of Presyterian state church in Scotland, Ireland, and England, **Sept. 25, 1643**.

Solferino, battle of, Austrians led by Emperor Franz Josef withdrew after bloody battle against French-Sardinian army of Napoleon III, **June 24, 1859**.

Solidarity, Polish labor union claiming 10 million members called strike, **Aug. 1980**, that led to unprecedented recognition of free trade unions by Soviet bloc country; operations suspended in military crackdown, **Dec. 13, 1981**.

solid-fuel rocket, invented, **1804**, by British inventor William Congreve [1772-1828].

solid hydrogen, production process developed, **1899**, by Scottish physicist Sir James Dewar [1842-1923].

Solomon Islands, island nation in s.w. Pacific, site of many battles in WW II; granted self-government by Britain, **Jan. 2, 1976**; gained complete independence, **July 7, 1978**.

Solway Moss, battle of, English forces of King Henry VIII [June 28, 1491-Jan. 28, 1547] defeated Scottish forces of King James V [Apr. 10, 1512-Dec. 14, 1542] at Solway Moss, **Nov. 25, 1542**.

Somalia, country on the Horn of Africa, divided into British protectorate, **1887**, and Italian protectorate, **1889**; British Somaliland granted independence, **June 26, 1960**, and joined with Italian Somaliland to form independent republic of Somalia, **July 1, 1960**; severe drought, **1975**; defeated in war with Ethiopia over Ogaden region, **1977-78**.

Somme River, battles of, Germans fought indecisive, bloody battle against British-French armies led by Marshal Joseph J. C. Joffre [Jan. 12, 1852-Jan. 3, 1931] and Marshal Ferdinand Foch [Oct. 2, 1851-Mar. 20, 1929]; German use of tanks for first time in battle, **July 1-Nov. 18, 1916**; British-French armies halted German offensive under Gen. Erich Ludendorff [Apr. 9, 1865-Dec. 20, 1937], **Mar. 21-Apr. 4, 1918**.

Somoza, assassination of, Anastasio Somoza [Feb. 1, 1896-Sept. 29, 1956], President of Nicaragua, shot in Leon, **Sept. 21, 1956**; died eight days later, **Sept. 29,**; Anastasio Somoza-Debayle [Dec. 5, 1925-Sept. 17, 1980], President of Nicaragua, fatally shot in La Paz, Bolivia, **Sept. 17, 1980**.

sonar, early device constructed, **1916**, by French physicist Paul Langevine [1872-1946].

sonata, musical composition, originated, from **c. 1635**, Italy; four movements standard, from **c. 1650**; zenith of sonata form **c. 1780-1820**.

Songhoy Empire, native kingdom founded by Berbers in w. Africa, **8th century**; conquered much of Mandingo Empire, **c. 1500**; declined after Moroccan invasion, **1591**.

Song of Roland, The (La Chanson de Roland), epic French poem, **c. 1050**, oldest manuscript, **c. 1250**.

Song of Songs (Song of Solomon) Old Testament book, probably written, **c. 300 B.C.**.

sonnet, fourteen-line poem, developed, Italy, from **1200s**; rules established, **c. 1275**, by Guittone D'Arezzo [c. 1225-1294]; perfected by Dante and Petrarch, **1300s**; became common poetic form after introduction into English, **c. 1530**, by Sir Thomas Wyatt [c. 1503-Oct. 11, 1542]

Sonnets from the Portuguese, series of 44 sonnets, **1850**, by English poetess, Elizabeth Barrett Browning, [Mar. 6, 1806-June 29, 1861].

Sonnets of Shakespeare, The, series of 144 sonnets by William Shakespeare, printed, **1609**, probably written, **1593-1601**.

Sons and Lovers, semi-autobiographical novel, **1913**, by English novelist D.H. Lawrence.

Sons of Liberty, secret groups formed in Boston and elsewhere in American colonies to protest against Stamp Act, **1765**; name adopted by the Knights of the Golden Circle during U.S. Civil War, **1864**.

Soor, (Sohr), battle of, well-disciplined Prussian army of Frederick II ("the Great") defeated larger Austrian army (at Soor in n. e. Bohemia) during the War of the Austrian Succession, **Sept. 30, 1745**. See **Hohenfriedenberg, battle of**.

sophists, school of ancient Greek philosophers and rhetoricians, opposed by Socrates, **from c. 450 B.C.**.

Sorbonne, college of University of Paris, founded, **c. 1257**, by confessor of St. Louis, Robert de Sorbon [Oct. 9, 1201-Aug. 15, 1274]; separate Sorbonne faculty abolished, **1882**.

Sorrow and the Pity, The (Le Chagrin et la Pitie), documentary film, **1969**, of France under German occupation, depicting active French collaboration, by German-French director Marcel Ophuls [Nov. 1, 1927-].

sound, first scientific study made, **c. 1600**, by Italian physicist and astronomer Galileo Galilei [1564-1642].

sound, absence of, in vacuum, demonstrated, **1660**, by British physicist and chemist Robert Boyle [1627-1691].

Sound and the Fury, The, novel, **1929**, by U.S. writer, 1949 Nobel Prize-winner William Faulkner.

sound in water, speed of, first accurately measured, **1826**, by French mathematician Jacques Sturm [1803-1855].

sound-motion picture, invented and first demonstrated, **1923**, by American inventor Lee De Forest [1873-1961].

Sound of Music, The, musical, opened, New York, **Nov. 16, 1959**, with Rodgers-Hammerstein music and lyrics written to Lindsay-Crouse book.

sound, stereophonic, method first developed and demonstrated, **1934**, by Bell Telephone Laboratories team of scientists headed by American physicist Harvey Fletcher [1885-1981].

sound, velocity of, calculated, **1687**, by English mathematician and physicist Sir Isaac Newton. [1642-1727].

South Africa Act, British parliament approved the creation of the Union of South Africa, uniting Transvaal, Natal, Cape Colony, and Orange River Colony (formerly Orange Free State), **Sept. 20, 1909**; went into effect, with Louis Botha [Sept. 27, 1862-Aug. 27, 1919] as first prime minister, **May 31, 1910**.

Southeast Asia Treaty Organization (SEATO), defense alliance established by U.S., Britain, France, Australia, New Zealand, Philippines, Thailand, and Pakistan, **Sept. 8, 1954**, to resist Communist intrusion in Southeast Asia.

South Carolina, one of Thirteen Colonies, ratified U.S. Constitution to become eighth state of the Union, **May 23, 1788**; first state to secede from the Union, **Dec. 20, 1860**; readmitted to the Union, **June 25, 1868**.

Southern Christian Leadership Conference (SCLC), U.S. civil rights organization established, **1957**, with Martin Luther King, Jr. as president.

South Dakota, part of territory acquired by Louisiana Purchase, admitted to the Union (U.S.) as 40th state, **Nov. 2, 1889**.

Southern Cross, **flight of the**, monoplane *Southern Cross*, piloted by Charles E. Kingsford-Smith [Feb. 9, 1897-Nov. 7-8, 1935], made great transpacific flight from Oakland, Calif., to Brisbane, Australia, **May 31-June 9, 1928**.

Southern Review, The, influential U.S. literary magazine, published, **1935-42**.

South Mountain, battle of, Union army of Gen. McClellan held the passes of South Mountain, Md., against Confederate attacks, **Sept. 14, 1862**.

South Pacific, musical, **1949**, that won Pulitzer and Tony awards for U.S. composers-writers Rodgers and Hammerstein; featured U.S. actress and singer Mary Martin [Dec. 1, 1913-];based on novel by James Michener, **1947**.

South Pole, southern-most end of the Earth, first reached by Norwegian explorer Roald Amundsen [July 16, 1872-June 1928], **Dec. 16, 1911**; reached by British explorer Robert F. Scott [June 6, 1868-c. Mar. 19, 1912], **Jan. 16, 1912**.

South Sea Bubble, speculation in the South Sea Company that assumed England's national debt and gained a monopoly of British trade in the South Seas and Spanish America, **1711-20**; bubble burst due to fraudulent schemes, **Jan. 1720**.

Southwold Bay, battle of, Dutch fleet

under Admiral Michel de Ruyter [Mar. 24, 1607-Apr. 29, 1676] defeated combined British and French fleets at Southwold Bay, n. of Thames River's mouth; French plans to invade Holland checked, **June 7, 1672**.

Soviet dissident trials, Russian dissidents exposing Soviet violations of human rights of 1975 Helsinki accord sentenced to prison and labor camps: Yuri F. Orlov, **May 18, 1978**; Aleksandr Ginzberg and Viktoras Petkus, **July 13, 1978**; Anatoly B. Shcharansky, **July 14, 1978**.

space walk, record (5 1/2 hours) achieved, **1966**, by American astronaut Edwin E. Aldrin [1930-] during *Gemini XII* earth orbital rendezvous mission.

Spa Conference, Germans signed disarmament agreement and reparations payments plan acceptable to Allies at meeting in town of Spa, e. Belgium **July 5-16, 1920**.

Spahis, loyal Turkish cavalry ordered by Sultan Mahmud II to kill the Janissaries, **June 16, 1826**.

Spanish-American War, U.S. supported Cuban rebels seeking independence from Spanish rule, **1898**; U.S. public opinion aroused by sinking of battleship *Maine* at Havana harbor, **Feb. 15, 1898**; U.S. declared Cuba independent, **Apr. 11, 1898**; Spain declared war on U.S., **Apr. 24, 1898**; U.S. fleet under Admiral Dewey defeated Spanish fleet at Manila Bay, **Apr. 31, 1898**; Spanish defeated at Santiago, Cuba, **July 3, 1898**; armistice signed, **Aug. 12, 1898**; Treaty of Paris freed Cuba, ceded Guam and Puerto Rico to U.S., and gave the Philippines to U.S. for $20 million, **Dec. 10, 1898**.

Spanish Civil War, conflict in which Nationalists overthrew republican government of Spain, **1936-39**; rightists and Nationalists rallied to revolt under Gen. Francisco Franco [Dec. 4, 1892-Nov. 20, 1975], **July 1936**; British-French proposed nonintervention pact signed by 27 nations, **Aug. 1936**; Nationalists, aided by Communists and the Falange, seized Catalonia and Barcelona, **Jan. 1939**; Nationalists entered Madrid, **Mar. 27, 1939**.

Spanish Inquisition, judicial court of the Roman Catholic Church established in Spain and headed by Tomas de Torquemada [1420-Sept. 16, 1498], noted for harsh treatment of Jews and Muslims, **15th century**, abolished in Spain, **1820**.

Spanish Succession, War of the, general European war fought for control of Spanish empire, caused by France's efforts to extend her power, **1701-14**; French defeated at Blenheim, **Aug. 13, 1704**; English captured Gibraltar, **1704**; allies defeated French at Ramillies, **May 23, 1706**; allied victories at Oudenarde, **July 11, 1708**; and at Malplaquet, **Sept. 11, 1709**; ended with Treaty of Utrecht, **Apr. 11, 1713**; with Treaty of Rastatt, **Mar. 6, 1714**, and with Treaty of Baden, **Sept. 7, 1714**.

Sparta, powerful military city-state of ancient Greece that rivaled Athens, **5th century B.C.**; won Peloponnesian War, **431-404 B.C.**; defeated by Thebes at Leuctra, **371 B.C.**; sacked by Goths, **395**.

Spartacus Party (Spartacists), radical German party, founded **Mar. 1916**, by Karl Liebknecht [Aug. 13, 1871-Jan. 15, 1919] and Rosa Luxemburg [Dec. 25, 1870-Jan.15, 1919]; became German Communist Party, **Jan. 1, 1919**; occupied Berlin government buildings until arrested and murdered, **Jan. 5-15, 1919**.

Specie Resumption Act, measure passed by U.S. Congress, **Jan. 14, 1875**, reduced circulating greenbacks to $300 million and provided for resumption of specie (coined money) payments, **Jan. 1, 1879**.

Speck murders, ex-convict Richard F. Speck [1942-] tried for the murder of eight student nurses in Chicago, **July 13, 1966**, and found guilty, **Apr. 15, 1967**.

Spectator, The, series of essays **1711-12**, by English essayist Joseph Addison [May 1, 1672-June 17, 1719] and Richard Steele.

spectroheliograph, invented, **1890**, by American astronomer George E. Hale [1868-1938]; used to photograph the sun.

spectroscope, diffraction-grating, invented, **1814**, by German physicist Joseph von Fraunhofer [1787-1826].

spectroscopic binary stars, first identified, **1889**, by American astronomer Edward C. Pickering [1877-1919].

spectroscopy, initiated, **1861**, by Swedish physicist Anders J. Angstrom [1814-1874].

spectrum analysis, first proposed, **c. 1845**, by American physicist David Alter [1807-1881].

Speyer, Diet of, diet convened by Holy Roman Emperor, **Feb. 21, 1529.**

Spingarn Medal, annual award by National Association for the Advancement of Colored People for outstanding achievement by an American black; established by Joel Elias Spingarn [May 17, 1875-July 26, 1939], **1913.**

spinning machine, invented, **1764,** by English textile engineer James Hargreaves [1720-1778].

spinning machine, power, first U.S. built, **1790,** by American millwright Sylvanus Brown [1747-1824].

spinning mule, devised, **1779,** by English inventor Samuel Crompton [1753-1827].

Spion Kop, battle of, British troops led by Gen. Redvers H. Buller [1839-June 2, 1908] crossed the Tugela River and captured Spion Kop from the Boers, **Jan. 25, 1900,** but were soon forced back. See **Boer War, Colenso, battle of.**

spiral hairspring (clock), developed, **c. 1658,** by English physicist Robert Hooke [1635-1703].

Spirit of Laws, The (L'Esprit des Lois), treatise, **1748,** by early French enlightenment philosopher Charles-Louis de Montesquieu.

Spithead mutiny, British sailors mutinied and won their demands for better wages and working conditions, **Apr. 15-May 17, 1797.**

Spock conspiracy case, Dr. Benjamin M. Spock [May 2, 1903-], William Sloane Coffin, Jr. [June 1, 1924-], and three others charged with conspiring to help young men evade U.S. draft, **Jan. 5, 1968;** Spock and four others found guilty, **June 14, 1968;** U.S. Court of Appeals overturned convictions, **July 11, 1969.**

spoils system, practice of awarding public offices to loyal party members, introduced into U.S. national politics by Pres. Andrew Jackson [Mar. 15, 1767-June 8, 1845], **1829;** corruption brought civil service reform, **1871.**

Spooner (Isthmian Canal) Act, U.S. Congress authorized, **June 28, 1902,** the building and financing of canal across isthmus of Panama or through Nicaragua.

Spotsylvania Courthouse, battle of, Union Army of the Potomac under Gen. Grant and Army of Northern Virginia under Gen. Lee engaged in series of indecisive attacks and counter-attacks during U.S. Civil War, **May 10-12, 1864.**

Spurs, battle of the, Flemish townspeople rebelled against French rule and totally defeated army sent by King Philip IV of France at Courtrai, **July 11, 1302;** English forces under King Henry VIII won victory over French at Guinegate in n. France, **Aug. 16, 1513.**

Sputnik I, first man-made satellite launched, **1957,** by Soviet scientists.

Sputnik II, first man-made satellite to carry live cargo launched, **1957,** by Soviet scientists; world's first space traveler, dog Laika.

Sri Lanka, island nation, formerly Ceylon, became independent republic, **May 22, 1972;** suffered large-scale uprising by extreme leftists, leaving thousands killed, **1971.**

Staffarda, battle of, French forces of King Louis XIV [Sept. 5, 1638-Sept. 1, 1715] won victory against Piedmontese forces of Victor Amadeus II [May 14, 1666-Oct. 31, 1732] at Staffarda during the War of the Grand Alliance, **Aug. 18, 1690.**

stainless steel, patented, **1919,** by American inventor Elwood Haynes [1857-1925].

Stalingrad (Volgograd), battle of, one of decisive battles of WW II; Russian army, after long bloody fighting, forced larger German army under Field Marshal Friedrich Paulus [Sept. 23, 1890-Feb. 1, 1957] to surrender; 300,000 German casualties; start of great Soviet offensive, **Aug. 23, 1942-Feb. 2, 1943.**

Stamford Bridge, battle of, Anglo-Saxons under King Harold I [1022-66] defeated Northumbrian-Norwegian forces of Tostig [d. 1066] and Harold III (Harold Hardrada) [d. 1066] in present-day n. England, **Sept. 25, 1066,** before rushing southward to meet invading Normans. See **Hastings, battle of.**

Stamp Act, British parliament passed act requiring American colonists to buy revenue stamps to be affixed to various pamphlets, newspapers, legal documents, etc., **Mar. 22, 1765**; act attacked by Patrick Henry [May 29, 1736-June 6, 1799] in his famous "treason speech", **May 29, 1765**; colonial delegates denounced act as unconstitutional at Stamp Act Congress, **Oct. 7-19, 1765**; repealed by parliament, **Mar. 18, 1766.**

Stamp Act Congress, famous meeting of colonial delegates at New York City hall to protest Stamp Act, **Oct. 7-19, 1765**; adopted Declaration of Rights and Grievances, drafted by John Dickinson [Nov. 8, 1732-Feb. 14, 1808], to be sent to British parliament, **Oct. 19.**

Stanford University, U.S. university, founded, Palo Alto, Calif., **1885.**

Stanley Cup competition, annual postseason playoffs of the National Hockey League (NHL) established to decide world's professional hockey champions, **1926.**

Stanley's African expeditions, New York *Herald* journalist Henry Morton Stanley [Jan. 28, 1841-May 10, 1904] discovered David Livingstone on Lake Tanganyika, uttering the famous line, "Dr. Livingstone, I presume?," **Nov. 10, 1871**; Stanley followed Congo River from its source to the Atlantic, **1874-77**; he helped establish Congo Free State, **1879-84**; he relieved German explorer Emin Pasha (Eduard Schnitzer) [Mar. 28, 1840-1892] during Mahdist uprising in Sudan, 1887-89.

Stanley Steamer, automobile designed,

1897, by American inventors Francis E. Stanley [1849-1918] and F. O. Stanley [1849-1940].

Stanwix (Schuyler), Fort, British loyalists allied with Mohawk Indians laid siege to Americans at Fort Stanwix on upper Mohawk River, **Aug. 3, 1777**; American column, seeking to relieve fort, defeated at Oriskany, **Aug. 6, 1777**; American volunteers under Gen. Benedict Arnold raised British siege and relieved fort, **Aug. 22, 1777.**

Stark effect, discovered, **1913**, by German physicist Johannes Stark [1874-1957].

Starry Night, The, painting, **1889,** by Dutch postimpressionist painter, Vincent van Gogh.

Star Spangled Banner, The, United States national anthem, written, **1814**, after watching British bombardment of Fort McHenry, Baltimore, by U.S. author and attorney, Francis Scott Key [Aug. 1, 1779-Jan. 11, 1843]; Congress adopted as national anthem, **March 3, 1931.**

stars, double, first recognized, **1803,** by English astronomer Sir William Herschel [1738-1822].

Star Trek, U.S. television adventure series, **1966-69, 1973-75,** since syndicated.

Star Wars, film, **1977**, a space fantasy about intergalactic war, conceived and directed by U.S. film director George Lucas.

State, U.S. Department of, oldest U.S. federal department created by Congress to oversee American foreign policy, **July 27, 1789**; Thomas Jefferson became first secretary of state, **Feb. 1790**; U.S. Foreign Service came under authority of secretary of state, **1954**; Peace Corps and Agency for International Development established as agencies within Department of State, **1961**.

States-General (Estates-General), French national assembly first summoned by Philip IV, **1302**; collapsed, **1358**; summoned by Louis XVI and met at Versailles, **May 5, 1789**; third estate declared itself the National Assembly, **June, 1789**.

St. Augustine, (Fla.), first permanent white settlement in U.S. founded by Spanish under Don Pedro Menendez de Aviles [1519-Sept. 17, 1574] at St. Augustine, Fla., **Sept. 8, 1565**; burned by English buccaneer Sir Francis Drake [c. 1540-Jan. 28, 1596], **July 1586**; passed to English at end of French and Indian War, **1763**.

Stavisky affair, Serge Alexandre Stavisky [Nov. 10, 1886-Jan. 8, 1934], Russian promoter of fraudulent bonds, fled to escape arrest by French police, **Dec. 1933**; Stavisky died mysteriously at Chamonix, **Jan. 1934**; riots by royalists and fascists against French republic at Paris, **Feb. 6-7, 1934**; long trial, involving politicians, allegedly linked to Stavisky, ended in acquittals, **1935-36**.

St. Bartholomew's Day massacre, general slaughter of Protestants throughout France precipitated fourth Huguenot War, **Aug. 24, 1572**.

St. Denis, battle of, French Catholic forces crushed the Protestant Huguenots but lost their leader Duke Anne de Montmorency [1493-Mar. 15, 1567] during the siege of Paris, **Mar. 1567**.

steady-state theory, proposed, **1948**, by Austrian-American astronomer Thomas Gold [1920-] and English astronomer Fred Hoyle [1915-].

steamboat, launched, **1787**, by American inventor John Fitch [1743-1798].

steam engine, alcohol-fueled, patented, **1797**, by English inventor Edmund Cartwright [1743-1823].

steam engine, condensing, invented, **1765**, by Scottish mechanical engineer James Watt [1736-1819]

steam engine, double-acting, invented, **1782**, by Scottish mechanical engineer James Watt [1736-1819].

steam engine, regenerative, invented, **1847**, by German-British inventor Sir William Siemens [1823-1883].

steam engine, U.S.-built, first stationary, high-pressure type produced, **1802**, by American inventor Oliver Evans [1755-1819].

steam hammer, patented, **1842**, by Scottish engineer James Naysmyth [1808-1890].

steam injector, patented, **1858**, by French aeronautical engineer Henri Giffard [1825-1882].

steam-propelled truck, developed, **1770**, by French military engineer Nicholas-Joseph Cugnot [1728-1804].

steam roller, invented, **1865**, by British inventor Thomas Aveling.

steam shovel, invented, **1835**, by American inventor William S. Otis [1811-1861].

steam snagboat, first launched, **1816**, by American steamboat captain and designer Henry M. Shreve [1785-1851]; called "Washington."

steam tractor, invented, **1832**, by English inventor John Heathcoat [1783-1861].

steam turbine, invented, **1629**, by Italian inventor Giovanni Branca.

steam turbine, compound, invented, c. **1884**, by English engineer Sir Charles Parsons [1854-1931].

stearic and oleic acids, method for isolating published, **1823**, by French chemist Michel E. Chevreul [1786-1889].

steel cable, developed, **1841**, by American engineer John A. Roebling [1806-1869].

steelmaking furnace, open-hearth, developed, **1857**, by German-British inventor Sir William Siemens [1823-1883].

Steinkirk (Steenkerke, or Steenkerque), battle of, French forces of King Louis XIV defeated English army of King William III [1650-1702] at village of Steinkirk, s. Belgium, during the War of the Grand Alliance, **July 24, 1692.**

Stella Dallas Show, The, long-running U.S. radio serial, **1937-55.**

stellar energy, source proposed, **1938,** as nuclear carbon cycle by German-American physicist Hans A. Bethe [1906-].

stellar spectra, photographic study established, **1885,** by American astronomer Edward C. Pickering [1877-1919], at Harvard College Observatory.

stereocomparator, invented, **1901,** by German scientist Carl Pulfrich [1858-1928].

stereoscope, invented, **1838,** by English physicist Sir Charles Wheatstone [1802-1875].

stereotype process, introduced, c. **1812,** by Scottish-American typefounder George Bruce [1781-1866].

sterilization (of surgical instruments), steam method pioneered, **1855,** by German physician Ernst von Bergmann [1836-1907].

stethoscope, invented, **1817,** by French physician Rene T. H. Laennec, [1781-1826].

St. Germain, Treaty of, elector of Brandenburg ceded to Sweden all his conquests in Pomerania, **June 29, 1679.**

St. Gotthard (Szentgotthard), battle of, Holy Roman Empire army under Count Raimund Montecuccoli [1608-Oct. 16, 1680] defeated the Ottoman Turks, **Aug. 1, 1664;** first serious blow to Turkish power in Hungary.

St. Gotthard Tunnel, first great railroad tunnel though the Alps (9 miles long), opened for goods and passenger traffic, **June 1, 1882.**

Stirling Bridge, site on Forth River where Scots under Sir William Wallace [1272?-1305] ambushed and wiped out vanguard of English army of Edward I [1239-1307], **Sept. 11, 1297.**

St. Lawrence Seaway, world's longest inland waterway, linking Great Lakes and Atlantic Ocean, authorized as U.S.-Canadian construction project by U.S. Congress, **May 13, 1954;** opened to shipping, **Apr. 25, 1959.**

St. Louis Exposition, U.S. exposition at St. Louis in honor of 100th anniversary of the Louisiana Purchase, **1903;** opening postponed, by delay in preparations, until **Apr. 30, 1904.**

St. Louis fire, great, more than 15 blocks of St. Louis, Mo. (400 buildings) destroyed by fire, **May 17, 1849.**

St. Mark's Basilica, five-domed basilica, Venice, built from **1063.**

Stockach, battle of, Austrians routed French under Marshal Jean Baptiste Jourdan [1762-1833], who retreated across the Rhine, **Mar. 25, 1799. See French Revolutionary Wars.**

Stock exchange, world's first stock exchange established at Antwerp, **1460.**

Stockholm, Peace of, ended hostilities between Britain and Sweden; Sweden ceded Bremen and Verden to George I (as elector of Hanover) for over one million rix-dollars, **Nov. 20, 1719.**

Stockholm, Treaty of, restored the status quo among Poland, Saxony, and Sweden before the Great Northern War; Prussia received Stettin (Szczecin) and w. Pomerania, **1720.**

stock market crash, decline in stock prices brought panic selling by U.S. investors and speculators, **Oct. 24, 1929,** and reached peak selling of shares, **Oct. 29, 1929,** beginning the Great Depression.

stock ticker, invented, **1869,** by American inventor Thomas A. Edison [1847-1931].

stock-ticker, rapid speed, invented, **1884,** by American inventor Stephen D. Field [1846-1913].

Stoicism, school of ancient philosophy,

founded, Athens, **c. 312 B.C.**, by Zeno of Citium [c. 336-264 BC].

Stolbovo, Treaty of, Russia ceded to Sweden towns on Gulf of Finland in return for Novgorod, **Feb. 27, 1617**.

stomach tube, for artificial feeding, introduced, **1790**, by Scottish surgeon John Hunter [1728-1793].

Stone Age, New (Neolithic Age), prehistoric period marked by advances in agriculture, domestic crafts, superior stone tools, and invention of the wheel and axle, **c. 5000-3000 B.C.**

Stone Age, Old (Paleolithic Age), prehistoric period during which Java Man, Peking Man, Neanderthal Man, and Cro-Magnon Man existed, **c. 500,000-10,000 B.C.**

storage battery, first practical invented, **1859**, by French physicist Gaston Plante [1834-1889].

St. Patrick's Cathedral, cathedral, New York, dedicated, **1879**.

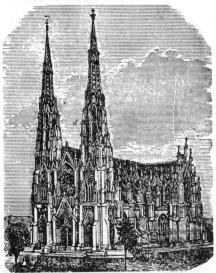

St. Paul's Cathedral, cathedral, London, begun, **1675**, completed, **1710**, by Sir Christopher Wren, on site of old cathedral destroyed by fire, **1666**—in turn completed, **1314**, on site of earlier cathedral burned, **1087**.

St. Petersburg (Leningrad), former capital of Russia, **1712-1918**; known as Petrograd, **1914-24**; withstood two-year German siege in WW II, **1941-43**.

St. Peter's Vatican Basilica, Christian church, metropolitan see of popes, begun, **1506**, under direction of Donato Bramante [1444-1514]; dome added, from **1547**, designed by Michelangelo; dedicated, **1627**.

Straits Settlements, former colonies of Penang, Singapore, and Malacca controlled by British East India Company, **1826-58**; became British crown colony, 1867; Labuan became fourth settlement in colony, **1912**; dissolved, **1946**.

Stralsund, siege of, Holy Roman Empire army under Gen. Wallenstein failed to take city of Stralsund on the Baltic after 10-week siege; heroic stand by citizens, **June-Aug. 1628**.

Stralsund, Treaty of, Denmark gave Hanseatic League control of trade in the Baltic and Scandinavian politics, **1370**.

Stranger, The (L'Etranger), novel, **1942**, by French writer Albert Camus, Nobel Prize-winner, **1957**.

Stratton Hill, battle of, British royalists defeated the parliamentarians in Devonshire, England, **May 16, 1643**. See **Civil War, English**.

Streetcar Named Desire, A, play, **1947**, by U.S. playwright Tennessee Williams; film, **1951**, based on Tennessee Williams' play, with Vivien Leigh, Marlon Brando [Apr. 3, 1924-] and Kim Hunter (born Janet Cole) [Nov. 12, 1922-].

street lights, first in Philadelphia devised, **1757**, by American statesman-scientist Benjamin Franklin [1706-1790].

ST. PAUL'S CATHEDRAL.

Street Offenses Act, British parliament made it an offense to loiter or solicit in a private or public place for the purpose of prostitution, **July 16, 1959.** See **Wolfenden Report.**

streltsy, revolt of the, Czar Peter the Great suppressed the streltsy (soldiers of the Moscow garrison), who revolted against Peter's modernization of armed forces and domestic reforms, **1698.**

Stresa Conference, France, Britain, and Italy protested Germany's rearmament in violation of Treaty of Versailles at meeting at Stresa, Italy, **Apr. 11-14, 1935.**

strontium, element No. 38; first isolated, **1808,** by English chemist Sir Humphry Davy [1778-1829] from carbonate compound mined in Scotland.

strychnine, isolated, **1818,** from nightshade plant by French chemists Joseph Bienaime Caventou [1795-1877] and Pierre Joseph Pelletier [1788-1842].

Stuart, House of, royal family that ruled Scotland, **1371-1603;** ruled England, **1603-1714.**

Student Nonviolent Coordinating Committee (SNCC), U.S. student organization involved in civil rights movement and opposed to Vietnam War, **1960s;** elected Stokely Carmichael, **1966,** who resigned, **1967,** to lead Black Panthers.

Student Peace Union (SPU), probably first national student political association in U.S., formed in Chicago, **1959;** dissolved, **1963.**

Students for a Democratic Society (SDS), U.S. student organization that demonstrated against Vietnam War and for civil rights, mid **1960s-early 1970s;** radicals formed Weather Underground, **1969.**

Studs Lonigan, fictional trilogy, **1932-35,** account of lower-middle-class Chicago milieu; includes *Young Lonigan,* **1932;** *Young Manhood of Studs Lonigan,* **1934;** and *Judgment Day,* **1935,** by U.S. novelist James T(homas) Farrell [Feb. 27, 1904-Aug. 22, 1979].

Study of History, A, theoretical study published in twelve volumes, **1934-61,** by English historian Arnold J(oseph) Toynbee [Apr. 14, 1889-Oct. 22, 1975.]

Sturm und Drang (storm and stress), movement in German romanticism, **c. 1770-**

1800, e.g.; Goethe's *Sorrows of Young Werther,* **1774,** Schiller's *The Robbers,* **1782.**

subatomic particles, discovered, **1947,** by U.S. physicist Luis W. Alvarez [1911-].

submarine, designed, **1898,** by Irish-American inventor John P. Holland [1840-1914]; successful, the *Holland* was purchased, **1900,** by Navy Department, becoming first U.S. Navy sub.

submarine, ballistic-missile, first U.S., the *George Washington,* launched, **1959,** at Groton, Conn.

submarine detector, invented, **1917,** by American mathematician Max Mason [1877-1961].

submarine quadruplex telegraph, invented and installed, **1879-1880,** by American inventor Stephen D. Field [1846-1913].

substage condenser, for microscopic work, invented, **1872,** by German physicist Ernst Abbe [1840-1905].

subways, pioneered, **1863,** by English engineers John Fowler [1817-1898] and Benjamin Baker [1840-1907] with the London opening of the first underground railway, called "the tube."

Sudan, Africa's largest country, proclaimed an independent republic, **Jan. 1, 1956;** Communist coup to topple government failed, **July 1971;** U.S. ambassador and charge d'affaires and Belgian diplomat killed by 8 Palestinian terrorists at Khartoum, **Mar. 2, 1973.**

Sudetenland, German-speaking region along borders of Bohemia and Moravia, Czechoslovakia, annexed by Nazi Germany under Hitler's orders, **Sept. 12-29, 1938;** Munich Pact allowed Germany to occupy Sudetenland **Sept. 30, 1938;** recovered by Czechoslovakia, **1945.** See **Munich Pact.**

Suez Canal, waterway of Egypt linking Mediterranean with Gulf of Suez built by

French engineer Ferdinand de Lesseps, **1859-69**; officially opened by many European celebrities and dignitaries, **Nov. 17, 1869**; blocked during war between Egypt and Israel, **Oct. 1956-Apr. 1957**; closed by Egypt during Arab-Israeli War, **1967-75**.

Suez Canal Convention, assembly of European powers declared Suez Canal free and open to all ships in time of war or peace, **Oct. 29, 1888**.

suffrage, woman, U.S. women's voting rights first proposed at Seneca Falls convention, N.Y., by Elizabeth Cady Stanton [Nov. 12, 1815-Oct. 26, 1902] and others, **July 19, 1848**; National Woman Suffrage Asssociation formed, led by Susan B. Anthony [Feb. 15, 1820-Mar. 13, 1906] and Stanton, merged with American Woman Suffrage Association, led by Lucy Stone [Aug. 13, 1818-Oct. 18, 1893], to form National American Woman Suffrage Association, **1890**; 19th Amendment to U.S. Constitution granted nation-wide suffrage to women, **Aug. 26, 1920**.

sugar, elementary composition determined, **1811**, by French chemists Joseph L. Gay-Lussac [1778-1850] and Louis J. Thenard [1777-1857].

Sugar Act, British parliament revised Molasses Act in hopes of forcing American colonies to help pay costs of maintaining British Empire, **Apr. 5, 1764**; James Otis [Feb. 5, 1725-May 23, 1783] opposed act at Boston, bringing up taxation-without-representation argument for first time, **May 24, 1764**; Boston merchants began non-importation of British goods, which spread to other colonies, **Aug. 1764**.

sugar beet, source of sugar discovered, **1747**, by German chemist Andreas Sigismund Marggraf [1709-1782].

Sugar Bowl, major U.S. collegiate football game played each Jan. 1 at New Orleans, La.; first Sugar Bowl game between Tulane and Temple, **1935**.

sugar-lactic acid transition, changes determined, between **1937 and 1941**, by Czech-American physicists Carl F. Cori [1896-] and Gerty T. Cori [1896-1957].

sulfonamide drug, first discovered, **1932**, by German physician Gerhard Domagk [1895-1964].

sulfuric acid, contact process patented, **1831**, by English chemist Perrigrine Phillips [c. 1800-?]; method still used.

Sullivan-Kilrain fight, last heavyweight championship fight with bare knuckles; John L. Sullivan beat Jake Kilrain [1859-1937] in 75 rounds at Richburg, Miss., **July 8, 1889**.

Sultana, Mississippi River steamboat *Sultana* sank after its boiler exploded near Memphis, Tenn.; c. 1450 persons died, **Apr. 27, 1865**.

Sumer, advanced agricultural civilization in ancient Mesopotamia, **4th-3rd mil. B.C.**; blended with Semite culture, **c. 2600 B.C.**; disappeared when Hammurabi ruled Babylonia, **18th century B.C.**

Summa contra Gentiles, treatise, **1258-64**, expounding Catholic doctrine, by medieval scholastic philosopher St. Thomas Aquinas.

Summa Theologica, treatise, **1265-74**, by medieval scholastic philosopher St. Thomas Aquinas.

Sumer is icumen in, poem, **c. 1200**, earliest extant English lyric, author unknown.

Sumter, Fort, fortification at entrance to harbor of Charleston, S.C., where Confederate bombardments ordered by Gen. Pierre G.T. Beauregard [May 28, 1818-Feb. 20, 1893] forced Union forces at Fort Sumter to surrender, beginning the U.S. Civil War, **April 11-12, 1861**; Union (U.S.) flag again raised over fort, **Apr. 14, 1865**.

Sun Also Rises, The, novel, **1926**, about

post-World War I expatriate Americans, by U.S. author Ernest Hemingway; Nobel Prize-winner, **1954**.

sundial, reportedly invented, **c. 590 B.C.**, by Greek mathematician Anaximander [611-547 B.C.]. First constructed in America, **1630**, by William Bowyer of New England Company for Gov. John Endicott [1589-1665].

sun, eclipse of, earliest known prediction, for **May 28, 585 B.C.**, by Greek astronomer Thales [640 B.C.-546 B.C.].

Sunflowers, painting, **1888**, presenting sunflowers in vase, by Dutch postimpressionist painter Vincent van Gogh.

Sung dynasty, ancient advanced Chinese dynasty, **960-1279**.

sun's magnetic field, structure first determined, **1977**, from data returned by U.S. Pioneer II spacecraft.

sun/moon dimensions, first estimated, **c. 130 B.C.**, by Greek mathematician and astronomer Hipparchus [160-120 B.C.].

sun valve, invented, **c. 1908**, by Swedish inventor Nils G. Dalen [1869-1937].

Super Bowl Game, major American professional football game between conference champions of National Football League; first game played at Los Angeles, **Jan. 15, 1967**.

superconductivity, discovered, **1911**, by Dutch physicist Heike Kamerlingh-Onnes [1853-1926].

superheterodyne circuit, radio receiver device invented, **1918**, by American electronics engineer Edwin Howard Armstrong [1890-1954].

super-laser, developed, **1969**, by French scientists at Lemeil Weapons Research Center near Paris.

supermagnet, first used around bubble chamber in high-energy research, **1966**, at Argonne National Laboratory.

supernova, research pioneered, **1937-41**, by Bulgarian-born Swiss astronomer Fritz Zwicky [1898-1974].

superregenerative detector circuit, patented, **1922**, by American radio engineer Edwin H. Armstrong [1890-1954].

Supper at Emmaus, painting, **1648**, by Dutch baroque painter Rembrandt.

Supreme Court, U.S., Congress passed Federal Judiciary Act, establishing Court with chief justice and five associate justices, **Sept. 24, 1789**; John Jay [Dec. 12, 1745-May 17, 1829] became first Chief Justice of U.S. Supreme Court, **Sept. 26, 1789**; nine members of Court, since **1869**.

Supreme Headquarters, Allied Powers in Europe (SHAPE), defensive organization established in Paris, **Apr. 4, 1951**, with Gen. Dwight D. Eisenhower in command.

surgery, breast, reconstructive, cosmetic surgery, developed, **c. 1920**, by American surgeon Max Thorek [1880-1960].

surgery, blood vessel, pioneered, **1902**, by French-American surgeon Alexis Carrel [1873-1944] with a method of suturing.

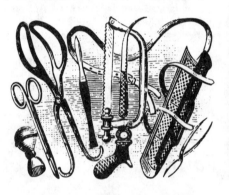

surgical knife, (electrical high-frequency) invented, **1907**, by American inventor Lee De Forest [1873-1961].

surgical mask, innovation, **1897**, of Polish surgeon Johann Mikulicz-Radecki [1850-1905].

Surinam, country on n.e. coast of South America, formerly Dutch Guiana, became independent republic, **Nov. 25, 1975**.

Surprise Symphony, symphony, **1791**, by Austrian composer Franz Joseph Haydn.

surrealism, movement in the arts, **1924-66**; launched by *Surrealist Manifesto*, **1924**, by French poet Andre Breton [Feb. 19, 1896-Sept. 28, 1966]; subsequent manifestos, **1930, 1935**.

survey maps, developed, **c. 23 B.C.**, by Roman general Marcus Vipsanius Agrippa [63 B.C.-12 B.C.].

Sutter's Mill, gold discovered on property of John A. Sutter [Feb. 15, 1803-June 18, 1880] in Sacramento Valley, Calif., **Jan. 24, 1848**.

Swaanendael, former Dutch settlement, now Lewes, Del., established on Delaware River, **1631**; inhabitants massacred by Indians, **1632**; sold to the Dutch West India Company, **1633**.

Swabian League, Swabian cities in Germany banded together for mutual protection of trade and peace, **1488-1534**; crushed knights' revolt led by Franz von Sickingen [1481-1523], **1522**; defeated the peasants in the Peasants' War, **1525**.

Swamp Fight, the, colonists from Massachusetts, Plymouth, and Connecticut led by Josiah Winslow [c. 1629-80] nearly wiped out the Narragansett Indians in a swamp in present-day South Kingston, R.I., **Dec. 19, 1675**.

Swan Lake, ballet, completed, **1876**, produced, Moscow, **1877**, with music by Tchaikovsky and choreography by Petipa.

Swaziland, kingdom in s. Africa, guaranteed autonomy by the British and Transvaal governments, **1881**; came under British administration, **1903**; became independent nation, **Sept. 6, 1968**.

Swearing of the Oath of Ratification of the Treaty of Munster, painting, **1648**, by Dutch painter Gerard Terborch [1617-Dec. 8, 1681]; artist's *Parental Admonition,* **1654-55**.

Sweden, Scandinavian country, site of Europe's earliest functioning parliament, the Riksdag, **1435**; rebelled successfully against Danish rule, **1521-23**; became great European power during latter part of Thirty Years' War, **1630-48**; Northern War ended in waning of Swedish power, **1700-21**; forced Denmark to cede Norway, **1814**; ended union with Norway, **1905**; 44-year Socialist government ended by conservative coalition, **Sept. 19, 1976**.

Swedish West India Company (South Company), trading and colonizing company established in Antwerp, **Oct. 1646**, under charter granted by King Gustavus II [1594-1632] of Sweden.

Sylphides, Les (The Sylphs), ballet first produced, Paris, **1909**, with music by French impressionist composer Claude Debussy and choreography by famous choreographer Michel Fokine.

Symbionese Liberation Army, radical terrorist group, Symbionese Liberation Army, kidnaped Patricia C. ("Patty") Hearst [Feb. 20, 1954-], **Feb. 4, 1974**, demanding $2-million ransom; FBI agents seized Patty with others in San Francisco, **Sept. 18, 1975**; Patty convicted of bank robbery charges while member of SLA, **Mar. 20, 1976**; William [Jan. 25, 1945-] and Emily [Feb. 11, 1947-] Harris sentenced to 10-year jail term for kidnapping of Patty, **Oct. 3, 1978**.

symbolic logic, developed, **1910**, by English mathematicians Bertrand A. Russell [1872-1970] and Alfred N. Whitehead [1861-1947] with their publication of *Principia Mathematica.*

symbolists, the, school of French poets, **1880-95**.

Symphonie Fantastique (Fantastic Symphony), romantic symphony, **1830**, adapting classical symphonic forms, by French orchestral composer, Hector Berlioz.

Symposium, philosophical dialogue, **c. 384 B.C.**, by Greek philosopher, Plato.

Synanon, U.S. organization, founded by Charles E. Dederich [Mar. 22, 1913-] in Ocean Park, Calif., **1958**; Dederich and others charged, **Dec. 1978**, with assassination attempt, **Oct. 1977**, of Los Angeles lawyer who had won $300,000 lawsuit for client against Synanon.

synchrocyclotron, proposed, **1945**, by American physicist Edwin M. McMillan [1907-]; frequency modulated cyclotron.

synthetic diamonds, announced, **1955,** by American physicists at General Electric Co..

synthetic graphite, produced, **1899,** by American industrial chemist Edward G. Acheson [1856-1931].

synthetic perfume, process discovered, **1868,** by English chemist Sir William Henry Perkin [1838-1907].

synthetic soil chemical, developed, **1951,** by Monsanto Chemical Co.

Syphilis, named, **1530,** by Italian physician Girolamo Fracastoro [1483-1553] in poem which also described the gumma lesion of tertiary (late-state) syphilis.

Syracuse, port-city in Sicily founded by Greeks, **734 B.C.;** defeated Athenian expedition sent by Alcibiades, **413 B.C.;** sacked by Romans in second Punic War, **212 B.C.**

syringe, hypodermic, first published description, **1853,** by physician C.G. Pravaz [1791-1853].

Taborites, radical Hussites who split from moderate Utraquists during Hussite Wars, **1434.**

Tacna-Arica controversy, dispute between Chile and Peru over legal ownership of provinces of Tacna and Arica, **1883-1929;** settled by U.S. proposal: Chile received Arica, Peru Tacna, **June 3, 1929.**

Taft-Hartley Act (Labor Management Relations Act), U.S. Congress enacted over Pres. Truman's veto, **June 23, 1947,** law that eliminated "excess" labor union advantages such as unconditional right to strike and closed shop, allowing 80-day government injunction against strike threatening national safety; amended by Landrum-Griffin Act, **Sept. 14, 1959.**

Taiping Rebellion, Chinese rebels led by mystic Hung Hsiu-ch'uan [Jan. 1, 1814-June 1, 1864] failed to overthrow Ch'ing dynasty and to create new dynasty, **1848-64.**

Taisho, reign of Japanese emperor carrying on reforms of Meiji restoration; Japan made great economic advances, **1912-26.**

Taj Mahal, monument-mausoleum, near Agra, India, built, **1630-48.**

Talavera, battle of, British forces fought indecisive battle against French during Peninsular War of the Napoleonic Wars, **July 28, 1809.**

Tale of Genji, The (Genji Monogatari),

Japanese novel, **c. 1010,** by writer and lady at court, Murasaki Shikibu [978?-1026].

Tale of Two Cities, A, novel, **1859,** a dramatic tale set in the French Revolution, by Victorian English novelist Charles Dickens.

Talladega, battle of, Tennessee militiamen under Gen. Andrew Jackson defeated Creek Indian warriors at Talladega, Ala., **Nov. 9, 1813.**

Tamburlaine, Elizabethan play in two parts, **1587,** by Christopher Marlowe.

Taming of the Shrew, The, comedy, **c. 1594.**

Tammany Hall, powerful central organization of New York City's Democratic Party established as benevolent Tammany Society, **1789;** dominated city's politics, **c. 1854-1932.**

tango, dance of Argentinian origin, developed, **c. 1880,** Buenos Aires.

tank, military, invented, **1914,** by British soldier-writer Sir Ernest D. Swinton [1868-1951].

Tannenberg, battles of, Poles, Russians, and Lithuanians, assembled by Polish King Ladislaus II (Ladislaus Jagiello) [1350?-1434], won great victory over Teutonic Knights at Tannenberg, e. Prussia, **July 15, 1410;** Germans under Marshal Paul von Hindenburg [Oct. 2, 1847-Aug. 2, 1934] and Gen. Ludendorff routed Russian army under Gen. Aleksandr V. Samsonov [1859?-Aug. 29, 1914], **Aug. 26-30, 1914**.

Tannhauser, opera, produced, Dresden, **1845**, revised Paris, **1861**; by German operatic composer Richard Wagner.

tantalum, element No. 73; discovered, **1802**, by Swedish chemist Anders G. Ekeberg [1767-1813].

Tanzania, country in Africa, established when Tanganyika (independent nation, **Dec. 9, 1961**) and Zanzibar (independent island nation, **Dec. 10, 1963**) merged to form single republic, **Apr. 26, 1964**; took present name, **Oct. 29, 1964**; 1,163-mile Tan-Zam RR between Dar-es-Salaam and Zambia opened, **Oct. 23, 1975**; closed border with Kenya over dispute of airlines, **1977**; warred successfully against Idi Amin's Ugandan troops, **1978-79**.

Taoism, Chinese religious system, developed from **c. 600 B.C.**

tape cassette, introduced, **1964**, by Netherlands-based firm, Phillips.

Tararori, battle of, mounted Muslim archers and legions of the principality of Ghor defeated the Hindu armies at Tararori, near Thanesar, **1192**.

Tariff of Abominations, U.S. Congress passed high, protective duties, resulting in increased bitterness between Northern mercantile and Southern agricultural interests, **May 13, 1828**; South Carolina adopted resolutions calling tariff unjust and unconstitutional, **Dec. 19, 1828**.

Tarleton's quarter, British mounted redcoats with sabers and bayonets, led by Col. Banastre Tarleton [1754-1833], slaughtered American revolutionary force led by Col. Abraham Buford [July 31, 1749-June 30, 1833] at Waxhaw Creek, S.C., **May 29, 1780**.

Tarnower murder case, millionaire developer of Scarsdale Diet, Dr. Herman Tarnower [1911-Mar. 10, 1980] shot to death in bedroom of his Purchase, N.Y., home, **Mar. 10, 1980**; former lover and headmistress of exclusive girl's school in Virginia, Jean Harris, found guilty of murder in the second degree, **Feb. 24, 1981**.

Tarsus, battle of, Christian knights led by Tancred [1076-1112] defeated Turks at city of Tarsus in Cilicia [s. Turkey] during first Crusade, **1097**.

Tartuffe, satiric comedy, **1664**, by French comic dramatist Moliere.

Tartu, Treaty of, Russia made peace with Finland and Estonia, **Oct. 14, 1920**.

Tarzan, fictional jungle hero, first appeared, **1914**, in *Tarzan of the Apes*, about orphaned child of English aristocrats raised by apes; 23 subsequent Tarzan books selling millions of copies written by U.S. author Edgar Rice Burroughs [Sept. 1, 1875-Mar. 19, 1950]; movie series comprised 19 films, **1930-50**.

Tatars (Tartars), name of peoples who laid waste to parts of Asia and Europe under Mongol leadership, **13th century**.

Tate-LaBianca murders, screen actress Sharon Tate Polanski [1943-Aug. 10, 1969] and four companions brutally murdered in her Bel-Air, Calif., home, **Aug. 10, 1969**; supermarket chain president Leno La Bianca [1925-Aug. 10, 1969] and his wife murdered in Los Angeles, **Aug. 10, 1969**.

Tauroggen, Convention of, Russian Field Marshal Yorck von Wartenburg [1759-1830] concluded on his own an agreement of neutrality with Russians, whereby Prussians withdrew from fighting, **Dec. 30, 1812**.

Taxation no Tyranny, famous pamphlet written by Dr. Samuel Johnson against the grievances of the American colonies, published in London, **1775**.

Tea Act, British passed act to save British East India Company from bankruptcy, allowing company to sell its tea duty-free in American colonies, **May 10, 1773**; undercut colonial merchants who held mass protest in Boston, **Nov. 29-30, 1773**; Boston Tea Party occurred, **Dec. 16, 1773**.

teaching machines, first self-scoring multiple-choice apparatus pioneered, **1924**, by American psychologist Sidney L. Pressey [1888-].

Teamsters, (International Brotherhood of Teamsters, Chauffeurs, Warehousemen, and Helpers of America), U.S. labor union established, **1903**, by merger of Teamsters National Union and Team Drivers International Union; expelled by AFL-CIO for corruption, **Dec. 6, 1957**; James R. Hoffa [Feb. 14, 1913-?] as Teamsters' president (1957-71); Hoffa imprisoned for fraud in union and jury tampering, **1967-71**; Hoffa disappeared, **July 30, 1975**.

Teapot Dome scandal, U.S. Senate investigation of Teapot Dome, Wyoming, and Elk Hills, California, oil lease transfers, **1923-27**, brought criminal prosecution of prominent officials; U.S. Secretary of the Interior Albert B. Fall [Nov. 26, 1861-Nov. 30, 1944] convicted of accepting bribes, **Oct. 25, 1929**, and jailed, **1931-33**.

technetium, element No. 43; discovered, **1937**, by Italian-American physicist Emilio Segre [1905-].

Tecumseh's confederacy, Shawnee chief Tecumseh attempted to form confederacy of Indian tribes in Northwest Territory, e. Mississippi valley, and the South, **c. 1795-1811**; confederacy fell apart with defeat of his brother, the Prophet [1775?-1837?], at Tippecanoe, **Nov. 7, 1811**.

telegraph method, patented, **1837**, by English physicist Sir Charles Wheatstone [1802-1875].

telegraph company, first in U.S. established, **1847**, by Magnetic Telegraph Company of Maryland.

telegraph, dial, invented, **1846**, by German electrical engineer Werner von Siemens [1816-1892].

telegraph, multiwire, invented, **1809**, by German scientist Samuel T. von Soemmerring [1755-1830].

telegraphone, invented, **1898**, by Danish electrical engineer Valdemar Poulsen [1869-1942]; device for recording and reproducing sound; forerunner of tape recorder.

telegraphy, electro-harmonic, patented, **1875**, by American inventor Elisha Gray [1835-1901]; transmitted musical tones.

telephone, invented, **1874**, by Scottish-born Alexander Graham Bell [1847-1922]. Patented **1876**.

telephone amplifier, invented, **1912**, by American inventor Lee De Forest [1873-1961].

telephone cable system, world's first transatlantic system began operating, **1956**, between Newfoundland and Scotland.

telephone relay network, first global system completed, **1969**.

telephone, string, invented, **1667**, by English scientist Robert Hooke [1635-1703].

telephotography, first transmission, **1904**, by German physicist Arthur Korn [1870-1945].

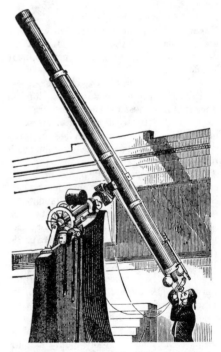

telescope, early model devised, **1608**, by Dutch spectacle maker Hans Lippershey [?-c. 1619]; one of first known to have been exhibited, **1609**, shown by Italian astronomer Galileo Galilei [1564-1642].

telescope, collimating, invented, **1785**, by American astronomer-mathematician David Rittenhouse [1732-1796].

telescope, reflecting, earliest form perfected and described, **1663**, by Scottish mathematician James Gregory [1638-1675] in his *Optica Promota*; first serviceable, invented, **1719**, by English mathematician John Hadley [1682-1744].

telescope, refracting, built, **c. 1670**, by Polish astronomer Johannes Hevelius [1611-1687]; led to discovery of four planets.

telescope, speculum, improved design developed, **1845**, by English astronomer William Parsons [1800-1867].

telescopic measuring device, invented, **1767**, by Scottish inventor James Watt [1736-1819].

telescopophone, invented, **1878**, by American inventor Thomas A. Edison [1847-1931] to concentrate sound from great distances.

television, first image transmitted, **1924**, by Scottish television pioneer John L. Baird [1888-1946].

television, color, first practical system developed, **1940**, by Hungarian-American Peter C. Goldmark [1906-1977].

television, filmless, demonstrated, **1951**, by American electronic engineers John T. Mullin [1913-] and Wayne R. Johnson [1922-].

television, transistorized, first introduced, **1959**, by Sony Corporation of Japan; black-and-white portable.

television with sound, pioneered, **1929**, by Scottish inventor John L. Baird [1888-1946] for British Broadcasting Company.

Tell-Tale Heart, The, psychological detective story, **1843**, in which murderer is revealed by ticking watch of his victim buried under the floor, by U.S. writer Edgar Allan Poe.

tellurium, element No. 52; discovered, **1782**, by Austrian chemist Franz J. Muller (von Reichenstein) [1740-1825].

temperance movements, organized efforts to induce persons to stop drinking liquor, **19th-early 20th century**; Woman's Christian Temperance Union formed in U.S., **1874**; Anti-Saloon League formed in U.S., **1895**; helped secure federal Prohibition in U.S., **1919-33**.

Tempest, The, last play of William Shakespeare, **c. 1611**.

Templars, Order of Knights, medieval military religious order, founded, **1118**, to protect pilgrims; approved by Rome, **1185**; ruled Cyprus, from **1191**; order suppressed by Rome, **1312**; Grand Master burned at stake, Paris, **1314**.

Temple, Jewish, sacred center of Jewish worship, built, Jerusalem, from **c. 950 B.C.**, by King Solomon [c. 970-931 B.C.]; destroyed by Babylonians, **586 B.C.**; rebuilt, **515 B.C.**; desecrated, **167 B.C.**; rededicated by Judas Maccabeus, **165 B.C.**; destroyed, **70**, by Romans.

Ten Commandments, The, film, **1923**, first religious extravaganza by Cecil B. De Mille; DeMille remake, **1956**, his longest film.

Ten, Council of, special emergency tribunal created to avert plots and crimes against the Venetian state, **1310**; made a permanent body, **1335**; most important governing body of Venice, **c. 1500-1797**.

Tennessee, formerly part of North Carolina, admitted to the Union (U.S.) as 16th state, **June 1, 1796**; seceded from the Union, **June 8, 1861**; readmitted to the Union, **June 24, 1866**.

Tennessee Valley Authority (TVA), U.S. Congress created, **May 18, 1933**.

Tenochtitlan, ancient capital of Aztec Empire, founded in the central valley of

Mexico, **c. 1345**; captured and razed by Spanish under Cortes, **Aug. 13, 1521**.

Ten Points, ten conditions outlined by Pres. Wilson, **Jan. 22, 1917**, under which he would urge U.S. to join international organization to maintain lasting peace.

Ten Thousand, retreat of the, torturous two-year and 4000 mi. retreat by defeated Greek mercenaries led by Xenophon [c. 431-c. 350 B.C.] after the battle of Cunaxa; only half the force survived, **401-399 B.C.**

Tenure of Office Act, measure passed, **Mar. 2, 1867**, by U.S. Congress over veto by Pres. Andrew Johnson [Dec. 29, 1808-July 31, 1875] prohibited the removal of any federal official without consent of the Senate; act repealed, **Mar. 5, 1887**; act declared unconstitutional by Supreme Court, **Oct. 25, 1926**.

Ten Year's War, conflict between Spain and Cuba seeking trade and governmental reform, **1868-78**; ended by Convention of El Zanjon, at which Spain promised reform, **Feb. 10, 1878**.

terbium, element No. 65; discovered, **1843**, by Swedish chemist Carl G. Mosander [1797-1858].

terrestrial magnetism observatory, first established, **1832**, by German mathematician Karl F. Gauss [1777-1855].

Teruel, battle of, Spanish loyalist forces drove insurgents from Teruel, central Spain, during bloody counter-offensive, **Dec. 5-19, 1937**.

Teschen, Congress of, ended the War of the Bavarian Succession; Austria retained only the Inn district in Bavaria, **May 13, 1779**.

Teschen dispute, armed conflict between Poland and Czechoslovakia over control of region of Teschen, **1919-20**; conference of ambassadors divided region, **July 28, 1920**, giving western part to Czechoslovakia and eastern part to Poland; Polish troops seized all Teschen, **Oct. 2, 1938**, after Munich Pact; status quo as of **July 28, 1920** reestablished, **1945**.

Tesla coil, invented, **1891**, by Yugoslavian-American inventor Nikola Tesla [1856-1943]; resonant air-core transformer.

Tess of the D'Urbervilles, novel, **1891**, in which a victimized servant girl driven to murder by a self-righteous husband finds tragic end herself, by English Victorian novelist and poet Thomas Hardy; film, **1981**.

Test Act, superseded Clarendon Code; excluded Roman Catholics from office; compelled duke of York to resign as Lord High Admiral, **Mar. 22, 1673**.

Test Acts, American revolutionary state governments passed laws requiring denial of loyalty to Britain, forcing many loyalists to flee to Canada and elsewhere, **1776-83**.

Tet Offensive, Vietcong and North Vietnamese forces made well-planned attacks on 30 provincial capitals in South Vietnam during Vietnam War, **Jan. 30-Feb. 24, 1968**; South Vietnamese recaptured city of Hue, **Feb. 24, 1968**.

Tettenhall, battle of, Edward the Elder [d. 924], son of Alfred the Great [849-Apr. 26, 899], won decisive battle against Northumbrian Danes, becoming ruler of all England s. of Humber River, **Aug. 5, 910**.

Teutoburger Wald (Teutoberg Forest), battle of, one of decisive battles of history; German barbarians under Arminius [d. 21] ambushed and destroyed Roman legions under Publius Quintilius Varus [d. 9]; n. limit of Roman Empire fixed, **9**.

Teutonic Knights (Teutonic Order), German military-religious order established during the Crusades, **1190-91**; conquered pagan Prussians, **c. 1226**; united with Livonian Knights, **1237-1525**.

Tewkesbury, battle of (*Bloody Meadow*), Yorkist army under Edward IV defeated

Lancastrians near Tewkesbury in w. central England during the Wars of the Roses, **May 4, 1471**.

Texan War of Independence, Mexican state of Texas declared itself an independent republic, **Mar. 2, 1836**; Mexicans captured the Alamo, **Mar. 6, 1836**; Texans won independence at battle of San Jacinto, **Apr. 21, 1836**.

Texas Annexation Treaty, U.S. Sec. of State John C. Calhoun [Mar. 16, 1782-Mar. 31, 1850] negotiated annexation of Texas to U.S. as territory, **Apr. 12, 1844**; rejected by Senate as slaveholders' plot, **June 8, 1844**.

Texas City disaster, most of Texas City, Tex., destroyed and 561 persons killed after S.S. *Grandcamp* blew up, **Apr. 16, 1967**.

Texas, former Mexican territory declared itself independent republic, **Mar. 2, 1836**; annexed to U.S. by joint resolution of Congress, **Mar. 1, 1845**; admitted to the Union as 28th state, **Dec. 29, 1845**; seceded from the Union, **Feb. 1, 1861**; readmitted to the Union, **Mar. 30, 1870**.

Texas-New Mexico Act, U.S. Congress established boundaries of Texas and territory of New Mexico, which was allowed to decide whether to be free or slave state, **Sept. 9, 1850**.

Texas Rangers, mounted police force established during Texas Revolution, **Nov. 24, 1835**; merged with Texas highway patrol, **1935**.

Texel, battles of, Dutch fleet under Admiral Maarten Tromp [1597-July 31, 1653] lost major naval battle against English fleet under Gen. George Monck [Dec. 6, 1608-Jan. 3, 1670] off Dutch island of Texel; last battle of first Dutch War, **July 31, 1653**; Dutch fleet under Admiral Michel de Ruyter checked larger English-French fleet at Texel during third Dutch War, **Aug. 20, 1673**.

thalassemia, first described, **1927**, by American pediatrician Thomas B. Cooley [1871-1945]; form of erythroblastic anemia, sometimes called Cooley's anemia.

thallium, element No. 81; discovered, **1861**, by English physicist Sir William Crookes [1832-1919].

Thames, battle of the, U.S. force under Gen. William Henry Harrison [Feb. 9, 1773-Apr. 4, 1841] defeated British army, aided by Indians under Tecumseh [Mar. 1768-Oct. 5, 1813], at Thames River in s. Ontario, **Oct. 5, 1813**.

Thanatopsis, poem, **1817**, seeking comfort for death in reflections upon unity of nature, by U.S. poet and newspaper editor William Cullen Bryant [Nov. 3, 1794-June 12, 1878].

Thapsus, battle of, Roman legions under Julius Caesar decisively defeated Numidians under Juba I [c. 85-46 B.C.], allied with Pompey's senatorial army, **Feb. 4, 46 B.C.**, ending all opposition to Caesar in Africa.

Thaw, The, novel, **1954**, by Russian writer and critic Ilya Ehrenberg [Jan. 27, 1891-Sept. 1, 1967].

Theatre Guild, acting company, founded, **1919**; produced some of best drama of the times; built Guild Theatre, **1925**; became Anta Theatre, **1951**.

Theater of the Absurd, type of modern drama depicting meaninglessness through the incongruous, originated with *The Bald Soprano*, **1950**, by Rumanian-French playwright Eugene Ionesco [Nov. 26, 1912-].

Thebes, capital of Middle Kingdom of ancient Egypt; center of Amon worship, **c. 2100-1800 B.C.**; sacked by Assyrians, **661 B.C.**; sacked by Romans, **29 B.C.**

Thebes, chief city of ancient Boeotia, freed from Spartan domination, **371 B.C.**; totally destroyed by Alexander the Great, **336 B.C.**

Theodosian Code, Theodosius II [401-50], emperor of the East, issued Roman legal code, **438**.

Theosophical Society of America, religious-philosophical-social society founded in New York City by Helena Petrovna Blavatsky [1831-May 8, 1891], **Nov. 17, 1875.**

thermal radiation, laws of, formulated, **1893, 1896**, by German physicist Wilhelm Wien [1864-1928].

thermionics, phenomena investigated, from **1900**, by English physicist Sir Owen W. Richardson [1879-1959].

thermometer, open-air, constructed, **1609**, by Italian physicist Galileo Galilei [1564-1642].

Thermopylae, battles of, about 300 Spartans under King Leonidas I [d. 480 B.C.] killed during heroic stand against invading Persian army of Xerxes at Thermopylae Pass, **480 B.C.**; Greeks temporarily halted invading Gauls under Brennus [d. 279 B.C.], **279 B.C.**; Syrians under Antiochus III ("the Great") [d. 187 B.C.] defeated by Roman legions at Thermopylae, **191 B.C.**

Thessalonians, Letter to the, New Testament books, believed written, c. **52-53**, by St. Paul the Apostle.

Thinker, The, well-known statue, **1880**, by 19th-century French sculptor Auguste Rodin.

Thin Man, The, "hard-boiled" U.S. detective novel, **1932**, introducing sleuth Nick Charles and wife Nora, by Dashiell Hammett; popular film series, **1934-47**, starring William Powell [July 29, 1892-] and Myrna Loy [Aug. 2, 1905-]; popular radio series, **1941-50**; television series, **1957-59.**

Third Class Carriage, The, painting, c. **1865**, depicting wretched conditions of poor French train riders, by French caricaturist, lithographer, and painter Honore Daumier.

Third International, Communist organization formed, **Mar. 2, 1919**, in Russia to spread Communist doctrine abroad to bring about world revolution.

Third Man, The, thriller, **1949**, by English novelist Graham Greene, who wrote screenplay for outstanding Carol Reed film, also **1949**.

Thirteenth Amendment to U.S. Constitution, ratified, **Dec. 18, 1865**, abolished slavery in U.S. and its territories.

13 Vendemiaire, Napoleon Bonaparte's cannonade, suppressed serious French uprising against Directory's power and won fame, **Oct. 5, 1795.**

Thirty Tyrants, oligarchic government installed by Spartan commander Lysander in ancient Athens, **404-403 B.C.**

Thirty Years' War, general European war fought mainly in Germany, **1618-48**; Czech Protestant forces defeated by forces of Holy Roman Empire and Holy League at White Mountain, **Nov. 8, 1620**; armies of Holy Roman Empire defeated at Breitenfeld, **Sept. 18, 1631**; at Lech, **Apr. 15, 1632**; at Lutzen, **Nov. 15-16, 1632**; Holy Roman army won victory at Nordlingen, **Sept. 6, 1634**; Swedish forces won brilliant victory at Jankau, **Mar. 7, 1645**; ended by Peace of Westphalia, **Oct. 24, 1648.**

Thomism, system of scholastic philosophy, developed, **1250-74**, by Dominican schoolman St. Thomas Aquinas; Thomism made official Catholic philosophy, **1879.**

Thomson-Urrutia Treaty, agreement concluding Panama's independence from Colombia, **1914**; U.S. Congress ratified treaty, **Apr. 20, 1921**; Colombia ratified treaty, **Dec. 22, 1921**, finally recognizing Panama's independence and establishing borders.

thorium, element No. 90; discovered, **1828,** by Swedish chemist Jons J. Berzelius [1779-1848].

Thorn (Torun), city on Vistula River, grew around fortress built by Teutonic Knights, **1231;** Swedish army under Charles XII captured fortress-city after gallant defense by Poles, **Sept. 22, 1703;** taken by Prussians, **1793, 1815;** passed to Poland, **1919.**

-STEAM THRASHING-MACHINE.

Thorn (Torun), Treaty of, temporarily settled the conflict between Poland and the Teutonic Knights, **Feb. 1, 1411;** Teutonic Knights evacuated w. Prussia, giving Poland access to the Baltic, **1466.**

three-dimensional chemical bonds, concept introduced, **1886,** by Dutch physical chemist Jacobus H. van't Hoff [1852-1911], to explain optical activity and asymmetry of organic compounds in solution.

3-D movies, announced, **1953,** by 20th-Century Fox.

Three Emperors' League, informal alliance formed among Germany, Austria-Hungary, and Russia to preserve the peace among them, **1872;** overridden by German-Austrian alliance, **1879.**

Threepenny Opera, The (Dreigroschenoper, Die), ballad opera, **1928,** based on Gay's *The Beggar's Opera*, **1728,** by German Marxist dramatist Bertolt Brecht; music by German-American composer Kurt Weill [Mar. 2, 1900-Apr. 3, 1950]; filmed, Germany, **1931.**

Three Sisters, The (Tri Sestry), play, **1901,** by Anton Chekhov.

Three Mile Island crisis, radioactive gases from nuclear reactor at Three Mile Island, Middletown, Penn., escaped; hydrogen bub-ble formed at top of reactor, **Mar. 28, 1979,** precipitating area evacuation; ended, **Apr. 9, 1979,** with clean-up to take many years.

Thresher, U.S. atomic-powered submarine *Thresher* mysteriously sank in Atlantic, e. of Boston; 129 persons perished in U.S. Navy's worst peacetime disaster in history, **Apr. 10, 1963.**

threshing machine, invented, **1784,** by Scottish millwright Andrew Meikle [1719-1811].

threshing machine (drum), patented, **1788,** by Scottish millwright Andrew Meikle [1719-1811].

Through the Looking Glass, fantasy adventure novel, **1872,** sequel to *Alice's Adventures in Wonderland*, **1865.**

Thoughts (Pensees), apology for Christianity, posthumously published, **1670.**

thulium, element No. 69; discovered, **1879,** by Swedish chemist and geologist Per T. Cleve [1840-1905].

Thus Spake Zarathustra, philosophical narrative, **1883-91,** by German philosopher Friedrich Nietzsche; symphonic poem, **1896,** composed by Richard Strauss.

Thyratron stimulator, developed, **1953,** by American scientists at Harvard University.

thyroid gland, studied, **1874,** by Swiss surgeon E. Theodor Kocher [1841-1917].

thyroxine, isolated and described, **1915,** by American physiochemist Edward C. Kendall [1886-1972].

Tiberias, town on Sea of Galilee became center of Jewish learning, **2nd century;** captured by Arabs, **637;** Turks under Saladin seized town, **July 4, 1187;** part of Ottoman Empire, **16th century;** joined Palestine, **1922.**

Ticonderoga, Fort, strategic location where French built Fort Carillon, **1755;** British forces under Gen. Jeffrey Amherst [Jan. 29, 1717-Aug. 3, 1797] took fort and renamed Fort Ticonderoga, **July 26, 1759;** seized by Green Mountain Boys under Ethan Allen [Jan. 21, 1738-Feb. 12, 1789] and troops under Benedict Arnold [Jan. 14, 1741-June 14, 1801], **May 10, 1775;** abandoned by Americans to British forces under Gen. John Burgoyne [1722-Aug. 4, 1792], **July 6, 1777.**

tidal effect of moon, first proposed, **c. 325 B.C.**, by Greek geographer Pytheas [4th century B.C.], after observing tides of the Atlantic Ocean..

Tientsin massacre, Chinese mob stormed and killed French consul and missionaries at Tientsin, China, **June 21, 1870**.

Tientsin, Treaties of, British and French won second Opium War; China opened 11 more ports, permitted legations (U.S., Russian, British, French, and others) at Peking, accepted Christian missions, and legalized opium importation, **June 26-29, 1858**.

Tiepolo rebellion, unsuccessful patrician plot against the Venetian oligarchy, **1310**.

Tillamook forest fire, great, one of worst forest fires in history totally destroyed 270,000 acres of forest in Tillamook region of Oregon; resulted in new ways to prevent forest fires and regulations, **Aug. 14, 1933**.

Till Eulenspiegel's Merry Pranks (Till Eulenspiegel's Lustige Streiche), tone poem, **1895**, based on German folklore first described in book Lubeck, **1500**, this musical version by composer Richard Strauss.

Tilsit, Treaties of, France made peace with Russia, which recognized the grand duchy of Warsaw and received a free hand with regard to Finland, **July 7, 1807**; France forced Prussia to give up all its territory w. of the Elbe River; duchy of Warsaw received Prussian Poland, **July 9, 1807**.

Timbuktu, important meeting place for nomadic people of the Sahara, established as a seasonal camp, **11th century**; became center of caravan trade on Saharan route between Morocco and Algeria, **14th century**; fl. as great Muslim cultural center, **15th-16th centuries**; destroyed by Moroccans, **1591**.

Time, U.S. newsmagazine, published from **1923**.

Time Machine, The, **1895**, pioneer science fiction novel by British author and historian H.G. Wells.

Time of Troubles, political crisis in Russia marked by the appearance of pretenders to the throne (false Dmitris), **1604-13**.

Times, The, London newspaper, founded **Jan. 1, 1785**, under name *Daily Universal Register*; became *Times*, **1788**; *Sunday Times* established, **1822**.

time zones, initiated, **1883**, by American astronomer, meteorologist Cleveland Abbe [1838-1916] of the Signal Bureau at Washington, D.C.

Timothy, Letters to, two New Testament books, ascribed to St. Paul and probably written, **64** and **67**, to his disciple Timothy.

tin can, patent applied for, **1810**, by English inventor Peter Durand.

Tin Lizzie (Model T), introduced, **1908**, by American carmaker Henry Ford [1863-1947].

Tippecanoe, battle of, U.S. troops under Capt. William Henry Harrison attacked and destroyed Shawnee Indian village at Tippecanoe Creek in Indiana, breaking Indian resistance in Northwest Territory, **Nov. 7, 1811**.

tipplers' revolt, unsuccessful revolt by Portuguese at Oporto against creation of wine monopoly by chief minister Sebastiao Jose de Carvalho e Melo, marques de Pombal [May 13, 1699-May 8, 1782], **1757**.

tires, solid rubber, introduced, **1847**, by English inventor Thomas Hancock [1786-1865].

Tiros I, first successful U.S. weather satellite sent into orbit, **1960**.

'Tis Pity She's a Whore, tragedy, **c. 1627**, drawing out fatal consequences of character's attraction for his own sister; ends in frenzy of killings at final banquet, by Jacobean dramatist John Ford [Apr., 1586-1640?].

tissue culture, first achieved, **1907**, by American anatomist Ross G. Harrison [1870-1959].

VIRGINIA TOBACCO

PIPES

Tisza River, battle of, Frankish army sent by Charlemagne destroyed Avar stronghold on Tisza River in central Europe; barbarian Avars vanished from history, **796.**

Titanic, British White Star liner "unsinkable" *Titanic,* on maiden voyage from England to U.S., struck iceberg and sank in North Atlantic, south of Newfoundland; 1517 persons perished, **Apr. 14-15, 1912.**

titanium, element No. 22; discovered, **1791,** by English mineralogist William Gregor [1761-1817].

Tithe War, Irish, Roman Catholics in Ireland openly and violently rebelled against enforced payments of tithes to support Protestant Church of England, **1831.**

Titus, Letter to, New Testament book, believed written, **65-66,** by St. Paul to his disciple Titus, traditional first bishop of Crete.

toaster, automatic electric, invented, **1918,** by American inventor Charles Strite.

Tobacco Plant-Cutters' War, low price of tobacco in colonial Virginia caused planters to cut down tobacco plants, leading to riots, arrest, and executions of ringleaders, **1680.**

Tobacco Road, novel, **1932,** by U.S. writer Erskine Caldwell; dramatized, **1933,** and

ran for 3,182 performances on Broadway.

tobacco smoking, evidence of dangers to health presented, **1954,** by American epidemiologists Edward C. Hammond [1912-] and Daniel Horn [1916-].

Tobruk, Mediterranean port in Libya captured by British in North African Campaign of WW II, **Jan. 22, 1941;** withstood repeated attacks by Germans under Gen. Rommel, **1941,** but fell to Rommel, **June 21, 1942;** recaptured by British, **Nov. 30, 1942.**

toccata, form of organ music, popular from **c. 1610,** emphasizing virtuosity of performer through elaborate runs.

Today Show, The, durable NBC television show, from **1952.**

Togo, country in w. Africa, first settled as a German colony (Togoland), **1884;** divided officially into British Togoland and French Togoland by mandates of the League of Nations, **1922;** both Togolands became UN trusteeships, **1946;** became independent republic of Togo, **Apr. 27, 1960.**

To His Coy Mistress, **1650,** English love lyric by metaphysical poet Andrew Marvell.

Tokugawa, Japanese family that held the shogunate and ruled Japan, **1603-1867.**

Tokyo fire, great, fire destroyed most of Edo (Tokyo) and its castles and killed more than 100,000 Japanese, **Jan. 18-19, 1657.**

Toleration Act, parliament excused England's nonconformists from church attendance; Protestant dissenters exempted if they had taken oaths of allegiance and supremacy, **May 24, 1689.**

Tom Jones, novel, **1749,** subtitled "history of a Foundling", by 18th-century English novelist Henry Fielding.

Tom Thumb, first steam locomotive built in U.S., **1830,** by American manufacturer-inventor Peter Cooper [1791-1879].

Tonga, 150-island archipelago in s.w. Pacific, united into a kingdom by Taufa'ahau Tupou (later King George Tupou I) [c. 1820-93] at end of civil war, **1845;** became a British protectorate, **1900;** gained full independence from Britain, **June 4, 1970.**

Tony Awards (Antoinette Perry Awards), annual awards in U.S. for outstanding performances and achievements in the Broadway theater, **1947.**

Topeka Constitution, Free State settlers

in Kansas framed new constitution outlawing slavery; Kansas had dual state government, **Oct. 23, 1855**.

Tordesillas, Treaty of, Spain and Portugal divided non-Christian world into two zones of influence; line of demarcation shifted west to give Portugal a claim to Brazil, **June 7, 1494**.

Torgau, battle of, Prussians under Frederick II defeated Austrians under Field Marshal Daun at German port city of Torgau during Seven Years' War, **Nov. 3, 1760**.

Torgau League, alliance of German Protestant princes to oppose Ferdinand I [Mar. 10, 1503-July 25, 1564] of Austria (later Holy Roman Emperor) and his Bavarian allies, **Feb. 27, 1526**.

torpedo, self-projecting, invented, **1866**, by English inventor Robert Whitehead [1823-1905].

Tosca, opera, first produced Rome, **1900**, about opera singer desired by Rome police chief, by Italian opera composer Giacomo Puccini.

To the Finland Station, landmark critical study, **1940**, of Socialist thought, by U.S. literary and social critic Edmund Wilson.

To the Lighthouse, novel, **1927**, written in poetic prose and stream-of-consciousness technique, by English writer Virginia Woolf.

Toulon, battles of, allied French and Spanish fleets checked British naval force off Toulon, France, **Feb. 22, 1744**; British fleet won victory over French, **Nov. 15, 1793**.

Toulouse, battle of, British forces of duke of Wellington defeated French under Nicolas Jean de Dieu Soult [Mar. 29, 1769-Nov. 26, 1851] at Toulouse in southern France during Napoleonic Wars, **Apr. 10, 1814**.

Tou Morong, battle of, major U.S. victory over North Vietnamese Communists in Vietnam War; U.S.-South Vietnamese units successfully relieved outpost of Tou Morong in n. Kontum province, **June 7-13, 1966**.

Tour de France, cyclists established famous annual international race, Tour de France, over 2500 mi.-road course in France, **1903**.

Tours (Poitiers), battle of, Moorish conquest of Europe halted; Franks under Charles Martel ("the Hammer") [688-741?] withstood furious Muslim cavalry attacks under Abd al Rahman [d. 732].

Tower of London, The, fortress-palace near Thames, London, built, from **1078**; served as royal residence and, later, through **1810**, as prison for such figures as Sir Thomas More, **1534-35**, and Sir Walter Raleigh, **1603-16**.

Townshend Acts, British passed acts requiring American colonists to pay duties on various imports and authorized agents to collect payment, **June 29, 1767**; Boston and other colonies began again non-importation of British goods, **Oct.-Dec. 1767**; John Dickinson called acts unconstitutional in *Letters from a Farmer in Pennsylvania*, **Nov. 5, 1767-Jan. 1768**; Boston Massacre occurred during protest, **Mar. 5, 1770**; acts repealed, except for duty on tea, **Apr. 12, 1770**.

tracheotomy, first successful operation performed, **c. 1545**, by Italian surgeon A. Musa Brasavolus [1500-1570].

tractor, invented, **1825**, by English inventor Robert Keeley.

tractor, Caterpillar, invented, **1900**, by American inventor Benjamin Holt.

Trafalgar, battle of, British fleet under Horatio Nelson won famous victory over French-Spanish fleet under Pierre de Villeneuve [1763-1806] off Cape Trafalgar, Spain; Nelson killed during this last great battle fought by sailing ships, **Oct. 21, 1805**.

Trail of Tears, forced march and resettlement of Indians to reservations w. of Mississippi River, **1830-43**; name derived from great suffering of Cherokees (about 4000 died) during U.S. army-led march, **1838**.

Trajan's Column, 150-feet-high carved column, Rome, erected, **113**.

tramway, electric, one of first opened **1883**; designed by German-British inventor Sir William Siemens [1823-1883].

tranquilizer drugs, introduced in U.S., **1954**, by Wallace Laboratories and Wyeth Laboratories.

transactional analysis, introduced, **1955**, by Canadian-American psychiatrist Eric Berne [1910-1970].

Transatlantic Review, important literary magazine, founded Paris, **1924**, to publish and sponsor important literary figures, by English novelist and editor Ford Maddox Ford.

Transcendentalism, U.S. philosophical movement, **c. 1840-80**; magazine, *The Dial*, **1840-44**, organ of the movement.

transfer-RNA, first isolated and structure determined, **1962** and **1965**, by American biochemist Robert W. Holley [1922-].

Transfiguration, painting, **c. 1480**, by Venetian founder of colorist painting Giovanni Bellini.

transformer, electric, invented, **1885**, by American electrical engineer William Stanley [1858-1916].

Trans-Iranian Railway, Iran built RR from Caspian Sea to Persian Gulf, **1927-1939**, using solely Iranian capital.

transistor, developed, **1948**, by American physicists John Bardeen [1908-], Walter H. Brattain [1902-], and William Shockley [1910-].

Transition, little magazine, published Paris, **1927-38**, promoting modern movement in literature and writers such as James Joyce and Gertrude Stein.

transit of Mercury, stellar phenomenon, first observed, **1631**, by French physicist-philosopher Pierre Gassendi [1592-1655].

Transit I, first ship navigation beacon in outer space, launched, **1960**, by American scientists.

Transportation, U.S. Dept. of, U.S. federal department established, **Oct. 15, 1966**, by Pres. Lyndon B. Johnson.

Trans-Siberian Railway, 4350-mi. railroad line connecting European Russia with Pacific coast (Vladivostok) built to open up Siberia, **1892-1905**.

transubstantiation, theological doctrine, defined, **1215**, Fourth Lateran Council, that bread and wine in the Eucharist are really transformed into body and blood of Christ.

Transvaal, South African region rich in natural resources, settled by the Boers, **1834-37**; British recognized Boer state called South African Republic, **1852**; British annexed region, **1877**; British again recognized region's independence, **1881**; foreign prospectors swarmed there after discovery of gold, **1886**; tensions increased between Boers and British following Jameson's Raid, **Dec. 29, 1895-Jan. 2, 1896**; Transvaal annexed by Britain, **1900**.

Trappists, Catholic religious order, branch of reformed Cistercians of Strict Observance, developed from **1662**, at LaTrappe, France (hence name).

Trasimeno, Lake, battle of, Carthaginians, Iberians, and Gauls led by Hannibal won one of bloodiest ambushes in history, destroying entire Roman army of Caius Flaminius [d. June 21, 217 B.C.], at Trasimeno in central Italy, **June 21, 217 B.C.**

Transkei, first Bantu (black African) "homeland" established by South African government for Xhosa tribe, **1963**; gained full independence, **Oct. 26, 1976**.

Travendal, Treaty of, King Charles XII [June 27, 1682-Dec. 11, 1718] of Sweden forced Denmark to abstain from war against Sweden, **Aug. 18, 1700**.

Traviata, La, Italian opera, **1853**, by romantic composer Giuseppe Verdi; based on play, *La Dame aux Camelias*, **1852**, by Alexander Dumas the Younger.

treadmill chain-band (horsepower), patented, **1834**, by American blacksmith-inventor Hiram A. Pitts [c. 1800-1860].

Treasure Island, romantic novel, **1883**, by Scottish writer Robert Louis Stevenson; film, **1934**.

Treasure of the Sierra Madre, The, film, **1948**, about greed inspired by gold-hunting fever in Mexico; John Huston won Oscars for writing and directing; Oscar for best supporting actor went to his father, Walter Huston (born Walter Houghston) [Apr. 6, 1884-Apr. 7, 1950].

Treasury, U.S. Department of, federal department created by Congress to advise U.S. president on fiscal policy and to collect taxes, **Sept. 2, 1789**; Alexander Hamilton became first secretary of the treasury, **Sept. 11, 1789**; Internal Revenue Service added to department, **1862**.

Trebbia River, battles of, Carthaginians under Hannibal defeated Romans at Trebbia River in n. Italy during second Punic War, **218 B.C.**; Russian-Austrian army routed French at Trebbia during French Revolutionary Wars, **June 17, 1799**.

Trek, Great, organized migration made by Dutch (Boer) farmers north to escape British domination and to settle in what became the Transvaal, Natal, and Orange Free State, **1835-36**.

Trent, Council of, Catholic Church general council, **1545-63**, that decreed series of reforms to meet challenge of Protestantism.

Trenton, battle of, Americans under Gen. Washington crossed ice-choked Delaware River and made successful surprise attack on Hessians at Trenton, N.J., **Dec. 25-26, 1776**.

Tresaguet road-building, method developed, **c. 1776**, by French civil engineer Pierre Tresaguet [1716-1796].

Trevi Fountain, baroque fountain, built Rome, **1762**.

TRH (thyrotropin releasing hormone), isolated, **1968-1969**, by American biochemist Andrew V. Schally [1926-] and American physiologist Roger Guillemin [1924-].

Trials for Treason Act, English parliament required two witnesses to prove an act of treason, **1696**.

Trial, The (Der Prozess), novel, **1925**, by Bohemian novelist Franz Kafka.

Trianon, Treaty of, Hungary signed peace treaty with Allies after WW I, giving Transylvania and e. Banat to Rumania, Slovakia and Ruthenia to Czechoslovakia, and Croatia, w. Banat, and Slavonia to Yugoslavia, **June 4, 1920**.

Trier, University of, leading European university at Trier, Germany, **1473-1797**.

Trieste problem, city of Trieste, claimed by Yugoslavia and Italy after WW II, made part of free territory of Trieste, **1947**, under UN protection; territory divided into Zone A and Zone B, placed under Italian and Yugoslav administration respectively by mutual agreement, **Oct. 5, 1954**.

trigonometric functions, abbreviations introduced, **c. 1631**, by English mathematician William Oughtred [1575-1660].

Trinidad and Tobago, island of Trinidad united with island of Tobago to become British colony, **1899**; joined West Indies Federation, **1958**; became an independent nation,

Aug. 31, 1962; became republic within the British Commonwealth of Nations, **Aug. 1, 1976**.

Trinity College, largest college of Cambridge University, founded, **1546**.

Trinity, Doctrine of the, Christian doctrine, that Godhead composed of three distinct persons; term coined, **c. 180**; doctrine defined by Councils of Nicaea, **325**, and of Constantinople, **381**.

triode, invented, **1906**, by American inventor Lee De Forest [1873-1961].

Triple Alliance, formed by England, Sweden, and Netherlands, against King Louis XIV [Sept. 5, 1638-Sept. 1, 1715], **Jan. 23, 1668**; formed by England, France, and Netherlands to strengthen the Treaty of Utrecht, **Jan. 4, 1717**.

Triple Alliance (Dreibund), formal alliance formed by and periodically renewed by Germany, Austria-Hungary, and Italy, **1882-1915**.

Triple Alliance, War of the, conflict between Paraguay and an alliance of Argentina, Brazil, and Uruguay, **1865-70**; ended with peace treaty, with Paraguay devastated, **June 20, 1870**.

Triple Crown, America's premier thoroughbred horse racing event to win the Kentucky Derby, the Preakness, and the Belmont Stakes in one year, accomplished by Sir Barton, **1919**; Gallant Fox, **1930**; Omaha, **1935**; War Admiral, **1937**; Whirlaway, **1941**; Count Fleet, **1943**; Assault, **1946**; Citation, **1948**; Secretariat, **1973**; Seattle Slew, **1977**; Affirmed, **1978**.

Triple Entente, informal, friendly understanding formed by Britain, France, and Russia to oppose the Triple Alliance, **1907**.

Tripolitan War, conflict between U.S. and Barbary States (pirates) of n. Africa, **1800—1805**; U.S. unsuccessfully blockaded port of Tripoli after pasha of Tripoli demanded more tribute, **June 1801**; Stephen Decatur and his men burned captured U.S. frigate *Philadelphia* in Tripoli's harbor, **Feb. 1804**; U.S. land forces captured Derna, port near Tripoli, **Apr. 26, 1805**; ended with peace treaty between U.S. and Tripoli, **June 4, 1805**.

Tristan and Isolde (Tristan und Isolde), opera, **1865**, by German composer Richard Wagner.

Tristram Shandy, novel, **1759—67**, in nine volumes, by English novelist Laurence Sterne.

Triumph of the Will (Triumph des Willens), film, **1934**, Nazi propaganda documentary, by German director Leni Riefenstahl [Aug. 22, 1902-].

Triumvirate, First, Julius Caesar, Pompey ("the Great") [106—48 B.C.], and Crassus established first three-man governing board in ancient Rome, **60 B.C.**

Triumvirate, Second, Augustus Caesar (Octavian) [Sept. 23, 63 B.C.—A.D. Aug. 19, 14], Marc Anthony [c. 83—Aug., 30 B.C.], and Marcus Aemilius Lepidus [d. 13 B.C.] formed three-man governing board in ancient Rome, **43 B.C.**

Troilus and Criseyde, long poem, **c. 1385**, based on Greek legend, by English poet Geoffrey Chaucer; inspired Shakespeare's play, same name, **c. 1601**.

Trojan War, Greek army led by Agamemnon conquered Trojans after 10-year siege of the city of Troy, **c. 1184 B.C.**

Trojan Women, The (Troades), Greek tragedy, **415 B.C.**, by Greek dramatist Euripides.

trolley railway, first modern one installed,

1887, in Richmond, Va. by American electrical engineer Frank J. Sprague [1857-1934].

Tropic of Cancer, novel, **1934,** with sequel, *Tropic of Capricorn,* **1939,** chronicling adventures of American expatriate in Paris of the 1930s; not published in U.S., until **1961,** because of explicitness; best-known works of U.S. writer Henry (Valentine) Miller [Dec. 26, 1891-June 7, 1980].

Troppau, Congress of, international conference failed to take action against liberal uprisings in the Two Sicilies and Spain, **Oct. 27-Dec. 17, 1820.**

Trotsky, assassination of, exiled Russian war minister Leon Trotsky [Oct. 26, 1879-Aug. 20, 1940] killed with an axe by Spanish-born Ramon Mercador [fl. 1930s-40s] near Mexico City, **Aug. 20, 1940.**

Troubadors, school of southern French poets, flourished, **c. 1100-1300.**

Trovatore, Il (The Troubador), opera, first produced, Rome, **1853,** by Italian operatic composer Giuseppe Verdi.

Troy (Ilion or Ilium), ancient Phrygian city in Asia Minor; made famous by Homer's account of the Trojan War, fl. **1200 B.C.**

Troyes, Treaty of, King Henry V of England became "heir of France," successor to Charles VI [Dec. 3, 1368-Oct. 21, 1422] of France, and the dauphin was disinherited, **May 21, 1420.**

Trucial States (Trucial Coast), seven sheikdoms on southern coast of Persian Gulf concluded truces with Great Britain, **1820;** known as Pirate Coast before accepting British protection, **1892;** merged to form independent United Arab Emirates, **Dec. 2, 1971.**

Trujillo, assassination of, Dominican dictator Rafael Leonidas Trujillo Molina [Oct. 24, 1891-May 30, 1961] shot to death by military officers near Ciudad Trujillo, **May 30, 1961.**

Truk, battles of, U.S. 5th Fleet and Task Force 58 devastated Japanese naval vessels and planes on Caroline island of Truk, **Feb. 17-18, 1944;** Task Force 58 returned to sink every Japanese ship at Truk, obliterating Japan's so-called "Gibraltar of the Pacific" in WW II, **Apr. 28-29, 1944.**

Truman Doctrine, principle of containing Soviet expansion and influence announced by U.S. Pres. Harry S. Truman, **Mar. 12, 1947.**

trumpet, brass instrument with valves, **c. 1815;** prior to **1700,** plain brass cylindrical bore; associated with military and ceremonial functions, from **c. 1300;** utilized in musical works, from **c. 1600.**

trytophane, amino acid discovered, **1901,** by English biologist Sir Frederick G. Hopkins [1861-1947] and English physiologist Sidney W. Cole.

Tsushima, battle of, major naval battle of Russo-Japanese War; Japanese fleet under Admiral Heihachiro Togo [1846-1934] sank, captured, or drove ashore entire Russian Baltic fleet in Tsushima Strait between China Sea and Sea of Japan, **May 27-28, 1905.**

tube, iconoscope, electronic scanner; invented, **1923,** by Russian-American physicist Vladimir K. Zwoykin [1889-].

tuberculosis, bacillus isolated, **1882,** by German physician Robert Koch [1843-1910].

tuberculosis sanitarium, first established, **1859,** by German physician Gustav Adolf Robert Hermann Brehmer [1826-1899].

Tubingen, University of, German university founded, **1477;** from **1534,** center of Protestant theological thought.

Tudeh Party, Iranian Communist Party created rebellion in province of Azerbaijan,

Nov. 18, 1945; Soviet-backed Tudeh rebels returned Azerbaijan to Iranian control, June 13, 1946; outlawed, Feb. 5, 1949, after attempt to kill Shah Muhammad Reza Pahlavi.

Tudor, House of, royal family that ruled England, 1485-1603.

Tuileries, former French palace in Paris, planned by Catherine de Medicis [Apr. 13, 1519-Jan. 5, 1589], c. 1560; French rebels forced King Louis XVI to move there from Versailles, 1789; stormed by French mob during French Revolution, Aug. 10, 1792; destroyed by fire, 1871.

tungsten, element No. 74; discovered, 1783, by Spanish mineralogist Don Fausto d'Elhuyar [1755-1833].

tungsten, ductile, production process, invented, 1908, by American physicist William D. Coolidge [1873-1975].

Tunisia, country on n. coast of Africa, became a French protectorate, May 12, 1881; site of serious fighting during WW II, 1942-43; won its independence from France, Mar. 20, 1956; proclaimed a republic, July 25, 1957.

tunnel (Esaki) diode, invented, 1958, by Japanese physicist Leo Esaki [1925-].

tunneling effect, theory developed, from 1958, by Japanese physicist Leo Esaki [1925-], Norwegian-American physicist Ivar

Giaever [1929-], and British physicist Brian D. Josephson [1940-].

tunnel-insulator, invented, 1960, by Norwegian American physicist Ivar Giaever [1929-].

Tunney-Dempsey fight, Gene Tunney [May 25, 1898-Nov. 7, 1978] defeated Jack Dempsey in 10th round at Philadelphia to win heavyweight boxing championship, Sept. 23, 1926; Tunney retired undefeated, July 26, 1928.

Tupac's rebellion, native Indian revolt under Tupac Amaru [1742?-81] crushed with difficulty by Spaniards in Peru, 1780-82.

Tupungato, Mt., second highest mountain in Western Hemisphere (22,300 ft.), on Chile-Argentina border, first climbed by Alpine guide Mattias Zurbriggen, Mar. 1897.

turbine, gas, invented, 1791, by British inventor John Barber.

turbine, hydraulic, invented, 1827, by French engineer Benoit Fourneyron [1802-1867].

Turbinia, launched, 1897; first vessel to be powered by turbine engine; designed by English engineer Charles Parsons [1854-1931].

turbojet engine, first built, 1937, by English engineer Sir Frank Whittle [1907-].

turbosupercharger, (for aircraft engines) developed, 1939, by American mechanical engineer Sanford A. Moss [1872-1946].

Turckheim, battle of, French army under Marshal Turenne routed Austrian army in surprise attack at Turckheim, regaining all of Alsace for France in a single battle, Jan. 5, 1675.

Turin, battle of, forces of Holy Roman Empire led by Eugene, Prince of Savoy, won major victory over French at Turin, ending French attempts to conquer n. Italy during the War of the Spanish Succession, Sept. 7, 1706.

Turkey, fall of Ottoman Empire, 1918, led to abolition of the Turkish sultanate, Oct. 1, 1922; the republic of Turkey formed with Mustafa Kemal, renamed Kemal Ataturk [1881-Nov. 10, 1938] as president, Oct. 29, 1923; abolished caliphate, Mar. 3, 1924; invaded Cyprus to help Turkish Cypriots, July 20, 1974.

Turkish Bath, The, painting, **1863**, by French neoclassical painter Jean-Auguste-Dominique Ingres.

Turkmanchai, Treaty of, ended war between Persia and Russia; Persia ceded part of Armenia, Erivan, and Nakhchivan, **Feb. 22, 1828**.

Turk-Sib Railroad, important RR linking Turkistan with Siberia opened to traffic, **1931**.

Turner's rebellion, Negroes under Nat Turner [Oct. 2, 1800-Nov. 11, 1831] killed 60 whites during unsuccessful rebellion in Southampton County, Virginia, **Aug. 21, 1831**.

Turnhout, battle of, Dutch army under Maurice of Nassau [1567-1625] surprised and defeated Spanish army at Turnhout, n.w. of Antwerp, boosting Dutch hopes for independence, **Aug. 22, 1597**.

turnip, introduced, **c. 1730**, as livestock fodder by English agriculturist Charles Townshend [1674-1738].

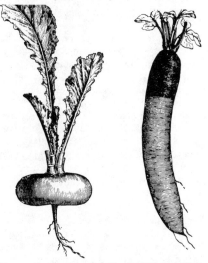

Turn of the Screw, The, **1898**, by U.S.-British novelist Henry James; dramatized as The Innocents, **1950**; made into opera, **1954**, by Benjamin Britten.

turret lathe, designed, **1849**, by American mechanical engineer Frederick W. Howe [1822-1891].

Turtle, first submarine used in warfare, became known later as American Turtle, designed by David Bushnell [1742?-1824]

unsuccessful against British flagship Eagle in New York Harbor, **Sept. 1776**.

Tuscarora War, Tuscarora Indians battled white settlers in Carolinas and Virginia, **1711-13**; Tuscarora massacred 200 settlers near Chowan and Roanoke rivers, N.C., **Sept. 22, 1711**; colonial militiamen killed 300 Tuscarora near Neuse River, N.C., **Jan. 28, 1712**; war ended after capture of Tuscarora stronghold (Tuscarora fled northward), **Mar. 23, 1713**.

Tuskegee Institute, one of first important Negro institutions for higher learning established, **July 4, 1881**, by Booker T. Washington [Apr. 5, 1856-Nov. 14, 1915].

TV Dinner, frozen meal originated, **1954**, by C. A. Swanson and Son of Omaha, Nebraska.

Tweed Ring, William Marcy ("Boss") Tweed [Apr. 3, 1823-Apr. 12, 1878] and his henchmen controlled Tammany Hall, **1868**; Tweed Ring charged with defrauding New York City of over $30 million, **Oct. 26, 1871**; Tweed convicted, **Nov. 19, 1873**; some henchmen fled to Europe with money, **1874**.

Twelfth Amendment to U.S. Constitution, ratified, **Sept. 25, 1804**, separated the voting for U.S. president and vice president.

Twelfth Night, or, What You Will, play, **c. 1600**, comedy revolving around resemblance of separated boy and girl twins, and containing some of best low comedy written by William Shakespeare.

Twelve, The (Dvenadtzat), poem, **1918**, about twelve Red Guards patrolling chaotic streets of revolutionary St. Petersburg; by Russian poet Alexander Alexandrovich Blok [Nov. 28, 1880-Aug. 9, 1921].

Twentieth Amendment to U.S. Constitution, ratified **Feb. 6, 1933**, abolished the so-called "lame duck" session of Congress and changed date of presidential inauguration from Mar. 4 to Jan. 20.

Twenty-fifth Amendment to U.S. Constitution, ratified **Feb. 10, 1967**, established plan for governing in case of U.S. president's incapacity and for choosing a vice president if office is vacant.

Twenty-first Amendment to U.S. Constitution, ratified, **Dec. 5, 1933**, repealed Eighteenth Amendment, or Prohibition.

Twenty-fourth Amendment to U.S. Constitution, ratified, **Jan. 23, 1964**, abolished poll tax as requirement for voting in national elections or primaries.

Twenty-one Demands, ultimatum secretly presented by Japan to China, **Jan. 18, 1915**, providing for Japan's control of Kiaochow, Manchuria, and Mongolia, of China's coal deposits, and of China's military and domestic matters.

Twenty-second Amendment to U.S. Constitution, ratified, **Feb. 26, 1951**, limited U.S. presidency to two terms.

Twenty-sixth Amendment to U.S. Constitution, ratified, **July 5, 1971**, lowered the voting age from 21 to 18 in all elections.

26th of July Movement, Cuban revolutionaries led by Fidel Castro [Aug. 13, 1926-] thoroughly defeated during attempt to seize government Moncada Fortress at Santiago, Cuba; Castro captured and imprisoned, **July 26, 1953**; revolutionary force under Castro and Che Guevara [June 14, 1928-Oct. 9, 1967] fought indecisive guerrilla war with government forces of Fulgencio Batista y Zaldivar [Jan. 16, 1901-Aug. 6, 1973] in Sierra Maestra, **June 28-Aug. 3, 1958**; Castro's army forced Batista into exile,

Dec. 31, 1958; Castro secured control of Havana, making Cuba first Communist nation in Western Hemisphere, **Jan. 1959**.

Twenty-third Amendment to U.S. Constitution, ratified, **Mar. 29, 1961**, allowed District of Columbia residents to vote in presidential elections.

Twenty Thousand Leagues Under the Sea (Vingt Mille Lieues sous les Mers), **1870**, early science fiction novel that foresaw the submarine, by French fiction writer Jules Verne.

Twice-Told Tales, collection of stories, first published, **1837**; enlarged, **1842**, by U.S. writer Nathaniel Hawthorne.

The Twilight Zone, television programs, **1959-65**, by U.S. writer-producer Rod Serling [Dec. 25, 1924-June 28, 1975].

Two Cultures, The, controversial speech and pamphlet, **1959**, by British novelist and scientist C.P. Snow.

Two Sicilies, the, kingdoms of Sicily and Naples during the Middle Ages; ruled by the Spanish line of Bourbons, **1759-1861**; officially merged into a single kingdom **1816**; became part of Italy, **1861**.

2001: A Space Odyssey, science-fiction film, **1968**, about search for extraterrestrial life; directed by Stanley Kubrick who co-authored script with British science-fiction writer Arthur C(harles) Clarke [Dec. 16, 1917-], whose *Sentinel*, **1951**, inspired film.

Two Treatises of Government, philosophical work, **1690**, written to advocate freedom and support of English Glorious Revolution, **1688**; basis of later philosophy of "liberalism," by English philosopher John Locke.

Tydings-McDuffie Act, U.S. Congress created, **Mar. 24, 1934**, Commonwealth of the Philippines under U.S. supervision; Philippines gained complete independence, **July 4, 1946**.

typecasting machine, invented, **1836**, by Scottish-American typefounder George Bruce [1781-1866].

Typee, first novel, **1846**, partly autobiographical, of a sojourn among Polynesian cannibals, by U.S. novelist Herman Melville.

typesetting machine, patented, **1822**, by American inventor William Church [1778-1863] in England.

typewriter, first practical model patented,

1868, by American inventor Christopher Sholes [1819-1890].

typewriter, Hammond, patented, **1880**, by American inventor Jabez D. Hammond [1839-1913].

typewriter, IBM Selectric, introduced, **1961**, by International Business Machines; designed by American engineer Eliot F. Noyes [1910-].

typewriter (with interchangeable type wheel), patented, **1880**, by American inventor James B. Hammond [1839-1913].

typewriter, (Remington) introduced, **1876**, by American manufacturer Philo Remington [1816-1889].

typhus, carrier of, determined, **1909**, by French physician Charles J. H. Nicolle [1866-1936].

typhus vaccine, method devised, **1940**, by American bacteriologist Hans Zinsser [1878-1940].

Tyre, great mercantile port of ancient Phoenicia built on an island, just off mainland, **c. 2800 B.C.**; achieved maritime supremacy in the Mediterranean, **1100 B.C.**; founded city of Carthage, **9th century B.C.**; sacked by Alexander the Great, **333-32 B.C.**; joined to Roman Empire, **64 B.C.**; destroyed by Muslims, **1291**.

tyrosine, amino acid discovered, **1846**, by German chemist Justus von Liebig [1803-1873].

Ubaid culture, prehistoric, primitive society in Sumer region; men did not know how to write and lived in isolated groups, **c. 5th mil. B.C.**

Uccialli, Treaty of, agreement between Italy and Ethiopia, whose Emperor, Menelik II [1844-1913] rejected in **1891** when he learned the Italian interpretation of treaty made Ethiopia a protectorate of Italy, **May 2, 1889**.

Uffizi Palace, Florentine structure, built, **1560-80**, to house office for Medici family; now art galleries designed by Florentine biographer of artists, mannerist painter and architect, Giorgio Vasari.

Uganda, country in Africa, formerly kingdom of Buganda, made a British protectorate, **1894**; became independent, **Oct. 9, 1962**; Gen. Idi Amin ousted Milton Obote and became dictator, **1971**; Israeli commando raid at Entebbe airport, **July 4, 1977**; Amin's dictatorship ended by combined Ugandan-Tanzanian force, **Apr. 11, 1979**.

Ugarit, ancient city of Canaan, dating from **5th mil B.C.**; under Egyptian and Hittite suzerainty, **14th-13th centuries, B.C.**

Uighur Empire, Asiatic-Turkish empire in Mongolia, **744-840**; Uighurs founded another empire in e. Turkistan that lasted until Mongol invasions, **13th century**.

Ulster massacre, some 30,000 killed in Ulster (n. Ireland) during Catholic uprising against Protestant masters, **Oct. 1641**.

ultracentrifuge, developed, **1923**, by

Swedish chemist Theodor H.E. Svedberg [1884-1971].

ultramicroscope, designed, **1903** by German chemist Richard Zsigmondy [1865-1929].

ultraviolet light, discovered, **1801,** by German physicist Johann Wilhelm Ritter [1776-1810].

ultraviolet microscope, developed, **c. 1915,** by English scientist Joseph E. Barnard [1870-1949].

Ulysses, novel, **1922,** by Irish writer, James Joyce; banned, U.S., until **1933.**

Unam Sanctam, papal bull, issued by Pope Boniface VIII, **November 18, 1302,** against French royal claims, declaring that there is only one, holy, Catholic and apostolic Church and that the pope is head of it.

Uncle Tom's Cabin, or Life among the Lowly, novel, **1852,** by U.S. writer Harriet (Elizabeth) Beecher Stowe [June 14, 1811-July 1, 1896]; dramatized, **1853.**

Uncle Vanya (Dyadya Vanya), play, **1899,** by Russian writer Anton Chekhov.

Underground Railroad, system of helping escaped Negro slaves from the South to reach free states or Canada, **c. 1820-61.**

Understanding Media: The Extensions of Man, book, **1964,** by Canadian writer and media theorist Marshall McLuhan.

underwater tunnel, first one built, **1825-1843,** by French-British engineer Marc I. Brunel [1769-1849] under Thames River.

Uniformity, Acts of, British parliamentary legislation, passed, **1549, 1552, 1559** and **1662,** by which doctrine and worship of the Church of England were established and regularized.

Union Act, British parliament united Upper and Lower Canada into one government, becoming Canada West and East respectively, **July 23, 1840.**

Union of American Hebrew Congregations, American Reform Jewish body, founded, Cincinnati, **1873;** headquarters in New York since **1951;** founded Hebrew Union College, **1875.**

Union of Orthodox Jewish Congregations of America, organization of U.S. orthodox synagogues, founded, **1898.**

Union or Death (The Black Hand), terrorist organization established by Bosnian and Serbian revolutionaries against Austrian government, **1911.**

Union Party, two different U.S. political parties; name of Republican Party that nominated Abraham Lincoln for president during U.S. Civil War, **June 7, 1864;** party opposed to New Deal and backed by National Union for Social Justice under Charles E. Coughlin [Oct. 25, 1891-Oct. 27, 1979] held national convention in Cleveland, **Aug. 14, 1936.**

Union stockyards, livestock center that grew into world's largest opened in Chicago, Ill., **1865.**

Unitarianism, religious belief in single person of Godhead; first Unitarian Church to break with Anglicanism, **1773;** first U.S. Unitarianism Church, Boston, **1785.**

United Arab Emirates, country on Persian Gulf, formed by union of the Trucial States or Sheikdoms, **Dec. 2, 1971.**

United Arab Republic, former political union of Egypt and Syria, **Feb. 1, 1958-Sept. 30, 1961,** with Gamal Abdal Nasser as president.

United Church of Christ, Christian communion, formed, **June 25, 1957,** in a uniting general synod between Congregational Christian Churches and Evangelical and Reformed Church; union came into effect, **1961.**

United Irishmen (United Irish Society), political organization established to secure separation of Ireland from England, **1791;**

became secret society, **1794**; defeated at Vinegar Hill, **June 21, 1798**.

United Mine Workers of America, labor union formed, **1890**, by merger of National Progressive Union, founded **1888**, and mine locals of Knights of Labor; John L. Lewis [Feb. 12, 1880-June 11, 1969] president of union, **1920-60**; joined CIO, **1935**; expelled from AFL, **1937**; withdrew from CIO, **1942**; readmitted to AFL, **Jan. 1946**, but expelled again, **1947**; W.A. ("Tony") Boyle [Dec. 1, 1904-] president of union, **1963-72**, convicted of murder of Joseph Yablonski [1910-Jan. 5, 1970], **1974**.

United Nations, charter first drafted at Dumbarton Oaks Conference, **Aug. 21-Oct. 7, 1944**; founding conference held in San Francisco, **Apr. 25-June 26, 1945**; UN Charter ratified, **Oct. 24, 1945**; first meeting of General Assembly at London, **Jan. 10, 1946**; UN accepted John D. Rockefeller's gift of $8.5 million to build permanent headquarters in New York City, **Dec. 14, 1949**; UN Building in New York City occupied, **1952**.

United Nations Educational, Scientific, and Cultural Organization, (UNESCO), special agency, founded **1945**, and joined United Nations, **July 30, 1946**, with headquarters in Paris.

United States Air Force Academy, established by U.S. Congress, **Apr. 1, 1954**; opened at Lowry Air Force Base at Denver, **1955**; permanent campus at Colorado Springs, Colo., opened, **1958**.

United States Civil War, (see Civil War, U.S.).

United States Coast Guard Academy, opened as U.S. Revenue Cutter Service

School of Instruction in New London, Conn., **1877**; took its present name, **1915**.

United States Golf Association (USGA), established as America's governing body for golf, **Dec. 22, 1894**; held its first amateur (National Amateur) and open (U.S. Open) championships in Newport, R.I., **1895**.

United States Lawn Tennis Association (USLTA), established at Newport, R.I., **Aug. 31, 1881**; inaugurated women's championship, **1887**; National Championship moved to West Side Tennis Club, Forest Hills, N.Y., **1915**; National Championship renamed U.S. Open, **1968**.

United States Military Academy, established by act of Congress at West Point, N.Y., **Mar. 16, 1802**; opened, **July 4, 1802**.

United States Naval Academy, established as the Naval School at Annapolis, Md., **Oct. 10, 1845**.

United States transatlantic crossing, U.S. passenger steamship *United States* established speed record (average speed of about 41 mph) on maiden voyage across Atlantic, eastbound from Ambrose to Bishop Rock in 3 days, 10 hours, and 40 minutes, **July 3-7, 1952**.

Unity and Security, Act of, King Gustavus III [1746-92] of Sweden strengthened his royal, despotic power, **Feb. 1789**.

Univac I (Universal Automatic Computer), completed, **1951**, by American physicist John W. Mauchly [1907-Jan. 8, 1981] and American electronics engineer J. Presper Eckert [1919-].

Universal Declaration of Human Rights, UN General Assembly declared all persons are born free and have equal rights, **1948**.

university wits, name for group of Elizabethan writers, **1580-95**, university-educated but devoted to literature and the theater; included Greene, Lyly, Marlowe, Nashe, and Peele.

Upanishads, collection of Hindu religious treatises on nature of man and universe, **c. 900 B.C.**

Upper Volta, country in w. Africa, made a French protectorate, **1896**; became self-governing Voltaic Republic, **1958**; took present name, **1959**; became independent republic, **Aug. 5, 1960**; suffered severe drought and famine, **1969-74, 1977-78**.

Uppsala, University of, Sweden's oldest university and one of world's great centers of learning, founded at Uppsala, **1477**; closed as a result of religious disputes, **1510-95**.

Ur, ancient city of Sumer, in s. Mesopotamia, **4th-3rd century B.C.**; fell to Elamites, **c. 1950 B.C.**; declined after **6th century B.C.**.

uranium, element No. 92, discovered, **1789**, by German chemist Martin H. Klaproth [1743-1817].

uranium, enriched, process developed, **1940**, by American physical chemist Philip Hauge Abelson [1913-].

uranium fission, discovered, **1938**, by German physicist Otto Hahn [1879-1968].

Uranus, discovered, **1781**, by German-English astronomer William Herschel [1738-1822]; satellites, discovered, **1851**, by English astronomer William Lassell [1799-1880].

Urban League, National, U.S. voluntary service agency established, **1910**.

Urbasi, Bengali poem, **1895**, by Bengali author Rabindranath Tagore; Nobel Prize-winner, **1913**.

urea, first organic compound synthesized from inorganic chemicals, **1828**, by German chemist Friedrich Wohler [1800-1882], by heating ammonium cyanate.

Ursulines, Catholic religious order, founded, Brescia, Italy, **1535**; papal approval, **1544**.

Uruguay, country on southeast coast of South America, declared an independent republic by the Thirty-three Immortals, **Aug. 25, 1825**; became sovereign nation of Uruguay, **Aug. 27, 1828**; joined Argentina and Brazil in War of the Triple Alliance against Paraguay, **1865-70**. See **Banda Oriental; Triple Alliance, War of the**.

U.S.S. *Nautilus,* (atomic submarine) first crossed under North Pole, **1958**.

U.S.S. *Triton,* world's largest, **c. 1960**, nuclear-powered submarine; stayed submerged, **1960**, for 34 days on round-the-world trip.

Utah, part of territory ceded to U.S. by Mexico, **1848**; admitted to the Union as 45th state, **Jan. 4, 1896**.

Utah Act, U.S. Congress created territorial boundaries and government for Mormon state of Deseret (Utah), which was allowed to decide slavery question on its own, **Sept. 9, 1850**.

Utah War, conflict between U.S. government and Mormons over non-Mormon settlement in Utah territory, **1857**; massacre of about 140 emigrants bound for California at Mountain Meadows, **Sept. 11, 1857**.

Ute Indians, North American tribe in Colorado and Utah, attacked Mexican settlements in San Luis Valley, Colo., early **1855**; subdued by U.S. troops, **1879**.

Utica, ancient city in North Africa founded by Phoenicians from Tyre, **c. 1100 B.C.**; became capital of Roman province of Africa, **146 B.C.**; destroyed by Arabs, **c. 700**.

utilitarianism, ethical doctrine, named, **1863**, by John Stuart Mill; first formulated by Jeremy Bentham, **c. 1788**.

Utopia, British steamship *Utopia* sank following collision off Gibraltar; 574 persons perished, **Mar. 17, 1891**.

Utraquists, moderate Hussites who were opposed to radical Taborites and were taken back into Catholic Church, **1433**.

Utopia, political romance, **1516**, by English writer, statesman and saint, Sir Thomas More.

Utrecht, Treaty of, ended War of the Spanish Succession; (Queen Anne's War in America), Louis XIV agreed not to unite France and Spain under one king, recognized Protestant succession in Britain and ceded some territories in North America to Britain, **Apr. 11, 1713**.

Utrecht, Union of, established by the seven provinces of n. Netherlands for their common defense, **Jan. 23, 1579**.

U-2 plane incident, U.S. photo-reconnaissance plane piloted by Francis Gary Powers [Aug 17, 1929-Aug. 1, 1977] shot down over Soviet territory, **May 1, 1960**; Soviets called Powers a spy, **May 7, 1960**; U-2 flights by U.S. suspended, **May 16, 1960**; Powers found guilty of espionage at Moscow trial, **Aug. 17-19, 1960** and imprisoned; Powers returned to U.S. in exchange for convicted Soviet spy Rudolf I. Abel [c., 1902-Nov. 15, 1971], **Feb. 10, 1962**.

Vaal Krantz, battle of, last major victory for Boers in Boer War; Transvaal-Orange forces forced British to relinquish Vaal Krantz, **Feb. 8, 1900**.

vaccination, devised, **1796**, by English physician Edward Jenner [1749-1863].
vaccine, multiple, developed, **1932**, by American pediatrician Louis W. Sauer [1885-1980].

vaccine, yellow fever, developed, **1937**, by South African-born American physician Max Theiler [1899-1972].
vacuum cleaner, suction-principle, first U.S. patented, **1869**, by American inventor I.W. McGaffey of Chicago, Ill; electric, invented, **1907**, by American inventor James M. Spangler.
vacuum flask, invented c. **1892** by Scottish chemist Sir James Dewar [1842-1923].
Vadimonian, Lake, battle of, Roman legions annihilated last Etruscan army and put Gauls to rout at Lake Vadimonian on Tiber River, **238 B.C.**
Vagabond King, The, operetta, opened, New York, **Sept. 21, 1925**, composed by Rudolf Friml.
Valenciennes, battle of, British forces won important victory over Germans at Valenciennes, n. France, **Nov. 1, 1918**.
Valladolid, University of, one of world's first universities founded at Valladolid, Spain; noted for its rich library and valuable manuscripts, **1346**.
Valley Forge, (Pa.), site of main camp of Continental Army during severe winter; where French Gen. Lafayette (Marquis de Lafayette) [Sept. 6, 1757-May 20, 1834]

and Prussian Gen. Steuben (Baron Friedrich Wilhelm Steuben) [Sept. 17, 1730-Nov. 28, 1794] helped Gen. Washington organize and train army, **Dec. 1777-June 1778**.
Valley of the Dolls, best-selling novel, **1960**, by U.S. writer Jacqueline Susann [Aug. 20, 1921-Sept. 21, 1974].
Valmy, battle of, French artillery halted advance of Prussian infantry at Valmy, **Sept. 20, 1792**.
Valois, dynasty of French kings, began with Philip VI [1293-Aug. 1350] of Valois and ended with Henry III [Sept. 19, 1551-Aug. 2, 1589], **1328-1589**.
Valparaiso, Treaty of, Chile and Bolivia signed indefinite truce, ending War of the Pacific, **Apr. 4, 1884**.
vanadium, element No. 23; discovered, **1830**, by Swedish chemist Nils G. Sefstrom [1787-1845].
Van Allen belts, high-energy radiation zones, discovered, **July 1958**, by American scientists.

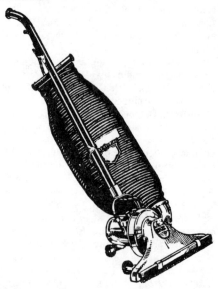

Vandals, ancient Germanic tribe that invaded Gaul, **406**; under Gaiseric [c. 390-477] captured Carthage, **439**; sacked Rome, **June 2-16, 455**.
Van Diemen's Land, former name of Tasmania, first discovered by Dutch explorer Abel Tasman [1603?-59] who named it Van Diemen's Land, **1642**; site of penal

colony, **1845**; last convicts transported there; renamed Tasmania, **1853**.

van der Waals equation, developed, **1873**, by Dutch physicist Johannes D. van der Waals [1837-1923].

Vanity Fair, novel, **1848**, by English novelist William Makepeace Thackeray.

vapor density, method for determining discovered, **1858**, by French chemist Jean B. A. Dumas [1800-1884] ; used to redetermine 30 atomic weights.

Variations on a Theme of Haydn, first major orchestral composition, **1873**, by German composer Johannes Brahms.

Varieties of Religious Experience, The, classic psychological study, **1902**, by U.S. philosopher and psychologist William James.

Variety, New York theatrical trade journal, from **1905**.

Varna, battle of, Turkish army massacred Christian army at Black Sea port of Varna, **Nov. 10, 1444**.

Varna Crusade, prompted by the pope, Christian army of Poles, Hungarians, and others advanced through Bulgaria to confront the Ottoman Turks, **1444**; Turks won decisive victory at Varna, **Nov.10, 1444**.

Vassar College, college for women founded, **1861**, at Poughkeepsie, New York.

Vatican, Roman hill, burial site of St. Peter, where basilica, **337**, and papal residence, **c. 500**, were erected; became principal papal residence, **1377**; independent state under papal rule, **1929**.

Vatican City, sovereign state under pope, whose temporal power was abrogated by the kingdom of Italy, **May 13, 1871**; regained sovereignty and independence by Lateran Treaty with Italy, **Feb. 11, 1929**.

Vatican Council I, Catholic ecumenical council, **1869-70**, defined pope's infallibility in deciding faith and morals in *Pastor Aeturnus*, **July 18, 1870**, decreed God could be known by reason in *Dei Filius*, **April 24, 1870**.

Vatican Council II, Catholic ecumenical council, **1962-65**, summoned by Pope John XXIII's *Humanae Salutis*, **Dec. 25, 1961**.

vaudeville, theatrical variety entertainment, founded, Boston, **1883**; heyday c. **1885-1930**.

velocity (of light), first determined as constant, **1676**, by Danish astronomer Olaus Roemer [1644-1710].

Venda, third black African "homeland" for one of nine Bantu groups gained full independence from South African government, **Sept. 13, 1979**.

Vendee, unsuccessful uprising by peasants in w. France, against French Revolution, **1793-96**.

vending machine, coin-operated, patented, **1929**, by American inventor Sebastiano Lando.

venereal disease, term first introduced, **1736**, by French surgeon Jean Astruc [1684-1766].

Venezuela, country in South America, declared its independence from Spanish rule, beginning 10-year war, **1811**; won independence at battle of Carabobo, **June 24, 1821**; established republic, separate from Greater Colombia, **1830**; nationalized oil industry with compensation to foreign companies, **Jan. 1, 1976**.

Venezuela Boundary Dispute, Venezuela and Britain over territorial boundary between British Guiana and Venezuela, Venezuela broke off diplomatic relations with Britain, **1887**; British rejected U.S.

offer to arbitrate, **Nov. 26, 1895**; Pres. Cleveland renounced Britain, **Dec. 17, 1895**; settled favorably to Britain, **Oct. 3, 1899**.

Veracruz, battle of, 13,000-man U.S. army under Gen. Winfield Scott landed at Veracruz, capturing the Mexican fortress and city after six-day artillery and naval bombardment, **Mar. 27, 1847**.

Verdun, battle of, longest and bloodiest battle of WWI; massive German offensive stopped by French under Gen. Henri Philippe Omar Petain [Apr. 24, 1856-July 23, 1951], **Feb. 21 - Dec. 18, 1916**.

Verdun, Treaty of, divided Charlemagne's empire among the sons of Louis I, Louis the German, Charles II, and Lothair I, **843**.

Vereeniging, Treaty of, Boers accepted British sovereignty in South Africa, were promised representative institutions, and given grants to rebuild farms after Boer War, **May 31, 1902**.

Vermont, declared itself an independent state, **Jan. 16, 1777**; admitted to the Union (U.S.) as 14th state, **Mar. 4, 1791**.

Verneuil, battle of, English longbowmen repulsed French-Scottish attack at Verneuil, **Aug. 17, 1424**.

vernier scale, devised, **c. 1631**, by French mathematician Pierre Vernier [1580-1637].

Verona, Congress of, international conference gave France mandate to use force to suppress Spanish rebellion against Ferdinand VII [Oct. 14, 1784-Sept. 29, 1833], **Oct. 20-Dec. 14, 1822**.

Verona, Diet of, German and Italian princes united in their holy war against the Saracen Turks, **983**.

Verrazano-Narrows Bridge, completed, **1964**, by Swedish-American engineer Othmar H. Ammann [1879-1965].

Versailles, Palace of, vast royal palace and grounds, constructed **1669-85**.

Versailles, Treaty of, major among five treaties that ended WWI, **June 28, 1919**.

Vervins, Treaty of, Philip II withdrew his Spanish troops from France, depriving Holy (Catholic) League of Spanish support, **May 2, 1598**.

Vesuvius, Mt., volcano erupted to bury the ancient cities of Pompeii, Herculaneum, and Stabiae, **Aug. 24, 79**.

Veterans Administration, U.S. Congress combined under one department all federal agencies servicing veterans, **July 3, 1930**.

Veterans of Foreign Wars (VFW), American organization created, **1899**, by Spanish-American War veterans at Columbus, Ohio; chartered by U.S. Congress, **1936**.

Vicar of Wakefield, The, novel, **1776**, about mild-mannered country vicar who undergoes trials of Job until all is righted by benevolent English gentleman by Anglo-Irish writer Oliver Goldsmith.

Vichy government, regime established by Marshal Henri Petain [Apr. 24, 1856-July 23, 1951] after Franco-German armistice that controlled unoccupied France and its colonies, **July 1940-May 7, 1945**; Vichy weakened after Hitler annulled armistice and occupied all of France, **Nov. 1942**.

Vicksburg, battle of, Union army under Gen. Grant captured city of Vicksburg, Miss., after long siege, and forced Confederates under Gen. Joseph E. Johnston [Feb. 3, 1807-Mar. 21, 1891] to retreat, **May 7-July 4, 1863**.

Victoria Cross, the, instituted in Great Britain, **Jan. 19, 1856**.

Victoria Falls, majestic waterfalls on Zambia-Zimbabwe border, discovered by David Livingstone [Mar. 19, 1813-May 1, 1873], **1855**.

Victorian, period in English literaure and culture **1837-1901**, coinciding with reign of Queen Victoria.

video telephone, experimental, first developed, **1927**, by Bell Telephone Laboratories.

Vienna, became seat of dukes of Austria, **12th century**; successfully defended itself during 58-day siege by Ottoman Turks, **July 14-Sept.12, 1683**; fl. as center of art, music, and science, **18th-early 20th centuries**.

Vienna, battle of, imperial and Polish forces led by John Sobieski (later King John III [June 2, 1624-June 17, 1696] of Poland) raised siege of Vienna and defeated larger Turkish army of Kara Mustapha [d. 1683], **Sept. 12, 1683**.

Vienna, Congress of, international assembly called to remake Europe after the first abdication of Napoleon and attended by Klemens Wenzel Nepomuk Lothar von Metternich [May 15, 1773-June 11, 1859] of Prussia, Charles Maurice de Talleyrand [Feb. 2, 1754-May 17, 1838] of France, and Robert Stewart Castlereagh [1769-1822] of Britain, **Sept. 1814-June 1815**; adopted constitution of new German Confederation, restored Austrian and Prussian monarchies, formed kingdoms of the Netherlands and Poland, reestablished Switzerland, **June 8, 1815**.

Vienna, Treaty of, peace treaty that settled the War of the Polish Succession, **Nov. 13, 1738**.

Vienne, Council of, Catholic ecumenical council, **1311-12**.

Vietnam Moratorium Day, millions of U.S. citizens held prayer vigils, candlelight marches, in protest against continuation of Vietnam War, **Oct. 15, 1969**; second moratorium day in U.S., **Nov. 14, 1969**, saw 250,000 antiwar marchers in Washington, D.C., and 100,000 in San Francisco.

Vietnam War, conflict in Southeast Asia, chiefly between U.S.-South Vietnam forces and Vietcong-North Vietnam forces, **1954-73**; Geneva Conference provided for partition of Vietnam pending reunification elections, **May 8-July 21, 1954**; Pres. Eisenhower offered U.S. aid to South Vietnam, **1954-55**; Communists formed National Liberation Front (Vietcong), **Dec. 1960**; South Vietnam's premier Ngo Dinh Diem [Jan. 3, 1901-Nov. 2, 1963] slain during military coup, **Nov. 1, 1963**; U.S. increased military advisers to South Vietnam, **1962-63**; U.S. destroyers allegedly attacked by North Vietnamese torpedo boats in Gulf of Tonkin, **Aug. 2, 1964**; Gulf of Tonkin Resolution authorized Pres. Lyndon Baines Johnson [Aug. 27, 1908-Jan. 22, 1973] to prevent further aggression, **Aug. 7, 1964**; U.S. planes bomb Hanoi-Haiphong area, **June 29, 1966**; almost 500,000 U.S. troops fought Vietcong during Tet Offensive, **Jan.-Feb. 1968**; first Paris peace talks began, **May 10, 1968**; massive antiwar protests in U.S., **1968-70**; U.S. presidential adviser Henry A. Kissinger [May 27, 1923-] conducted secret peace talks, **June 1971-Jan. 1972**; Pres. Richard M. Nixon [Jan. 9, 1913-] ordered intensive bombing of North Vietnam, **Apr. 15, 1972**; U.S., Vietcong, North and South Vietnam signed peace pacts in Paris, ending longest war in U.S. history, **Jan. 27, 1973**; last U.S. troops evacuated from Vietnam, **Mar. 29, 1973**.

View of Toledo, landscape painting, **1608**, by Greek-Spanish painter, El Greco.

Vijayanagar Empire, centered at ancient city of Vijayanagar, s.e. India, fl. **c. 1510-30**; destroyed by Muslims, **c. 1565**.

Vikings (Norsemen or Varangians), Scandinavian warriors who raided the coasts of Europe, British Isles, and North America, **9th-11th centuries**.

Village Blacksmith, The, poem, **1839**, celebrating New England blacksmith, by U.S. poet Henry W. Longfellow.

Vilnius (Vilna) dispute, conflict between Poles and Lithuanians over claim to city of Vilnius, **1919-22**; Curzon Line set by Allies, **Dec. 8, 1919**, left Vilnius to Lithuanians; Poles drove Bolshevik-supported Lithuanians out, **Oct. 9, 1920**; Vilnius incorporated into Poland, **Apr. 18, 1922**, after plebiscite; Soviets captured city, **1939**, and made it part of Soviet-held Lithuania, **1940**.

Vimeiro, battle of, British army led by Wellington defeated French army led by Androche Junot [1771-1813] at Vimeiro, ending first French invasion of Portugal during Peninsular War, **Aug. 21, 1808**.

Vinaroz, battle of, Spanish insurgents (Franco's forces) defeated loyalists at port of Vinaroz during Spanish Civil War, **Apr. 15, 1938**.

Vincennes, (Ind.), historic site where French built strategic Fort Vincennes to guard entrance to Mississippi Valley, **c. 1724**; colonial forces led by George Rogers Clark [Nov. 19, 1752-Feb. 13, 1818] captured British Fort Sackville on site, **Feb. 1779**.

Vinegar Hill, battle of, British forces routed Irish rebels at Vinegar Hill, Enniscorthy, virtually ending rebellion by United Irishmen, **June 21, 1798**.

Vinland (Vineland or Wineland), name of n.e. coast of North America discovered by Vikings under Leif Ericsson (Ericson), **c. 1000**; briefly colonized by Thorfinn Karlsefni, **c. 1002-1010**.

viola, member of violin family, developed **c. 1600**.

violin, four-stringed instrument played with bow, developed, Brescia and Cremona, **1550-1600**; chin rest added, **1800**.

Virginia and Kentucky Resolutions, declared Alien and Sedition Acts unconstitutional and "of no effect," **Nov.-Dec. 1798**.

Virginia, one of Thirteen Colonies, ratified U.S. Constitution to become tenth state of the Union, **June 25, 1788**; seceded from the Union, **Apr. 17, 1861**; readmitted to the Union, **June 26, 1870**.

Virginia Plan, plan of union providing for popular election of lower house of Congress, submitted by Gov. Edmund J. Randolph [Aug. 10, 1755-Sept. 12, 1813] of Virginia, **May 19, 1787**, at Constitutional Convention revising Articles of Confederation; adopted **June 19, 1787**.

Virgin Islands of the United States, purchased by U.S. from Denmark, **Jan. 17, 1917**, for $25 million; U.S. Dept. of Interior took over their administration, **1954**.

Virginius, steamer *Virginius* flying U.S. flag and transporting arms to Cuban rebels captured by Spanish, **Oct. 31, 1873**.

virus and enzyme synthesis (genetic control), discovered, **c. 1958**, by French chemist Jacques L. Monod [1910-], French biologist Andre Lwoff [1902-], and French geneticist Francois Jacob [1920-].

virus, cancer-causing, first discovered (in chickens), **1910**, by American physician F. Peyton Rous [1879-1970].

Visconti, Italian Ghibelline family that ruled Milan successively as lords, imperial vicars, and dukes, **c. 1250-1447**.

Visigoths, ancient Germanic tribe that sacked Rome under Alaric I [c. 370-410], **Aug. 14 (or 24), 410**; defeated by the Franks at Vouille, **507**.

vision physiology, research developed, from **1940s**, by American biochemist George Wald [1906-], American physiologist Haldan K. Hartline [1903-]; and Swedish physiologist Ragnar A. Granit, [1900-].

vitamin A, discovered, **1912**, by English biologist Frederick G. Hopkins [1861-1947].

vitamin B, thiamine, isolated, **1933**, by American chemist Robert R. Williams [1886-1965]; synthesized **1936**.

vitamin B requirement, human requirement determined, **1934**, by American physician George R. Cogwill [1893-].

vitamin B₁, discovered, **1897**, by Dutch physician Christiaan Eijkman [1858-1930].

vitamin B₂, riboflavin, synthesized, **1935**, by Russian-Swiss chemist Paul Karrer [1889-1971].

vitamin B₁₂ structure determined, **c. 1960**, by British chemist Dorothy M. Hodgkin [1910-].

vitamin C (ascorbic acid), first obtained in pure form, **1932**, by Hungarian-American physician Albert Szent-Gyorgyi [1893-].

vitamin C, isolated, **1932**, by American biochemist Charles G. King [1896-].

vitamin C, synthesized, **1933**, by Swiss chemist Tadeus Reichstein [1897-] who also discovered method to produce it commercially, **1933**.

vitamin D, discovered, **1922**, by American physiological chemist Elmer V. McCollum [1879-1967].

vitamin E, discovered, **1922**, by American physician Herbert M. Evans [1882-1971].

vitamin K, discovered, **1939**, by Danish biochemist Carl P. Dam [1895-] and American biochemist Edward A. Doisy [1893-].

Vitoria, battle of, British-Portuguese army under Wellington defeated French at Vitoria, northeast of Madrid, during Napoleonic Wars, **June 21, 1813**.

Vittorio Veneto, battle of, Italian armies under Gen. Armando Diaz [Dec. 5, 1861-Feb. 29, 1928] overwhelmed Austrian forces at Vittorio Veneto in n. Italy, which led to Austro-Hungarian surrender during WWI, **Oct. 24-Nov.3, 1918**.

Volstead Act, Prohibition amendment (Eighteenth) to U.S. Constitution ratified, **Oct. 28, 1919**; repealed by Twenty-first Amendment, **Dec. 5, 1933**.

Voltaic pile, invented, **1800**, by Italian physicist Alessandro Volta [1745-1827]; earliest form of battery.

Von Pirquet's Test, devised, **1907**, by Austrian physician Clemens Peter Von Pirquet [1874-1929] as a skin test to show the presence of tuberculosis; also known as the cutaneous tuberculin reaction, it proved particularly valuable in detecting the disease in children.

Voorhis Act, U.S. Congress authorized, **Oct. 17, 1940**, registration of all foreign organizations with political or military activities in U.S.

vorticism, avant-garde movement in literature and art, **1912-20**, launched by British writer Wyndham Lewis; two annuals, *Blast*, **1914** and **1915**, published verse by poets such as Eliot and Pound.

Vostok I, first manned spacecraft launched, **1961**, by Soviet scientists; carried first human in outer space, Russian cosmonaut Yuri A. Gagarin [1934-1968].

vote-recorder, electrographic, patented, **1869**, by American inventor Thomas A. Edison [1847-1931].

voting machine, electric, invented, **1869**, by American inventor Thomas A. Edison [1847-1931]; first used in election, **1892**.

Voting Rights Act, U.S. Congress authorized federal authorities to begin registering black voters in Alabama, Louisiana, and Mississippi, **Aug. 10, 1965**; amended and applied also to Northern cities or counties where literacy tests are required for voters, **1970**; extended for 7 years, **1975**.

Vouille, battle of, Frankish army of King Clovis I [c. 466-511] Visigothic army of Alaric II [d. 507] (who was slain); Visigoths abandoned Gaul and retreated across Pyrenees, **507**.

V-2 rocket, first successful long-range missile designed, **1942**, by German rocket pioneer Wernher von Braun [1912-1977]; weapon used by Germans in WWII.

vulcanization process, cold, discovered, **1841,** by English chemist Alexander Parkes [1813-1890].

Vulgate, The, Latin version of the Bible officially accepted by the Catholic Church; New Testament translated from Greek, **c. 384,** Old Testament from Hebrew, **405,** by St. Jerome [c. 345-Sept. 30, 420]; definitive revised *Vulgate* issued, Rome, **1980.**

Vyborg, (Viborg), battle of, Finnish White Army supported by Germans defeated Russian Red Army at Vyborg, n.w. of Leningrad, driving Bolsheviks out of Finland, **Apr. 29, 1918.**

Vyborg Manifesto, public declaration issued by Russian Constitutional Democratic Party, criticizing the government and calling upon the people to refuse to pay taxes, **July 21, 1906.**

Wade-Davis Manifesto, document issued by radical Republicans in U.S House of Representatives, criticizing Pres. Abraham Lincoln's "lenient" reconstruction plan for the South, late **July 1864,** after Lincoln's veto of "severe" Wade-Davis Bill for South's reconstruction, **July 8, 1864.**

Wafd, Egyptian political party founded by Saad Zaghlul Pasha [c.1850-1927], **1919,** to free Egypt from British influence and to bring socio-economic reform; controlled

Egyptian parliament **1924-52;** disappeared after Gamal Abdel Nasser [Jan. 15, 1918-Sept. 28, 1970] set up one-party system, **1956.**

Wages and Hours Act (Fair Labor Standards Act), U.S. Congress set scale of minimum wages and maximum hours for workers and prohibited child labor in industries engaged in interstate commerce, **June 25, 1938;** upheld by U.S. Supreme Court, **Feb. 3, 1941.**

Wagon Box Fight, American forces successfully defended themselves against repeated Sioux and Cheyenne Indian attacks at Fort Phil Kearny on the Bozeman Trail in Montana, **Aug. 1867;** Indians destroyed Fort Phil Kearny immediately after it was evacuated by army forces, **1868.**

Wagram, battle of, French forces of Napoleon won important victory over Austrians at Wagram, Austria, **July 5-6, 1809.**

Wahabis, puritanical Arab Muslims who controlled Saud tribe, began holy war against other Muslim tribes, **c. 1763;** ruled all Arabia, except Yemen, **1811;** driven out, **1818;** ruled Persian Gulf coast of Arabia, **1821-33;** Ibn Saud [c. 1880-Nov. 9, 1953] reconstituted kingdom of Hejaz and Nejd as Saudi Arabia, **Sept. 22, 1932.**

Wahehe War, conflict between Germans and African natives in German East Africa, **1891-93.**

Waitangi, Treaty of, British guaranteed to the Maoris full control of their lands in return for Maori recognition of British sovereignty in New Zealand, **Feb. 6, 1840.**

Waiting for Godot (En Attendant Godot), play, **1952,** by Irish-born French-English playwright, Samuel Beckett; Nobel Prize-winner, **1969.**

Wakarusa War, Border Ruffians camped on Wakarusa River halted their attack against Free State forces at Lawrence, Kansas, **Nov. 26, 1855.**

Wakefield, battle of, Lancastrians decisively defeated Yorkists at Wakefield in n. central England; duke of York, earl of Rutland, earl of Salisbury killed, extinguishing old generation of nobles and deepening hatred of both sides during the Wars of the Roses, **Dec. 30, 1460.**

Walden, book, **1854,** by U.S. poet, prose

stylist, essayist and naturalist, Henry David Thoreau.

Waldensians, Christian community, founded Piedmont, **c. 1175**; excommunicated, **1185**; persisted, making common cause with Protestants, **1532**; granted tolerance by Kingdom of Piedmont, **1848**.

Walker expedition, group under American adventurer William Walker [1824-Sept. 12, 1860] overthrew government of Nicaragua; Walker became country's ruler, **June-Oct. 1855**; U.S. Pres. Franklin Pierce [Nov. 23, 1804-Oct. 8, 1869] recognized Walker as president of Nicaragua, **1856**; Walker forced out by Cornelius Vanderbilt [May 27, 1794-Jan. 4, 1877] whose company in Nicaragua was threatened, **May 1857**; Walker's invasion and takeover of Honduras failed, **Aug.-Sept. 1860**.

walking, mechanism of, researched, **1833**, by German physicist Wilhelm E. Weber [1804-1891] and German anatomist Eduard F. Weber [1806-1871].

Wallace, shooting of, Alabama Gov. George C. Wallace [Aug. 25, 1919-] shot **May 15, 1972**, by Arthur H. Bremer [1951-] at political rally in Laurel, Md.

Waller's Plot, conspiracy instigated by English poet Edmund Waller [Mar. 3, 1606-Oct. 21, 1687] to secure the city of London for King Charles I, **1643**; discovered by parliament, which banished Waller.

Walter Winchell Show, The, broadcast program, on radio (*Walter Winchell's Journal*), **1932-55**, on television, **1952-56**, **1960**.

waltz, three-quarter-time popular dance, emerged, German lands, **1770-80**.

Wankel-engine, first designed, **1954**, by German engineer Felix Wankel [1902-].

War and Peace (Voina i Mir), novel, **1864-69**, by Russian writer, Count Leo Tolstoy; opera, **1944**, by Russian composer Sergei Prokofiev. 3½-hour film, **1956**, with Henry Fonda, Audrey Hepburn, and U.S. actor Mel Ferrer [Aug. 25, 1917-]; 7-hour Russian film, **1968**; television series, **1973-74**.

Warburg, battle of, British cavalry won victory against French during Seven Years' War; French forced back to Rhine, **July 31, 1760**.

War Department, U.S., Congress created department of federal government to run U.S. military establishment, **Aug. 7, 1789**; reformed as Department of the Army, **July 26, 1947**.

War Measures Act, Canadian Prime Minister Pierre Elliott Trudeau [Oct. 18, 1919-] invoked measures to deal with terrorists of Front de Liberation du Quebec, **Oct. 16, 1970**, that had kidnapped the Quebec minister of labour and a British trade official, **Oct. 5, 1970**; replaced by Public Order Act, temporary measure to permit police to arrest and hold suspects without warrant, **Dec. 1, 1970**.

War of 1812, armed conflict between U.S. and Britain, partly over shipping rights and neutrality, **1812-15**; U.S. Capt. Oliver Hazard Perry won battle of Lake Erie, **Sept. 10, 1813**; Gen. William Henry Harrison won battle of the Thames, **Oct. 5, 1813**; British halted at Fort McHenry, **Sept. 12-14, 1814**; ended by Treaty of Ghent, **Dec. 24, 1814**; British decisively defeated by Americans at New Orleans, **Jan. 8, 1815**.

War of the Three Henrys (eighth Huguenot War), Henri of Guise [1550-88], Henri III [1551-89] of Valois, and Henry of Navarre (later Henry IV [1553-1610]) fought for the French throne, **1585-89**; Henry of Navarre won at Coutras, **Oct. 20, 1587**;

Henry of Navarre defeated Holy League at Arques, **Sept. 21, 1589**; and at Ivry, **Mar. 14, 1590**.

War of the Worlds, The, story, **1898**, by pioneer science-fiction writer, novelist H.G. Wells; radio dramatization by Orson Welles, **1938**, caused widespread panic; film version **1953**.

War Production Board (WPB), former U.S. government agency established, **Jan. 16, 1942**, by Pres. F.D. Roosevelt to oversee all war production and supply; abolished **Nov. 1945**, after supervising production of $185 billion worth of weapons and supplies.

Warren Commission, special commission under Chief Justice Earl Warren [Mar. 18, 1891-July 9, 1974] to investigate the assassination of U.S. Pres. John F. Kennedy, established by Pres. Lyndon B. Johnson, **Nov. 29, 1963**; commission's final report delivered, **Sept. 24, 1964**, maintaining Lee Harvey Oswald acted alone as assassin and Jack Ruby was innocent of conspiracy; commission's findings attacked, since **1964**.

Warsaw Pact, mutual defense alliance established in Warsaw, Poland, **May 14, 1955**, by Albania, Bulgaria, Czechoslovakia, E. Germany, Hungary, Poland, Rumania, and U.S.S.R.; Albania withdrew, **1968**.

washing machine, pioneered, **1907**, by American manufacturer Frederick L. Maytag [1857-1937].

washing machine (electric), marketed, **1907**, by Hurley Machine Co., Chicago, Ill..

washing machine (manual), invented **1851**, by American inventor James T. King.

Washington, formerly part of Oregon Territory, admitted to the Union (U.S.) as 42nd state, **Nov. 11, 1889**.

Washington Conference, international assembly of naval powers resulted in Five-Power Treaty that set tonnage of aircraft carriers and capital ships, Four-Power Treaty in which Britain, France, U.S., and Japan agreed to respect each other's rights in Pacific, two Nine-Power treaties guaranteed China's territorial integrity (all treaties to remain in force, until **Dec. 31, 1936**), **1921-22**.

Washington, D.C., became capital of U.S., **June 1800**; first Congress convened there, **Nov. 17, 1800**; Thomas Jefferson became first U.S. president inaugurated there, **Mar. 4, 1801**; captured and burned by British, **Aug. 24, 1814**.

Washington's *Farewell Address*, statement by U.S. Pres. George Washington warning Americans against "permanent alliances" with foreign nations, dated **Sept. 17, 1796**; never delivered orally but published in Philadelphia paper, **Sept. 19, 1796**.

Washington, Fort, about 8000 British and Hessian troops assaulted American-held Fort Washington at n.e. end of Manhattan Island, forcing 2837 Americans to surrender at start of American Revolution, **Nov. 16, 1776**; British under Gen. Cornwallis crossed Hudson River and seized companion position of Fort Lee, **Nov. 18, 1776**.

Washington Mining Company, first silver-mining company in U.S. began operations at Silver Hill Mine, Lexington, N.C., **1842**.

Washington Square, novel, **1881**, by U.S. novelist Henry James.

Washington, Treaty of, U.S. and Britain signed treaty, **May 8, 1871**, that provided for international arbitration to settle *Alabama* claims and San Juan Islands dispute.

Washita, battle of the, U.S. 7th Cavalry under Lt. Col. George Custer attacked without warning Cheyenne and Arapahoe camp on Washita River, killing more than 100

Indians and their chief Black Kettle [d. Nov. 27, 1868], **Nov. 27, 1868**.

Wassermann test, (for syphilis) devised, **1906**, by German bacteriologist August von Wassermann [1866-1925].

Waste Land, The, complex, allusive poem, **1922**, by U.S.-British poet and literary arbiter, T.S. Eliot, Nobel Prize-winner, **1948**.

Watauga Association, first independent local government in America formed when British turned present-day area of Tennessee over to five-man governing committee, **1772**.

Watergate scandal, five men arrested for breaking into Democratic National Committee headquarters in Watergate complex, Washington, D.C., **June 17, 1972**; Pres. Nixon accepted responsibility, but not blame, for break-in, **Apr. 30, 1973**, with resignations from his Chief of Staff H.R. Haldeman [Oct. 27, 1926-], John D. Ehrlichman [Mar. 20, 1925-], and John W. Dean, III [Oct. 15, 1938-], who testified, **June 25, 1973**, to widespread cover-up of Watergate break-in; White House taping of all conversations in Pres. Nixon's offices revealed, **July 16, 1973**; *Saturday Night Massacre*, **Oct. 20, 1973**; seven former White House and campaign aides indicted for Watergate cover-up, **Mar. 1, 1974**; in televised hearings, **July 24-30, 1974**,

House Judiciary Committee recommended three articles of impeachment against Pres. Nixon; U.S. House of Representatives voted to accept articles of impeachment, **Aug. 20, 1974**; Pres. Nixon resigned, **Aug. 9, 1974**, and was pardoned by new U.S. Pres. Gerald R. Ford [July 14, 1913-], **Sept. 8, 1974**; Haldeman, Ehrlichmann, and former Att. Gen. John N. Mitchell [Sept. 5, 1913-] found guilty of Watergate cover-up, **Jan. 1, 1975**.

watch manufacturing, pioneered, **c. 1850**, by American horologist Aaron L. Dennison [1812-1895].

watch, self-winding, invented, **1791**, by French inventor Abraham-Louis Breguet [1747-1823].

water-closet system, patented, **1778**, by English engineer Joseph Bramah [1748-1814].

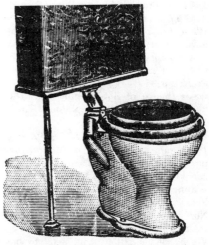

water fluoridation, tested, **1952**, in Newburgh, N.Y.; New York State Health Commission reported 47% drop in tooth decay among school children.

Waterloo, battle of, British under Wellington, supported by Prussians, routed French army at Waterloo, near Brussels, ending Hundred Days rule of Napoleon and 23 years of war between France and other European powers, **June 18, 1815**.

Water Music, The, suite of airs, dances, and fanfares for orchestra, **1717**, by George Frederick Handel.

water tunnel, one of earliest known, built

c. 520 B.C. by Greek engineers, 6th cent. B.C., on the Aegean island of Samos..

water turbine, invented, 1849, by English-American hydraulic engineer James B. Francis [1815-1892].

waterwheel, improved, patented, 1844, by American inventor Theodore R. Timby [1822-1909].

waterwheel, turbine, developed, 1884, by American inventor Uriah Atherton [1804-1879].

Watson, Fort, capture of, Fort Watson, commanding the road from Camden to Charleston, S.C., captured from the British by American revolutionaries under Gen. Francis Marion [c. 1732-Feb. 27, 1795], Apr. 23, 1781.

Watts riot, 6-day riot in Negro section of Los Angeles, Aug. 11-16, 1965.

wave character of particles, proposed, 1924, by French physicist Prince Louis V. de Broglie [1892-].

Waverly Novels, The, name under which novels of Sir Walter Scott, written 1814-32, first published; name from author's first novel, *Waverly*, 1814, about Stuart Pretender.

wave theory of light, established, 1800, by English physician and physicist Thomas Young [1773-1829].

Way Down East, silent film melodrama, 1920, directed by D.W. Griffith; heroine played by U.S. actress Lillian Gish (born Lillian de Guiche) [Oct. 14, 1896-].

Wayne, Fort, hostile Indians (Shawnee, Potawatomi, Miami, and Chippewa) in Northwest Territory inflicted two humiliating defeats on U.S. forces at modern Fort Wayne, Indiana, thus continuing to block settlement of the territory, Oct. 18, 1790, Oct. 22, 1790.

Waynesboro, battle of, 10,000 Union cavalrymen under Gen. Philip H. Sheridan won victory, capturing many men, weapons, wagons, and supplies of Confederate Gen. Jubal A. Early at Waynesboro, Va., Mar. 2, 1865.

Way of the World, The, play, 1700, a comedy detailing tricks required for successful marriage suit, with famous scene of "contract" between bride and groom, work of English Restoration dramatist William Congreve.

Ways and Means Committee, standing committee of U.S. House of Representatives formed, 1795, to supervise all financial legislation; gained authority over all legislation for raising revenue, 1865.

weather forecasting, started, U.S., 1871, by Cleveland Abbe, [1838-1916].

weather reports, daily, initiated, 1869, by American astronomer and meteorologist Cleveland Abbe [1838-1916] at Cincinnati Observatory.

Weather Underground, U.S. radicals called Weathermen, part of Students for a Democratic Society, mid-1960's; broke away from SDS to establish Weather Underground, 1969, that protested against Vietnam War through bombings.

Webster-Ashburton Treaty, U.S. and Britain agreed on fixed Canadian border between Maine and Lake of the Woods of n. Minnesota, Aug. 9, 1842.

Webster-Hayne debates, famous debates between Sen. Robert Y. Hayne [Nov. 10, 1791-Sept. 24, 1839] of South Carolina, advocate of states' rights, and Sen. Daniel Webster [Jan. 18, 1782-Oct. 24, 1852] of Massachusetts, advocate of sovereign national government, Jan. 21-27, 1830.

Webster's Spelling Book, school textbook, 1783, also called *Blue-Backed Speller*.

Weimar Republic, German republic, part of Second Reich, established by constitutional assembly at Weimar, East Germany, and dissolved when Nazis under Hitler took power, July 31, 1919-Mar. 23, 1933.

Weinberg-Salam theory of weak interactions, developed, 1967, by American physicist Steven Weinberg [1933-] and Pakistani physicist Abdus Salam [1926-].

welding, electric, invented, **1877**, by American inventor Elihu Thomson [1853-1937].

Well-Tempered Clavier, The (Das Wohltemperierte Clavier), 48 preludes and fugues, **1744**, by German composer Johann Sebastian Bach.

Wends, pagan Slavs who were Germanized and Christianized by ruling German princes, **c. 1147-1200**.

Wereloe, Treaty of, King Gustavus III of Sweden formed a defensive alliance with Russia, **1790**.

Wessex, kingdom of, kingdom established by Saxons under Cerdic [d. 534], **495**; gained control of other kingdoms—Mercia, Kent, and Northumbria—under reign of Alfred the Great [849-99], late **9th century**; kings of Wessex gained control over all of England, **10th century**; Danish rule established under Canute [995?-1035], **1016**.

Western Reserve, tract of land in present-day Ohio reserved by Connecticut when she ceded her western territory to U.S., **1786**; Connecticut citizens burned out in American Revolution given "firelands" in Western Reserve, **1792**; Moses Cleaveland, agent of Connecticut Land Company that bought rest of Reserve, **1795**, established first permanent settlement, Cleaveland (Cleveland), **1796**; included in Northwest Territory,

1800; Connecticut gave up title to it, **1801**.

West Florida controversy, boundary dispute between U.S. and Spain over territory in Florida, **1795-1813**; Pres. James Madison [Mar. 16, 1751-June 28, 1836] annexed w. part of West Florida (s. parts of Mississippi, Alabama, and Louisiana), **Oct. 27, 1810**, U.S. occupied e. part, **Apr. 15, 1813**.

West Gate Bridge disaster, great, one of worst disasters in bridge-building history; huge two-section 393 ft. span of 8500 ft. West Gate Bridge buckled during construction, then fell 160 ft. into Yarra River, Melbourne, Australia, **Oct. 15, 1970**.

West Indies Associated States, Antigua, St. Kitts-Nevis, Dominica, Grenada, St. Lucia, and St. Vincent formed Associated States of the United Kingdom, **Feb.-June 1967**; full independence for Grenada, **Feb. 7, 1974**, for Dominica, **Nov. 3, 1978**, for St. Lucia, **Feb. 22, 1979**, for St. Vincent and the Grenadines, **Oct. 27, 1979**. See **West Indies Federation**.

West Indies Federation, 10 British territories in the West Indies formed federation, **Jan. 3, 1958**, with seat of government at Port-of-Spain, Trinidad; Jamaica withdrew from federation **Sept. 19, 1960**, and gained full independence, **Aug. 6, 1962**; Trinidad-Tobago withdrew, **Jan. 15, 1962**, and gained full independence, **Aug. 31, 1962**; dissolved, **Feb. 6, 1962**.

Westminster Abbey, London abbey, founded **c. 616**; medieval church built adjoining, from **c. 1050**.

Westminster, Treaty of, ended Anglo-Dutch war; English took back New York and Delaware (captured by Dutch in 1673), **Feb. 9, 1674**.

Westphalia, kingdom of, Napoleon created kingdom of Westphalia, for his brother Jerome Bonaparte [Nov. 15, 1784-June 24, 1860] to rule as king, **Aug. 1807**; kingdom collapsed, **Oct. 1813**.

Westphalia, Peace of, ended Europe's Thirty Years' War and left the German states destitute, **Oct. 24, 1648**.

West Side Story, musical, opened, **Sept. 26, 1957**, music by Leonard Bernstein; lyrics by U.S. lyricist-composer Stephen (Joshua) Sondheim [Mar. 22, 1930-]; film version, **1961**.

West Virginia, part of Virginia territory, broke away during Civil War and admitted to the Union (U.S.) as 35th state, **June 20, 1863**.

wet collodion process, (in photography) invented, **1851**, by English sculptor Frederich S. Archer [1813-1857].

Wexford, battle of, Oliver Cromwell's army attacked and massacred Irish and English royalists at Irish seaport of Wexford, **Oct. 11, 1649**.

What Price Glory?, play, **1924**, by U.S. playwrights Maxwell Anderson and Laurence Stallings [Nov. 25, 1894-Feb. 28, 1968]; film version, **1926, 1952**.

What's My Line?, long-running U.S. television series, **1950-67**.

Wheatstone bridge, fundamental form discovered, **1833**, by English mathematician Samuel H. Christie [1784-1865]; potential recognized, **1843**, by English physicist Sir Charles Wheatstone [1802-1875].

When Lilacs Last in the Dooryard Bloom'd, poem, **1867**, free-verse elegy in which poet mourns death of Abraham Lincoln with return of lilacs in Spring, by U.S. poet Walt Whitman.

Whig Party, U.S. political party formed by those opposed to Pres. Andrew Jackson and his policies, **1834**; joined with National Republican Party, **1836**; struggle between pro- and antislavery factions ended party, **1852**.

Whirlwind computer, completed, **1953**, by Massachusetts Institute of Technology.

Whiskey Rebellion, violent rebellion in w. Pennsylvania against excise taxes on whiskey imposed by federal government, **July 1794**; 15,000 militiamen, on orders of Pres. Washington, put down rebellion, **Sept. 24, 1794**.

Whiskey Trust, about 80 U.S. liquor distilleries combined to control production, price, and profits, **1886**.

Whiskey War, Ohio women stood before liquor dealer's stores and denounced the sale of all alcoholic beverages, **1874**.

Whitby, Synod of, ecclesiastical synod, England, **664**, in which Church in England decided to follow Rome and Council of Nicaea in celebrating Easter.

Whitechapel murders, savage mutilation murders of at least 14 persons in London's East End, attributed to killer who dubbed himself "Jack the Ripper," **Aug.-Nov. 1888**.

White Christmas, Christmas song, **1942**, written by U.S. composer and lyricist Irving Berlin; from film *Holiday Inn*.

White Eagle, Order of, famous Polish decoration for chivalry instituted by King Ladislaus I [1260-1333] on the marriage of his daughter to Grand Duke of Lithuania, **1325**.

White Lotus Rebellion, anti-Manchu rebellion in China that occurred during corrupt Ch'ing dynasty; many Chinese beheaded by Manchus, **1796-1804**.

White Mountain, battle of, armies of Holy Roman Empire and Catholic League under Count of Tilly (Johannes Tserklaes) [1559-1632] routed Bohemian Protestant army under Christian of Anhalt [1568-1630] on White Mountain; battle ended independence of Bohemia for 300 years and was first battle of Thirty Years' War, **Nov. 8, 1620**.

White Plains, battle of, British under Gen. William Howe captured Chatterton's Hill at White Plains, N.Y., **Oct. 28, 1776**.

Whitney, Mt., highest mountain of contiguous states of U.S. (14,494 ft.), in Sierra Nevada, Calif., first climbed by American expedition, **Aug. 18, 1873**.

Who's Afraid of Virginia Woolf?, play, **1962**, by U.S. playwright, Edward Albee; film, **1966**, featured Elizabeth Taylor and Richard Burton.

Wide-Awakes, the, political group in Republican Party formed, **1860,** in support of Abraham Lincoln for the presidency; famous for their torch-light parades.

Wiesloch, battle of, revolutionary forces under Ernst von Mansfeld [1580-Nov. 29, 1626] defeated imperial forces of Catholic League under Johannes Tserklaes, Count of Tilly [1559-1632], during Thirty Years' War, **Apr. 16, 1622.**

Wightman Cup tournament, annual U.S.-British women's tennis tournament inaugurated by a Philadelphia sportswoman, **1923.**

Wilderness Campaign, series of battles fought between Union and Confederate forces in Wilderness region of Virginia, **May-June 1864;** Army of the Potomac under Gen. Grant and Army of Northern Virginia under Gen. Lee fought indecisive battle at Spotsylvania Courthouse, **May 10-12, 1864;** Grant failed to dislodge Lee's entrenched army at Cold Harbor, **June 3, 1864.**

Wilderness Road, major route used by American frontiersmen and pioneers on westward migration over Appalachians, **c. 1790-1840;** Daniel Boone blazed road further, through Cumberland Gap, into present-day Kentucky, **1775.**

Wilderness Society, U.S. organization founded by conservationists, **1935,** to preserve wilderness areas and wildlife through educational and scientific programs.

Wilhelm Gustloff and General Steuben disaster, German liner *Wilhelm Gustloff* loaded with war refugees and hospital ship *General Steuben* sunk by Soviet submarine off Danzig; 6800 persons perished in world's greatest marine disaster, **Jan. 30, 1945.**

Willard-Johnson fight, Jess Willard [Dec. 29, 1883-Dec. 15, 1968] knocked out Jack Johnson in 26 rounds in Havana, Cuba, to become world heavyweight boxing champion, **Apr. 5, 1915.**

William and Mary, College of, college, founded Williamsburg, Virginia, **1693,** second oldest in U.S.; main building designed, **1695,** by Sir Christopher Wren.

William Henry, Fort, French and Canadian troops under Gen. Montcalm, allied with Indians, forced British and colonials to surrender at Fort William Henry near south end of Lake George, N.Y., during French and Indian War, **Aug. 9, 1757.**

William Tell, opera, **1829,** about Swiss national hero, by Italian composer Gioacchino Rossini; play, **1804,** by German poet Friedrich von Schiller; Tell legend first written in ballad form, **1474.**

Will to Believe, The, philosophical essays, **1896,** holding that men have right to accept idealistic beliefs that lead to desirable action, by U.S. pragmatist, philosopher, and psychologist William James.

Wilmington, (Del.), first Swedish settlers built Fort Christina there, **Mar. 1638;** captured by Dutch, **1655;** captured by British, who renamed it, **1664;** Eleuthere Irenee Du Pont [June 24, 1771-Oct. 31, 1834] established gunpowder manufacturing mill there, **1802.**

Wilmington Ten, ten civil rights activists arrested and imprisoned for allegedly fire-bombing grocery store in Wilmington, N.C., **Feb. 6, 1971;** highly publicized post-conviction hearing, with N.C. governor affirming his belief in their guilt, **Jan. 23, 1978,** but reducing their sentences with early paroles.

Wilmot Proviso, amended bill passed by U.S. House of Representatives but ignored by Senate, excluding slavery from any territory acquired from Mexico; North-South bitterness increased, **Aug. 1846-Mar. 1847.**

Wimbledon, British lawn tennis championships established by All England Croquet Club at Wimbledon, England, **1877.**

Wimpfen, battle of, Spanish and Catholic League forces, led by count of Tilly, defeated German Protestant army at Wimpfen near Neckar River during Thirty Years' War, **May 6, 1622.**

Windfall **profits oil tax,** U.S. tax on "windfall" profits of oil industry proposed by Pres. Jimmy Carter, **Apr. 1979;** U.S. House of Representatives passed oil tax bill, **Mar. 13, 1980;** U.S. Senate passed compromise version of bill, **Mar. 27, 1980;** Pres. Carter signed Crude Oil Windfall Profit Tax Act, **Apr. 2, 1980.**

Windhoek, battle of, South African-British forces under Gen. Louis Botha [Sept. 27, 1862-Aug. 27, 1919] defeated German forces at Windhoek, German South West Africa (Namibia) during WW I, **May 12, 1915.**

windmill, known in Babylon, **c. 1700 B.C.**, as water pump for irrigation; earliest known post mill, **1191**, in Bury St. Edmunds, England; first vertical sail windmills in Europe, **c. 1180**; first in America built, **1621**, by Virginia colonial official Sir George Yeardley [1582-1627].

Windsor, House of, royal, reigning family of Great Britain, **since 1901**; family name of Wettin (family name of Albert of Saxe-Coburg-Gotha [Aug. 26, 1819-Dec. 14, 1861] was changed to Windsor by George V [June 3, 1865-Jan. 20, 1936], **1917**.

Windsor Treaty, secret agreement between Britain and Portugal; Portugal agreed not to allow armaments to pass through Delagoa Bay to the Transvaal or to declare neutrality during Boer War, **Oct. 14, 1899**.

wind tunnel, invented, **1923**, by American inventor Max M. Munk.

Wings, film, **1927**, about American pilots in World-War I France, with U.S. stars Clara Bow [Aug. 6, 1905-Sept. 26, 1965] and Buddy Rogers [Aug. 13, 1904-].

Winnebago Indians, warred against Illinois Indians, **1671**; suppressed by Gen. Anthony Wayne, **1793-94**, warred against Ojibwa Indians, **1827**.

Winnie-the-Pooh, children's novel, **1926**, by English humorist A(lan) A(lexander) Milne [Jan. 18, 1882-Jan. 31, 1956].

Winter Battle, German forces overwhelmed Russians in Masurian Lakes region, northern Poland, during WW I, **Feb. 4-22, 1915**.

wireless telegraphy, developed, **1896**, by Italian physicist Guglielmo Marconi [1874-1937] and German physicist Karl F. Braun [1850-1918]. Transmitted message across the Atlantic, **1901**.

wirephoto, invented, **1881**, by English inventor Shelford Bidwell [1848-1909].

Wisconsin, formerly part of Northwest Territory, admitted to the Union as 29th state, **May 29, 1848**.

Wittelsbach, Bavarian dynasty whose family lands were split by Holy Roman Emperor into two main lines (Palatinate and Bavaria), **1329**; family lands reunited under single Wittelsbach ruler, **1799**; dynasty deposed, **1918**.

Wittstock, battle of, Swedish-German army won major victory over Saxon-Holy Roman Empire army at Wittstock, n.e. of Berlin, **Oct. 4, 1636**.

Wizard of Oz, The Wonderful, classic children's novel, **1900**, first and best-known of a long series about Oz, by U.S. writer L(yman) Frank Baum [May 15, 1856-May 6, 1919]; film, **1939**, of Frank Baum's children's novel, with Judy Garland as Dorothy supported by actors Bert Lahr, Ray Bolger [Jan. 10, 1904-], and Jack Haley (born John Joseph Haley) [Aug. 10, 1899-June 6, 1979].

Wolcott-Charles fight, Joe Wolcott [1914-] knocked out Ezzard Charles in seventh round at Pittsburgh to become heavyweight boxing champion, **July 18, 1951**.

Wolf Mountain, battle of, U.S. troops under Gen. Nelson A. Miles [Aug. 8, 1839-May 15, 1925] routed Sioux warriors under Chief Crazy Horse on Wolf Mountain in Montana, avenging the massacre at Little Bighorn, **Jan. 7, 1777**.

Woman Bathers (Grandes Baigneuses), painting, **1905**, one of series of bathers, presenting nudes in planes and colors rather than realistically; precursor to 20th-century non-representational art, by post-impressionist painter, Paul Cezanne.

Women Appointed for Voluntary Emergency Service, (WAVES), U.S. Congress formed, **July 30, 1942**, women's reserve unit of U.S. navy; women enlisted in regular navy, **1948**, but retained name "Waves."

Women's Army Corps (WAC), U.S. Congress formed, **May 14, 1942,** as Women's Army Auxiliary Corp (WAAC); WAAC changed to WAC, **1943**; WAC made part of regular army, **1948**.

Women's Christian Temperance Union (WCTU) formed in Cleveland, **1874**; World WCTU organized, **1883**.

Women's Reserve of U.S. Coast Guard (SPARS), U.S. Congress formed, **Nov. 23, 1942,** demobilized, **1946**; reactivated, **1965**.

Women's Reserve of U.S. Marine Corps (WM), U.S. Congress formed, **Feb, 13, 1943**.

wood, edible, method developed, **1917,** by German chemist Friedrich Bergius [1884-1949]; converts wood into digestible sugar-type carbohydrates.

wool-combing machine, invented, **1789,** by English inventor Edmund Cartwright [1743-1823].

Woolens Act, British parliament forbade colonists in America to ship wool or woolen products from one colony to another, **1698**.

Worcester, battle of, Oliver Cromwell's army destroyed English royalist and Scottish army at Worcester in w. central England, forcing Charles II to flee for his life during English Civil War, **Sept. 3, 1651**.

word processor, first introduced, **1964,** by International Business Machines (IBM).

Workhouse Test Act, parliament established workhouses in England where the poor could support themselves by work, **1722**.

Works Projects Administration (WPA), U.S. federal agency created by order of Pres. Franklin D. Roosevelt, **Apr. 8, 1935,** as Works Progress Administration; redesignated, **1939**, abolished, **Dec. 4, 1942**.

World Council of Churches, ecumenical organization for Christian unity, proposed, **1937,** Edinburgh, at Faith and Order Conference; constitution drafted, **1938,** Utrecht; ratified, Amsterdam, **Aug. 22, 1948**.

World Cup competition, quadrennial international tournament to decide soccer supremacy, inaugurated at Montevideo, Uruguay, by Federation Internationale des Associations Football, **1930**.

World Health Organization (WHO), special agency of the United Nations established, **1946**.

World Series, annual series of games between National and American league champion teams, established to decide baseball's world championship, **1903**.

World War I (the Great War), general conflict between Allies (Britain, France, Russia, U.S., Belgium, Serbia, Montenegro, and Japan) and Central Powers (Germany, Austria-Hungary, and Ottoman Empire), **1914-18**; Serbian nationalist assassinated Archduke Francis Ferdinand [Dec. 18, 1863-June 28, 1914] at Sarajevo, **June 28, 1914**; French won first battle of the Marne, **Sept. 6-8, 1914**; indecisive, bloody trench warfare on Western Front, **1914-17**; Germans defeated Russians at Tannenberg on Eastern Front, **Aug. 26-30, 1914**; Allies failed to oust Ottoman Empire from war during Gallipoli Campaign, **Apr. 1915-Jan. 1916**; Germans and Austrians routed Italians at Caporetto, **Oct. 24-Nov. 12, 1917**; French held Germans at Verdun, **Feb. 21-Dec. 18, 1916**; German unrestricted submarine warfare brought U.S. into war, **Apr. 6, 1917**; Central Powers signed peace Treaty of Brest-Litovsk with Russia, **Mar. 3, 1918**; German counteroffensive stopped at second battle of the Marne, **July 15-17, 1918**; Italians won major victory at Vittorio Veneto, **Oct. 24-Nov. 3, 1918**; armistice signed at Compiegne, **Nov. 11, 1918**.

World War II, general world conflict between Axis Powers (chiefly Germany, Italy, and Japan) and the Allies (chiefly U.S., Britain, France, Australia, Russia,

China, Belgium, and the Netherlands), **1939-45**; Germany under Adolf Hitler [Apr. 20, 1889-Apr. 30, 1945] attacked Poland, without declaring war, **Sept. 1, 1939**; Britain and France declared war on Germany, **Sept. 3, 1939**; German forces overran Luxembourg, Netherlands, Belgium, and France, **May-June 1940**; Vichy government of France established after French signed armistice with Germany, **June 22, 1940**; Germans failed to bomb Britain into submission (battle of Britain), **Aug-Oct. 1940**; British fought Italians and Germans in North African Campaign, **1940-43**; Germans began invasion of Russia, **June 22, 1941**; Japanese attacked U.S. at Pearl Harbor, **Dec. 7, 1941**; U.S. declared war on Japan, **Dec. 8, 1941**; British victory at El Alamein, **Nov. 2, 1942**; German offensive checked at Stalingrad, **Feb. 2, 1943**; allied conquest of Sicily and Italy, **July-Aug. 1943**; Italy surrendered, **Sept. 8, 1943**; U.S. forces won back Japanese-held Pacific islands, **1942-45**; Allies landed in Normandy, **June 6, 1944**; Allies won battle of the Bulge, **Dec. 1944-Jan. 1945**; Germany surrendered, **May 7, 1945**; U.S. dropped atomic bomb on Hiroshima, **Aug. 6, 1945**; on Nagasaki, **Aug. 9, 1945**; Japan surrendered, **Aug. 14, 1945** (formally signed, **Sept. 2, 1945**).

World Zionist congresses, first World Zionist Congress for creation of Jewish state in Palestine, called by Theodor Herzl [Mar. 2, 1860-July 3, 1904] at Basel, Switzerland, **1897**; World Zionist Congress split, favoring Palestine over British offer of homeland in Uganda, **1905**; congress led by Chaim Weizmann [Nov. 27, 1874-Nov. 9, 1952], **1920-29**; **1935-46**; World Zionist Congress adopted Peel Report to partition Palestine into Jewish, Arab, British states, **Aug. 1937**; World Zionist Congress demanded admission of one million Jews to Palestine, **Aug. 13, 1945**.

Worms Cathedral, romanesque cathedral, begun, **1081**, completed, **c. 1250**; double-choired, and double-towered.

Worms, Concordat of, Holy Roman Emperor Henry V [1081-May 23, 1125] renounced the right of investiture and recognized freedom of election of the clergy, **Sept. 1122**.

Worms, Diet of, called by Holy Roman Emperor Charles V [Feb. 24, 1500-Sept. 21, 1558] to discuss imperial matters and the teachings of Martin Luther [Nov. 10, 1483-Feb. 18, 1546], **1521**; Luther refused to retract his teachings, **Apr. 17, 1521**; officially pronounced Martin Luther an outlaw and a heretic, **May 25, 1521**.

Worth, battle of, Prussian army temporarily checked by French using center-fire rifle, the chassepot, and the first machine-gun, the mitrailleuse, but managed to win victory at Worth during Franco-Prussian War, **Aug. 6, 1870**.

Wounded Knee, battle of, last major Indian battle in the West; U.S. 7th Cavalry massacred Sioux warriors, women, and children at Wounded Knee Creek, S. Dak., **Dec. 29, 1890**.

Wounded Knee takeover, about 300 militants of American Indian movement seized trading post and church at Wounded Knee, S.D., **Feb. 27, 1973**, demanding full investigation of U.S. government treatment of Indians; negotiations brought agreement, **May 5, 1973**; U.S. charges against Indian leaders dropped, **Sept. 16, 1974**.

Wurzberg, battle of, Austrian forces won victory over French under Jean Victor Moreau at Wurzburg, Bavaria, **Sept. 3, 1796**.

Wusterhausen, Treaty of, Prussia broke alliance with Britain and France and joined Austria, **Oct. 12, 1726**.

Wuthering Heights, novel, **1847**, by Emily (Jane) Bronte [July 30, 1818-Dec. 19, 1848]; Laurence Olivier film version, **1939**.

Wyndham Act, British parliament resolved Irish Land Question, **1903**; Irish tenants aided by Amended Land Purchase Act, **1909**.

Wyoming, part of territory acquired by Louisiana Purchase, admitted to the Union (U.S.) as 44th state, **July 10, 1890**.

Wyoming Valley massacre, Indians under chief Joseph Brant and British loyalists under Walter Butler [1752?-81] massacred settlers at Wyoming Valley, Penn., scalping many of them, **July 4, 1778**.

Wyszynski's imprisonment, Polish Roman Catholic Cardinal Stefan Wyszynski [Aug. 3, 1901-May 28, 1981], opponent of Stalin's policies, arrested and imprisoned, **Dec. 1953- Oct. 29, 1956**.

Xaquixaguana, battle of, Pedro de la Gasca [c., 1485-1567?] defeated Gonzalo Pizarro [c. 1506-48] to take control of Spanish Peru, **1548.**

xenon, element No. 54; discovered, **1898,** by Scottish chemist Sir William Ramsay [1852-1916] and English chemist Morris W. Travers [1872-1961].

xerography, dry-printing process pioneered, **1937,** by American inventor Chester Carlson [1906-1968]; fully developed, self-contained machine, **1960.**

x-ray diffraction, discovered, **1912,** by German physicist Max von Laue [1879-1960].

x-ray photograph, first taken in U.S., **1896,** by Yugoslavian-American physicist Michael I. Pupin [1858-1935].

x-rays, genetic effects first reported, **1927,** by American biologist Hermann J. Muller [1890-].

x-ray scattering, discovered, **c. 1904,** by English physicist Charles G. Barkla [1877-1944].

x-ray spectroscopy, pioneered, **c. 1920,** by Swedish physicist Karl M. Siegbahn [1886-1978].

x-ray tube, hot-filament, invented, **1913,** by American physical chemist William D. Coolidge [1873-1975].

xylophone, percussion instrument, developed **c. 1850;** first orchestral use: Saint-Saens' *Danse Macabre,* **1874.**

XYZ Affair, U.S. representatives, led by Charles Cotesworth Pinckney [Feb. 25, 1746-Aug. 16, 1825], sought treaty of commerce and amity with France, **May 31, 1797;** French agents (XYZ) failed to bribe U.S. representatives and to acquire U.S. loan to France, as France's price for making treaty, **Oct. 4, 1797.**

Yablonski murder, United Mine Worker official Joseph Yablonski [1910-Jan 5, 1970], his wife, and their daughter found shot to death, **Jan. 5, 1970;** deposed UMW president W.A. ("Tony") Boyle convicted of ordering the killings, **Apr. 11, 1974.**

Yale University, famous American university established as collegiate school in Killingworth, Conn., **1701;** moved to New Haven, **1716;** renamed Yale College in honor of its benefactor, Elihu Yale [1649-July 8, 1721], **1718;** became a university, **1887.**

Yalta Conference, U.S. Pres. F.D. Roosevelt, British Prime Minister Winston Churchill, and Soviet Premier Joseph Stalin [Dec. 21, 1879-Mar. 5, 1953] met at Yalta in the Crimea, **Feb. 4-11, 1945.**

Yamassee War, conflict between Yamassee Indians and British settlers in Carolinas, Georgia and Florida, **1715-28;** main Yamassee village near St. Augustine, Fla., destroyed by British, **1727.**

Yandabo, Treaty of, ended British-Burmese war over border areas, **Feb. 24, 1826.**

yankee, term of unknown origin applied from **c. 1730,** to New Englanders; prior to that it had been applied to Dutch New World settlers only.

Yankee Doodle, popular song of patriot soldiers in American Revolution, first heard,

c. **1755**; first known manuscript version dated, **1775**; earliest printed version, **1778**; had hundreds of verses.

Yankee Stadium, baseball park opened, **Apr. 18, 1923**, in New York City to become home field of New York Yankees.

Yarmuk, battle of, Muslim Arabs defeated Byzantines at Yarmuk River, **636**, seizing Syria and Jerusalem, **637**, Mesopotamia, **639**, and Egypt, **640-42**, during Arab conquest of Middle East.

Yazoo City, (Miss.), city wrested from Confederates by Gen. Francis J. Herron [1837-1902] and 5000 Union troops, **July 13, 1863**; many city buildings burned by Unionists, **May 1864**.

Yellow Book, The, illustrated quarterly, published, **1894-97**, that carried some of principal writers and artists of the day: among them, Aubrey Beardsley, Max Beerbohm, and Henry James.

Yellowstone National Park, oldest and largest U.S. national park first reached by Lewis and Clark, **1806**; established as public park, **1872**.

Yemen (Yemen Arab Republic), country in s.w. Arabia, became independent of Ottoman rule, **1918**; joined United Arab Republic (Egypt and Syria) to establish United Arab States, **1958**; long civil war between republicans and royalists ended in republican victory, **1962-69**; war with Southern Yemen, **Feb. 24-March 19, 1979**.

Yemen, Southern (People's Democratic Republic of Yemen),, waged war against British and local dynastic leaders, to gain independence, **Nov. 30, 1967**; war with neighboring Yemen, **Feb. 24-Mar. 19, 1979**.

"Yes, Virginia, there is a Santa Claus", New York *Sun* editorial; editor Francis P. Church [Feb. 22, 1839-Apr. 11, 1906] wrote one of most memorable editorials in newspaper history in answer to question by eight-year-old Virginia O'Hanlon [1890-May 13, 1971], **Dec. 1897**.

Yippies (Youth International Party), radical U.S. antiwar political group founded by Jerry Rubin [1938-], Abbie Hoffman [1936-], and others, **1968**.

York, battle of, Danes routed Saxons, killed Northumbrian kings, and ended Saxon power in n. Britain, **867**.

Yorkshire Ripper murders, 13 women murdered in the north of England, **1975-80**; truck driver Peter Sutcliffe [1947-] admitted to being Yorkshire Ripper and pleaded guilty to manslaughter but innocent to charges of murder, **April 29, 1981**; Yorkshire Ripper Sutcliffe convicted for murders and sentenced to life imprisonment, **May 22, 1981**.

Yorktown, battle of, British redcoats under Gen. Cornwallis, blockaded at Yorktown, Va., by French fleet under Admiral de Grasse (Francois Joseph Paul, comte de Grasse) [Sept. 13, 1722-Jan. 11, 1788], forced to surrender after American siege by Gen. Washington, aided by French forces under Marshal Rochambeau (Jean Baptiste Donatien de Vimeur, comte de Rochambeau) [July 1, 1725-May 10, 1807], **Oct. 6-19, 1781**.

You Bet Your Life, broadcast quiz show, on radio, **1947-59**, on television, **1950-61**.

You Can't Go Home Again, novel, **1940**, by U.S. writer, Thomas Wolfe.

Young America movement, movement chiefly by Democrats to unite U.S. behind good leaders, open the country to the world, play down sectionalism, and evolve American values, **1840-60**.

Young Italy (Giovine Italia), secret society, founded by Giuseppe Mazzini [June 22, 1805-Mar. 10, 1872], **1831**.

Young Men's Christian Association (YMCA), established in London, **1844**; first U.S. chapter at Boston, **1851**.

Young Men's Hebrew Association, U.S. organization for young Jewish men founded first chapter in New York City, **Mar. 22, 1874**.

Young Plan, revision of the Dawes Plan prepared by international committee headed by Owen D. Young [Oct. 27, 1874-July 11, 1962], went into effect **June 7, 1929**.

Young Turks, reformist and strong nationalist movement forced the restoration of Turkish constitution of 1876, **July 24, 1908**; helped parliament depose the sultan, **Aug. 1909**; gained control of government by coup d'etat, **Jan. 23, 1913**.

Young Women's Christian Association (YWCA), established in London, **1855**; first YWCA in U.S. as Ladies' Christian Union in New York City, **1858**.

Your Hit Parade, series, on radio, **1935-59**, on television, **1950-59, 1974**.

Ypres, battles of, British forces stopped German "race for the sea" (North Sea and English Channel) at Ypres, Belgium, in WWI, **Oct. 30-Nov. 24, 1914**; Allied forces and Germans (who used poison gas for first time) fought indecisive battle at Ypres, **Apr. 22-May 25, 1915**; British failed to break through German line at third battle of Ypres (or Passchendaele) and had about 400,000 casualties, **July 31-Nov. 10, 1917**. See **World War I**.

ytterbium, element No. 70; discovered, **1878**, by Swiss chemist Charles de Marignac [1817-1894].

yttrium, element No. 39; discovered, **1794**, by Finnish chemist Johan Gadolin [1760-1852].

Yuan dynasty, ancient Chinese dynasty, founded by Mongol Emperor Kublai Khan [1216-94], **1260-1368**.

Yukon, Canadian territory, first explored by fur traders of the Hudson's Bay Company, **1840s**; administered as part of Northwest Territories, **1870-95**; gold strikes on Klondike River brought prospectors, **1890s**; made separate district, **1895**; became separate territory, **1898**; rejected union with British Columbia, **1937**.

Yungay, battle of, Chilean army won important victory over Peruvian-Bolivian army at Yungay, Chile, ending the Peruvian-Bolivian Confederation's domination of Chile, **Jan. 20, 1839**.

Zama, battle of, decisive and final battle of second Punic War; Romans under Scipio Africanus Major [234-183 B.C.] defeated Carthaginians under Hannibal at Zama in present-day Tunisia, **202 B.C.**

Zambia, country in s. central Africa, ruled as Northern Rhodesia by British South Africa Company, **1889-1924**; administered by British government, **1924-53**; part of federation of Rhodesia and Nyasaland, **1953-63**; became independent republic of Zambia within the British Commonwealth, **Oct. 24, 1964**.

Zamora, Treaty of, arranged by the pope between Portugal and Castile, the latter recognized Portugal's independence, **1143**.

Zealandia, Fort, Ming dynasty loyalists led by Chinese pirate-general Koxinga [1624-62], failing to overthrow Ch'ing (Manchu) dynasty, besieged Dutch-held Fort Zealandia on Formosa (Taiwan) and forced it to surrender, ending Dutch rule of Formosa, **1661-62**; Koxinga's independent kingdom on Formosa fell to the Manchus, **1683**.

Zechariah, The Book of, Old Testament book, written, **520-18 B.C.**.

Zeeman effect, discovered, **1896**, by Dutch physicists Pieter Zeeman [1865-1943] and Hendrik A. Lorentz [1865-1928].

zemstvo, Russian system of provincial self-government, **1864-1917**; replaced by Soviet system, **1917**.

Zen Buddhism, branch of Buddhism, originated, China, and brought to Japan, **c. 1200**.

Zenger case, newspaper journalist and publisher John Peter Zenger [1697-July 28, 1746] of New York *Weekly Journal* arrested and imprisoned on libel charges, **Oct. 1734**; Zenger acquitted when his attorney Andrew Hamiton [1676-1741] successfully established truth as absolute defense against libel, **1735**.

Zephaniah, The Book of, Old Testament book, **c. 630-25 B.C.**, by Zephaniah, 9th of the minor prophets.

Zephyr, introduced, **1934**, by Chicago, Burlington, and Quincy Railroad.

Zero Population Growth, U.S. organization established, **1968**.

ziggurat, built c. **2300 B.C.**, by Mesopotamian civilization.

Zimbabwe, republic of Rhodesia in south central Africa became independent black nation of Zimbabwe, **Apr. 17, 1980.**

Zimmerman note, message from German Foreign Affairs Minister to German Ambassador in Mexico intercepted by British and U.S., **Feb. 1917.**

zinc, element No. 30; discovered, **1746**, by German chemist Andreas S. Marggraf [1709-1782].

zinc rolling-mill, first built in U.S., **1866**, by German-American metallurgist Frederick W. Matthiessen [1835-1918].

Zinjanthropus, discovered, **1959**, by British anthropologist Louis S.B. Leakey [1903-1972] in Olduvai Gorge of Tanzania; 1,750,000-year-old evidence of man's first appearance in Africa.

zipper, originally patented, **1893**, as a "clasp locker" for fastening shoes, by American inventor Whitcomb L. Judson.

zirconium, element No. 40, discovered, **1789**, by German chemist Martin H. Klaproth [1743-1817].

zodiacal light, first studied systematically, c. **1668**, by Italian-French astronomer Giovani D. Cassini [1625-1712].

Zoopraxiscope, invented, c. **1884**, by English motion-picture pioneer Eadweard Muybridge [1830-1904]; device for reconstituting movement from still photographs.

Zorba the Greek (Alexis Zorbas), novel, **1946**, celebrating passionate, Dionysian approach to life embodied in hero Zorba, by modern Greek writer, Nikos Kazantzakis; Greek film, **1965.**

Zorndorf, battle of, Prussian cavalry of Frederick II ("the Great") won major victory over Russians, half of whom were casualties (21,000); Prussians lost 13,000 men, **Aug. 25, 1758.**

Zoroastrianism, religion, dominant in Western Asia, from c. **550 B.C.-A.D. c. 650.**

Zuravno, Treaty of, ended 4-year war between Poland and Ottoman Empire, which received part of Ukraine and Podolia, **Oct. 16, 1676.**

Zurich, battles of, Austrian forces defeated French under Army Marshal Andre Massena [May 6, 1758-Apr. 4, 1817] at Zurich, Helvetic Republic (Switzerland), during French Revolutionary War, **June 4-7, 1799**; Massena won victory over Russian army at Zurich, **Sept. 26, 1799.**

Zutphen, battle of, Dutch supported by English unsuccessfully beseiged Spanish-held city of Zutphen in e. Netherlands (Dutch liberated city five years later), **Sept. 22, 1586.**

Laurence Urdang, Inc., headed by Laurence Urdang, is one of the most prestigious reference research groups in the U.S. and England. Urdang books (over 80 titles in the past ten years) include *The Facts on File Dictionary of Astronomy* and *The Synonym Finder* (both selected by the American Library Association as best reference books of 1979), *The Random House Dictionary of the English Language*, *The New Dictionary of Physics*, *The New Century Shakespeare Handbook*, *The Hamlyn Junior Science Encyclopedia*, *The New Penguin Dictionary of Electronics*, and parts of the *Encyclopaedia Britannica 3*.